SCI ACTIVITIES
FOR MIDDLE SCHOOL STUDENTS

Second Edition

George C. Lorbeer
California State University
Northridge

Boston Burr Ridge, IL Dubuque, IA Madison, WI New York San Francisco St. Louis
Bangkok Bogotá Caracas Lisbon London Madrid
Mexico City Milan New Delhi Seoul Singapore Sydney Taipei Toronto

McGraw-Hill Higher Education

A Division of The **McGraw-Hill** *Companies*

SCIENCE ACTIVITIES FOR MIDDLE SCHOOL STUDENTS, SECOND EDITION

Copyright © 2000, 1996 by The McGraw-Hill Companies, Inc. All rights reserved. Printed in the United States of America. Except as permitted under the United States Copyright Act of 1976, no part of this publication may be reproduced or distributed in any form or by any means, or stored in a data base or retrieval system, without the prior written permission of the publisher.

 This book is printed on recycled, acid-free paper containing 10% postconsumer waste.

1 2 3 4 5 6 7 8 9 0 QPD/QPD 0 9 8 7 6 5 4 3 2 1 0

ISBN 0–07–229916–9

Editorial director: *Jane E. Vaicunas*
Sponsoring editor: *Beth Kaufman*
Developmental editor: *Teresa Wise*
Marketing manager: *Daniel M. Loch*
Project manager: *Mary E. Powers*
Senior production supervisor: *Sandra Hahn*
Designer: *K. Wayne Harms*
Senior photo research coordinator: *Carrie K. Burger*
Compositor: *Shepherd, Inc.*
Typeface: *10/12 Times Roman*
Printer: *Quebecor Printing Book Group/Dubuque, IA*

Cover designer: *Sean M. Sullivan*
Cover photograph: *Luis Castaneda/Image Bank*
Photo research: *Mary Reeg Photo Research*

Page: 1; © PhotoDisc, Inc.; p. 57: PhotoDisc, Inc.; p. 61: PhotoDisc, Inc.; p. 128: PhotoDisc, Inc.; p. 143: George Lorbeer; p. 167: George Lorbeer; p. 180: George Lorbeer; p. 206: Photo Disc, Inc.; Photographer: Jeremy Woodhouse; p. 281: George Lorbeer: p. 289: George Lorbeer; p. 290: PhotoDisc, Inc.; p. 324: Dr. Nelson; p. 367: Dr. Nelson; p. 393: Photo courtesy of NASA; p. 395: Dr. Nelson; p. 409: PhotoDisc, Inc.

Some of the laboratory experiments included in this text may be hazardous if materials are handled improperly or if procedures are conducted incorrectly. Safety precautions are necessary when you are working with chemicals, glass test tubes, hot water baths, sharp instruments, and the like, or for any procedures that generally require caution. Your school may have set regulations regarding safety procedures that your instructor will explain to you. Should you have any problems with materials or procedures, please ask your instructor for help.

Library of Congress Cataloging-in-Publication Data

Lorbeer, George C.
Science activities for middle school students / George C. Lorbeer.—
2nd ed.
p. cm.
Includes index.
ISBN 0–07–229916–9
1. Science—Study and teaching (Middle school) I. Title.
Q181.L84 2000
507′. 1′2—dc21 99–35891
CIP

www.mhhe.com

To my wife, Dottie, THANKS.

Without her continuous moral support this book would never have been completed.

Contents

Part V: Health

Section E: Public Health

Section F: First Aid

Section G: Safety

Part VI: Ecology

Section A: Ecosystems

Section B: Conservation

Section C: Pollution

Section D: Pollution Solutions

Part VII: Earth and Space

Section A: Universe

Preface

Science Activities for Middle School students has been designed for students in grades 5 through 9. Each Activity includes current, vital information that would enrich the lives of Middle School students. The Activities cover all areas of General Science that teachers will find highly beneficial in planning and conducting effective science lessons. Key areas include matter, energy, plants, animals, health, ecology, Earth, and space travel.

In addition to teachers, curriculum workers, science supervisors, university and college methods instructors, and other school officials will find this Middle School Science book an invaluable aid in planning and helping students become more enlightened in the area of science. Parents, too, who want to help their children expand their knowledge of science will find that this "Science Activities for Middle School Students" is filled with interesting and motivating Activities.

The repair of the Hubble Telescope in space, discoveries in the structures of the genes, the finding of the last quark, the predictions of population growth, the findings of new planets and galaxies in our expanding, known universe, the cloning of animals, the critical loss of wildlife, and the launching of several sections of the new international space station are only a few of the scientific events that have been incorporated in this book for Middle School students.

Not since Sputnik has there been so much emphasis on science. We are living in a scientific and technological world, and judging by the current trend, it will soon be essential for all people to understand the areas covered in this text in order to maintain even the basic understanding of life. Unfortunately, we are not providing our students with the fundamental scientific background and problem-solving skills they need to live in this complex world. (See the Table of Contents.)

The major emphasis of this edition is still a hands-on, minds-on approach. John Dewey's statement, "We learn by doing," is the focal point of this book. Students learn best by direct, firsthand experiences. While teachers' scientific explanations of natural phenomena may be interesting, they often lack substance and meaning for the students. This book has been designed to provide teachers, student teachers, teachers' aides, and students with many complete Activities presented so that even the neophyte science teacher can perform them successfully. The materials needed are mostly common, inexpensive items found in the home, local market, or the classroom. Activities can be used as student experiments, group activities, and/or teacher demonstrations. This book provides many ideas to enrich present school science curricula.

What is Science?

1. *Science is the study of the environment.* It includes the biological environment from the tiniest living organisms to the largest living creatures, and the physical environment from the smallest speck of matter to the immense universe.
2. *Science is a method of solving problems.* It requires using all the materials and procedures necessary and available. It is not a predetermined, sequential step-by-step process. If this were so, all of the world's problems would have been solved a long time ago. Science includes hypothesizing, investigating, collecting, and interpreting data. It is a continuous refinement of each problem studied by testing, narrowing the hypotheses in numbers and scope, retesting, and so on until conclusions based on objective evidence are reached. Since "The Scientific Method" is so important and can be used in a multitude of Activities found throughout this book, the following are some of the steps that could also be included using this procedure.
   a. Sensing problems of a scientific nature
   b. Inquiring into strategies for problem solving
   c. Seeking assistance from others who are considered experts
   d. Clarifying problems and subproblems
   e. Speculating on possible hypotheses
   f. Using books, periodicals, and other materials as sources for information
   g. Selecting promising alternative(s) for testing
   h. Experimenting and observing in order to gather data
   i. Using new tools and techniques
   j. Gathering facts under controlled conditions
   k. Looking for irregularities, deviations, or exceptions
   l. Checking cause-and-effect relationships
   m. Measuring and recording findings
   n. Interpreting and organizing data
   o. Verifying findings with reliable sources
   p. Reporting findings accurately
   q. Predicting outcomes on the bases of gathered information
   r. Testing results with new applications
   s. Developing "models"
3. *Science is an art.* It requires creativity and provides internal satisfactions. A student who constructs a simple telegraph or organizes a collection of butterflies feels the same internal satisfaction as a

student who composes a basic melody or paints a simple picture. Science activities can produce intrinsic satisfactions that are as enjoyable and productive as any other art form. Do not discount this phase of science education.

4. *Science is an attitude based on facts.* The ability to understand and interpret natural phenomena alleviates misconceptions and unreasoning fears. The student who knows the cause of thunder, and has achieved this understanding in a meaningful way by popping a paper bag, is less likely to be frightened during a storm. When a student learns that animals are not apt to sting or bite except in self-defense, he/she is less apt to fear animals.
5. *Science is a pragmatic philosophy.* We all need a sound philosophy of life. Science can play an important role in this development by yielding information about life itself, the difference between living and nonliving things, the elements that make a healthy organism, and the dangers to living individuals from external sources or self-imposed deleterious substances and behaviors.

Objectives of Science Education

In planning any science program, the first step for the teacher is to determine the objectives that should be achieved for *each* individual student. While the individual teacher may want to develop a personal list of goals, the following objectives are highly recommended.

1. *Developing personal strengths.* This includes not only the basics of reading, writing, and arithmetic skills, but also communication skills, social activities, critical attitudes of work, problem-solving skills, and satisfying psychological needs such as recognition, affection, security, and belonging, etc.
2. *Becoming aware of the natural environment and social realities.* Students are naturally curious about their environment, and they are anxious to learn about it—*if* we don't stifle individual initiative. Students are continually asking, "Why?" "How?" "When?" "What?" The informed teacher can direct students down the path of discovery to develop personal skills and acquire basic scientific knowledge. We, as educators, should use this natural curiosity as a prime motivating device in science and in all the other disciplines as well.
3. *Having fun in games, contests, hobbies, and recreation.* Science is fun! Students enjoy creating projects and performing experiments. Much scientific knowledge can be acquired through games and contests. Many students have hobbies that involve science such as collecting rocks, raising pets, building model airplanes, and performing crafts. Recreational activities—swimming, backpacking, surfing, skating, and so on—all have scientific implications which should be utilized by the classroom teacher in every possible lesson.
4. *Enjoying artistic experience.* There are many satisfying science implications in all art forms. Colors in painting, sounds in music, and movements in dance all interrelate with science.
5. *Living healthfully and safely.* Science educators can help students by teaching them about food, rest, exercise, accident prevention, first aid, causes of disease and so on. Indoctrination about the dangers of using drugs and smoking cigarettes can spell the difference between health and sickness, life and death, even to very young students.
6. *Learning that science is involved in all vocations.* Science is involved in all walks of life, from performing general menial tasks to working with nuclear energy.
7. *Acquiring the basic facts about the biological and physical environments.* By building on basic facts, students will begin to develop fundamental concepts which expand with each related new fact; concepts are developed from facts, not vice versa. One of the major problems in teaching science is the selection of appropriate facts which will develop desired concepts.
8. *Developing a scientific attitude.* Students begin to learn cause-and-effect relationships, increase their natural curiosity, suspend judgment, develop the desire to search for valid answers, approach problems with an open mind, and accept "The Scientific Method" as a basic approach to solving *factual* problems. A scientific attitude can eliminate superstitions, remove unfounded fears, and prevent individuals from jumping to erroneous conclusions.
9. *Using "The Scientific Method".* This method cannot, and is not intended to solve all the problems people face; however, learning the basic procedures in "The Scientific Method" can help individuals solve many of the problems they encounter. It will enable students to become aware of problems, hypothesize about them, devise possible solutions, conduct tests, make accurate observations, collect data, avoid misleading clues, and find the correct answers, if not on the first attempt, then on subsequent studies of the problem(s). While "The Scientific Method" can help discover facts, it can never solve problems on the level of values. Science can never determine what is good or bad, right or wrong, better or worse—these are value judgments. Scientists deal with facts; philosophers with values. Problems stimulate thinking, and never before in our history has critical thinking been so sorely needed.
10. *Building a sound personal, pragmatic philosophy of life* This is the summation of all the previous objectives. It leads to wisdom and social concerns based on facts, concepts, a scientific attitude, and the knowledge and use of the "The Scientific Method."

Ideals of Science Education (Professional Recommendations)

Many excellent recommendations regarding science education have been noted in the professional field, and many of these have been incorporated in this book. Some of the most important are:

1. *Bloom's Taxonomy of Educational Objectives:* recommendations that begin with specific bits of information and lead toward abstract relations
2. *National Research Council, Teaching Standards:* recommendations about orchestrating student involvement in each Activity
3. *National Science Education Standards:* emphasizes student participation
4. *California Academic Standards Commission, Science Standards:* recommendations concerning scope and sequence of science content
5. *American Association for the Advancement of Science (AAAS):* benchmarks for Science Literacy
6. *National Science Teachers Association:* recommendations for Science Literacy

A composite of the above guidelines (or "Standards") and my own recommendations for science teaching would include:

1. Incorporating student experiences
2. Challenging students to predict the outcome of each Activity
3. Focusing on the student rather than on the subject content
4. Planning for the diversity of students
5. Designing lessons to permit student designs of investigations
6. Focusing on the scientific methods for solving problems
7. Stimulating student discussions on each step of the procedure
8. Promoting skepticism
9. Considering the teacher to be a resource person, not just a dispenser of information
10. Rewarding curiosity
11. Using as many resources as practical: multisensory aids, reference materials, and knowledgeable personnel in and out of school
12. Encouraging extended investigations
13. Ensuring a safe working environment
14. Developing small group activities
15. Making each Activity open-ended and not giving students the answers prematurely in planning, investigating, or reaching conclusions
16. Evaluating all phases of the learning process, not just factual accumulation

One of the major problems facing new science teachers is the element of time. It would be ideal if students could raise problems, plan the investigations, conduct the tests, collaborate with other students and resource specialists, do the necessary research, collect the data, interpret the findings, and be completely satisfied with the entire process, as defined in most professional "standards." However, there is not enough classroom time available, and consequently, teachers must balance the "ideals of standards" with the "realities of time, resources, and desired objectives."

The Design of the Book

The physical makeup of the book has been designed to make it easy for teachers to use. It is divided into eight major Parts. Each Part contains many carefully pretested Activities. (See Table of Contents.) Each Activity has nine major divisions. Each Activity is significant because it is related to other Activities and to life itself. To make each Activity more meaningful to the student, it should be taught in units with other Activities and not taught in isolation.

1. Problem
   Each Problem is stated in the form of a typical question which might be raised by an inquiring student. This enables the teacher to select the appropriate Activity and helps in lesson planning.
2. Materials Needed
   In Materials Needed, the supplies and equipment needed to perform the Activity are listed. Most materials are simple, inexpensive, and easy to obtain.
3. Procedure
   This is a step-by-step process that can be used to develop each Activity. The focus is on the student. It combines the utilization of:
   a. The process approach
   b. Open-mindedness
   c. Hands-on, minds-on focus
   While this book focuses on one set of procedures, the students should be encouraged to establish their own methods of solving the problem raised. Their procedures could well be just as accurate and even more motivating and educational. The students should not be discouraged if failure results. The only failure in science is the student who won't try again. Failure is not terminal; it is a step in the solution of almost every problem. It is not an insurmountable fence. If students' procedures repeatedly lead to failure, the procedures cited in the text can be utilized. Students should be continuously lauded for their attempts whether successful or not.
4. Results
   The Results are the observed conclusions of the Procedure. Other results of different procedures may be obtained, and they may yield the correct answer(s) to the particular problem or question raised in the Activity.
5. Basic Facts and Supplemental Information
   The teacher and/or student is provided with additional background information that will help to complete the understanding of the particular

problem involved. It includes scientific principles, handy hints, and safety precautions.

6. Thought Questions for Classroom Discussions
   These are included so that teachers may add thought-provoking questions, especially if they prefer the *inquiry* techniques to challenge students to think about possible solutions to other practical problems. This encourages teachers and students to do more critical thinking. Critical thinking is at the heart of all scientific testing, and consequently, it is a vital part of each Activity.
7. Related Ideas For Further Inquiry
   This section has been included to enrich each Problem. Activities can be correlated to show the interrelationships of science topics and investigations, and consequently the students will gain a better comprehension of each area and not view each Activity as an isolated one. Teachers who prefer "teaching units" will find this most helpful.
8. Vocabulary Building—Spelling Words
   We need to help students in every way possible to improve their language skills, and science instruction can be one of the vehicles for the student to develop in this area. This section, Vocabulary Building—Spelling Words, has been included to integrate science and language arts, particularly, spelling. The "Glossary," too, is another example of integrating science and language arts.
9. Thought For Today
   These statements are essentially philosophical and/or humorous in nature and have been added to provide enjoyment as well as "food for thought" for the teacher and the students. These "thoughts" have been used in classrooms for years and have proven to be an excellent initiatory activity. Statements can be modified, depending on the level and understanding of the students.

There are three main parts of every successful lesson:

1. Objectives—what you hope to accomplish
2. Activities—how you are going to accomplish the objectives
3. Evaluation—how well the objectives were accomplished

This book focuses on the Activities (the "HOW") which are at the heart of every science lesson.

In summary, science helps us understand our environment. It enables us to solve problems with an open mind, helps us appreciate the natural order and beauty of the universe, aids us to live in a more intelligent manner, teaches us respect for all creatures and our natural, physical environment, and encourages us to conserve our resources now and for future generations.

For the student, science should be a "rediscovery of the known by the uninformed." Students are not like sponges—they do not automatically absorb knowledge. They are individuals who learn best by firsthand, hands-on experiences. All of the Activities in this book were developed to raise and answer scientific questions that might arise in daily living.

The science teacher should be a director of learning, an agent of interaction, a motivator, a guide, a resource person, and rarely, if ever, a "storyteller." The teacher must recognize that students differ in experiences, learning rates, interests, abilities, backgrounds, etc., and must take each of these factors into consideration.

This book is not designed to cover all the science content for any one grade. Instead, it offers typical, effective, proven Activities from the various areas of science to give a teacher sufficient ideas to initiate a meaningful program of science education with a feeling of confidence. A teacher at any level of instruction can modify any Activity, making it either easier or more complex, depending on the age and intellectual level of the students. It must be remembered that these Activities are for young students who have a high level of curiosity and who like to have fun while learning.

Reviewers

I am grateful to the following reviewers for their helpful comments and suggestions:

Ryda D. Rose—The University of Pennsylvania
Michael Martinez—The University of California—Irvine
Dr. William Boone—The University of Indiana—Bloomington
Robert E. Kilburn—Boston University

George C. Lorbeer

PART I
PHYSICAL WORLD

SECTION A: MATTER

Activity I A 1

A. Problem: *How Does Living Matter Differ from Nonliving Matter?*

B. Materials Needed:

1. Books
2. Pencils
3. Rocks
4. Small plants
5. Classroom animals
6. Pictures of students' pets
7. Plastic items (comb, ruler, etc.)
8. Miscellaneous items

C. Procedure:

1. Have class make a list of:
   a. nonliving things
   b. plants
   c. animals
2. List the characteristics of each group.
3. Compare and contrast their differences.

D. Results:

1. The pupils will recognize the differences between living and nonliving things and between plants and animals.
2. Students will understand that most known living things are classified as either plants or animals.
3. Students will learn that many scientists today classify all living things in five main kingdoms: 1) Monera, 2) Protista, 3) Fungi, 4) Plants, and 5) Animals.

E. Basic Facts and Supplemental Information:

1. Living things are alike in some respects and different in others.
2. Nonliving things have very few characteristics of living things.
3. Animals move about; plants do not.
4. Animals have senses for locating food and the means of locomotion to obtain it.
5. Most plants make their own food.
6. Living things will have the following characteristics: they reproduce, feed, react to stimuli (irritability), grow, develop, acquire energy, have cells (or are one cell), respire (breathe), have complex structure (protoplasm), die (may omit for younger students).
7. All living matter can be divided into three main classes:
   a. Producers (plants, fungi, algae)
   b. Consumers (most animals including people)
   c. Reducers, decomposers (bacteria)

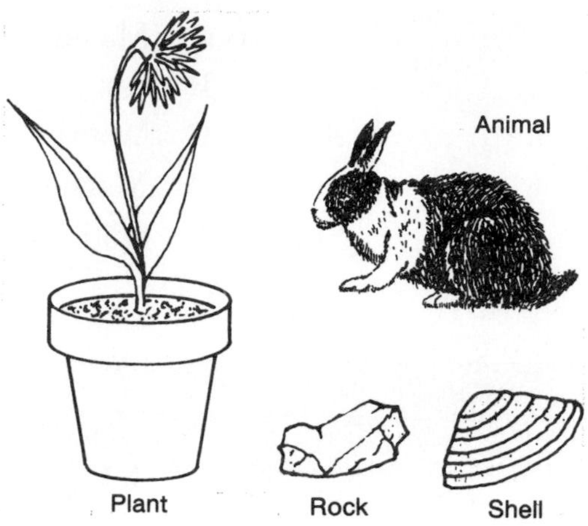

8. If it weren't for reducers-decomposers we would be living in one big garbage pile.

F. Thought Questions for Class Discussions:

1. How do some nonliving things move?
2. What is the biggest living thing you know about? the smallest?
3. What is the largest nonliving thing? the smallest?
4. Do nonliving things ever affect other nonliving things?

G. Related Ideas for Further Inquiry:

1. Look at some nonliving things with a microscope or magnifying glass.
2. Do some research on the biggest and smallest living things and nonliving things.
3. Younger students can collect pictures of plants and animals.
4. Study Activity IV-A-2, "What is the triangle of life?"
5. Study Activity III-A-1, "How do we classify living things?"
6. Study Activity IV-A-1, "What are some characteristics of all living things?"

H. Vocabulary Builders—Spelling Words:

1) **nonliving** 2) **locomotion** 3) **stimuli** 4) **respiration** 5) **protoplasm** 6) **irritability**

I. Thought for Today:

"One of the secrets of a long and fruitful life is to forgive everybody everything every night before you go to bed."—Ann Landers

Activity I A 2

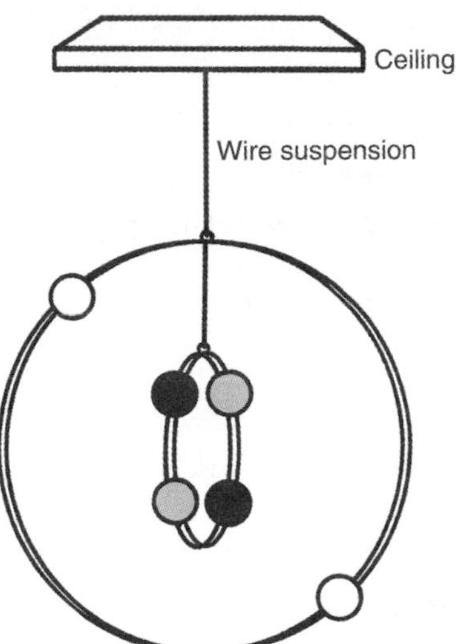

A Helium "Atom Mobile"
Electrons in outer orbit
Protons (light-colored) and
Neutrons (dark-colored) in
inner portion (nucleus)

A. Problem: *What Are Atoms? Molecules?*

B. Materials Needed:

1. Styrofoam balls
2. Water paints
3. Thin wire
4. Iron
5. Zinc
6. Reference material(s) showing the electrons, protons, and neutrons of atoms
7. Copper
8. Water
9. Salt
10. Baking soda

C. Procedure:

1. Briefly explain the three different states of matter: solids, liquids, and gases.
2. Define and describe atoms and molecules.
3. Show sketches or models of atoms such as iron, copper, zinc, etc.
4. Show sketches or models of molecules such as water, salt, baking soda, oxygen gas (O_2), nitrogen gas (N_2).
5. Have students blow against their hands and describe what they feel. Tell them that they are feeling molecules in motion.
6. Have each student build a mobile of a different atom using the reference materials as a guide.
   a. Cut out styrofoam balls for protons, neutrons, and electrons using a different color for each. (Electrons could be painted red; protons, blue; and neutrons, orange.)
   b. Arrange the protons and neutrons in a small, inner circle as shown in the drawing. Use any means of attachment to the wire that is convenient. This inner circle represents the nucleus where the protons and neutrons are bunched together.
   c. Attach "styrofoam electrons" to the larger, outer-wire circle. These should be spaced equidistantly, and the number must be the same as the number of protons in the nucleus.
   d. Attach the "nucleus ring" to the "electron ring."
   e. Affix this "mobile" to the ceiling or a high point in the room.

D. Results:

1. When students blow air against their hands they are making air molecules move.
2. Students will learn about atoms through actual construction and display of mobiles.

E. Basic Facts and Supplemental Information:

1. Atoms are the basic components of molecules.
2. Molecules are combinations of atoms.
3. There are now 115 known elements; 92 occur naturally and the rest have been synthesized in the laboratory.
4. A million atoms or molecules are about the size of the period at the end of this sentence.
5. Molecules are so small that we cannot see them.
6. Molecules are in constant motion regardless of whether they are in a solid, liquid, or gaseous state.
7. The smallest particle of matter that can be divided and still retain the properties of matter is called a molecule.

F. Thought Questions for Class Discussions:

1. If molecules didn't move, could laundry be dried outside?
2. Is all matter composed of molecules?
3. If all molecules are in motion, why don't all solids dissipate and disappear?

G. Related Ideas for Further Inquiry:

1. Study Activity I-A-4, "What is the 'Periodic Table'?"
2. Study Activity I-A-5, "What is the difference between a physical change and a chemical change?"
3. Study Activity I-A-11, "What are the tiniest pieces of matter?"

H. Vocabulary Builders—Spelling Words:

1) **atoms** 2) **molecules** 3) **elements**
4) **electrons** 5) **protons** 6) **neutrons**
7) **orbits** 8) **evaporation**

I. Thought for Today:

"Do not put off until tomorrow what you can do today."

Activity IA3

A. Problem: *What Is the "Periodic Table"?*

B. Materials Needed:

1. Large piece of construction paper (the larger the better)
2. Yardstick or meterstick
3. Rulers (12")
4. Pencils (several)
5. Black ink
6. Reference materials describing the Periodic Table. (There are now 115 known elements.) (See next page for Periodic Table.)

C. Procedure:

1. Study all the reference materials to learn about the main characteristics of each element that are usually included in that element's "box." For each element this should include:
   a. name
   b. symbol
   c. atomic number
   d. atomic weight
2. Each element belongs to a specific "group." Locate the group for each element.
3. Develop your own "Periodic Table." A sample is shown. (See drawing.)
4. Chart your Periodic Table on the construction paper.
5. Optional follow-up activities could include individual or group studies on the characteristics of each group.

D. Results:

1. A meaningful Periodic Table will be constructed.
2. Students will learn many basic facts about elements and groups of elements.

E. Basic Facts and Supplemental Information:

1. There are now 115 known elements.
2. Ninety-two of these elements occur naturally on Earth.
3. Eight elements make up 99% of the Earth's crust:

ELEMENT	PERCENT	ELEMENT	PERCENT
Oxygen	46.6	Sodium	2.9
Silicon	27.7	Potassium	2.6
Aluminum	8.1	Magnesium	2.1
Iron	5.0	All others	1.4
Calcium	3.6		

4. The smallest part of an element is the atom. Study Activity I-A-2, "What are atoms? molecules?"
5. The Periodic Table is vital to chemists.

Basic Facts about the Periodic Table

1. The atomic number is the total number of electrons of each atom.
2. Oxygen, number 8 in the Periodic Table, has 8 electrons.
3. Electrons surround the nucleus of each atom and are arranged in "orbits" or "shells" around the nucleus.
4. The innermost shell can hold only 2 electrons; the next shell, 8; the next shell, 18; etc. The shells (orbits) are designated in rows in the Periodic Table—e.g., hydrogen and helium have 1 and 2 electrons, respectively.
5. The second shell, or row, begins with lithium and ends with neon.
6. Each column of atoms has similar properties because they have an equal number of electrons in their outermost shell.
7. The atomic weight of oxygen has been assigned "16." The atomic weights of all other elements are proportional to the weight of oxygen.

F. Thought Questions for Class Discussions:

1. What are the main parts of atoms?
2. What are molecules? compounds?
3. Can elements in the same group combine to form a new molecule?
4. Are the lower atomic numbers solids, liquids, or gases?

G. Related Ideas for Further Inquiry:

1. Create mobiles of an atom from each atomic group.
2. Study about atomic energy.
3. Have students give reports on the atomic bombs that were dropped on Hiroshima and Nagasaki. They were different types of atomic bombs.
4. Study about atomic energy and nuclear power plants.

H. Vocabulary Builders—Spelling Words:

1) **element** 2) **compound** 3) **molecule**
4) **atomic** 5) **weight** 6) **number**
7) **structure** 8) **valence** 9) **Periodic Table**

I. Thought for Today:

Age is a matter of mind. If you don't mind, it doesn't matter."

TABLE OF CHEMICAL ELEMENTS

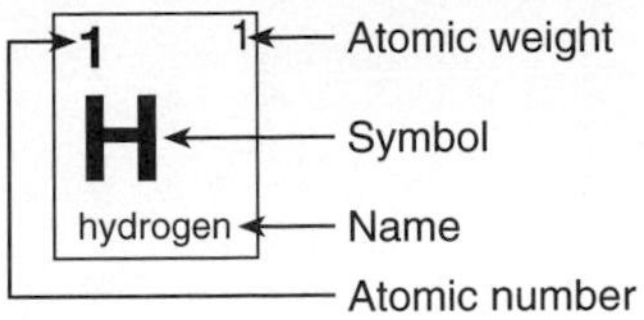

1 1.008 **H** hydrogen																	2 4.003 **He** helium
3 6.941 **Li** lithium	4 9.012 **Be** beryllium											5 10.811 **B** boron	6 12.011 **C** carbon	7 14.01 **N** nitrogen	8 16.000 **O** oxygen	9 18.998 **F** fluorine	10 20.183 **Ne** neon
11 22.990 **Na** sodium	12 24.312 **Mg** magnesuim											13 26.982 **Al** aluminum	14 28.09 **Si** silicon	15 30.974 **P** phosphorus	16 32.064 **S** sulfur	17 35.453 **Cl** chlorine	18 39.948 **Ar** argon
19 39.10 **K** potassium	20 40.08 **Ca** calcium	21 44.956 **Sc** scandium	22 47.90 **Ti** titanium	23 50.942 **V** vanadium	24 51.996 **Cr** titanium	25 54.938 **Mn** manganese	26 55.847 **Fe** iron	27 58.933 **Co** cobalt	28 58.71 **Ni** nickel	29 63.54 **Cu** copper	30 65.37 **Zn** zinc	31 69.72 **Ga** gallium	32 72.59 **Ge** germanium	33 74.922 **As** arsenium	34 78.96 **Se** selenium	35 79.90 **Br** bromine	36 83.80 **Kr** krypton
37 85.47 **Rb** rubidium	38 87.62 **Sr** strontium	39 88.905 **Y** yttrium	40 91.22 **Zr** zirconium	41 92.9 **Nb** niobium	42 95.94 **Mo** molybdenum	43 98 **Tc** technetium	44 101.07 **Ru** ruthenium	45 102.905 **Rh** rhodium	46 106.4 **Pd** palladium	47 107.9 **Ag** silver	48 112.40 **Cd** cadmium	49 114.82 **In** indium	50 118.7 **Sn** tin	51 121.8 **Sb** antimony	52 127.60 **Te** tellurium	53 126.904 **I** iodine	54 131.30 **Xe** xenon
55 132.905 **Cs** cesium	56 137.34 **Ba** barium	57–71 (See Row 57–71 Below)	* 72 178.49 **Hf** hafnium	73 180.948 **Ta** tantalum	74 183.85 **W** tungsten	75 186.2 **Re** rhenium	76 190.2 **Os** osmium	77 192.2 **Ir** iridium	78 195.09 **Pt** platinum	79 196.967 **Au** gold	80 200.59 **Hg** mercury	81 204.37 **Tl** thallium	82 207.19 **Pb** lead	83 208.980 **Bi** bismuth	84 (209) **Po** polonium	85 (210) **At** astatine	86 222 **Rn** radon
87 223 **Fr** francium	88 226 **Ra** radium	89–103 (See Row 89–103 Below)	* 104 (Wt. N.A.) **Rf** rutherfordium	105 (Wt. N.A.) **Db** dubnium	106 (Wt. N.A.) **Sg** seaborgium	107 (Wt. N.A.) **Bh** bohrium	108 (Wt. N.A.) **Hs** hassium	109 (Wt. N.A.) **Mt** meitnerium	110 Unnamed as of this writing	111 Unnamed as of this writing	112 Unnamed as of this writing	*					

* 57–71 Lanthanides	57 138.9 **La** lanthanum	58 140.12 **Ce** cerium	59 140.907 **Pr** praseodymium	60 144.24 **Nd** neodymium	61 145 **Pm** promethium	62 150.35 **Sm** samarium	63 151.96 **Eu** europium	64 157.25 **Gd** gadolinium	65 158.924 **Tb** terbium	66 162.50 **Dy** dysprosium	67 164.930 **Ho** holmium	68 167.26 **Er** erbium	69 168.934 **Tm** thulium	70 173.04 **Yb** ytterbium	71 174.97 **Lu** lutetium
* 89–103 Actinides	89 227 **Ac** actinium	90 232.038 **Th** thorium	91 231 **Pa** protactinium	92 238.03 **U** uranium	93 237 **Np** neptunium	94 244* **Pu** plutonium	95 243* **Am** americium	96 247* **Cm** curium	97 247* **Bk** berkelium	98 251* **Cf** californium	99 252* **Es** einsteinium	100 257* **Fm** fermium	101 258* **Md** mendelevium	102 259* **No** nobelium	103 260* **Lr** lawrencium

* Three new elements have synthesized in the laboratory as this book is going to press. They are atomic numbers 118,116,and 114.

Activity I A 4

A. Problem: *What Are Elements? Compounds? Mixtures?*

B. Materials Needed:

1. Glass jar
2. Bits of paper
3. Paperclips
4. Spoon
5. Water
6. Marbles
7. Tacks
8. Sand
9. Salt
10. Sugar
11. Iron filings
12. Copper pennies
13. Magnifying glass
14. Reference materials, including Periodic Table (See Activity I-A-3.)

C. Procedure:

1. Define terms:
   a. **Element**—basic unit of matter of atom consisting of electrons, protons, and neutrons.
   b. **Compound**—basic unit of molecule with atoms in fixed chemical proportions.
   c. **Mixture**—any physical combination of substances without changing chemical compositions.
2. Identify each of the substances listed in Materials Needed as to whether it is an element, a compound, or a mixture.
3. Look at the sand with a magnifying glass. Do all particles look the same?
4. Look at the sugar with a magnifying glass. Do all particles look the same?
5. Put the paper clips, bits of paper, marbles, and tacks in a half-filled glass of water.
6. Stir vigorously. Did the materials in item 5 above change in appearance?

D. Results:

1. The sand particles were varied in appearance.
2. The sugar particles were identical in appearance.
3. All of the materials in the glass retained their individual identities.

E. Basic Facts and Supplemental Information:

1. Common elements found in the home are products that consist of copper, zinc, lead, iron, etc.
2. Common compounds found in the home are salt, baking soda, ammonia, water, etc.
3. Common mixtures found in the home are liquid soap, detergents, paints, soups, salad dressings, milk, etc.
4. A mixture is a combination of two or more ingredients, not in a fixed proportion, with each part retaining its identity.

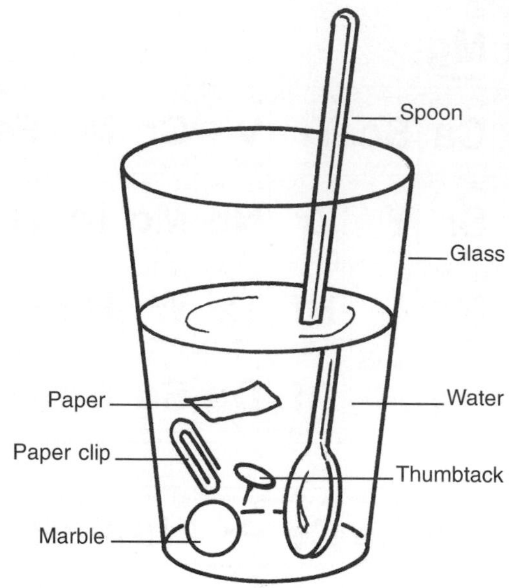

F. Thought Questions for Class Discussions:

1. Is a mixture the result of a physical change or a chemical change?
2. How does a mixture differ from a solution?
3. How many mixtures can you name?
4. Is air a mixture or a compound?

G. Related Ideas for Further Inquiry:

1. Have students make a chart of the first 10 elements in the Periodic Table showing differences in atomic number, weight, number of protons, number of electrons, number of neutrons, and the number of electrons in the outer ring.
2. Discuss what elements, compounds, and mixtures are found in sea water.
3. Make a list of 10 compounds found in the home.
4. Make a list of 10 mixtures found in the home.
5. Make a list of 5 elements found in the home.
6. Study Activity I-A-2 "What are atoms? molecules?"
7. Study Activity I-A-3, "What is the 'Periodic Table'?"
8. Study Activity I-A-11, "What are the tiniest pieces of matter?"
9. Study Activity I-A-12, "What is a solution?"

H. Vocabulary Builders—Spelling Words:

1) **elements** 2) **compounds** 3) **mixtures** 4) **iron** 5) **copper** 6) **sand** 7) **sugar** 8) **marbles**

I. Thought for Today:

"Education is not training but rather the process that equips you to entertain yourself, a friend, and an idea."

A. Problem: *What Is the Difference Between a Physical Change and a Chemical Change?*

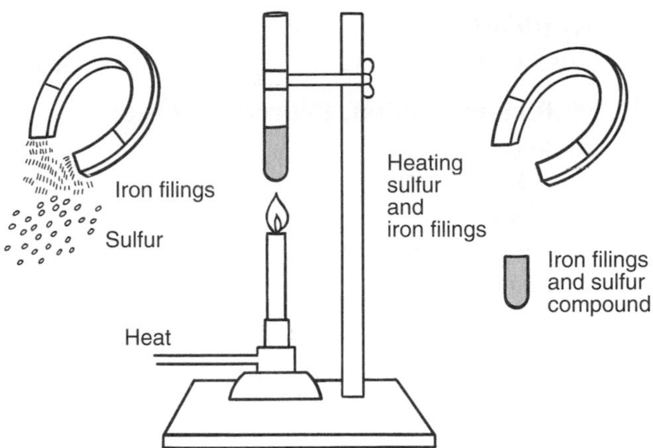

B. Materials Needed:

1. Sulfur powder
2. Iron filings
3. Two test tubes
4. Magnet
5. Saucer
6. Ring stand
7. Paper towels
8. Hammer
9. Hot plate or Bunsen burner
10. Goggles

C. Procedure:

1. Mix sulfur and iron filings in a test tube.
2. Shake the two elements together.
3. Pour them into a saucer.
4. Using a magnet, separate the iron filings from the sulfur.
5. Put twice as much sulfur as iron filings into a second test tube.
6. Heat this test tube over a hot plate or Bunsen burner. (Only the teacher or older student under the supervision of the teacher should do this part.)
7. Let cool.
8. Wrap the test tube in paper towels.
9. With hammer, break it as *carefully* as possible.
10. Using the magnet, try to separate the iron filings from the sulfur.

D. Results:

1. When the iron and sulfur were mixed in the first test tube, the magnet attracted all the iron filings.
2. When the iron and sulfur were mixed in the second test tube and heated, a change in color occurred. The magnet was unable to separate the iron filings from the sulfur. They had chemically combined to form iron sulfide.

E. Basic Facts and Supplemental Information:

1. A mixture is the placing together of two or more elements with each element retaining its individual properties. A compound is the union of two or more elements by chemical change, with each element no longer retaining its original characteristics.
2. A solution is a special kind of mixture. It usually consists of solid materials dissolving in a liquid. Salt water is a good example of this type of mixture. A liquid can be combined with another liquid to form a solution by a "physical change." Adding milk to a cup of coffee would be a good example of a "physical change." Two liquids could be combined by a chemical change. Mixing an acid with a base would yield this kind of "combination."

F. Thought Questions for Class Discussions:

1. How do we know a chemical change has taken place?
2. When water evaporates into the air, is this a physical or a chemical change?
3. Why won't the magnet attract the iron sulfide compound?

G. Related Ideas for Further Inquiry:

1. Study home food recipes for mixtures.
2. Study mineral ores for compounds.
3. Study Activity I-A-2, "What are atoms? molecules?"
4. Study Activity I-A-3, "What is the 'Periodic Table'?"
5. Study Activity I-A-4, "What are elements? compounds? mixtures?"

H. Vocabulary Builders—Spelling Words:

1) **materials** 2) **combine** 3) **elements** 4) **compounds** 5) **mixtures** 6) **ores** 7) **magnet** 8) **sulfur** 9) **filings**

I. Thought for Today:

"Those who do not learn from the mistakes of the past are condemned to repeat them."

Activity I A 6

A. Problem: *Can a Solid and a Liquid Make a Gas? Can a Solid Change Directly to a Gas?*

B. Materials Needed, Procedure One:

1. Rubber balloon
2. Soft drink bottle
3. Baking soda (2 teaspoons)
4. Vinegar (one-quarter cup)
5. Spoon

Materials Needed, Procedure Two:

1. Glass tray or casserole dish
2. Dry ice
3. Tongs

C. Procedure One:

1. Spoon the baking soda into the balloon.
2. Carefully pour the vinegar into the bottle.
3. Affix the balloon to the top of the bottle keeping the baking soda at the bottom of the balloon.
4. Lift the bottom of the balloon with the baking soda over the top of the bottle.
5. Release the balloon.

Procedure Two:

1. Discuss with class the three states of matter.
2. Explain the fact that any substance is a solid, liquid, or gas depending on the amount of energy (heat) it holds.
3. As an example, water is a solid when its temperature is below 0°C.; a liquid from 0° C. to 100° C; and a gas above 100°C.
4. Show the class the dry ice.
5. Inform them that dry ice is solid carbon dioxide.
6. Using the tongs, place the dry ice on the glass tray or in the casserole dish.

D. Results:

1. The balloon will become inflated over the bottle.
2. The dry ice will change directly to gaseous carbon dioxide.

E. Basic Facts and Supplemental Information:

1. Procedure One involves a chemical change. The baking soda reacts with vinegar to form two new substances, one of which is carbon dioxide, a gas that inflates the balloon.
2. Procedure Two involves a physical change. Solid ice acquires heat from the air and changes directly to a gas. There is no chemical change. It starts out as solid carbon dioxide and ends up as gaseous carbon dioxide. This is called "sublimation."

F. Thought Questions for Class Discussions:

1. Is carbon dioxide ever used in the home?
2. When gasoline burns in an automobile engine is carbon dioxide involved?
3. Is carbon dioxide involved in photosynthesis?

G. Related Ideas for Further Inquiry:

1. Study "sublimation," the changing of a substance from a solid directly to a gas.
2. Study Activity I-A-4, "What are elements? compounds? mixtures?"
3. Study Activity I-A-5, "What is the difference between a physical change and a chemical change?"

H. Vocabulary Builders—Spelling Words:

1) **carbon dioxide** 2) **baking soda** 3) **vinegar** 4) **sublimation** 5) **transfer** 6) **expand** 7) **gaseous** 8) **substance**

I. Thought for Today:

"The only disability in life is a bad attitude."

Procedure One

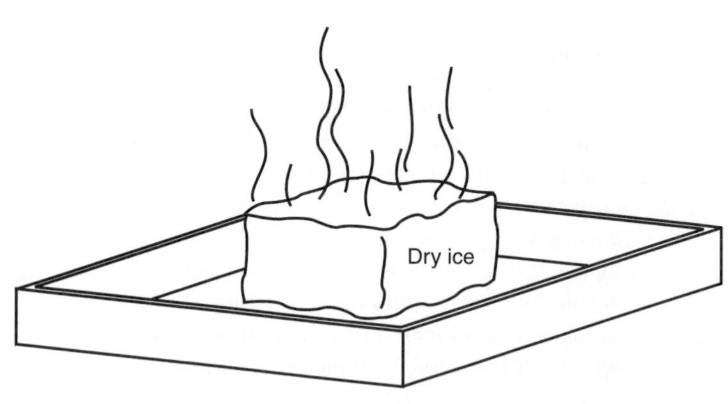

Procedure Two

Activity IA7

A. Problem: *What Is the Difference Between Weight and Volume?*

B. Materials Needed:

1. Volleyball, football, or softball
2. Weighing device
3. Balancing board with fulcrum
4. Balloon
5. Weights

C. Procedure:

1. Blow up the balloon to the approximate size of the ball.
2. Weigh the balloon.
3. Record the weight of the balloon.
4. Weigh the ball.
5. Record the weight of the ball.
6. Place the fulcrum in the center of the balancing board.
7. Try to balance the balloon and ball without weights on the balloon side.
8. Add weights to the side of the balloon to see if you can balance them. You might have to adjust the fulcrum.
9. Discuss these three terms:
   a. mass (aggregate of matter)
   b. weight (heaviness of matter)
   c. volume (size of mass)

D. Results:

1. The ball and the balloon weigh different amounts.
2. The ball is heavier than the balloon.
3. The balancing board will not balance without any weights.
4. The balancing board can be balanced with the addition of weights and possibly an adjustment of the fulcrum.

E. Basic Facts and Supplemental Information:

1. Any mass has both weight and volume.
2. Common weight measurements of objects are ounces, pounds, and tons, or in the metric system, grams, kilograms, and metric tons. A metric ton is equal to 1.1 tons (short ton).
3. Common volume measurements of solids are reported in cubic inches, cubic feet, and cubic yards, or in the metric system, cubic centimeters, cubic meters, and cubic kilometers.
4. Common volume measurements of liquids are ounces and quarts and in the metric system, milliliters and liters.
5. Weight is the gravitational pull of an object.

Placing the ball and balloon on the fulcrum like this:

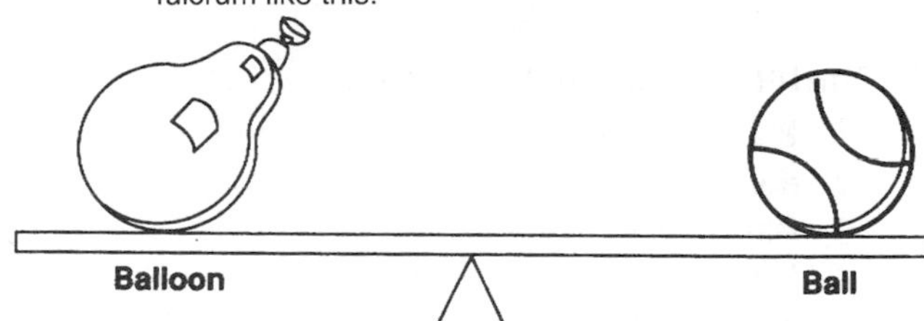

will cause this:

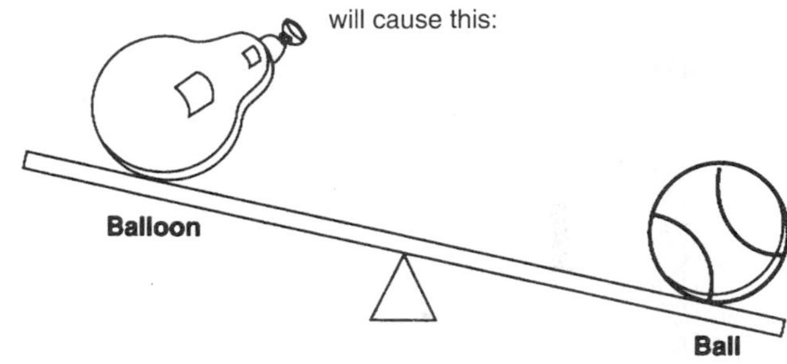

F. Thought Questions for Class Discussions:

1. Could you weigh an object if it were lighter than air?
2. How could you determine the volume of any object?
3. How could you determine the mass of any object?

G. Related Ideas for Further Inquiry:

1. Weigh objects of different sizes and shapes.
2. Compute the volume of regularly shaped three-dimensional objects.
3. To find the volume of irregularly shaped objects:
   a. Pour water into a container, allowing enough space so that the object can be immersed without the water overflowing.
   b. Measure this amount of water and record this volume.
   c. Immerse the object in the water.
   d. Record the new volume of water with the immersed object in it.
   e. The volume of the object is the difference between the volume of water with the object in it and the volume of water without the object in it.

H. Vocabulary Builders—Spelling Words:

1) **mass** 2) **weight** 3) **balance** 4) **ball** 5) **balloon** 6) **fulcrum** 7) **resistance**

I. Thought for Today

"Approach problems with an open mind."

Activity I A 8

A. Problem: *What Matter Is Acidic? What Matter Is Alkaline?*

B. Materials Needed:

1. Three water glasses
2. Red litmus paper
3. Blue litmus paper
4. Vinegar
5. Ammonia or baking soda solution
6. Salt (one-half teaspoon)
7. Water

C. Procedure:

1. Prepare a saltwater solution by mixing one-half teaspoon salt in a glass of water.
2. Dip a piece of red and a piece of blue litmus paper into the solution.
3. In a second glass pour a small amount of vinegar.
4. Dip a piece of blue litmus paper into the solution.
5. In a third glass pour a small amount of ammonia or baking soda (about one-quarter teaspoon).
6. Dip a piece of red litmus paper into this solution.
7. Repeat steps 4 and 6 using other colored litmus paper.

D. Results:

1. In the saltwater solution the red and blue litmus papers did not change color.
2. In the vinegar solution the blue litmus paper turned red.
3. In the ammonia or baking soda solution the red litmus paper turned blue.
4. See Basic Facts and Supplemental Information for other test results.

E. Basic Facts and Supplemental Information:

1. Ions are atoms or molecules that have gained or lost electrons from their original outer shell.
2. Solutions usually have hydrogen or hydroxide ions. If they have hydrogen ions they are acidic. If they have hydroxide ions they are alkaline (basic).
3. Litmus paper turns blue in the presence of alkaline solutions and red in the presence of acids. We can conclude that vinegar is acidic and that ammonia is alkaline (basic). Other liquids can be tested to determine if they are acidic or basic.

Salt water

Red and blue litmus paper remain the same

Vinegar

Blue litmus paper turns red

Ammonia

Red litmus paper turns blue

4. Some tap water may be naturally acidic or basic, and if so, then bottled or distilled water will have to be used for the procedure.

F. Thought Questions for Class Discussions:

1. Why do we need to know whether a substance is acid or alkaline?
2. If acid is spilled, how can we prevent it from causing damage?
3. What would happen if we placed red litmus paper in the vinegar? Blue litmus in the ammonia or baking soda solution?

G. Related Ideas for Further Inquiry:

1. Test other liquids to determine if they are acidic or alkaline.
2. Research other chemical tests for determining acidity or alkalinity of liquids.
3. If you put blue litmus paper in lemon juice, it turns red, showing that lemon juice is acidic.
4. If you put red litmus paper in a test solution and it turns blue, this proves the solution is alkaline (basic).
5. Study Activity I-A-2 "What are atoms? molecules?"
6. Study Activity I-A-12, "What is a solution?"

H. Vocabulary Builders—Spelling Words:

1) **acidic** 2) **alkaline** 3) **alkalinity** 4) **basic** 5) **litmus paper** 6) **vinegar** 7) **ammonia** 8) **baking soda**

I. Thought for Today:

"If people learn from their mistakes, many are getting a fantastic education."

Activity

A. Problem: *How Does a Fire Extinguisher Work?*

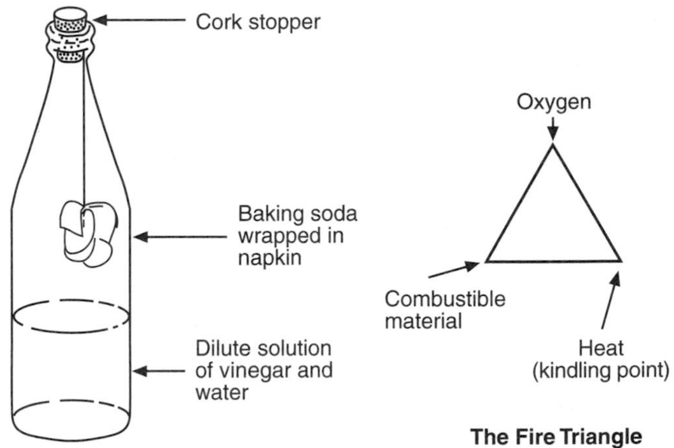

The Fire Triangle

B. Materials Needed:

1. Clear pint or quart bottle
2. Cork stopper
3. Vinegar water (one tablespoon vinegar in one cup water)
4. Baking soda
5. Paper napkin, small
6. Spoon and cup for measuring
7. Thread
8. Paper towels

C. Procedure:

1. Fill bottle about one-third full of diluted vinegar.
2. Wrap one teaspoonful of baking soda in a napkin.
3. Tie thread around napkin and suspend by fitting cork to neck of bottle.
4. Place cork in bottle so that it may be removed with minimum effort.
5. Wrap bottle with several thickness of paper towels as a safety precaution.
6. Keep class members at least six feet away from bottle.
7. When fire extinguisher is set to use, point the top of the bottle toward the ceiling or toward a solid wall. *Be very careful not to point it toward anything which might break or cause injury.*
8. Invert the bottle momentarily and the solution will soften the napkin; the baking soda will be released to drop into the vinegar solution.
9. Quickly aim the bottle at the ceiling or wall.

D. Result:

When the vinegar reacts with the baking soda, carbon dioxide is given off. The carbon dioxide builds up pressure and the cork is forced out of the bottle with great force.

E. Basic Facts and Supplemental Information:

1. Carbon dioxide does not support combustion.
2. Carbon dioxide drives out some of the oxygen that is needed for combustion.
3. Three items are required for fires (burning): (a) combustible material, (b) oxygen, and (c) heat. This is called the "Fire Triangle."
4. If any one of the three items is removed, then no burning can take place.
5. In a real fire, the fire extinguisher should be aimed at the edge of the fire, not the center.
6. Carbon dioxide does not support combustion because it is not a part of the "Fire Triangle." It slows down burning by replacing the oxygen with carbon dioxide.

F. Thought Questions for Class Discussions:

1. Why do we wrap the baking soda in a paper napkin?
2. How does carbon dioxide stop fires from burning?
3. Do all gases slow down fires?

G. Related Ideas for Further Inquiry:

1. Design a fire extinguisher using different materials or procedures.
2. Have a fire department representative talk to class.
3. Show the class a real fire extinguisher. Explain how it operates.
4. Study Activity I-A-5, "What is the difference between a physical change and a chemical change?"
5. Study Activity VI-D-6, "How can we protect our recreational areas?"

H. Vocabulary Builders—Spelling Words:

1) **extinguisher** 2) **vinegar** 3) **napkin**
4) **fire** 5) **oxygen** 6) **combustible**

I. Thought for Today:

"He who hesitates is sometimes saved."

Activity I A 10

A. Problem: *What Is Diffusion?*

B. Materials Needed, Procedure One:

1. Water glass
2. Medicine dropper
3. Food coloring
4. Water

Materials Needed, Procedure Two:

1. Water glass or beaker
2. Coffee crystals
3. Water

Materials Needed, Procedure Three:

1. Two glass jars or clear plastic containers with tops
2. Mothballs

Materials Needed, Procedure Four:

1. Bulletin board
2. 100 cutout disks
   a. red color preferred
   b. about 1 1/2 inches in diameter
3. 100 straight pins

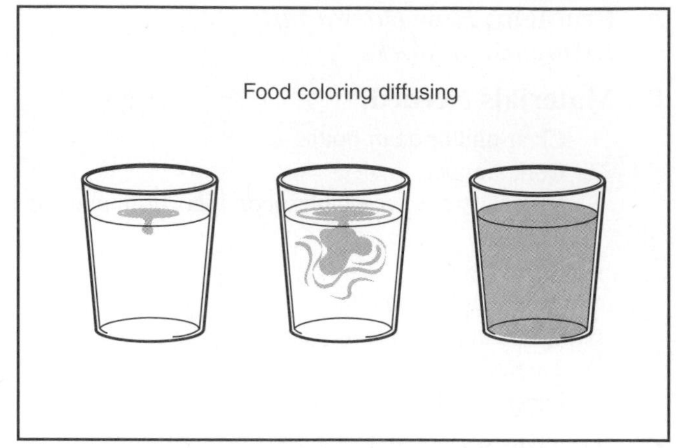

Procedure One

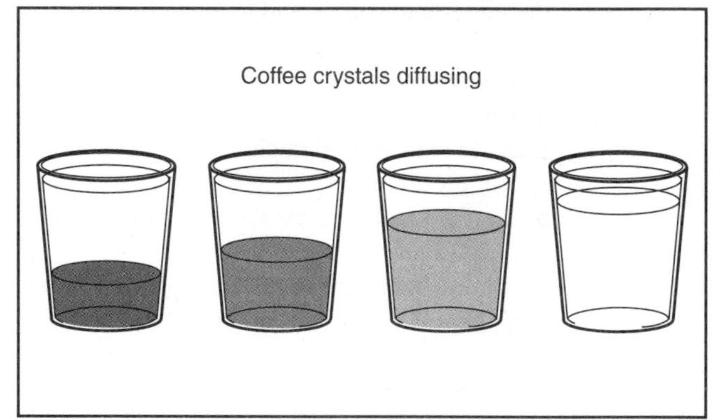

Procedure Two

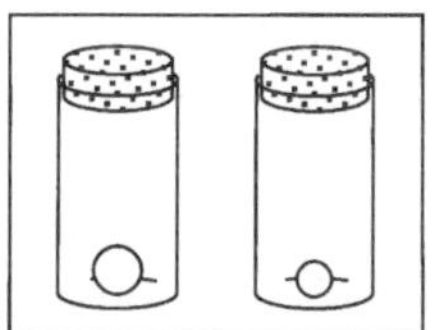

The mothball in the capped jar becomes smaller.

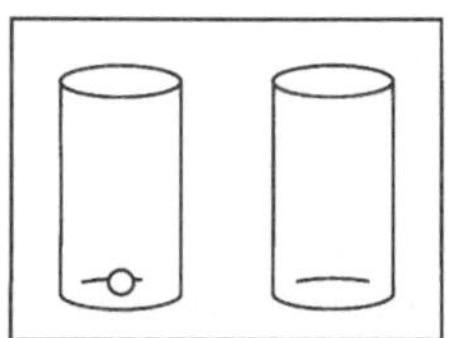

The mothball in the uncapped jar disappears.

Procedure Three

C. Procedure One:

1. Fill one of the glasses two-thirds full of water.
2. Put some food coloring in the medicine dropper, and place several drops on the surface of the water.
3. Set glass aside and observe after several hours.

Procedure Two:

1. Place some coffee crystals in a water glass or beaker.
2. Slowly pour water over the crystals and let stand. Observe results immediately and again after several hours.

Procedure Three:

1. Place one mothball in each of two containers, capping one of them.
2. Let stand for several days or weeks and note any changes.

Procedure Four:

1. Pin 100 disks on the bulletin board in 10 rows of 10 disks to a row closely packed together (see drawing). Do not discuss this with anyone.
2. On day 2, spread the disks apart leaving about an inch between each of the disks. Again avoid any conversations regarding them.
3. On day 3, move the disks so that there are 3 or more inches between the disks.
4. On the fourth day, pin the disks all over the bulletin board in random fashion. Now discuss what has been happening. Diffusion!!!
5. Ask the students if they know what "diffusion" is.
6. Challenge the students to teach others about "diffusion."
7. Pin one of the disks on the clothing of each student; have students wear the disk for one school

day. When anyone asks them what it is, tell the students they will have to explain "diffusion" to that person. To verify that this is being done, the "nonclass" person who asked what the disk was for would be requested to initial the back of the disk. When a student has five initials on his/her disk, it can be taken off.

The author knows of one teacher who was promoted primarily on the basis of this Activity. Everyone in that teacher's school knew the meaning of "diffusion."

D. Results:

1. When drops of food coloring are placed on the surface of the water, the molecules in a liquid state (food coloring) move through the water.
2. When some coffee crystals are placed in a glass of water, the molecules in a solid state (coffee) move through water.
3. In the activity with mothballs, the mothball in the uncovered jar will eventually disappear. The mothball in the covered jar will become smaller. Mothballs change to a gas and dissipate over a period of time.
4. In Procedure Four, everyone learns the meaning of "diffusion."

E. Basic Facts and Supplemental Information:

1. Molecules are so small that we cannot see them.
2. Molecules are in constant motion regardless of whether they are in a solid, liquid, or gaseous state.
3. In these activities we can think of the food coloring, coffee crystals, or mothballs as clumps of molecules.

F. Thought Questions for Class Discussions:

1. Why do clothes dry faster outside?
2. Where does all the water go when it rains?
3. Would perfume be valuable if it didn't diffuse?

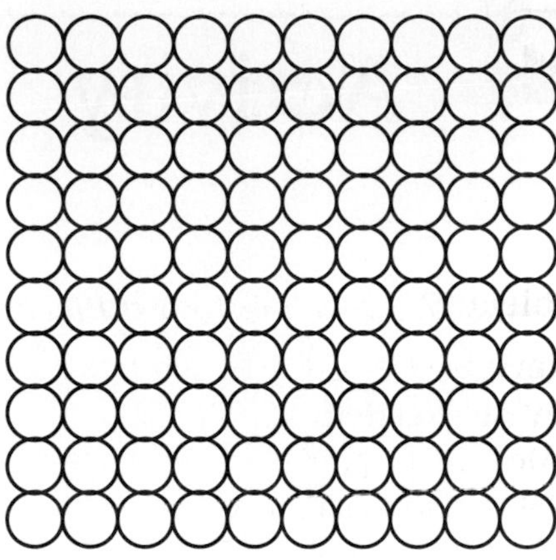

Diffusion disks

Procedure Four

G. Related Ideas for Further Inquiry:

1. Study Activity I-A-2, "What are atoms? molecules?"
2. Study Activity I-A-3, "What is the 'Periodic Table'?"
3. Study Activity I-A-5, "What is the difference between a physical change and a chemical change?"
4. Study Activity I-A-12, "What is a solution?"

H. Vocabulary Builders—Spelling Words:

1) **diffusion** 2) **mothballs** 3) **coffee** 4) **crystals** 5) **disks** 6) **dissolving** 7) **evaporation** 8) **molecules** 9) **physical** 10) **chemical**

I. Thought for Today:

"Do not put off until tomorrow what you can do today."

Activity I A 11

A. Problem: *What Are the Tiniest Pieces of Matter?*

B. Materials Needed:

1. Paper
2. Pencils (black and colored)
3. Drawing compasses
4. Reference materials on atomic structure

C. Procedure:

1. Describe and define atoms and their subatomic particles.
2. Have students read about atomic structure.
3. Have students draw the four sketches after they have read the characteristics of each.
4. Using whatever color code you wish, color the various parts of each drawing.
5. Mount the better drawings on the bulletin board.

D. Results:

1. Students will learn about the tiniest pieces of matter by studying and drawing the present information we have on atomic structure.
2. Students will learn that matter is composed of large pieces which can be broken down into smaller and smaller pieces.

E. Basic Facts and Supplemental Information:

1. Scientists have determined that atoms are the smallest particle of matter that still retain the characteristics of the larger piece of matter.
2. Atoms are composed of protons and neutrons in a nucleus and electrons orbiting around the nucleus.
3. Neutrons and protons collectively are called "nucleons."
4. All nucleons consist of quarks and leptons.
5. A proton consists of a(n):
   a. electron (charged lepton)
   b. electron neutrino (neutral lepton)
   c. up quarks (two of them)
   d. down quark (one of them)
6. A neutron consists of a(n):
   a. electron (charged lepton)
   b. electron neutrino (neutral neutrino)
   c. down quarks (two of them)
   d. up quark (one of them)
7. Gluons bind the quarks together.
8. Over 100 types of atomic particles have been identified.
9. Scientists have been able to identify different particles by pictures taken in "atom smashers."

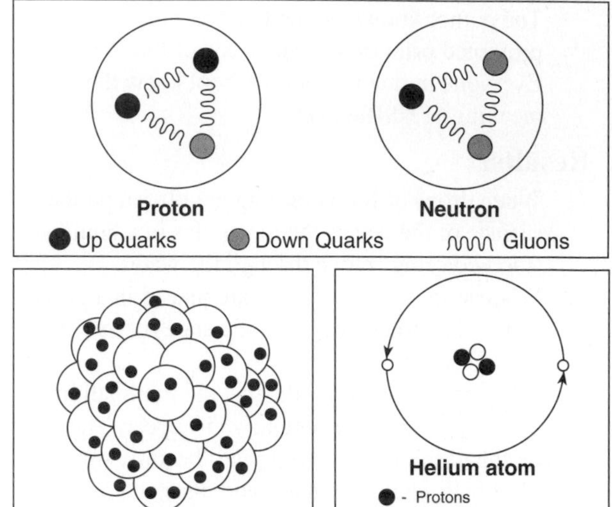

10. Many of these particles exist only for a fraction of a second.
11. We still don't know all the subatomic particles and how they are related to each other.
12. In German "quark" means "cottage cheese."

F. Thought Questions for Class Discussions:

1. Do you think that leptons and quarks can be subdivided? New evidence suggests this can be done.
2. Do our bodies contain leptons and quarks?
3. Is there anything that doesn't contain leptons and quarks?
4. How do scientists find out about subatomic particles, particles that are too small to be seen with the naked eye?

G. Related Ideas for Further Inquiry:

1. Study the different "families" of matter.
2. Students can make models of atoms by using clay, styrofoam, or paper mobiles.
3. Study Activity I-A-2, "What are atoms? molecules?"
4. Study Activity I-A-3, "What is the 'Periodic Table'?"
5. Study Activity I-A-4, "What are elements? compounds? mixtures?"

H. Vocabulary Builders—Spelling Words:

1) **atoms** 2) **electrons** 3) **protons** 4) **neutrons** 5) **leptons** 6) **quarks** 7) **neutrinos** 8) **gluons**

I. Thought for Today:

"The impossible is often untried."

Activity I A 12

A. Problem: *What Is a Solution?*

B. Materials Needed:

1. Water glass
2. Water, warm
3. Teaspoon
4. Sugar
5. Measuring cup

C. Procedure:

1. Fill the water glass with warm water using the measuring cup to fill the glass to the brim, but not overflowing.
2. Fill the teaspoon with sugar.
3. Slowly and carefully add the sugar to the water.
4. Wait until it dissolves completely.
5. Add a second teaspoon of sugar slowly and carefully.
6. Sometimes a third teaspoon of sugar can be added depending on the size of the glass and the warmth of the water.
7. Ask the class, "Where did the sugar go? Why doesn't the water overflow?"

D. Results:

1. The first teaspoon of sugar will dissolve quickly.
2. The second teaspoon of sugar will dissolve but it will take a little more time.
3. Usually, the third teaspoon of sugar will cause the water to overflow.

E. Basic Facts and Supplemental Information:

1. A solution is a liquid containing a dissolved substance. The substance can be a solid, liquid, or a gas.
2. In solids, molecules are packed tightly together.
3. In liquids, molecules are wider apart, thus leaving "holes" or "openings."
4. In gases, molecules become disconnected and they will dissipate anywhere they can.
5. In this Activity, the solid sugar molecules find the "holes" or "openings" and do not take up any more volume.
6. When these are full, the water can no longer hold any more sugar, so the volume increases and the water overflows.
7. The warmer the water, the larger the "holes" or "openings," and the more sugar can be added.

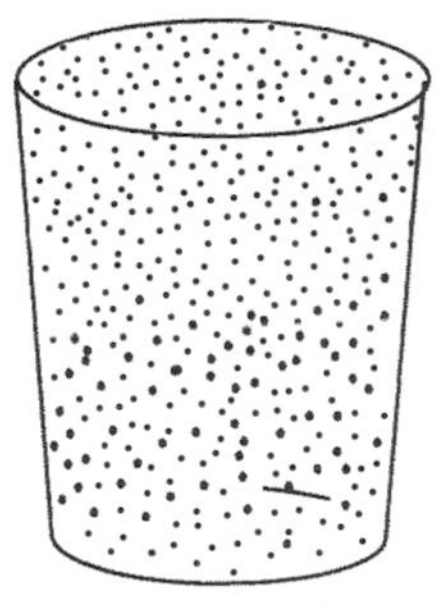

Sugar dissolving in water

8. Whenever a solid substance is homogeneously mixed with a liquid and does not precipitate out, it is known as *dissolving* the substance in the liquid. The resulting liquid is a combination of the original liquid, plus the solid, which has been dissolved in it. This is known as a solution. Liquids can hold only so much dissolved material for each temperature.
9. There are many solutions we come in contact with daily in our homes, in our schools, and in our neighborhoods. In our homes, liquid detergents, hair sprays, liquid medicines, and bleaches are good examples of solutions. Soft drinks, chocolate milk, and some salad dressings are solutions.

F. Thought Questions for Class Discussions:

1. What would happen in a "saturated solution" if the liquid solvent were cooled?
2. Can air hold water? Can water hold air?
3. Is a solution a "mixture"?

G. Related Ideas for Further Inquiry:

1. Study solutions found in the home.
2. Study why some solutions are thicker or thinner (viscosity).
3. Study Activity I-A-2, "What are atoms? molecules?"
4. Study Activity I-A-4, "What are elements? compounds? mixtures?
5. Study Activity I-A-10, "What is diffusion?

H. Vocabulary Builders—Spelling Words:

1) **solution** 2) **solvent** 3) **solute** 4) **dissolve** 5) **molecules** 6) **movement** 7) **teaspoon** 8) **sugar**

I. Thought for Today:

"Chemistry is no field for people with shaky hands."

A. Problem: *What Color Marble Sinks Faster?*

B. Materials Needed:

1. Five tall water glasses (clear)
2. Five marbles, all different colors
3. Rubbing alcohol
4. Water
5. Salad oil
6. Mineral oil
7. Light color corn syrup
8. Paper towels
9. Five spoons

C. Procedure:

1. Tell the class, "We want to have a contest to see which color marble sinks faster."
2. Select five students as contestants.
3. Select three other students as judges.
4. Fill the water glasses to within a half inch of the top with the liquids cited in "Materials Needed," one with water, one with alcohol, etc.
5. Place the glasses far enough apart so that students won't bump into each other.
6. Hand each student one marble.
7. Tell them that each of them is to place his or her marble just above the surface of the liquid. Then when you say "GO," each is to release the marble to see which marble is heavier and sinks faster.
8. When everything is set, say "GO."
9. You may have to have several contests to determine the winner and the rankings.
10. Retrieve the marbles from the liquids using spoons.
11. Wipe off the marbles with the paper towels after each contest.
12. You can also change contestants. Tell the class that different people have different reaction times, i.e., time between a stimulus and the reaction to it.

D. Results:

1. The marbles will sink at different rates.
2. The thicker the liquid, the slower the descent of the marble.

E. Basic Facts and Supplemental Information:

1. The speed of descent of each marble will depend on the viscosity (density or thickness) of the fluid, not the color of the marble.
2. Many scientific investigations are like this one. The real factor is hidden; the obvious one is called a "red herring," which has nothing to do with the item under study.

Colored marbles in different liquids

3. Viscosity is the resistance to flow.
4. Viscosity plays a major role any time liquids are involved in lubricating, spraying, etc.
5. Long slender jars can be substituted for water glasses.
6. If tall graduates are available, they make excellent test equipment. (Graduates are glass or plastic measuring devices for determining quantities of liquids.)

F. Thought Questions for Class Discussions:

1. What other liquids could be tested in this experiment?
2. What determines whether an object sinks or floats?
3. Do heavier things sink faster?

G. Related Ideas for Further Inquiry:

1. Study all Activities in this Section I-A, "Matter," and in Section I-C, "Water."
2. Study Section VII-C, "Earth's Crust."

H. Vocabulary Builders—Spelling Words:

1) **viscosity** 2) **density** 3) **thickness**
4) **marbles** 5) **liquid** 6) **reaction time**

I. Thought for Today:

"If you are going around in circles, you are cutting too many corners."

Section B: Air

Activity I B 1

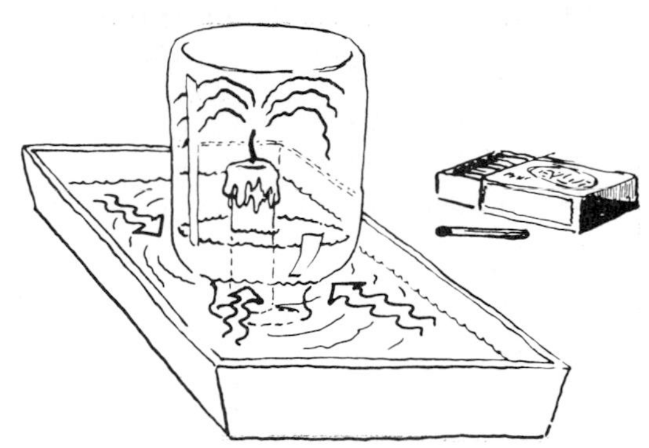

A. Problem: *How Much Oxygen Is in the Air?*

B. Materials Needed:

1. Widemouth jar (quart size)
2. Pyrex dish or metal pan
3. Matches
4. Candle
5. Water to fill dish halfway
6. Food coloring

C. Procedure:

1. Light candle.
2. Set candle on melted drippings in the center of dish or pan.
3. Fill pan half-full of water.
4. Add food coloring to water for better effect.
5. Place widemouth jar over lighted candle.
6. Observe results.

D. Results:

1. The candle will cease burning.
2. Water will rise in the jar.

E. Basic Facts and Supplemental Information:

The candle flame has removed most of the oxygen from the air in the jar. The pressure of the air left inside the jar has been reduced below that of the air outside. Carbon dioxide, CO_2, is also formed. Air heated by the candle escapes under the lip of the jar. Water rises in the jar about one-fifth of the way so that we can conclude that oxygen makes up about 20% of the air. This is a rough estimate only since there are several other factors which must be taken into account such as heat, incomplete combustion, etc. Much of the remaining air is nitrogen, which makes up about 79% of the normal air constituency. Other gases found in the air in small quantities are carbon dioxide, neon, krypton, argon, xenon, and ozone.

F. Thought Questions for Class Discussions:

1. Why does the candle go out?
2. Why does the water rise in the jar?
3. Is there any change in water level if the jar partially filled with water is allowed to remain for a while? Why? Mark level(s) by placing rubber band(s) around the jar.
4. What are the "products of combustion"? Do they have any effect in this activity?

G. Related Ideas for Further Inquiry:

1. Study and give examples of the "Fire Triangle"—the three requirements needed for combustion to take place.

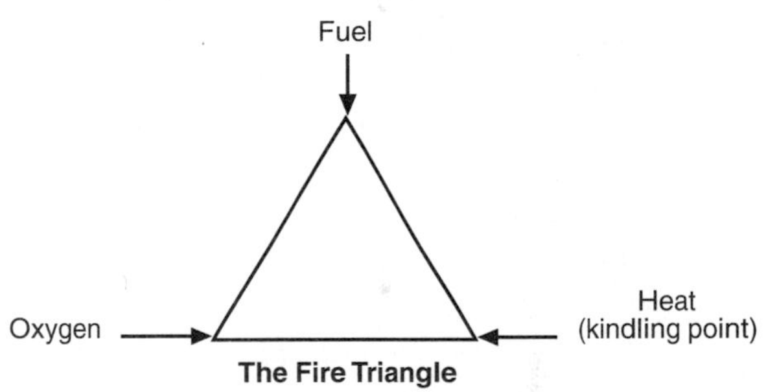

2. Using the "Fire Triangle," cite some examples of how combustion could be controlled or eliminated in practical situations such as: forest fires, home fires, picnic fires, etc.
3. Discuss how welders use oxygen.
4. Discuss how oxygen is a vital factor in space exploration.
5. Study Activity I-B-3, "How can we make carbon dioxide? How can we detect carbon dioxide?"
6. Study Activity I-B-4, "Can air pressure crush a can?"
7. Study Activity I-B-5, "Can a shelled hard-boiled egg be put into a small-mouthed bottle without breaking the egg?"

H. Vocabulary Builders—Spelling Words:

1) **oxygen** 2) **nitrogen** 3) **carbon** 4) **escapes** 5) **combustion** 6) **rises** 7) **estimate** 8) **Pyrex**

I. Thought for Today:

"Education makes people easy to lead but difficult to drive: easy to govern but impossible to enslave."

Activity I B 2

A. Problem: *How Does Air Pressure in a Bicycle Tire Hold Up the Bicycle?*

B. Materials Needed:

1. Bicycle with inflated tires
2. Hand tire pump

C. Procedure:

1. Deflate one bicycle tire.
2. Feel the tire.
3. Attach hose of hand pump to air valve of deflated tire.
4. Inflate the tire using hand pump.
5. Stop when inflated tire has normal appearance.
6. Have students feel the bicycle tire and the tire pump.

D. Results:

1. Students can see and feel that air pressure does hold up the bicycle tire.
2. The pump, not the handle, gets hot due to the compression of the air by the pump.

E. Basic Facts and Supplemental Information:

1. Automobile tires function in the same way as bicycle tires.
2. Air pressure can hold up heavy objects. Some types of lifts use this principle. If time permits, you may wish to have students study how an air pump works.

F. Thought Questions for Class Discussions:

1. Why does a bicycle tire get flat only on the bottom?
2. What might cause a tire to go flat?
3. Is the air pressure in the tire greater than the air pressure outside the tire?
4. How is air pressure measured?

G. Related Ideas for Further Inquiry:

1. Try the same test with an automobile tire tube if one is available.
2. Try the same test with an air mattress.
3. Try the same test with a beach ball.
4. Study Activity I-B-9, "In which direction does air pressure exert the greatest force?"
5. Study Activity I-B-4, "Can air pressure crush a can?"

H. Vocabulary Builders—Spelling Words:

1) **bicycle** 2) **tire** 3) **inflate** 4) **deflate** 5) **attach** 6) **automobile** 7) **compression**

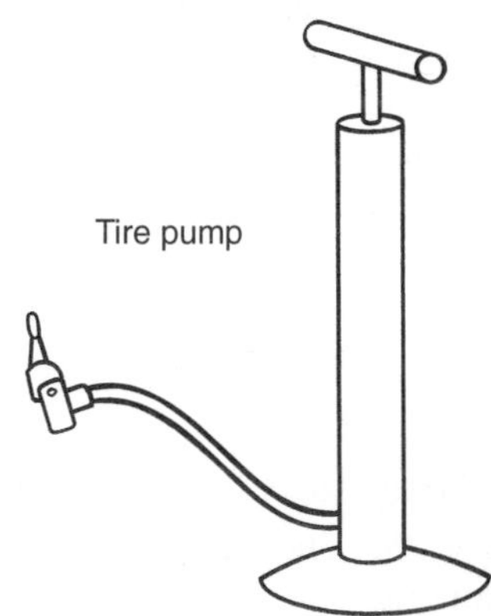

I. Thought for Today:

"A mistake is evidence that someone has tried to do something."

Activity

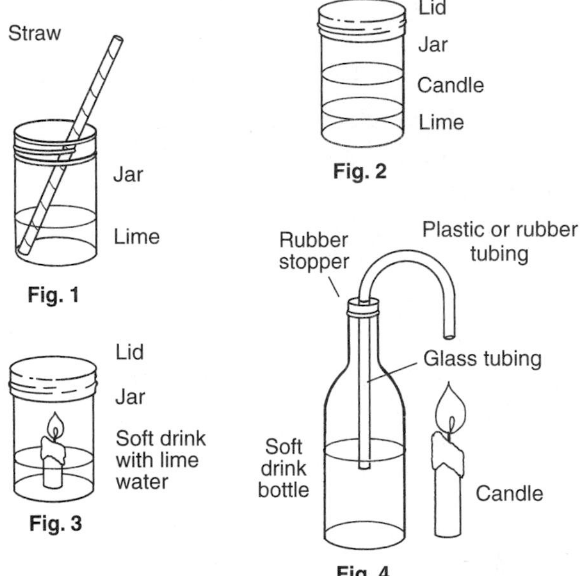

A. Problem: *How Can We Make Carbon Dioxide? How Can We Detect Carbon Dioxide?*

(Four Activities; may do one or more.)

B. Materials Needed:

1. Limewater or slaked lime (purchase at a lumber yard or pharmacy)
2. Water
3. Clear soft drink (carbonated)
4. Plastic or glass jar with cover
5. Small candle
6. Small bottle
7. Plastic tubing
8. Rubber stopper, one hole (to fit into top of soft drink bottle)
9. Glass tubing
10. Drinking straw
11. Tablespoon

C. Procedure:

1. Use limewater or dissolve a tablespoon of slaked lime in a quart of water. Shake well. Let stand till nearly clear; remove and pour off the clear solution leaving the white solid in the bottom undisturbed.
2. Place a one inch layer of this lime solution in the jar and blow through the solution with the drinking straw. (Figure 1).
3. Place a candle in a glass jar; light the candle; and place the lid over the jar. (Figure 2).
4. As soon as the candle goes out, remove the lid and candle and quickly add one-quarter inch of the lime solution. Cap the jar and shake well.
5. Add half of the soft drink to the jar with the limewater solution. Shake well. (Figure 3).
6. Wet the rubber stopper and insert tubing.
7. Place the stopper in the bottle that is half-filled with soft drink. (Figure 4).
8. Attach the plastic tubing to the glass tubing.
9. Shake well holding the plastic tubing tightly; then release it over the candle.

D. Results:

1. If carbon dioxide is present in sufficient strength, it will turn the limewater milky due to the formation of calcium carbonate.
2. Exhaled air from the human body contains carbon dioxide and will turn limewater milky or cloudy.
3. A burning candle gives off carbon dioxide; carbon dioxide does not support combustion.
4. The carbon dioxide present in a soft drink will turn milky in the presence of limewater.
5. Carbon dioxide displaces oxygen and will extinguish the candle.

E. Basic Facts and Supplemental Information:

1. Most soft drinks contain carbonic acid produced by dissolving carbon dioxide in water.
2. When oxygen and a substance containing carbon are heated to the kindling point, oxidation takes place and carbon dioxide is formed.
3. Limewater is calcium hydroxide. When calcium dioxide is added to this, calcium carbonate is formed. Since this does not dissolve well, it precipitates out; hence, the liquid becomes milky.

F. Thought Questions for Class Discussions:

1. What is the source of carbon dioxide in all these experiments?
2. What are some properties of carbon dioxide?
3. Is carbon dioxide heavier than air?
4. In fighting fires, is this an advantage or disadvantage?

G. Related Ideas for Further Inquiry:

1. Study the characteristics of carbon dioxide.
2. Study the effects of adding extra carbon dioxide to the atmosphere.
3. Study other Activities in Parts I and VI, especially I-B-1, "How much oxygen is in the air?" and VI-A-9, "What is the carbon cycle?"

H. Vocabulary Builders—Spelling Words:

1) **detect** 2) **carbon dioxide** 3) **limewater** 4) **dissolve** 5) **solution** 6) **calcium carbonate**

I. Thought for Today:

"All that is necessary for evil to triumph is for good men to do nothing."—Edmund Burke

Activity I B 4

A. Problem: *Can Air Pressure Crush a Can?*

B. Materials Needed:

1. One-gallon tin can
2. Stopper to fit can
3. Pair of pot holders
4. Hot plate, gas burner, or canned heat
5. Water

C. Procedure

1. Put approximately one-quarter inch of water in the can.
2. Heat the can over the heat source until the water reaches the boiling point and steam comes out of the opening.
3. Using pot holders, carefully remove the can from the heat and close the opening with the stopper; make sure this is an airtight fit. *This is very important.*
4. Watch carefully as the can cools after it has been removed from the heat source.

D. Result:

The can will slowly crinkle and collapse.

E. Basic Facts and Supplemental Information:

1. The air pressure inside and outside were equal at the start, when the water was added, and when the water was steaming.
2. The steam forces most of the air out of the can.
3. After the can was sealed and allowed to cool, the steam condensed causing a partial vacuum. The volume of air and steam was reduced causing a reduction in pressure inside the can. One cc (cubic centimeter) of water will make 1500 cc of steam and vice versa.
4. The condensation reduces the pressure inside, and the outside pressure, being greater, crushes the can.
5. If any outside air is let into the can, a balance of forces will take place, causing the can to remain intact.

F. Thought Questions for Class Discussions:

1. How is a partial vacuum created on the inside of a can?
2. Why is it necessary to boil the water before sealing the can?
3. Why must the can be airtight?
4. If air has a pressure of 14.7 pounds per square inch, how much pressure was exerted on this can? (Hint: How many surfaces does a can have?)

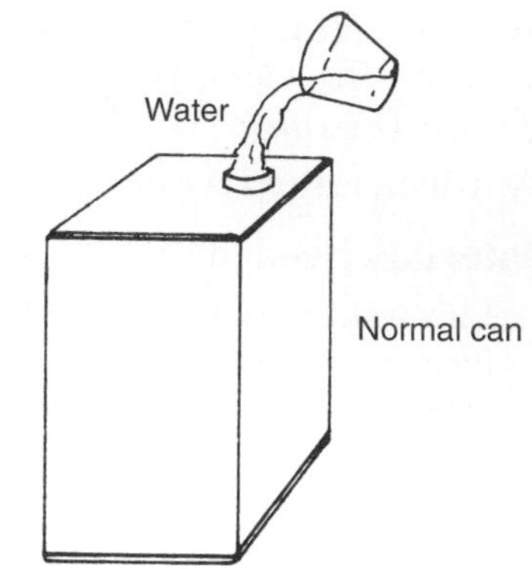

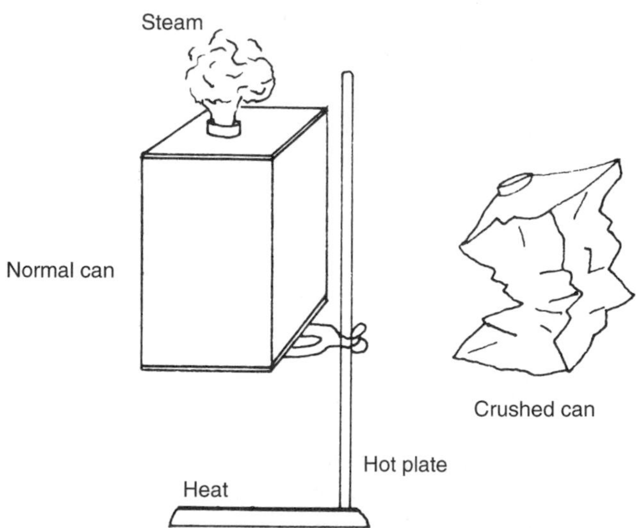

G. Related Ideas for Further Inquiry:

1. Pour several ounces of water in a can with a push-down top or use a loosely fitted cork. Place over heat source. Take precautions, for the cork will be blown out of can.
2. Study Activity I-B-9, "In which direction does air pressure exert the greatest force?"
3. Study Activity I-B-10, "What is sideways air pressure?"

H. Vocabulary Builders—Spelling Words:

1) **partial** 2) **vacuum** 3) **condensation** 4) **steam** 5) **precautions** 6) **boiling point** 7) **heat**

I. Thought for Today:

"It is harder to conceal ignorance than to acquire knowledge."

Activity

A. Problem: *Can a Shelled Hard-boiled Egg Be Put into a Small-Mouthed Bottle Without Breaking the Egg?*

B. Materials Needed:

1. Small-mouthed bottle (slightly smaller than the egg)
2. Medium-sized wad of paper
3. Matches
4. Hard-boiled egg with shell removed

C. Procedure:

1. Show the pupils that the egg will not fit into the bottle without being crushed.
2. Light the wad of paper and carefully insert it into the bottle.
3. Place the egg into the mouth of the bottle immediately.
4. Have students observe the results.

D. Result:

The egg will bob up and down, then slowly descend into the neck of the bottle, and finally pop into the bottle with a loud "plunk."

E. Basic Facts and Supplemental Information:

1. The bobbing up and down of the egg is due to the fact that as the heated air expands, the air bubbles out from beneath the egg. When the paper stops burning, the air within the bottle cools and the inside pressure is reduced. However, the normal air pressure on the top and sides of the egg remains unchanged. The egg, therefore, is forced into the bottle.
2. A good challenging question is how to get the egg back out without breaking the egg. This can be accomplished by inverting the bottle and blowing hard into its mouth; the increased air pressure on the inside will force the egg out. (Don't forget to duck or move head quickly to the side.)
3. The teacher can start this Activity with an unshelled egg first and then compare results. The unshelled egg will not move because the air pressure is not strong enough to compact the egg, and there is always a little pressure seepage. With the shelled egg, the fit becomes very tight, so the outside pressure is allowed to act on it.
4. Air pressure equals 14.7 pounds per square inch (at sea level).
5. Air pressure acts in all directions—down, up, sideways, every way.

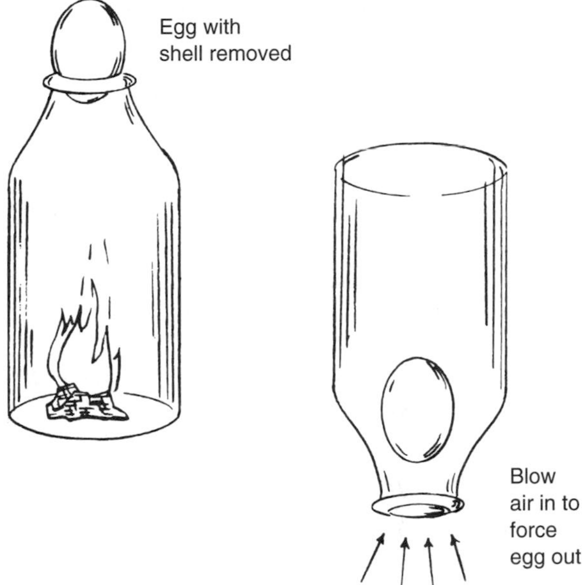

F. Thought Questions for Class Discussions:

1. What would happen to the egg if you tried to push it into the bottle with your hands?
2. Is the egg "sucked" into the bottle or is it pushed in by the outside air pressure?
3. Why aren't soft items crushed by the great air pressure that surrounds them?

G. Related Ideas for Further Inquiry:

1. Place the base of a small candle in a shelled, hard-boiled egg. Light the candle and place an inverted bottle over the egg and the lighted candle.
2. Study Activity I-B-4, "Can air pressure crush a can?"
3. Study Activity I-B-9, "In which direction does air pressure exert the greatest force?"
4. Study Activity I-B-2, "How does air pressure in a bicycle tire hold up the bicycle?"
5. Study Activity I-B-10, "What is sideways air pressure?"

H. Vocabulary Builders—Spelling Words:

1) **expand** 2) **descend** 3) **bottle** 4) **hard-boiled** 5) **breaking** 6) **wad** 7) **shelled** 8) **force**

I. Thought for Today:

"Education is what survives when what was learned has been forgotten."—B. F. Skinner

A. Problem: *How Does a Siphon Work?*

B. Materials Needed:

1. Three feet of plastic or rubber tubing
2. Two glass jars
3. Water

C. Procedure:

1. Fill one jar with water.
2. Put about one inch of water in the other jar.
3. Place the full jar at a higher level than the other one. (See drawing.)
4. Fill the plastic or rubber tubing with water. (Must be completely filled.)
5. Cover each end of the tubing with your thumbs.
6. Insert one end of the tubing into the higher-level jar and the other end into the lower-level jar. Be sure the tubing in the lower-level jar is below the level of the water level in the higher jar.
7. Take thumb away from tubing in the lower-level jar; then take thumb away from tubing in the higher-level jar.

D. Result:

The water will flow from the jar filled with water into the jar containing one inch of water until the water is at the same level even though the quantity in the jars will not be the same.

E. Basic Facts and Supplemental Information:

1. In the "Before" drawing, the water will flow downward due to the force of gravity and the atmospheric pressure, P. As the water flows down, this will create a partial vacuum in the tube. The atmospheric pressure P exerted on the surface of the water L, will force water up the tube and along the tube in direction D. This will cause a continuous flow of water as long as the level of M is lower than the level of L.
2. It is often stated that water cannot run uphill. Well, this Activity disproves this concept. What does the water do in this siphoning activity from the start of the siphoning from the water level in the top of the first jar to the top of the tubing? It runs uphill. Actually it is "pushed" uphill by atmospheric air pressure.

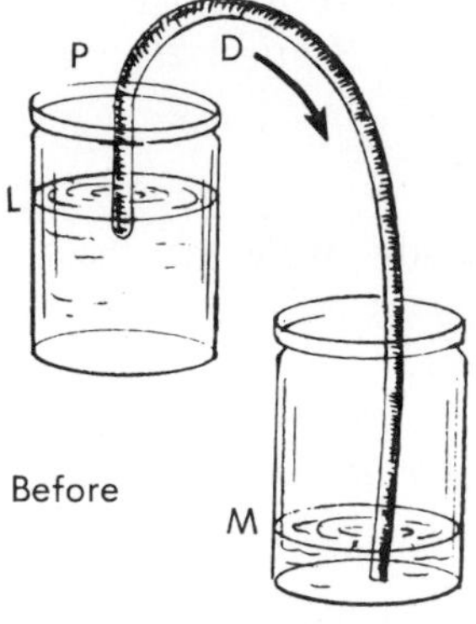

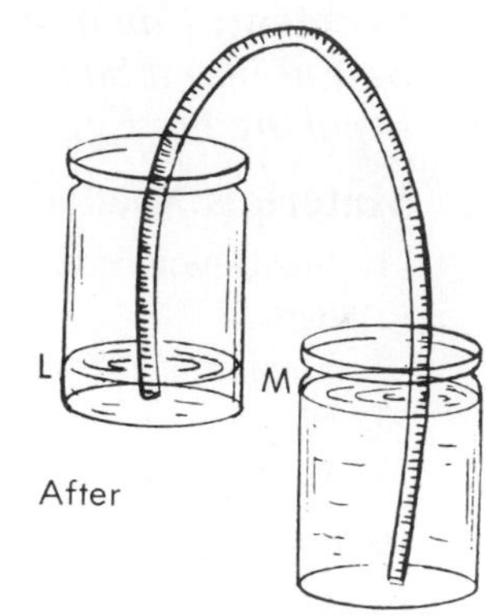

3. Siphons are a main part of many water supply systems for municipalities and outlying areas. Large pumps are used to initiate the siphoning action and to keep the water flowing.

F. Thought Questions for Class Discussions:

1. What will happen if the jars are alternately raised and lowered?
2. Will this siphon work if one of the jars becomes empty?
3. Why won't the siphon work if some air gets into the tubing?
4. How do water pumps use this principle?
5. Are there other ways to start a siphon?

G. Related Ideas for Further Inquiry:

1. Practice siphoning your classroom aquarium when it needs cleaning.
2. Discuss the dangers of siphoning gasoline from an automobile.
3. Study Activity I-B-7, "How can we make a fountain siphon?"
4. Study Activity I-B-8, "Can air pressure hold water in a covered can with holes in its sides?"
5. Study Activity I-B-12, "How does an atomizer work?"

H. Vocabulary Builders—Spelling Words:

1) **siphon** 2) **vacuum** 3) **pressure** 4) **plastic** 5) **tubing** 6) **thumb** 7) **gravity** 8) **atmosphere**

I. Thought for Today:

"School is a place where children live."

Activity I B 7

A. Problem: *How Can We Make a Fountain Siphon?*

B. Materials Needed:

1. Two glass jars or flasks
2. Two-hole stopper to fit one jar or flask
3. Two pieces of glass tubing (one long with pointed end, one short)
4. Two pieces of plastic tubing to fit glass tubing
5. Water colored with food coloring
6. Ring stand
7. Pan or bucket

C. Procedure:

1. Wet double-holed stopper.
2. Insert long piece of glass tubing in one hole of the stopper with pointed end up as shown in drawing.
3. Work tubing up by slowly twisting it back and forth until it almost touches the top of the jar or flask.
4. Repeat the procedure with the second piece of tubing until equal lengths project above and below the jar or flask.
5. Put colored water in both jars.
6. Attach a piece of plastic tubing on the bottom of the long piece of glass tubing so that it will almost reach the bottom of the lower jar or flask.
7. Attach a long piece of tubing to the bottom of the shorter glass tubing so that it will reach into the pan or bucket.
8. Place the bottom jar or flask on the desk or table top.
9. Place the ring stand in the position shown in the drawing.
10. Set the pan or bucket on the other side and below the level of the bottom jar or flask.
11. Pinching the long tubing so that water will not run out, attach the stopper to the upper jar or flask as shown in the drawing.
12. When your preliminary explanations have been made and you are ready to go, release the tubing.

D. Result:

Water will run out of the long plastic tubing and at the same time other water will spurt into the upper jar from the lower jar.

E. Basic Facts and Supplemental Information:

The weight of the water in the upper jar or beaker will make the water flow downward into the lower pan or

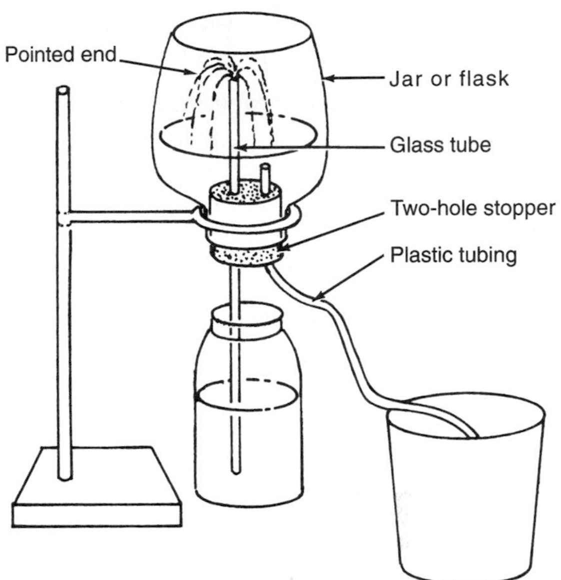

bucket, leaving a partial vacuum in the upper jar or flask. The outside air pressure will force the water upward through the tubing. Water comes up with such force that it forms a spray in the open space in the upper jar or flask. Colored water is used to make the water more visible to the students.

F. Thought Questions for Class Discussions:

1. Can this fountain siphon be made to operate indefinitely?
2. If no water is added to the supply in the jar, when will the fountain stop operating?
3. With a sink and running water available, how could this run continuously?

G. Related Ideas for Further Inquiry:

1. Study Activity I-B-6, "How does a siphon work?"
2. Study Activity I-B-9, "In which direction does air pressure exert the greatest force?"
3. Study Activity I-B-4, "Can air pressure crush a can?"

H. Vocabulary Builders—Spelling Words:

1) **siphon** 2) **fountain** 3) **pressure** 4) **stream** 5) **tubing** 6) **plastic** 7) **colored** 8) **pointed**

I. Thought for Today:

"How a person feels is more important than what a person knows."

Activity

Procedure One

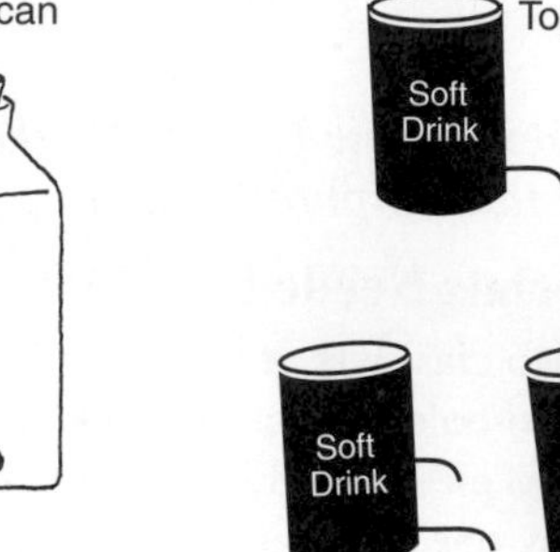

Procedure Two

A. Problem: *Can Air Pressure Hold Water in a Covered Can with Holes in Its Side?*

B. Materials Needed, Procedure One:

1. Small metal can or plastic bottle with removable top or cork
2. Water
3. Awl
4. Sink, tray, or bucket to catch water

Materials Needed, Procedure Two:

1. Empty soft drink can
2. Awl
3. Adhesive, cellophane, or duct tape
4. Sink, tray, or bucket to catch water

C. Procedure One:

1. Punch a small hole near bottom of the plastic bottle or metal can.
2. Put finger over hole and fill bottle or can with water.
3. With top off, remove finger from hole and watch water flow from it in a steady stream.
4. Refill bottle or can with finger over the hole.
5. Fasten top to it securely. (Finger must be over hole while refilling.)
6. Remove finger from hole and observe results.

Procedure Two:

1. In soft drink can punch three small holes vertically, one near the bottom, one near the middle, and one near the top.
2. Tape the holes securely.
3. Fill the can with water.
4. Place can near sink, tray, or bucket.
5. Remove bottom tape and observe results.
6. When empty, replace bottom tape, fill the can, and quickly remove bottom and middle tapes. Observe results.
7. When empty, replace both tapes, fill the can, and quickly remove all the tapes. Observe results.

D. Results One:

1. On first attempt with top off the bottle, water flows from the hole in a steady stream.
2. On second attempt with top on the bottle, water does not flow from the hole.

Results Two:

1. When can is full of water and all holes are taped, nothing happens.
2. When the bottom tape is removed, water streams out the bottom hole.
3. When the middle and bottom tapes are removed, water streams out both holes with the lower stream being stronger (it shoots out further).
4. When all the tapes are removed water streams out of all holes with the bottom one being stronger, the middle one next, and the top one the weakest.

E. Basic Facts and Supplemental Information:

1. In Procedure One, when the bottle has no top on it the weight of the water and air pressure will force the water out of the small hole in a steady stream. When the top is on, the air pressure cannot exert a downward force on the water in the can or bottle. Air pressure acting against the water in the hole does not permit any water to escape.
2. In Procedure Two, the air pressure is the same in all trials but the weight of the water adds to the force of the stream so that the bottom stream has a total greater force acting on it, and so the stream is longer and stronger.

F. Thought Questions for Class Discussions:

1. Does altitude have any effect on this experiment?
2. Why do we punch two holes on the top of any can holding a liquid?
3. Can water ever run uphill?
4. How do they get water from low valleys over high mountains?

G. Related Ideas for Further Inquiry:

1. Punch holes in a horizontal line and test.
2. Punch horizontal holes close together and squeeze the streams. The streams will flow together and appear as a knot.

H. Vocabulary Builders—Spelling Words:

1) **atmospheric** 2) **pressure** 3) **stream** 4) **punched** 5) **finger** 6) **soft drink** 7) **cork**

I. Thought for Today:

"Without experience one gains no wisdom."

A. Problem: *In Which Direction Does Air Pressure Exert the Greatest Force?*

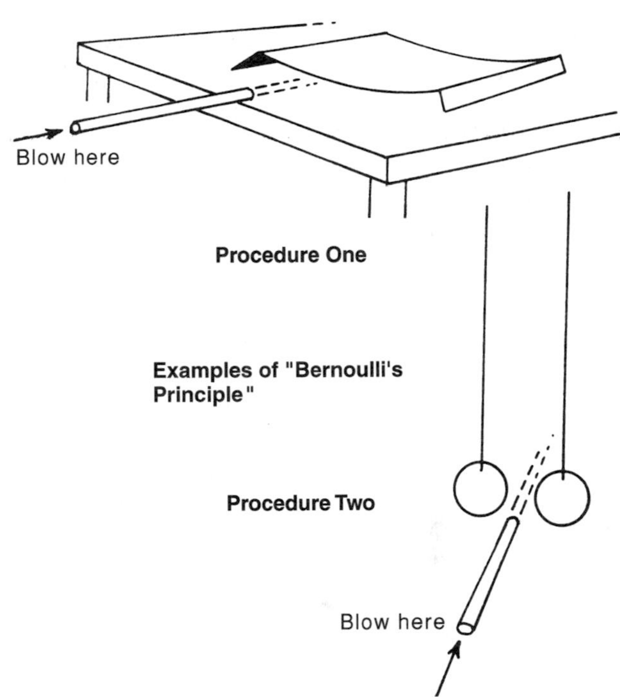

B. Materials One, Procedure One:

1. 5″ × 7″ index card
2. Soda straw
3. Table or desk top

Materials Two, Procedure Two:

1. Two ping-pong balls
2. Cellophane tape
3. Thread
4. Book
5. Table or desk top

C. Procedure One:

1. Fold the card so that one-half inch at each end of the card is perpendicular to the card itself.
2. Place the card on the desk or table so that the folded card makes a little platform.
3. Using the soda straw, blow vigorously through the straw and under the card.

Procedure Two:

1. Tape a piece of thread to each ping-pong ball. (See drawing.)
2. Let them hang down from the desk or table top by placing the threads under the book so that the ping-pong balls will be separated by about one inch.
3. Have a student, using the soda straw, blow vigorously between the two ping-pong balls to try to blow them apart.

D. Results One:

The harder one blows, the faster the air moves under the card and the more the card bends down toward the current of air.

Results Two:

The harder one blows between the ping-pong balls, the closer they will move together.

E. Basic Facts and Supplemental Information:

1. In Procedure One, a rapidly moving current of air reduces the sideways pressure under the card, thus the normal pressure above is greater and pushes the card downward.
2. In Procedure Two, the normal pressure between the ping-pong balls is reduced; consequently, the outside pressure is greater, causing the balls to come closer together. This is called "Bernoulli's Principle." It is the same principle that operates in Activity I-B-10, "What Is Sideways Air Pressure?"

F. Thought Questions for Class Discussions:

1. What would happen to a person who stands too close to a moving train?
2. What would happen if a person got too close to the jet stream of an airplane?
3. What happens when two automobiles moving in opposite directions pass close together?

G. Related Ideas for Further Inquiry:

1. Hold a sheet of paper in front of your lips, let it droop, and then blow briskly over the top.
2. How does this principle affect airplanes?
3. Study other Activities in this section, especially I-B-8, "Can air pressure hold water in a covered can with holes in its side?" I-B-10, "What is sideways air pressure?" and I-B-12, "How does an atomizer work?"

H. Vocabulary Builders—Spelling Words:

1) **Bernoulli** 2) **principle** 3) **direction**
4) **exert** 5) **pressure** 6) **ping-pong**
7) **thread** 8) **vertical** 9) **moving**

I. Thought for Today:

"It is useless to try to reason a person out of a thing that a person was never reasoned into."

A. Problem: *What Is Sideways Air Pressure?*

B. Materials:

1. Wooden spool
2. Thin cardboard
3. Common pin or thumbtack

C. Procedure:

1. Cut a piece of cardboard approximately 2" square.
2. Push the pin or tack through the center of the cardboard.
3. Place this over one end of the spool with the pin inside the hole in the spool. (This keeps the card from sliding sideways.)
4. Blow a steady stream of air into the opposite end of the spool as card is held as shown in drawing.
5. Release the cardboard but continue to blow.

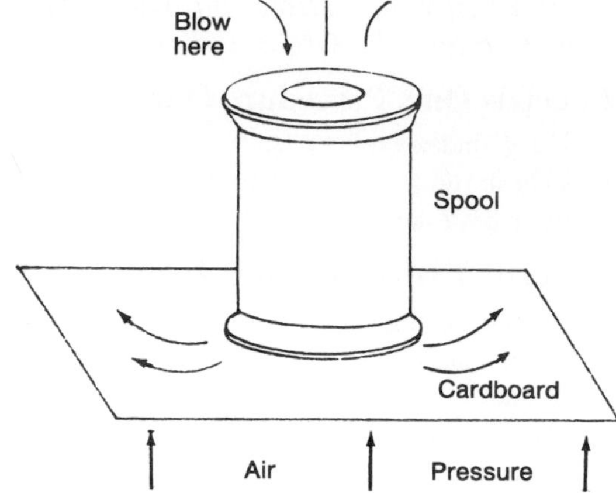

D. Results:

1. The cardboard seems to cling to the spool.
2. The harder you blow, the tighter the cardboard clings to the spool.
3. When the blowing stops, the cardboard falls.

E. Basic Facts and Supplemental Information:

The blown air moves out the sides between the spool and cardboard, and not downward. The more air going out the side, the less pressure is exerted downward. The normal air pressure from below pushes upward, keeping the cardboard near the spool. When the blowing is stopped, the weight of the cardboard causes it to drop because the air pressure above and below is then equal and gravity takes over.

Bernoulli's Principle has become one of the basic laws of science. In essence it states that the faster a stream of gas moves in one direction, the less is the pressure of the gas in a perpendicular or "sideways" direction. This activity is a prime example of Bernoulli's Principle.

F. Thought Questions for Class Discussions:

1. Is this experiment related to two passing trains?
2. If two automobiles pass too close to each other, what might happen?
3. Would children on passing bicycles be affected by this phenomenon?

G. Related Ideas for Further Inquiry:

1. Look up "Bernoulli's Principle" in an encyclopedia or science book and describe it in simple terms.
2. Place a ping-pong ball in a funnel with the stem below and pointing straight upward. Try to blow the ping-pong ball out of the funnel.
3. Place a ping-pong ball in an inverted funnel with the stem on top, and while holding the ball in the cup blow steadily on the stem and release the ball.
4. Another exciting activity is to place a fully inflated balloon in an airstream created at the exhaust end of a vacuum cleaner with the airstream pointing straight up.
5. Study Activity I-B-4, "Can air pressure crush a can?"
6. Study Activity I-B-9, "In which direction does air pressure exert the greatest force?"
7. Study Activity I-B-12, "How does an atomizer work?"
8. Study Activity I-B-13, "How does a vacuum cleaner work?"

H. Vocabulary Builders—Spelling Words:

1) **sideways** 2) **pressure** 3) **spool**
4) **wooden** 5) **thumbtack** 6) **cardboard**
7) **upward** 8) **Bernoulli**

I. Thought for Today

"Give a man a fish and he eats for a day; teach him to fish and he eats for a lifetime."

Activity I B 11

A. Problem: *Can You Keep a Plastic Ball in an Airstream?*

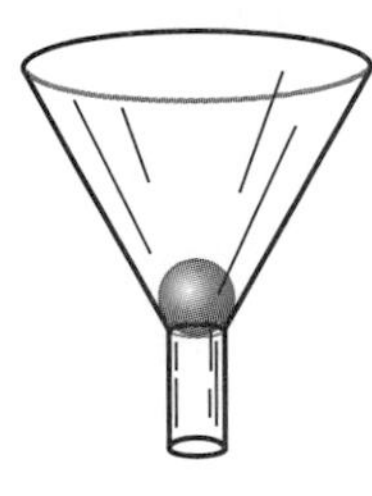

B. Materials Needed:

1. Large funnel
2. Plastic ball (6" to 12" in diameter)
3. Ping-pong ball
4. Hair dryer

C. Procedure:

1. Place the ping-pong ball in the mouth of the funnel.
2. Challenge a student to blow the ping-pong ball out while keeping the funnel in an upright position.
3. Again with the ping-pong ball in the mouth of the funnel, challenge another student to try to blow the ball out of the funnel by blowing vigorously into the neck of the funnel, with the funnel inverted so that the neck is up and the mouth (large part) is facing down.
4. Show the plastic ball to the class.
5. Secure the hair dryer so that the airstream is pointed directly up.
6. Ask the class what they think might happen if the plastic ball were placed in the middle of the airstream.
7. After the responses, put the plastic ball in the middle of the airstream.

D. Results:

1. The ping-pong ball will remain in the neck of the funnel when the funnel is pointed up and blowing is continuous.
2. The ping-pong ball will remain in the neck of the funnel when it is pointed down and blowing is continuous.
3. The plastic ball will remain in the airstream.

E. Basic Facts and Supplemental Information:

1. These activities are a demonstration of Bernoulli's Principle.
2. This principle states that as air, or any other gas, moves in one direction, the sideways pressure is reduced.
3. In these Procedures when the air is moving in one direction, its sideways pressure is reduced, thus allowing the external pressure to force the ping-pong ball or the plastic ball closer to the airstream.

F. Thought Questions for Class Discussions:

1. Where would a moving airstream be dangerous?
2. If two cars were running parallel to each other and they came close together would "sideways air pressure" have any effect on them?
3. Is "lift" on an airplane a form of "sideways air pressure?"

G. Related Ideas for Further Inquiry:

1. Hold two pieces of paper close together and try to blow them apart.
2. Try different size and weight balls using the same size funnel.
3. Keeping the hair dryer in an upright position, move it slowly to the right, then to the left.
4. Keeping the hair dryer in an upright position, reduce the airstream by turning the hair dryer's power down.
5. Study Activity I-B-2, "How does air pressure in a bicycle tire hold up the bicycle?"
6. Study Activity 1-B-9, "In which direction does air pressure exert the greatest force?"
7. Study Activity I-B-13, "How does a vacuum cleaner work?"

H. Vocabulary Builders—Spelling Words:

1) **funnel** 2) **ping-pong** 3) **airstream**
4) **balloon** 5) **pressure** 6) **Bernoulli**

I. Thought for Today:

"The average person is one who thinks he/she isn't."

Activity I B 12

A. Problem: *How Does an Atomizer Work?*

B. Materials Needed:

1. Drinking straw
2. Scissors
3. Small bowl
4. Water

C. Procedure:

1. Fill the bowl about half full with water.
2. Cut off about 2″ of the drinking straw with the scissors.
3. Insert this piece into the bowl of water holding it slightly off the bottom of the bowl.
4. Hold the remainder of the straw (the long piece) in a horizontal position directly over the top of the short piece as shown in the drawing. It must be close to, but not touching the top of the short piece.

D. Result:

When the straws are positioned properly and a student blows through the long straw, a mist or spray will form. Several trials are usually necessary for adjusting the straws.

E. Basic Facts and Supplemental Information:

1. This model atomizer operates because the stream of air moving over the top of the short straw reduces the pressure over the straw in the bowl of water. Normal air pressure, therefore, forces the water up the straw. When it gets to the top it is blown off in tiny droplets producing the desired spray. A spray gun works on the same principle. Bernoulli's Principle states that when air is moving rapidly in one direction, the sideways air pressure is reduced.
2. Perfume atomizers work in the same way except instead of a person blowing over the top of the perfume container, a bulb of air is squeezed to perform the same blowing action—only this time over perfume instead of water.

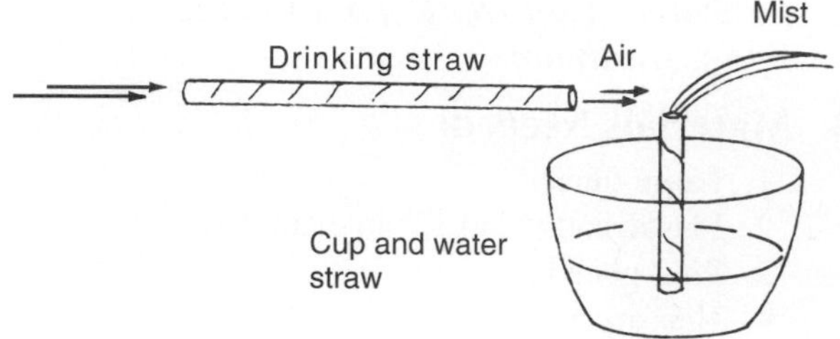

F. Thought Questions for Class Discussions:

1. Why does the liquid rise vertically in the straw?
2. Why doesn't the stream of air force the liquid back down into the straw?
3. Could other liquids be used?

G. Related Ideas for Further Inquiry:

1. Examine a commercial air sprayer. Does it work the same way?
2. Do all sprayers work this way?
3. Study Activity I-B-2, "How does air pressure in a bicycle tire hold up the bicycle?"
4. Study Activity I-B-10, "What is sideways air pressure?"
5. Study Activity I-B-9, "In which direction does air pressure exert the greatest force?"
6. Bring an empty perfume atomizer to class and have the class "feel" the air in motion from squeezing the air bulb.

H. Vocabulary Builders—Spelling Words:

1) **atomizer** 2) **mist** 3) **droplets**
4) **sideways** 5) **velocity** 6) **drinking**
7) **adjust** 8) **mist** 9) **blowing**

I. Thought for Today:

"The only thing you can get in a hurry is trouble."

Activity I B 13

A. Problem: *How Does a Vacuum Cleaner Work?*

B. Materials Needed:

1. Electric fan
2. Two thin strips of paper
3. Chalkboard
4. Chalk
5. Table or desk
6. Small hand vacuum cleaner
7. Bits of paper, confetti size
8. Shavings from pencil sharpener
9. Large piece of cardboard

C. Procedure:

1. Draw a simple outline of a vacuum cleaner on the board as shown in drawing.
2. Set the electric fan on the table or desk top.
3. Hold the two strips of paper in front of the fan.
4. Turn the fan on.
5. Observe the results.
6. Discuss the results.
   a. The fan pushes the air forward.
   b. This concentrates the air in front of the fan creating a high-pressure area.
   c. The air in back of the fan is thinned, creating a low-pressure area.
   d. Air always moves from high-pressure areas to low-pressure areas.
7. Turn on the small hand vacuum cleaner.
8. Dump some bits of paper and pencil-sharpening debris on the large piece of cardboard.
9. Pick up the paper and debris with the vacuum cleaner.
10. Have students design a vacuum cleaner using the principle of air movement demonstrated in the first six steps of this activity. They must include in their drawing:
    a. inlet hose
    b. outlet
    c. fan (with motor)
    d. porous bag

D. Results:

1. Students will learn about low and high air pressure forces and how they are created.
2. Students will have designed a vacuum cleaner.

E. Basic Facts and Supplemental Information:

1. High and low pressures (of air) are caused by the pushing of the air by the fan.
2. As air is pushed out of the vacuum cleaner new air is forced in by external air pressure.
3. A vacuum cleaner is simply a fan with a hose attached to the low-pressure side and a porous bag on the high-pressure side to collect the dirt and prevent it from blowing back into the room.

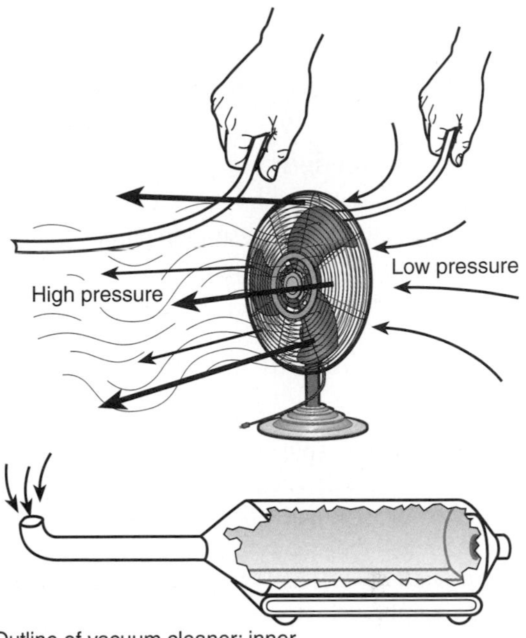

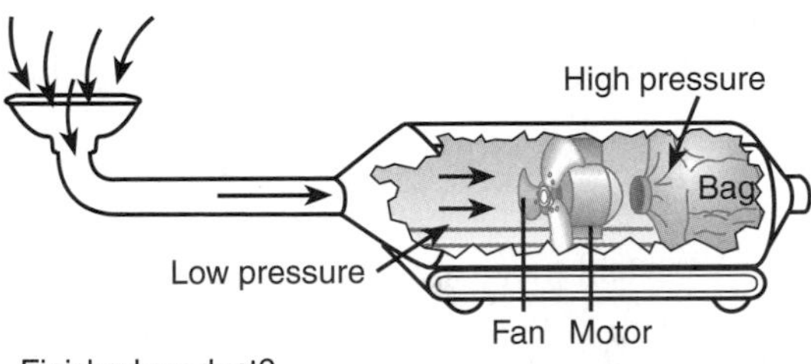

Outline of vacuum cleaner; inner workings to be designed by students.

High pressure
Bag
Low pressure
Fan Motor

Finished product?

F. Thought Questions for Class Discussions:

1. Is there a real "vacuum" in a vacuum cleaner?
2. Does an automobile car pump use a "vacuum"?
3. How does a thermos bottle work to keep liquids either hot or cold?

G. Related Ideas for Further Inquiry:

1. Study Activity I-B-6, "How does a siphon work?"
2. Study Activity I-B-9, "In which direction does air pressure exert the greatest pressure?"
3. Study Activity I-B-12, "How does an atomizer work?"

H. Vocabulary Builders—Spelling Words:

1) **vacuum** 2) **cleaner** 3) **pressure** 4) **hose** 5) **electric** 6) **strips** 7) **debris** 8) **newspaper**

I. Thought for Today:

"Beware of the half-truth; it may be the wrong half."

Activity I B 14

A. Problem: *How Does a Baseball Pitcher Throw a Curve Ball?*

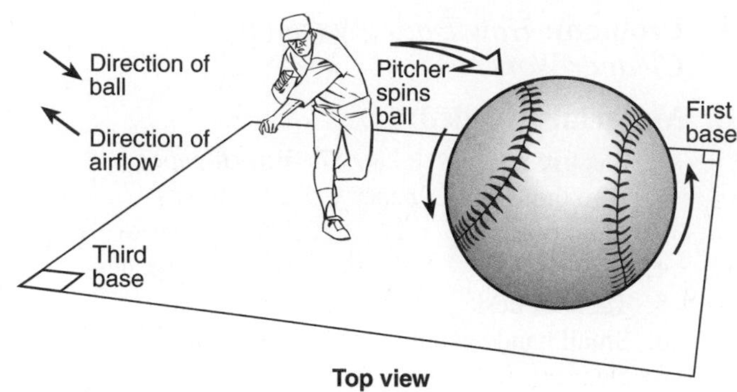

B. Materials Needed:

1. Several baseballs
2. Large ball (for demonstration purposes)
3. Marking pen
4. Chalkboard
5. Chalk

C. Procedure:

1. Draw a simple baseball infield and enlarged baseball with spin arrows on the chalkboard. (See drawing.)
2. Draw arrows on the large ball on opposite sides depicting the direction of the spin on the ball.
3. Review several activities showing Bernoulli's Principle such as those Activities in I-B-9, I-B-10, I-B-11, and I-B-12.
4. Cite these important facts regarding a curving, pitched ball:
   a. The baseball has raised stitches which close the cover snugly.
   b. These stitches drag a thin layer of air with the ball.
   c. The ball rotates 15 to 25 times on the way to home plate depending on the velocity of the pitch.
   d. If we were looking down on the ball pitched, and the ball were rotating counterclockwise:
      1) The air on the third base side would be traveling against the flow of the ball.
      2) The air on the first base side would be traveling with the flow of the ball.
      3) The speed of the air relative to the surface of the ball would be different on each side.
      4) In this case the air pressure on the first base side would be lower than that on the third base side, causing the ball to curve toward the first base side.
5. Students can practice spinning baseballs by twisting their wrists and shoulder joints. *Students should be warned that throwing a curve ball can cause permanent damage if done too frequently or too vigorously.*

D. Results:

1. Students will learn that pitching a curve in baseball is based on Bernoulli's Principle.
2. Students will learn to throw a curve ball by imparting a spin on the ball.

E. Basic Facts and Supplemental Information:

1. This principle is involved in airplane flights, the flight of birds, ski jumping, drag racing, etc.
2. It takes years for pitchers to develop a good curve ball.

F. Thought Questions for Class Discussions:

1. Does pitching "sliders" involve the same principle?
2. Are all rotating objects in air affected by unequal air pressures?
3. Do faster spinning objects curve more or less than slower spinning ones?

G. Related Ideas for Further Inquiry:

Study the Activities cited in step 3 of the Procedure.

H. Vocabulary Builders—Spelling Words:

1) **baseball** 2) **curve** 3) **pressure** 4) **clockwise** 5) **counterclockwise** 6) **traveling** 7) **spinning**

I. Thought for Today:

"Come baseball time and I'll defend this proposition to the end; 'A diamond is a boy's best friend.' "

Section C: Water

Activity

I C 1

A. Problem: *When Water Freezes Does It Expand or Contract?*

B. Materials Needed, Procedure One:

(Can be done at school or home)

1. Two jars
2. Water
3. Refrigerator
4. Heating device

Materials Needed, Procedure Two:

(Good homework assignment)

1. Two small cans
2. Labels or marking pens
3. Refrigerator

C. Procedure One:

1. Fill one jar with hot water, the other with cold.
2. Label one jar "HOT" and the other "COLD."
3. Cover both bottles.
4. Place aside and observe the following day.

Procedure Two:

1. Fill the two cans exactly to the top.
2. Place one can in the freezing compartment of a refrigerator.
3. Place the second can in the cold (regular) compartment.
4. Let the cans stand until the next day (or until the one placed in the freezing compartment is frozen).

D. Results:

1. In Procedure One, the jar marked "HOT" will show a lower water level than the one marked "COLD."
2. In Procedure Two, the water placed in the cold (regular) compartment of the refrigerator will have contracted so it is not quite to the top of the can. The water that was frozen will be pushed out so that it extends above the top of the can.

E. Basic Facts and Supplemental Information:

Water expands slightly when heated and contracts slightly when it is cooled. In cooling, the molecules move closer together. When the temperature gets down to 4° C. or 39°F., water begins to expand rather than contract further. From this point to the freezing point it can cause damage to containers such as water pipes, radiators, batteries, etc.

F. Thought Questions for Class Discussions:

1. Why does ice float if water normally contracts and gets heavier (per volume) as it cools?

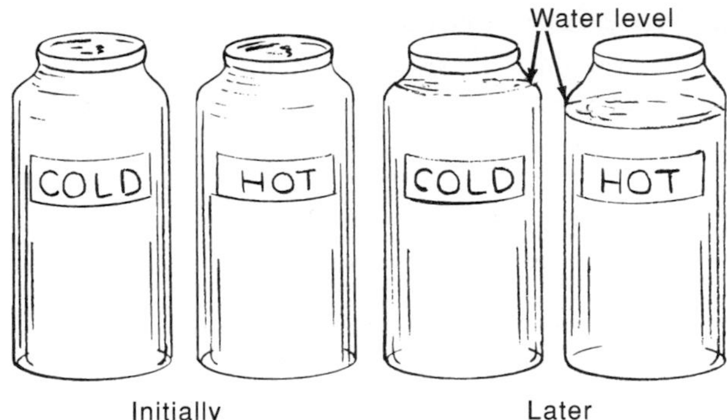

Procedure One

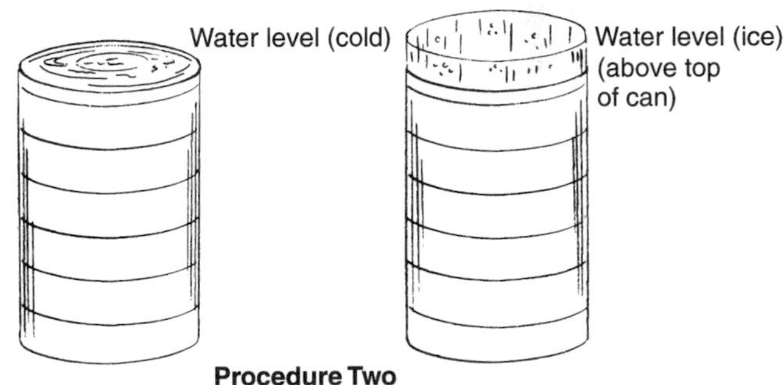

Procedure Two

2. What happens when water in an automobile radiator freezes?
3. What does antifreeze do when added to water in an automobile radiator?
4. Why do icebergs float?
5. What causes some water pipes to break in cold weather?

G. Related Ideas for Further Inquiry:

1. Have students check the level of any liquids in the refrigerator and then again when they have warmed up to room temperature.
2. Repeat Procedure Two using old capped jars enclosed in heavy duty freezer bags.
3. Discuss how ice cream is made at home and why salt is added to the ice.

H. Vocabulary Builders—Spelling Words:

1) **liquid** 2) **bottle** 3) **freezing** 4) **temperature** 5) **contract** 6) **expand** 7) **refrigerator** 8) **molecules** 9) **Celsius** 10) **Fahrenheit**

I. Thought for Today:

"The art of teaching is the art of assisting discovery."—Mark Van Doren

Activity I C 2

A. Problem: *What Makes a Submarine Go Up and Down?*

B. Materials Needed:

1. Tall glass or one-quart canning jar
2. Eyedropper
3. Water
4. Rubber balloon
5. Rubber band

C. Procedure:

1. Fill the glass or jar with water up to about one-half inch from the top.
2. Place the eyedropper in the water with enough water in it so that it barely floats. (You'll have to make several trials to adjust it properly.)
3. Observe the air pocket inside.
4. Cut the balloon and make a rubber cap for the jar. Secure with a rubber band.
5. Push cap down and keep it depressed.
6. If "diver" (eyedropper) sinks, release pressure on top of glass or jar.

D. Result:

The eyedropper goes into a dive when the rubber top is depressed. When the rubber top is released, the eyedropper will almost rise to near the surface of the water.

E. Basic Facts and Supplemental Information:

1. The increase in air pressure forces more water into the eyedropper, making it heavier, and consequently it sinks to the bottom. When the cap is elevated, the air pressure is decreased in the jar. The air in the eyedropper then forces the water out, and the eyedropper becomes lighter and consequently rises.
2. The floatation device is called a "cartesian diver." It can be made with a piece of glass tubing and a cork that fits on the top of the tubing. It is necessary to adjust the size of the cork so that the diver just barely floats. This can be accomplished by using a large cork and gradually filing off small pieces until the diver just floats. To make this device more visible to the students, make circles on the tubing with red fingernail polish.
3. A third type of "diver" can be fashioned by using the top of a ball point pen and a piece of clay for "ballast."

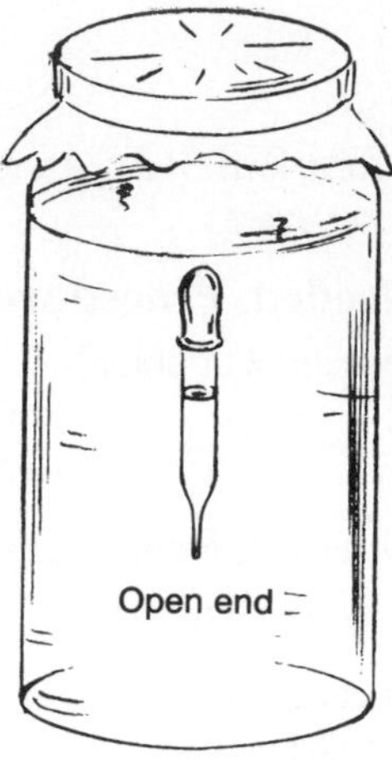

Cartesian diver

F. Thought Questions for Class Discussions:

1. Why is it important to adjust the eyedropper so that it just barely floats at the beginning of the experiment?
2. Can you do this experiment without having a little air in the eyedropper?
3. How do submarines use this principle?
4. What happens to the water level in the eyedropper?

G. Related Ideas for Further Inquiry:

1. Discuss what makes any object sink or float.
2. Study deep sea diving and how divers descend and ascend.
3. Interview scuba divers.
4. Study Activity I-C-4, "What makes the cork move? What makes the string move?"
5. Study Activity I-C-6, "The sailor's dilemma."
6. Study Activity I-C-8, "How does a hydrometer work?"
7. Study Activity I-C-11, "Does an object weigh the same in water as it does in air?"

H. Vocabulary Builders—Spelling Words:

1) **submarine** 2) **eyedropper** 3) **rubber** 4) **ascend** 5) **descend** 6) **cartesian diver** 7) **surface**

I. Thought for Today:

"Every adult needs a child to teach; it's the best kind of adult education."

Activity

A. Problems: *What Is "Surface Tension"?*

B. Materials Needed:

1. Long tall jar or graduate
2. Water glass or bowl
3. Needle
4. Soap or detergent
5. Metal paper clips
6. Water

C. Procedure One:

1. Fill a tall jar or graduate to about one-quarter inch from the top with water.
2. Looking at the jar or graduate at eye level, look at the spot where the water meets the sides of the jar or graduate. (See Figure 1.)
3. Ask the students to determine if this surface of the water is flat, curved up, or curved down.

Procedure Two:

1. Fill the drinking glass or bowl to the very top of the container making the water as level with the top of the container as possible.
2. Carefully place a needle on the surface of the water carefully lowering it slowly and horizontally. (See Figure 2.)
3. Wait for one minute and observe results.
4. After the needle has floated for about a minute, slowly touch the surface of the water with a bit of soap or a drop of liquid detergent.
5. Observe results.

Procedure Three:

1. Add water to a jar or glass until the water level is even with the edge of the top.
2. Ask the students to estimate how many paper clips they think can be added to the water without the water spilling over the edge.
3. Add paper clips carefully to the jar or glass full of water until the water runs over the top. (See Figure 3.)
4. Note the angle of the water with the edge of the jar or graduate at various times.

D. Results:

1. Procedure One: The water will curve up at the sides of the glass.
2. Procedure Two: The needle will float until the soap or detergent is added. Then it will sink.
3. Procedure Three: Many paper clips can be added until the water rises in the center and curves down where the water touches the glass. Then it will overflow.

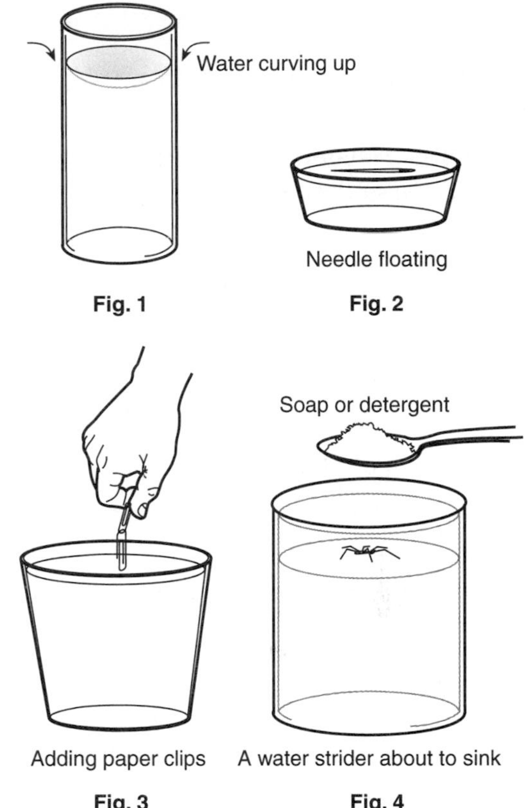

Fig. 1 Fig. 2 Fig. 3 Fig. 4

E. Basic Facts and Supplemental Information:

Surface tension is the attraction of molecules to each other by cohesion and adhesion. The following three Activities in this Section will explain surface tension in more detail.

F. Thought Questions for Class Discussions:

1. Are ocean-going ships partially buoyed up by surface tension?
2. What does a chip of soap or a few drops of liquid detergent do to surface tension?
3. Do all liquids have surface tension?

G. Related Ideas for Further Inquiry:

1. Razor blades and paper clips can also float on the surface of the water if the surface tension is not broken.
2. Water striders use surface tension to keep afloat. If the surface tension is broken with soap or detergent, these animals will sink and drown unless rescued. (See Figure 4.)

H. Vocabulary Builders—Spelling Words:

1) **surface** 2) **tension** 3) **attraction**
4) **cohesion** 5) **adhesion** 6) **needle**

I. Thought for Today:

"There's a big difference between giving good advice and lending a helping hand."

Activity I C 4

A. Problem: *What Makes the Cork Move? What Makes the String Move?*

B. Materials Needed, Procedure One:

1. Water glass
2. Water
3. Small cork
4. Measuring cup

Materials Needed, Procedure Two:

1. Clear glass or plastic bowl
2. String
3. Water
4. Soap or detergent
5. Scissors or knife

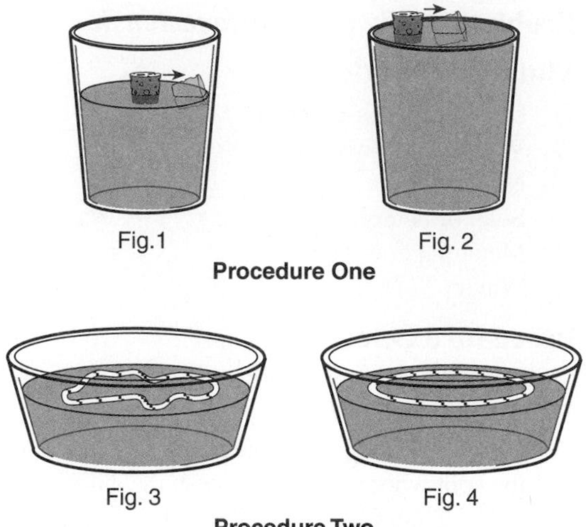

C. Procedure One:

1. Fill the glass about two-thirds full of water.
2. Place the cork in the water.
3. Observe the position when it finally comes to rest. (See Figure 1.)
4. With the measuring cup, carefully and slowly add water until the water reaches its highest point without spilling. (See Figure 2.)
5. Observe the final position of the cork.

Procedure Two:

1. Fill the glass or plastic bowl about two-thirds full of water.
2. Cut the string so that you can tie the ends and make a loop that will fit into the bowl comfortably. (See Figure 3.)
3. Place the loop of string in the bowl.
4. Let stand for a minute or two.
5. Touch the water inside the loop of string with a piece of soap or a drop of detergent.
6. Observe results.

D. Results:

1. In Procedure One, the cork will move from the center of the glass to one of its edges. As more water is added and the water is just above the brim, the cork will float to the center of the glass.
2. In Procedure Two, the string will appear to be in an irregular loop to start. After soap or detergent is added to the center of the loop, it will become a near-perfect circle.

E. Basic Facts and Supplemental Information:

1. Both of these activities involve surface tension. Surface tension is the mutual attraction of adjacent molecules.
2. The attraction of the surface molecules is less than the attraction of those below the surface. Consequently, the water molecules near the edge of the glass have less force acting on them downward, and therefore remain higher. In the string Activity (see Procedure 2), the soap or detergent breaks the surface tension inside the loop causing water molecules outside to exert greater "pull" on the string.

F. Thought Questions for Class Discussions:

1. What affect does the soap or detergent have on the molecules of water?
2. Do you know why atoms cling to others to form molecules?

G. Related Ideas for Further Inquiry:

1. Study Activity I-C-3, "What is 'surface tension'?"
2. Study Activity I-C-5, "What is 'capillarity'?"

H. Vocabulary Builders—Spelling Words:

1) **surface** 2) **tension** 3) **adhesion** 4) **cohesion** 5) **attraction** 6) **movement**

I. Thought for Today:

"Whatever is worth doing is worth doing well."

Activity I C 5

A. Problem: *What Is "Capillarity"?*

B. Materials Needed, Procedure One:

1. Plate, ceramic or plastic
2. Six wooden matches (or toothpicks)
3. Water

Materials Needed, Procedure Two:

1. Bowl, ceramic or plastic
2. Water
3. Cube of sugar
4. Piece of soap or liquid detergent
5. Ten wooden matches

C. Procedure One:

1. Break five matches half through at the middle.
2. Arrange the five matches symmetrically on the dry plate around a circle about three-quarters of an inch in diameter. (See Figure 1.)
3. Dip a sixth match into water and use it to wet each of the five matches where they are bent, with a drop or two of water.
4. Leave the matches on the plate for a short time.

Procedure Two:

1. Fill the bowl about two-thirds full of water.
2. Let settle for a minute or two.
3. Carefully arrange the matches in a circle as shown in Figure 3.
4. While holding the cube of sugar, slowly lower it about halfway into the center of the matches.
5. Observe results.
6. Next, dip the soap into or add a drop of detergent to the center of the match circle.

D. Results:

1. Procedure One: The matches partially straighten out and form a five-pointed star.
2. Procedure Two: The matches will move toward the center when the cube of sugar is touched to the water. When the soap or detergent is added, the matches will scatter to the edges of the bowl.

E. Basic Facts and Supplemental Information:

1. Water enters the dry wood cells in the bent parts of the matches and swells the cells. This swelling and movement in turn tends to straighten the matches. This type of movement is called "capillarity."

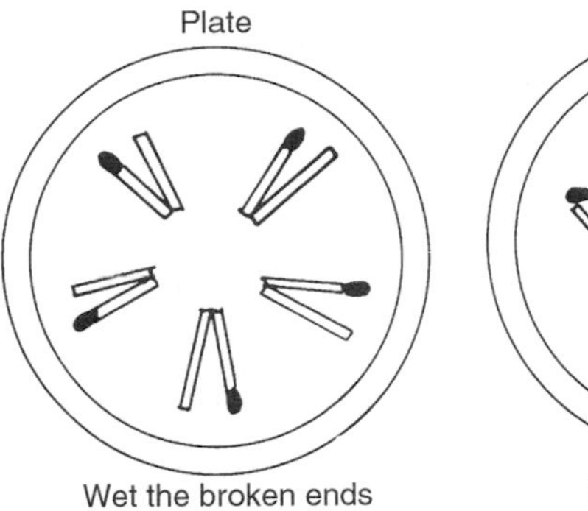

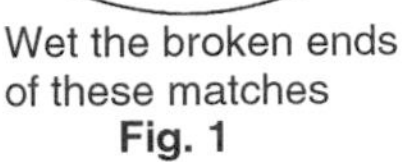

Wet the broken ends of these matches
Fig. 1

Matches form a five-pointed star
Fig. 2

Fig. 3

Fig. 4

Fig. 5

2. When the cube of sugar is touched to the water, a little water is absorbed by the cube setting up a little current which draws the matches to the center. When soap or detergent is added, this breaks the surface tension of the water, and the outer water molecules exert more drawing power and move the matches to the edges of the bowl.

F. Thought Questions for Class Discussions:

1. What are the relationships among the terms "capillarity," "osmosis," and "surface tension"?
2. Is there any "magic" involved in these Activities?

G. Related Ideas for Further Inquiry:

1. Study Activity I-C-3, "What is 'surface tension'?"
2. Study Activity I-C-4, "What makes the cork move? What makes the string move?"

H. Vocabulary Builders—Spelling Words:

1) **capillarity** 2) **osmosis** 3) **surface**
4) **tension** 5) **expansion** 6) **detergent**

I. Thought for Today:

"If you want children to improve, let them hear the nice things you say about them to others."—Haim Ginott

Activity I C 6

A. Problem: *The Sailor's Dilemma*

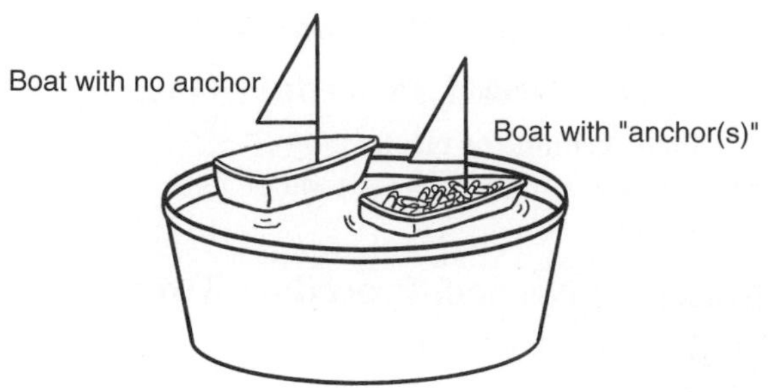

B. Materials Needed:

1. Toy sailboat
2. Modeling clay
3. Large bowl or aquarium
4. Water
5. Tall, widemouthed jar
6. Tall, narrow can that will fit inside jar
7. Weights (paper clips, nails, or metal tacks)
8. Marking pen or pencil

C. Procedure:

1. Show the sailboat to the class.
2. Place the sailboat in the large bowl or aquarium.
3. Fashion a small boat of clay simulating the sailboat.
4. Partially fill it with weights.
5. Place this weighted boat in the large bowl or aquarium.
6. Now pose this "challenging dilemma" to the class: "If this were a real boat on a real lake, and instead of nails and paper clips there were a real anchor in the boat, would the water level of the lake rise, fall, or remain the same if its anchor were taken out of the boat and dropped into the lake?"
7. After the class has made "guesses" (hypotheses), the guesses can be tested by using the tall jar as the lake, the can as the sailboat, and the weights as the anchor.
8. Float the area with weights inside in the tall jar, marking the water level.
9. Dump the weights in the bottom of the jar and with the can still floating mark the new water line.
10. Compare levels.

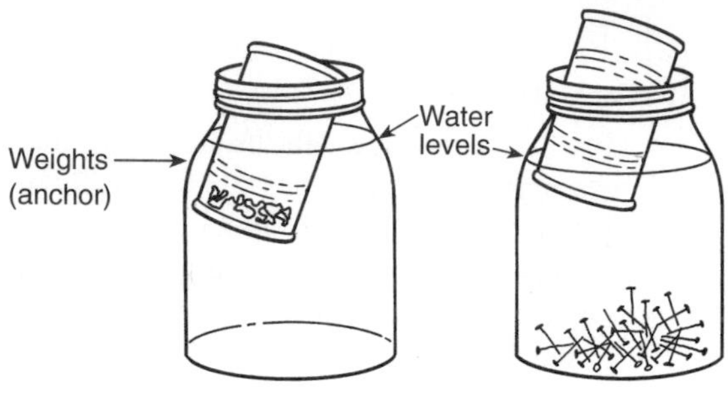

D. Result:

The water level in the jar will *drop*!

E. Basic Facts and Supplemental Information:

1. When the anchor is in the boat, the weight of the anchor will displace water equal to the weight of the anchor. If the anchor weighs 100 grams, the weight of the volume of water displaced would be 100 grams.
2. Water weighs 1 gram per cubic centimeter.
3. 100 grams of water would occupy 100 cubic centimeters.
4. When the "anchor" is dropped overboard, the anchor still weighs 100 grams but it displaces the volume of water occupied by the anchor. If the "anchor" weighs twice as much as the water, the water displaced would be only 50 grams or 50 cubic centimeters.
5. This being so, the water level would be less when the anchor is in the water. Originally the water level would be the level of the lake plus 100 cubic centimeters. With the anchor overboard the water level would be the level of the lake plus 50 cubic centimeters.

F. Thought Questions for Class Discussions:

1. How can heavy ships float?
2. Do cargo ships have to worry about weights?
3. Could a boat sink if only water were added to its weight? Why?

G. Related Ideas for Further Inquiry:

1. Study Activity I-C-2, "What makes a submarine go up and down?"
2. Study Activity I-C-8, "How does a hydrometer work?"
3. Study Activity I-C-11, "Does an object weigh the same in water as it does in air?"

H. Vocabulary Builders—Spelling Words:

1) **sailor** 2) **dilemma** 3) **displace** 4) **weights** 5) **volume** 6) **mass** 7) **gram** 8) **centimeter**

I. Thought for Today:

"It is easier to build a child than to repair a man or woman."

Activity

A. Problem: *What Is Chromatography?*

B. Materials Needed:

1. White blotting paper or filter paper
2. Saucepan or tray
3. Water
4. Inks (different colors) and/or
5. Dyes (different colors) and/or
6. Food colorings
7. Dowel
8. Clothespins
9. Supporting device

C. Procedure:

1. Cut blotting paper or filter paper into strips, one inch wide and twelve inches long.
2. Arrange the supporting device as shown in drawing.
3. Place the saucepan or tray below the supporting device.
4. Fill the saucepan or tray with water.
5. Hang the strips of paper with clothespins so that the ends are about one inch below the water line.
6. Add about a teaspoonful of ink, dye, or food coloring to the tray of water.
7. Let stand.

D. Results:

1. The paper strips will become wet.
2. Soon colored streaks will appear on the paper.
3. The colored streaks will spread up the paper.
4. If the ink, dye, or food coloring contains multiple colors, each will appear on the strips.

E. Basic Facts and Supplemental Information:

1. When the color has nearly reached the top, remove the strip from the tray and let it dry.
2. Some inks, dyes, and coloring matter contain only one color, but others are a mixture of two or more colors.
3. Chromatographic techniques are used to test a wide range of substances.
4. The water carries the test material through the paper.
5. Part of the test is concerned with the color and the other part is concerned with the movement of the color. Some liquids, inks, dyes, and food coloring, are absorbed more quickly and spread up the strips more quickly than others.

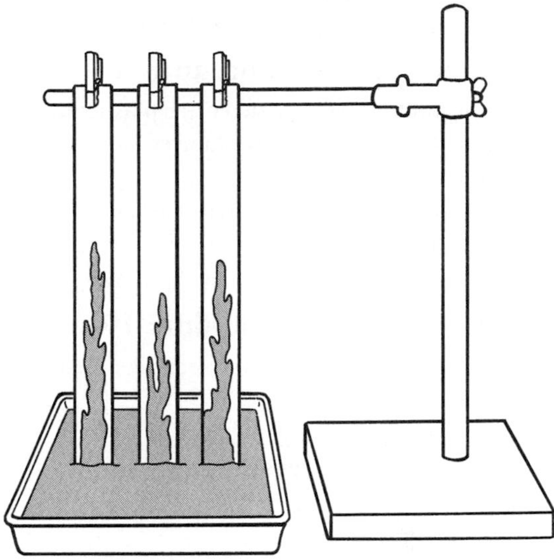

Chromatographs

6. Three strips of paper are normally used to check results. Ideally they should yield identical results, but differences in the mixing with water, grade of paper, and time all play a role in the final chromatograph.

F. Thought Questions for Class Discussions:

1. Would this technique be valuable to detectives? to chemists?
2. Does the speed of absorption depend on the specific color or the specific substance?
3. Is there any relationship between this test and with the way plants get their food?

G. Related Ideas for Further Inquiry:

1. Study Activity III-E-1, "How do roots absorb water?"
2. Study Activity I-C-5, "What is 'capillarity'?"
3. Study Activity II-C-12, "How can we make our own dyes?"

H. Vocabulary Builders—Spelling Words:

1) **blotting** 2) **strips** 3) **saucepan** 4) **dowel** 5) **absorption** 6) **capillarity** 7) **inks** 8) **dyes** 9) **coloring** 10) **clothespins** 11) **streaks**

I. Thought for Today:

"Politicians talk themselves red, white, and blue in the face."

Activity

A. Problem: *How Does a Hydrometer Work?*

B. Materials Needed, Procedure One:

1. Two water glasses or two clear plastic glasses
2. Two covers for water containers
3. Water
4. Two wooden pencils with rubber erasers
5. Two thumbtacks
6. Salt

Materials Needed, Procedure Two:

1. Two water glasses or two clear plastic glasses
2. Water
3. Two hard-boiled eggs
4. Spoon (to handle eggs)

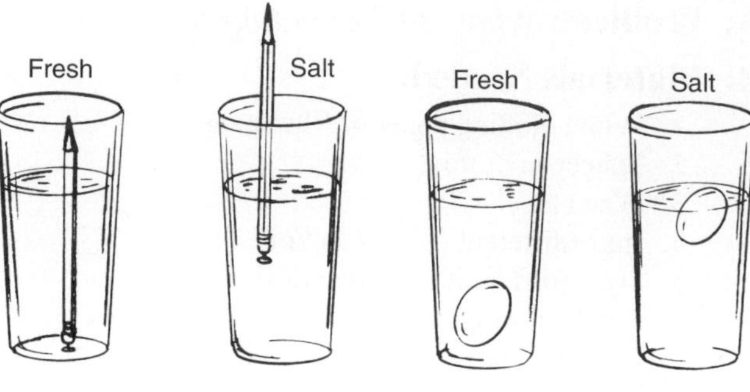

Pencils with thumbtacks
Procedure One

Chicken eggs
Procedure Two

C. Procedure One:

1. Fill both glasses about two-thirds full of water.
2. Stick thumbtacks in the eraser ends of both pencils.
3. Add one-half teaspoon of salt to one glass.
4. Place one pencil in the fresh water, tack end down.
5. Place the second pencil in the salt water, tack end down. (You may have to test various lengths of the pencil for best results.)
6. Observe the results.

Procedure Two: (to test hydrometer)

1. Fill both glasses about two-thirds full of water.
2. Dissolve the salt in one of the glasses.
3. With spoon, gently lower the eggs, one in each glass.
4. Observe the results.

D. Results:

1. In Procedure One, the pencil in the salt water will float higher than the one in fresh water.
2. In Procedure Two, the egg in the fresh water will sink, but the egg in the salt water will be partially buoyed up.
3. These are examples of how a hydrometer works.

E. Basic Facts and Supplemental Information:

1. A hydrometer is a device for measuring the density of a liquid. The denser the liquid, the greater the buoyancy.
2. Buoyancy is determined by the density of the liquid involved. Battery hydrometers use this principle. The denser the liquid, the stronger the battery.

F. Thought Questions for Class Discussions:

1. Is salt water denser (heavier) than fresh water?
2. Is salt water denser (heavier) than an egg?
3. Why is salt water heavier than fresh water?
4. Why is water mixed with alcohol lighter than fresh water?

G. Related Ideas for Further Inquiry:

1. Have class relate experiences in swimming in salt water and fresh water.
2. Compare densities of different liquids: oil, molasses, alcohol, mercury, etc.
3. Make a simple hydrometer using a plastic straw, sealing it at one end, and adding sand to it until it does what the pencil (or egg) described in this Activity did.

H. Vocabulary Builders—Spelling Words:

1) **buoyancy** 2) **density** 3) **hard-boiled**
4) **afloat** 5) **tablespoon** 6) **hydrometer**
7) **thumbtack**

I. Thought for Today

"A school is a building with four walls with tomorrow inside."—Len Waters

Activity

A. Problem: *What Makes Popcorn Pop?*

B. Materials Needed:

1. Unpopped corn kernels
2. Heat source
3. Frying pan with lid
4. Cooking oil

C. Procedure:

1. For a treat, the class can make popcorn.
2. Put some cooking oil in the frying pan.
3. Put some kernels in the frying pan.
4. Put lid on the frying pan.
5. Turn on heat source.
6. When popcorn has finished popping, ask class what makes the popcorn pop.
7. Discuss the possible causes.
8. Compare corn seeds to other types of seeds.
9. Discuss various kinds of snack foods.
10. Compare the food value of corn with wheat, barley, oats, etc.
11. Discuss the various ways that popcorn is flavored.

D. Results:

1. The popcorn will pop.
2. Students will learn why and how popcorn pops. (See Basic Facts and Supplemental Information.)
3. Students will learn that seeds differ in many ways.
4. Students will learn that cereals vary in many ways and that packaged cereals have many additives.

E. Basic Facts and Supplemental Information:

1. The reason the popcorn pops is that the water in the corn kernels changes to steam and literally blows the kernels apart.
2. When water is converted to steam it expands 1,500 times its original volume.

F. Thought Questions for Class Discussions:

1. What other methods are used for cooking foods?
2. Does water play a part in cooking all foods?

Popcorn popping

3. Is popping corn a physical or chemical change?
4. Why so some kernels remain unpopped?

G. Related Ideas for Further Inquiry:

1. Discuss how a pressure cooker works.
2. Compare primitive and modern methods of cooking.
3. Have the students study how foods are preserved.
4. Study Activity I-B-4, "Can air pressure crush a can?"
5. Study Activity II-B-7, "Is water a good conductor of heat?"
6. Study Activity II-B-9, "What happens to gases when they are heated? cooled?"
7. Study Activity V-C-5, "What is the importance of fiber in our diet?"

H. Vocabulary Builders—Spelling Words:

1) **popcorn** 2) **kernels** 3) **frying**
4) **cooking** 5) **popping** 6) **steam**

I. Thought for Today:

"The biggest coward in the world is the person who is afraid of a new idea."

Activity I C 10

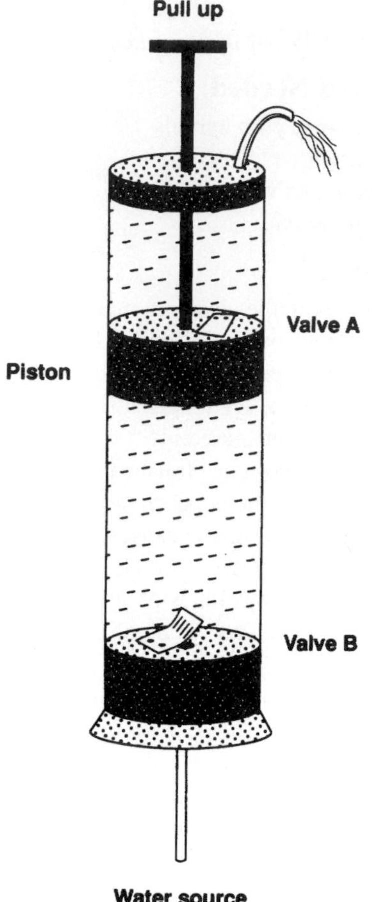

A. Problem: *How Does a Pump Work?*

B. Materials Needed:

1. Glass cylinder
2. Three large pieces of cork
3. Bent glass tubing (spout)
4. Rubber balloon strips (or inner tube strips from an automobile tire)
5. Metal rod with handle
6. Water
7. Pins, bent paper clips, or stapler
8. Bucket or pail
9. Instrument for making holes in cork (round file, drill, etc.)

C. Procedure:

1. Cut top cork so that it has two holes in it; one in the center for the metal plunger and one off to the side for the bent glass tubing.
2. Cut middle cork the same way except the offset hole should have a valve (balloon or tire tube strip) over it fastened with pins or bent paper clips or stapled as shown in the drawing.
3. The third cork should have a center hole and a valve in it opening to a water supply (bucket or pail).
4. Fill the cylinder with water as shown in the drawing.
5. When the pump is fully assembled, push the plunger down and pull up gently several times.

D. Results:

A hand pump is made which clearly shows the actions of the various components.

E. Basic Facts and Supplemental Information:

1. When the plunger has been pushed all the way down and then moved up, it creates a partial vacuum and the water is drawn up from the water source.
2. When the plunger is pushed down, the valves open, allowing the water to flow through the glass cylinder.
3. On the next upward stroke, the valve in the piston head closes and the water is forced out of spout.
4. These actions are repeated as the pump moves up and down.
5. The atmospheric pressure on the water in the bucket or pail forces the water up into the cylinder.
6. All the inside parts of the pump are called the "piston."

F. Thought Questions for Class Discussions:

1. Does an air pump work the same way as a water pump?
2. Where else could water pumps be used?
3. Are "inertia" and "momentum" involved in air and liquid pumps?

G. Related Ideas for Further Inquiry:

1. A regular hand tire pump can be taken apart and the corresponding parts studied.
2. Cutaway drawings or pictures of other pumps can be studied.
3. Study Activity I-B-6, "How does a siphon work?"
4. Study Activity I-B-7, "How can we make a fountain siphon?"

H. Vocabulary Builders—Spelling Words:

1) **pump** 2) **spout** 3) **piston** 4) **valve** 5) **tubing** 6) **cylinder**

I. Thought for Today:

"Never be afraid to answer a question promptly even if it is, 'I don't know!'"

A. Problem: *Does an Object Weigh the Same in Water as It Does in Air?*

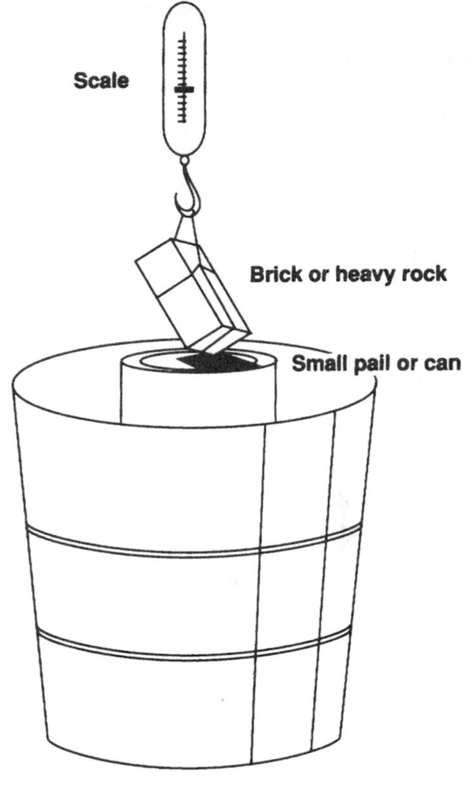

B. Materials Needed:

1. Scale
2. String
3. Brick
4. Small pail or can
5. Large pail
6. Water

C. Procedure:

1. Weigh the brick and record its weight.
2. Place small pail or can in large pail.
3. Add water to the small pail or can until it is completely filled.
4. Tie string around the brick so that it can be supported by scale.
5. Attach brick to scale.
6. Lower brick supported by string and scale into the water until it is just submerged but not touching the bottom. Some of the water will flow into the larger pail.
7. Check the reading on the scale.
8. Ask class if reading is the same.
9. Since the reading will be different, ask why.

D. Results:

1. The difference in the weight of the brick in the air and in the water is due to the buoyancy of the water.
2. The volume of the water displaced is equal to the volume of the brick.

E. Basic Facts and Supplemental Information:

1. If any object floats in water it displaces a certain volume of water. The weight of the water displaced is equal to the weight of the object.
2. This is Archimedes' Principle. Archimedes was a Greek mathematician who lived in the third century B.C. He observed this principle when he was taking a bath and the water overflowed!

F. Thought Questions for Class Discussions:

1. Is there much buoyancy on a big ship?
2. Would Archimedes' Principle be valid if oil were substituted for water?
3. If you added water to a swimming pool aboard a big ship would it change the buoyancy of the ship?
4. Would the weight be the same in air and water if a sponge were used instead of a brick?

G. Related Ideas for Further Inquiry:

1. Test to determine if there is any change in buoyancy if salt water is used.
2. Discuss how you can determine the buoyancy of submarines.
3. Study other Activities in this Section.

H. Vocabulary Builders—Spelling Words:

1) **buoyancy** 2) **submerged**
3) **Archimedes' Principle** 4) **object** 5) **supported**

I. Thought for Today:

"This time, like all times, is a very good one, if we know what to do with it."—Ralph Waldo Emerson

Activity I C 12

A. Problem: *Does Water Always Flow Downhill?*

B. Materials Needed:

1. Two large glass jars
2. Three feet of plastic tubing
3. Water
4. Clothespin

C. Procedure:

1. Ask students if they have ever seen water flowing and in which direction it was flowing: up, down, sideways.
2. Tell the class: "We are going to test to see if water ever flows uphill."
3. Fill one jar with water and place it on a level higher than the other jar.
4. Fill plastic tubing with water.
5. Cover each end with one thumb.
6. Insert one end of tubing into the water in the one jar, and the other end into the other jar. Permit no air to enter tubing.
7. Be sure that the end of the tube in the empty jar is below the water level in the water jar.
8. Remove thumb from the end of the tube.
9. Place a clothespin in the middle of the tubing to control the flow of water.
10. Remove the clothespin and let the water flow.
11. Always keep the levels of water in the jars so that they never permit air to enter into the tubing.
12. Alternate the position of the jars, raising the lower one to the higher position.
13. Control the flow as desired with the clothespin.

D. Results:

1. In this Activity water flows *up* from the supply container to the top of the tubing and then *down* to the receiving container.
2. When the containers' positions are reversed, the old receiving container becomes the supply container and the old supply container becomes the new receiving container.

E. Basic Facts and Supplemental Information:

1. Water will always flow down except in a few unusual cases where it is enclosed in a container and air pressure forces it up against gravity. This is what happens in this Activity.

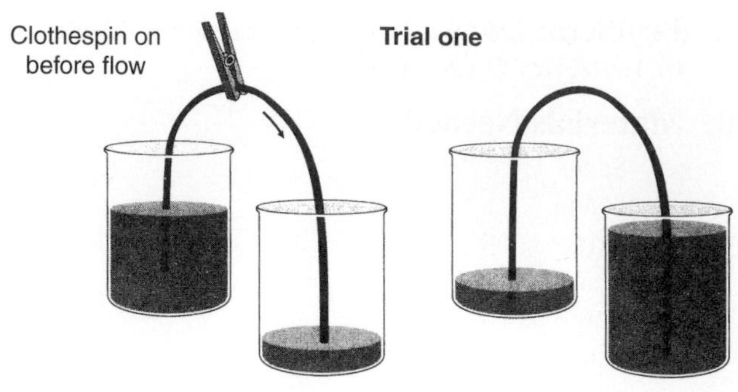

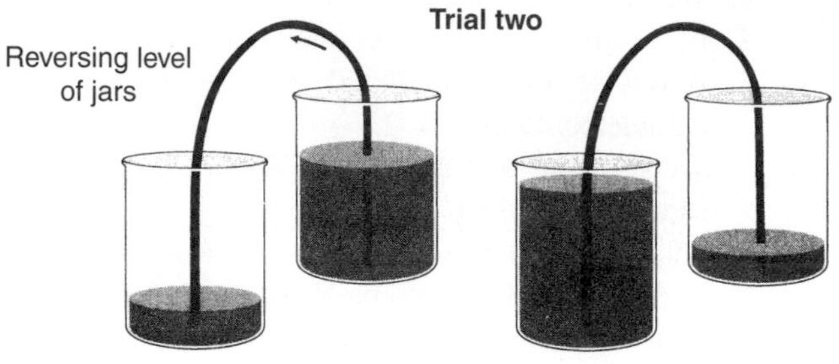

2. This demonstration shows how a siphon works.
3. Normally all liquids flow the same way water does—down.
4. Water must be pumped over mountains. It can never flow up naturally.

F. Thought Questions for Class Discussions:

1. Do rivers only run downhill?
2. How does water get to high elevations?
3. How do water pumps work?

G. Related Ideas for Further Inquiry:

1. Study your community's source of water.
2. Discuss what makes water flow downhill.
3. Study other Activities in this Section.

H. Vocabulary Builders—Spelling Words:

1) **uphill** 2) **downhill** 3) **level** 4) **carton** 5) **aquarium** 6) **suction**

I. Thought for Today:

"It's not the hair on top of the head but what is under it that counts."

Activity

A. Problem: *Is Hot Water Heavier or Lighter Than Cold Water?*

B. Materials Needed:

1. Large glass or clear plastic bowl
2. Ice
3. Small container
4. Water, room temperature
5. Water, warm or hot
6. Food coloring or ink
7. String

C. Procedure:

1. Add room temperature water to the large bowl.
2. Add ice to the bowl.
3. Stir and let stand until the ice is melted.
4. Tie a string around the neck of the small container.
5. Add hot water to this container.
6. Add several drops of food coloring or ink to this container.
7. Carefully lower this small container into the large bowl.

D. Results:

1. The colored water will rise like a volcano.
2. It will slowly spread throughout the water in the bowl.

E. Basic Facts and Supplemental Information:

1. The molecules of hot water are more spread out than the molecules of cold water.
2. Hot water is lighter than cold water; consequently, it will rise.
3. When the temperatures become equal, the waters will mix and the color will become consistent throughout.

F. Thought Questions for Class Discussions:

1. If different liquids were mixed, would this change the results of this Activity?

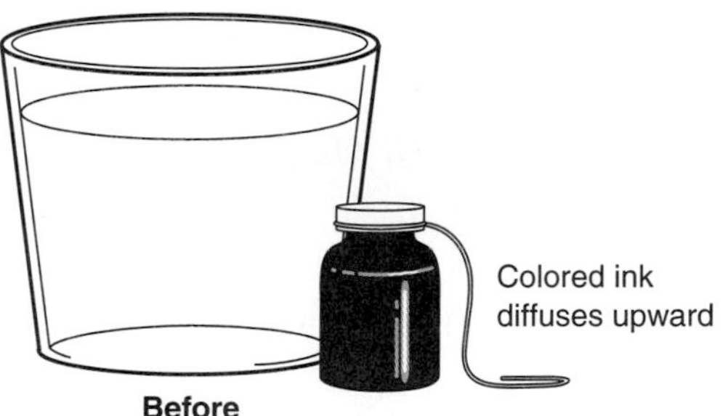

Before

After

2. What is a solution? Is this a physical mixture or a chemical mixture?
3. Does hot and cold air have the same effects as hot and cold water?

G. Related Ideas for Further Inquiry:

1. Study Activity VII-C-4,"What causes a volcano to erupt?"
2. Study Activity I-C-12, "Does water always flow downhill?"
3. Study Activity I-C-10, "How does a pump work?"

H. Vocabulary Builders—Spelling Words:

1) **convection** 2) **conduction** 3) **coloring**
4) **temperature** 5) **bowl** 6) **molecules**

I. Thought for Today:

"TV is a medium because it is rare that it is well done."

Section D: Magnetism

Activity I D 1

A. Problem: *What Is a Magnetic Field of Force?*

B. Materials Needed:

1. Bar magnet
2. Sheet of paper or thin cardboard
3. Iron filings
4. Compass
5. Table
6. Pencil

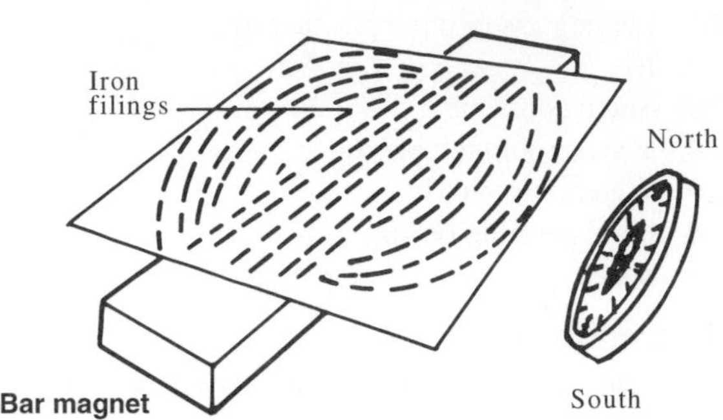

Compass to check direction

C. Procedure:

1. Place the compass near the edge of the table.
2. Place the bar magnet so that the north pole of the magnet is pointing north as indicated on the compass. The north pole of the magnet is the "north-seeking" pole.
3. Confirm poles by checking with compass.
4. Cover the magnet with a thin cardboard or paper.
5. Sprinkle iron filings evenly on the cardboard.
6. Shake or tap the paper or cardboard lightly.
7. With pencil, draw lines alongside iron filings.
8. Remove iron filings and study pencil lines.

D. Results:

1. The iron filings will arrange themselves along the magnetic lines of force.
2. The lines will look like those in the drawing.
3. The filings point toward the poles.
4. When equal attractions from the poles occur, the lines will appear as shown in the middle of the drawing. Note that the filings seem to stand on end at the poles of the magnet.

E. Basic Facts and Supplemental Information:

1. A magnet has a field of force. This will be shown by the iron filings being drawn together in lines, extending along the magnet. A little farther away from the magnet the iron filings will look just as they did when they were sprinkled on the cardboard. The force of the magnet did not move them. The force on the filings becomes weaker the farther the filings get from the magnet, finally becoming so weak it will not move the filings at all.
2. When a bar magnet is bent into a "U" shape it is called a "horseshoe magnet." This type of magnet has greater attraction power because the two poles are closer together. By using iron filings near a magnet it can be shown that the lines of force are closer together nearer the magnet.

F. Thought Questions for Class Discussions:

1. Does the strength of the magnet have any effect on the magnetic field?
2. How does the magnetic field of the bar magnet differ from that of the horseshoe magnet?
3. Where in your home can you find practical uses for magnets?

G. Related Ideas for Further Inquiry:

1. Repeat test with a horseshoe magnet.
2. Pencil or ink lines can be drawn near iron filings for a permanent record.
3. Study Activity I-D-5, "Is the Earth a magnet?"
4. Study Activity I-D-6, "What is magnetic declination?"
5. Study Activity I-D-2, "Through what kinds of substances do magnetic lines of force pass?"

H. Vocabulary Builders—Spelling Words:

1) **iron filings** 2) **magnetic field** 3) **compass** 4) **horseshoe** 5) **bar** 6) **sprinkle** 7) **direction**

I. Thought for Today:

"Part of the problems of the world is that people mistake sex for love, money for brains, and television for living."

Activity I D 2

A. Problem: *Through What Kinds of Substances Do Magnetic Lines of Force Pass?*

B. Materials Needed:

1. U-shaped magnet, small
2. Paper clip
3. Large widemouthed glass or jar.
4. Thin pieces of wood, glass, plastic, leather, iron, rubber, paper, cloth, copper, steel, aluminum, etc.
5. Iron filings
6. Water
7. Cup hook
8. Piece of string

C. Procedure One:

1. Make a wooden support as shown in Fig. 1.
2. Attach cup hook to the top.
3. Attach thread or string to the base.
4. Attach a paper clip about halfway to the top with thread or string from the wooden support.
5. Hang horseshoe (U-magnet) from the top so that there is a strong attraction to the paper clip but still enough room to insert test materials.
6. Insert test materials between the magnet and the paper clip.

Procedure Two:

1. Place filings in glass and cover with water to a depth of several inches. (The depth will depend on the strength of the magnet.) See Fig. 2.
2. Hold magnet just above the water.

D. Results:

1. Procedure One:
   a. The magnet will attract through paper, cloth, glass, plastic, thin plywood, rubber, and nonferrous materials.
   b. The magnet will not attract materials through iron, steel, nickel, or cobalt.
2. Procedure Two: The iron filings will be attracted through the water to the magnet.

E. Basic Facts and Supplemental Information:

1. Several other metals besides iron are capable of becoming magnetized. Among them are cobalt and nickel.
2. Most metals are not magnetic.
3. Sometimes magnetic boards are used in a classroom. If a teacher wants to make a combination magnet and flannel board, steel screening can be placed behind the flannel. Because magnetic lines of force travel through the flannel, magnets can still be used on the flannel board. To stimulate curiosity, you may want to combine this Activity with Activity I-D-5, "Is the earth a magnet?"

F. Thought Questions for Class Discussions:

1. Why will a magnet attract an iron object through a piece of paper?
2. Can you think of any places in your home where there are magnets?

G. Related Ideas for Further Inquiry:

1. Many commercial products use magnets. Have students do some research in this area.
2. Discuss how iron and steel objects could be located under water.
3. Study Activity I-D-1, "What is a magnetic field of force?"
4. Study Activity I-D-4. "What is magnetic soccer?"

H. Vocabulary Builders—Spelling Words:

1) **attract** 2) **lines of force** 3) **support**
4) **iron filings** 5) **paper clip** 6) **magnetic**

I. Thought for Today:

"The primary purpose of a liberal education is to make one's mind a pleasant place in which to spend one's leisure."

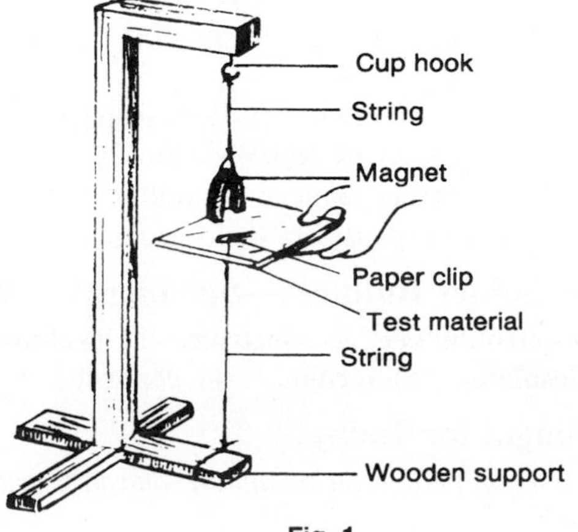

Fig. 1

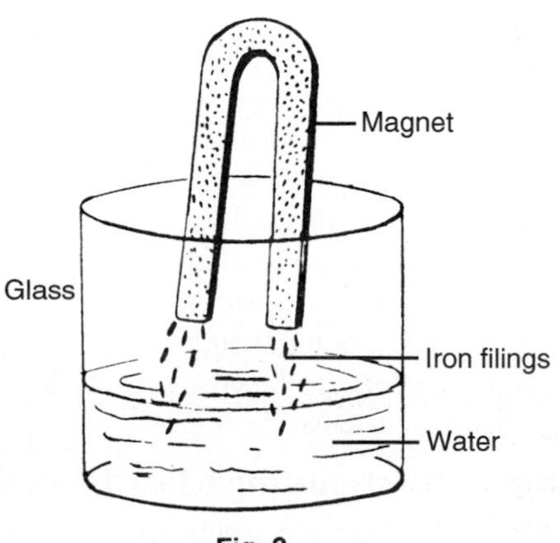

Fig. 2

Activity I D 3

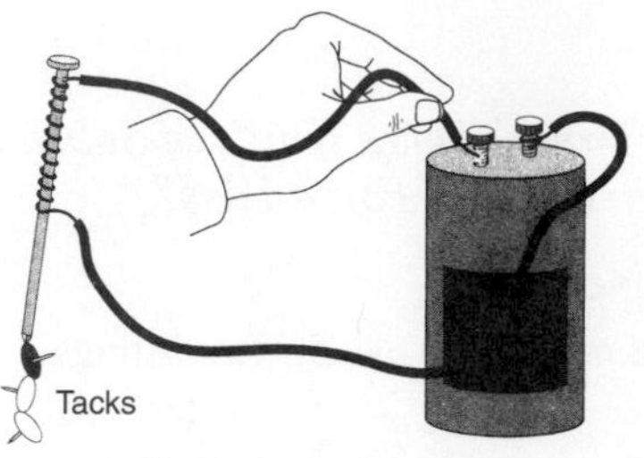

A simple electromagnet

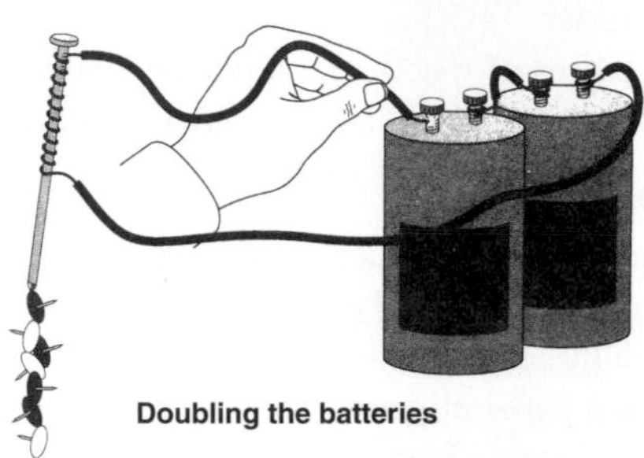
Doubling the batteries

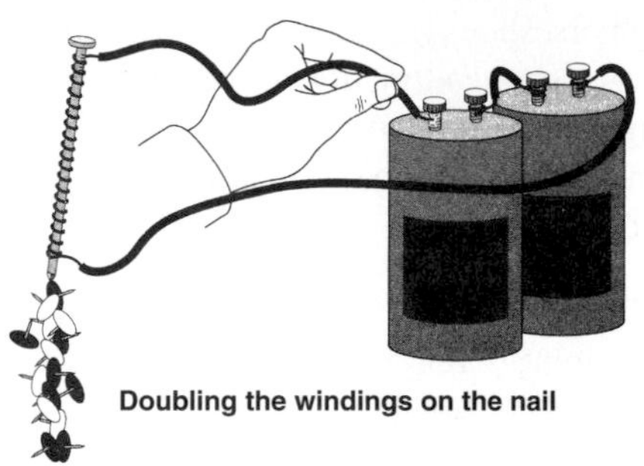
Doubling the windings on the nail

A. Problem: *How Can We Make an Electromagnet?*

B. Materials Needed:

1. Large nail
2. Two batteries
3. Insulated wire, #18
4. Metal thumbtacks

C. Procedure:

1. Wrap the nail with about seven or eight turns of the wire leaving about one foot of wire on either end.
2. Connect one end of the wire to one terminal of the battery.
3. Place the thumbtacks in a pile.
4. Holding the other end of the wire complete the circuit by touching it to the other terminal.
5. Lower the nail into the pile of thumbtacks.
6. Lift as many tacks as you can from the pile.
7. Move these to one side and release the wire from the terminal.
8. Count the number of tacks the electromagnet picked up.
9. Repeat the experiment using two batteries.
10. Repeat the experiment using one battery and twice as many turns of wire around the nail.
11. Repeat the experiment with twice the number of turns as the first experiment and with two batteries.

D. Results:

1. In the first experiment the electromagnet will pick up a number of thumbtacks.
2. Using two batteries will increase the strength of the electromagnet.
3. Increasing the number of turns of the wire will increase the strength of the electromagnet.
4. Increasing the number of batteries and the number of turns of the wire will increase the strength of the electromagnet.

E. Basic Facts and Supplemental Information:

1. Electromagnets are used very frequently in homes and business operations.
2. In homes they are used in doorbells or chimes, telephones, electric appliances, electric toys, etc.
3. In business they are used in electric motors, electric switches, electric typewriters, computers, manufacturing equipment, etc.
4. Electromagnets can be created with direct or alternating currents.

F. Thought Questions for Class Discussions:

1. Can you find any electromagnets in your home?
2. Are there any electromagnets in your classroom?
3. Where do you think electromagnets would be used in automobiles?

G. Related Ideas for Further Inquiry:

1. Study all Activities in Section I-E, "Static Electricity."
2. Study Activity I-D-4, "What is magnetic soccer?"
3. Blow up balloons. Rub them briskly on your clothing. Place them on flat walls. Most of them will cling because of "static electricity."

H. Vocabulary Builders—Spelling Words:

1) **electromagnet** 2) **electrons** 3) **protons**
4) **insulated** 5) **terminal** 6) **connect**

I. Thought for Today:

"If you don't climb the mountain you can't see the view."

Activity

A. Problem: *What Is Magnetic Soccer?*

B. Materials Needed:

1. Four dry cell batteries
2. Four feet of #18 wire
3. Tagboard, approximately 18″ × 30″
4. Two large nails
5. Pen and pencil
6. Ruler
7. Two small blocks of wood, each approximately 1″ × 2″ × 4″
8. 12 metal thumbtacks
9. Two large tacks
10. Two large steel screws
11. Empty tin can
12. Metal cutter
13. Desk or tabletop

C. Procedure:

1. Make two simple knife switches. Each is constructed by:
   a. Screwing a large screw into one end of the wooden block.
   b. Cutting out a metal strip from the tin can with a metal cutter. This serves as the "clapper." (Be careful cutting the strip.)
   c. Bending the strip as shown in the drawing. This serves as the "key" that completes the circuit.
   d. Cutting and attaching wires to the key and the batteries as shown in the drawing.
2. Make two electromagnets. Each is constructed by:
   a. Wrapping each nail with wire as shown in the drawing with enough left over on either end to attach to the key and one of the batteries.
   b. Stripping ends of wires to remove insulation from ends to make good connections.
3. Join the wires from the nail to the key apparatus. The wiring should be long enough so that the tip of the nails on the completed electromagnets can reach the center of the playing field.
4. Draw a soccer field on the tagboard with pen or pencil. (See drawing.)
5. Lay the tagboard soccer field on top of the table or desk.
6. Line up the 12 metal thumbtacks along the center line.
7. Select two players.
8. Instruct the players as to the rules of the game.
   a. On the command "Go," each player will close the knife switch and try to pick up a tack from the center line and deposit it in his/her goal.

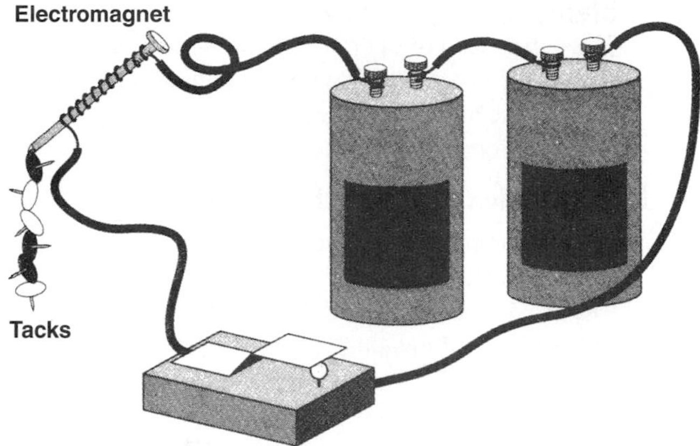

Knife switch connected to batteries

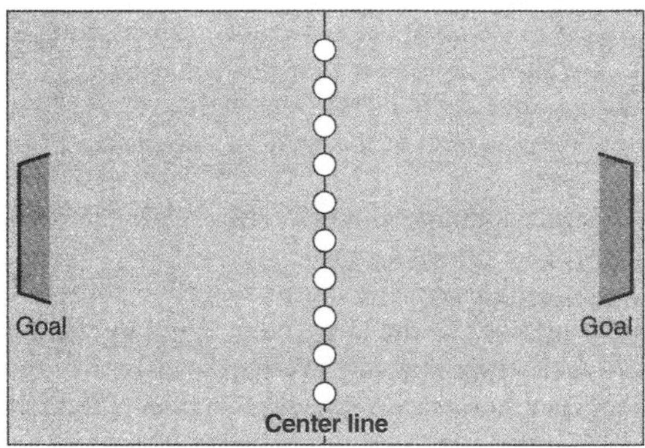

Soccer field

   b. When a tack is placed in a goal, the player must immediately open his/her knife switch to stop the action of the electromagnet, otherwise the tack will leave the goal, and if this happens, the score does not count.
   c. The winner is the one who gets the most tacks in his/her goal.

D. Results:

1. Students will construct a knife switch.
2. Students will construct an electromagnet.
3. Students will have a lot of fun playing a game while learning how an electromagnet operates.

E. Basic Facts and Supplemental Information:

1. Electromagnets are used in junkyards to move large iron or steel objects.
2. Electromagnets are used in doorbells and door chimes.
3. Electromagnets are also used in telephones, generators, and many other electrical items.

4. Scientists still do not have an adequate knowledge of the cause of "attraction" and "repulsion" of magnets.
5. If you magnetize a steel needle and then cut it in half, each half becomes a magnet.

F. Thought Questions for Class Discussions:

1. Will increasing the number of batteries help or hurt the speed of operation in the soccer game?
2. Does the direction the wire is wound around the nail make any difference?
3. Does a doorbell operate like a knife switch?

G. Related Ideas for Further Inquiry:

1. Other games can be constructed in a similar manner.
2. Railroad tracks can be drawn; linked paper clips make an ideal magnetic train.
3. Differences between a temporary and a permanent magnet should be discussed.
4. Study Activity I-D-1, "What is a magnetic field of force?"
5. Study Activity I-D-2, "Through what kinds of substances do magnetic lines of force pass?"
6. Study Activity I-D-3, "How can we make an electromagnet?"

H. Vocabulary Builders—Spelling Words:

1) **electromagnet** 2) **attraction** 3) **repulsion** 4) **knife switch** 5) **circuit** 6) **soccer** 7) **batteries** 8) **scoring** 9) **tacks**

I. Thought for Today

"It's nice to be important but it is more important to be nice."

Activity I D 5

A. Problem: *Is the Earth a Magnet?*

B. Materials Needed:

1. Map of magnetic poles
2. Ball of yarn
3. Bar magnet
4. Long knitting needle

C. Procedure:

1. Work the bar magnet through the ball of yarn so that equal ends are protruding.
2. With the bar magnet slanting slightly to one side insert the knitting needle through the center of the ball of yarn. This is a model of the Earth and its magnetic poles.
3. Discuss true north direction. (We can determine by the North Star.)
4. Discuss magnetic north direction. (We can determine by a compass.)
5. Discuss variation. (This is the difference in degrees between true north and magnetic north.)
6. Show the class the "model" of the Earth.
7. Explain that the knitting needle represents the axis of the Earth on which the Earth rotates.
8. Point to the bar magnet and tell the class that the Earth acts very much like the bar magnet having a north pole, a south pole, and a magnetic field.
9. Study the map on the following page.

D. Results:

1. Students will find that the Magnetic North Pole lies about 15° south of the True North Pole and the Magnetic South Pole lies about 24° north of the True South Pole.
2. Students will learn that the variation varies greatly and there is no regular pattern.
3. Pupils will find that while most variations are small, some are very large—over 100° of longitude.

E. Basic Facts and Supplemental Information:

1. Even the magnetic poles are not fixed.
2. The magnetic poles are believed to be caused by the mineral deposits within the earth.
3. The magnetic poles even change during the Earth's revolution.
4. Variations are measured in degrees east or west of the true direction.

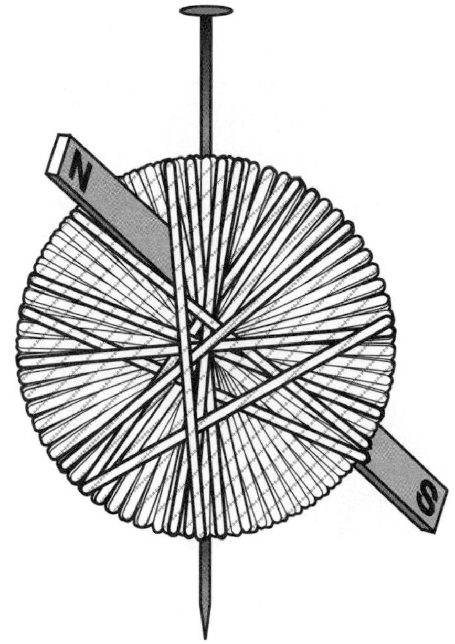

5. The North Pole of a magnet is so named because it points to magnetic north.
6. The Earth's magnetic North Pole is in the Canadian Arctic about 1,000 miles (1,600 kilometers) from the true or geographic North Pole.
7. The Earth's magnetic South Pole is in Adelie Land about 1,500 miles (2,400 kilometers) from the geographic South Pole in Central Antarctica.
8. The Earth's magnetism is produced by molten metal deep within the Earth's core. As the Earth spins, electric currents produce the Earth's magnetic force.

F. Thought Questions for Class Discussions:

1. Do you think early sailors had trouble navigating?
2. What are gyrocompasses?
3. Would magnetic compasses be effective on the moon?
4. Are we living on a huge magnet?

G. Related Ideas for Further Inquiry:

1. Study Section I-A, "Matter."
2. Study Section VII-C, "Earth's Crust."
3. Study Activity I-D-1, "What is a magnetic field of force?"
4. Study Activity I-D-2, "Through what kinds of substances do magnetic lines of force pass?"

5. Study Activity I-D-6, "What is magnetic declination?"

H. Vocabulary Builders—Spelling Words:

1) **North Pole** 2) **South Pole** 3) **magnetic**
4) **variation** 5) **deviation** 6) **Arctic**
7) **Antarctic**

I. Thought for Today:

"Imagination was given to us to compensate for what we are not, and a sense of humor to console us for what we are."

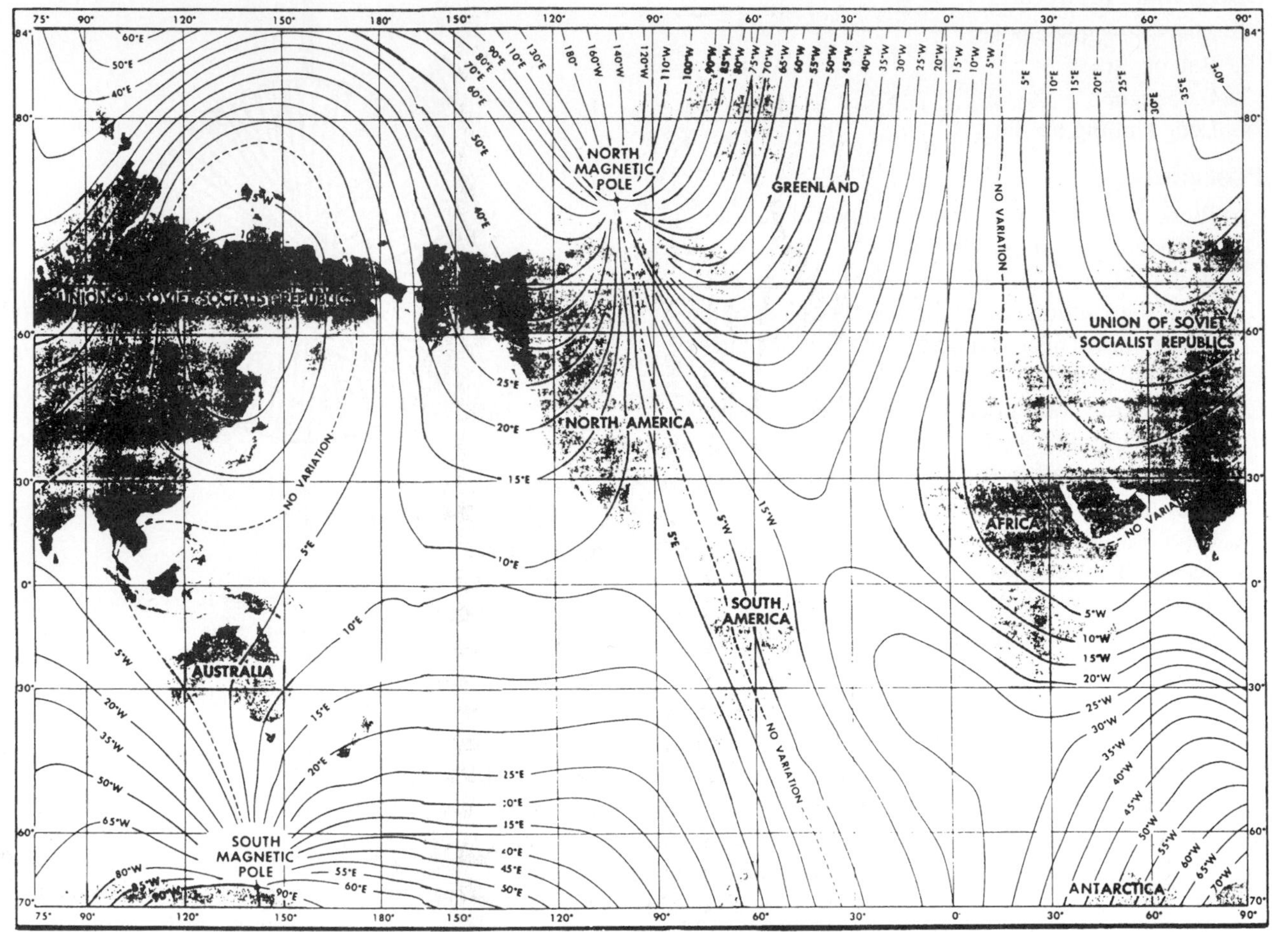

The earth's magnetic poles do not correspond to the regular north and south poles. The difference is called "variation."

Activity

A. Problem: *What Is Magnetic Declination?*

B. Materials Needed:

1. Long steel needle
2. Two small needles
3. Styrofoam ball
4. Two water glasses
5. Rectangular block of wood
6. Protractor
7. Pliers
8. Cellophane tape
9. Bar magnet

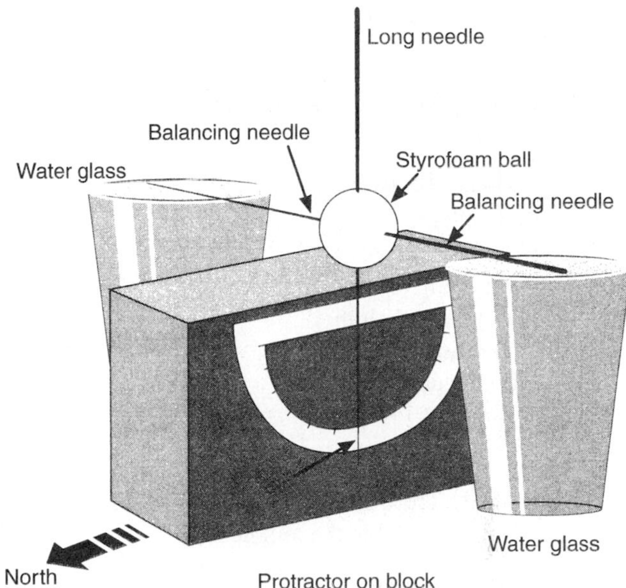

C. Procedure:

1. With pliers, carefully insert the large steel needle through the center of the styrofoam ball.
2. With pliers, carefully insert the two smaller needles, one on each side of the styrofoam ball at right angles to the large needle.
3. Attach the protractor to the block of wood with cellophane tape so that the flat edge of the protractor will be on the top in a horizontal position. (See drawing.)
4. Place the two glasses, one on either side of the block, so that the small needles will rest on their top edge facing the block.
5. The block of wood with the protractor should be pointing toward the north.
6. You might have to use a book or other device to adjust the height of the block or glasses so that the needle will be allowed to swing freely and at the right position so that readings of the large needle pointing can be read on the protractor.
7. Test the needle to see if it points straight down.
8. Remove the ball and the needles from the edge of the glasses.
9. Magnetize the point of the large needle by stroking it in one direction with the south pole of the bar magnet.
10. Replace the ball and needle on the edges of the glasses.
11. Note the change in the angle of the "pointer."

D. Results:

1. The needle pointed straight down before it was magnetized.
2. The needle will point in a northerly direction in the second trial after the needle becomes magnetized.

E. Basic Facts and Supplemental Information:

1. The point of the large needle is now a "north-seeking compass."
2. A regular compass will point along a horizontal plane to the Earth's magnetic north pole.
3. If this apparatus were placed directly over the Earth's magnetic north pole, the needle would point straight down.
4. If the needle were placed near the Earth's magnetic equator and perfectly balanced, it would be horizontal and point north.
5. The angle of dip (declination) is a result of the Earth's magnetic pole. The "pointer" usually points toward the north and a little off center.

F. Thought Questions for Class Discussions:

1. What metals can become magnetized?
2. Can nearby metal objects interfere with the accuracy of these tests?
3. After the needle has become magnetized is it a temporary or permanent magnet?

G. Related Ideas for Further Inquiry:

1. Test the attraction or repulsion of the poles of two bar magnets.
2. Test the magnetic fields of a bar magnet by sprinkling iron filings on a card placed over a bar magnet.
3. Repeat this experiment with a horseshoe magnet.

H. Vocabulary Builders—Spelling Words:

1) **magnet** 2) **magnetized** 3) **styrofoam** 4) **pliers** 5) **protractor** 6) **pointer**

I. Thought for Today:

"It's the person who waits for his ship to come in that's always missing the boat."

Section E: Static Electricity

Activity I E 1

A. Problem: *What Makes These Balloons "Lovable"?*

B. Materials Needed:

1. Red balloon
2. Blue balloon
3. Light string or thread
4. Piece of wool cloth
5. Supporting device
6. Marking pens

C. Procedure:

1. Inflate the balloons.
2. Draw a picture of a girl on the red balloon with her lips painted in the middle.
3. Draw a picture of a boy on the blue balloon with his lips painted in the middle.
4. Tie a knot in each end of the balloon or tie a short piece of string or thread around the neck of the balloons to keep them inflated.
5. Tie a long piece of string or thread to each balloon.
6. Secure the other ends to a supporting device so that when the balloons are hanging the "pictures" are facing each other and are about two inches apart.
7. Tell the students that you have some magical love potion on the piece of cloth.
8. Rub one of the faces of the balloon near its mouth with the piece of wool cloth.
9. Keeping the balloons separated, ask the class what they think will happen.
10. Slowly bring the rubbed balloon close to the other.
11. When the balloons appear to be kissing ask, "Why?"

D. Results:

1. The electrons are removed from the balloon that was rubbed and it becomes positively charged.
2. The electrons on the second balloon move closer to the first balloon because unlike charges attract each other.
3. Consequently, the "faces" (the nearest surface) of both balloons have unlike charges and attract each other. They appear to "kiss."

E. Basic Facts and Supplemental Information:

You can separate the balloons carefully, but they will still hold their charges and try to "kiss" again.

F. Thought Questions for Class Discussions:

1. Where did the electrons go?
2. Could other objects be used to produce static electricity?
3. What is the difference between static electricity and current electricity?

G. Related Ideas for Further Inquiry:

1. Have some students comb their hair briskly and determine why it crackles.
2. Ask students if after they walked on a carpet or rug and then touched a metal object, if they felt an "electric shock."
3. Have other balloons in class that students can inflate and secure at the opening. Have students rub these balloons briskly on their clothes, then place them against a wall. The balloons will cling to any vertical, flat surface.
4. Study Activity I-E-2, "What makes these plastic strips 'unlovable'?"
5. Study Activity I-E-3, "Do you have electricity in your hair?"

H. Vocabulary Builders—Spelling Words:

1) **static** 2) **electricity** 3) **electrons**
4) **attraction** 5) **repulsion** 6) **rubbing**

I. Thought for Today:

"A boy becomes a man when he decides it's more fun to steal a kiss than second base."

Activity I E 2

A. Problem: *What Makes These Plastic Strips "Unlovable"?*

B. Materials Needed:

1. Two plastic strips, one inch wide
2. Two pieces of wool cloth
3. Thread
4. Supporting device

C. Procedure:

1. Tie two pieces of thread to the supporting device about an inch apart.
2. Tie the two plastic strips to the ends of each piece of thread so that the strips hang down freely, about one inch apart. (See drawing.)
3. Select two students. Have them move several feet apart.
4. Give each of them a piece of wool cloth.
5. Have each of them rub his/her plastic strip downward rather briskly, being sure not to break the thread.
6. Have both students carefully move their strips to the original positions and release them.

D. Results:

1. The two plastic strips will move away from each other.
2. In time, they will return to their original positions.

E. Basic Facts and Supplemental Information:

1. The plastic strips were originally electrically neutral.
2. When rubbed with wool the outer electrons are rubbed off.
3. The two plastic strips now have the same charge.
4. Like charges repel; unlike charges attract.

F. Thought Questions for Class Discussions:

1. Where do you think the electrons went?
2. What is the relationship between electron movement and current electricity?
3. Have you ever combed your hair briskly and heard it "crackle"? If so, what do you think caused this?

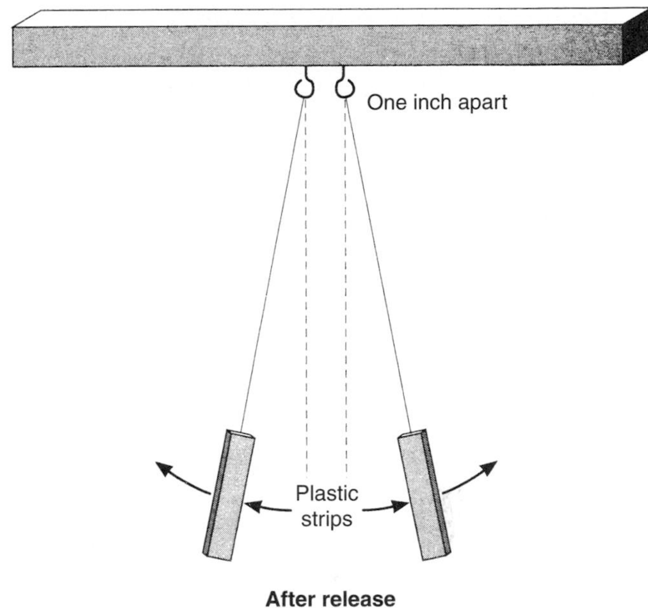

After release

G. Related Ideas for Further Inquiry:

1. At home, after dark, have the students turn out the lights in a room and shuffle their feet briskly on a rug or carpet. Immediately touch a doorknob. They should feel a little shock and see a spark.
2. Study Activity I-E-1, "What makes these balloons 'lovable'?"
3. Study Activity I-E-3, "Do you have electricity in your hair?"
4. Study Activity I-E-4, "Does static electricity affect water flow? attract bits of paper?"
5. Study Activity I-E-5, "What is an electroscope?"

H. Vocabulary Builders—Spelling Words:

1) **plastic** 2) **electrons** 3) **briskly**
4) **repulsion** 5) **attraction** 6) **strips**

I. Thought for Today:

"An opinion is often a minimum of facts combined with prejudice and emotion."

A. Problem: *Do You Have Electricity in Your Hair?*

B. Materials Needed:

1. Student with fine, dry hair
2. Comb

C. Procedure:

1. Have the student comb his/her hair briskly.
2. Have the student place the comb just above the top of his/her hair.

D. Results:

1. The student's hair will become electrically charged.
2. The hair will have a tendency to stand up straight near the comb.

E. Basic Facts and Supplemental Information:

1. When the hair is combed briskly, the electrons are rubbed off and the hair becomes positively charged.
2. The comb becomes negatively charged collecting the electrons.
3. Because opposite charges attract each other the hair follicles move toward the comb.
4. This works well with students who have regular, dry hair; fine hair is even better.

F. Thought Questions for Class Discussions:

1. Where else have you seen evidence of static electricity?
2. What is the difference between static electricity and current electricity?
3. How can you tell if an object is positively or negatively charged?

G. Related Ideas for Further Inquiry:

1. Obtain a lodestone. Test it for its magnetic properties.
2. Study Section I-D, "Magnetism."
3. Study Activity I-A-2, "What are atoms? molecules?"
4. Study Activity I-E-1, "What makes these balloons 'lovable'?"
5. Study Activity I-E-2, "What makes these plastic strips 'unlovable'?"
6. Study Activity I-E-5, "What is an electroscope?"

H. Vocabulary Builders—Spelling Words:

1) **briskly** 2) **comb** 3) **attraction** 4) **positively** 5) **negatively** 6) **charged** 7) **electrons**

I. Thought for Today:

"There is only one quality worse than hardness of the heart and that is softness of the head."

Activity I E 4

A. Problem: *Does Static Electricity Affect Water Flow? Attract Bits of Paper?*

B. Materials Needed, Procedure One:

1. Plastic comb
2. Small stream of water from faucet
3. Student with dry hair

Materials Needed, Procedure Two:

1. Plastic comb
2. Bits of tissue paper
3. Student with dry hair

C. Procedure One:

1. Adjust the faucet stream so that it flows steadily in a small stream.
2. Have student vigorously comb his/her hair.
3. Have the student hold the comb near the stream of water.
4. Observe the flow of water.
5. Have the student move the comb horizontally toward and then away from the stream of water.
6. Observe any changes in the flow of water.

Procedure Two:

1. Lay the bits of paper on a table or desk top, scattering them slightly.
2. Have the student comb his/her hair briskly and then immediately hold the comb near the bits of paper.
3. Observe results.
4. Move comb slowly around the bits of paper.
5. Again observe any changes.

D. Results:

1. When the comb is rubbed it will become negatively charged.
2. In Procedure One, the stream of water will bend toward the comb as long as the comb is nearby.
3. In Procedure Two, when the comb is placed near the bits of paper, the bits of paper will "jump up" to the comb and adhere to it briefly.

E. Basic Facts and Supplemental Information:

1. Static electricity is caused by rubbing the electrons of atoms of one material and causing them to move towards other materials that have fewer electrons closer to them.
2. Running water has neutral charges. When the negatively charged comb is placed near the water, the electrons on the atoms of the water move to the opposite side, leaving the side nearest the comb positively charged. The attraction between the negatively charged comb and the positively charged side of the atoms of the water causes the water to "bend" toward the comb.

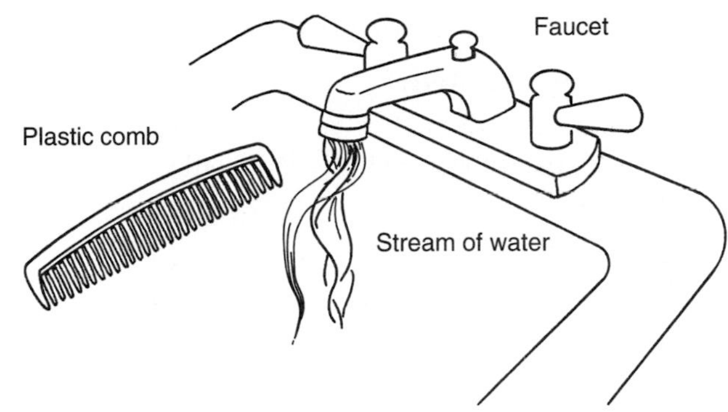

Procedure One

Procedure Two

F. Thought Questions for Class Discussions:

1. How do lightning rods work?
2. Where does the electricity come from that is in the clouds?
3. Can you make a balloon cling to a wall by rubbing it briskly against your clothing and then placing it on a wall?

G. Related Ideas for Further Inquiry:

1. Study Activity I-E-1, "What makes these balloons 'lovable'?"
2. Study Activity I-E-2, "What makes these plastic strips 'unlovable'?"
3. Study Activity I-E-5, "What is an electroscope?"
4. Study Section II-G, "Current Electricity."

H. Vocabulary Builders—Spelling Words:

1) **static** 2) **comb** 3) **faucet** 4) **vigorously** 5) **briskly** 6) **stream** 7) **negatively** 8) **positively**

I. Thought for Today:

"The bigger a person's head gets, the easier it is to fill his/her shoes."—Anne Bancroft

Activity I E 5

A. Problem: *What Is an Electroscope?*

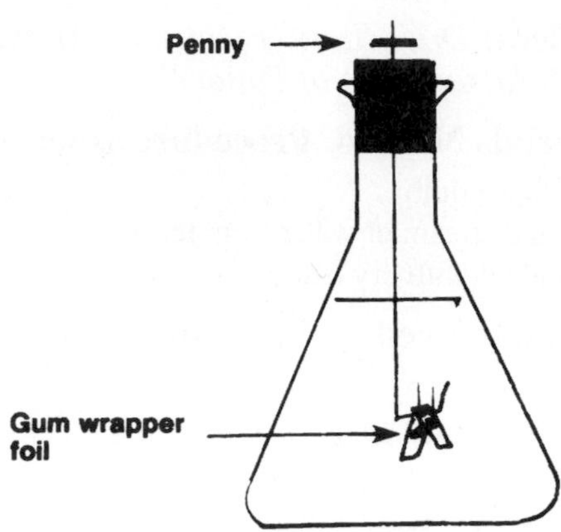

B. Materials Needed:

1. Flask or bottle
2. Cork (not rubber) to fit flask or bottle
3. Penny
4. Soldering iron
5. Solder
6. Chewing gum wrapper foil
7. Rubber cement
8. Copper wire
9. Piece of silk
10. Piece of wool

C. Procedure:

1. Tell the students about or have them make an electroscope.
2. To make an electroscope:
   a. Very carefully solder a penny to a piece of copper wire (or have a competent person do this).
   b. Push the wire through the cork.
   c. Make a flat hook bend in the wire about one-half inch from the end.
   d. Cut a strip of foil from the gum wrapper about one-quarter inch wide and two inches long.
   e. Hang this over the flat hook part so that it balances.
   f. Put the wire apparatus in the flask or bottle.
3. Run the following tests:
   a. Rub a hard rubber or plastic comb over a piece of wool or briskly through your hair, and then touch the penny with the comb.
   b. Rub a glass or plastic rod with a silk cloth, and then touch the penny with the glass or plastic rod.
   c. Charge the electroscope by bringing a luminous dial from a watch near the penny.

D. Results:

1. In test one (3a), the foil becomes negatively charged; the foil ends will separate.
2. In test two (3b), the foil becomes positively charged; the foil ends will separate.
3. In test three (3c), the detector was charged, but lost its charge when the watch was placed nearby, thus causing the foil ends to drop.

E. Basic Facts and Supplemental Information:

1. Electrons are on the outer parts of atoms, encircling the nucleus.
2. Most of an atom consists of space because the electrons are at a great relative distance from the nucleus.
3. Because of this great distance, electrons are easily moved by rubbing the atoms of which they are apart.
4. We used to think that atoms were composed of three basic elements: protons, neutrons, and electrons. We now have identified over 100 different atomic particles.
5. Most of these particles have been discovered by using "atom smashers," and these particles exist for only a short period of time.

F. Thought Questions for Class Discussions:

1. What are electrons?
2. How can we tell that electrons are negatively charged?
3. Is lightning a form of static electricity?
4. What are lightning rods?

G. Related Ideas for Further Inquiry:

1. Study Activity I-E-1, "What makes these balloons 'lovable'?"
2. Study Activity I-E-2, "What makes these plastic strips 'unlovable'?"
3. Study Activity I-E-3, "Do you have electricity in your hair?"
4. Study Activity I-E-4, "Does static electricity affect water flow? attract bits of paper?"

H. Vocabulary Builders—Spelling Words:

1) **electroscope** 2) **electrons** 3) **static** 4) **electricity** 5) **soldering** 6) **repulsion**

I. Thought for Today:

"It's hard to teach kids the alphabet these days. They all think that 'V' comes after 'T'."

PART II
ENERGY

$E=mc^2$

SECTION A: SOURCES

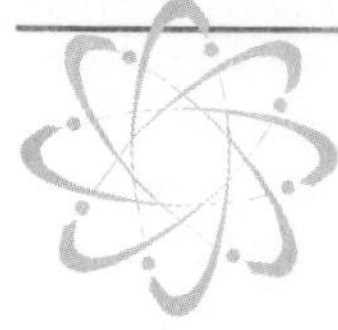

Activity II A 1

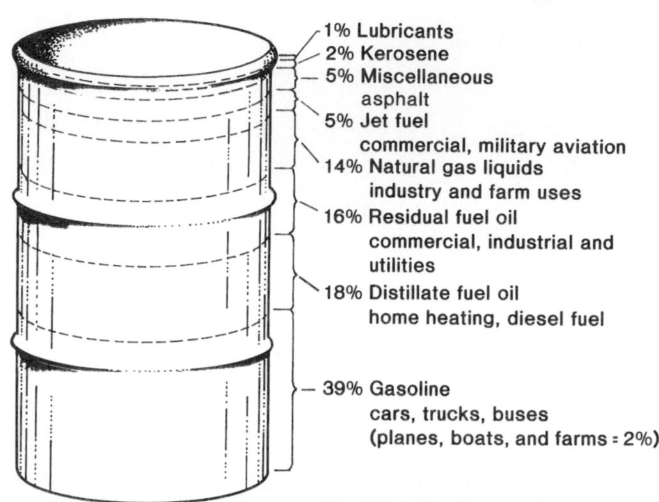

How our crude oil is separated

A. Problem: *Is There an Energy Crisis?*

B. Materials Needed:

1. Can of motor oil
2. Pictures of gas appliances
3. Piece of coal or picture of coal
4. Picture of dam
5. Picture or model of a nuclear power plant
6. Picture of the sun
7. Pictures of cars, planes, buses, etc.

C. Procedure:

1. Discuss these energy problems:
   a. Dependence on foreign oil
   b. Costs of foreign oil
   c. Demand for more energy by Americans (7% more each year)
   d. Estimated sources of present energy supplies:
      1) oil—40%
      2) nuclear—18%
      3) coal—28%
      4) natural gas—10%
      5) hydroelectric—4%
   e. We are running out of oil in the continental United States and we have limited supplies in Alaska.
   f. Many "poor" countries are burning their natural biomass for energy, which is deteriorating their living standards.
2. Describe how oil is being used:
   a. gasoline
   b. home heating diesel fuel
   c. industry, utilities
   d. natural gas (industry, farms)
   e. jet fuel
   f. kerosene
   g. lubricants
   h. plastics
   i. miscellaneous
3. Describe how we might get future energy supplies.
   a. Increase coal production.
   b. Increase nuclear power plants.
   c. Develop shale oil industry.
   d. Increase drilling explorations for oil and gas.
   e. Offshore drilling on our continental shelves.
   f. Reclaim oil wells that were formerly too costly.
4. Describe ways of more efficient use of energy resources.

D. Result:

Students will learn that we are in an energy crisis condition and that we have little prospect of easing the situation in the immediate future. As the world's population increases, the demands for energy will increase and the "nonrenewable" sources will decrease.

E. Basic Facts and Supplemental Information:

1. New sources of energy that could be most helpful are solar, geothermal, ocean tides, ocean waves, and winds.
2. At the present rate of use, Arabian oil is expected to last only about 35 years.
3. Every day over four kilowatt hours of solar energy fall on each square foot on our planet at the latitude of Los Angeles. This could provide clean energy with no pollution and no destruction of land resources if we learn to harness it economically.

F. Thought Questions for Class Discussions:

1. Do we need to think about conserving our energy as well as producing more?
2. Do you think the use of nuclear energy should be increased or decreased?
3. How would you solve the energy crisis?

G. Related Ideas for Further Inquiry:

1. Study Section II-G, "Current Electricity."
2. Study Part VI, "Ecology."
3. Study all other Activities in this Section.

H. Vocabulary Builders—Spelling Words:

1) **oil** 2) **coal** 3) **hydroelectric** 4) **nuclear** 5) **natural** 6) **energy** 7) **crisis** 8) **uses**

I. Thought for Today:

"There are three ways to get things done: do it yourself, hire someone to do it, or forbid your kids to do it."

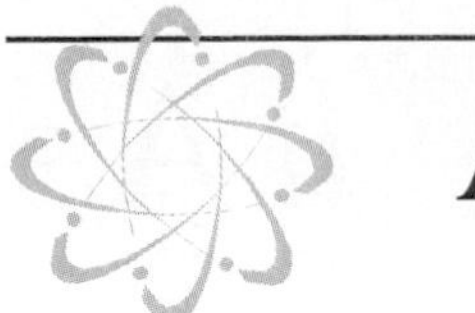

Activity

A. Problem: *What Are Fossil Fuels?*

B. Materials Needed:

1. Piece of coal
2. Kerosene or lighter fluid
3. Can of oil
4. Picture of shale, tar, sand (optional)
5. Candle or heat source

C. Procedure:

1. Display the materials and show how each is related to energy, and specifically, fossil fuels.
2. Describe burning. All fire (burning) require: a) fuel, b) high temperature, and c) oxygen. These are called the "Fire Triangle." Remove one of these and there is no fire (burning).
3. Discuss our need for energy.
4. Burn a candle and tell the students that the wax comes from fossil fuels.
5. Carefully warm some water over a heat source and describe how the energy came from fossil fuels.
6. Discuss how fossil fuels originated from the decomposition of organic materials (plants and animals).

D. Results:

1. Students will learn there are many kinds of fossil fuels.
2. Burning, warming, and heating all require energy, and most of it comes from fossil fuels.

E. Basic Facts and Supplemental Information:

1. Fossil fuels consist primarily of oil and gas. Oils are refined by a process called "fractional distillation," in which oil is heated and the lighter, more volatile substances are removed first, followed by each consecutive product.
2. Gasoline is refined during this process, and several additives are added to make it more efficient for internal combustion engines.
3. Coal, a fossil fuel, is found abundantly in the United States, which has two-thirds of the free world's supply.
4. The United States has about 3.3 trillion (3,300,000,000,000) tons of coal, but about 70 billion (70,000,000,000) tons lie so close to the Earth's surface that it must be "strip-mined."

F. Thought Questions for Class Discussions:

1. Think of a hard manual task. Could you devise a means of using energy to do this?
2. What will happen to our world when the Earth's fossil fuels run out?
3. Is gasoline inexpensive now? Will it always be inexpensive?

G. Related Ideas for Further Inquiry:

1. Study Section II-B, "Fire and Heat."
2. Study Section VI-B, "Conservation."
3. Study Part III "Plants" and Part IV "Animals."
4. Study Activity II-A-1, "Is there an energy crisis?"
5. Study Activity II-A-3, "How beneficial is solar energy?"

H. Vocabulary Builders—Spelling Words:

1) **volatile** 2) **fossil fuels** 3) **fractional distillation** 4) **gasoline** 5) **kerosene**

I. Thought for Today:

"It's an odd thing but, internationally speaking, oil seems to cause a lot of friction."

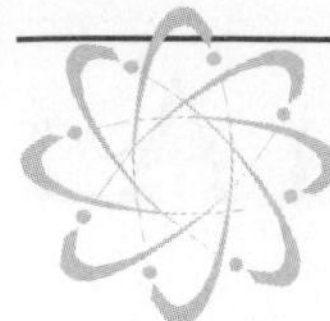

Activity II A 3

A. Problem: *How Beneficial Is Solar Energy?*

B. Materials Needed:

1. Two cans (medium-sized)
2. Aluminum foil
3. Black construction paper
4. Two thermometers
5. Cellophane or masking tape
6. Water
7. Ice pick

C. Procedure:

1. Fill both cans with water.
2. Wrap one can with aluminum foil (sides and top).
3. Secure with cellophane or masking tape.
4. Wrap the other can with black paper (sides and top).
5. Secure with cellophane or masking tape.
6. Using the ice pick, punch a hole in each top (aluminum foil and black paper).
7. Insert a thermometer in the hole on top of each can.
8. Leave thermometers in cans for a few minutes.
9. Record temperature readings in both cans.
10. Place both cans in the sun.
11. Let the cans stay in the sun as long as possible.
12. Observe new readings.
13. Compare changes in readings.
14. Remove both thermometers.

D. Results:

1. In the first part of the procedure (see 9 above), the temperature readings will be the same in both cans.
2. In the second part of the procedure (see 12 above), the temperature in both cans will be increased, and the can wrapped in black paper will show the greater rise.

E. Basic Facts and Supplemental Information:

1. The basic source of our energy is from the sun (solar energy).
2. Solar energy costs nothing to produce, but is expensive to harness.
3. The sun's energy will last for 5 billion years (the anticipated life of the sun).
4. The sun gives off many kinds of radiation.
5. Basically, it is the infrared rays that produce heat.
6. Solar energy is now being used to warm air in homes, water in homes, swimming pools, etc.
7. Solar energy is nonpolluting.

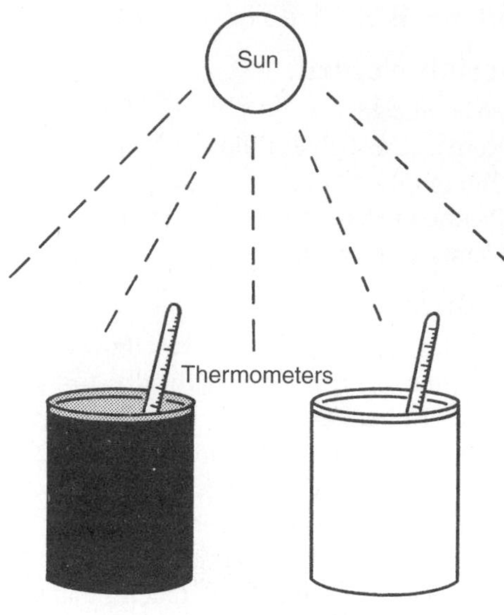

Solar energy

8. We could stretch solar cells across barren desert lands to produce needed energy.
9. Solar photovoltaic cells can generate electric current when exposed to the sun.
10. Virtually every spacecraft and satellite developed since 1958 has used this kind if energy.

F. Thought Questions for Class Discussions:

1. How can solar energy be stored for use when the sun does not shine?
2. In what areas would solar energy devices be most efficient?
3. Can we use solar energy to generate steam?

G. Related Ideas for Further Inquiry:

1. Study Activity II-A-1, "Is there an energy crisis?"
2. Study Activity II-A-2, "What are fossil fuels?"
3. Study Activity II-A-5, "What is hydroelectric power?"
4. Study Section II-B, "Fire and Heat."
5. Study Section VII-B, "Solar System."

H. Vocabulary Builders—Spelling Words:

1) **solar** 2) **radiation** 3) **panel** 4) **readings** 5) **air conditioners** 6) **radiant** 7) **heat** 8) **deserts** 9) **energy** 10) **infrared**

I. Thought for Today:

"In 40 minutes the sun delivers to the Earth's surface as much energy as humans use in a year."

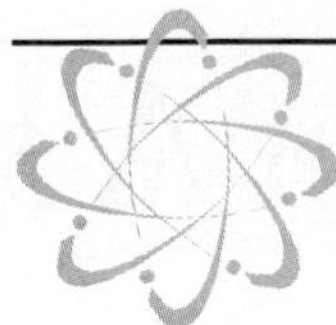

Activity II A 4

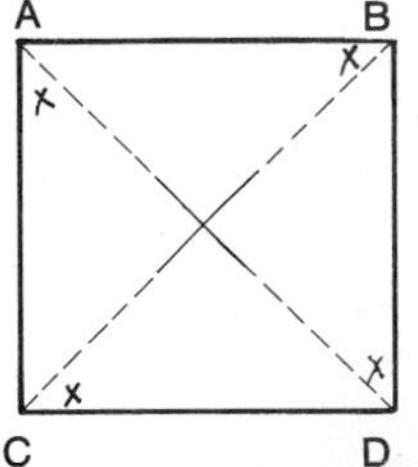

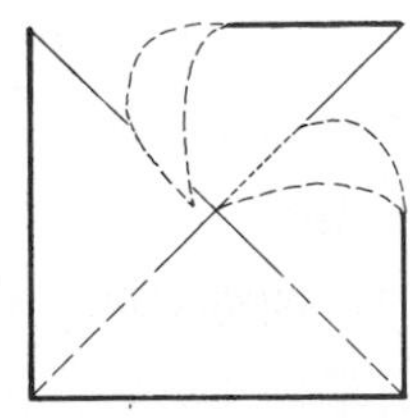

A. Problem: *Is Wind a Good Source of Energy?*

B. Materials Needed:

1. Wooden dowel or stick about 6 inches long
2. Straight pin
3. Construction paper

C. Procedure:

1. Cut a piece of construction paper making a 6-inch square.
2. Draw diagonal lines from A to D and from B to C. (See drawing.)
3. Cut to within one-half inch of center point from four corners along these diagonal lines.
4. Fold points X to center and put the pin through the center where lines cross.
5. Attach this pinwheel to the end of the wooden dowel or stick by forcing the point of the pin into the dowel or stick.
6. Blow into the center of the pinwheel or hold pinwheel in any current of air.

D. Result:

Students will learn to make a small paper windmill.

E. Basic Facts and Supplemental Information:

1. Wind (moving air) causes pinwheel to whirl.
2. When the same principle is used on a large scale, the wind can be used to do beneficial work.
3. In some areas where winds are prevalent, many windmills have been constructed for providing energy to nearby communities.
4. Wind power is inexhaustible, clean, efficient, and free, and does not pollute the atmosphere.
5. Wind power generators are more efficient than present-day solar, nuclear, or fossil fuel generators.
6. The major drawbacks of wind power are the capriciousness of the winds and the limited areas where the winds are continually strong enough to supply more than a fraction of our total needs.
7. Windmills have been used in the past to grind wheat into flour, pump water, and do other jobs.
8. The modern windmill converts wind power into electricity.

F. Thought Questions for Class Discussions:

1. How does wind make this paper windmill operate? What makes it turn?
2. Is this kind of windmill able to do work?
3. What kinds of work are ordinarily done by regular windmills?
4. Where do sailboats get their energy to move?

G. Related Ideas for Further Inquiry:

1. Study Activity II-A-1, "Is there an energy crisis?"
2. Study Activity II-A-2, "What are fossil fuels?"
3. Study Activity II-A-5, "What is hydroelectric power?"
4. Study Activity II-A-6, "Can we get sufficient energy from geothermal sources?"
5. Study Activity II-A-8, "Is nuclear energy harmful or safe?"
6. Study Part VI, "Ecology."

H. Vocabulary Builders—Spelling Words:

1) **windmill** 2) **construction** 3) **diagonal**
4) **center** 5) **pinwheel** 6) **generator**
7) **capricious** 8) **weather** 9) **vane**

I. Thought for Today:

"The most called-upon prerequisite of a friend is an accessible ear."

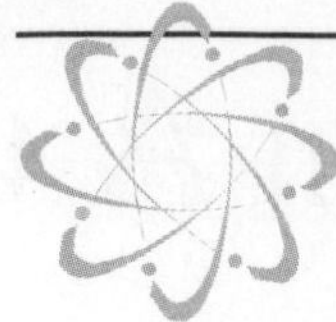

Activity

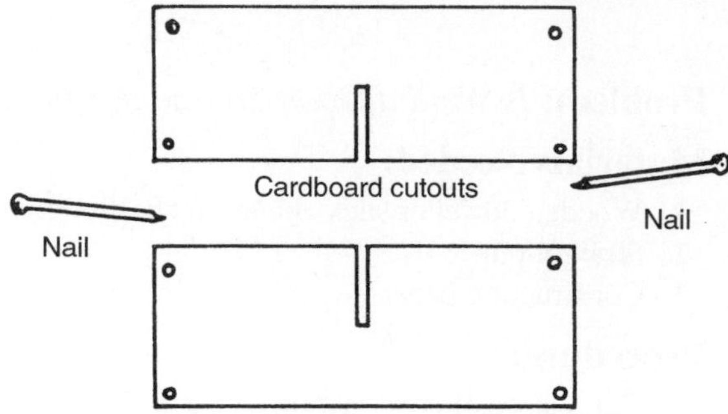

A Problem: *What Is Hydroelectric Power?*

B. Materials Needed:

1. Cardboard, two pieces about 4″ × 6″
2. String
3. Water
4. Pitcher
5. Basin
6. Nails (small)
7. Scissors
8. Punch
9. Water glass

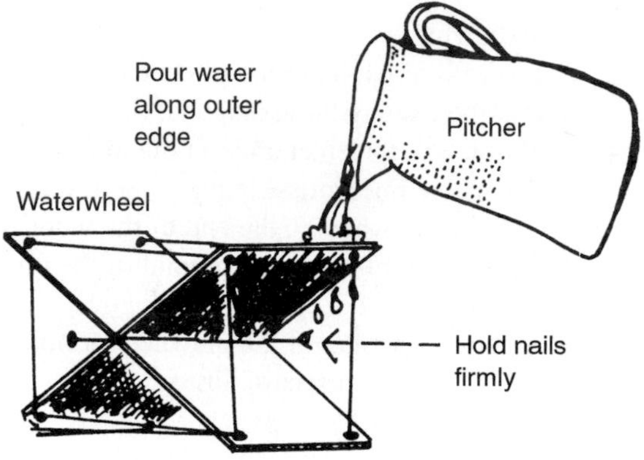

C. Procedure:

1. Cut notches in cardboard as shown in drawings.
2. Punch holes in edges as shown in drawings.
3. Slip pieces together at notches.
4. Secure pieces in stable position by looping string through punched holes.
5. Mount the nails through the cardboard as "axles." (You might want to secure them fully with cellophane tape.)
6. Have two students work with each set of apparatus.
7. Have one student hold the "axle" and the other fill the pitcher with water and slowly pour water along the outer edges of each "paddle."
8. Let students feel the force of water from a running faucet, drinking faucet, or the pouring of a glass of water.

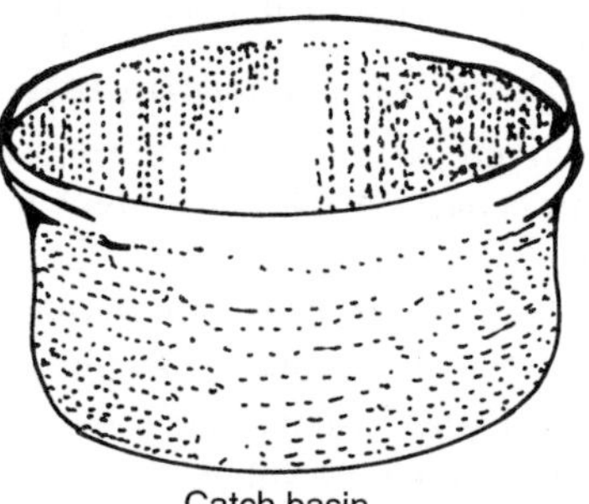

D. Result:

The waterwheel will turn.

E. Basic Facts and Supplemental Information:

Hydroelectric power is produced through falling water turning huge generators in many dams that have been constructed for this purpose. Hydroelectric power, if utilized to the fullest, could only supply 30% of our energy needs. Sediment builds up behind the dams so that each dam has a relatively short lifespan. The negative environmental factors for constructing new dams are:

1. Small animals lose their homes.
2. Croplands are destroyed.
3. Rivers need to be rerouted.
4. Valleys are filled with silt.
5. Fish die from "thermal pollution."

F. Thought Questions for Class Discussions:

1. Do you think we should build more dams?
2. How valuable is the silt that builds up behind the dams?
3. Is energy generated by hydroelectric power the same as that generated by fossil fuels?

G. Related Ideas for Further Inquiry:

1. If any students have visited dams, have them discuss their visits with the class.
2. Study Part VI, "Ecology."
3. Study other Activities in this Section.

H. Vocabulary Builders—Spelling Words:

1) **hydroelectric** 2) **generator** 3) **dams**
4) **paddle wheel** 5) **pitcher** 6) **sediment**

I. Thought for Today:

"There is no end to what may be done if it matters not who gets the credit."

Activity II A 6

A. Problem: *Can We Get Sufficient Energy from Geothermal Sources?*

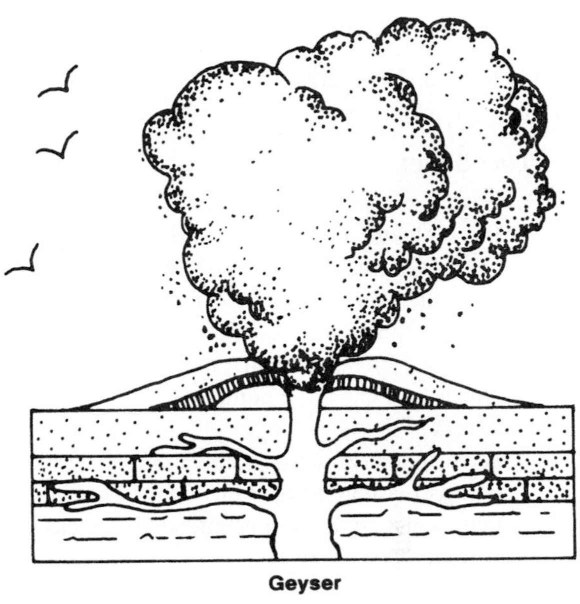

Geyser

B. Materials Needed:

1. Rocks (small)
2. Tongs
3. Heat source
4. Old pan
5. Water
6. Metal pail or can

C. Procedure:

1. Put rocks in can.
2. Heat rocks with heat source.
3. Carefully heat rocks for about five minutes.
4. Put a small amount of water in metal pail or can.
5. *Carefully* lift rocks with tongs and place in water.

D. Result:

Rocks will warm the water and may even cause the water to boil.

E. Basic Facts and Supplemental Information:

1. The center of the Earth is a molten mass. See Activity VII-B-9, "What is in the center of the Earth?"
2. Some surfaces of the Earth contain hot rocks. Scientists have plumbed more than 2 1/2 miles down in New Mexico and discovered hot rocks. They pumped 290 gallons of water down this system every minute and the hot rocks changed to steam at a temperature of 357° F.
3. Theoretically, if you dug deep enough anywhere in the world you could produce steam to turn generators to produce energy.

F. Thought Questions for Class Discussions:

1. What causes "Old Faithful" in Yellowstone National Park to send forth geysers of hot water and steam?
2. What other sources of energy can we get from water?
3. What might be some dangers in using geothermal energy?

G. Related Ideas for Further Inquiry:

1. Check with students to find out if any of them have ever visited natural hot springs. If so, have them describe what they have seen.
2. Study Section VII-C, "Earth's Crust."
3. Study Section II-B, "Fire and Heat."
4. Study Activity II-A-1, "Is there an energy crisis?"
5. Study Activity II-A-2, "What are fossil fuels?"
6. Study Activity II-A-3, "How beneficial is solar energy?"
7. Study Activity II-A-4, "Is wind a good source of energy?"
8. Study Activity II-A-5, "What is hydroelectric power?"

H. Vocabulary Builders—Spelling Words:

1) **geothermal** 2) **converts** 3) **geyser**
4) **energy** 5) **plumbed** 6) **Old Faithful**

I. Thought for Today:

"Genius is 1% inspiration and 99% perspiration."

Activity II A 7

A. Problem: *What Is a Chain Reaction?*

B. Materials Needed:

Many dominoes

C. Procedure:

1. Have students line up the dominoes in one straight line on their edges so that when one domino falls over it will make the next one tumble until all the dominoes can be made to fall down in sequence.
2. Have a student push the first domino over.
3. Discuss with students that this is what is called a "linear action." (One domino acts on another in a line.)
4. Have another group of students set up a second group of dominoes as shown in the drawing so that when one domino is tumbled it knocks down several more.
5. Discuss atomic energy and atomic bombs, citing that in order to get energy out of atomic piles, a chain reaction is necessary where neutrons of atoms act like the dominoes in this setup.
6. Have another student push the first domino over.
7. Describe that in a real chain reaction, one neutron splits an atom and releases several additional neutrons.

Linear reaction

Chain reaction

D. Results:

1. Students will build a "linear reaction" and see how it operates.
2. Students will build a "chain reaction" and see how it operates.

E. Basic Facts and Supplemental Information:

1. A chain reaction is necessary to set off an atomic bomb.
2. Nuclear material is constantly giving off neutrons.
3. In order to have a chain reaction, we have to increase the size of the atomic material until it becomes about the size of a softball. This is called the "critical mass." At this point the free neutrons start a chain reaction, resulting in an atomic explosion.
4. In a nuclear power plant the chain reaction is controlled by strontium rods inserted into an atomic pile to absorb the free electrons and thus prevent an explosion.

F. Thought Questions for Class Discussions:

1. Where do the neutrons come from?
2. What are the by-products of a uranium pile?
3. Where are we going to put the radioactive wastes from nuclear power plants?

G. Related Ideas for Further Inquiry:

1. Have students do research on X-rays.
2. Some teachers have successfully demonstrated a "chain reaction" by placing many mouse traps in a large box with a cellophane front for viewing and placing ping-pong balls on each "set" mouse trap and then dropping a single ping-pong ball down from the top of a closed cover with only space enough to insert the first ping-pong ball.
3. Study Part VI, "Ecology."
4. Study Activity II-A-8, "Is nuclear energy harmful or safe?"

H. Vocabulary Builders—Spelling Words:

1) **dominoes** 2) **atomic pile** 3) **neutron** 4) **linear** 5) **action** 6) **chain reaction**

I. Thought for Today:

"Live in such a way that you would not be ashamed to sell your parrot to the town gossip."

Activity II A 8

A. Problem: *Is Nuclear Energy Harmful or Safe?*

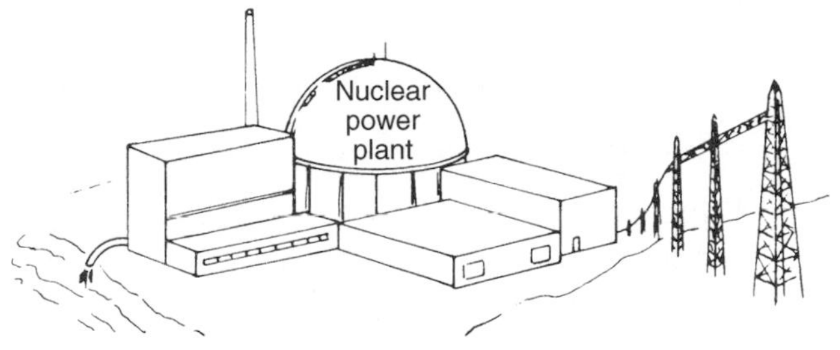

B. Materials Needed:

1. Newspaper articles about nuclear energy
2. Radio and television reports
3. Magazine write-ups

C. Procedure:

1. Make a collection of articles discussing nuclear energy.
2. Discuss these articles.
3. If possible, bring in a film or outside speaker to discuss nuclear energy for peaceful purposes.

D. Results:

1. Students will find that there are many accounts of nuclear energy in the public media.
2. Students will learn that there are many differences of opinion regarding nuclear energy.
3. Some accounts state that nuclear energy is harmful while others state that it is beneficial and safe.

E. Basic Facts and Supplemental Information:

1. We need energy. Nuclear energy is one source of energy.
2. There are inherent problems in producing nuclear energy.
3. The material used in producing nuclear energy can be used for nuclear weapons.
4. With India's recent nuclear testing, all of the major countries now have or could easily make atomic bombs.
5. There have been several major accidents at nuclear plants involving radiation and subsequent deaths.
6. The disposal of radioactive wastes is a serious problem because these wastes remain radioactive for thousands of years. The United States is planning on "disposing" some radioactive wastes in a salt mine in New Mexico about 2,000 feet below the desert surface.
7. There are two major types of nuclear energy: fission and fusion. Fission is the splitting of atoms to release energy, which we have achieved. Fusion is the joining of two atoms to produce energy, which we have not yet achieved for practical purposes.
8. There are about 400 nuclear power plants operating around the world. They don't last forever and have to be retired. The problem is what to do with them.
9. A study by psychiatrists William Beardslee and John Mack has shown that American children become aware of nuclear war before age 12. Half of them say that it affects their future plans. They said that a significant number were "deeply disturbed," "profoundly pessimistic," and "just plain scared."
10. Nuclear energy is America's third leading source of electricity.
11. As of this writing, there are approximately 25,000 nuclear warheads stockpiled in the world's arsenal.

F. Thought Questions for Class Discussions:

1. How should we dispose of old nuclear power plants? (They are radioactive.)
2. What should we do with the radioactive wastes that are being continually produced?
3. Would you like to live close to a nuclear power plant?

G. Related Ideas for Further Inquiry:

1. Study Activity II-A-7, "What is a chain reaction?"
2. Study Activity II-A-1, "Is there an energy crisis?"
3. Study Activity II-A-2, "What are fossil fuels?"
4. Study Section V-G, "Safety."
5. Study Part VI, "Ecology."
6. Study Section VII-C, "Earth's Crust."

H. Vocabulary Builders—Spelling Words:

1) **nuclear** 2) **reactors** 3) **fusion**
4) **fission** 5) **newspaper** 6) **radio**
7) **television** 8) **retired** 9) **disposal**

I. Thought for Today:

"It's a confusing world—we are running out of electricity and we don't even know what it is."

Section B: Fire and Heat

Activity II B 1

A. Problem: *What Is the Fire Triangle?*

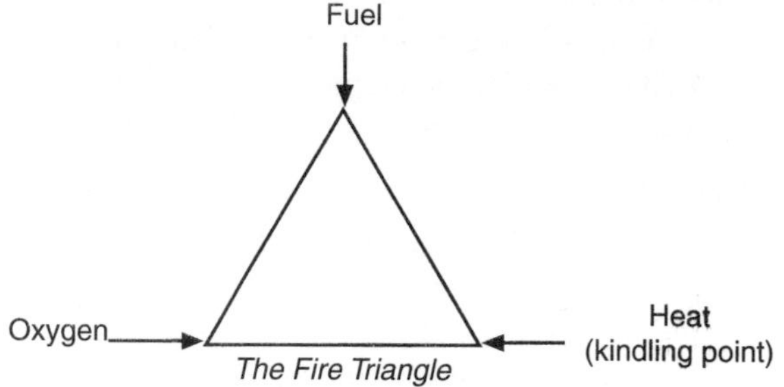

B. Materials Needed:

1. Baking pan
2. Nonburnable protective pad
3. Sheet of newspaper
4. Matches
5. Large glass jar or metal pail

C. Procedure:

1. Discuss local fire accidents.
2. Have students relate any fires that they are aware of that were serious in nature.
3. Place protective pad on desk or table.
4. Place baking pan in the center of the protective pad.
5. Tear several small strips of paper from the newspaper.
6. Crumple them into a small ball.
7. Carefully ignite the paper ball.
8. Let it burn for several seconds.
9. Before it burns itself out, carefully cover the fire with glass jar or metal pail.
10. After the fire is extinguished, ask the class why the fire went out.
11. Discuss with the class how firefighters put out fires.
12. Have the class list and discuss the three main elements that are needed for a fire:
    a. fuel (combustible material)
    b. heat
    c. oxygen

    These make up the "Fire Triangle." (See drawing.)

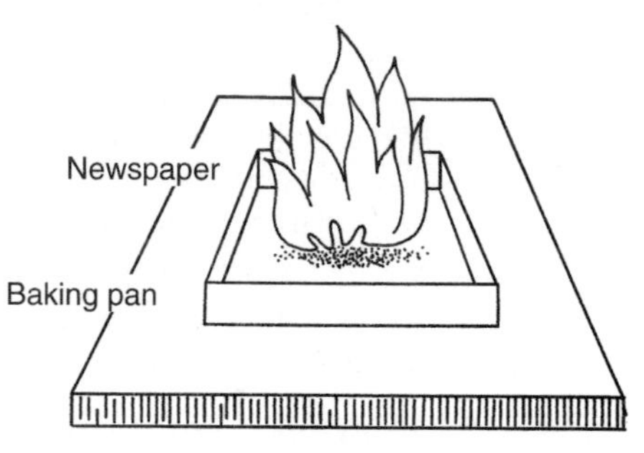

D. Results:

1. When ignited, the newspaper will burn.
2. When the oxygen supply is diminished, the fire will go out.
3. Students will learn the three elements that compose the "Fire Triangle."

E. Basic Facts and Supplemental Information:

1. The removal of any one of the three elements of the "Fire Triangle" will cause the fire to be extinguished.
2. Firefighters use water to reduce the "heat" of the fire below its "kindling point."
3. In some cases, firefighters also use foam to cut off the fire's oxygen supply.
4. Another method of fighting small fires is to use a fire extinguisher. This works because it reduces the oxygen supply.

F. Thought Questions for Class Discussions:

1. Do all substances burn?
2. What are some causes of fires in homes?
3. What are some of the causes of forest fires?
4. What are some safety precautions that we can take to prevent fires in our homes, at school, and in our community?

G. Related Ideas for Further Inquiry:

1. Study Activity II-B-2, "Does heat travel in solids?"
2. Study Activity II-B-4, "Do some substances conduct heat faster than others?"
3. Study Activity VI-D-6, "How can we protect our recreational areas?"

H. Vocabulary Builders—Spelling Words:

1) **triangle** 2) **combustion** 3) **oxygen**
4) **temperature** 5) **extinguish** 6) **kindling**

I. Thought for Today:

"The difficulties of life are intended to make us better, not bitter."

Activity II B 2

A. Problem: *Does Heat Travel in Solids?*

B. Materials Needed

1. Clamping device
2. Thin steel rod
3. Wax (paraffin or candle)
4. Heat source

C. Procedure:

1. Support the thin steel rod in the clamping device as shown in the drawing.
2. Make several small balls of wax and stick them on the underside of rod at equal intervals.
3. Hypothesize (guess) if the time between dropping of adjacent wax balls will be more, less, or the same if heat is applied to the outer end of the rod.
4. Carefully apply heat to the unsupported end of the rod.
5. Record the time it takes each wax ball to drop from the rod.
6. Calculate the amount of time it took between dropping of adjacent wax balls.

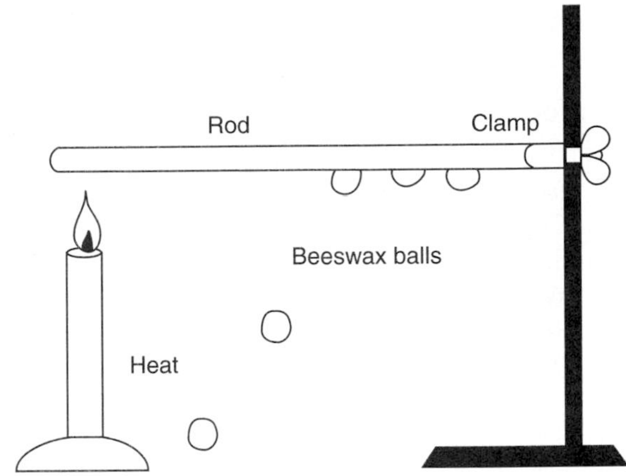

D. Results:

1. As the heat is conducted along the rod, the paraffin or candle wax balls will start to melt and drop off.
2. The time between the dropping of the wax balls increases as they are located farther and farther away from the heat source.

E. Basic Facts and Supplemental Information:

1. Heat is conducted more rapidly near the flame (heat source) but more slowly as it is carried farther and farther away, because of heat loss due to radiation. For this reason, if a rod is long enough, a point will be reached where no wax balls will fall off.
2. If the melting point of the wax is known, it is possible to calculate the speed of conduction from point to point (one wax ball to another).
3. Heat is a form of energy.
4. Heat can never be destroyed.
5. Heat can be transferred from one object to another by conduction, convection, or radiation.
6. In this Activity, heat is transferred from the heating source to the steel rod by convection, then to the wax by conduction.
7. When the wax absorbs enough heat to reach its melting point, it becomes a liquid and drops off the steel rod.

F. Thought Questions for Class Discussions:

1. Does all wax melt at the same temperature?
2. What kinds of waxes are used in our homes?
3. Do solids hold their heat very long?
4. If a piece of wood and a piece of metal are exposed to sunlight, which becomes hotter? Is one hotter or just *feels* hotter? Why?
5. Do the wax balls drop from the rod because the wax changes to a liquid?

G. Related Ideas for Further Inquiry:

1. Study Activity II-B-1, "What is the Fire Triangle?"
2. Study Activity II-B-4, "Do some substances conduct heat faster than others?"
3. Study Activity I-A-2, "What are atoms? molecules?"
4. Study Activity I-A-4, "What is the 'Periodic Table'?"
5. Study Activity I-A-10, "What is diffusion?"

H. Vocabulary Builders—Spelling Words:

1) **conduction** 2) **radiation** 3) **solids** 4) **wax** 5) **dropping** 6) **hypothesize** 7) **time** 8) **adjacent**

I. Thought for Today:

"A person without dreams is an individual without a future."

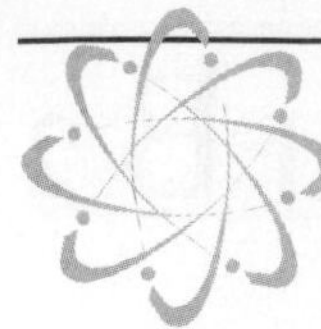

Activity II B 3

A. Problem: *Do all Metals Conduct Heat at the Same Rate?*

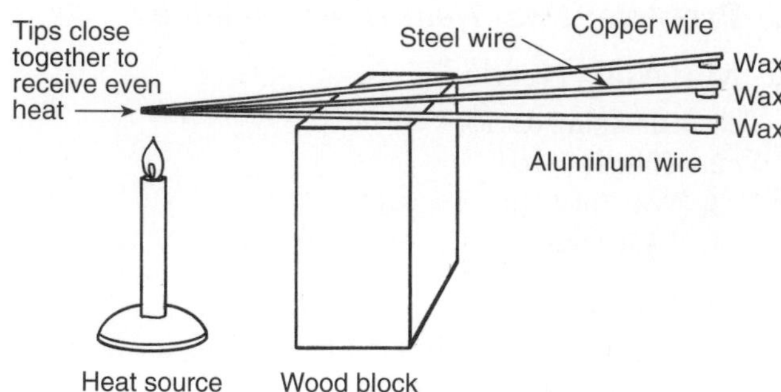

B. Materials Needed:

1. Heat source
2. Aluminum wire
3. Copper wire
4. Steel wire
5. Wood block, 2″ × 2″ × 6″
6. Staples
7. Paraffin or candle wax

C. Procedure:

1. Staple wires to the top of the wood block as shown in sketch.
2. Attach wax balls to the underside of each wire.
3. *Carefully* apply heat to the joined ends of the wire. Heat source should be about an inch below the wires.

D. Results:

1. The wax ball at the end of the aluminum wire will drop off first.
2. The wax ball at the end of the copper wire will drop off second.
3. The wax ball at the end of the iron or steel wire will drop off last.

E. Basic Facts and Supplemental Information:

1. Of the three metals tested, aluminum conducts heat the fastest, and steel, the slowest.
2. Conduction of heat is correlated to the conduction of electricity.
3. Metals expand when they are heated and contract when they are cooled.
4. Expansion and contraction are vital factors in the production and uses of metal objects, especially when they are in contact with other metal materials.
5. Airplanes and space shuttles must take into account these properties when the metal parts in contact with the air causes them to heat up because of friction with the air.
6. Many safety devices in machines are designed to account for the expansion and contraction of metals.

F. Thought Questions for Class Discussions:

1. How can you hang a wire clothesline to be sure it is taut?
2. What causes telephone lines and electric power lines to sag?
3. What kinds of metals are used in electric cords?
4. Where are electric wires used in homes?

G. Related Ideas for Further Inquiry:

1. Test other materials for conduction such as ceramics, glass, lead, etc.
2. Study Activity I-A-4, "What is the 'Periodic Table'?"
3. Study Activity I-A-10, "What is diffusion?"
4. Study Activity II-B-1, "What is the Fire Triangle?"
5. Study Activity II-B-2, "Does heat travel in solids?"
6. Study Activity I-A-5, "What is the difference between a physical change and a chemical change?"

H. Vocabulary Builders—Spelling Words:

1) **conduction** 2) **radiation** 3) **heat**
4) **aluminum** 5) **copper** 6) **iron** 7) **steel**
8) **staples** 9) **block** 10) **wires** 11) **candle**

I. Thought for Today:

"It is a great thing to win the admiration of people, but a greater thing to gain their love."

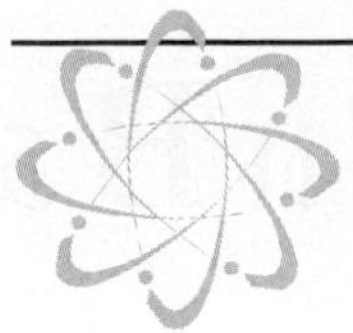

Activity

II B 4

A. Problem: *Do Some Substances Conduct Heat Faster Than Others?*

B. Materials Needed:

1. Ceramic cup
2. Aluminum cup
3. Thermometer (high level or cooking)
4. Wood bowl
5. Boiling water
6. Crushed ice
7. Heat source

C. Procedure:

1. *Carefully* pour boiling water in each of the three containers.
2. *Carefully* feel the outside of the containers.
3. Place the thermometer in one of the containers.
4. Record the temperature and dry the thermometer carefully. Repeat this step with each of the other two containers.
5. Allow the containers to stand for 15 minutes.
6. Record temperatures every 5 minutes.
7. Compare the readings.
8. Determine facts on the rates of conduction of these materials.
9. *Carefully* empty all containers, dry them, and put an equal amount of crushed ice in each.
10. After the ice has started to melt, insert the thermometer in each container and record the temperatures every 5 minutes.
11. Compare the readings.

D. Results:

1. With the boiling water:
   a. all containers will have an equal starting temperature but will feel different as time elapses.
   b. the aluminum cup will lose its temperature the fastest, the ceramic cup the next, and the wooden bowl the slowest.
2. With the crushed ice:
   a. all containers will have an equal starting temperature after the ice has melted but will feel different as time elapses.
   b. the aluminum cup will gain heat the fastest, the ceramic cup the next, and the wooden bowl the slowest.

E. Basic Facts and Supplemental Information:

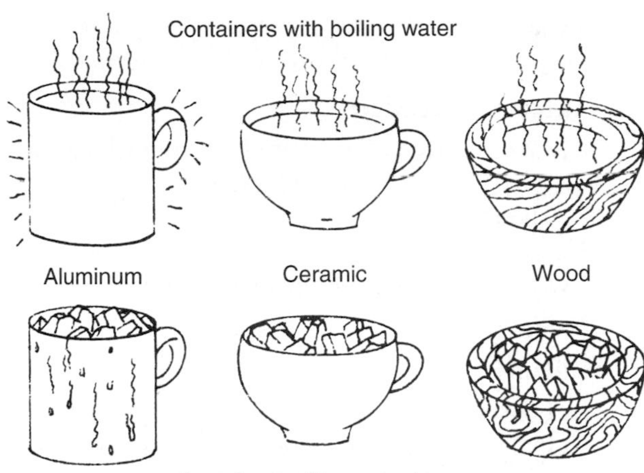

1. Aluminum is a better conductor of heat than either ceramic or wood; consequently, it will gain (or lose) heat the fastest.
2. Ceramic is a better conductor of heat than wood.
3. Wood is the poorest conductor of heat of these three materials; consequently, it will gain (or lose) heat the slowest.
4. Coldness is the lack of heat.

F. Thought Questions for Class Discussions:

1. If you want coffee to stay hot, would you put it in an aluminum cup?
2. Why does hot coffee, when served in a metal cup, seem hot at first, but much cooler after a few minutes?
3. Will a cold drink stay cold longer in a metal can or a wooden bowl?
4. How does a thermos bottle keep hot liquids hot and cold liquids cold?

G. Related Ideas for Further Inquiry:

1. Study the differences between a Celsius (Centigrade) thermometer and a Fahrenheit thermometer.
2. Study Activity II-B-5, "Will water temperature rise if water is heated while it has ice in it?"
3. Study Activity II-B-6, "Can water be heated in a paper container?"
4. Study Activity II-B-7, "Is water a good conductor of heat?"
5. Study Activity II-B-2, "Does heat travel in solids?"

H. Vocabulary Builders—Spelling Words:

1) **aluminum** 2) **ceramic** 3) **wood** 4) **heat** 5) **plastic** 6) **steel** 7) **conduct** 8) **container**

I. Thought for Today:

"Experience should be a guiding post not a hitching post."

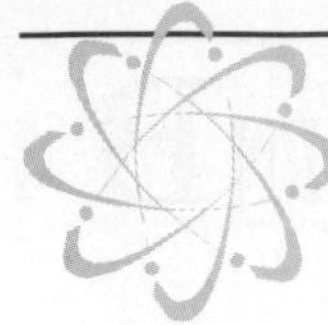

Activity II B 5

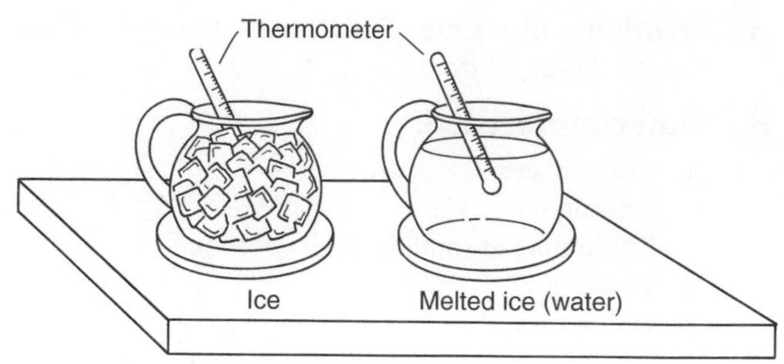

A. Problem: *Will Water Temperature Rise if Water Is Heated While It Has Ice in It?*

B. Materials Needed:

1. Pyrex coffee pot or other glass jar in which water can be heated easily and safely
2. Thermometer
3. Supply of ice
4. Electric hot plate or other heat source
5. Spoon

C. Procedure:

1. Put some water in the coffee pot or glass jar.
2. Put a generous supply of ice in the water.
3. Dip the thermometer in the ice water and keep stirring it until the temperature on the thermometer goes down to 32° F. or 0° C. (freezing point of water).
4. Apply heat slowly to the ice water.
5. Carefully keep stirring the ice water gently with spoon until all the ice is gone.
6. Record the temperature every half minute.
7. When the ice has melted, note if there are any temperature changes for 3 or 4 minutes.

D. Results:

1. The temperature will not rise until the ice has melted.
2. When the ice has melted, the temperature will rise.

E. Basic Facts and Supplemental Information:

1. The reason why the temperature doesn't rise can be found in the conditions that govern the freezing of water and the melting of ice. We have to have enough heat removed from the water to change its state from liquid to solid. The reverse is also true. We must add heat to change from a solid to a liquid. It requires 80 calories of heat for each gram of water to melt the ice. This is why the temperature will not rise until all the ice has been melted.
2. We must add heat to change any solid to a liquid.
3. We must add heat to change any liquid to a gas.
4. In this Activity we are adding heat, but not enough to change the temperature because the container still has ice in it. As long as there is ice present, it lacks enough heat to change the ice (solid) to a liquid (water).

F. Thought Questions for Class Discussions:

1. What causes the bubbles in a carbonated drink when ice is added to the drink?
2. Will an ice-cold drink on a hot day be warmer than an ice-cold drink on a cold day?
3. Does the temperature remain constant as a solid changes to a liquid? as a liquid changes to a gas?
4. What is the temperature of melting snow?
5. What is the temperature of boiling water?
6. Where does the crushed ice get its heat to melt?
7. Can you see steam? (No; what one sees are small droplets of liquid water.)

G. Related Ideas for Further Inquiry:

1. Study Activity I-C-1, "When water freezes does it expand or contract?"
2. Study Activity I-C-13, "Is hot water heavier or lighter than cold water?"
3. Study Activity II-B-6, "Can water be heated in a paper container?"
4. Study Activity II-B-7, "Is water a good conductor of heat?"
5. Study Activity VII-E-9, "How can we measure humidity in the air? How can we build a hygrometer?"

H. Vocabulary Builders—Spelling Words:

1) **temperature** 2) **melt** 3) **liquid** 4) **freezing** 5) **solid** 6) **stirring** 7) **ice-cold** 8) **calories**

I. Thought for Today:

"Many minds are like concrete—all mixed up and permanently set."

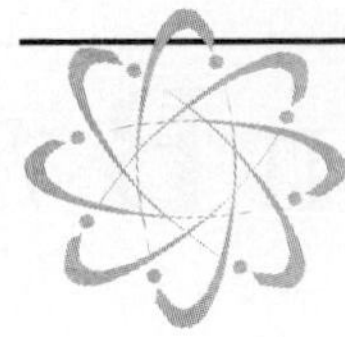

Activity II B 6

A. Problem: *Can Water Be Heated in a Paper Container?*

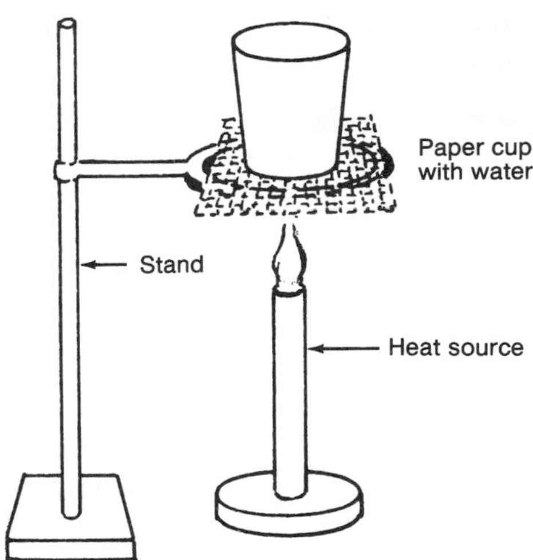

B. Materials Needed:

1. Paper cup, nonwaxed
2. Ring stand
3. Clamp support
4. Wire screen
5. Water
6. Candle, burner, or Sterno
7. Safety pail
8. Tongs

C. Procedure:

1. Discuss what conditions must be present in order to have burning:
   a. fuel
   b. oxygen
   c. high temperature (kindling point of fuel)
2. Place the wire screen on the ring stand.
3. Place the cup on the wire screen.
4. Fill the cup about one-third full of water.
5. Carefully light the candle or burner and place below the cup so that the tip of the flame is just touching the bottom of the cup.
6. Have class observe the activity.
7. Discuss what conditions were present.
8. Remove the water from the cup.
9. Have tongs and a safety pail handy to carefully dispose of burning paper if necessary.
10. Apply the flame again as in step 5 above.
11. Observe the results.
12. Discuss what conditions were present.

D. Results:

1. The paper cup might char but will not burn as long as there is water in the cup because the water keeps the cup below its kindling point and conducts heat away from the paper cup.
2. When the water is removed, the cup burns.

E. Basic Facts and Supplemental Information:

1. There are three elements in the "Fire Triangle." Remove any one of the three elements and there can be no fire. (Study Activity II-B-1, "What is the 'Fire Triangle'?")
2. This demonstration should be conducted over a sink or some other surface that will not be hurt by spilling water or by burning paper. Students should be kept at a safe distance.

F. Thought Questions for Class Discussions:

1. What conditions are necessary for wood to burn? gas to burn?
2. Would it make any difference if a waxed carton were used instead of a plain paper cup?
3. If something is burning, what "condition(s)" must be removed to stop the burning?

G. Related Ideas for Further Inquiry:

1. Study the differences between a Celsius (Centigrade) thermometer and a Fahrenheit thermometer.
2. Study Activity II-B-2, "Does heat travel in solids?"
3. Study Activity II-B-4, "Do some substances conduct heat faster than others?"
4. Study Activity II-B-5, "Will water temperature rise if water is heated while it has ice in it?"
5. Study Activity II-B-7, "Is water a good conductor of heat?"

H. Vocabulary Builders—Spelling Words:

1) **kindling point** 2) **ring stand** 3) **oxygen**
4) **fuel** 5) **heat source** 6) **triangle**
7) **screen** 8) **combustion** 9) **convection**

I. Thought for Today:

"If something goes wrong it is more important to talk about who is going to fix it than who is to blame."

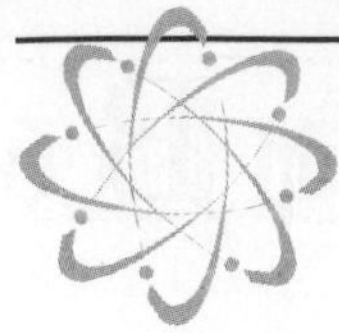

Activity II B 7

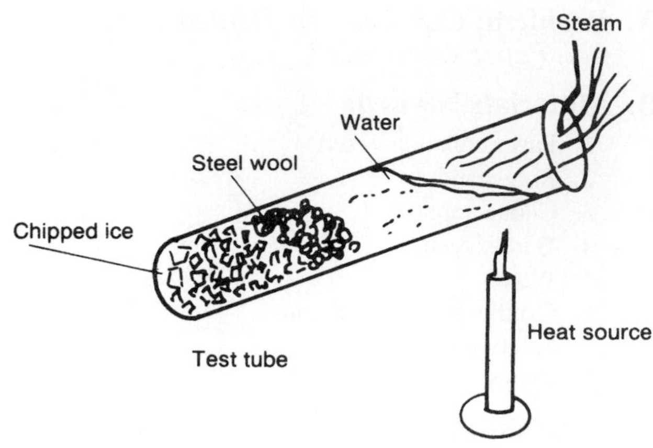

A. Problem: *Is Water a Good Conductor of Heat?*

B. Materials Needed:

1. Test tube
2. Crushed ice
3. Steel wool
4. Water
5. Bunsen burner or heat source
6. Tongs

C. Procedure:

1. Place crushed ice in the bottom of the test tube.
2. Place steel wool on top of the crushed ice. This keeps the crushed ice in place.
3. Fill the test tube about half full of water.
4. Heat the top of the water by carefully holding the test tube over the flame with tongs at an angle similar to that shown in the drawing.

D. Results:

1. The water will change to steam.
2. The ice will remain as ice.

E. Basic Facts and Supplemental Information:

1. Water is a poor conductor of heat, as shown in this experiment; otherwise, heat would have been conducted through the water, causing the ice to melt.
2. Metals are good conductors of heat.
3. Glass is a poor conductor of heat.
4. Air is a very poor conductor of heat, especially if the air is not moving.
5. Many substances are poor conductors of heat because they contain many trapped air bubbles: cork, felt, wood, sawdust, sponges, etc.
6. Wool clothing traps the air, therefore it is a good insulator and is worn in many cold climates.

F. Thought Questions for Class Discussions:

1. How are automobile engines kept cool?
2. Do women wear wool coats to keep warm?
3. What do Eskimos wear? Why?
4. What kinds of materials do we use to insulate our homes?
5. Are we concerned with insulation when we air-condition our homes?

G. Related Ideas for Further Inquiry:

1. Study why the gas company wants people to insulate their water heaters.
2. Study Section I-C, "Water."
3. Study Activity II-B-5, "Will water temperature rise if water is heated while it has ice in it?"
4. Study Activity II-B-6, "Can water be heated in a paper container?"
5. Study Activity II-B-2, "Does heat travel in solids?"

H. Vocabulary Builders—Spelling Words:

1) **conductor** 2) **test tube** 3) **steel wool**
4) **crushed ice** 5) **steam** 6) **temperature**
7) **sponges** 8) **half** 9) **source**

I. Thought for Today:

"The biggest problem today is that everybody's fixing the blame and nobody is fixing the trouble."

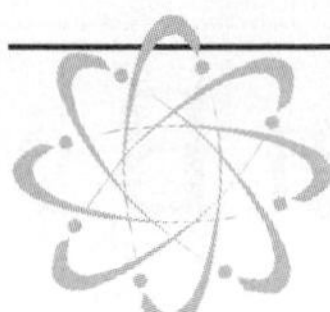

Activity

A. Problems: *Is Carbon Dioxide Heavier than Air? Will Carbon Dioxide Gas Support Combustion?*

B. Materials Needed:

1. Large glass jar
2. Baking soda and vinegar or dry ice (solid form of carbon dioxide)
3. Three candles
4. Wood or cardboard trough (See drawing.)
5. Small water glass
6. Tongs (if dry ice is used) (Dry ice will "burn" the hands if handled without tongs!)

C. Procedure:

1. Attach candles in trough as shown in drawing. (Bottom of candles can be trimmed so that they will stand upright easily.)
2. Use prop to tilt one end.
3. *Carefully* light candles.
4. If you are using baking soda and vinegar, place several teaspoons of baking soda in glass.
5. Add a half cup of vinegar. (Carbon dioxide is formed when soda and vinegar are mixed.)
6. Place jar over the glass, or, if a piece of dry ice is used, place the dry ice in the jar with tongs and cap the jar.
7. Wait several minutes so that the jar will fill with carbon dioxide.
8. Remove the lid and gently "pour" the carbon dioxide gas out of the jar and just over the top candle as shown in the drawing.

D. Result:

As the carbon dioxide floats down the trough, the candles go out one by one.

E. Basic Facts and Supplemental Information:

1. Carbon dioxide is heavier than air and thus can be "poured" from the jar. Carbon dioxide is effective as a fire extinguisher because it is heavier than air and settles around the flame, shutting off the oxygen supply. This is what happens when the carbon dioxide is poured down the trough.
2. This Activity demonstrates two principles:
   a. Carbon dioxide is heavier than air.
   b. Carbon dioxide does not support combustion.

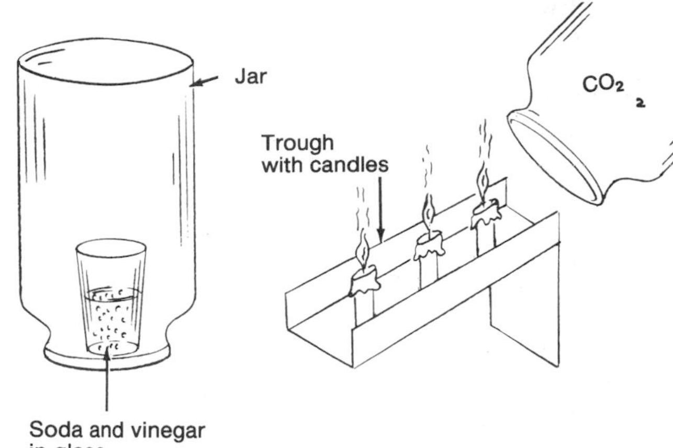

F. Thought Questions for Class Discussions:

1. Why is carbon dioxide applied above the flame instead of below the flame?
2. If you knew an excess of carbon dioxide was in the air, would it be better to breathe near the ceiling or near the floor of the room? Why?
3. Do you know any other way of making carbon dioxide?
4. Do our bodies give off carbon dioxide?
5. What would happen if oxygen was used in this Activity instead of carbon dioxide?

G. Related Ideas for Further Inquiry:

1. Study the carbon dioxide cycle, especially as it relates to plants.
2. Study Activity II-B-1, "What is the Fire Triangle?"
3. Study Activity II-B-4, "Do some substances conduct heat faster than others?"
4. Study Activity II-B-2, "Does heat travel in solids?"
5. Study Activity VI-C-6, "What is global warming (the Greenhouse Effect)?"

H. Vocabulary Builders—Spelling Words:

1) **support** 2) **carbon dioxide** 3) **combustion** 4) **vinegar** 5) **baking soda** 6) **trough** 7) **jar** 8) **extinguished** 9) **candles** 10) **pour**

I. Thought for Today:

"The key to wisdom is a knowledge of our own ignorance."

Activity II B 9

A. Problem: *What Happens to Gases When They Are Heated? Cooled?*

B. Materials Needed:

1. Narrow-necked bottle
2. One-holed stopper (rubber or cork)
3. Water, cold
4. Glass or plastic tubing, 15 centimeters (6″) long
5. Red food coloring
6. Fingernail polish
7. Thermometer
8. Heating device (optional)

C. Procedure:

1. Add about one-half inch water to the bottom of the bottle.
2. Add red food coloring until the water becomes colored and can be easily seen.
3. Wet the stopper so that the tubing can be inserted easily by slowly twisting.
4. Insert the tubing into the stopper so that the bottom of the tubing will rest halfway between the bottom of the bottle and the surface of the water.
5. Show the class the regular thermometer.
6. Discuss the uses of thermometers.
7. Note the level of the water in the tubing.
8. Place the apparatus in the sun or carefully use a heating device to warm the air in the bottle.
9. Note the changes in the height of the liquid in the tubing at selected intervals of time.
10. Next, cool the apparatus by bringing it out of the sun or by cooling it by placing it in cool water.

D. Results:

1. When the water is heated, the water will rise in the tubing.
2. When the water is cooled, the water level in the tubing will fall.

E. Basic Facts and Supplemental Information:

1. Gases, like liquids, expand when heated and contract when cooled.
2. When gases are heated the molecules move farther apart.
3. In this Activity, the molecules of gas (air) expand and increase the pressure on the water, thus causing the water to rise higher in the tubing.

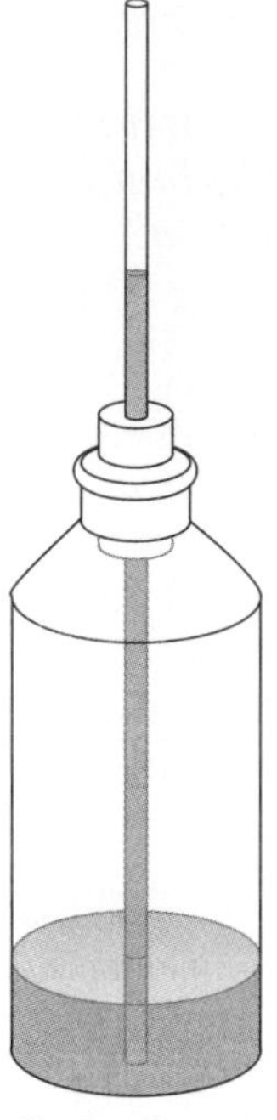

Bottle, air, and colored water

F. Thought Questions for Class Discussions:

1. What happens to a pump when it is used to inflate a bicycle or car tire?
2. Do all gases change to liquids at the same temperature?
3. Why are some gases helpful while others are very dangerous?
4. Where do we get our natural gas?

G. Related Ideas for Further Inquiry:

1. Study Activity II-B-2, "Does heat travel in solids?"
2. Study Activity II-B-4, "Do some substances conduct heat faster than others?"
3. Study Activity II-B-5, "Will water temperature rise if water is heated while it has ice in it?"
4. Study Activity II-B-6, "Can water be heated in a paper container?"
5. Study Activity VII-E-9, "How can we measure humidity in the air? How can we build a hygrometer?"

H. Vocabulary Builders—Spelling Words:

1) **gases** 2) **tubing** 3) **molecules**
4) **heated** 5) **cooled** 6) **thermometer**

I. Thought for Today:

"Remember—even if you are on the right track, you'll get run over if you just sit there."

SECTION C: LIGHT AND COLOR

Activity II C 1

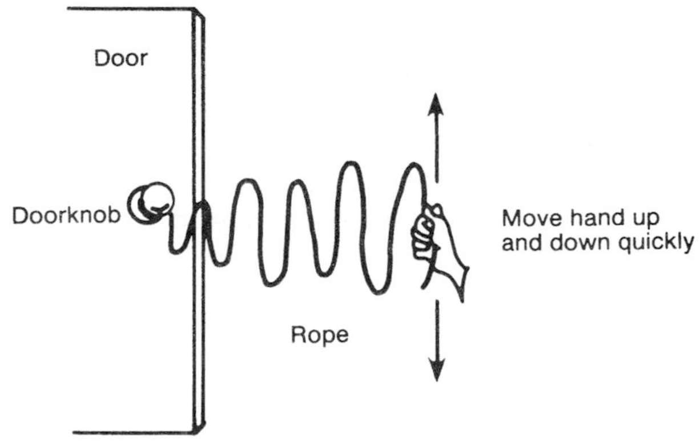

Rope moves in one plane (direction).
Real light waves move in all planes (directions).

A. Problem: *What Is Light?*

B. Materials Needed:

1. Rope, 6′ to 8′ long
2. Cookie sheet
3. Small rock
4. Candle
5. Fixed objects (like doorknob)
6. Flashlight
7. Matches
8. Water
9. Classroom lights

C. Procedure:

1. Turn on the classroom lights.
2. Turn on flashlight.
3. Light the candle.
4. Ask students what these three activities have in common.
5. You might ask: "What do we get from the sun?" (Hopefully, their answers will be "heat" and "light.")
6. Ask: "What is light?"
7. Tell the students that we really don't know, but we do know some of its characteristics.
8. Attach the rope to a doorknob or fixed object.
9. Vacillate it so that it moves in waves.
10. Pour water in the cookie sheet until it is half full.
11. Drop the rock in the water in the cookie sheet.
12. Darken the room; shine the flashlight on the wall.

D. Results:

1. Light moves like the waves on the rope and rock tests.
2. Light appears to be very tiny particles from the flashlight. Scientists call these particles "photons."

E. Basic Facts and Supplemental Information:

1. Light is a form of energy.
2. Light travels through space like heat energy.
3. Light is the kind of energy that our eyes can see.
4. Light travels very, very fast. Its speed is 186,000 miles per *second.* In the metric system, that's equivalent to 300,000 kilometers per second.
5. Because of light we can see. Light strikes our eyes and our brain interprets these sensations as pictures.
6. White light is really a combination of all the colors of the rainbow.

F. Thought Questions for Class Discussions:

1. How do the primary colors of light differ from the primary colors of art?
2. What are primary colors?
3. What is color blindness?

G. Related Ideas for Further Inquiry:

1. Study Activity II-C-2, "Is light a form of energy?"
2. Study Activity II-C-3, "What is the difference between direct light and reflected light?"
3. Study Activity II-C-8, "What is the difference between a concave lens and a convex lens?"

H. Vocabulary Builders—Spelling Words:

1) **direct** 2) **indirect** 3) **incandescent** 4) **reflection** 5) **photons** 6) **particles**

I. Thought for Today:

"We can easily forgive a child who is afraid of the dark; the real tragedy of life is when people are afraid of the light."

Activity II C 2

A. Problem: *Is Light a Form of Energy?*

B. Materials Needed:

1. Magnifying glass
2. Piece of paper
3. Bright sunlight
4. Classroom lights
5. Metal tray or nonscorchable surface

C. Procedure:

1. Review Activity II-C-1, "What is light?"
2. Locate a position in the classroom where the sun comes in directly or conduct this Activity outside when the sun is shining brightly.
3. Lay the piece of paper on the tray or nonscorchable surface.
4. Hold the magnifying glass between the bright sunlight and the piece of paper.
5. Move the magnifying glass up and down until the smallest point of light focuses on the paper.
6. Hold it in this position for a few moments.

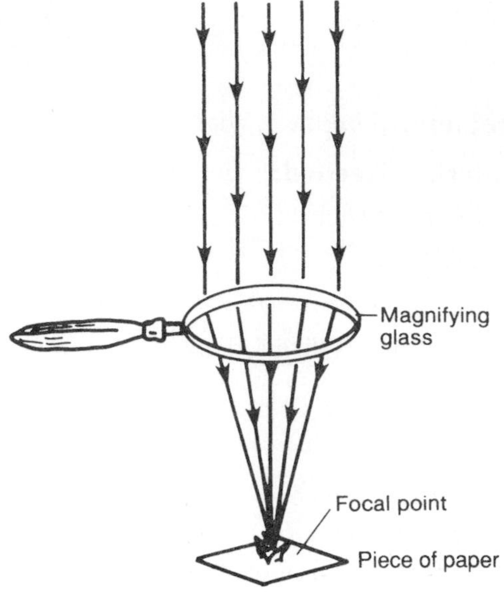

D. Results:

1. Students will learn from the previous Activity that light can be considered "waves" or "photons."
2. The paper will start to smolder, then scorch, and may even burst into flames.

E. Basic Facts and Supplemental Information:

1. Energy is the ability to do work.
2. In this Activity the sun shining through the magnifying glass does work to raise the temperature of the paper to its kindling point.
3. Explain to the class that because the glass lens has a curved surface, the light rays are bent as they go through the lens. All rays are brought to a point when sunlight passes through the magnifying glass, and because the sun's rays have energy or heat, all rays combined at this point will cause the paper to burn. The bending of light rays as they pass through a glass lens is due to the difference in density produced by the lens's curved surface. Light rays are a form of energy. A magnifying glass concentrates this energy at the one point.
4. Light travels at about 186,000 miles per second. As the sun is about 93,000,000 miles away, light from the sun takes about 8 minutes to reach us. Light travels best in a vacuum.

F. Thought Questions for Class Discussions:

1. Is a magnifying glass thicker in the middle or at the edges? Why?
2. Why does a magnifying glass make objects look larger?
3. Will a glass that is curved the opposite way make objects appear smaller?
4. Do you think solar energy is a good potential source for energy?

G. Related Ideas for Further Inquiry:

1. Study Activity II-A-3, "How beneficial is solar energy?"
2. Study Activity II-C-8, "What is the difference between a concave lens and a convex lens?"
3. Study Activity II-C-4, "How can we make a periscope? Can light be bent?"

H. Vocabulary Builders—Spelling Words:

1) **rays** 2) **magnifying** 3) **focal point**
4) **sunlight** 5) **energy** 6) **radiation**

I. Thought for Today:

"Show me your notebook and I'll show you the state of your mind."

Activity II C 3

A. Problem: *What Is the Difference between Direct Light and Reflected Light?*

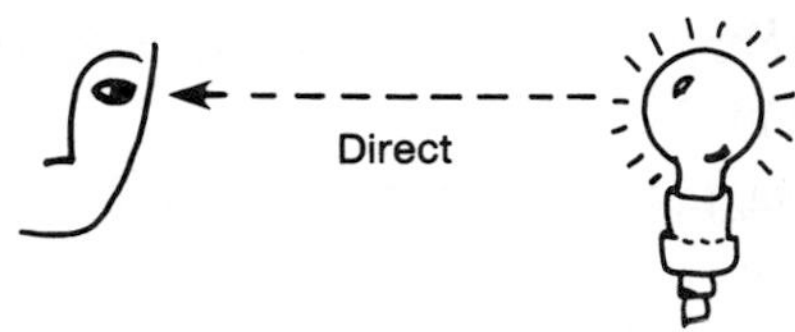

Fig. 1

B. Materials Needed:

1. Light bulb
2. Mirror
3. Reflector for the light bulb

C. Procedure:

1. Tell the students that you are going to show them two different types of light.
2. Demonstrate source light by lighting the light bulb and having the students look directly (very briefly) at the light.
3. Next, using the reflector to hide the light bulb from the students' view, turn the bulb so that the light is reflected by the mirror.
4. Have the students look at the mirror.
5. Discuss the differences involved in direct light and reflected light.

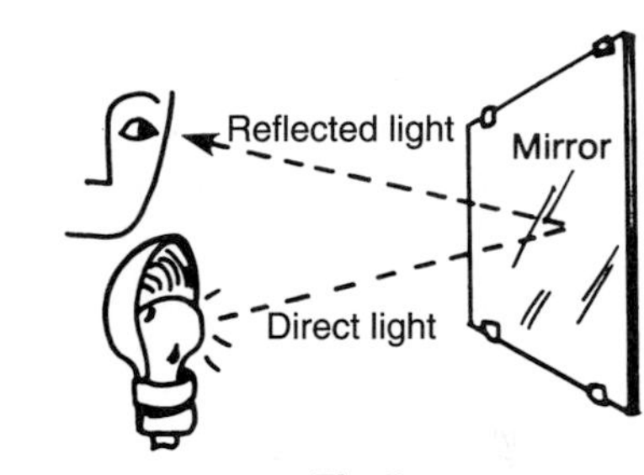

Fig. 2

D. Results:

1. The light will come directly from the bulb.
2. The light from the mirror will be reflected light from the bulb.

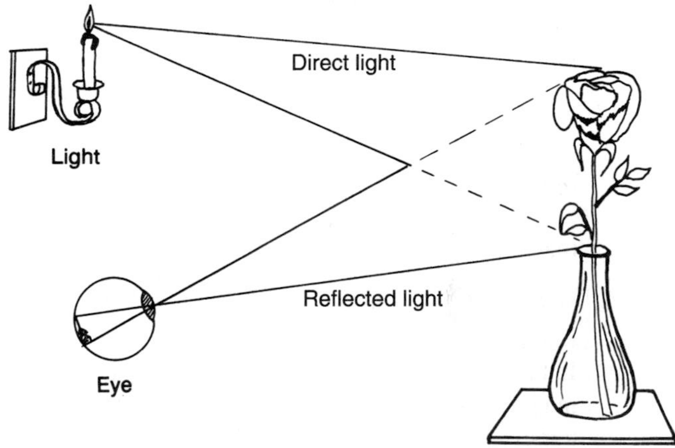

Fig. 3

E. Basic Facts and Supplemental Information:

1. We receive light by two means: direct and reflected. This Activity will help students understand direct light and indirect light. Many things are visible because they give off their own light—e.g., the sun, electric light, candles, flashlights, etc. (These are all luminous.)
2. Most substances are visible because they reflect light from one of the luminous sources. We can see in the light because of reflections from luminous objects, but we can't see the same objects in the dark.

F. Thought Questions for Class Discussions:

1. Why is reflected light from the mirror practically the same strength as direct light?
2. Is the sun's light direct light?
3. Is moonlight direct or reflected light?

G. Related Ideas for Further Inquiry:

1. Have students draw Figure 2 as accurately as possible. Have them discuss the differences between direct (source or luminous) and reflective (indirect) light.
2. Study Activity II-C-1, "What is light?"
3. Study Activity II-C-2, "Is light a form of energy?"
4. Study Activity II-C-4, "How can we make a periscope? Can light be bent?"

H. Vocabulary Builders—Spelling Words:

1) **source** 2) **reflected** 3) **emit** 4) **direct** 5) **indirect** 6) **luminous** 7) **bulb** 8) **mirror**

I. Thought for Today:

"Bad officials are elected by people who don't vote."

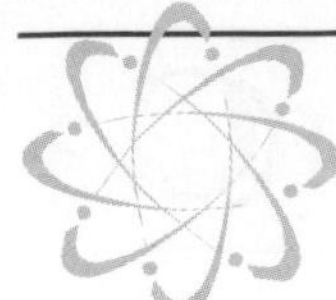

Activity II C 4

A. Problem: *How Can We Make a Periscope? Can Light Be Bent?*

B. Materials Needed, Procedure One:

1. Cardboard
2. Scissors or single-edged razor blade
3. Two small pocket mirrors
4. Cellophane tape

Materials Needed, Procedure Two:

1. Cardboard box
2. Scissors or single-edge razor blade
3. Small candle or flashlight
4. Matches if using candle
5. Four small pocket mirrors

C. Procedure One:

1. Fold the cardboard and cut diagonal slots in it as shown in the drawing.
2. Place the mirrors in the slot as shown and fasten them securely with cellophane tape. These should be at 45° angles.
3. Cut a square hole for the viewing section.

Procedure Two:

1. Cut cardboard box as shown in the drawing.
2. Attach mirrors with cellophane tape with reflecting surfaces facing the inside of the box at 45° angles.
3. Put the top on the box.
4. Shine the flashlight or the candle in front of one opening.

D. Results:

1. In Procedure One, a periscope will be created as shown in the top drawings.
2. In Procedure Two, students will be able to "see through" a solid object.

E. Basic Facts and Supplemental Information:

1. Light travels in straight lines if unhindered.
2. Light rays can be reflected by mirrors.
3. Silver plastic material from greeting cards or other sources may be substituted for mirrors.

F. Thought Questions for Class Discussions:

1. How tall can we make a periscope?
2. Does light travel *from* our eyes or *to* our eyes? How can this be proved?
3. Where can periscopes be used?
4. Where are mirrors used?

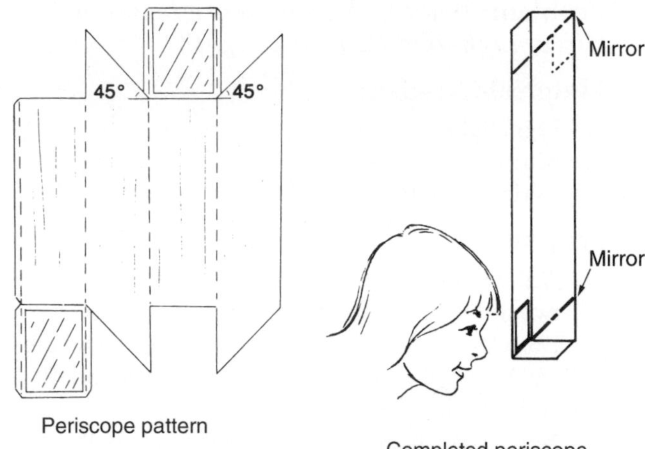

Procedure One

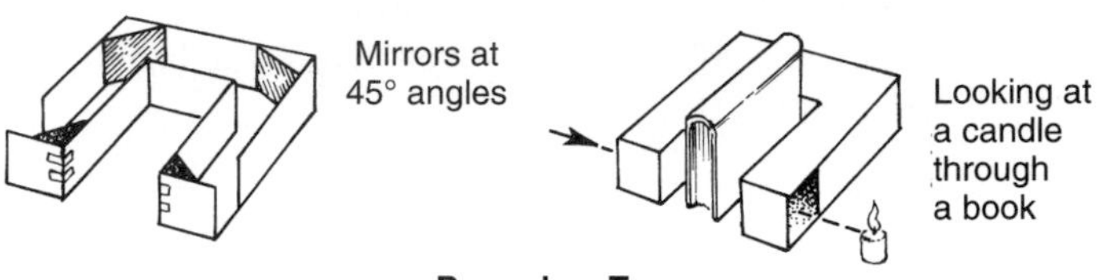

Procedure Two

G. Related Ideas for Further Inquiry:

1. If you hold the periscope sideways, you can see around a corner.
2. Study Activity II-C-1, "What is light?"
3. Study Activity II-C-2, "Is light a form of energy?"
4. Study Activity V-B-2, "How well do we see?"
5. Study Activity V-B-6, "Do our eyes ever deceive us?"
6. Study Activity V-B-8, "Are you right-eyed or left-eyed?"

H. Vocabulary Builders—Spelling Words:

1) **periscope** 2) **mirror** 3) **apparent** 4) **angle** 5) **pattern** 6) **diagonal** 7) **viewing** 8) **locking**

I. Thought for Today:

"It is better to keep your mouth shut and appear to be stupid than open it and remove all doubts."

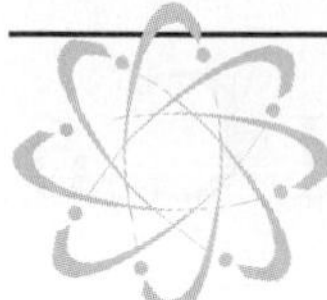

Activity II C 5

A. Problem: *How Can We Project a Rainbow on the Ceiling?*

B. Materials Needed (Figure 1):

1. Prism
2. Window
3. Strong sunlight
4. Any movable flat surface

Materials Needed (Figure 2):

1. Overhead projector
2. Water glass
3. Water
4. Small book or toweling

C. Procedure:

1. Select window with strong sunlight passing through.
2. Place the prism so that the sunlight can pass through it, and adjust the movable surface until the "rainbow" appears clear.

D. Result:

Sunlight will split into the following sequence of colors: red, orange, yellow, green, blue, indigo, and violet. An easy way to remember this sequence of colors is by the mythical character ROY G BIV.

E. Basic Facts and Supplemental Information:

1. From an experiment such as this one, it can be shown that white light, such as sunlight, is composed not of a single color but of many colors. Whenever light passes at an angle from one substance into another of different density, it is bent; that is, its direction is changed. The different colors are bent differently, with the violet being bent most and the red least. Hence, when the light comes out of the prism, the different colors are traveling in somewhat different directions, and they do not strike the flat surface in the same place. This is how the rainbow is produced. The droplets of falling water have the same effect as the prism. All the colors in combination are called the spectrum.
2. Sunlight and light from a light bulb, flashlight, or projector appear colorless, but they are actually composed of seven basic colors. When blended under normal circumstances it is called "white light." These individual colors can be separated by a prism, water, glass, or any transparent substance with differences in thickness. Two other kinds of light, ultraviolet and infrared, are also present but can't be seen with the naked eye.

F. Thought Questions for Class Discussions:

1. How can we see various colors?
2. Are there other kinds of light rays that we don't see?

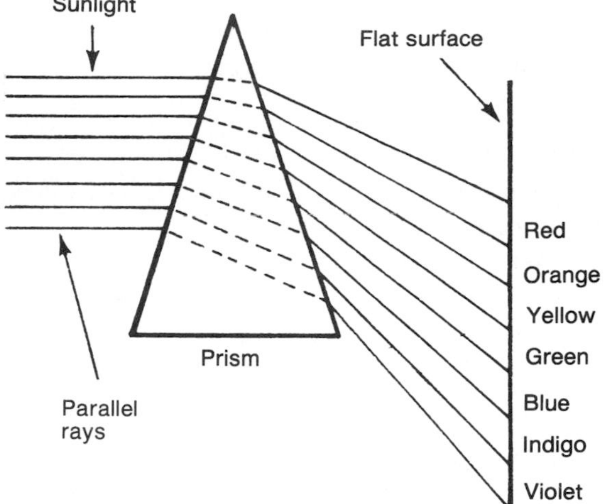

Fig. 1

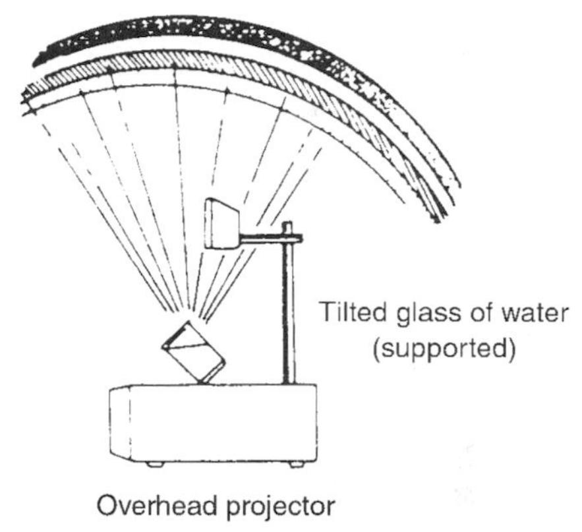

Fig. 2

3. If we put two prisms together in opposite directions, what color(s) of light would appear?

G. Related Ideas for Further Inquiry:

1. Another fun Activity is shown in Figure 2. Place a glass of water tilted to the brim on an overhead projector and support it in any way you can. When the projector is turned on, the glass of water acts like a prism and a rainbow can be seen on the wall or ceiling.
2. Study Activity II-C-1, "What is light?"
3. Study Activity II-C-2, "Is light a form of energy?"
4. Study Activity II-C-4, "How can we make a periscope? Can light be bent?"

H. Vocabulary Builders—Spelling Words:

1) **prism** 2) **refraction** 3) **rainbow** 4) **angles** 5) **spectrum** 6) **ultraviolet** 7) **infrared**

I. Thought for Today:

"Some speakers who don't know what to do with their hands should clamp them over their mouths."

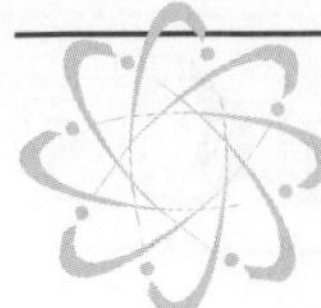

Activity II C 6

A. Problem: *What Is an Image?*

B. Materials Needed:

1. Mirror (any size)
2. Wooden supports (See drawing.) (Books can be used.)
3. Water glass or quart jar
4. Water
5. Candle
6. Matches
7. Window glass (about 12″ square)
8. Card with student's name printed on it
9. Candle holder or small block of wood

C. Procedure:

1. Have student look at him/herself in the mirror.
2. Have student wink his/her right eye.
3. Observe which eye winks in the mirror.
4. Have student salute with his/her left hand.
5. Observe which hand saluted in the mirror.
6. Put student's name card in front of mirror.
7. Observe how card looks in mirror.
8. Place pane of glass between wooden supports or secure with books. (Handle glass carefully.)
9. Fill glass or quart jar with water.
10. Place the jar or glass about 10 inches in back of the pane of glass.
11. Light the candle (carefully).
12. Place candle in holder or on block of wood with candle wax.
13. Place candle about 10 inches in front of the pane of glass.
14. Look at the jar or glass through the pane of glass.

D. Results:

1. The image's left eye winked.
2. The image's right hand saluted.
3. The letters of the name appeared upside down and backwards but in proper order.
4. The candle appears to be burning in the water-filled glass or jar.

E. Basic Facts and Supplemental Information:

1. An image is a likeness, copy, or picture reflected by a mirror or lens.
2. Images are vital phenomena of cameras, binoculars, telescopes, and our eyes.
3. All light originates from some source, such as the sun or a light bulb.
4. If light strikes an object at an angle, it bounces off that object at the same angle, and if the object is curved, some weird distortions are seen.

F. Thought Questions for Class Discussions:

1. Does the surface of a clear pond or lake act like a mirror?
2. What would you see if you placed a mirror directly behind you while looking at a mirror in front of you?
3. How do automobile mechanics use mirrors?

G. Related Ideas for Further Inquiry:

1. Study Activity II-C-3, "What is the difference between direct light and reflected light?"
2. Study Activity II-C-7, "What causes an image to change shape, size, and/or position?"
3. Study Activity II-C-8, "What is the difference between a concave lens and a convex lens?"

H. Vocabulary Builders—Spelling Words:

1) **image** 2) **reflected** 3) **apparent**
4) **opposite** 5) **upside down** 6) **distortion**

I. Thought for Today:

"You shouldn't go through life looking for something soft; you might find it under your hat."

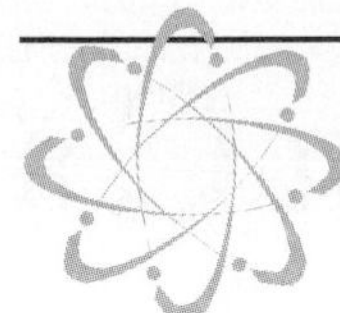

Activity II C 7

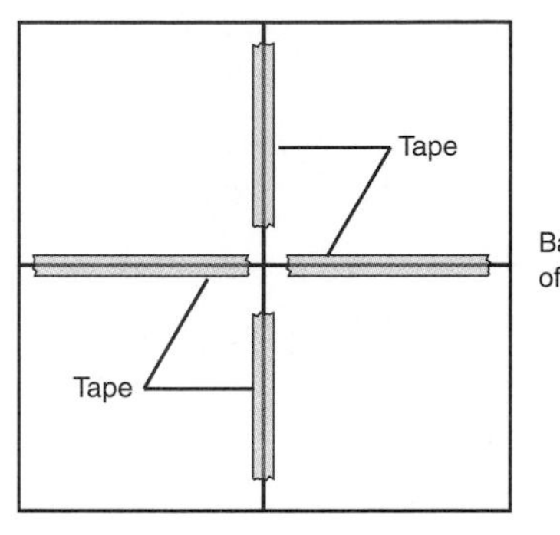

Fig. 1

A. Problem: *What Causes an Image to Change Shape, Size, and/or Position?*

B. Materials Needed:

1. Four square mirrors, all the same size
2. Thick cellophane or masking tape
3. Various objects to be placed in front of mirrors
4. Colored pictures

C. Procedure:

1. Put tape on the back of the mirrors, leaving a little room to maneuver the mirrors. (See Figure 1.)
2. Holding the taped mirrors in a flat, upright position have several students look at themselves in the mirrors and report what they have seen.
3. Bending the mirrors vertically only have several other students look into the mirrors and report what they have seen. (See Figure 2.)
4. Bending the mirrors horizontally only, have several other students look into the mirrors and report what they have seen. (See Figure 3.)
5. Bending the mirrors both vertically and horizontally, have several other students look into the mirrors and report what they have seen.
6. Continue to maneuver the mirrors with various objects and colored pictures and have students report on the distortions.

Fig. 2

Fig. 3

D. Results:

1. Students will have a lot of fun viewing the distorted images of their faces and objects.
2. Some images appeared fatter, thinner, shorter, or taller than the original object.
3. Some parts of the object disappeared.
4. Many distortions occurred.

E. Basic Facts and Supplemental Information:

1. Light travels in a straight line.
2. Light can be bent or angled. If light strikes a reflective object at a certain angle, it will bounce off that object at an equal angle.
3. The speed of light remains constant before and after striking a reflective object.

F. Thought Questions for Class Discussions:

1. Have you seen "tricky" mirrors in an amusement park or at a circus?
2. Could you make the image of the object disappear entirely?
3. What would happen if the light source were a single color?

G. Related Ideas for Further Inquiry:

1. Study Activity II-C-3, "What is the difference between direct light and reflected light?"
2. Study Activity II-C-6, "What is an image?"
3. Study Activity II-C-2, "Is light a form of energy?"

H. Vocabulary Builders—Spelling Words:

1) **image** 2) **reflected** 3) **distortion** 4) **mirrors** 5) **direction** 6) **bending**

I. Thought for Today:

"Ideas are a dime a dozen. People who put them into action are priceless."

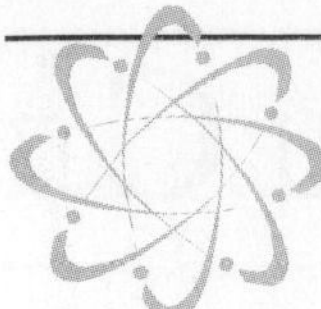

Activity

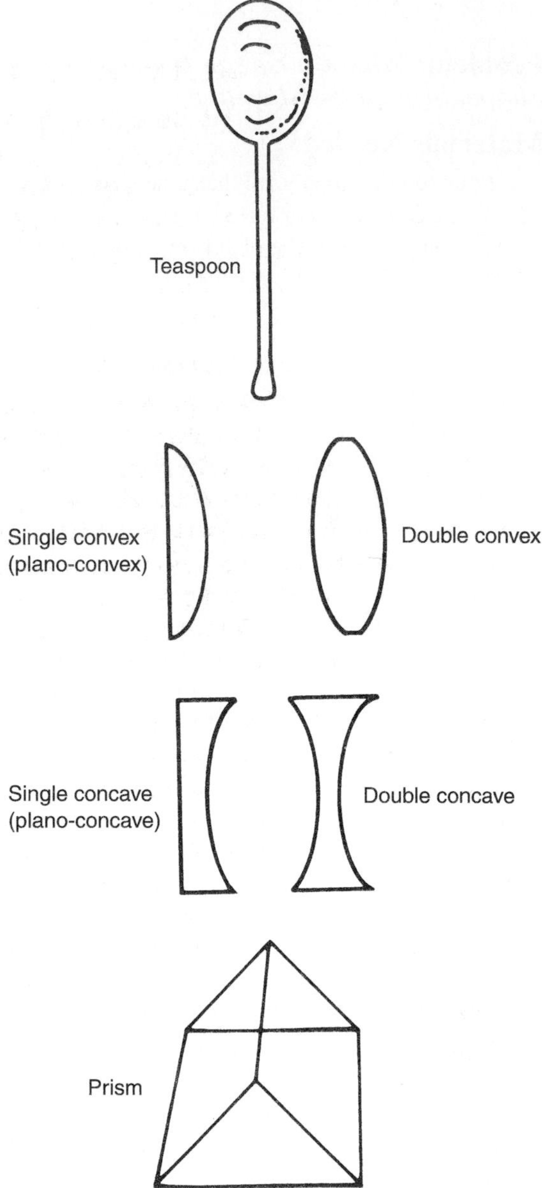

A. Problem: *What Is the Difference between a Concave Lens and a Convex Lens?*

B. Materials Needed:

1. Highly polished spoons
2. Magnifying glass(es)
3. Different lens types (if available)
4. Objects to view with magnifying glass

C. Procedure:

1. If a spoon does not have a high sheen, polish it.
2. Pass out spoons to class members. (May have to share if insufficient numbers.)
3. Have pupils look at their image on the inside part of the bowl of the spoon starting at arm's length and slowly moving the spoon closer to their eyes. (Closing one eye and moving towards the other one gives better results.)
4. Have students note changes in images.
5. Have students repeat, only this time have them rotate spoons so they are looking at the backs of the bowls.
6. Have students note changes in images.
7. Look at several objects through the magnifying glass moving it closer to and then away from the objects, noting changes in images.
8. The depth and time spent on studying lenses will depend on the maturity level of the students. Younger students can study spoons and draw the lines where light enters the spoon and the angle(s) where it leaves. Middle students can study simple concave and convex lenses. Older students can study complex lenses.
9. Light is reflected off an object at the same angle it enters the object.

D. Results:

1. In the first part, the image inside the bowl will appear upside down and grow larger until it fills the whole surface.
2. On the back side of the spoon, the image will start out small and will be right side up and get larger as the spoon is moved closer and closer to the eye. It will also have an oval appearance.
3. With a magnifying glass, the image will only appear larger and right side up.

E. Basic Facts and Supplemental Information:

1. Convex lenses bend the light inward.
2. Concave lenses bend the light outward.
3. Magnifying glasses use double convex lenses.
4. Slide projectors and film projectors use double convex lenses.
5. Telescopes also use double convex lenses for greater magnification.

6. Double convex lenses appear thicker in the middle and thinner on the edges.
7. Double concave lenses are used in the eyeglasses of nearsighted people.
8. Double concave lenses appear thinner in the middle and thicker on the ends.
9. An "image" is what we see indirectly as our "image" in the mirror.
10. A prism is also a type of lens.
11. A lens that is flat on one side and curved on the other is called "plano-concave" or "plano-convex."

F. Thought Questions for Class Discussions:

1. What kind of lenses are used in binoculars?
2. Some automobile headlights have complicated lenses. What major types of lenses would they have?
3. Where else might lenses be used?
4. The following statement appears on most side-view mirrors on automobiles: "Objects in the mirror are closer than they appear." Why is this? What kind of lens is being used?

G. Related Ideas for Further Inquiry:

1. Examine eyeglasses.
2. Examine projector lenses.
3. Examine flashlight lenses.
4. The magnifying power of a convex lens can be measured by looking at some thin-lined paper and comparing the number of lines outside to the number of lines viewed inside. If, for example, there are five spaces outside to one space inside, the magnifying power is five times. This magnification occurs in all directions.
5. Study Activity II-C-1, "What is light?"
6. Study Activity II-C-2, "Is light a form of energy?"
7. Study Activity II-C-3, "What is the difference between direct light and reflected light?"
8. Study Activity II-C-4, "How can we make a periscope? Can light be bent?"
9. Study Activity II-C-6, "What is an image?"

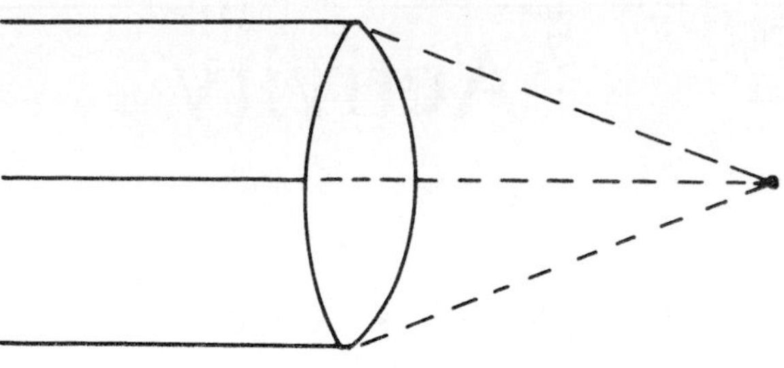

Convex lens makes rays converge.

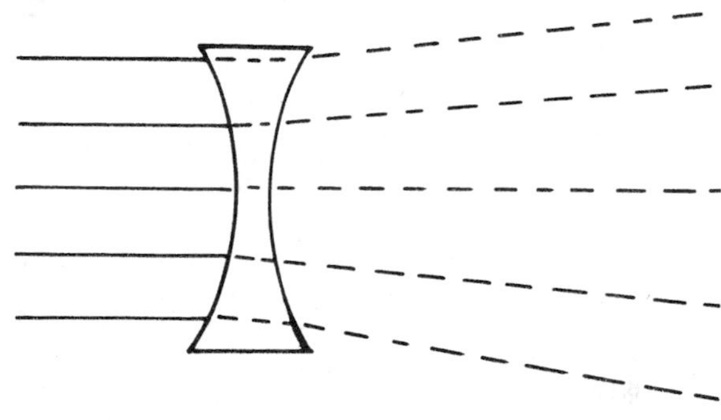

Concave lens makes rays diverge.

H. Vocabulary Builders—Spelling Words:

1) **concave** 2) **convex** 3) **plano-concave**
4) **plano-convex** 5) **image** 6) **double concave**
7) **double convex** 8) **prism** 9) **converge**

I. Thought for Today:

"Hardening of the attitudes starts a long time before hardening of the arteries."

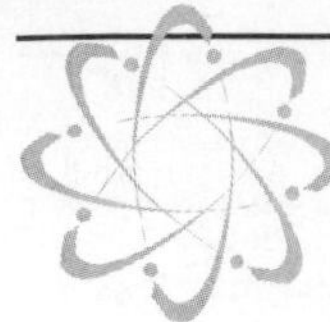

Activity

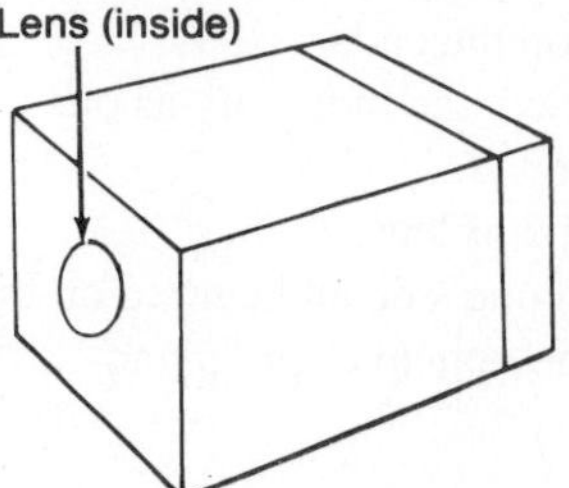

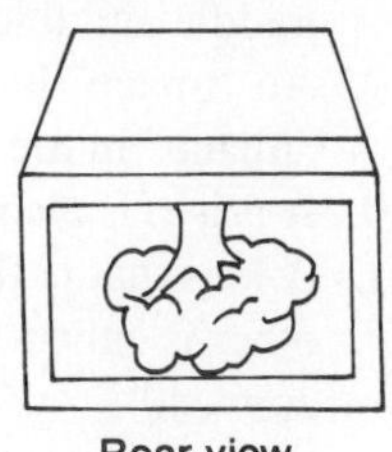

Procedure One

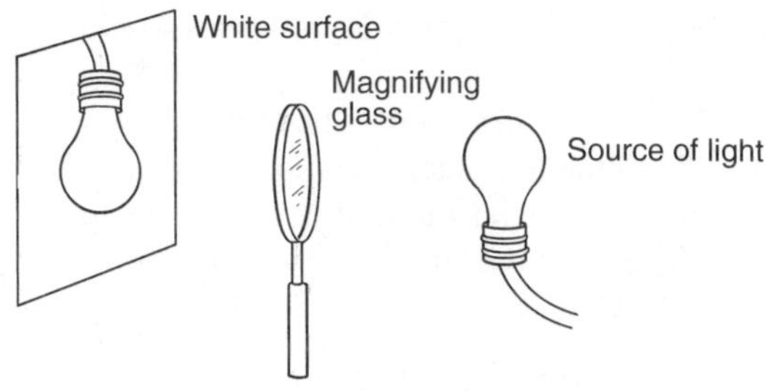

Procedure Two

A. Problem: *How Does a Camera Work?*

B. Materials Needed, Procedure One:

1. Convex lens
2. Small cardboard box
3. Masking tape
4. Ground glass or thin white tissue paper (translucent)
5. Black paint
6. Paint brush
7. Scissors

Materials Needed, Procedure Two:

1. White surface (sheet or wall)
2. Darkened room
3. Source of light (either an open window or an electric light)

C. Procedure One:

1. Paint the inside of the cardboard box black.
2. Cut a small round hole about the size of a pencil in one end of the box.
3. Tape a lens in the box behind the hole. (Be sure that the tape does not overlap into the hole.)
4. Put the ground glass or piece of translucent paper in the opposite end of the box.
5. Point the end of the box which contains the lens toward a tree or other object and see what happens on the ground glass or translucent paper.

Procedure Two:

1. Put the lens directly between the source of light and the white surface.
2. Move the lens toward the white surface until the source of light focuses on the white surface. This may require moving the lens backward and forward a little until an exact focus is obtained.

D. Results:

1. You will see the image from the outside of the box. *Note:* You may have to put a hood over your head in order to make the object appear darker and clearer on the ground glass or translucent paper.
2. The exact image of the source of light will be focused on the white surface.
3. The images will be reversed and will appear upside down and left to right.

E. Basic Facts and Supplemental Information:

1. Light travels in straight lines through the same media.
2. Light rays can be made to bend if they pass through lenses. This is because the glass of the lens varies in thickness (density).

F. Thought Questions for Class Discussions:

1. Why are distant objects always in focus and close-up objects not in focus?
2. How could you make the image larger? smaller?
3. Can you explain why the image is upside down, right to left, and left to right?
4. Does the power of the lens have anything to do with the size of the image that appears on the white surface?

G. Related Ideas for Further Inquiry:

1. Take a polished spoon and observe the image in the bowl of the spoon.
2. Turn the spoon over and observe the back of the spoon. Explain what was observed.

H. Vocabulary Builders—Spelling Words:

1) **focus** 2) **camera** 3) **inverted** 4) **transparent** 5) **translucent** 6) **image** 7) **reverse** 8) **source**

I. Thought for Today:

"The world's most disappointed people are those who get what's coming to them."

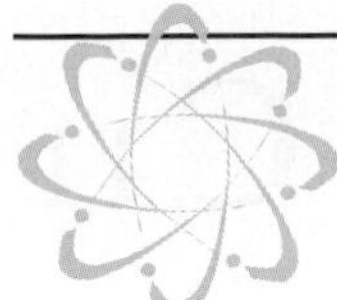

Activity II C 10

A. Problem: *How Can We Make a Pinhole Camera?*

B. Materials Needed:

1. Two paper or styrofoam cups (Cylindrical cartons can be used.)
2. Safety pin or punch (for making a tiny hole)
3. Translucent paper
4. Cellophane tape

C. Procedure:

1. Punch a small hole in the center of the bottom of one paper cup (cup 1).
2. Cover the open end of this paper cup with a piece of translucent paper, taping it to the cup.
3. Cut the bottom out of a second paper cup and place the large end next to the translucent paper and cellophane tape the two cups together. (See drawing.)
4. Point the first cup (the one with the tiny hole in the end) at a well-lighted object and look at the translucent paper, using the second cup as a shade for the paper.

D. Result:

An image of the object will show on the translucent paper. The image will be upside down, left to right, and right to left.

E. Basic Facts and Supplemental Information:

1. This illustrates the principle of the camera. The light is reflected from the object, through the hole, and onto the translucent paper. The light rays are stopped by the paper and the image becomes visible.
2. Light travels in a straight line so that the light from the top of the object will pass through the pinhole and strike the bottom of the translucent paper. The light from an object on the right side will pass through the pinhole and strike the left side of the translucent paper.
3. To make the image darker, put a hood over your head to eliminate much of the external lighting.
4. This is a fun project, and all the students can become involved either individually or in pairs.

F. Thought Questions for Class Discussions:

1. Could you design a "pinhole camera" so that the image would not be reversed?
2. Why does the object appear upside down on the translucent paper?
3. If the lenses in our eyes work the same way, why don't we see everything upside down?

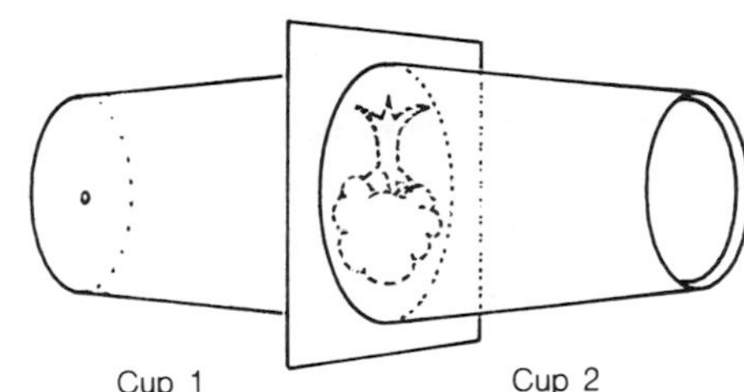

G. Related Ideas for Further Inquiry:

1. Study different types of lenses and how they change the appearance of the objects.
2. Study lenses in microscopes, telescopes, and magnifying glasses.
3. Look through some reading glasses. How do they change the appearance of things?
4. Study side-view mirrors on automobiles.
5. Study Activity II-C-1, "What is light?"
6. Study Activity II-C-3, "What is the difference between direct light and reflected light?"
7. Study Activity II-C-6, "What is an image?"
8. Study Activity II-C-8, "What is the difference between a concave lens and a convex lens?"
9. Study Activity II-C-9, "How does a camera work?"

H. Vocabulary Builders—Spelling Words:

1) **camera** 2) **pinhole** 3) **translucent** 4) **image** 5) **cellophane** 6) **paper** 7) **reversed** 8) **object**

I. Thought for Today:

"Children are like wet cement; whatever falls on them makes an impression."

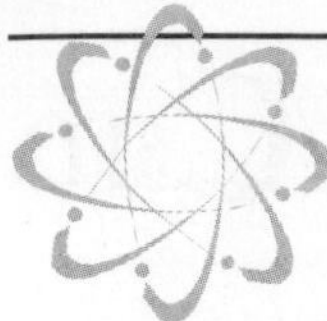

Activity II C 11

A. Problem: *Now Can We Make a Simple Telescope?*

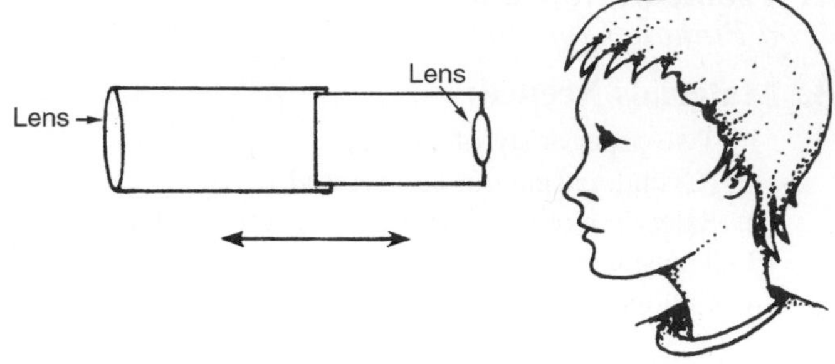

B. Materials Needed:

1. Two convex lenses (Lenses that are thicker in the middle)
2. Two different sizes of cardboard tubing (Smaller one should just fit in the larger one.) (Tubing should be about 20″ long to start.)
3. Heavy cardboard if needed (See Procedure Step 1.)
4. Tape (cellophane, filament, or masking)

C. Procedure:

1. If lens is a different size than the tubing, place lens on heavy cardboard and cut out so that cardboard will fit into tubing and lens can be secured to heavy cardboard with tape.
2. Repeat with both pieces of tubing, securing a lens at the end of each tubing.
3. Fit the two pieces of tubing with lenses together.
4. Look at objects 12 feet to 18 feet away.
5. Slide tubing back and forth.
6. The length of tubing, to have a correct focus, will depend on the strengths of the lenses. If unable to focus, cut off about 2 inches from the ends of each piece of tubing and try to focus again.
7. If still not able to focus, repeat step 6 until able to do so.
8. Tubing can be made from construction paper and coiled to make desired length and diameter of each tube.

D. Result:

A simple telescope will be constructed.

E. Basic Facts and Supplemental Information:

1. A convex lens is one that is thick in the middle and thin at the edges, while a concave lens is thin in the middle and thick at the edges.
2. Rays of light enter one lens of the telescope and are bent to form a small image. This image is then magnified by the other lens. This is the principle of a refracting telescope. A reflecting telescope is different. It uses a large concave mirror and a small convex lens.

F. Thought Questions for Class Discussions:

1. Can you see farther at night or during the day?
2. How can we measure the distance of planets by using a telescope?
3. Are binoculars a pair of telescopes?

G. Related Ideas for Further Inquiry:

1. Study Activity II-C-1, "What is light?"
2. Study Activity II-C-3, "What is the difference between direct light and reflected light?"
3. Study Activity II-C-4, "How can we make a periscope? Can light be bent?"
4. Study Activity II-C-6, "What is an image?"
5. Study Activity II-C-8, "What is the difference between a concave lens and a convex lens?"
6. Study Activity II-C-9, "How does a camera work?"

H. Vocabulary Builders—Spelling Words:

1) **refracting** 2) **reflecting** 3) **telescope** 4) **focus** 5) **simple** 6) **lens** 7) **lenses**

I. Thought for Today:

"Nothing is opened more by mistake than the mouth."

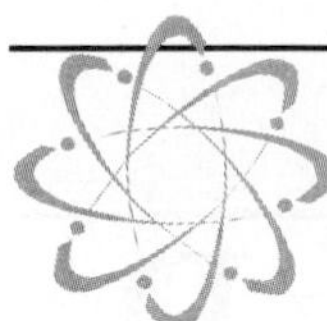

Activity

II C 12

A. Problem: *How Can We Make Our Own Dyes?*

B. Materials Needed:

1. Samples of:
   a. Water-based paint
   b. Oil-based paint
   c. Emulsion paint
2. Saucepan
3. Hot plate
4. Water
5. Scraps of white cloth
6. Items used in Procedure step 5
7. Apron or protective clothing
8. Tongs

C. Procedure:

1. Show samples of the different kinds of paints.
2. Briefly explain what makes color. (White light is a combination of all colors.)
3. Discuss with students their favorite color(s).
4. Decide on what colors(s) and test materials you want to use.
5. The following color list gives a few good examples:

Color:	*Test Material:*
Red	Red cabbage, cherries, beetroot or beets
Green	Spinach, birch leaves, grass
Yellow	Onion skins, daffodil flowers, hickory bark or chips
Blue	Iodine (slowly add drops for a few minutes)
Brown	Tea, coffee, walnut shells

6. Fill the pan half-full of water.
7. Add the test material to the water.
8. Carefully simmer for about 15 minutes.
9. Allow water to cool.
10. Soak the scrap of cloth in the solution for about 5 minutes.
11. Remove cloth from solution with tongs.
12. Check the color to see if you have the color and shade you want.
13. You will probably have to practice to get the color and shade you want.

D. Results:

1. The piece of cloth will be dyed.
2. Students will learn how some dyes are made.

E. Basic Facts and Supplemental Information:

1. Be sure that this activity is done with adult supervision as simmering water can be dangerous.

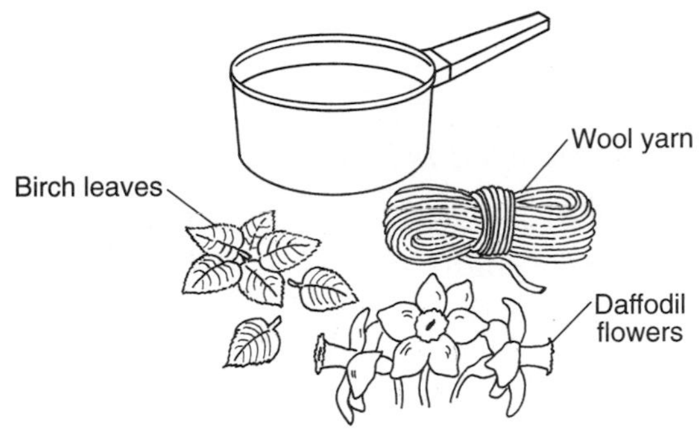

2. We live in a colorful world.
3. Dyes color our clothing, paper, leather, and even our food products.
4. There are natural dyes made from plants and animals, and synthetic dyes made from chemicals.
5. Pigments are colored particles that do not dissolve in water.
6. Paints contain a pigment, a binder to hold the pigment in place, and a solvent to make the paint flow easily.

F. Thought Questions for Class Discussions:

1. What is white light?
2. What are primary colors?
3. How do the primary colors of light and paints differ?
4. What are secondary colors?

G. Related Ideas for Further Inquiry:

1. Study how the cuttlefish uses a squirt of black ink to ward off its predators.
2. Study how dyes are used in cosmetic products.
3. Study other sources of dyes:
   a. Red clay (iron oxide) gives a reddish-brown color.
   b. Copper salts yield green colors.
   c. White colors can be created with many lead compounds.
4. Study the colors of minerals.

H. Vocabulary Builders—Spelling Words:

1) **dye** 2) **color** 3) **paints** 4) **cosmetics** 5) **cloth** 6) **water-based** 7) **oil-based** 8) **colors** (Also use words cited in Procedure, Step 5, Test Material.)

I. Thought for Today:

"Why is a blackberry red when it's green?"

SECTION D: SOUND

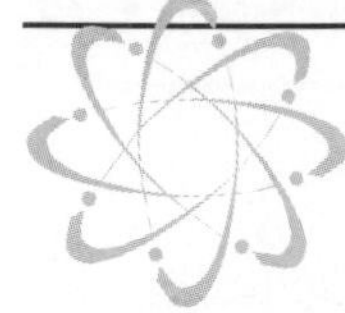

Activity II D 1

A. Problem: *What Is Sound?*

B. Materials Needed:

1. Blade of grass
2. Strip of paper
3. Toy guitar, or other stringed musical instrument
4. Any noisemaker (dried gourd, tonette, rattle, whistle, blocks of wood)
5. Tissue paper over comb
6. Rubber band

C. Procedure:

1. Have students hold a blade of grass or strip of paper between their thumbs and blow.
2. Have students place tissue paper over a comb, hold it to their lips, and hum.
3. Stretch a rubber band around some object, pluck it, and listen to it.
4. Stop the vibrations and listen again.
5. Pluck a stringed instrument, listen to it; stop its vibrations and listen again.
6. Make sounds with noisemaker(s).
7. Ask the class if they know what all these sounds have in common.

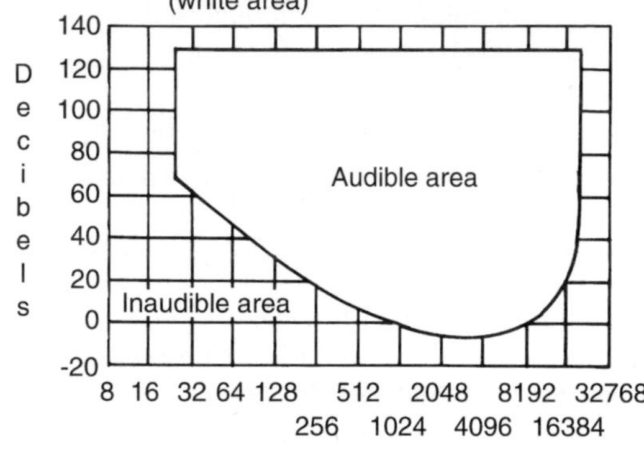

D. Results:

1. These test materials will produce vibrations which cause sound.
2. When vibrations cease, sounds will stop.

E. Basic Facts and Supplemental Information:

1. Sounds travel in air at about 1,600 feet per second.
2. Sound travels faster in liquids and solids.
3. One aspect of sound is *frequency* or *pitch.* It is the number of vibrations (cycles) per second. The more vibrations or cycles, the higher the pitch.
4. Another characteristic of sound is *intensity* or *amplitude.* The greater this is, the louder the sound.
5. The average person has a very limited hearing range and scope.
6. The normal hearing range is between 20 and 20,000 vibrations per second.

F. Thought Questions for Class Discussions:

1. What other vibrating objects will cause sound?
2. Are noises caused by vibrations?
3. Are there any vibrations we can't hear?
4. What is an echo?

G. Related Ideas for Further Inquiry:

1. Study the sounds of music.
2. Listen to the sounds of birds, insects, and other animals.
3. Place finger on throat and hum.
4. Study Activity II-D-8, "Can we see sound? feel sound?"
5. Study Activity II-D-6, "What makes sounds differ in volume (intensity)?"
6. Study Activity II-D-7, "What makes sounds differ in quality (harmonics or overtones)?"
7. Study Activity II-D-5, "How does a stethoscope work?"

H. Vocabulary Builders—Spelling Words:

1) **frequency** 2) **pitch** 3) **intensity** 4) **sound** 5) **vibrations** 6) **cycles** 7) **amplitude** 8) **listen**

I. Thought for Today:

"Learning is the original and greatest of all 'do it yourself' projects."

Activity

II D 2

A. Problem: *How Can We Make a Simple Telephone?*

B. Materials Needed:

1. Two empty cans
2. String (or waxed dental floss)
3. Wax (not necessary, but helpful)
4. Two buttons
5. Ice pick or can opener

C. Procedure:

1. Punch a small hole in the center of each can at the bottom.
2. Cut string desired length and run wax up and down the string.
3. Put waxed string through the holes in the cans.
4. Tie a button on each end of the string to hold them firmly in the cans.
5. Keep the strings taut.
6. Have one student talk into one can and another student listen at the other can.

D. Result:

When a student talks into the can, the vibrations from the vocal cords cause the air to vibrate and this makes the bottom of the can vibrate. These vibrations are carried along the waxed string. When they reach the other can, the bottom of the can vibrates causing the adjacent air to vibrate. When the vibrations reach a person's eardrum at the other end of the string, they reproduce the sound of the voice.

E. Basic Facts and Supplemental Information:

1. Sound must have a medium to vibrate. In this activity we can trace the vibrations through the different media from the vocal cords to the air to the can to the string to the other can to the eardrum.
2. Other equipment can be substituted and the results will be the same. Plastic or paper cups can be used instead of tin cans. Thin wire or very heavy thread can be used in place of the string. Large knots can be tied in lieu of buttons.

F. Thought Questions for Class Discussions:

1. Why does it help to wax the string in order to make this "tin can telephone"?
2. Would fine wire, stretched between the cans, work better than the string?
3. Would this telephone work around corners? Why?
4. What causes sounds to increase when we raise our voices or turn up the volume on the radio, stereo, CD player, or television?

G. Related Ideas for Further Inquiry:

1. Have students place their thumb and fingers on their throats. Have them talk, sing, or hum and they will feel vibrations.
2. Discuss how vibrations cause sounds in musical instruments, stereos, radios, television, and telephones.
3. In a storm when it is thundering and we see lightning, can we tell how far away a storm is if we know that sound travels about 5 miles per second and light travels about 186,000 miles per second (almost negligible in this problem because sound travels so fast)?
4. Study Activity II-D-1, "What is sound?"
5. Study Activity II-D-4, "Does sound travel in a vacuum?"
6. Study Activity II-D-5, "How does a stethoscope work?"
7. Study Activity II-D-6, "What makes sounds differ in volume (intensity)?"
8. Study Activity II-D-8, "Can we see sound? feel sound?"

H. Vocabulary Builders—Spelling Words:

1) **string** 2) **waxed** 3) **listen** 4) **taut** 5) **center** 6) **vocal cords** 7) **vibrations** 8) **speak**

I. Thought for Today:

"In quarreling, the truth is always lost."

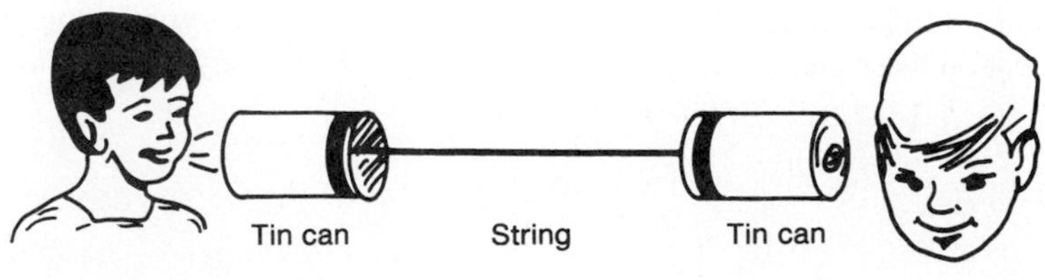

Activity

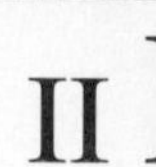

II D 3

A. Problem: *How Do Vibrating Wires Make Different Sounds?*

B. Materials Needed:

1. Four wires of the same length
   a. Two steel wires, same thickness (A and B)
   b. One steel wire, thinner than above two (C)
   c. One copper wire, same thickness as single steel wire (D)
2. Frame as illustrated in drawing
3. One light weight and three heavier weights to keep wires taut

C. Procedure:

1. Arrange the four wires on a frame like the one in the drawing. A and B are made of steel of the same length and thickness. A has the light weight on it; B has a heavier weight. When the wire is stretched, we say it has tension. C is also made of steel wire but is not as thick as A or B. D is made of copper wire which is lighter than steel wire.
2. Pluck the various wires and note the differences in pitch produced.
3. Pluck any one wire and remember the pitch.
4. Press the same wire firmly to the table with your finger and pluck it again.
5. Repeat with the other wires. Listen carefully.

D. Result:

Different pitches will be produced.

E. Basic Facts and Supplemental Information:

1. We know now that four different characteristics regulate the pitch of vibrating strings:
   a. *The tension*—The higher the tension, the higher the pitch (same thickness, length, and materials).
   b. *The thickness*—The thicker the wire, the lower the pitch (same material, same length and tension).
   c. *The material*—The lighter the wire, the higher the pitch (same length, tension, and thickness).
   d. *The length*—The shorter the wire, the higher the pitch (same material, thickness, and tension).
2. The proper tuning of any stringed musical instrument is dependent on these characteristics.

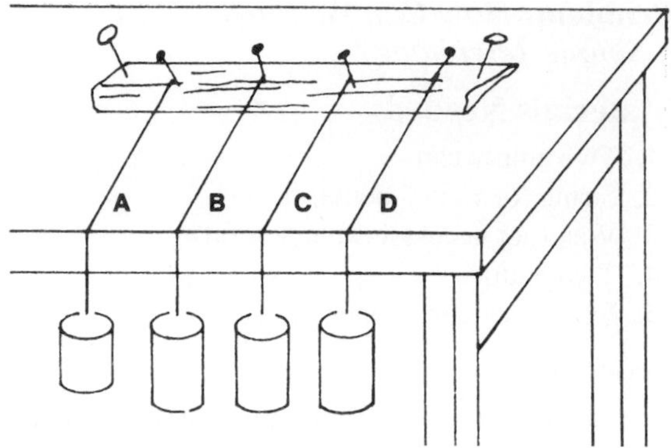

F. Thought Questions for Class Discussions:

1. Does this experiment have anything to do with tuning a piano? Pianos have wires that are struck.
2. If we double the weight, do we double the volume? pitch? (See drawing.)
3. Do we hear the strings vibrating or the air molecules moving?

G. Related Ideas for Further Inquiry:

1. Study how sounds vary with different musical instruments such as:
   a. violin
   b. guitar
   c. banjo
   d. harp, etc.
2. Study Activity II-D-1, "What is sound?"
3. Study Activity II-D-2, "How can we make a simple telephone?"
4. See Activity II-D-6, "What makes sounds differ in volume (intensity)?"
5. Study Activity II-D-7, "What makes sounds differ in quality (harmonics or overtones)?"
6. Study Activity II-D-8, "Can we see sound? feel sound?"

H. Vocabulary Builders—Spelling Words:

1) **vibrating** 2) **tension** 3) **material** 4) **length** 5) **width** 6) **thickness** 7) **wires** 8) **size**

I. Thought for Today:

"The only reason some people listen to reason is to give them time for a rebuttal."

Activity

II D 4

A. Problem: *Does Sound Travel in a Vacuum?*

B. Materials Needed:

1. Flask or large bottle
2. One-holed rubber or cork stopper
3. Wooden dowel or rod
4. Miniature bells
5. Rubber band or masking tape
6. Source of heat (candle or hot plate)
7. Half cup of water
8. Gloves or tongs

C. Procedure:

1. Wet one-holed stopper.
2. Work dowel or rod through the stopper so that just a small part sticks above stopper.
3. Secure bells to the dowel or rod with a rubber band or masking tape. See drawing for positioning.
4. Fit stopper snugly into the flask or bottle.
5. Shake the jar and listen.
6. Remove stopper and put one-third cup of water in bottom of flask.
7. Boil water in the bottle for several minutes without stopper. Steam drives the air out leaving only a little liquid water and steam.
8. With gloves or tongs, carefully remove bottle from the source of heat and immediately plug it with the prepared stopper, making sure the bells are in the wide part of the bottle. (See drawing.)
9. After cooling, shake the bottle and listen.

D. Results:

1. Sound will be heard when there is air in flask.
2. Sound will not be heard (or will be faintly heard) when flask contains a partial vacuum.

E. Basic Facts and Supplemental Information:

1. Sound is the vibrations of molecules that travels through solids, liquids, and gases. When a vacuum (no molecules) is present, sound cannot travel because there is no medium to carry it. In this Activity, if sound could pass through a vacuum, some sound would be heard, even if the glass flask "masked" some of it.
2. When people communicate, the medium through which sounds travel is air. If we had no air, there would be no medium to carry our voices.

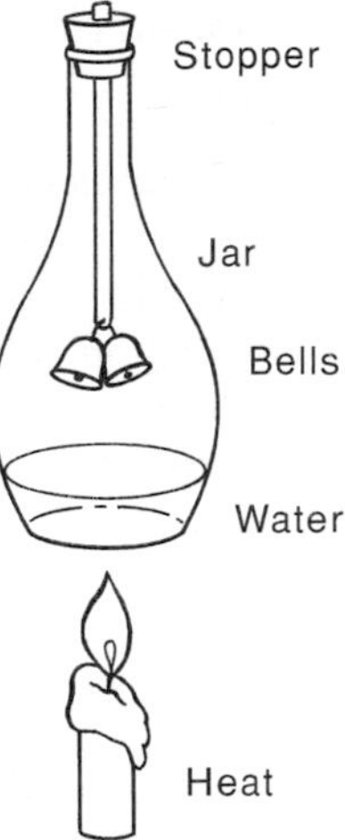

F. Thought Questions for Class Discussions:

1. Why is it necessary to seal the bottle after it has been removed from the heat?
2. Could this be a test for a "vacuum"?
3. Can we see steam? (No, we see molecules of liquid water.)
4. Could people talk to each other in outer space without any hearing devices?
5. How do we communicate with astronauts in space?

G. Related Ideas for Further Inquiry:

1. Shake contents of a thermos bottle. Why can't you hear any noise inside?
2. Study Activity II-D-1, "What is sound?"
3. Study Activity II-D-2, "How can we make a simple telephone?"
4. Study Activity II-D-3, "How do vibrating wires make different sounds?"
5. Study Activity II-D-5, "How does a stethoscope work?"
6. Study Activity II-D-6, "What makes sounds differ in volume (intensity)?"
7. Study Activity II-D-7, "What makes sounds differ in quality (harmonics or overtones)?"

H. Vocabulary Builders—Spelling Words:

1) **flask** 2) **vacuum** 3) **snugly** 4) **steam** 5) **bottle** 6) **heat** 7) **gloves** 8) **tongs**

I. Thought for Today:

"Nothing lowers the level of conversation more than raising the voice."

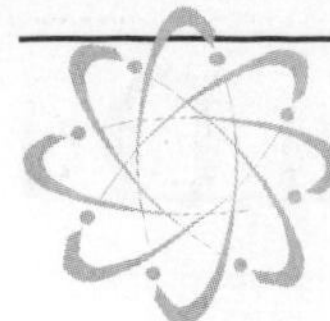

Activity

A. Problem: *How Does a Stethoscope Work?*

B. Materials Needed:

1. Three pieces of rubber or plastic tubing, each 8″ long
2. Three medium-sized funnels
3. "Y" joint (glass or plastic tubing)
4. String, rubber bands, or tape
5. Sound makers (harmonica, whistle, tuning forks, etc.)

C. Procedure:

1. Take one piece of rubber or plastic tubing and attach it to one of the funnels on one end.
2. Follow the same procedure for the other two tubing ear pieces (funnels).
3. Now join the three pieces of tubing with the funnels together, using the "Y" joint; fasten all connections with string, rubber bands, or tape.
4. Have students listen to sound makers with this homemade stethoscope. The ear pieces can be held by other students or by an extra large rubber band fitted over the head and under the chin.
5. Listen to a student's heartbeat.
6. Have a student jog in place for 2 minutes and listen to his/her heartbeat again.
7. Make the apparatus as shown in Figure 2.
8. Make a noise in one part of the room that is closer to one funnel than the other.
9. Have student guess where the sound originated.

D. Results:

1. The funnels and tubes will intensify the vibrations of the heart by channeling sound waves through the tubes directly to the ears and eliminating outside noises. Students will get a better concept of how sound can be channeled and intensified.
2. The students will learn that the heart beats more frequently (and louder) after exercise.
3. In reversing funnels, sounds appear to be coming from the opposite direction of the source of the sound.
4. Our brains interpret the sounds our ears hear.

E. Basic Facts and Supplemental Information:

1. Through experiments with the stethoscope, students will learn about sound.
2. They will learn more about their heart rates before and after exercise.
3. Perhaps it will lessen fears of some children when their doctors use stethoscopes during an examination.

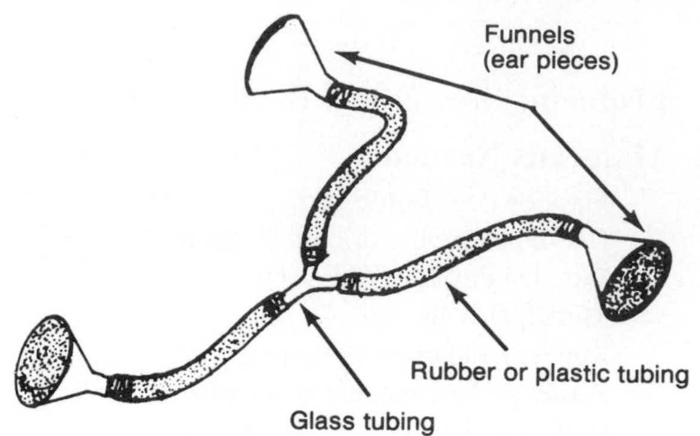

Fig. 1

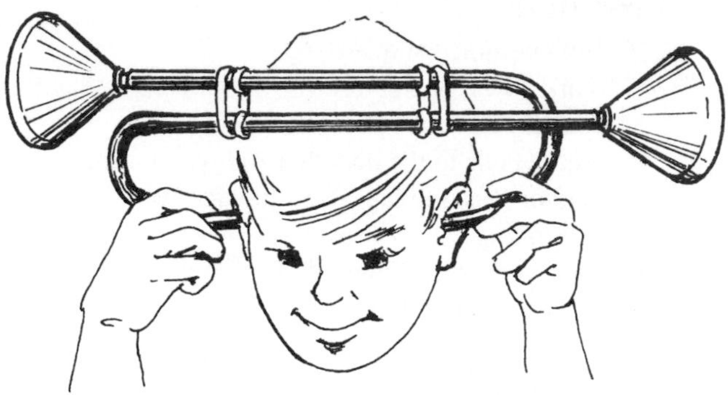

Fig. 2

F. Thought Questions for Class Discussions:

1. How does this instrument (Figure 1) compare with a doctor's stethoscope?
2. How do you think stethoscopes help doctors?
3. Do all sounds coming through this stethoscope have the same volume? pitch? quality?

G. Related Ideas for Further Inquiry:

1. Study Activity II-D-1, "What is sound?"
2. Study Activity II-D-2, "How can we make a simple telephone?"
3. Study Activity II-D-4, "Does sound travel in a vacuum?"
4. Study Activity II-D-6, "What makes sounds differ in volume (intensity)?"
5. Study Activity II-D-7, "What makes sounds differ in quality (harmonics or overtones)?"
6. Study Activity V-B-11, "How well do we hear?"

H. Vocabulary Builders—Spelling Words:

1) **stethoscope** 2) **tubing** 3) **funnel**
4) **plastic** 5) **rubber** 6) **tape**
7) **doctor** 8) **ears** 9) **hearing**

I. Thought for Today:

"Nature gave us two ears and one mouth so that we would listen twice as much as we talk."

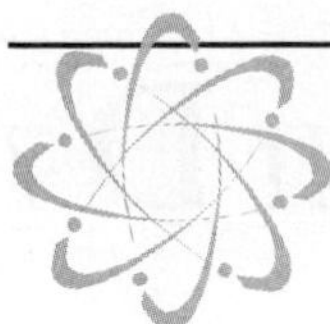

Activity

A. Problem: *What Makes Sounds Differ in Volume (Intensity)?*

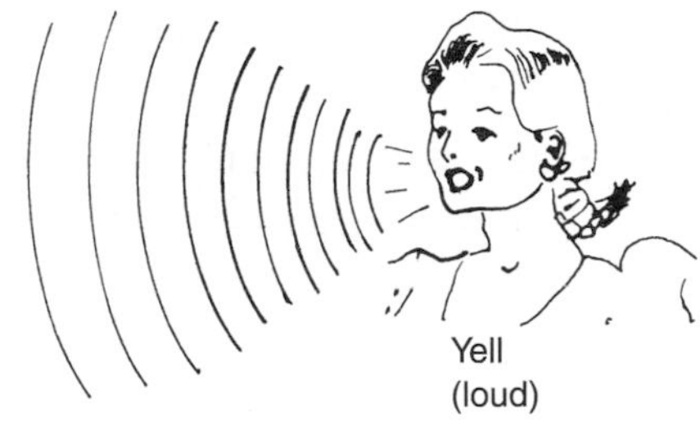

B. Materials Needed:

1. Students' voices
2. Household objects that make noise
3. Cassette player
4. Open windows to hear:
   a. street traffic noises
   b. schoolyard noises
   c. other noises

C. Procedure:

1. Have students whisper to each other.
2. Have students converse in normal tones.
3. Turn on cassette player with volume down.
4. Gradually increase its volume.
5. Listen to any exceptionally loud noises outside of classroom (planes, factories, grass-mowers, etc.).
6. Ask class what causes loud noises.

D. Results:

1. Students will note that sound is produced by vibrations.
2. When vibrations are increased the sound becomes louder due to the faster movement of air molecules.

E. Basic Facts and Supplemental Information:

1. Study intensity scale.
2. One major problem confronting our youth is the loudness of their music. This damages the nerve fibers and they do not regenerate. This leads to a greater and greater loss of hearing, and by the time the individual realizes what has happened, it is too late to do anything about it. Hearing aids will help some, but these cannot restore natural hearing.

INTENSITY SCALE:

DECIBELS:	TYPICAL EXAMPLES:
0	Zero point of hearing
0–10	Ordinary breathing
11–20	Whispers
21–30	Household sounds
31–40	Classroom sounds
41–50	Automobiles; vacuum cleaners
51–60	Noisy offices; stores
61–70	Normal conversations; television
71–80	Heavy street traffic
81–90	Assembly lines; heavy traffic
91–100	Air compressors; boiler factories
101–110	Jet planes, thunder
111–120	Feeling of pain
190	Loudest estimate, volcano

F. Thought Questions for Class Discussions:

1. How can we protect our hearing from loud noises?
2. What are some sources of loud noises?
3. How do people working near airplanes protect their hearing?
4. Why do we use a megaphone?
5. Why do we use an amplifier?
6. What would life be like without our sense of hearing?

G. Related Ideas for Further Inquiry:

1. Study the difference between "nerve deafness" and "bone deafness."
2. How do deaf or hard-of-hearing people communicate?
3. Study the means of communication we use for long distances.
4. Study Activity II-D-1, "What is sound?"
5. Study Activity II-D-2, "How can we make a simple telephone?"
6. Study Activity II-D-4, "Does sound travel in a vacuum?"
7. Study Activity II-D-8, "Can we see sound? feel sound?"
8. Study Activity V-B-11, "How well do we hear?"

H. Vocabulary Builders—Spelling Words:

1) **intensity** 2) **volume** 3) **vibrations** 4) **whisper** 5) **nerve deafness** 6) **factory** 7) **protection**

I. Thought for Today:

"The surest way to gain respect is to earn it by good conduct."

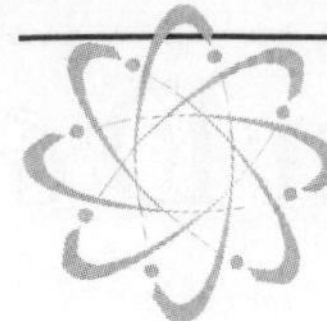

Activity II D 7

A. Problem: *What Makes Sounds Differ in Quality (Harmonics or Overtones)?*

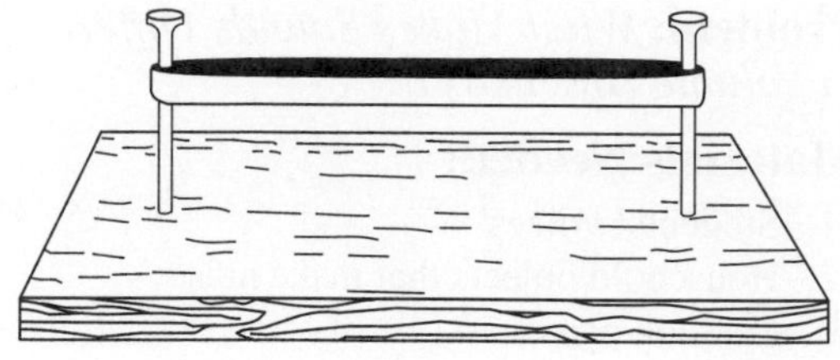

Sounding board

B. Materials Needed:

1. Baseboard one-half inch thick, any convenient length and width
2. Two tall nails with large heads
3. Hammer
4. Several wide rubber bands
5. Cassette player
6. Stringed musical instrument

C. Procedure:

1. Construct the sounding board:
   a. Hammer the two nails in the baseboard about two inches from either end. (See drawing.)
   b. Stretch one wide rubber band between the two nails. The second one is a spare.
2. Divide the class into three or four groups.
3. Have one student in each group talk to the other members of his/her group in a normal speaking voice.
4. Have other members of each group talk to his/her group members.
5. Have each group discuss how the voices of its members varied in speech characteristics.
6. Play several short recordings on the cassette player that contain voice recordings.
7. Compare these recordings with the voices of the students.
8. Have a "talented" student play the stringed musical instrument for a few minutes.
9. Pluck the rubber band on the sounding board.
10. Holding the rubber band tightly in the middle, pluck it again.
11. Compare all the sounds from all the sources.

D. Results:

1. Students will learn to recognize differences in sounds by:
   a. volume or intensity
   b. pitch
   c. quality
2. Students will realize that tone quality gives richness to music and voices.

E. Basic Facts and Supplemental Information:

1. Sound is caused by vibrations.
2. Sounds vary in volume (intensity).
3. Sounds vary in pitch (frequency of vibrations).
4. Sounds vary in quality (harmonics or overtones). This is the result of secondary vibrations from parts vibrating along with the main wire, cord, rubber band, etc.

F. Thought Questions for Class Discussions:

1. Why do musical instruments that play the same note differ in sound?
2. How do people's voices differ?
3. What is the difference between "sound" and "noise"?

G. Related Ideas for Further Inquiry:

1. Study Activity II-D-1, "What is sound?"
2. Study Activity II-D-2, "How can we make a simple telephone?"
3. Study Activity II-D-3, "How do vibrating wires make different sounds?"
4. Study Activity II-D-5, "How does a stethoscope work?"
5. Study Activity II-D-8, "Can we see sound? feel sound?"
6. Study Activity II-D-9, "How can we make our own musical instruments?"
7. Study Activity V-B-11, "How well do we hear?"

H. Vocabulary Builders—Spelling Words:

1) **harmonics** 2) **overtones** 3) **vibrations** 4) **listening** 5) **pluck** 6) **quality** 7) **communication** 8) **hearing**

I. Thought for Today:

"Very often the chip on a person's shoulder is just bark."

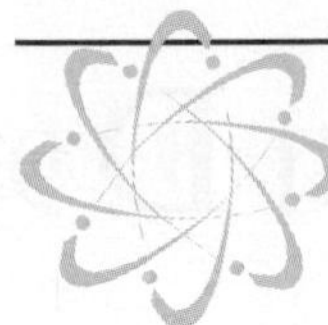

Activity

A. Problem: *Can We See Sound? Feel Sound?*

B. Materials Needed:

1. Knitting needle or ruler
2. Rubber band, wide
3. Table
4. Sounding board (flat board with one nail head protruding upwards toward each end—see drawing)

C. Procedure:

1. Define the word "vibration" before the activity is started.
2. Give several examples of vibrations and vibrating objects.
3. Stretch a rubber band between the two nails. Notice if there is any sound.
4. Pluck the rubber band and listen. Notice if there is any sound.
5. Lay one end of a knitting needle or ruler on the edge of the table.
6. Holding the end on the table with one hand, snap the needle or ruler up or down with the other hand.
7. Feel the air just above the needle without touching the needle.
8. Put your fingers on your throat when you talk.

D. Results:

1. The rubber band will produce no sound until it has vibrated.
2. Students will see the needle vibrating.
3. Students will feel the air moving above the needle.
4. Students observe that sound vibrations are produced in different ways.

E. Basic Facts and Supplemental Information:

1. Sound vibrations can be seen and felt. They can also be heard.
2. Sounds vary in pitch, volume, and quality (harmonics).
3. When the needle or ruler vibrates, it causes the air molecules to vibrate in unison with it. What the students see is the object moving. What the pupils feel is the movement of the air.
4. A harp can be made from pieces of metal coat hangers stapled to a wooden block for amplification. To play, pluck wires. (See bottom drawing.)

F. Thought Questions for Class Discussions:

1. Can an object vibrate so fast that the ear will not hear the sound produced?
2. How can we find out the vibration range of the normal ear?
3. What three senses are involved in this activity?

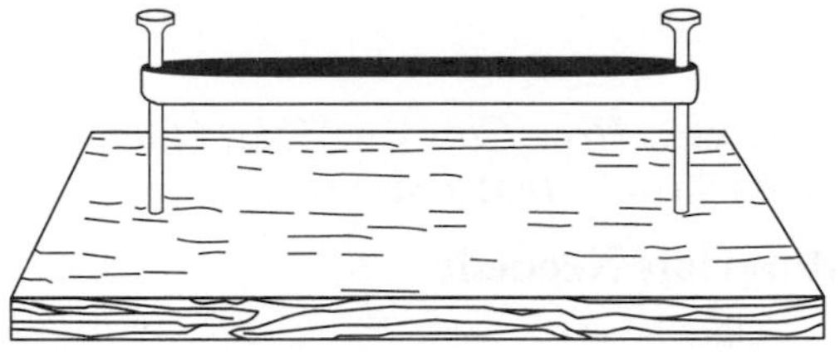

Sounding board

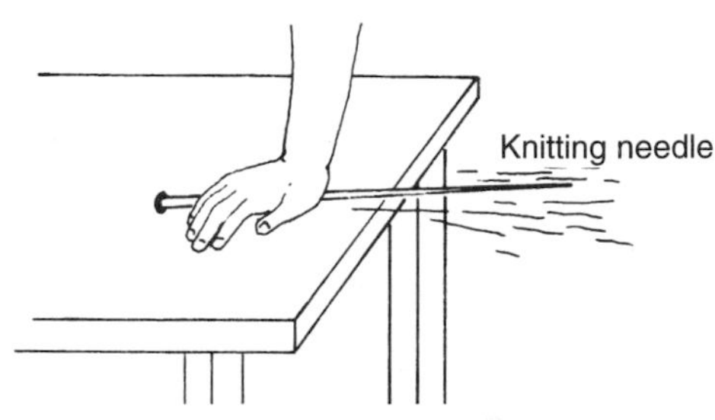

Knitting needle on table

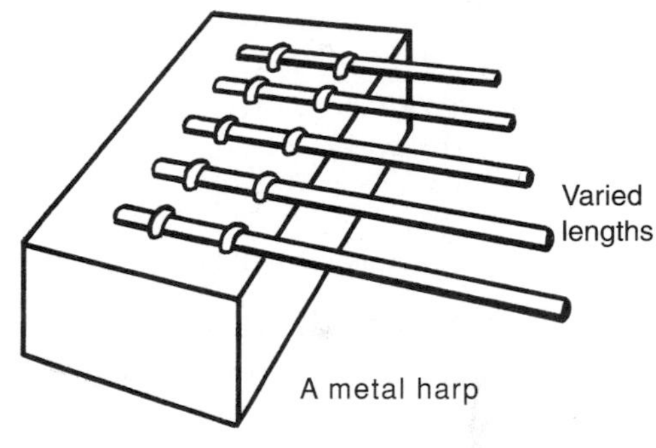

A metal harp

G. Related Ideas for Further Inquiry:

1. Study Activity II-D-1, "What is sound?"
2. Study Activity II-D-6, "What makes sounds differ in volume (intensity)?"
3. Study Activity II-D-3, "How do vibrating wires make different sounds?"
4. Study Activity V-B-11, "How well do we hear?"

H. Vocabulary Builders—Spelling Words:

1) **vibrations** 2) **harmonics** 3) **needle** 4) **ruler** 5) **pluck** 6) **sounding board** 7) **rubber band** 8) **stretch** 9) **coat hangers** 10) **pitch**

I. Thought for Today:

"If at first you don't succeed, you're like most other people."

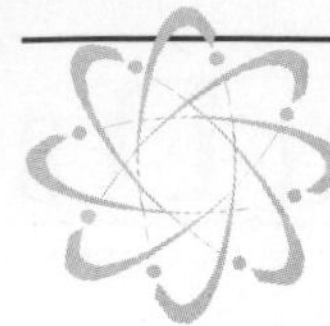

Activity — II D 9

A. Problem: *How Can We Make Our Own Musical Instruments?*

B. Materials Needed:

1. Cigar boxes
2. Wooden slats
3. Wires
4. Small nails and tacks
5. Straws
6. Screw eyes
7. Tin cans
8. Small boxes
9. Paper clips
10. Bells
11. Balloon pieces, etc.

C. Procedure:

1. Have each student decide on what kind of instrument he/she would like to make. (See drawings.)
2. Supply the materials.
3. Let them go to work.

D. Result:

A supply of musical instruments will be constructed.

E. Basic Facts and Supplemental Information:

1. Stringed instruments can be made with cigar boxes, wooden slats, and some wires.
2. Flutes can be made out of straws with ends cut at angles and pinched.
3. Percussion instruments can be created from tin cans covered with balloon pieces.
4. Tamborines can be made with small boxes filled with paper clips.
5. Bells can be used as is.
6. Other toy musical instruments can be created depending on the creativity of the individual student.

F. Thought Questions for Class Discussions:

1. How do these instruments differ from regular ones?
2. What causes sound?
3. What is the difference between "music" and "noise"?

G. Related Ideas for Further Inquiry:

1. Form a class orchestra.
2. Integrate with music lessons.
3. Make other instruments.

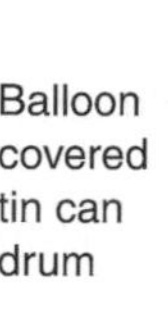

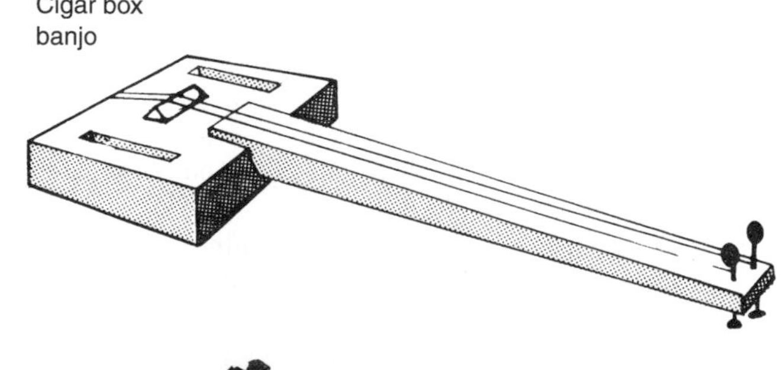

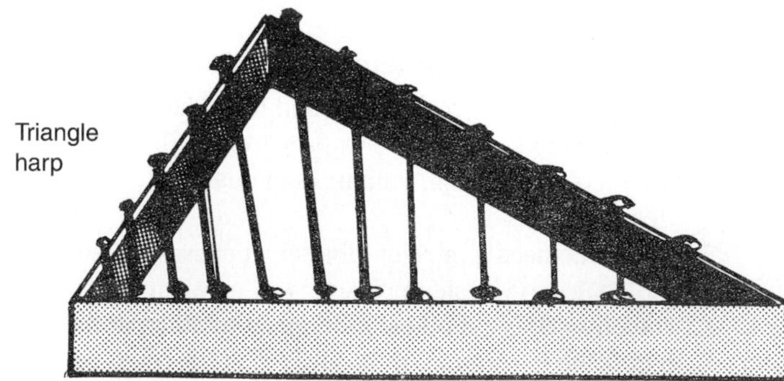

H. Vocabulary Builders—Spelling Words:

1) **instruments** 2) **percussion** 3) **wind**
4) **cigar** 5) **slat** 6) **music** 7) **balloons**

I. Thought for Today:

"A closed mouth gathers no foot."

Section E: Simple Machines

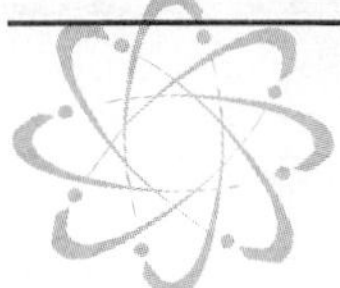

Activity

II E 1

Types of simple machines

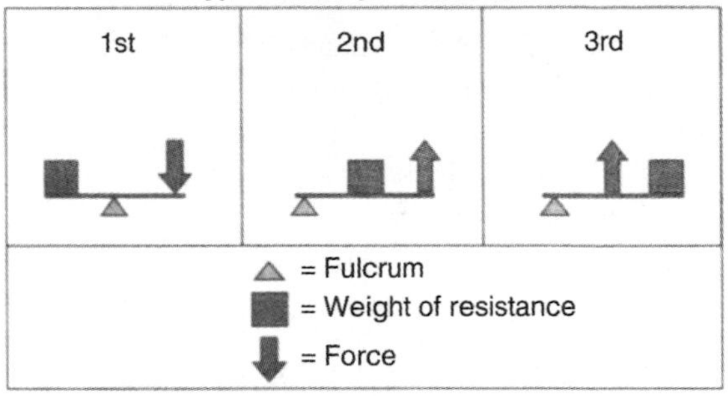

1st	2nd	3rd

▲ = Fulcrum
■ = Weight of resistance
⬇ = Force

Lever (three classes)

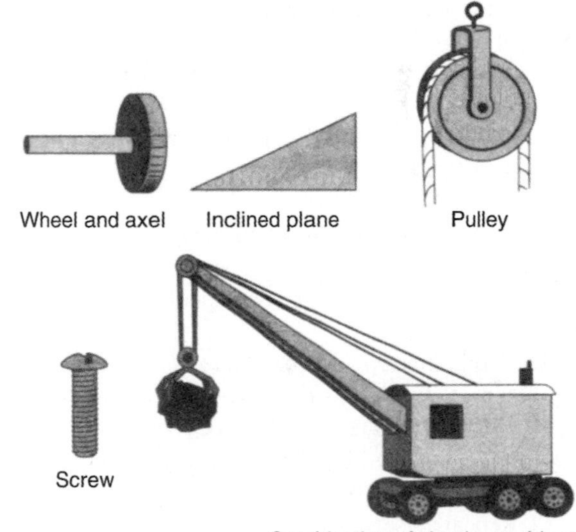

Combination of simple machines

A. Problem: *Can You Identify Some Simple Machines?*

B. Materials Needed:

1. Pictures of simple machines
2. Models of simple machines
3. Objects that are or contain simple machines such as:
   a. Hammer
   b. Eggbeater
   c. Pliers
   d. Tweezers
   e. Watch
   f. Toy bicycle
   g. Toy car
   h. Skateboard
   i. Pencil sharpener

C. Procedure:

1. Define a simple machine: "A device or apparatus that makes work easier."
2. Briefly describe how all machines help us.
3. Show pictures, models, or objects of the following types of simple machines:
   a. levers (three classes)
   b. pulleys
   c. inclined planes
   d. wheel and axle
   e. gears
   f. screws
   g. wedges
4. Have the students identify each simple machine in the pictures, models, or objects.

D. Results:

1. Students will be able to identify each simple machine.
2. Students will realize that much of our modern machinery is really a combination of many simple machines.

E. Basic Facts and Supplemental Information:

1. Machines help us to work.
2. Machines require some energy source to work.
3. Machines help us to do work easier.
4. Some work could not be done without the use of machines.

F. Thought Questions for Class Discussions:

1. How many simple machines can you name that are found in your home?
2. How many simple machines can you name that are found in an automobile?
3. Is time a concern in using simple machines?

G. Related Ideas for Further Inquiry:

1. Identify some simple machines found in our bodies.
2. Study a bicycle and determine how many simple machines it has.
3. Study the effects of friction in using simple machines.

H. Vocabulary Builders—Spelling Words:

Use the terms of the simple machines cited in Procedure, step 3.

I. Thought for Today:

"No dream comes true until you wake up and go to work."

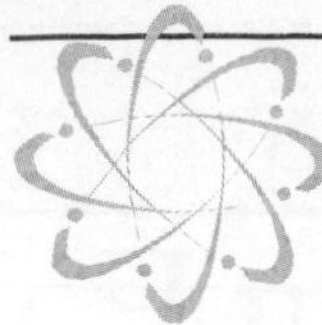

Activity II E 2

A. Problem: *How Do Gears Work?*

B. Materials Needed:

1. Baseboard, approximately 8″ × 10″
2. Nails (four large finishing)
3. Rubber bands
4. Spools (four the same size; two, different)
5. Hammer

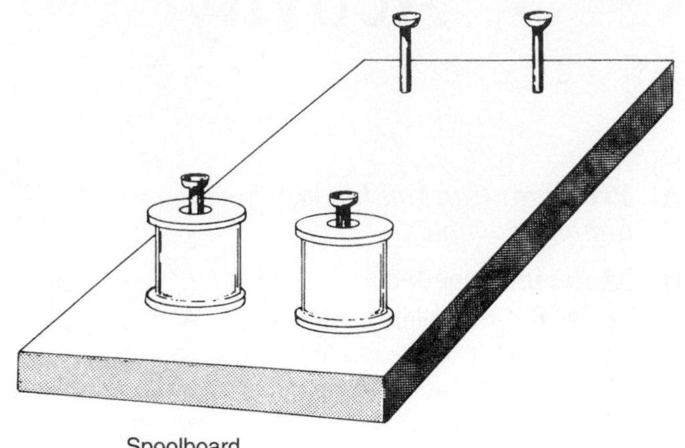

Spoolboard

C. Procedure:

1. Hammer the nails in the baseboard to create a "spoolboard." (See drawing.)
2. Place two spools in adjacent positions.
3. Place a rubber band over these two spools.
4. Turn one spool manually and note the directions of turn of the two spools.
5. Make a figure 8 out of this rubber band over the spools.
6. Turn one spool manually and note directions of turn of the two spools.
7. Add a third spool.
8. Place two rubber bands on the three spools so that one rubber band turns two spools, the second rubber band also turns two spools and there are no figure 8's.
9. Using three spools, make one figure 8 over two spools. Turn one spool and note the direction and speed of all three spools. (See setup 4.)
10. Experiment with different configurations of rubber bands and different numbers of spools.
11. Repeat all setups but vary the size spools noting directions and speed of rotation.

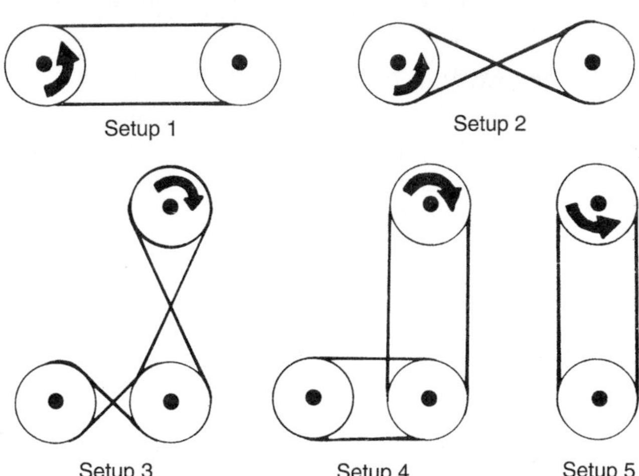

D. Results:

1. In the first part, both spools turn in the same direction and at the same speed.
2. Every time a figure 8 is added, the direction of movement changes.
3. Different size spools change the speed of rotation.

E. Basic Facts and Supplemental Information:

1. A gear is a toothed wheel.
2. The action of gears is identical to the action of the spools.
3. Interlocking gears placed at right angles to each other are called "beveled gears."
4. Gears can be moved by a threaded rod.
5. There are many combinations of gears which can change direction, power, and/or speed.

F. Thought Questions for Class Discussions:

1. What would happen if gears became progressively larger? progressively smaller?
2. How does the pedal gear on a bicycle affect the rear wheel?
3. What are some other advantages of gears?

G. Related Ideas for Further Inquiry:

1. Students can design gears out of heavy cardboard, creating different movements by changing sizes.
2. Study all Activities in this Section.

H. Vocabulary Builders—Spelling Words:

1) **gears** 2) **ratio** 3) **teeth** 4) **rotation** 5) **clockwise** 6) **counterclockwise** 7) **beveled**

I. Thought for Today:

"Do not engage mouth unless brain is in gear."

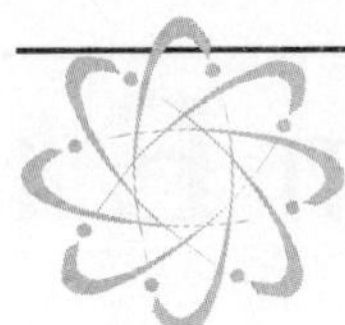

Activity

II E 3

A. Problem: *How Do We Measure Work? (Newton's Second Law of Motion)*

B. Materials Needed:

1. Weight, approximately 5 pounds
2. Spring scale to measure weight
3. Yardstick or metal tape measure
4. Stopwatch preferred (or watch with a second hand)
5. Rope or heavy cord

C. Procedure:

1. Weigh the weight.
2. Lift the weight up about one foot from the floor or desk.
3. Place the weight on the floor.
4. Measure off a distance of 10 feet.
5. Have one student push the weight over the measured distance.
6. Tell the class that work is measured in foot-pounds (kilogram-meters in the metric system) whether it is lifted vertically or moved horizontally.
7. Write the formula on the board and tell the students it is easy to use:

   $F = W \times D$ (F is the Force of Work,

   W = Weight, and D = Distance)
8. Ask students to compute the amount of work done in lifting the weight.
9. Ask them to compute the amount of work done in moving the weight horizontally.
10. Challenge students to compute the amount of work done when playing Hop-Scotch, if a player jumps or hops ten times, one foot high, and covers a distance of ten feet. (See drawing.)

D. Results:

1. When the weight is lifted off the floor one foot, the amount of work done will be one foot times the weight in pounds. The answer will be in "foot-pounds."
2. The weight will be moved 10 feet and the amount of work done will be 10 times the weight in pounds.
3. All students will become aware of the term "horsepower" and the older or more mature students can compute the horsepower used.

E. Basic Facts and Supplemental Information:

1. The formula for finding horsepower can be written on the chalkboard. It is:

   Work (in foot-pounds) = distance (in feet) × weight (pounds).
2. The work done in lifting 5 pounds one foot is "5 foot-pounds."
3. The work done in pushing a 5-pound weight over a 10 foot distance would be $10 \times 5 = 50$ foot-pounds.
4. Horsepower involves work and time.

   $$\text{Power} = \frac{\text{Work}}{\text{Time}}$$
5. $$\text{Horsepower} = \frac{\text{550 Foot-Pounds}}{\text{Second}}$$
6. In the second activity, if a 5-pound weight was pushed 10 feet in 4 seconds, we would compute the horsepower by first dividing 20 by 4. This gives us 5. To determine what part 5 is of 550 we must divide 5 by 550. This gives us 1/110 or .009 horsepower.

F. Thought Questions for Class Discussions:

1. Could a person ever work as hard as a horse?
2. What is the main difference between work and horsepower?
3. If water is cascading over a dam, is it doing work?

G. Related Ideas for Further Inquiry:

1. Study Activities in this Section on "Simple Machines."
2. Study Activities in Part II, "Energy."
3. Study other Activities in this Section.

H. Vocabulary Builders—Spelling Words:

1) **work** 2) **power** 3) **horsepower** 4) **Newton** 5) **foot-pounds** 6) **distance** 7) **kilogram-meters**

I. Thought for Today:

"Children need strength to lean on, a shoulder to cry on, and an example to learn from."

Activity II E 4

A. Problem: *Is the Screwdriver a Simple Machine?*

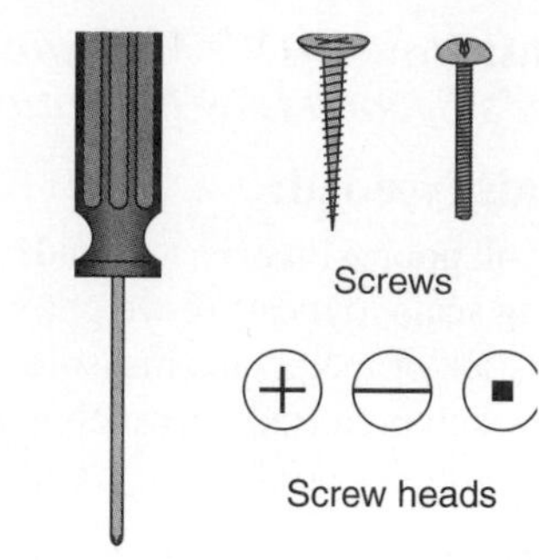

B. Materials Needed:

1. Assortment of screwdrivers
2. Assortment of screws
3. Dozen pieces of soft wood
4. Three or four hammers
5. Small nails
6. Pictures of different lengths and types of screws. (These can sometimes be obtained from local hardware stores)

C. Procedure:

1. Define a simple machine as a device or apparatus that makes work easier.
2. Cite examples of other simple machines:
   a. levers
   b. pulleys
   c. inclined planes
   d. wedges
   e. wheel and axles
   f. gears
3. Discuss how each of these makes work easier.
4. Tell students you want to put a screw in a block of wood for some specific reason such as to affix a hanger for a coat, hat, cup, etc. Ask if they could do this without using a screwdriver.
5. Divide the class into groups and let them use a screwdriver and a screw.
   a. First use a hammer and small nail to make a small hole to get the screw started straight.
   b. Use the screwdriver and a screw to work the screw into the wood.
6. Show the class the various sizes, types, and lengths of screws.
7. Discuss the uses and benefits of each.

D. Results:

1. Students will realize that it is very difficult to use a screw without a screwdriver.
2. Since a screwdriver makes work easier, a screwdriver is a simple machine.

E. Basic Facts and Supplemental Information:

1. A screw is really a circular inclined plane. (See Related Ideas for Further Inquiry)
2. There are many types of screwdrivers.
3. Screws vary in size, thread, material, and purpose of use.

F. Thought Questions for Class Discussions:

1. Why are screws more effective than nails?
2. Where are screws used in your home?
3. Are screws used on bicycles, skateboards, in-line skates, etc.?

G. Related Ideas for Further Inquiry:

To show that a screw is an inclined plane, take a sheet of paper and cut it diagonally in two. Starting with the original width wrap it around a long wooden pencil. Examine the "paper threads" and compare them to a screw's thread.

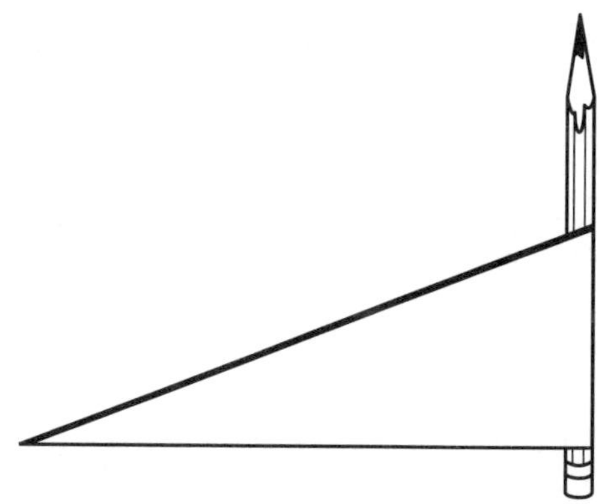

H. Vocabulary Builders—Spelling Words:

1) **screw** 2) **screwdriver** 3) **simple** 4) **machine** 5) **inclined** 6) **easier**

I. Thought for Today:

"Some folks are like blisters. They show up after the work is done."

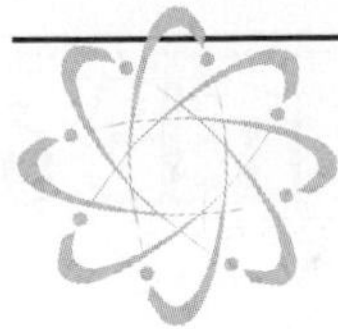

Activity

A. Problem: *How Can We Improve the Simple Screwdriver?*

B. Materials Needed:

1. Screwdriver
2. Assortment of screws
3. Block of soft wood
4. Hammer
5. Small nails
6. Chalkboard
7. Chalk

C. Procedure:

1. Discuss different kinds of simple machines.
2. Show the ordinary screwdriver and some regular screws to the class.
3. Briefly describe how they are used.
4. Demonstrate how the screwdriver is used, citing some of the problems that a person might encounter. Punch a tiny hole in the soft block with the hammer and small nail to get the screw started.
5. Tell the students that you want them to be creative and redesign screwdrivers so they can work better and have more uses.
6. List the suggestions on the chalkboard.

D. Results:

1. The students may surprise you and come up with a lot of new ideas.
2. Students may propose some of the following "creative" ideas:
   a. bigger handles
   b. shorter stems
   c. spoke in handle for easier turning
   d. magnetize the stem
   e. grooved handles
   f. battery operated
   g. rachet
   h. holder in handle for loose screws, etc.

E. Basic Facts and Supplemental Information:

1. This has been used in many classes and is mentally stimulating and challenging even for students in the lower grades.
2. Other simple machines can be studied and "improved" in a like manner.
3. Some ideas may not be new, but the students should be encouraged to discuss them anyway.
4. The screw is really a circular inclined plane.

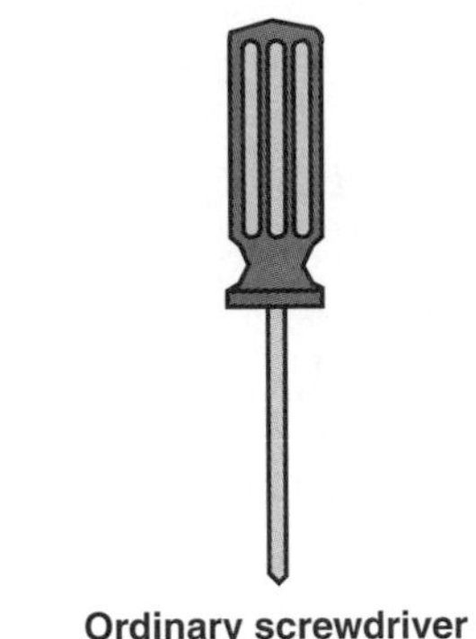

Ordinary screwdriver

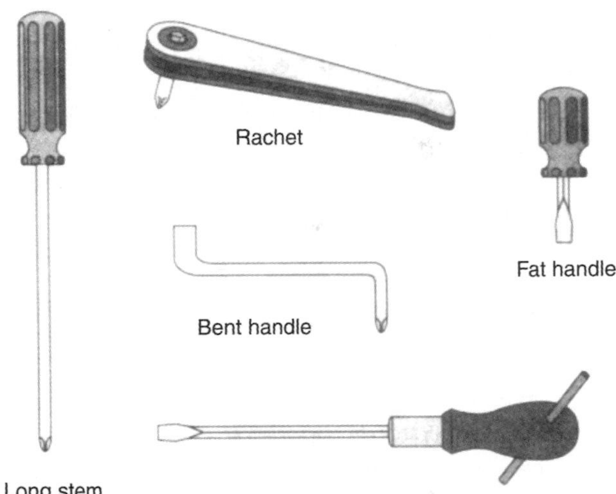

Improved versions

F. Thought Questions for Class Discussions:

1. Can the hammer be improved?
2. Can pliers be improved?
3. What other means of joining materials together can be used besides using screws?

G. Related Ideas for Further Inquiry:

1. Study Activity II-E-1, "Can you identify some simple machines?"
2. Study Activity II-E-2, "How do gears work?"
3. Study Activity II-E-6, "What is a wedge? How does it help us?"

H. Vocabulary Builders—Spelling Words:

1) **screwdriver** 2) **machine** 3) **work**
4) **inclined** 5) **force** 6) **chalkboard** 7) **handle**
8) **screws**

I. Thought for Today:

"A smile is the magic language of diplomacy that motivates students."

Activity II E 6

A. Problem: *What Is a Wedge? How Does It Help Us?*

B. Materials Needed:

1. Wedge, wooden
2. Seven or eight books
3. String or light cord
4. Plyboard, 12″ × 24″ (approximately)
5. Hammer or soft mallet

C. Procedure:

1. Tie the books together in a stack with the string or cord.
2. Place the wedge's tip slightly under one edge of the plyboard.
3. Place the books on the plyboard over the same edge as the wedge. (See drawing.)
4. Discuss the other types of simple machines:
   a. what they are
   b. what they do
   c. how they help us do work
5. Discuss the wedge:
   a. It is an inclined plane that moves under or into an object.
   b. It moves an object up or splits it, usually into two parts.
   c. It helps us do a job that would be difficult or impossible to do without some kind of external help.
6. Lightly tap the wedge with the hammer or mallet so that it will lift the board bearing the stack of books.
7. Continue to tap the wedge until it is completely under the board.

D. Results:

1. The board will slightly rise with the first tap.
2. It will continue to rise with each subsequent tap.

E. Basic Facts and Supplemental Information:

1. Wedges vary in size, thickness, angle of penetration or lift, and material.
2. The thinner the wedge, the less energy is required to move the wedge, however more attempts will be required to do the work, e.g., splitting a log or raising an object.
3. The thickness of the wedge determines the maximum distance that an object can be lifted or moved.

Lifting a stack of books the easy way.

4. One of the biggest problems when using a wedge is the great amount of friction involved and consequently a greater amount of work is necessary.
5. Practical uses of the wedge are found in many tools such as the chisel, axe, knife, nail, pin, tack, staple and, of course, the wedge itself.

F. Thought Questions for Class Discussions:

1. Have you ever used a wedge? How did it help you?
2. Does friction play a major role in the use of a wedge?
3. Does a wedge save work or just make work easier?

G. Related Ideas for Further Inquiry:

1. Study Activity II-E-1, "Can you identify some simple machines?"
2. Study Activity II-E-3, "How do we measure work? (Newton's Second Law of Motion)"
3. Study Activity II-F-1, "What are Newton's Laws of Motion?"
4. The teacher or adult associate could actually split a real log with a wedge, making sure that students are kept at a safe distance in case of flying pieces of wood.

H. Vocabulary Builders—Spelling Words:

1) **wedge** 2) **lift** 3) **force** 4) **inclined** 5) **split** 6) **plyboard** 7) **hammer** 8) **work**

I. Thought for Today:

"The mighty oak was once a little nut that stood its ground."

SECTION F: MOVEMENT AND RESISTANCE

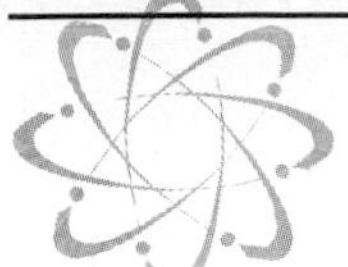

Activity II F 1

A. Problem: *What Are Newton's Laws of Motion?*

B. Materials Needed:

1. Book
2. Marbles
3. Desk or table

C. Procedure:

1. Discuss how things move.
2. Describe how nice it would be if we could predict movements.
3. Lay the book on the table.
4. Ask if there are any forces acting on it.
5. Push a marble along a table top or the floor.
6. Ask if there are any forces acting on it when it is in motion.
7. Push down on the desk.
8. Ask if there are any forces acting if there is no movement.
9. Discuss "Newton's Three Laws of Motion." Simplify the laws appropriately for the level of your students.

D. Results:

1. Students will learn that the three activities portrayed are examples of Newton's Laws of Motion.
2. Each "Law" is cited with a specific number.

E. Basic Facts and Supplemental Information:

1. Sir Isaac Newton (1642–1727) was a physicist who formulated these laws to explain movements of celestial bodies in space as well as movements on Earth.
2. The three laws are:
   a. A body continues in a state of rest, or in motion at a constant speed in a straight line, except when this state is changed by forces acting upon it. (First Law)
   b. Force is equal to mass multiplied by acceleration. In other words, a given force on a given mass will produce a given acceleration. On twice the mass, it will produce half the acceleration. If the force on a given mass is doubled, the acceleration will double too. (Second Law)
   c. To every action, there is an equal and opposite reaction. (Third Law)

F. Thought Questions for Class Discussions:

1. Are there forces acting on everything all the time?
2. Do you know any exceptions to these Laws of Motion?
3. If an arrow is shot in the air, does it obey the laws of motion?

G. Related Ideas for Further Inquiry:

1. Have a student on skates or a skateboard push against the side of a desk and note results.
2. Drop some nonbreakable objects. Have students explain movement.
3. Have a student ride a bicycle and discuss performance in terms of the Laws of Motion.
4. Study all Activities in this Section.

H. Vocabulary Builders—Spelling Words:

1) **motion** 2) **constant** 3) **speed**
4) **force** 5) **mass** 6) **acceleration**
7) **action** 8) **reaction** 9) **Laws of Motion**

I. Thought for Today:

"One small schoolboy to another: 'It might be unconstitutional but I always pray before a test.' "

Book (at rest)

Marble (in motion)

Action and reaction

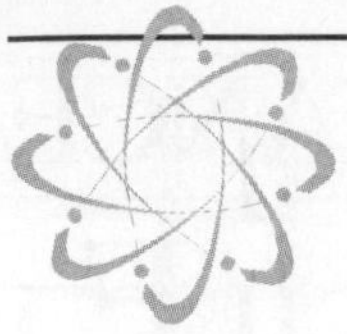

Activity II F 2

A. Problem: *What Is Acceleration? Deceleration?*

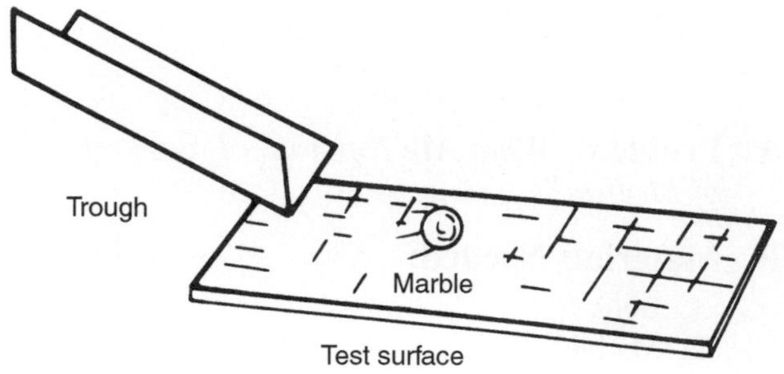

B. Materials Needed:

1. Cardboard strip
2. Marble
3. Desk or tabletop
4. Sandpaper
5. Strip of cloth
6. Small block of wood (or book)

C. Procedure:

1. Bend cardboard to make a trough.
2. Place trough at one end of desk or table.
3. Raise one end of trough with block of wood or book about one inch (2 1/2 centimeters).
4. Place marble in trough and release.
5. Repeat, only this time, let it roll on sandpaper.
6. Repeat again, only this time, let the marble roll over the strip of cloth.
7. Place book at the end of cloth strip.
8. Place marble in trough and release again.
9. Increase height of trough and repeat all marble releases.
10. Ask class about the speed of the marble at various points during each release. Was the marble:
    a. stopped?
    b. gaining speed?
    c. losing speed?

D. Results:

1. In all experiments, the marble is at rest initially but starts moving and gains speed as it moves down the trough.
2. The marble then decelerates (slows down) as it travels over the desk or table top, sandpaper, or cloth.
3. The marble slows down faster over the cloth, then the sandpaper, then the desk or table top.

E. Basic Facts and Supplemental Information:

1. The problems of acceleration and deceleration affect our lives tremendously. Every movement we make involves these factors. Without movement there would be no life.
2. Some of the biggest problems in our space program concern the control of acceleration and deceleration.
3. Newton's First Law of Motion states that a body in motion stays in motion unless acted on by an external force, and a body at rest stays at rest unless acted on by an external force.
4. The external forces in these tests are
   a. the trough
   b. the test surface
   c. gravity
5. A falling object in "free fall" would accelerate at the rate of 32.2 feet (9.8 meters) per second per second.

F. Thought Questions for Class Discussions:

1. What can cause acceleration?
2. What can cause deceleration?
3. What role does gravity play in acceleration? deceleration?

G. Related Ideas for Further Inquiry:

1. Toss a ball in the air. Discuss its acceleration and deceleration.
2. Have a student ride a skateboard or a bicycle, or use skates. Discuss the problems of acceleration and deceleration.
3. Study Section VII-D, "Gravity."
4. Study Activity II-F-1, "What are Newton's Laws of Motion?"
5. Study Activity II-F-7, "Are there forces acting without movement of objects?"
6. Study Activity II-F-12, "How does friction vary with pressure?"

H. Vocabulary Builders—Spelling Words:

1) **acceleration** 2) **deceleration** 3) **trough** 4) **sandpaper** 5) **downward** 6) **across**

I. Thought for Today:

"You can't fool all the people all the time—quite a few of them are fooling you."—Danny Thomas

Activity

II F 3

A. Problem: *What Is the Conservation of Matter?*

B. Materials Needed: Cookies

Cookies for class

C. Procedure:

1. Discuss matter. Study Part I, "Physical World," Section A, "Matter."
2. Discuss the ingredients (pieces of matter) that are needed to make cookies:
   a. flour
   b. eggs
   c. butter
   d. milk, etc.
3. Discuss where these pieces of matter originated.
4. Discuss how each of these items had parts and no matter was lost anywhere to get to its present state.
5. Discuss how cookies were made and how no "matter" was lost in their preparation, A little liquid was changed to a gas. It was *Conserved.* The remaining materials were physically mixed or chemically changed but no "matter" was lost anywhere.
6. Pass out cookies to the students and give them permission to eat them if they wish.
7. Tell the class that our bodies will change the cookies to useful food and energy and the remaining portions will be eliminated. No atoms or molecules (matter) will ever be lost.
8. Since no matter is ever lost, scientists call this phenomenon "The Conservation of Matter."

D. Results:

1. Cookies were eaten.
2. No matter was lost; it only changed its characteristics.

E. Basic Facts and Supplemental Information:

1. Matter cannot be created or destroyed.
2. Energy cannot be created or destroyed.
3. Matter can be converted to energy. This is accomplished in nuclear power plants and atomic bombs.
4. Energy can be converted to matter.
5. Actually energy and matter are two forms of the same thing.
6. Matter is found everywhere.
7. Matter is found in our bodies, food, trees, airplanes, boats, elevators, baseballs, snow, chocolate candy, books, stars, etc.—in everything and everywhere.

F. Thought Questions for Class Discussions:

1. Is the atom the smallest piece of matter that we know?
2. When a small piece of newspaper burns up, what happens to the matter that was originally the newspaper?
3. Is carbon dioxide "matter"?

G. Related Ideas for Further Inquiry:

1. Study Activity I-A-2, "What are atoms? molecules?"
2. Study Activity I-A-3, "What are elements? compounds? mixtures?
3. Study Activity I-A-5, "What is the difference between a physical change and a chemical change?"
4. Study Activity I-A-11, "What are the tiniest pieces of matter?"

H. Vocabulary Builders—Spelling Words:

1) **matter** 2) **conservation** 3) **destroyed**
4) **created** 5) **originated** 6) **physical**

I. Thought for Today:

"Many kids think a balanced diet is a hamburger in each hand."

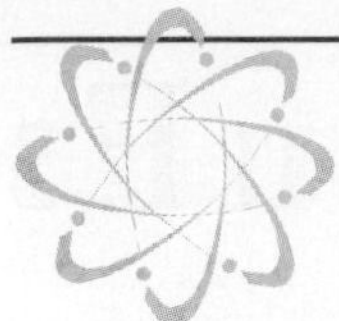

Activity II F 4

A. Problem: *What Is the Conservation of Energy?*

B. Materials Needed:

1. Pitcher
2. Water
3. Water glass

C. Procedure:

1. Partially fill the pitcher with water.
2. Pour some water from the pitcher into the glass, drawing an analogy from this demonstration to water flowing over a dam.
3. Discuss energy. (Study Part II, "Energy.")
4. Discuss the flow of energy:
   a. The water behind the dam has potential energy.
   b. When the water is released, the potential energy is converted to kinetic energy.
   c. The flowing water drives the turbines.
   d. The turbines spin and are now a source of kinetic energy. Some energy has been changed because of friction and has been converted to heat and sound. No energy was lost—it just changed form.
   e. The energy from the turbines in the generators convert mechanical energy into electrical energy.
   f. The electrical energy is delivered to our homes.
   g. In our homes we change electrical energy into heat, light, sound, and mechanical energy to run our washing machines, dishwashers, etc.
   h. No energy is ever lost in the process. This is what we mean by "The Conservation of Energy."

D. Results:

1. Water was poured from the pitcher into the glass, simulating the flow of water from the dam to the turbines in the generators.
2. Students will realize that no energy was lost in converting energy from a dam to electricity used in the homes such as electric lights, dishwashers, refrigerators, computers, television, can openers, etc.

E. Basic Facts and Supplemental Information:

1. Energy cannot be created or destroyed.
2. Matter cannot be created or destroyed.
3. Matter can be converted to energy. This is accomplished in nuclear power plants.
4. Energy can be converted to matter.

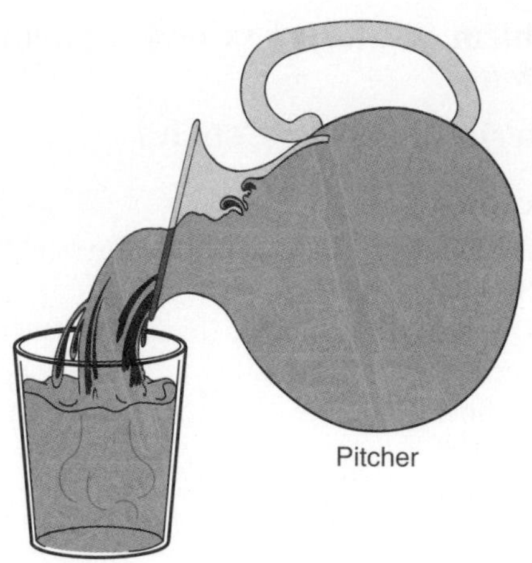

5. Actually energy and matter are two forms of the same thing.
6. There are two main forms of energy:
   a. potential energy—energy at rest
   b. kinetic energy—energy in motion
7. There are many kinds of energy:
   a. heat
   b. light
   c. sound
   d. mechanical
   e. electrical
   f. chemical, etc.

F. Thought Questions for Class Discussions:

1. What is the difference between potential energy and kinetic energy?
2. Is the atom the smallest piece of matter that we know?
3. When a small piece of newspaper burns, what happens to the matter the newspaper originally contained?

G. Related Ideas for Further Inquiry:

1. Study all Activities in this Part.
2. Study Activity I-A-2, "What are atoms? molecules?"
3. Study Activity I-C-9, "What makes popcorn pop?"

H. Vocabulary Builders—Spelling Words:

1) **energy** 2) **conservation** 3) **destroyed** 4) **created** 5) **kinetic** 6) **potential** 7) **electrical**

I. Thought for Today:

"It's easy to tell when you are on the right road—it's all uphill."

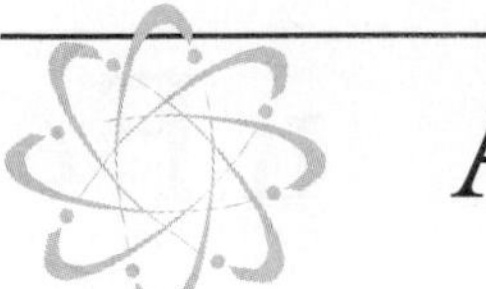

Activity II F 5

A. Problem: *Why Does This Can Keep Rolling Back?*

Fig. 1

Fig. 2

B. Materials Needed:

1. Heavy plastic cylindrical container
2. Tight-fitting plastic lid
3. Hammer
4. Large nail
5. Long rubber band or elastic cord
6. Heavy nut or other weight

C. Procedure for Construction:

1. Punch two holes in the bottom of the container, on opposite ends. (See Figure 1.)
2. Punch two holes in the lid on opposite sides to match the holes in the bottom of the container.
3. Thread the rubber band or elastic cord through the lid, then to the bottom of the container, then to the second hole in the bottom of the container, and return to the lid so that the rubber band or cord makes a figure 8. (See Figure 2.)
4. Knot the ends of the rubber band or the elastic cord on the outside of the lid.
5. Carefully remove the lid and secure the weight to the center crossing of the rubber band or cord making sure that the weight does not slip when the rubber band is tightened.
6. Replace the lid carefully making sure that the weight is in the center and the rubber band or elastic cord is still crossing.

Procedure for Using:

1. Briefly discuss inertia and momentum.
2. Briefly discuss the effects of gravity.
3. Tell class that you have an unusual container that defies part of Newton's First Law of Motion: "A body at rest will stay at rest unless acted on by some external force."
4. Roll the container slowly away from you.
5. When it is "at rest," release the container and it will come back to you.
6. Ask the class, "Why?"

D. Results:

1. The container will return to you.
2. The class should be perplexed.

E. Basic Facts and Supplemental Information:

1. Newton's First Law of Motion states: A body continues in a state of rest or in motion at a constant speed in a straight line, except when this state is changed by forces acting on it.
2. This Activity seems to defy the first part of Newton's First Law of Motion.
3. Actually it does not. The force moving the container is the energy that was stored up in the twisted rubber band or elastic cord.
4. Make several trial runs before the demonstration to make sure the apparatus is working properly.

F. Thought Questions for Class Discussions:

1. What force starts an automobile moving when it is at rest?
2. What force starts a bicyclist moving when the bicycle is at rest?
3. What force starts a space shuttle in its takeoff?

G. Related Ideas for Further Inquiry:

1. Study Activity II-F-1, "What are Newton's Laws of Motion?"
2. Study Activity II-F-2, "What is acceleration? deceleration?"
3. Study Activity II-F-4, "What is the conservation of energy?"
4. Study also Part II, Section E, "Simple Machines."

H. Vocabulary Builders—Spelling Words:

1) **container** 2) **elastic** 3) **inertia**
4) **momentum** 5) **gravity** 6) **rolling**

I. Thought for Today:

"By asking for the impossible we obtain the possible."—Italian Proverb

A. Problem: *What Will Happen in This Egg Experiment?*

B. Materials Needed:

1. Widemouth jar
2. Small tube (cylinder)
3. Cake pan
4. Broom
5. Egg, hard-boiled
6. Table or desk top
7. Water

C. Procedure:

1. Place the jar on the edge of table or desk top.
2. Fill the jar with water.
3. Place the cake pan over the jar with rim up.
4. Place the tube in the center of cake pan.
5. Place the egg on the tube.
6. Discuss inertia.
7. Discuss momentum.
8. Place broom about 6 inches from the table edge on the floor in an upright position.
9. Push down on the broom so that the broom straws bend away from table.
10. Step on the straws.
11. Bend broom handle towards you and away from apparatus.
12. Release.

D. Results:

1. The broom will hit the cake pan.
2. The cake pan will move sideways carrying the tube with it.
3. The egg, now unsupported, will fall into the jar of water.
4. The water will splash.

E. Basic Facts and Supplemental Information:

1. This demonstrates
   a. inertia
   b. momentum
   c. Newton's First Law of Motion
2. Gravity is the force that acts on the egg.
3. Inertia is the tendency of a body to remain in the state it is in. If it is still, to remain still; if it is in motion, to remain in motion unless acted on by some outside force.

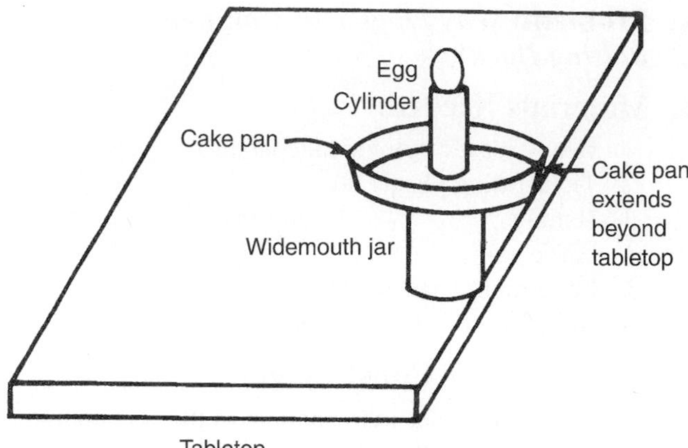

4. Momentum is the force with which a body moves; mathematically, it is expressed by mass times acceleration.
5. The egg should rest only on the edge of the tube, not too far down.
6. After practice and successful trials, you may substitute a fresh egg.

F. Thought Questions for Class Discussions:

1. Does a thrown baseball have inertia? momentum?
2. Does our planet have both inertia and momentum?
3. Do all moving objects have inertia and momentum?

G. Related Ideas for Further Inquiry:

1. Study Activity II-F-1, "What are Newton's Laws of Motion?"
2. Study Activity II-F-2, "What is acceleration? deceleration?"
3. Study Activity II-F-4, "What is the conservation of energy?"
4. Study Activity II-F-5, "Why does this can keep rolling back?"
5. Study Section VII-D, "Gravity."

H. Vocabulary Builders—Spelling Words:

1) **inertia** 2) **momentum** 3) **force** 4) **Newton** 5) **cylinder** 6) **gravity** 7) **broom** 8) **motion**

I. Thought for Today:

"It is not every question that deserves an answer."

Activity

II F 7

A. Problem: *Are There Forces Acting without Movement of Objects?*

B. Materials Needed:

1. Book
2. Desk

C. Procedure One:

1. With arms at chest level, have students hook their index fingers. (See drawing.)
2. Have them try to pull their arms apart while still keeping their fingers hooked.

Procedure Two:

1. Have each student hook an index finger with another student.
2. Have them try to keep their fingers hooked while gradually applying force towards themselves but keeping hooked fingers from moving.

Procedure Three:

1. Have a student sit on a desk for a moment.
2. Have the student get off the desk.
3. Place a book on the desk.
4. Remove the book.
5. Ask class what is similar in these actions.
6. Explain force (pushing or pulling on an object).
7. Explain that if forces are equal, there is no movement.

D. Results:

1. In Procedure One, no movement resulted even though forces were applied.
2. In Procedure Two, no movement resulted even though forces were applied.
3. In Procedure Three, there was no apparent movement of the person sitting on the desk or the book lying on the desk, even though there were forces acting in both cases.

E. Basic Facts and Supplemental Information:

In Procedure Three when a person sits on the desk, he/she is exerting a downward force. The desk reacts by pushing upward with an equal force. The same is true of the book. The book pushes down and the desk pushes up with an equal force. It is difficult to believe that the desk can exert differences of force, but that is exactly what happens or there would be movement somewhere.

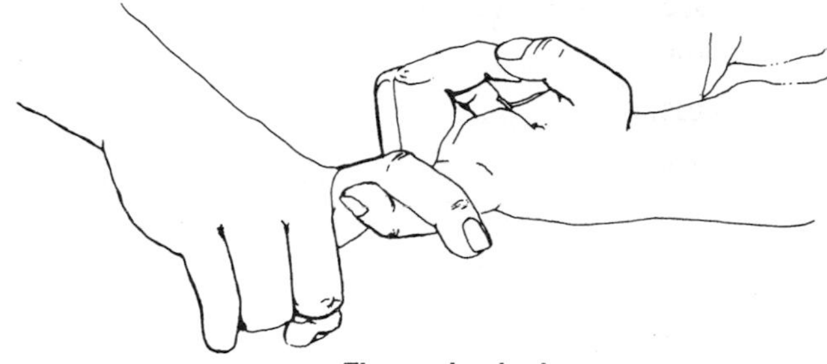

Fingers hooked

F. Thought Questions for Class Discussions:

1. Are there forces acting on a parked car?
2. Why do automobiles and bicycles have brakes?
3. Does it take more force to move a car from a dead stop or to stop it when it is in motion?

G. Related Ideas for Further Inquiry:

1. Have one student place his/her hands on the wall and push. Explain forces.
2. Have one student stand about 2 feet from the wall, facing it, and have him/her place his/her two hands on the wall with outstretched arms.
3. Have three other students line up with each facing the back of the one in front. Have each place arms outstretched on the shoulders of the one in front. Challenge the three to see if they can collapse the arms of the student with the hands on the wall. Discuss with students why they were unsuccessful.
4. Study Activity II-F-1, "What are Newton's Laws of Motion?"
5. Study Activity II-F-4, "What is the conservation of energy?"
6. Study Activity II-F-2, "What is acceleration? deceleration?"
7. Study Activity II-F-6, "What will happen in this egg experiment?"

H. Vocabulary Builders—Spelling Words:

1) **stationary** 2) **stationery** 3) **force** 4) **desk** 5) **reaction** 6) **equal** 7) **opposite**

I. Thought for Today:

"Science arises from the discovery of identity amidst diversity."

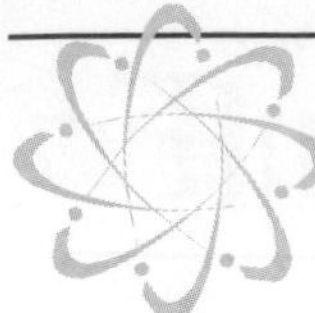

Activity

A. Problem: *Does Steam Exert a Tremendous Force?*

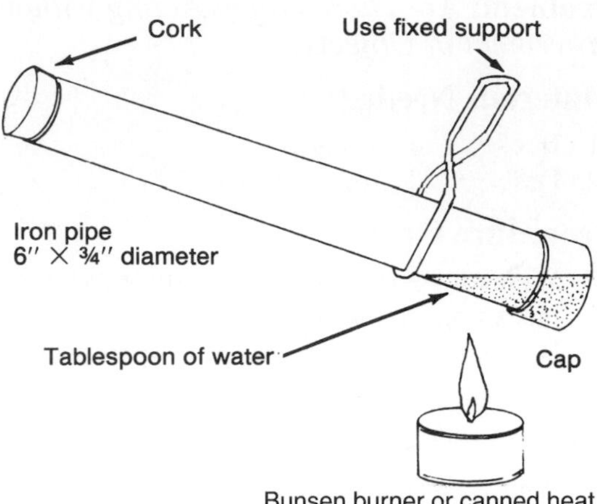

B. Materials Needed:

1. Piece of three-quarter-inch metal pipe 6″ long and threaded on at least one end.
2. Cap to fit the threaded end
3. Cork to fit in the other end
4. Bunsen burner or canned heat
5. Tablespoon of water
6. Ring stand and clamps

C. Procedure:

(Use extreme caution.)

1. Tighten the cap securely on one end of the pipe.
2. Place a tablespoon of water in the pipe. (See drawing.)
3. Place a cork stopper firmly but not too tightly in the opening of the other end.
4. *Be sure to point the pipe away from people, windows, or other fragile objects. Never hold pipe in hand.*
5. Secure the pipe at an angle to the stand with a clamp.
6. Heat the pipe at the capped end containing the water.
7. Aim corked end of the pipe toward a padded box, safe wall, or outside.

D. Result:

When the pipe has been heated, it will change the water to steam. The steam pressure creates a terrific pressure which forces the stopper out of the "cannon," usually with a loud noise and moderately high velocity.

E. Basic Facts and Supplemental Information:

1. Steam exerts tremendous force.
2. One cannot be too cautious working with steam.
3. One cubic centimeter of water will convert to 1,500 cubic centimeters of steam. This explains why there is such force behind steam.
4. It is the force of steam that makes corn kernels explode and become popcorn.
5. Because of the power of steam, old railroad engines were driven by steam.
6. Automobiles were tested with steam-driven engines but they proved to be impractical.

F. Thought Questions for Class Discussions:

1. What causes the cap on an automobile radiator to blow off?
2. How do they keep a hot-water heater from exploding?
3. How is steam harnessed for our benefit?

G. Related Ideas for Further Inquiry:

1. Boil water in a tea kettle without stopping up the spout.
2. Boil water in a pot with a lid on it.
3. An excellent activity to show the force of steam is to make some popcorn. Popcorn is made when the water in corn kernels is heated to steam. It is the steam that explodes the kernels. When water changes to steam it expands greatly and the steam literally bursts the kernels.
4. Study Activity II-F-1, "What are Newton's Laws of Motion?"
5. Study Activity II-F-2, "What is acceleration? deceleration?"
6. Study Activity II-F-3, "What is the conservation of matter?"
7. Study Activity II-F-4, "What is the conservation of energy?"
8. Study Activity II-F-9, "How does a steam turbine work?"

H. Vocabulary Builders—Spelling Words:

1) **threaded** 2) **safety** 3) **precautions** 4) **force** 5) **steam** 6) **cannon** 7) **cork** 8) **careful**

I. Thought for Today:

"The foundation of every nation is the education of its youth."

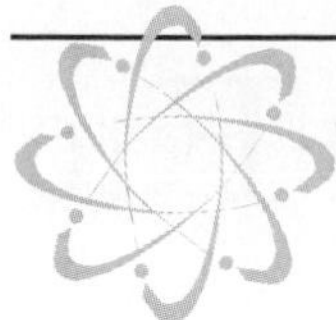

Activity

II F 9

A. Problem: *How Does a Steam Turbine Work?*

B. Materials Needed:

1. Three-inch cork disk
2. Eight strips of tin (1/2″ by 1 1/2″)
3. Flat board (4″ square)
4. Long nail or dowel
5. Glass test tube
6. Gas burner or heat source
7. Glass tube bent at right angles
8. Rubber cork, single hole
9. Pyrex bottle
10. Tripod
11. Water
12. Pliers

C. Procedure:

1. Bend the strips of tin so that they are slightly curved horizontally.
2. Using pliers to avoid injury, carefully insert the strips of tin into the cork disk which will be the vanes to catch the steam.
3. Assemble the rest of the materials as shown in the drawing. Remember to wet the stopper before inserting it into the glass tube.
4. Adjust the glass tube so the end is as close to the vanes as possible.
5. Fill Pyrex bottle half-full of water.
6. Heat the water.

D. Result:

The steam will be forced out of the flask and against the vanes, causing the "turbine" to rotate.

E. Basic Facts and Supplemental Information:

1. The steam turbine is capable of developing a great amount of power. Steam generators use this principle to produce electricity. The generators in atomic plants use steam turbines to turn the generators. The steam comes from water heated by the nuclear reactors.
2. Not only is steam pressure dangerous, but also steam temperature. Water is converted to steam at 100° C. or 212° F.; consequently, one should avoid coming in contact with steam in the home when cooking or ironing.
3. Hot-water tanks in the homes all have thermostats to control the water temperature, and safety valves for added protection.

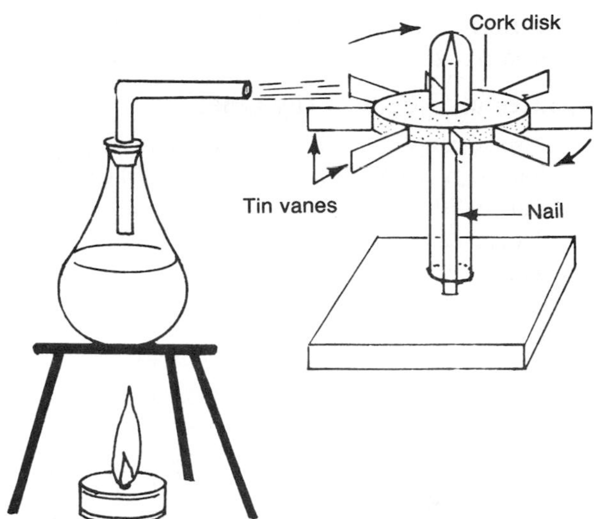

F. Thought Questions for Class Discussions:

1. Why do the blades on the turbine have to be curved?
2. Why does the jet of steam need to be played on the turbine at an angle?
3. What other uses could steam turbines have?
4. Is inertia and/or momentum involved in this activity?
5. What causes car radiators to overheat?

G. Related Ideas for Further Inquiry:

1. Compare steam generators to gasoline engines.
2. Visit a steam generator power plant at a local utility.
3. A steam kettle and a hot plate can be substituted for the "steam generator."
4. Study Activity II-F-1, "What are Newton's Laws of Motion?"
5. Study Activity II-F-3. "What is the conservation of matter?"
6. Study Activity II-F-4, "What is the conservation of energy?"
7. Study Activity II-F-8, "Does steam exert a tremendous force?"

H. Vocabulary Builders—Spelling Words:

1) **turbine** 2) **vanes** 3) **generate** 4) **power** 5) **Pyrex** 6) **steam** 7) **nail** 8) **force** 9) **disk**

I. Thought for Today:

"A soft answer turns away wrath."

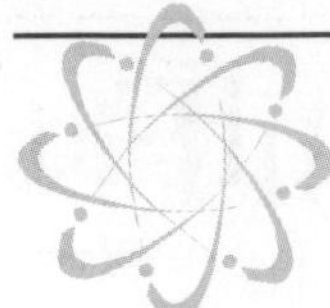

Activity

A. Problem: *How Can We Make Steam-Propelled Toys?*

B. Materials Needed, Toy One:

1. Small can with screw-type lid
2. Soap dish
3. Small candle
4. Pipe cleaners or wires
5. Water
6. Large dishpan or sink
7. Awl
8. Matches

Materials Needed, Toy Two:

1. Hollow eggshell
2. Coat hanger or heavy wire
3. Piece of thin plyboard or heavy cardboard
4. Candle
5. Matches
6. Toy wheels
7. Awl
8. Water
9. Tape (to seal hole in egg)

C. Procedure One:

1. With an awl, punch a small hole near the top edge of the bottom of the can.
2. Place some water in the can. Place lid on can.
3. Mount the can so that it will stand horizontally by twisting the pipe cleaner stems or wires around the can in such a way that they will support the can in the soap dish. (See drawing.)
4. Place this (steam boiler) carefully over a candle in the soap dish boat.
5. Place the soap dish on the water in the dishpan or sink.
6. Light the candle.

Procedure Two:

1. Construct toy as shown in drawing using an awl to make one small hole on each end of the egg, puncturing the yolk and then blowing or using a light stream of water to empty its contents. One hole should then be sealed with any strong tape.
2. Fill the eggshell half-full of water.
3. Place the candle under the supported eggshell.
4. Place the apparatus in an open space.
5. Light the candle.

D. Results:

1. As the candle heats the water in the can it will change the water to steam. The steam squirts out the hole in the can which causes the whole float to move in the opposite direction.
2. The toy eggmobile will scoot around.

E. Basic Facts and Supplemental Information:

The reason the "steamboat" moves forward is because the steam shooting out from the can creates a propulsion force which causes the steamboat to move in the opposite direction. This is the same principle that permits a rocket to lift off from a launching pad. The fuel in the rocket pushes down on the pad with force which propels the rocket up into space.

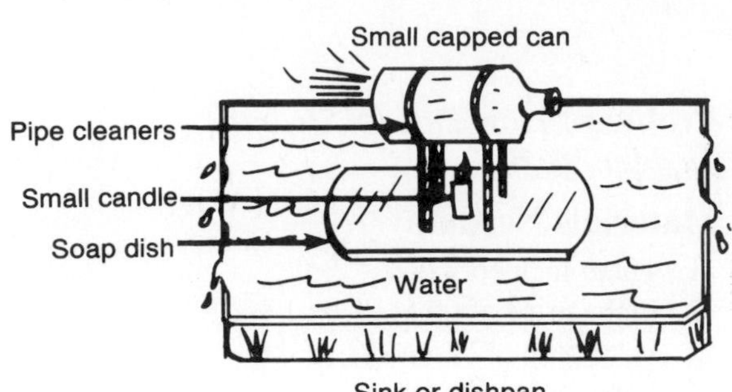

Steamboat (Toy One)

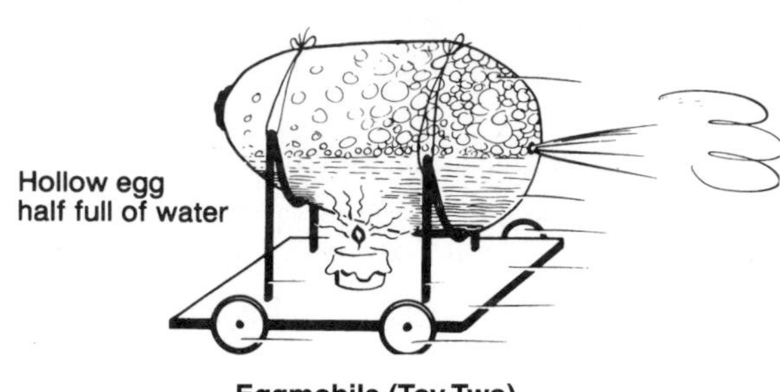

Eggmobile (Toy Two)

F. Thought Questions for Class Discussions:

1. What are the different ways people use to transport themselves?
2. What kinds of propellant systems are used?
3. Do people use the same systems for propelling themselves on land, on water, and in the air?

G. Related Ideas for Further Inquiry:

1. Study Newton's Third Law of Motion: "For every action there is an equal and opposite reaction."
2. Study different means of transportation.
3. Study Activity II-F-1, "What are Newton's Laws of Motion?"
4. Study Activity II-F-8, "Does steam exert a tremendous force?"
5. Study Activity II-F-9, "How does a steam turbine work?"

H. Vocabulary Builders—Spelling Words:

1) **steam** 2) **force** 3) **action** 4) **reaction** 5) **propulsion** 6) **water** 7) **needle** 8) **eggmobile**

I. Thought for Today:

"We judge ourselves by what we are capable of doing, while others judge us by what we have already done."—Longfellow

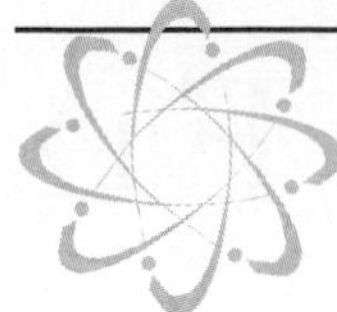

Activity

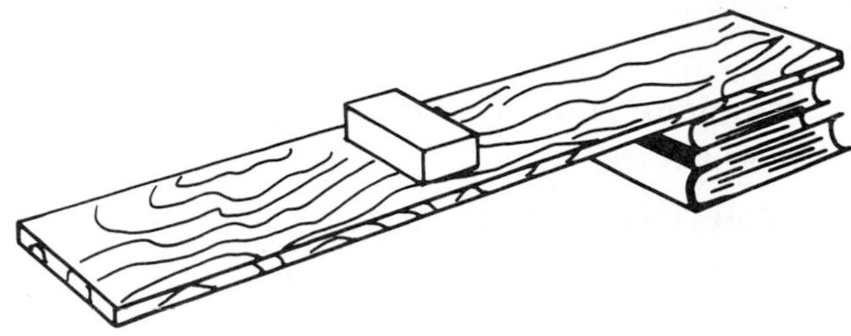

Sliding friction

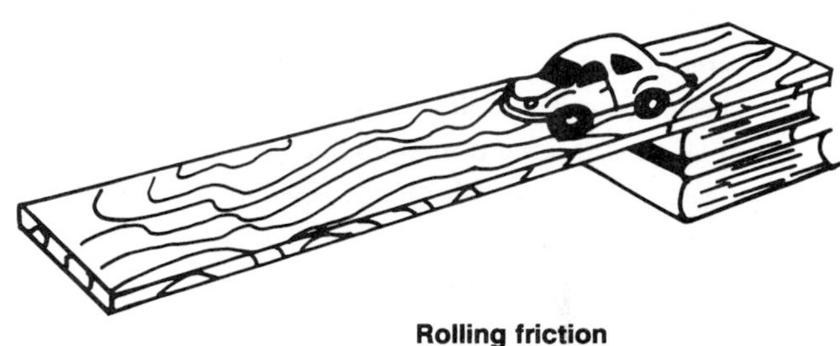

Rolling friction

A. Problem: *How Can Friction Be Reduced?*

B. Materials Needed:

1. Sandpaper
2. Matches
3. Two books for support
4. Toy car
5. Flat board
6. Soap or wax
7. Small wood block (same size as toy car)
8. Two wooden blocks (3″ × 4″)

C. Procedure:

1. Hold hands in front of you, palms facing each other, and rub hands together.
2. Strike a match.
3. Rub a piece of sandpaper on a block of wood.
4. Slide the two blocks of wood together.
5. Rub surfaces of blocks with soap or wax, and repeat above operation.
6. Place a flat board in a position so that one end is higher than the other.
7. Place a wooden block about the same size as the car on the top of the flat, inclined board.
8. Place a toy car on the higher end and release the car.

D. Results:

1. Your hands will become warm.
2. The match will ignite.
3. The blocks will require more force without the use of soap or wax.
4. The block will not slide on the flat board.
5. The car will roll freely.

E. Basic Facts and Supplemental Information:

1. Friction produces heat and causes wear.
2. Lubrication reduces friction.
3. Rolling friction is less than sliding friction because there is less surface area contact.
4. Ball bearings and roller bearings are examples of using rolling objects to reduce friction.
5. Rolling friction is present with ball bearings, roller bearings, and rotating wheels.

F. Thought Questions for Class Discussions:

1. What are some other experiments you can devise to compare rolling friction to sliding friction?
2. Why does lubrication reduce friction?
3. Can water be used as a lubricant?
4. How is friction lessened in engines?
5. Do ships have to overcome friction?

G. Related Ideas for Further Inquiry:

1. Study a roller skate, skateboard, or in-line skate and note how they reduce friction by using wheels.
2. Repeat experiment with single block of wood, but use a lubricating oil on its base.
3. Increase the angle of the board. Discuss how this affects friction on the blocks of wood and car.
4. Can you find ways that friction helps us?
5. Study Activity II-F-2, "What is acceleration? deceleration?"
6. Study Activity II-F-12, "How does friction vary with pressure?"
7. Study Activity II-F-13, "How do ball bearings work?"

H. Vocabulary Builders—Spelling Words:

1) **friction** 2) **block** 3) **lubrication** 4) **rolling** 5) **wooden** 6) **board** 7) **incline** 8) **wax**

I. Thought for Today:

"Science solves everything. When they found out they couldn't open windows on railroad cars, they air-conditioned the whole train."

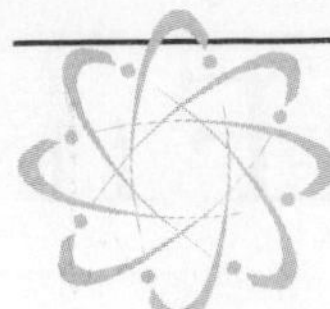

Activity II F 12

A. Problem: *How Does Friction Vary with Pressure?*

B. Materials Needed:

Yardstick or meterstick

C. Procedure:

1. Have one student spread his/her hands about 20 inches apart and then have another student place the yardstick or meterstick on top of the first student's index fingers so that the stick is as balanced as possible (See drawing.)
2. Estimate at what point which end of the stick will fall off the student's fingers if he/she moves both hands together slowly at exactly the same rate of speed for each hand.
3. After the estimate is made, have the student move his/her hands together very slowly.
4. Remove the stick from the student's fingers.
5. Discuss what happened.
6. Have another student place his/her fingers several inches apart in a horizontal position and have another student place the yardstick or meterstick on these two fingers.
7. Again guess what will happen if the student slowly moves his/her fingers apart.
8. After the guesses have been made, have the student holding the stick slowly move his/her fingers apart.

D. Results:

1. When the fingers are moved toward the center the stick will be continually balanced and the fingers will meet in the center without the stick falling in either direction.
2. When the fingers are moved outward, the fingers will both reach the ends of the stick without the stick falling in either direction.

E. Basic Facts and Supplemental Information:

The heavier the weight the greater the friction. The side that is longer (and heavier) will remain stationary until the other side becomes heavier. Then this (the other side) will move until the first side becomes heavier. This will continue until the index fingers meet in the exact center of the yardstick or meterstick or on its edges when the fingers are moved outward.

F. Thought Questions for Class Discussions:

1. Why does the stick slide faster over one hand than the other?
2. Can you make the hands not meet in the center of the stick by putting a little oil on one side of the stick or putting a little oil on one side of one finger that comes in contact with the stick?
3. What do you think will happen if you start with three fingers on one side and one finger on the other side?
4. What do you think will happen if you place a little weight in the middle of the stick before you start?

G. Related Ideas for Further Inquiry:

1. Study Activity II-F-2, "What is acceleration? deceleration?"
2. Study Activity II-F-7, "Are there forces acting without movement of objects?"
3. Study Activity II-F-4, "What is the conservation of energy?"
4. Study Activity II-F-11, "How can friction be reduced?"
5. Study Activity II-F-13, "How do ball bearings work?"

H. Vocabulary Builders—Spelling Words:

1) **meterstick** 2) **friction** 3) **pressure** 4) **fingers** 5) **stationary** 6) **apart** 7) **together** 8) **balanced** 9) **sliding** 10) **yardstick**

I. Thought for Today:

"The recognition of ignorance is the first spark of enlightenment."

Activity II F 13

A. Problem: *How Do Ball Bearings Work?*

B. Materials Needed:

1. 15 or 20 marbles, all of the same size
2. Heavy book
3. Large coffee can lid
4. Small can lid
5. Desk or table
6. Roller skate, skateboard, or in-line skate

C. Procedure:

1. Put the book on the desk or table and try to spin it.
2. Put the large lid on the desk or table.
3. Place the smaller lid inside the larger one.
4. Place marbles between the rims of the lids.
5. Place book on this apparatus.
6. Spin the book.
7. Examine ball bearing wheels on a skateboard or a roller skate.

D. Results:

1. The book will not spin when placed on the table or desk.
2. When placed on the improvised "ball bearing apparatus" the book will spin freely.
3. Students will see how a ball bearing is constructed.

How ball bearings are made

Ball-bearing frame

Ball-bearing frame with balls

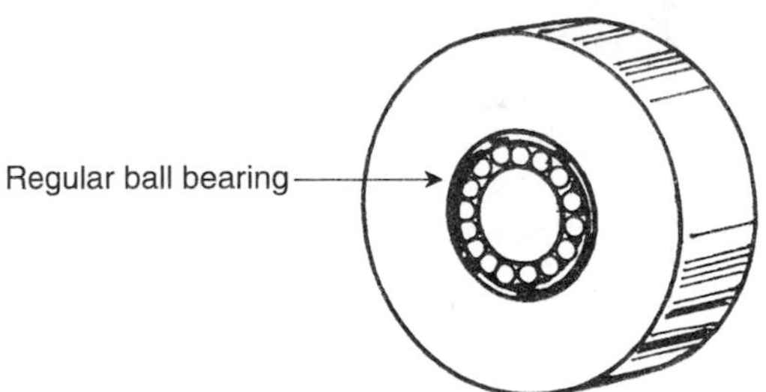

E. Basic Facts and Supplemental Information:

There is a lot of friction between the book and the desk or table top because of large surface area contact. When ball bearings are used, the surface contact is reduced and the book spins more freely. This kind of friction is called "rolling friction." This principle of overcoming friction has direct application in thousands of machines.

F. Thought Questions for Class Discussions:

1. How does a ball bearing apparatus differ from a wheel and axle?
2. Where are the ball bearings located in an automobile?
3. Does a bicycle use rolling friction in some of its moving parts?
4. What kind of friction do ice skaters need? rolling friction? sliding friction? no friction?

G. Related Ideas for Further Inquiry:

1. If this apparatus is strong enough, have a student place an old book or board on it, have him/her stand on it, and have another student carefully and slowly turn him/her.
2. Pipes, spools, pencils, and dowels can also be used in many ways to demonstrate "rolling friction."
3. Study Activity II-F-2, "What is acceleration? deceleration?"
4. Study Activity II-F-11, "How can friction be reduced?"
5. Study Activity II-F-12, "How does friction vary with pressure?"
6. Study Activity II-F-15, "What is centrifugal force? centripetal force?"

H. Vocabulary Builders—Spelling Words:

1) **rolling** 2) **friction** 3) **marbles** 4) **apparatus** 5) **spinning** 6) **cover** 7) **skateboard**

I. Thought for Today:

"Confidence is that feeling you have before you understand the situation."

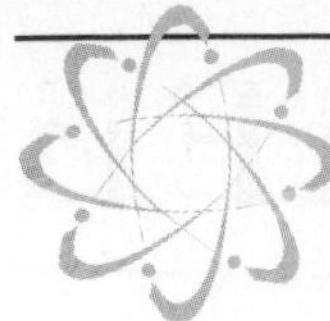

Activity II F 14

A. Problem: *How Do Pendulums Work?*

B. Materials Needed:

1. High support (top of chalkboard)
2. Various lengths of string
3. Enlarged protractor drawn on board
4. Proportionate weights (e.g., 5, 10, 15 grams)
5. Chart like that shown in drawing
6. Watch with a second hand

C. Procedure:

1. Attach longest string to the top of support with the enlarged protractor behind it.
2. Attach the largest weight to the other end.
3. Raise the weight in about a 90° arc.
4. Release the weight.
5. Time the number of swings it makes in one minute.
6. Record the swings in chart.
7. Repeat using the next heaviest weight.
8. Repeat with lighter and lighter weights.
9. Use a second string about three-fourths the length of the first and repeat with all the weights, timing all the swings and recording data.
10. Repeat with shorter and shorter lengths of strings.
11. Repeat with smaller and smaller arcs such as: 75°, 60°, 45°, and 30°.

Pendulum Swing Time:

Length of String:		*Weight:*		
90° Arc	10	5	10	15
	20			
	40			
	80			
75° Arc	10	5	10	15
	20			
	40			
	80			
60° Arc	10	5	10	15
	20			
	40			
	80			
30° Arc	10	5	10	15
	20			
	40			
	80			

D. Results:

1. Weights do not affect swing time.
2. Arcs do not affect swing time.
3. Lengths of string do affect swing time.

E. Basic Facts and Supplemental Information:

1. Have students form groups with each group working on one constant.
2. Pendulums will always swing in a straight line unless left for a long period of time when they would begin to rotate due to the rotation of the Earth.
3. Grandfathers' clocks use pendulums with double arms to correct for expansion and contraction due to changes in room temperature.
4. The longer the pendulum, the greater the swing time.

F. Thought Questions for Class Discussions:

1. How does gravity affect the motion of a pendulum?
2. If you wanted a pendulum to swing slower what would you do?
3. At what point does the pendulum weight have maximum kinetic energy? maximum potential energy?

G. Related Ideas for Further Inquiry:

1. Study Section VII-D, "Gravity."
2. Study Section II-E, "Simple Machines."
3. Study Activity II-F-1, "What are Newton's Laws of Motion?"
4. Study Activity II-F-2, "What is acceleration? deceleration?"
5. Study Activity II-F-4, "What is the conservation of energy?"
6. Study Activity II-F-5, "Why does this can keep rolling back?"

H. Vocabulary Builders—Spelling Words:

1) **pendulum** 2) **swing time** 3) **length** 4) **arc** 5) **angle** 6) **kinetic** 7) **potential** 8) **energy**

I. Thought for Today:

"If you can keep your head while everybody else is losing theirs, you'll be a head taller."

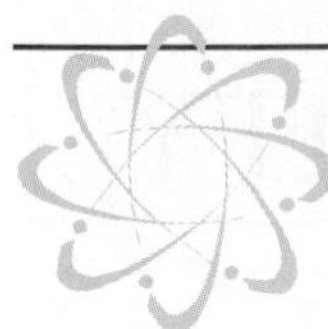

Activity

A. Problem: *What Is Centrifugal Force? Centripetal Force?*

B. Materials Needed:

1. Large spool
2. Heavy string
3. Old tennis ball
4. Weight
5. Ice pick

C. Procedure One:

1. *Carefully* punch two holes in the tennis ball.
2. Work heavy string through the tennis ball.
3. Have a student swing tennis ball horizontally in a small circle as shown in Figure 1.
4. Have the student describe any forces acting on the ball and/or force exerted by him/her.

Procedure Two:

1. With the string still attached to the tennis ball, thread the string through the spool.
2. Attach the weight on the other end.
3. Have another student slowly swing the tennis ball horizontally in a small circle with ball and weight in balance as shown in Figure 2.
4. Have the student describe any forces acting on the apparatus or exerted by him/her.
5. Have the student increase the speed of rotation of the tennis ball.
6. Have the student describe the forces involved.
7. Have the student describe any changes in the forces.

D. Results:

1. In Procedure One the teacher should make the student aware that he/she is pulling the ball toward him/her all the time the ball is in a circular motion.
2. In the first part of Procedure Two the ball and weight should reach a balanced condition with the student again realizing that he/she is exerting an inward pull.
3. As the ball is swung faster, the student should realize that he/she is exerting a greater pull and the weight should rise closer to the spool.

E. Basic Facts and Supplemental Information:

1. When the ball is swinging, the student must exert a pull toward the center of the circle. This inner pull is centripetal force.
2. There is no such thing as centrifugal force per se. Actually the term "centrifugal force" is nothing more than the inertia of a body in motion.

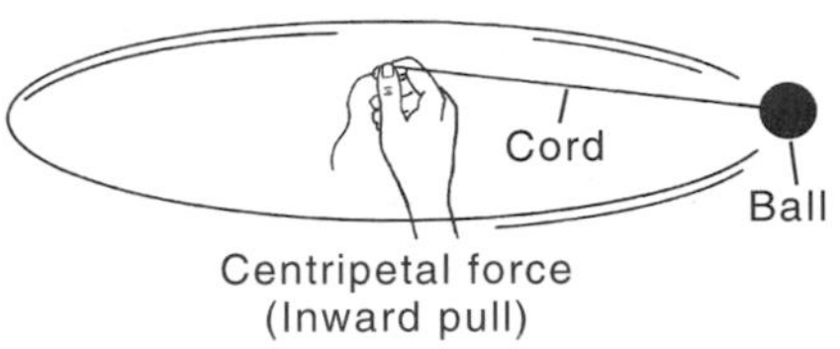

Fig. 1

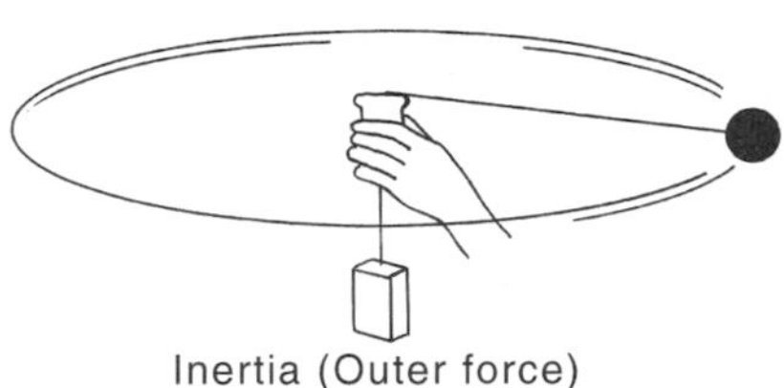

Fig. 2

3. It is very convenient to use the term centrifugal force and assume it is an outward pull. The only outward pull is the inertia of the ball.
4. If the ball were released in Procedure One, the ball would fly off in a straight line acted upon only by the force of gravity.

F. Thought Questions for Class Discussions:

1. Does it require a greater force to swing a heavy object or a light one?
2. Would there be any change in forces if the ball were swung vertically instead of horizontally?
3. If these procedures were conducted in a spaceship, would the results be the same?

G. Related Ideas for Further Inquiry:

1. Study the forces acting on a bicycle rider going around in a circle.
2. Study what happens when a fast moving car goes into a slide while going around a corner.
3. Study Activities II-F-1, II-F-2, VIII-B-1, and VIII-B-3.

H. Vocabulary Builders—Spelling Words:

1) **centrifugal** 2) **centripetal** 3) **inertia**
4) **pull** 5) **force** 6) **weight** 7) **momentum**

I. Thought for Today:

"People who go around in circles are never big wheels."

SECTION G: CURRENT ELECTRICITY

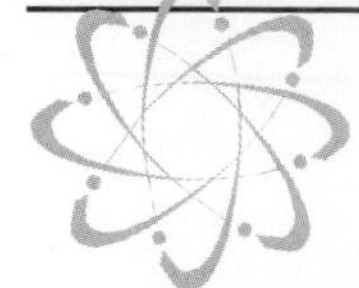

Activity II G 1

A. Problem: *How Is Electricity Made for Our Homes?*

B. Materials Needed:

1. Horseshoe magnet
2. Tube that is wider than the horseshoe magnet
3. Compass
4. Electric wire, #20, 30″
5. Small model home
6. Small model telephone pole
7. Dowel, thin, about 10″ long

C. Procedure:

1. Wrap about forty (40) turns of the electric wire around the dowel or tube leaving several feet at each end to complete model apparatus.
2. Slip the wire off the dowel and run the ends of wire on model telephone pole to the model home.
3. Place magnet in coil and rotate by hand.
4. Tie magnet to thin dowel.
5. (Optional.) Place magnet near coil and check compass pointer as the magnet is rotated.

D. Results:

1. A model electric system to the home has been constructed.
2. If the compass was used, the pointer will move showing that a magnetic field has been created around an electrical system.

E. Basic Facts and Supplemental Information:

1. In real life, the magnet is spun by a turbine creating a generator.
2. As the magnet spins around, it forces electrons on the wires to move along the wires.
3. When the magnet is in one position the electrons flow one way; when it moves to the opposite side, the electrons flow in the other direction, consequently producing alternating current.
4. There are alternating currents and direct currents.
5. Direct currents are produced by all forms of batteries. These currents run in one direction.
6. Electricity is produced by the flow of electrons from one atom to the next. It is like a bee jumping from flower to flower.

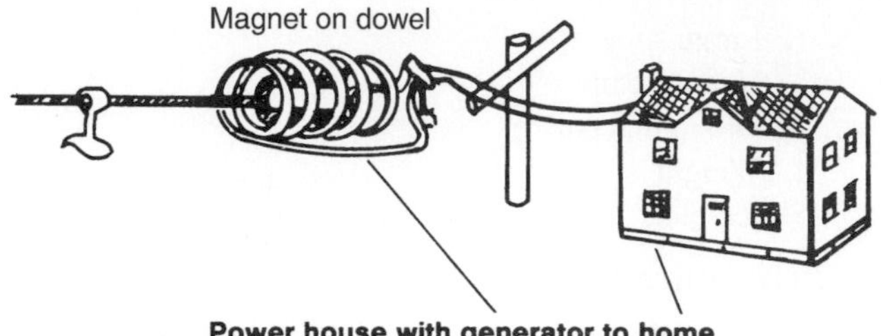

7. The hope for the future is that electrical demands will be met by solar energy.
8. Solar energy can be "caught" by photovoltaic cells, which convert solar energy directly into electrical energy.

F. Thought Questions for Class Discussions:

1. What is the difference between alternating and direct current?
2. What would homes be like without electricity?
3. What are some safety precautions we should take into account when using electricity in our homes?

G. Related Ideas for Further Inquiry:

1. Learn what the terms "voltage," "watts," and "ohms" mean.
2. Study Activity II-G-2, "How much electricity, gas, and water do we use in our homes?"
3. Study Activity II-G-3, "Does an electric current produce a magnetic field?"
4. Study Activity II-G-6, "What is electrical resistance?"
5. Study Activity II-G-7, "How can we make a current detector (homemade galvanometer)?"
6. Study Activity II-G-8, "How can we make an electric motor?"

H. Vocabulary Builders—Spelling Words:

1) **generator** 2) **voltage** 3) **ohms**
4) **watts** 5) **precautions** 6) **electricity**

I. Thought for Today:

"How strange to use 'You only live once' as an excuse to throw it away."—Bill Copeland

Activity

II G 2

A. Problem: *How Much Electricity, Gas, and Water Do We Use in Our Homes?*

B. Materials Needed:

1. Mock-up electric meter
2. Mock-up gas meter
3. Mock-up water meter

C. Procedure:

1. Discuss the use of electricity in the home.
2. Discuss the use of water in the home.
3. Discuss the use of gas in the home.
4. Discuss how we measure these.
5. Show the gauges for the mock-up electric meter.
6. Show students how to read the meters noting that gas and water dials are numbered clockwise and electric dials are numbered counterclockwise.
7. Have the students read their electric meters at home.
8. Repeat these steps for reading the water meter.
9. Repeat these steps for reading the gas meter.

D. Result:

Students will learn how to read their electric, gas, and water meters.

E. Basic Facts and Supplemental Information:

1. Some meters are read once per month; some meters are read every two months.
2. Electricity is reported in "kilowatt hours" (KWH).
3. Water is reported in cubic feet (CU FT).
4. Gas is reported in therms.
5. Gallons of water can be determined by multiplying cubic feet by 7.5.
6. If gas and/or water meter has a "one" dial system the gauge(s) will be different than those shown.
7. Remember how the dials move; some move clockwise, some counterclockwise.

F. Thought Questions for Class Discussions:

1. Can a person check the accuracy of a utility bill?
2. Where do we get our electricity? gas? water?
3. How can we conserve our use of these utilities?

G. Related Ideas for Further Inquiry:

1. Study Section I-C, "Water."
2. Study Section VI-B, "Conservation."
3. Study Activity II-G-1, "How is electricity made for our homes?"

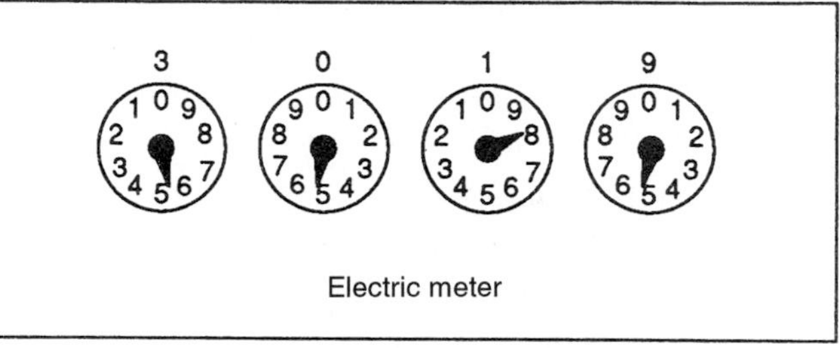

This meter reads 5585

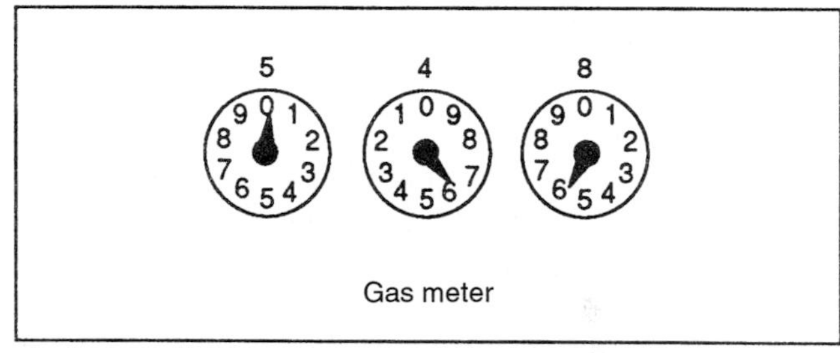

This meter reads 066

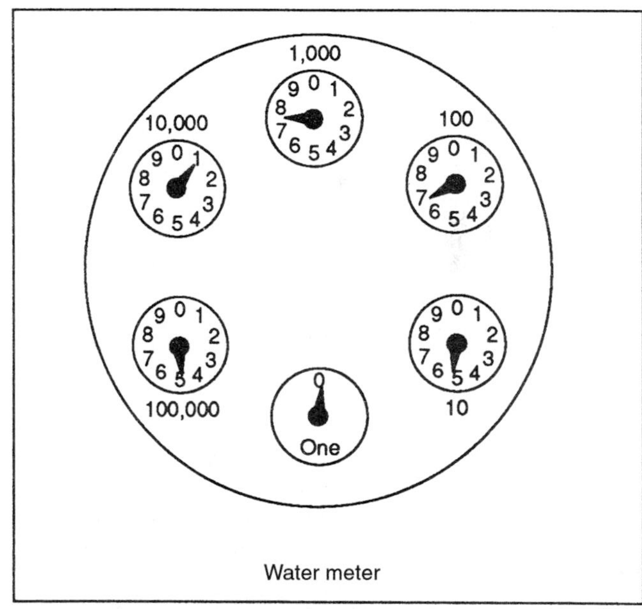

This meter reads 51765

H. Vocabulary Builders—Spelling Words:

1) **cubic feet** 2) **kilowatts** 3) **dials** 4 **meters** 5) **clockwise** 6) **counterclockwise** 7) **therms**

I. Thought for Today:

"We had no matches, gas or electricity until the 19th century."

Activity II G 3

A. Problem: *Does an Electric Current Produce a Magnetic Field?*

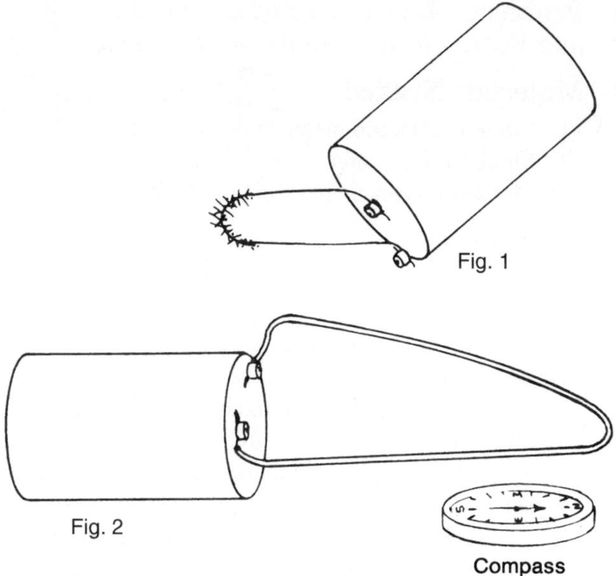

B. Materials Needed:

1. Piece of heavy copper wire, 6 to 10 inches long (#10 or #12)
2. Iron fillings
3. Dry cell battery (1.5 volts)
4. A three-foot piece of #22 insulated wire
5. Small magnetic compass
6. Cutting pliers

C. Procedure One:

1. Strip ends of wire with cutting pliers.
2. Connect the heavy piece of copper wire directly across the terminals of a dry cell making a loop as shown in drawing.
3. Quickly dip this loop of wire into a small pile of iron filings. (See Figure 1.)
4. After about four or five seconds disconnect one of the wires from a terminal; otherwise it will "short-circuit" the battery.

Procedure Two:

1. Connect a 3 foot piece of #22 insulated wire across the terminals of a dry cell. Arrange the wire so that one length of it is either vertical or horizontal. (See Figure 2.)
2. Move a small magnetic compass around this wire.
3. Switch the wires on the poles.
4. Move the compass around again.
5. Observe results.
6. Disconnect wire from terminals.

D. Results:

1. In the Procedure One, the iron filings are attracted because of the magnetic field around the current.
2. When the current is broken, the iron filings fall off the wire.
3. In the Procedure Two, the compass will point to or away from the wire. The magnetic compass shows that the region around an electric current contains a magnetic field.
4. When the current is reversed, the compass pointer will also be reversed.

E. Basic Facts and Supplemental Information:

1. Do not permit the wire to complete the circuit for prolonged periods of time, as this will damage the dry cell by reducing its electrical potential.
2. Every electric current produces a magnetic field around the flow of electricity.

F. Thought Questions for Class Discussions:

1. What will happen if the wire is too fine?
2. What will happen if the wires are left connected to the battery?
3. Why did the compass reverse directions in the second half of Procedure Two?

G. Related Ideas for Further Inquiry:

1. Study Activity II-G-1, "How is electricity made for our homes?"
2. Study Activity II-G-2, "How much electricity, gas, and water do we use in our homes?"
3. Study Activity II-G-6, "What is electrical resistance?"
4. Study Activity II-G-7, "How can we make a current detector (homemade galvanometer)?"
5. Study Activity II-G-8, "How can we make an electric motor?"

H. Vocabulary Builders—Spelling Words:

1) **electric** 2) **compass** 3) **short-circuit** 4) **reverse** 5) **current** 6) **terminal** 7) **connect** 8) **copper** 9) **filings** 10) **attracted** 11) **field**

I. Thought for Today:

"There is no comparison between that which is lost by not succeeding and that which is lost by not trying."

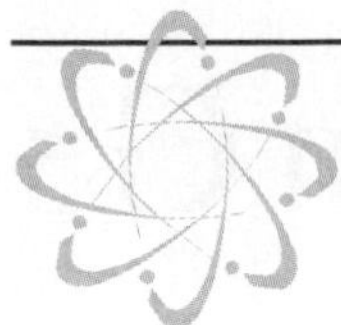

Activity

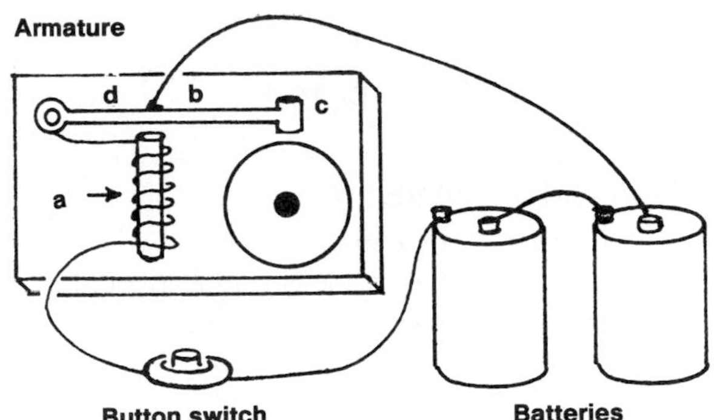

A. Problem: *How Does an Electric Doorbell Work?*

B. Materials Needed:

1. Electric doorbell (or chalkboard drawing)
2. Push button
3. Two dry cells
4. Electric wire (#16 to #22)
5. Stripping pliers

C. Procedure:

1. Remove the cover of the doorbell so that working parts can be observed.
2. After stripping the ends of all wires, connect the two dry cells in series to the doorbell and the push button. (See drawing.) (Note that the center terminal of one dry cell is connected to the outside terminal of the second.) The push button can be placed anywhere in the circuit. A knife switch can be used instead of a push button.
3. Depress the push button and hold for several seconds.

D. Result:

1. When the button switch is pushed down, the current is flowing and the electromagnet will become magnetized and attract the iron bar (armature) (d).
2. The armature is pulled toward the electromagnet and the clapper (c) hits the bell.
3. As the armature is pulled down and away from the fixed contact (b) the circuit is broken.
4. Since there is no current flowing through the electromagnet, the armature is no longer attracted to the electromagnet and it returns to its original position.
5. When the armature returns, the contact points touch again and the circuit is completed.
6. When the circuit is completed the current again flows, and the electromagnet becomes active and the whole cycle of operations is repeated. This continues rapidly as long as the button switch is held down and the batteries are strong.

E. Basic Facts and Supplemental Information:

1. This electric doorbell is one of the most common examples of what happens in creating and destroying magnetic lines of force with electricity. When the current flows, there is a magnet. Without the current, the magnetic lines of force disappear. Alternately applying the current and removing it thus makes the hammer vibrate. This principle is applied to many other household and commercial objects.
2. The one key point with electricity is that there must be a complete circuit for the electricity to flow. The flow is the movement of electrons to adjoining atoms. Anything that disrupts the flow will break the circuit and prevent electricity from flowing. A light switch does nothing more than break the circuit.

F. Thought Questions for Class Discussions:

1. How many things can you think of that use electromagnets in their operation?
2. How can you increase the rapidity with which the vibration takes place?
3. How does a doorbell differ from a door chime in operation?

G. Related Ideas for Further Inquiry:

1. Repeat Activity but vary the number of batteries.
2. Repeat Activity but vary the number of winds on the armature.
3. Study Activity II-G-1, "How is electricity made for our homes?"
4. Study Activity II-G-2, "How much electricity, gas, and water do we use in our homes?"
5. Study Activity II-G-6, "What is electrical resistance?"
6. Study Activity II-G-7, "How can we make a current detector (homemade galvanometer)?"
7. Study Activity II-G-8, "How can we make an electric motor?"

H. Vocabulary Builders—Spelling Words:

1) **doorbell** 2) **push button** 3) **terminal** 4) **clapper** 5) **switch** 6) **contact** 7) **electric** 8) **electromagnet** 9) **operation** 10) **circuit**

I. Thought for Today:

"Horse sense is found in stable situations."

Activity II G 5

A. Problem: *How Do We Make a Doorbell Chime?*

B. Materials Needed:

1. Electric Wire (#16 to #22)
2. Small hollow tube made of cardboard or plastic
3. Long finishing nail
4. Dry cell battery
5. Knife switch
6. Small metal plate (chime)
7. Supporting device for coil

C. Procedure:

1. Wind the wire around the hollow tube of cardboard or plastic leaving two long ends.
2. Place the hollow tube over the finishing nail (one with a small head), which is about as long as the plastic or paper tube.
3. Strip the ends of both wires.
4. Attach one of the end wires to the battery and the other wire to the switch. (See drawing.)
5. Complete the circuit by adding a wire from the push button or knife switch to the remaining terminal of the battery.
6. Suspend the plate above the finishing nail.
7. Close the switch and observe the action of the nail.

D. Result:

When the coil is connected to a dry cell (or toy transformer), the nail will first be pulled upward as shown by the dotted line striking the plate and making a metallic sound (chime). Then it will return to a resting position with the center of the nail nearly at the center of the coil.

E. Basic Facts and Supplemental Information:

1. Magnetic lines of force created by the electric current pull the nail with such force that it jumps. We can make an electric chime by placing a device so that the nail will strike it as it is pulled up by the electrified coil. Most musical door chimes use this principle.
2. A push button can be substituted for the knife switch.

F. Thought Questions for Class Discussions:

1. If the terminals are reversed, will it change the direction of the movement?
2. If the nail is reversed, will it change the direction of the movement?
3. In what other ways could we use this apparatus?

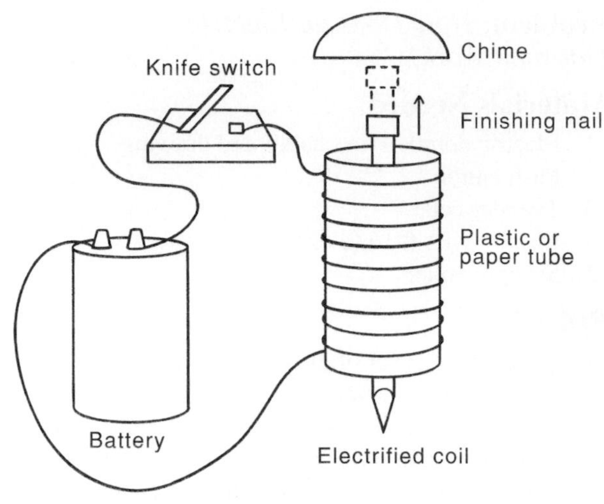

A doorbell chime

G. Related Ideas for Further Inquiry:

1. Make a simple electrified xylophone using this method.
2. Study Activity II-G-1, "How is electricity made for our homes?"
3. Study Activity II-G-2, "How much electricity, gas, and water do we use in our homes?"
4. Study Activity II-G-3, "Does an electric current produce a magnetic field?"
5. Study Activity II-G-4, "How does an electric doorbell work?"
6. Study Activity II-G-6, "What is electrical resistance?"
7. Study Activity II-G-9, "How can we make an electric identifier?"

H. Vocabulary Builders—Spelling Words:

1) **electric** 2) **finishing nail** 3) **knife switch** 4) **chime** 5) **cardboard** 6) **plate** 7) **battery**

I. Thought for Today:

"The most beautiful thing we can experience is the mysterious. It is the source of true art and science."— Albert Einstein

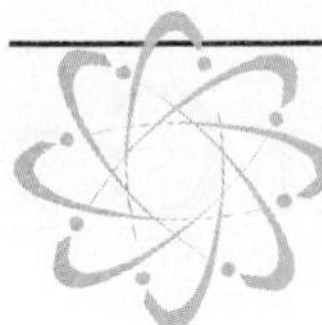

Activity II G 6

A. Problem: *What Is Electrical Resistance?*

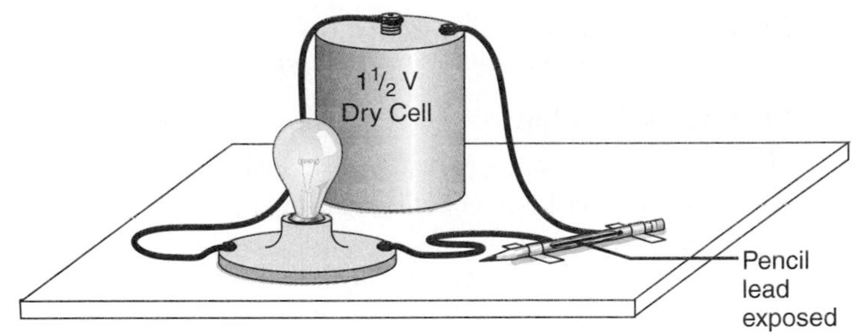

B. Materials Needed:

1. Dry cell (1.5 volts)
2. Small light socket
3. Bulb to fit socket
4. Baseboard
5. Two screws
6. Screwdriver
7. Long wooden pencil
8. Binding tape
9. Pocket knife
10. Electric wire #16
11. Stripping pliers

C. Procedure, Construction:

1. Carefully screw the socket to the middle of the baseboard.
2. Carefully remove one half of the wood from the middle two-thirds of the pencil. (See drawing.)
3. Secure the ends of the pencil to the baseboard with the binding tape so that the pencil cannot move.
4. Cut one length of wire about 12 inches long. Strip about 3/4 inch of insulation from each end.
5. Attach this wire to one terminal of the dry cell and the other end to one terminal of the light bulb socket.
6. Cut two more lengths of wire 12 inches long. Strip about 3/4 inch of insulation from each of the four ends.
7. Attach one wire to the other terminal of the battery.
8. Attach the second wire to the other end of the light bulb socket.
9. Place the light bulb in the socket.

Procedure, Use:

1. Discuss the word "resistance" and give several nonelectrical examples such as pushing a stalled car or running water through a hose.
2. Discuss how electricity flows and meets resistance:
   a. type of material
   b. source of power
   c. temperature, etc.
3. Take one wire in each hand; holding each wire on the insulated part, touch the exposed pencil lead (graphite) at its farthest points.
4. Observe the light.
5. Slowly drag the wires closer together.
6. Observe the light.

D. Results:

1. At first the light burns dimly.
2. As the wires got closer and closer together the light burned brighter and brighter.

E. Basic Facts and Supplemental Information:

1. The more lead in the pencil that the electricity must travel through, the greater the "resistance."
2. The more energy it takes to overcome resistance, the less energy is available for light.
3. Graphite (carbon) conducts electricity but not as efficiently as copper or steel.
4. A rheostat is a device that controls the flow of electricity.

F. Thought Questions for Class Discussions:

1. Where could rheostats be used?
2. Where would we want to vary the amount of electricity?
3. Do theaters use rheostats?

G. Related Ideas for Further Inquiry:

1. Study Activity II-G-1, "How is electricity made for our homes?"
2. Study Activity II-G-7, "How can we make a current detector (homemade galvanometer)?"
3. Study Activity II-G-8, "How do we make an electric motor?"

H. Vocabulary Builders—Spelling Words:

1) **resistance** 2) **current** 3) **graphite** 4) **flow** 5) **electric** 6) **pencil** 7) **battery** 8) **terminal**

I. Thought for Today:

"The kindness planned for tomorrow doesn't count today."

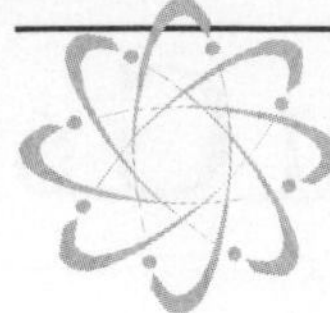

Activity

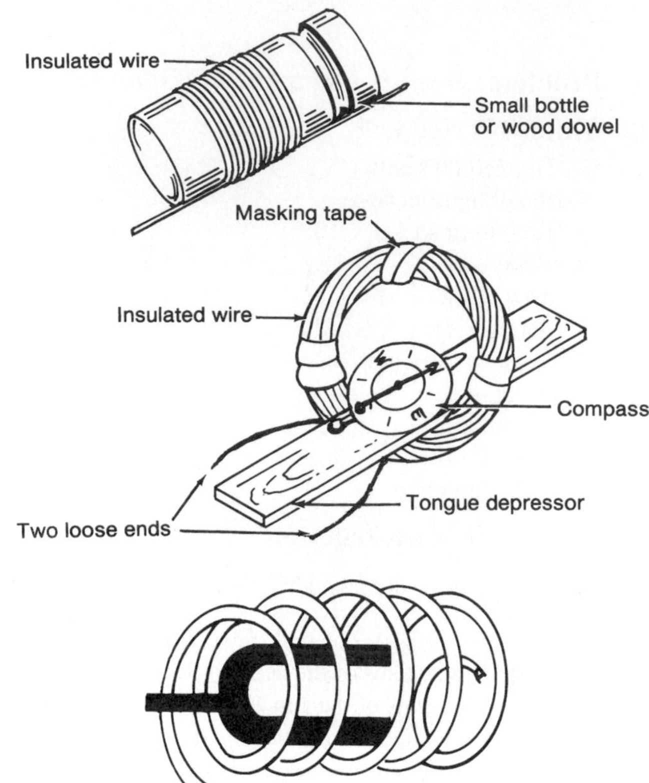

Simple galvanometer

A. Problem: *How Can We Make a Current Detector (Homemade Galvanometer)?*

B. Materials Needed:

1. Twenty feet of #28 or smaller insulated wire
2. Adhesive, masking, or cellophane tape
3. Tongue depressor
4. Small pocket-size compass
5. Small bottle or wood dowel about an inch in diameter
6. Battery (1.5 volts)
7. Stripping pliers

C. Procedure:

1. Wrap about 50 turns of the insulated wire around the small bottle or dowel. Wrap this in one direction only and wrap loosely. Leave enough of the two ends exposed so they can be connected to the battery.
2. Carefully slide the coil of wire from the bottle or dowel and put three strips of tape around the coil as shown in drawing.
3. Place a compass in the center of the coil as shown in the drawing.
4. Strip the wire ends.
5. Momentarily connect the terminals of the battery to the ends of the wire coil.
6. Observe the compass.
7. Disconnect one wire from the battery.

D. Result:

When the electric current passes through the coil, a magnetic field will be created which will deflect the compass needle from its starting position.

E. Basic Facts and Supplemental Information:

1. When the electric current passes through the coil, the magnetic field which is created causes a deflection in the needle of the compass. The same technique can be used to detect any kind of electric current.
2. A galvanometer is an instrument for detecting or measuring a small electric current by movement of a magnetic needle or of a coil in a magnetic field.
3. The electricity we use in our homes, schools, and businesses is created in power stations.
4. Power stations burn coal or oil to create the heat which converts water into steam. The steam drives turbines. The turbines turn dynamos called generators. The generators produce electricity.

F. Thought Questions for Class Discussions:

1. Can this technique be used to find out if a battery is dead or not?
2. Is this the principle on which commercial current detectors is based?
3. Which way did the compass needle point? Why?

G. Related Ideas for Further Inquiry:

1. Run the same test using a bar magnet instead of a horseshoe magnet. Were the results the same?
2. Trace electricity from the nearest power station to your school.
3. Study Activity II-G-4, "How does an electric doorbell work?"
4. Study Activity II-G-8, "How can we make an electric motor?"
5. Study Activity II-G-9, "How can we make an electric identifier?"

H. Vocabulary Builders—Spelling Words:

1) **galvanometer** 2) **current** 3) **detector** 4) **compass** 5) **cylinder** 6) **coil** 7) **tongue** 8) **insulated** 9) **wiring** 10) **electricity**

I. Thought for Today:

"A father is usually more pleased to have his son look like him than act like him."

Activity

II G 8

A. Problem: *How Can We Make an Electric Motor?*

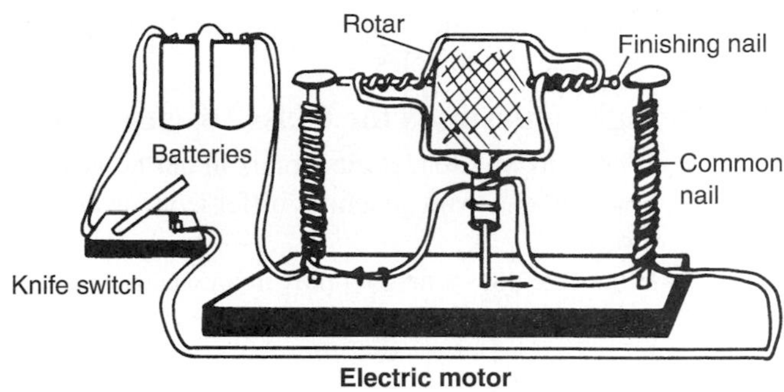

Electric motor

B. Materials Needed:

1. Glass tubing
2. Large cork
3. Two large finishing nails
4. Cork borer or cork screw
5. Thin electric wire, #18 or #20
6. Two large common nails
7. Baseboard
8. Two dry cell batteries
9. Knife switch
10. Stripping pliers
11. Stapler
12. Light hammer
13. Heat source (with flame)
14. Electric tape

C. Procedure:

1. Round off glass tubing by placing tip above flame and carefully rotating tubing until the end is rounded and closed.
2. With cork borer or cork screw drill a hole in the wide base of cork about two-thirds of the way.
3. Insert rounded-off portion of tubing into the cork so that there is a tight fit. A round file or pocket knife might be helpful for fitting.
4. Insert one of the finishing nails horizontally through the top of the cork, about one-third of an inch from the top, so that equal lengths of the nail are protruding from each side.
5. Using 3 feet of the wire, strip three-quarters of an inch from each end.
6. Tape one end of the wire to the spindle (the bottom part of the glass tubing) in a vertical position with the end of the wire pointing downward.
7. Run this wire to the one end of the finishing nail and wrap the wire tightly around the nail, then over the top of the cork, and to the other side of the nail, ending up on the spindle in a vertical position with the end pointing downward. Make sure that the wire on both sides of the finishing nail is wound in the same direction.
8. Tape this end to the opposite side of the spindle where the first end was secured. This part is called the "rotor."
9. Remove the first tape (see step C-6) and then tape both ends of the wire to the glass spindle so that the bare ends are exposed on opposite sides of the spindle.
10. Hammer two common nails to the baseboard so that the tops of the nails are just a little higher than the armatures (finishing nails).
11. Hammer a finishing nail exactly halfway between these two nails through the baseboard so that the point of the nail is in the up position.
12. Check the rotor to be sure that it is positioned correctly and turns freely.
13. Cut a 4 foot length of wire in half and strip all four ends.
14. Wind each wire around one of the common nails leaving enough at each end to connect to the battery or knife switch and the other to the commutator (the bare wires and the spindle). One wire is wound in one direction; the second wire is wound in the other direction. This is vital; otherwise the motor will not run. These are the poles of the electromagnet.
15. Place rotor on finishing nail and adjust wires so that good contacts are made between the rotor and these wire ends. Usually this takes several adjustments.
16. When final adjustments are made, staple lead wires to the board.
17. Connect wires to knife switch and batteries as shown in drawing.
18. When all is set, close knife switch, and with proper adjustments, motor will run!

D. Result:

An electric motor will have been constructed.

E. Basic Facts and Supplemental Information:

1. Don't worry if motor doesn't run on first trial. Adjustments with the brushes (contact points) are usually necessary.
2. The nails are wound in opposite directions so they will have unlike poles.

F. Thought Questions for Class Discussions:

1. Where do we use electric motors in our homes?
2. How does a steam generator differ from an electric motor?
3. What role does a magnet play in an electric motor?

G. Related Ideas for Further Inquiry:

1. Study Activity II-G-1, "How is electricity made for our homes?"
2. Study Activity II-G-6, "What is electrical resistance?"
3. Study Activity II-G-9, "How can we make an electric identifier?"

H. Vocabulary Builders—Spelling Words:

1) **brush** 2) **commutator** 3) **motor** 4) **armature** 5) **electric** 6) **knife switch** 7) **stripping**

I. Thought for Today:

"Sometimes a majority simply means that all the fools are on the same side."

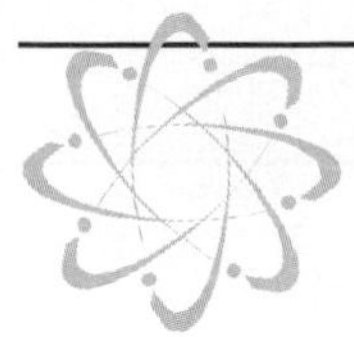

Activity

A. Problem: *How Can We Make an Electric Identifier?*

(An electric identifier is an electrical device made up of two separate lists, side by side, of scrambled items to be paired.)

B. Materials Needed:

1. Plyboard (1′ × 2′)
2. Copper wire
3. Wire strippers
4. Battery
5. Bulb holder
6. Bulb
7. Hand drill and bit
8. Nuts and bolts (one-half inch)
9. Small cards for questions; others for answers
10. Rubber cement or glue
11. Felt tip pens

C. Procedure:

1. Decide the kind and number of items you want on each list. They must be equal in numbers.
2. Draw outlines of card placement on plyboard.
3. Drill holes to fit nut and bolts to the center of plyboard as shown in drawing.
4. Plan each item in the question column to match an answer in the answer column, being sure to vary the locations of questions and answers. (These can be changed later if you wish.)
5. Cut the number of wires you have in the question column so that they will reach the answer position with some length to spare (for the reverse side).
6. Cut two wires long enough to reach the terminals from the battery and the light.
7. Strip the ends of each of these wires.
8. Insert the bolts so that the heads will be in the front of the plyboard.
9. Turn the board over and wrap the wires around the bolts; then secure with the nuts. (See drawing.)
10. From the battery, run one wire to the bulb socket.
11. From the other bulb terminal attach the second long wire.
12. Students are now ready to use the "electric identifier."
13. When the correct answer wire is matched with the correct question wire, the circuit is completed and the light will go on.

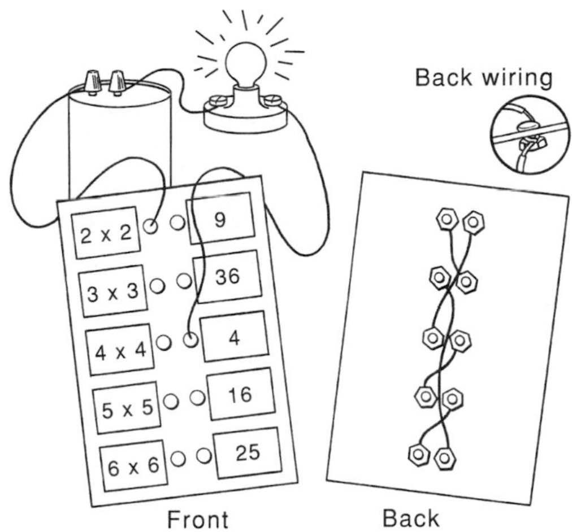

D. Results:

1. This is an excellent motivating device. Students enjoy playing with it, but more important, matching items on the electric identifier is a learning experience.
2. They will also learn about electric circuitry.

E. Basic Facts and Supplemental Information:

1. Vary the connections on the back because students soon learn the positions.
2. Some teachers have made stands for these; others have enclosed them in a box with the questions on the top of the box.
3. Be sure all wires are secure and terminals clean.

F. Thought Questions for Class Discussions:

1. What other class subjects could be used with the identifier?
2. What is the difference between an alternating current and a direct current such as this device uses?
3. Could a buzzer be used instead of a light? (Teachers that have used them say they are too noisy.)

G. Related Ideas for Further Inquiry:

Study the following related Activities: II-G-1, II-G-3; II-G-6, and II-G-7.

H. Vocabulary Builders—Spelling Words:

1) **electric** 2) **identifier** 3) **nuts** 4) **bolts** 5) **connections** 6) **pairing** 7) **matching** 8) **bulb**

I. Thought for Today:

"Questions are never indiscreet; answers sometimes are."

PART III

PLANTS

Section A: Parts and Classification

Activity III A 1

A. Problem: *How Do We Classify Living Things?*

B. Materials Needed:

1. Pictures of bacteria, fungi, and algae
2. Pictures of a wide variety of plants
3. Pictures, specimens, and stuffed animals

C. Procedure:

1. Describe the five main living kingdoms and give examples of each:
   a. **Monera**—bacteria, some blue-green algae
   b. **Protista**—amoebas, diatoms, euglena
   c. **Fungi**—molds, mildews, mushrooms
   d. **Plants**—mosses, liverworts, ferns, shrubs, trees
   e. **Animals**—jellyfish, worms, mollusks, centipedes, frogs, fish, rodents, birds, mammals
2. Have students try to classify any group of things such as books, hats, shoes, or clothing in any subclassifications they choose (size, color, weight, function).
3. Have the students prepare their own classification of animals.
4. Describe how scientists classify living things in the following subclassifications:
   kingdom
   phylum
   class
   order
   family
   genus
   species
5. The depth of classification should be determined by the age of the students. Older students may want a book on plant and animal taxonomy (technical classifications). Younger students can use common, general subdivisions as those mentioned above in Procedure. Middle grade students may want to subdivide these a little further.

D. Result:

Students will become aware of the complex nature of plant and animal classification.

E. Basic Facts and Supplemental Information:

1. Classification is a very difficult task and all scientists are not agreed as to classification schemes. Most problems of classification concern tiny organisms.
2. The science of classification is called "taxonomy."

F. Thought Questions for Class Discussions:

1. Can all living things be classified?
2. Can automobiles be classified?
3. Can rocks be classified?

G. Related Ideas for Further Inquiry:

1. Study Activity IV-A-3, "What are the scientific classifications of dogs, cats, and human beings?"
2. Study Activity IV-A-2, "What is the triangle of life?"
3. Study Activity IV-A-1, "What are some characteristics of all living things?"
4. Study Activity III-A-3, "How do plants reproduce?"

H. Vocabulary Builders—Spelling Words:

1) **kingdoms** 2) **phylum** 3) **order** 4) **class** 5) **family** 6) **genus** 7) **species** 8) **living**

I. Thought for Today:

"A child, like your stomach, doesn't need all you can afford to give it."

Activity III A 2

A. Problem: *What Are the Main Parts of a Flower?*

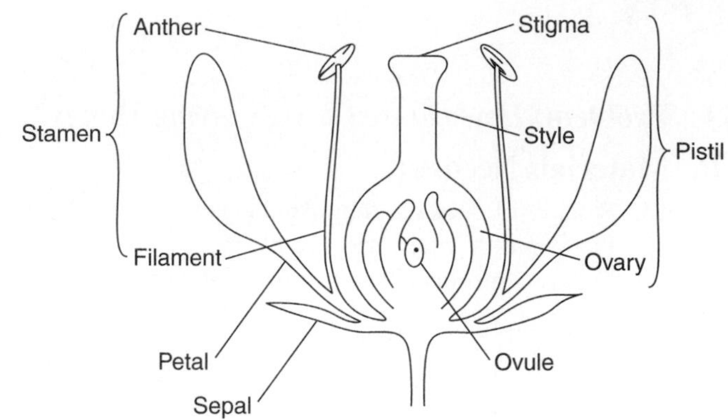

B. Materials Needed:

1. Pictures of flowers
2. Specimens of flowers (A specimen is part of a real object.)
3. Reference books on flowers
4. Multisensory aids about flowers
5. White typing paper
6. Clear plastic sheets
7. Transparent tape
8. Magnifying glasses

C. Procedure:

1. Present an overview of plants in general.
2. Show any appropriate multisensory aids.
3. Discuss the role of the part of the plant called "flower."
4. Assign students the task of collecting flower specimens.
5. Discuss the various parts of the flower. (See drawing.)
6. Have each student examine his/her specimen to see if he/she can locate the main parts of flowers.
7. Have each student open his/her flower fully and study it further.
8. Mount the flower parts on a sheet of white typing paper.
9. Label the parts that can be easily identified.
10. Enclose with plastic sheets and transparent tape.
11. Display on bulletin board or science table.

D. Results:

1. Flowers will be collected, mounted, and displayed.
2. Students will learn the various parts of flowers and their functions.

E. Basic Facts and Supplemental Information:

1. Plants are found almost everywhere in the world.
2. They exist in all kinds of environments: water, mountains, cold, hot, etc.
3. Flowers are the reproductive parts of plants.
4. Flowers exist for a short period of time.
5. Part of the flower becomes a fruit with seeds.
6. The seeds produce a new generation of plants.
7. A typical flower has four main parts which are attached to the stem of the flower:
   a. *Sepals:* green leaflike structures which enclose and protect the other parts.
   b. *Petals:* colorful part, many with sweet odors or nectar to attract insects.
   c. *Stamen:* male organ of the flowers with anthers on top that form the sperm or male reproductive cells.
   d. *Pistil:* female organ located in the middle of the flower. At the base is the ovary.

F. Thought Questions for Class Discussions:

1. How important is it for flowers to attract insects?
2. Is it necessary for flowers to attract a particular kind of insect?
3. Where are the prettiest flowers located in your community?

G. Related Ideas for Further Inquiry:

1. Students can practice arranging flowers.
2. If flowers are available nearby, take a school campus walk or short field trip.

H. Vocabulary Builders—Spelling Words:

1) **sepal** 2) **petal** 3) **stamen** 4) **pistil**
5) **flower** 6) **attract** 7) **insects** 8) **ovary**

I. Thought for Today:

"Flowers are the most beautiful things that nature ever created."

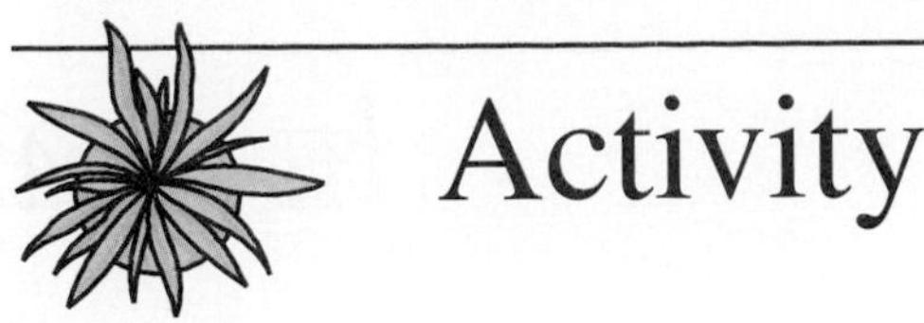

Activity III A 3

A. Problem: *How Do Plants Reproduce?*

B. Materials Needed:

1. Large drawing of a pistil of a flower
2. Large drawing of a stamen of a flower
3. Reference books on plant reproduction
4. Multisensory aids on plant reproduction if available
5. Specimens of flowers (students can collect)

C. Procedure:

1. Present an overview of plants in general.
2. Show any appropriate multisensory aids.
3. Review previous Activity III-A-2, "What are the main parts of a flower?"
4. Discuss the main parts of the stamen, the male reproductive organ. It is located inside the petals. It consists of:
   a. stalk or filament
   b. anther, which is an enlarged tip at the top of the filament
5. Discuss the main parts of the pistil, the female reproductive organ. It is located in the very center of the flower. It consists of:
   a. ovary, which is at the base of the pistil
   b. style, which is a tender stalk arising from the ovary
   c. stigma, which is the enlarged portion at the top of the style
6. Show the specimens collected and point out the main parts of a flower's reproductive system.
7. Discuss typical reproductive processes of flowers.

D. Results:

1. Students will collect specimens.
2. Students will learn the main parts of a flower's reproductive system.
3. Students will learn the process of flower reproduction.

E. Basic Facts and Supplemental Information:

1. Pollen grains are produced by the anthers.
2. These grains will form the sperm, which are the male reproductive cells.

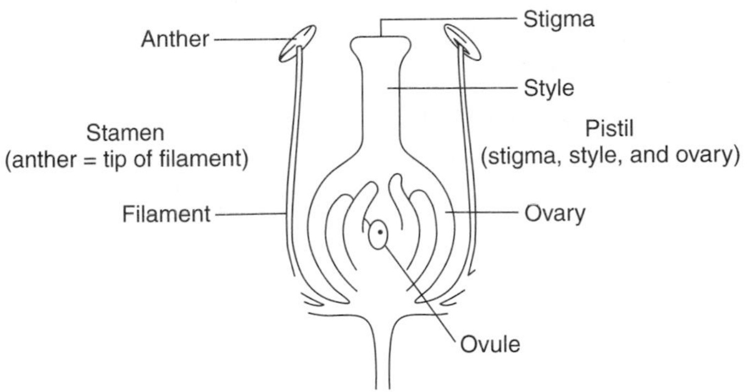

3. To create seeds, pollen must get from the anther on the filament to the tip (stigma) of the pistil.
4. This process is called "pollination."
5. Pollination may occur on one flower, which is called "self-pollination," or between two flowers, which is called "cross-pollination."
6. Pollination is the first step in seed development.
7. The sperm, which is formed from the pollen grain, travels to the ovary, where it fertilizes the egg and forms a seed.

F. Thought Questions for Class Discussions:

1. How are insects important to flowers?
2. How are insects detrimental to flowers?
3. Are flowers important to animals?

G. Related Ideas for Further Inquiry:

1. Study Activity III-A-1, "How do we classify living things?"
2. Study Activity III-A-2, "What are the main parts of a flower?"
3. Study Activity III-A-5, "Can we make a vegetable garden?"

H. Vocabulary Builders—Spelling Words:

1) **pollen** 2) **grain** 3) **sperm** 4) **ovary** 5) **reproduction** 6) **fertilization** 7) **style**

I. Thought for Today:

"He that climbs a ladder must begin at the first rung."

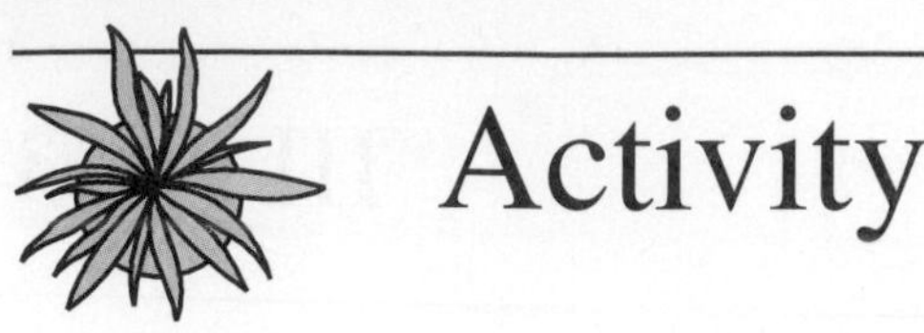

Activity

III A 4

A. Problem: *What Kinds of Trees Are Found in Our Neighborhood?*

B. Materials Needed:

1. Area at or near school where some trees are found
2. Reference materials on trees

C. Procedure:

1. Examine the trees you see and answer the following questions:
   a. What is a tree?
   b. Do all trees have the same shape?
   c. Do they have the same kinds of leaves?
2. Have students draw sketches of different kinds of trees.
3. Discuss how trees differ from other plants.
4. See Basic Facts and Supplemental Information.

D. Result:

Students learn that there are many species, sizes, shapes, etc. of trees.

E. Basic Facts and Supplemental Information:

1. A tree is a special kind of green plant. It has a wooden stem covered with bark. We call the tree stem a trunk. Each species of tree has a different shape.
2. Trees differ in height, leaves, buds, twigs, bark, etc. Some trees are deciduous, while others are evergreen.
3. Deciduous trees lose their leaves every year; evergreens do not.
4. Trees are the biggest plants on our earth. Sequoia trees are giant plants found in California.
5. Trees provide homes for animals, especially birds.
6. Trees provide seeds, nuts, and fruit for people and animals.
7. Some trees live to be thousands of years old.
8. Horizontal cuts in tree trunks show "rings." Each ring represents a year's growth.
9. Some trees have stamens and pistils in their blossoms. Some tree blossoms have pistils only; some have stamens only. In these, two different trees are needed for reproduction.
10. Trees vary in the shape of their leaves from thin pine needles to broad leaves like those of willows and sycamores.
11. Fruits and seeds are other means of identification. These could vary from apples on an apple tree to acorns on an oak tree.
12. Trees provide us with about 25% of our fresh oxygen supply.

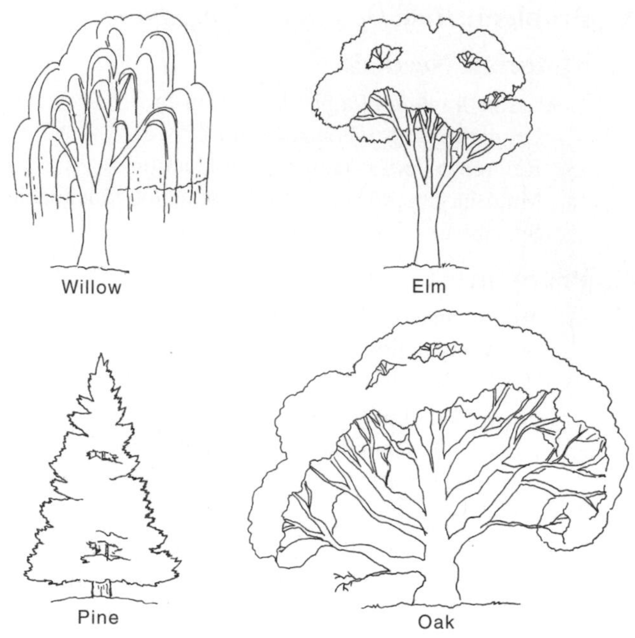

F. Thought Questions for Class Discussions:

1. How do trees differ from each other?
2. Do some trees stay green all year?
3. Why do some trees lose their leaves in the fall?
4. What causes trees to become uprooted?

G. Related Ideas for Further Inquiry:

1. Compare deciduous and evergreen trees.
2. Have students discuss forests and hiking experiences concerning trees.
3. Discuss the value of fruit trees.
4. Discuss forest fires. See Activity VI-D-6, "How can we protect our recreational areas?"
5. Study Activity III-A-1, "How do we classify living things?"
6. Study Activity III-A-2, "What are the main parts of a flower?"
7. Study Activity III-A-3, "How do plants reproduce?"

H. Vocabulary Builders—Spelling Words:

1) **deciduous** 2) **evergreen** 3) **elm** 4) **trees** 5) **oak** 6) **poplar** 7) **willow** 8) **bark** 9) **rings**

I. Thought for Today:

"There are two ways to get to the top of an oak tree. You can climb it or sit on an acorn."

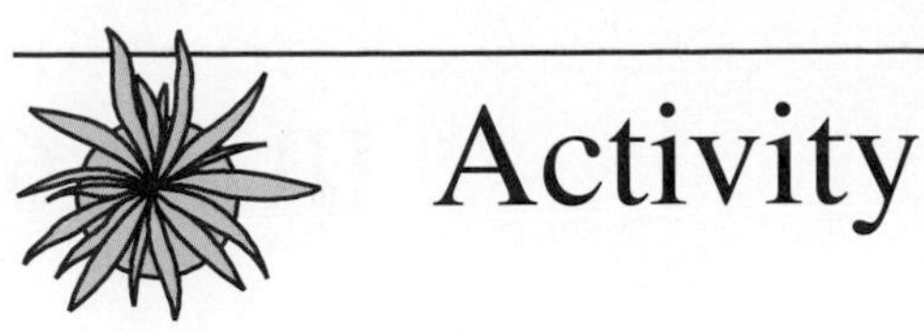

Activity III A 5

A. Problem: *Can We Make a School Vegetable Garden? (The Best Time Is in the Spring.)*

B. Materials Needed:

1. Garden spot (Need about 100 square feet)
2. Reference materials on gardening
3. Vegetable seeds or young plants
4. Stakes
5. Hammer
6. Spade, rake, hoe
7. Trowels
8. Organic fertilizers (compost)
9. Water
10. Buckets or plastic bags (to carry off weeds and vegetables)
11. String

C. Procedure:

1. Decide on the amount of time you want to spend on this project (short term or full season). (Best to start short-term program and use quick-maturing vegetables.)
2. Plot your garden in rows, noting spacing between planting seeds (or young plants) and distances between rows. (Vegetables are excellent to start a school garden.)
3. Use string and stakes to mark off columns and rows.
4. Prepare soil; use compost if possible.
5. Plant seeds or young plants according to instructions, making sure of growing time and expected harvest time.
6. Water as necessary.
7. Frequent care is needed to eliminate weeds and insects.

D. Result:

A rich harvest. Vegetables will grow under the careful care of the students.

E. Basic Facts and Supplemental Information:

1. Class can be divided into groups and each group can plot, plan, and plant a row. (Don't plan anything elaborate. Keep it simple.)
2. There are many excellent books about home gardens at nurseries and seed departments in garden supply stores.
3. This is an exciting activity and one that builds up extreme anticipation with time.

F. Thought Questions for Class Discussions:

1. What kinds of vegetables grow best in your locality?
2. What kinds of problems might you have in developing a vegetable garden?
3. How do soils vary in composition?
4. How can you protect your garden from insects?
5. Is your soil rich or does it need fertilization?

G. Related Ideas for Further Inquiry:

1. Study Section V-C, "Nutrition."
2. Study Section VI-B, "Conservation."
3. Experiment with vertical gardens on trellises and wire fences.
4. Study Activity III-A-1, "How do we classify living things?"
5. Study Activity III-A-2, "What are the main parts of a flower?"
6. Study Activity III-A-4, "What kinds of trees are found in our neighborhood?"

H. Vocabulary Builders—Spelling Words:

1) **vegetable** 2) **garden** 3) **stakes** 4) **seeds** 5) **fertilizer** 6) **plot** 7) **rows** 8) **columns** 9) **harvest** 10) **trowel** 11) **growing**

I. Thought for Today:

"There is no better demonstration of faith than a person planting seeds in a field."

Activity III A 6

A. Problem: *How Fast Do Bacteria Grow?*

Bacteria grow fast.

B. Materials Needed:

1. Fresh, green grass clippings
2. Two bushel baskets
3. Two tall thermometers
4. Old rags or newspapers
5. Reference materials on composting and bacteria

C. Procedure:

1. Study reference materials on composting.
2. Discuss composting.
3. Discuss bacteria.
   a. Formerly considered part of the plant kingdom.
   b. In the new five divisions of living matter, bacteria are classified as "Monera."
   c. The other "kingdoms" are:
      1) Protista
      2) Fungi
      3) Plants
      4) Animals
4. Fill one basket with old rags or crumpled newspaper.
5. Fill the second one with the fresh green grass clippings.
6. Place a long thermometer in each of the baskets.
7. Record the initial readings.
8. Let stand overnight and take second readings the following day.
9. Repeat procedure on the third day.

D. Results:

1. Both temperatures should read the same initially.
2. Usually on the second day the temperature in the "grass cuttings" basket will read several degrees higher.
3. On the third day this basket should show an increase of 10 to 20 degrees.

E. Basic Facts and Supplemental Information:

1. Fresh grass clippings will attract a lot of bacteria.
2. Bacteria begin acting on cuttings at once.
3. Bacteria will eat the grass and produce heat as they eat, grow, and multiply.
4. Bacteria act in a similar fashion with composts.
5. The "grass basket" will feel warm to the touch.
6. Compost piles have been known to produce enough heat to start a fire.
7. This rapid rise in temperature shows that bacteria do grow very fast.
8. Bacteria are nearly everywhere: they are in the food we eat, the water we drink, and the air we breathe.
9. They grow best in warm, damp, and dark environs.
10. There are thousands of different kinds of bacteria.
11. Some bacteria take nitrogen from the air and add it to the soil. Green plants can then use it.
12. Bacteria never die of old age. It may take about 20 minutes for them to mature and divide into two bacteria.

F. Thought Questions for Class Discussions:

1. How can farmers protect freshly cut hay from possibly raising its temperature high enough to burn?
2. Are bacteria good or bad?
3. What is acidophilus?

G. Related Ideas for Further Inquiry:

1. Study the five kingdoms of living organisms.
2. Ask a medical professional about bacteria caused diseases.
3. Study how bacteria reproduce (fission).
4. Study other Activities in this Section.
5. Study Activity V-D-2, "Why should we wash our hands frequently?"

H. Vocabulary Builders—Spelling Words:

1) **bacteria** 2) **monera** 3) **bushel** 4) **basket** 5) **thermometer** 6) **rags** 7) **newspapers** 8) **heat**

I. Thought for Today:

"Cultivate health instead of treating disease."

Section B: Seeds and Reproduction

Activity III B 1

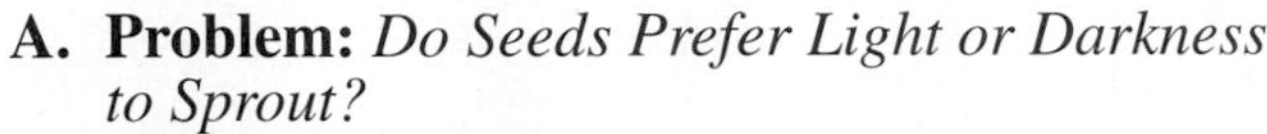

A. Problem: *Do Seeds Prefer Light or Darkness to Sprout?*

B. Materials Needed:

1. Two large water glasses
2. Two blotters or sponges
3. Lima bean seeds
4. Water
5. Dark paper bag or cover

C. Procedure:

1. Place one blotter or sponge in the bottom of each glass, curving along the sides as shown in the drawing.
2. Soak the lima bean seeds overnight. (Soaking helps them sprout faster.)
3. Place each lima bean seed at various intervals between the glass and the blotter or sponge.
4. Add just enough water in the glasses so the blotters or sponges will become moist.
5. Cover one glass with a dark paper bag. Let the other remain exposed to light.
6. Observe each glass daily.
7. Keep blotters or sponges moist continually by adding water as needed.

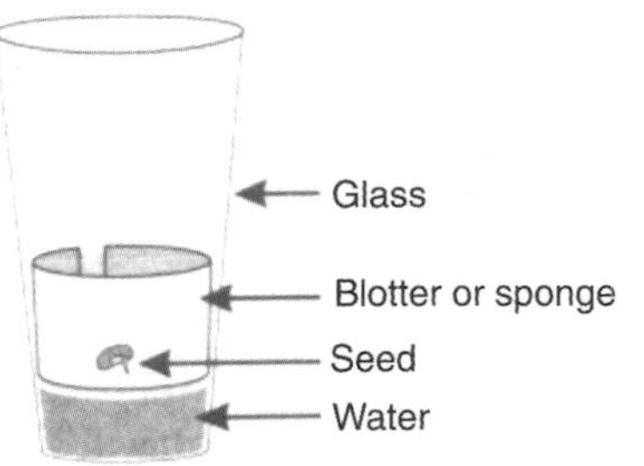

Plant a seed between glass and blotter or sponge — *Watch it grow*

In darkness

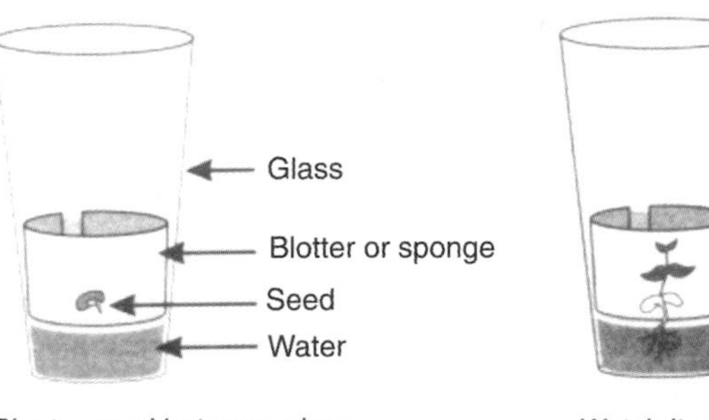

Plant a seed between glass and blotter or sponge — *Watch it grow*

In light

D. Results:

1. After several days the seeds will begin to sprout.
2. No difference in the sprouting times will be noted by the seeds in the glass which is covered and the one left exposed to light.

E. Basic Facts and Supplemental Information:

1. Seeds do not need light to sprout.
2. Light is needed for plant growth, not seed sprouting.
3. Most seeds sprout in the absence of light.

F. Thought Questions for Class Discussions:

1. What would happen if the blotters or sponges were not kept moist?
2. What would happen if the blotters or sponges and the seeds were kept under water?
3. Could other type seeds be tested in this manner?

G. Related Ideas for Further Inquiry:

1. Compute the germination rate of the seeds tested (percent of seeds that sprouted).
2. Test to see if seeds planted in soil would germinate faster than the ones in this experiment.
3. Test different types of soil for speediest germination rate.
4. Study Activity III-B-2, "How many different kinds of seeds can we collect?"
5. Study Activity III-C-3, "How do we test germination percentages of seeds?"

H. Vocabulary Builders—Spelling Words:

1) **lima beans** 2) **sprouting** 3) **moist**
4) **germination** 5) **intervals** 6) **sponges**

I. Thought for Today:

"The most important things in life are not things."

Activity

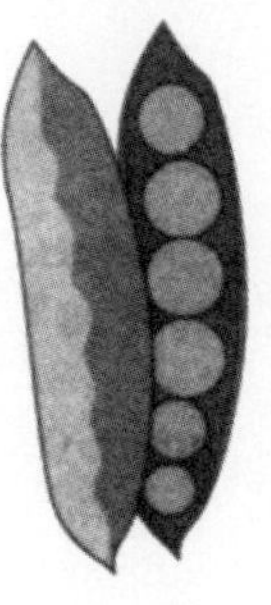
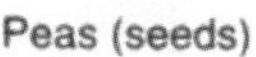
Peas (seeds)

Tomato seeds

Strawberry seeds

Seeds

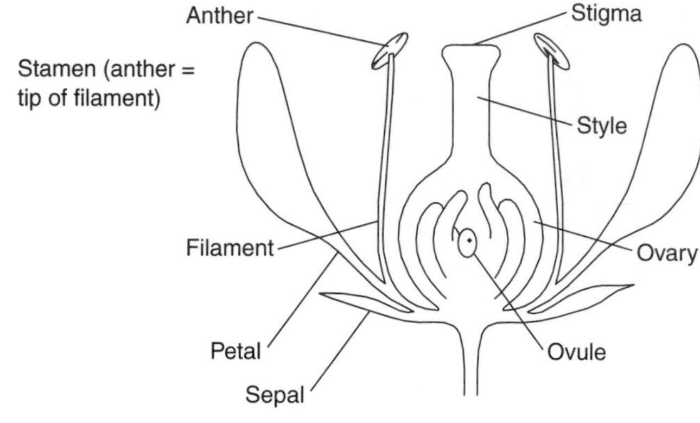

A flower

A. Problem: *How Many Different Kinds of Seeds Can We Collect?*

B. Materials Needed:

1. Pictures of flowers, fruits, and seeds
2. Books or printed materials for research of the above
3. Seeds that students bring to class
4. Magnifying glasses and/or microscope

C. Procedure:

1. Have students bring in seeds that they have found in their homes and neighborhood.
2. Collect and label the source of all the seeds. Labels should include seed type, date, and the name of the collector.
3. Students should study how seeds differ in size, color, shape, etc. This could be done individually or in groups.
4. Have students report their findings to the class.
5. Smaller seeds can be studied under a magnifying glass or microscope.

D. Results:

1. No pun intended—this will be a very fruitful activity.
2. Students enjoy collecting things.
3. They will become junior taxonomists.
4. They will realize the importance of plants as a necessity of life.

E. Basic Facts and Supplemental Information:

1. Flowers are reproductive organs by which plants reproduce their own kind.
2. Seeds are eggs.
3. Flowering plants (angiosperms) require eggs to be fertilized by sperm.
4. Plants produce spores.
5. Egg and sperm cells develop from the spores.
6. Most flowers contain four main parts: sepals, petals, stamen, and pistil.
7. The sepals are the outermost leaflike structures.
8. The petals are the "showy" part of the flower.
9. The stamen and the pistil are the reproductive parts of the flower.
10. The stamen is the next innermost part consisting of a long filament on which the anthers rest. It is next to the pistil.
11. The anthers produce pollen grains which become sperm cells.
12. The pistil is the centermost part of the flower. It is like a small stalk with an elongated lower part (the ovary) and a stigma which rests on top to catch the pollen grains.
13. Many flowers have numerous, complex parts.
14. The pollen reaches the ovule in many ways. Often it absorbs water, swells, and breaks and then works its way down to the ovule.
15. The ovule develops into seeds.
16. Within the seed is a miniature plant.

F. Thought Questions for Class Discussions:

1. In what ways can pollen be carried to other plants?
2. Have you ever seen seed dispersal in action?
3. Have you ever picked up seeds on your clothing?

G. Related Ideas for Further Inquiry:

1. Study Activity III-A-2, "What are the main parts of a flower?"
2. Study the factors that help the growth of plants.
3. What factors prevent a plant from developing?
4. Study the relationship of plants and animals.

H. Vocabulary Builders—Spelling Words:

1) **seeds** 2) **sepals** 3) **petals** 4) **stamens** 5) **pistils**

I. Thought for Today:

"Fear of the future is a great waste of the present."

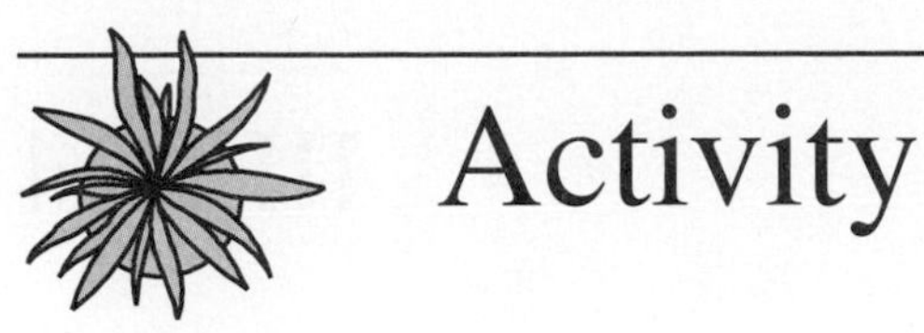

Activity III B 3

A. Problem: *What Conditions Lead to Mold Growth?*

B. Materials Needed:

1. Slice of bread
2. Water
3. Cellophane, or some other airtight covering
4. Magnifying glass
5. Pictures, drawing, or samples of mold on bread

C. Procedure:

1. Ask the students if they have ever seen any mold. Tell them what it looks like.
2. Discuss their experiences with the mold.
3. Mutually plan to test the various factors in mold development:
   a. Take two moist samples of bread. Seal one in cellophane; expose the other to air.
   b. Expose two more samples of bread, one in strong light, one in the dark.
   c. Expose two more samples of bread; keep one very dry, the other moderately moist.
   d. Expose two more samples of bread, one in a warm dark place, the other in a cold dark place such as a refrigerator.
   e. Examine the bread samples each day with a magnifying glass and record any changes in appearance.

D. Results:

1. Students will share their experiences with molds they have seen.
2. Students will help plan the means of determining mold growth.
3. Molds grow best in warm, dark, moist environments.
4. Molds will develop on some of the samples.

E. Basic Facts and Supplemental Information:

1. Molds are part of the classification of fungi.
2. Black mold is probably the best known example of fungi.
3. Sometimes the tests designed in Procedure above are slowed because of preservatives now added to bread and other foodstuffs.

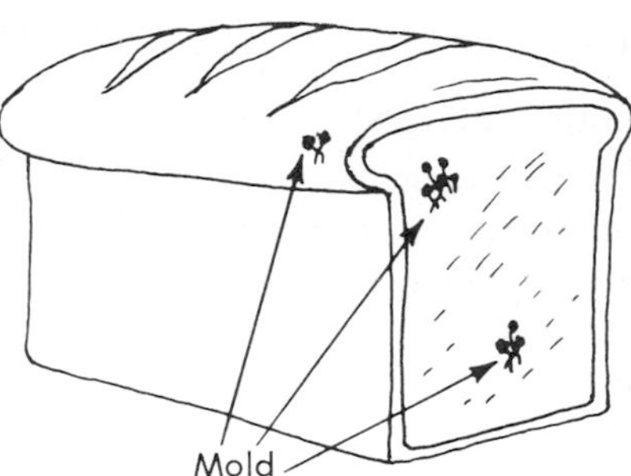

F. Thought Questions for Class Discussions:

1. Where and how should bread be stored to keep it free from molds?
2. What other foods do you think might develop molds if left exposed?
3. What methods do people use to preserve their foods?
4. Are all plants green?
5. How do mold seeds get on food? (Answer: They are airborne.)

G. Related Ideas for Further Inquiry:

1. Discuss other food products on which molds grow.
2. Discuss ways of preserving food.
3. Have students examine molds under a magnifying glass and then draw pictures of the molds.
4. Study Activity III-A-1, "How do we classify living things?"
5. Study Activity III-A-2, "What are the main parts of a flower?"
6. Study Activity III-A-3, "How do plants reproduce?"
7. Study Activity III-A-6, "How fast do bacteria grow?"
8. Study Activity III-D-3, "How does temperature affect growth?"

H. Vocabulary Builders—Spelling Words:

1) **molds** 2) **moist** 3) **samples** 4) **fungi** 5) **magnifying** 6) **dark** 7) **warm** 8) **conditions**

I. Thought for Today:

"A person who asks a question is a fool for five minutes. A person who does not, is a fool forever."

Activity III B 4

A. Problem: *What Is "Grafting"?*

B. Materials Needed:

1. Plant stock (main body)
2. Scions (cuttings or clippings)
3. Wedge (spreader)
4. Grafting wax
5. Hand clippers
6. Knife
7. Saw

C. Procedure:

1. Discuss with class various means of plant reproduction.
2. Tell the students that the one way that you are going to demonstrate plant reproduction is by grafting (attaching one kind of plant to another).
3. Cut off the top of the branch or trunk on which the grafting is to be done.
4. Split the branch or trunk down the center with a knife. (*Be careful.*)
5. Cut the scions from the desired buds with enough left over to make a wedge that will be inserted into the branch or trunk.
6. Shape the base of one scion with a knife to form a long narrow wedge. (*Be careful.*)
7. Repeat this process with a second scion. It's always better to insert two scions in each graft.
8. Insert the two scions into the outer edges of the main stock (cambrium layers). These are the growing sections of the stock.
9. Seal the slit in the stock and the top of the scion with grafting wax.
10. Observe its development.

Scions (cuttings)

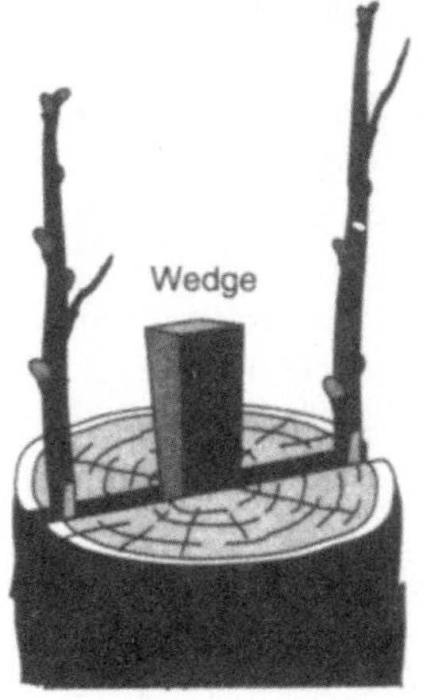

Match cambrium layers of each scion to the cambrium layer of branch or trunk.

Grafting wax covers all exposed areas.

D. Results:

1. Usually only one of the scions will grow. If both do grow, cut off the weaker one.
2. Students will learn another form of plant reproduction and growth.

E. Basic Facts and Supplemental Information:

1. There are many other types of grafting.
2. Other means of obtaining new plants are by dividing and layering.
3. It is a good idea to ask a nursery person the best time to graft for the particular plant you want.

F. Thought Questions for Class Discussions:

1. What are the advantages of grafting?
2. Can unrelated species be grafted? (No!)
3. Can animal parts be grafted? (Yes!)

G. Related Ideas for Further Inquiry:

1. Study all Activities in this Section.
2. Study Section III-C, "Soils and Germination."
3. Study Section III-D, "Growth."

H. Vocabulary Builders—Spelling Words:

1) **grafting** 2) **scion** 3) **knife** 4) **wedge** 5) **cambrium** 6) **stock** 7) **reproduction**

I. Thought for Today:

"Our national flower is the concrete cloverleaf."

SECTION C: SOILS AND GERMINATION

Activity III C 1

A. Problem: *What Can We Find in Our Soil?*

B. Materials Needed:

1. Trowel
2. Paper cups (6)
3. Newspapers
4. White typing paper
5. Magnifying glass
6. Marking pencil or pen
7. Old spoon
8. Microscope (optional)

C. Procedure:

1. Find six different places around the campus where the soil varies.
2. Have students collect paper cups full of soil by digging straight down for about 3 inches and putting the soil in the paper cups.
3. Label where the soil was found.
4. Bring the samples to the classroom.
5. Lay out six work stations.
6. Place a sheet of newspaper on each work station.
7. Place sheets of white typing paper on the newspaper.
8. Empty the soil on the white typing paper.
9. With the old spoon, separate the soil into its different parts.
10. Have students identify as many different materials as possible.
11. Use the magnifying glass for better identification.
12. Microscopic examination could also be conducted (optional).
13. Keep record of findings in a notebook.
14. Have each group report on its findings.

D. Results:

1. Students will become junior geologists.
2. They will learn that the soil contains many materials. Some of these might be:
   a. rocks, pebbles, stones
   b. soils (humus, clay, sand, loam)
   c. plant debris (leaves, stems, etc.)
   d. animal debris (skeletons, parts, etc.)
   e. live plants and animals

Six samples of soil

E. Basic Facts and Supplemental Information:

1. Plants need soil, water, and many minerals to fully develop.
2. The elements needed for plant growth are nitrogen, phosphorus, sulphur, potassium, iron, manganese, zinc, boron, calcium, magnesium, and molybdenum.
3. Soils vary depending on where the samples were taken.

F. Thought Questions for Class Discussions:

1. How did the soils differ?
2. Did you find any remnants of man-made products: paper, plastics, etc?
3. How do insects help the soil?

G. Related Topics and Activities:

1. Study photosynthesis.
2. Study plants that grow in different types of soil.
3. Study other Activities in this Part, "Plants."

H. Vocabulary Builders—Spelling Words:

1) **humus** 2) **loam** 3) **clay** 4) **debris** 5) **materials** 6) **mineral** 7) **magnifying**

I. Thought for Today:

"Freedom is the right of all people to be as happy as they can."

Activity III C 2

A. Problem: *Are Some Soils Better than Others for Holding Water?*

B. Materials Needed:

1. Five clay flowerpots, same size
2. Five glass jars big enough for flowerpots to be set in. (See drawing.)
3. Soils:
   a. Clay
   b. Silt
   c. Sand
   d. Loam
   e. Humus
4. Measuring cup
5. Water
6. Watch with second hand

C. Procedure:

1. Place each type of soil in a different flowerpot.
2. Place flowerpots in the glass jars.
3. Pour equal amounts of water into each flowerpot.
4. Observe the amount of water that runs off from each pot, the amount of dirt carried through with the water, and the length of time for the water to seep through.

D. Results:

1. With clay, little soil is washed off; it has little holding power.
2. With silt, a lot of soil is washed off; it has little holding power.
3. With sand, a lot of sand is lost; it has little holding power.
4. With loam, a lot of loam is lost; it has little holding power.
5. With humus, little soil is washed off; it is the best soil for holding water.

E. Basic Facts and Supplemental Information:

1. Soil with vegetation will hold water longer and tends to prevent erosion. Leaf matter and remains from trees hold water and becomes the best watershed materials.
2. The five test soils are:
   a. *Sand*—fine particles of disintegrated rock or seashells.

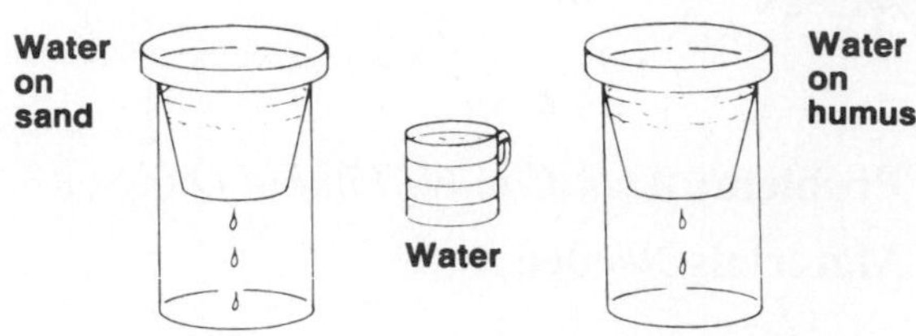

   b. *Humus*—remains of dried plants and animals.
   c. *Loam*—composition of gravel, sand, and clay.
   d. *Silt*—very fine soil and sand deposited by running streams and rivers.
   e. *Clay*—stiff, sticky kind of earth that can be molded.
3. The first eight inches of most farms' soils is called "topsoil." It takes about five hundred years to make one inch of topsoil. Modern farming practice is causing the loss of some topsoil.

F. Thought Questions for Class Discussions:

1. What is a watershed?
2. How important is watershed to us?
3. Can farmers with steep slopes on their farms change their soil type?

G. Related Ideas for Further Inquiry:

1. Study soil erosion and methods of prevention.
2. Study how farmers enrich or improve their soils.
3. See Section VII-C, "Earth's Crust."
4. Study Activity III-C-1, "What can we find in our soil?"
5. Study Activity III-C-3, "How do we test germination percentages of seeds?"
6. Study Activity III-C-4, "What is composting?"
7. Study Activity III-C-6, "How can we improve our soils?"
8. Study Activity III-E-6, "What is photosynthesis?"

H. Vocabulary Builders—Spelling Words:

1) **humus** 2) **loam** 3) **clay** 4) **silt** 5) **sand** 6) **water** 7) **rate** 8) **topsoil**

I. Thought for Today:

"A weed is a plant whose virtues are yet to be discovered."

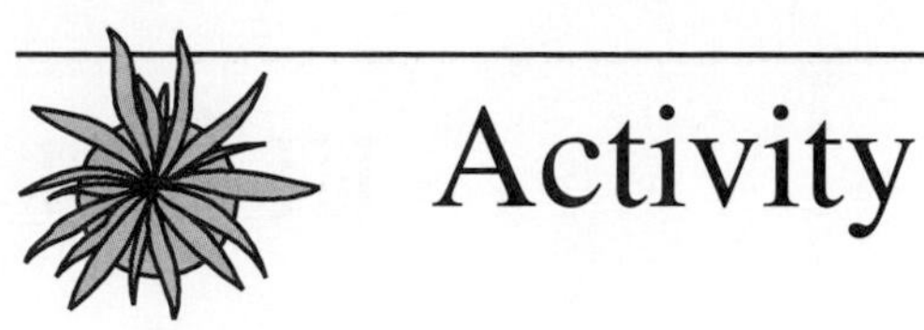

Activity III C 3

A. Problem: *How Do We Test Germination Percentages of Seeds?*

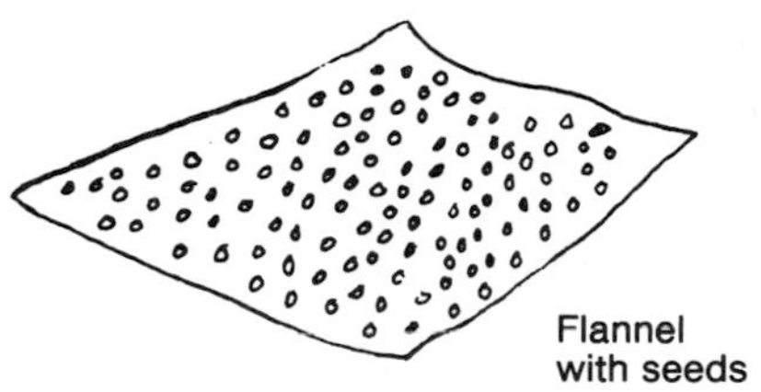

Flannel and seeds rolled

Procedure One

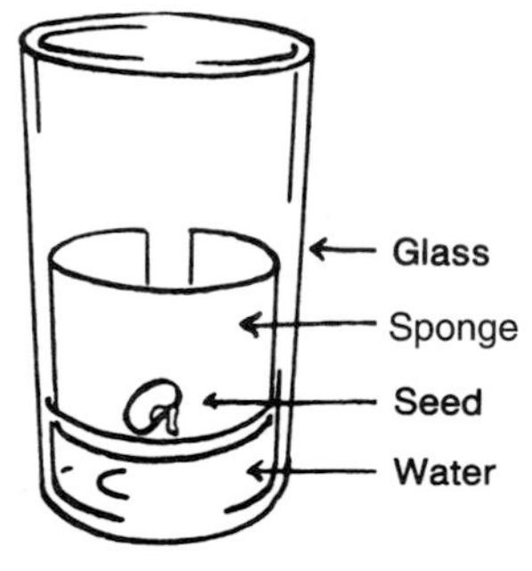

Plant a seed between glass and blotter.

Watch it grow.

Procedure Two

B. Materials Needed, Procedure One:

1. One square foot of cotton flannel
2. Radish seeds (50–100)
3. Pan of water

Materials Needed, Procedure Two:

1. Water glass or clear plastic tumbler
2. Sponge that will fit into container (See drawing.)
3. Lima bean seeds
4. Water

C. Procedure One:

1. Dampen flannel with water.
2. Place the radish seeds over the flannel.
3. Roll flannel into rather loose roll.
4. Place one end of roll in a pan of water.
5. Place this in an open window for 10 days, adding water as needed.
6. After 10 days unroll flannel and count the number of seeds that have sprouted and the number of seeds that have not.
7. Compute the percentage of seeds that have sprouted.

Procedure Two (Test for Larger Seeds):

1. Soak the lima beans in water overnight for easier germination.
2. Place the sponge on the inside of the container, curving it to fit the glass or tumbler.
3. Place the lima beans between the container and the sponge.
4. Water slightly until the sponge becomes moist and there is a little water on the bottom to ensure an adequate water supply.
5. Place in a lighted area.
6. Keep a supply of water on the bottom of glass or tumbler.
7. Observe daily.

D. Results:

1. In Procedure One, some of the seeds have sprouted, some have not.
2. In Procedure Two, the seeds will start to germinate.

E. Basic Facts and Supplemental Information:

The ratio of the seeds that have sprouted to the total number of seeds planted can be determined. By finding the ratio it can be determined how many seeds would sprout if actually planted. This would tell the condition of the seeds and their growth expectation. This could lead to a discussion of how farmers estimate the amount of seed to plant under various circumstances. Also, many seed distributors report in percent the guaranteed germination of seeds if planted before a given date.

F. Thought Questions for Class Discussions:

1. Do all seeds need to be fresh to germinate?
2. Do all seeds of similar age have the same germination potential?
3. Where do farmers get their seeds?

G. Related Ideas for Further Inquiry:

1. Test other kinds of seeds: radish, squash, apple, grapefruit, etc.
2. Study Section III-B, "Seeds and Reproduction."
3. Study the other Activities in this Section.

H. Vocabulary Builders—Spelling Words:

1) **germination** 2) **percentages** 3) **ratio**
4) **thermometer** 5) **radish** 6) **blotter** 7) **growth**

I. Thought for Today:

"The rooster that crows the loudest is the first to lose its head."

Activity III C 4

A. Problem: *What Is Composting?*

B. Materials Needed:

1. School lunch leftovers
2. Grass clippings
3. Old leaves
4. Other organic materials
5. Reference materials on composting, home gardening, etc.
6. Gardening tools (hoe, rake, shovel, etc.)

C. Procedure:

1. Locate an area on the school campus where the class might start a school vegetable garden.
2. Discuss the types of plants that the class would like to grow.
3. Discuss the soil where the school garden will be developed.
4. Enrich the soil with materials from a compost pile or compost bin:
   a. Place a layer of school lunch leftovers: bread, egg shells, apple cores, etc. down first.
   b. Over this place a layer of grass cuttings (school gardener might help with this).
   c. On top of these, place a layer of old leaves. (Earthworms decompose these to basic ingredients. Obtain worms after a good rain.)
   d. These three layers will provide a natural compost that will decay and furnish an excellent natural fertilizer.
5. Turn the soil over. It should be kept moist and crumbly.
6. Spread some compost over the garden area.
7. Mix this with the regular soil, raking it back and forth.
8. Plant the seeds that you have selected according to planting instructions.
9. Keep garden well-watered.
10. The garden should be kept free of weeds.

D. Results:

1. Students will learn how to develop a compost pile or make a compost in a bin.
2. Students will enjoy creating their own garden.

E. Basic Facts and Supplemental Information:

1. Stress and encourage natural procedures.
   a. Weeds can be kept in check by covering the planting area with straw, hay, or sawdust.
   b. Insects can be controlled by dusting the garden with ashes and ground limestone.
   c. Natural insect repellants include onion, cloves, garlic, and hot pepper. Any of these can be placed in hot water and then drained. The drained solution can be used as a spray.

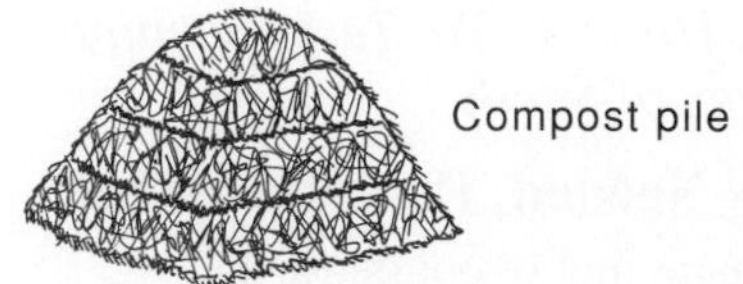

Compost pile

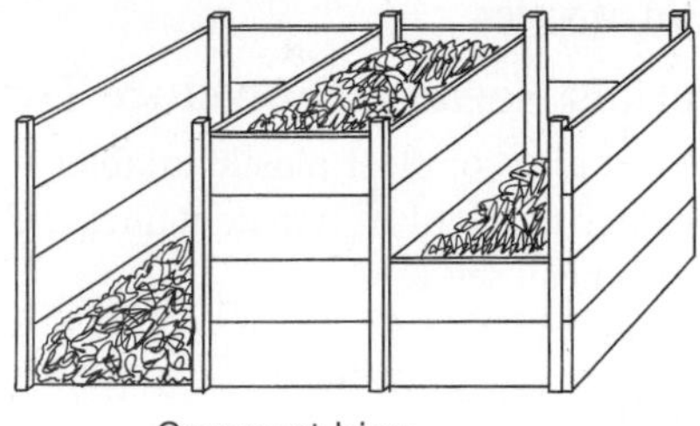

Compost bins

2. Composting is a means of returning a large amount of humus material to the soil that would be wasted otherwise.
3. Composting is the sandwiching of various levels of organic materials.
4. It is an excellent source of nitrogen, which is needed for all plant growth.
5. Do not place greasy materials in the compost pile or bin.
6. Keep compost pile moist.

F. Thought Questions for Class Discussions:

1. Is composting worth the time and trouble it takes?
2. Which is better, chemical fertilizers or compost materials?
3. Is there any environmental damage caused by composting? chemical fertilizers?

G. Related Ideas for Further Inquiry:

1. Study Section VI-D, "Pollution Solutions."
2. Study Section VII-C, "Earth's Crust."
3. Study Activity III-C-5, "How are our soils being changed?"
4. Study Activity III-C-6, "How can we improve our soils?"
5. Study Activity III-A-5, "Can we make a school vegetable garden?" (Best time is in the spring.)

H. Vocabulary Builders—Spelling Words:

1) **compost** 2) **humus** 3) **layers** 4) **moist** 5) **garden** 6) **clippings** 7) **leaves** 8) **grass**

I. Thought for Today:

"Gardens are not made by singing 'Oh how beautiful' and sitting in the shade."

Activity III C 5

A. Problem: *How Are Our Soils Being Changed?*

B. Materials Needed:

1. Simulated chemicals
2. Electric fan
3. Toy tractor
4. Box, cardboard (about 12″ × 20″)
5. Loose dirt
6. Sprinkling can
7. Water
8. Talcum powder

C. Procedure:

1. Fill the box with loose dirt and make dioramas to demonstrate how our soils are being changed. (Dioramas are three-dimensional scenes in a box.)
2. Demonstrate the specific ways that our soils are being modified by:
   a. wind (use the fan)
   b. rain (use sprinkling can)
   c. chemicals (use talcum powder)
   d. farming techniques, good and bad (use tractor)

D. Result:

Students will learn that soils are being continuously changed by nature and people.

E. Basic Facts and Supplemental Information:

1. Natural changes in our soils are occurring constantly (wind, rain, temperature changes, snow, ice, etc.)
2. People change soil conditions by:
   a. cutting down trees to make room for cities and roads
   b. adding chemicals
   c. tractoring
   d. crop rotation
   e. wastes
3. Soils are vital to our existence, and any loss or destruction of them could mean starvation for millions of people.

F. Thought Questions for Class Discussions:

1. Have people helped or hurt the soils?
2. Should we protect our soils and particularly our topsoils?
3. Will we have enough good soil to provide planting to feed future generations?

G. Related Ideas for Further Inquiry:

1. Study Section VI-A, "Ecosystems."
2. Study Section VI-B, "Conservation."
3. Study Section VII-C, "Earth's Crust."
4. Study Activity VI-B-1, "How can we conserve our soils and our lands?"
5. Study Activity VI-B-2, "How can we conserve our food sources?"
6. Study Activity VI-B-5, "How can we conserve our natural resources?"
7. Study Activity VI-C-10, "What is soil erosion?"
8. Study Activity VI-D-2, "What is 'sustainability'?"

H. Vocabulary Builders—Spelling Words:

1) **chemicals** 2) **pesticides** 3) **population**
4) **topsoil** 5) **generation** 6) **fertilizers**

I. Thought for Today:

"The thing most commonly raised on city land is taxes."

Activity III C 6

A. Problem: *How Can We Improve Our Soils?*

B. Materials Needed:

1. Models, pictures of soil erosion
2. Pictures of farming techniques
3. Books, pamphlets on soil composition
4. Research materials on gardening techniques
5. Research materials on soil conservation

C. Procedure:

1. Discuss the value of plants to all animal life.
2. Discuss the uses of plants to people.
3. Discuss the problems of soil erosion.
4. Look for statistics on soil loss. (We are gradually losing our topsoil.)
5. Have students research techniques that prevent soil erosion.
6. Have students research methods of enriching the soil.

D. Results:

1. Students will learn that our topsoil is being reduced by nature and people.
2. Students will learn that food supplies are going to become more and more critical as our population mushrooms and our agricultural lands decrease because of urban sprawl.
3. Students will realize that soil erosion can be retarded or stopped.
4. Students will learn that the remaining soils can be enriched through artificial fertilizers.

E. Basic Facts and Supplemental Information:

1. Soil is composed of weathered rocks which have become small particles and decayed particles of organic life.
2. Soils are continually being changed by physical and chemical processes, from weathering to animal activities, including the activities of people.
3. Winds, rains, and rivers move our soils.
4. Farmers can prevent some of this loss by:
   a. contour farming
   b. terracing
   c. wind breaks
   d. wattling process (prevents gulleying)
   e. crop rotation practices
5. Farmers can enrich their soils by:
   a. watering (dissolving materials)
   b. aerating

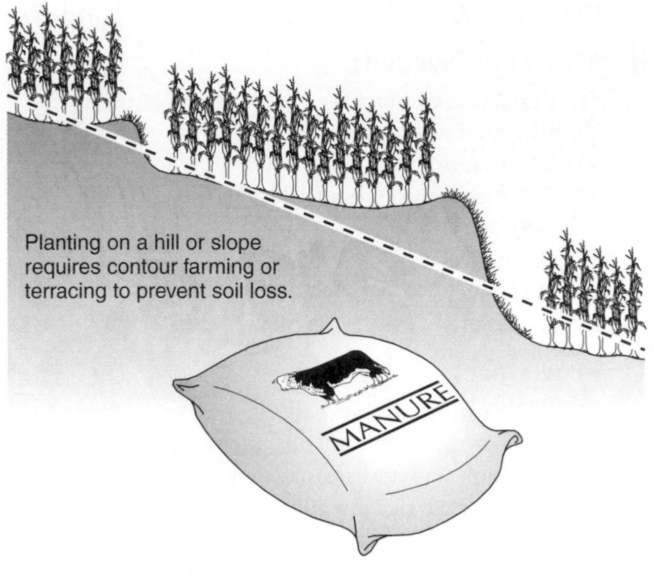

   c. adding fertilizers
   d. rotating crops
   e. using animal manure
   f. using cover crops (saves soil in off-seasons)
   g. utilizing land for best suited crops

F. Thought Questions for Class Discussions:

1. What are the main types of soils?
2. What are the main items found in agricultural soils?
3. Do all good soils contain water and air?

G. Related Ideas for Further Inquiry:

1. Study Activities in Part III, "Plants."
2. Study Activities in Part IV, "Animals."
3. Study Activities in Section VII-C, "Earth's Crust."
4. Study Section VI-C, "Pollution."
5. Study Activity III-C-1, "What can we find in our soil?"
6. Study Activity III-C-4, "What is composting?"
7. Study Activity III-C-5, "How are our soils being changed?"

H. Vocabulary Builders—Spelling Words:

1) **erosion** 2) **conservation** 3) **rotation** 4) **terracing** 5) **fertilizers** 6) **wattles**

I. Thought for Today:

"A gentleman farmer raises nothing but his hat."

Section D: Growth

Activity

III D 1

A. Problem: *How Can We Improve Crop Growth?*

B. Materials Needed:

1. Water
2. Commercial manure (samples)
3. Chemicals used in fertilizers (compounds containing ammonia, calcium, phosphorus, potassium)
4. Lime (helps acidity, nitrogen-fixation)
   a. Calcium carbonate—$CaCO_3$
   b. Calcium hydroxide—$Ca(OH)_2$
   c. Calcium oxide—CaO
5. Pictures of green plants that can be used in tillage: beans, vetches, lupines, legumes (peas, beans, clover, etc.)
6. Pictures showing methods of growing crops

C. Procedure:

1. Study local agricultural crops.
2. If possible, invite a local farmer to show how he/she aids plant growth.
3. If time permits, have the students develop a vegetable garden.
4. Study the problems of soils, fertilizers, soil erosion, pollution, etc.

D. Results:

1. Students will learn that farming is a scientific adventure and requires more than just planting seeds and harvesting.
2. Students will appreciate the food that they purchase at the markets.
3. Students will become aware of the efforts needed to produce the food for our expanding population.

E. Basic Facts and Supplemental Information:

1. The basic elements of plant food are nitrogen, phosphorus, and potassium.
2. When added to the soil, the calcium products release potassium.
3. Nitrogen is supplied by ammoniates derived from animal and plant sources.
4. Science has provided farmers with techniques for analyzing soils so that farmers can determine what their soils contain and what are the best additives for maximum production.
5. Early settlers in America moved to new virgin lands when soils became depleted and crops worsened. Today's farmers add the necessary chemicals to replenish those lost from prior crops.

Scientific farming includes:

Soil type
Moisture
Irrigation
Drainage
Lime
Organic matter
Manure
Tillage
Mulching
Chemicals
Weather
Seasons
Crop rotation
Disease Control

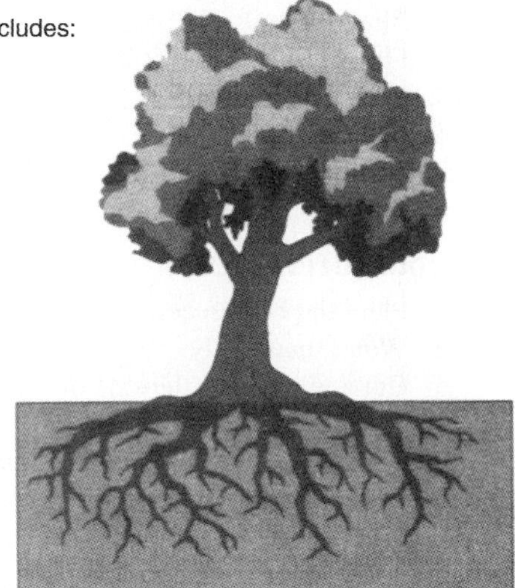

6. Too much or too little fertilizer can reduce soil fertility potential.
7. Most farming areas have representatives from the United States Department of Agriculture to help the farmer with soil testing.
8. The main considerations for maximum yield are:
   a. soil's organic matter
   b. soil type
   c. crop(s) desired
   d. water supply
   e. drainage/irrigation
   f. climate
   g. season
   h. potential diseases
   i. tillage

F. Thought Questions for Class Discussions:

1. Are we losing our topsoil?
2. Is food going to be a bigger and bigger concern as our population increases?
3. Where are most new houses, commercial buildings, highways, and industries built? on agricultural lands?

G. Related Ideas for Further Inquiry:

1. Study soil types.
2. Study weather conditions for various crops.
3. Study population trends in the United States and the world to determine future food requirements.

H. Vocabulary Builders—Spelling Words:

1) **fertilizers** 2) **mulching** 3) **phosphorus**
4) **nitrogen** 5) **potassium** 6) **ammonia**

I. Thought for Today:

"Americans have more food to eat than any other people on earth, and more diets to keep them from eating it."

Activity III D 2

A. Problem: *Do Plants Grow Toward Light?*

B. Materials Needed:

1. Bean seeds
2. Flowerpot or plastic cup
3. Soil, humus
4. Cardboard box
5. Knife
6. Water

C. Procedure:

1. Plant the bean seeds in flowerpot or plastic cup.
2. Water them daily.
3. Cut a window in the side of the box. (See drawing.)
4. After the seeds have sprouted and have grown 2 to 4 inches, place the pot in the light box. The light box should be completely closed except for the one window in the side.
5. The light box should be placed in a position to receive strong sunlight.
6. Observe daily.

D. Results:

1. The plant will grow toward the window.
2. The plant will continue to grow toward the window and the light.

E. Basic Facts and Supplemental Information:

1. When school plants are placed near windows they should be turned occasionally to prevent one-sided growth.
2. The tendency of plants to grow towards light is called "phototropism."
3. When moths are attracted to light, this too, is called "phototropism."
4. Light is essential to plants.
5. Plants use light in the process of photosynthesis.
6. The word "photosynthesis" means putting together by light.
7. Plants take carbon dioxide and water in the presence of sunlight and make glucose a simple sugar.
8. Plants use glucose to provide fuel for their cells.
9. Plants also give off oxygen in the process of photosynthesis.
10. The chemical equation for photosynthesis is:

$6\ CO_2 + 6\ H_20 \rightarrow C_6H_{12}0_6 + 6\ O_2$

Light box

F. Thought Questions for Class Discussions:

1. What would happen to the plant if the pot were rotated 180° after the first few weeks?
2. What would happen if the window in the box were sealed?
3. What would happen if colored cellophane were placed over the window?

G. Related Ideas for Further Inquiry:

1. Cut several holes at various places in the box. Open only one hole at a time until there is plant movement. Then close this hole and open another one.
2. Study Activity III-D-1, "How can we improve crop growth?"
3. Study Activity III-D-3, "How does temperature affect growth?"
4. Study Activity III-D-5, "Do plants give off carbon dioxide in darkness?"
5. Study Activity III-D-6, "How can plants be transplanted?"

H. Vocabulary Builders—Spelling Words:

1) **phototropism** 2) **humus** 3) **rotated** 4) **box** 5) **sprout** 6) **photosynthesis** 7) **flowerpot** 8) **plastic**

I. Thought for Today:

"Rivers and people get crooked by following the line of least resistance."

Activity III D 3

A. Problem: *How Does Temperature Affect Growth?*

B. Materials Needed:

1. Three young plants in separate flowerpots
2. Water
3. Soil, humus

C. Procedure:

1. Have students place one pot in a very cold place.
2. Have students place one pot in a moderately cool place.
3. Have students place the third pot in a warm place.
4. Label or classify these pots as cold, cool, and warm.
5. Pour enough water in each pot to keep the soil moist.
6. Keep other environmental factors equal.

D. Results:

1. After about one week, differences in sizes of plants will be noticed.
2. In the cold climate the plant will have shown very little growth and even signs of dying.
3. In the cool climate the plant will have shown some growth but not as much as in the warm climate.
4. In the warm climate, the young plant will have grown the most.

E. Basic Facts and Supplemental Information:

Plants grow differently in varying conditions. A thermometer can be used to record the temperature in each pot. Try to use water at the same temperature the plant is located to reduce variables.

F. Thought Questions for Class Discussions:

1. Will seeds germinate in a cold environment?
2. Do all plants thrive better in warm climates?
3. Do all animals thrive better in warm climates?

G. Related Ideas for Further Inquiry:

1. If possible, place another potted plant in a very hot place, such as next to a heater or heat register.
2. Check seeds for germination by varying temperature.
3. Study Activity III-D-1, "How can we improve crop growth?"
4. Study Activity III-D-2, "Do plants grow toward light?"
5. Study Activity III-D-6, "How can plants be transplanted?"
6. Study Activity III-D-8, "What are biological controls used to help plants?"

H. Vocabulary Builders—Spelling Words:

1) **temperature** 2) **growth** 3) **extremely** 4) **moderately** 5) **environment** 6) **warm** 7) **cool** 8) **cold** 9) **plants** 10) **climate**

I. Thought for Today:

"One sure way to lose ground is by slinging mud."

Activity III D 4

Fig. 1

Fig. 2

Fig. 3

Procedure One

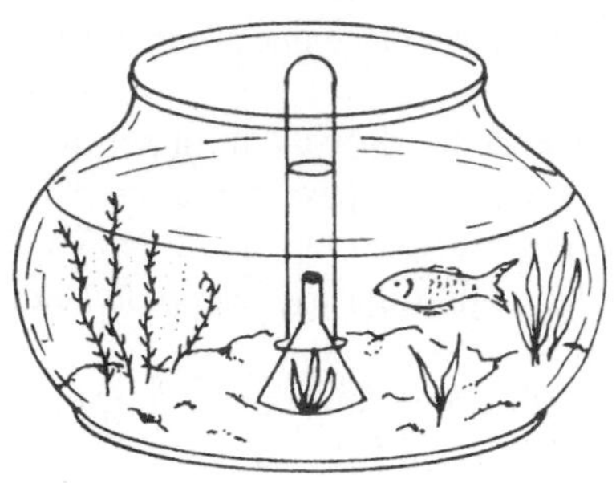
Fig. 4
Procedure Two

A. Problem: *Do Land Plants and/or Water Plants Give Off Oxygen?*

B. Materials Needed:

1. Two large glass jars
2. Live potted plants
3. Two candles
4. Matches
5. Aquarium with water plant
6. Several splinters of wood
7. Grease or wax
8. Glass funnel
9. Test tube

C. Procedure One (Land Plants):

1. Place a lighted candle in an inverted jar. It will soon go out, indicating that most of the oxygen has been chemically combined. (See Figure 1.)
2. To prove this, raise the jar and insert a glowing splinter. Notice that it will quickly go out.
3. Place a live, green plant in another inverted jar in a sunlit area. (See Figure 2.)
4. Place a lighted candle beside the plant.
5. When the candle goes out, put grease or wax around the mouth of the jar to keep air from seeping in. (See Figure 3.)
6. After 3 or 4 days, quickly insert the glowing end of a splinter to test for oxygen.

Procedure Two (Water Plants):

1. Place a glass funnel over the plants in the aquarium. (See Figure 4.)
2. Over the funnel put a test tube completely filled with water.
3. Wait until about one-third of the water has been displaced by gas in the tube. (See Figure 4.)
4. Burn the end of a splinter and then blow out the flame so that the end is still glowing.
5. Remove test tube carefully and insert the glowing end of the splinter into it quickly.

D. Results:

1. In Procedure One:
   a. In the first part, the candle will be extinguished.
   b. In the second part, the plant will generate new oxygen.
2. In Procedure Two:
   In the water plant test, oxygen will be generated. (See Figure 4.)
3. Both the land plant and the water plant gave off oxygen.

E. Basic Facts and Supplemental Information:

1. Glowing splinters will burst into flame in the presence of oxygen.
2. Since both splinters burst into flames, it is evident that both land and water plants give off oxygen.
3. All animals require oxygen for survival.

F. Thought Questions for Class Discussions:

1. Do plants give off oxygen at night when there is no sunshine?
2. Would the splinter burst into flame if the test tube contained air? carbon dioxide?
3. What special characteristics do plants have that live in water?

G. Related Ideas for Further Inquiry:

1. Study how plants reproduce in water.
2. Study Section I-B, "Air."
3. Study Activity III-D-1, "How can we improve crop growth?"
4. Study Activity III-D-2, "Do plants grow toward light?"
5. Study Activity III-D-5, "Do plants give off carbon dioxide in darkness?"
6. Study Activity III-D-8, "What are biological controls to help plants?"

H. Vocabulary Builders—Spelling Words:

1) **potted** 2) **wax** 3) **grease** 4) **test tube** 5) **inverted** 6) **flaming** 7) **splinter** 8) **burst**

I. Thought for Today:

"Never close your lips to those to whom you have opened your heart."

Activity

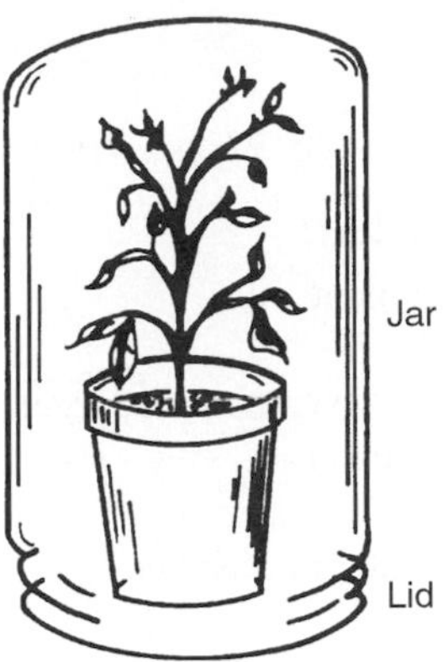

A. Problem: *Do Plants Give Off Carbon Dioxide in Darkness?*

B. Materials Needed:

1. Large canning jar (gallon size preferable) with lid
2. Potted plant (should almost touch top of jar)
3. Limewater
4. Cup
5. Lightproof cover for jar (tagboard or heavy cloth)

C. Procedure:

1. Place the potted plant under the large canning jar and allow it to remain in darkness for a day. (Cover it during daylight.)
2. Carefully remove the jar, and then quickly invert it. Pour limewater in the bottom of the container and replace the lid on it.
3. Shake well.

D. Result:

The limewater turns milky due to the presence of carbon dioxide.

E. Basic Facts and Supplemental Information:

Plants give off oxygen during the day and carbon dioxide when placed in darkness. These processes are called respiration. This process is necessary for the plants to use the food they have produced.

The simplified formula is:

sugar (food) + oxygen → carbon dioxide (to the air) + water + energy

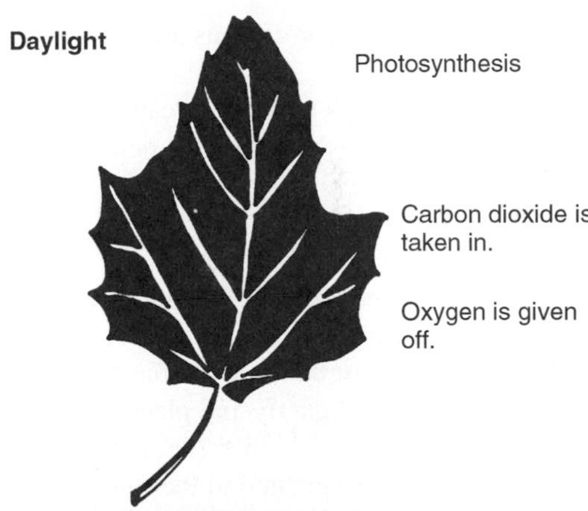

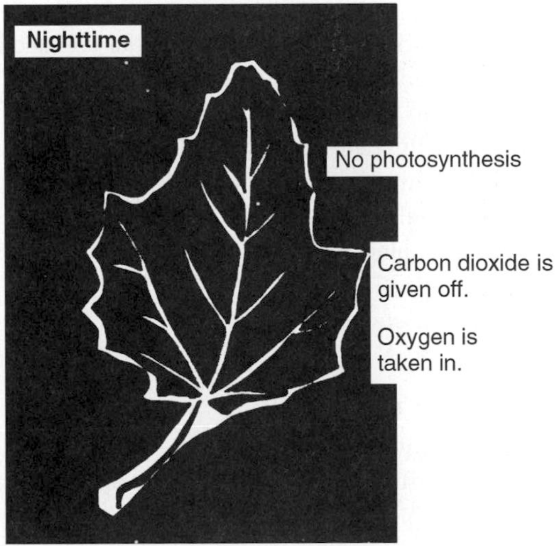

F. Thought Questions for Class Discussions:

1. Where does the carbon come from in carbon dioxide?
2. Do you know what solid carbon dioxide is?
3. Can you name any other gases by their chemical names?

G. Related Ideas for Further Inquiry:

1. Study Activity I-B-3, "How can we make carbon dioxide? How can we detect carbon dioxide?"
2. Study Activity III-D-2, "Do plants grow toward light?"
3. Study Activity III-D-4, "Do land plants and/or water plants give off oxygen?"

H. Vocabulary Builders—Spelling Words:

1) **respiration** 2) **carbon dioxide** 3) **oxygen**
4) **limewater** 5) **darkness** 6) **photosynthesis**

I. Thought for Today:

"Nature gave us two ends—one to sit on and one to think with. Man's success or failure is dependent on the one he uses most."

Activity III D 6

A. Problem: *How Can Plants Be Transplanted?*

B. Materials Needed:

1. Small potted plant
2. Potting soil
3. Suitable place on campus or larger indoor pot for transplanting plant
4. Trowel
5. Shovel (If outdoor transplant)
6. Water

C. Procedure:

1. Select a larger pot or campus area for transplanting.
2. Make a hole in the new pot or campus area that is about 1 1/2 times the depth and height of the old plant.
3. Fill the hole about one-third with the potting soil.
4. Slightly moisten the potting soil.
5. Soften or cut the edges of the plant's container so that the plant and the roots can be removed with a minimum of disturbance to the plant's root system.
6. Remove the plant gently and place it in the new spot, keeping the roots intact. Spread the roots gently as they are planted in their new place. Keep as much of the original soil around the plant as possible.
7. Make a mixture of about half regular soil and half potting soil to fill the hole.
8. Gently tap the new mixture around the plant firmly, filling any large air holes.
9. The level of the new ground should be the same as the original.
10. When the plant is firmly placed in the new spot, moisten gently.
11. If the new container is indoors, place it near sunlight.

D. Results:

1. The plant will be transplanted.
2. With careful handling and care the plant should take root in its new surroundings.

E. Basic Facts and Supplemental Information:

1. Most plants can be transplanted rather easily.
2. The best time to transplant is in the spring when the root system is the healthiest.
3. Do not overwater.

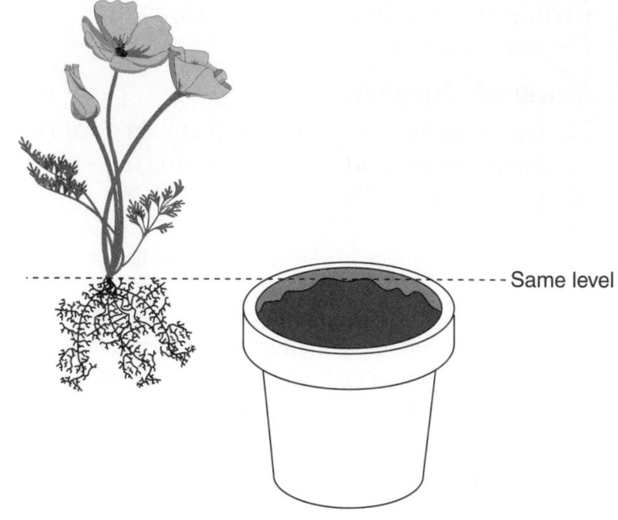

4. Many different kinds of plants can be transplanted:
   a. trees
   b. shrubs
   c. roses
   d. garden flowers
   e. houseplants
   f. vegetables
   g. fruits

F. Thought Questions for Class Discussions:

1. What season is the best for transplanting?
2. Can plants be overfertilized?
3. Can plants be overwatered?

G. Related Ideas for Further Inquiry:

1. Study Section III-B, "Seeds and Reproduction."
2. Study Section III-C, "Soils and Germination."
3. Study Activity III-D-1, "How can we improve crop growth?"
4. Study Activity III-D-2, "Do plants grow toward light?"
5. Study Activity III-D-4, "Do land plants and/or water plants give off oxygen?"

H. Vocabulary Builders—Spelling Words:

1) **transplant** 2) **flowers** 3) **trowel** 4) **shovel** 5) **potting** 6) **root system** 7) **moisture**

I. Thought for Today:

"Don't be envious of the grass that is greener on the other side of the fence. It is also harder to mow."

Activity

A. Problem: *How Do Clippings Grow into Plants?*

B. Materials Needed:

1. Water glass or jar
2. Aluminum foil
3. Rubber band or string
4. Knife
5. Pencil
6. House or garden plant(s)
7. Scissors

C. Procedure:

1. Have each student bring a water glass or jar to school.
2. Have each student prepare a clipping for testing.
3. Tell each student how to prepare a clipping.
   a. Select plant
   b. Cut off a young, healthy, leafy stem about 6–10 inches long near the top of the plant.
   c. Trim off the leaves from the bottom half only. (It's always a good idea to have extra clippings on hand. The school gardener could probably supply these.)
4. Fill the glass or jar with water to about one-half inch from the top.
5. Place the aluminum foil over the top of the glass or jar.
6. Cut the foil in a large circle so that there will be enough to fold down over the edge of the glass or jar.
7. Fold the foil down over the edge.
8. Secure with the rubber band or string.
9. With closed scissors, punch two or three holes in the top of the foil.
10. Place each cutting in one of the holes.
11. Place each cutting that is in a glass or jar in the classroom where there is sunlight and ventilation.
12. Observe daily for possible changes.

D. Results:

1. The clippings will begin to sprout new leaves.
2. The old leaves will begin to enlarge.

E. Basic Facts and Supplemental Information:

1. Many plants can be started in this manner.
2. Containers with rich soil should be ready so that clippings can be planted after they have sprouted.
3. Gardeners often use clippings or cuttings in their work.
4. Many plants may be propagated from stem cuttings. Some common ones are:
   a. roses
   b. chrysanthemums
   c. dracaenas
   d. philodendrons
   e. hydrangeas

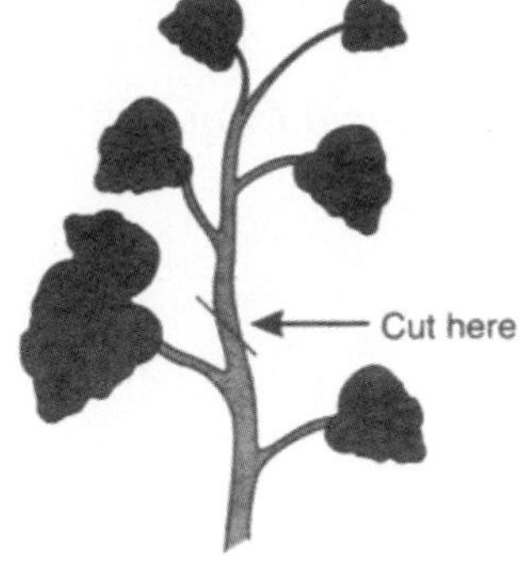

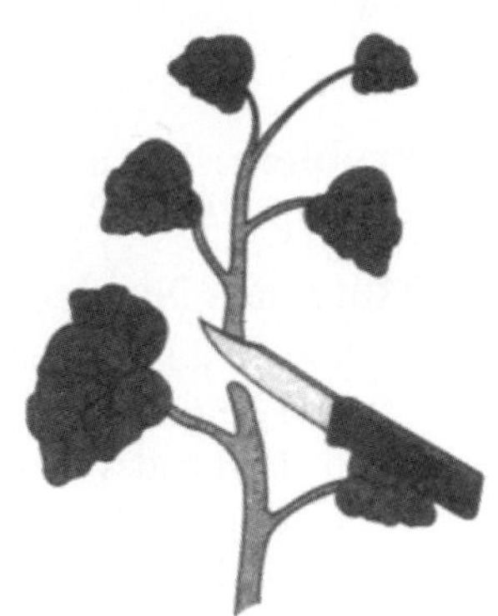

Cut at a 45° angle below the node

Place clipping in water

Watch it grow

F. Thought Questions for Class Discussions:

1. What would happen if the air hole(s) were covered?
2. What would happen if the cutting was kept out of sunlight?
3. What would happen if you left the cutting in the water for a long period of time?

G. Related Ideas for Further Inquiry:

1. Check with the school gardener and/or local nursery people for plants in your community that would be best suited for this Activity.
2. Study Activity III-D-1, "How can we improve crop growth?"

H. Vocabulary Builders—Spelling Words:

1) **cuttings** 2) **clippings** 3) **aluminum** 4) **trimming** 5) **scissors** 6) **plantings**

I. Thought for Today:

"Wise sayings often fall on barren ground, but a kind word is never thrown away."

Activity III D 8

A. Problem: *What Are "Biological Controls" to Help Plants?*

B. Materials Needed:

1. Reference materials on:
   a. Pesticides
   b. Herbicides
   c. Insecticides
   d. Biological controls
2. Specimens or pictures of plant damage in your local community

C. Procedure:

1. Interview farmers, local nursery people, and parents about local plant damage.
2. Collect information from the public media regarding plant pests.
3. Study the reference materials cited above.

D. Results:

1. Students will learn that pests cause substantial damage to plants, particularly to food crops.
2. Students will learn that there are many types of controls for pests:
   a. chemical—spraying with DDT, DDE
   b. biological—using natural preys on insects
   c. physical—covering plants
   d. cultural—moral and ethical choices involving plants and their controls
   e. quarantines

E. Basic Facts and Supplemental Information:

1. Chemical controls of insects and other animals usually prove hazardous to the environment and our health.
2. Biological controls use natural enemies of the pests rather than harsh and hazardous chemicals.
3. Ladybug beetles have been used in the control of aphids on orange groves.
4. Wasps have been used successfully in the decimation of gypsy moth caterpillars.
5. Pheromones, which have powerful scents, have been used against the cabbage worm, alfalfa caterpillar, grubs of Japanese beetles, etc.
6. Some large animals have been directly harmful to people: lions, tigers, bears, poisonous snakes, etc.
7. Some smaller organisms are major nuisances to people: fleas, ticks, flies, algae, earwigs, etc.

8. Farmers have to make choices as to what kind(s) of insect controls to use. These decisions are based on:
   a. costs
   b. effectiveness
   c. reaction to the crops
   d. reaction to the environment, short-range and long-range
9. The United States is producing over 300 million pounds of herbicides and 25 million pounds of insecticides, fungicides, and fumigants every year. There are great concerns over these as health hazards.
10. Methyl bromide, a pesticide, is not only damaging to insects and harmful to people, it is 50 times more damaging to our ozone layer than CFC's (chloroflurocarbons).

F. Thought Questions for Class Discussions:

1. Where do the chemicals end up that are used in insecticides and fertilizers?
2. Do chemicals do more harm than good?
3. Are people pests to some organisms?

G. Related Ideas for Further Inquiry:

1. Study Section IV-C, "Insects and Spiders."
2. Study Section VI-D, "Pollution Solutions."
3. Study Activity III-D-1, "How can we improve crop growth?"
4. Study Activity III-D-6, "How can plants be transplanted?"

H. Vocabulary Builders—Spelling Words:

1) **biological** 2) **controls** 3) **pesticides** 4) **insecticides** 5) **herbicides** 6) **specimens**

I. Thought for Today:

"A weed is a plant whose virtues are yet to be discovered."

Section E: Roots, Stems, and Leaves

Activity III E 1

A. Problem: *How Do Roots Absorb Water?*

B. Materials Needed:

1. Water glass
2. Water
3. Molasses or syrup
4. Large raw carrot
5. Glass tube
6. One-hole stopper
7. Apple corer
8. Wax (or paraffin)
9. Three toothpicks

C. Procedure:

1. Remove the top of the carrot.
2. With apple corer, cut hole down from the top of the carrot about three-fourths of its length and about one-half its diameter (to fit the one-hole stopper).
3. Fill the hole almost to the top, allowing for the stopper, with syrup or molasses. This becomes food which would normally come from the roots.
4. Insert the long glass tube through the one-hole stopper by first wetting the stopper and then rotating the glass tube back and forth; apply gentle pressure on the tube at the point of insertion.
5. Insert the tube and stopper in the carrot. (See drawing.)
6. Carefully seal the rubber stopper in the carrot by using melted wax or paraffin around the rim.
7. Place the carrot in a glass of water with the water covering about three-quarters of the carrot.
8. Insert three toothpicks in the carrot to support it. (See drawing.)
9. Observe the results daily.

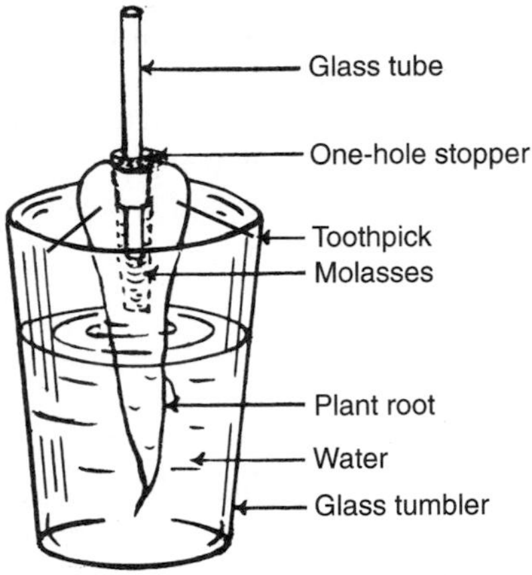

D. Result:

Over a period of several hours to a few days the water from outside the root (see drawing) will be absorbed (by osmosis) by the root and will cause the liquid to move up the tube.

E. Basic Facts and Supplemental Information:

1. There are many ways of setting up a demonstration of root absorption of water (osmosis). We are interested in learning about osmosis in plant roots because our food crops depend on it.
2. Osmosis is the diffusion (movement) of a solvent through a partially permeable membrane that tends to equalize the concentrations of the solutions on either side of the membrane. In this Activity the molasses or syrup is "heavily concentrated" and there is little or no concentration of the molasses or syrup in the glass tube.
3. Turnips work equally well in this Activity. The one precaution in this Activity is to make sure the stopper is sealed tight; otherwise, the liquid will not rise in the tube.

F. Thought Questions for Class Discussions:

1. Do our bodies use osmosis?
2. Do other liquids have the same kind of action?
3. What would happen if the top of this capillary tube were sealed?

G. Related Ideas for Further Inquiry:

1. Study Section I-C, "Water."
2. Study Activity III-E-2, "In which direction do roots grow?"
3. Study Activity III-F-2, "How can we make a carrot basket?"
4. Study Activity I-C-5, "What is 'capillarity'?"

H. Vocabulary Builders—Spelling Words:

1) **molasses** 2) **syrup** 3) **corer** 4) **wax** 5) **paraffin** 6) **osmosis** 7) **movement** 8) **concentration**

I. Thought for Today:

"What kind of roots does a mathematical plant have?" (Square roots)

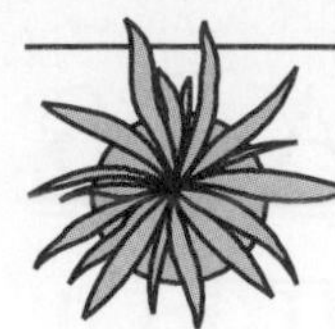

Activity III E 2

A. Problem: *In Which Direction Do Roots Grow?*

B. Materials Needed:

1. Small rectangular glass or clear plastic container
2. Small, young plant
3. Piece of cardboard large enough for one horizontal side of container (See drawing.)
4. A second piece of cardboard to cover top of container if soil is loose
5. Potting soil or humus
6. Water
7. Tape

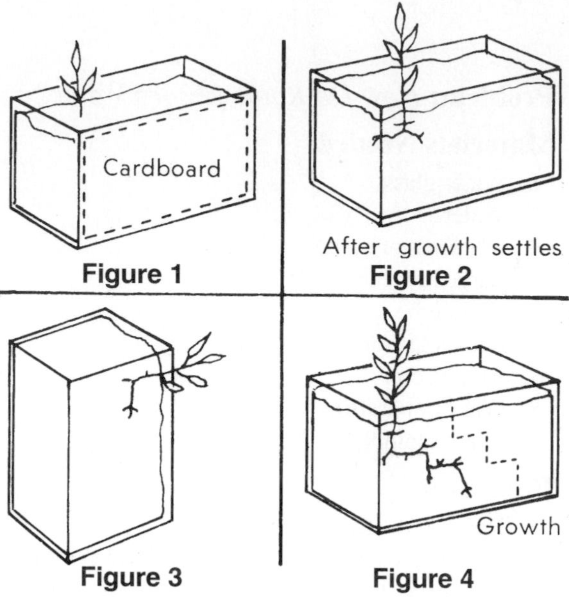

Figure 1
Figure 2
Figure 3
Figure 4

C. Procedure:

1. Fill container with potting soil or moist humus.
2. Place plant in soil close to one side of the container. (See Figure 1.)
3. Tape the cardboard to the outside of the container to protect roots from light.
4. After four days turn container on its side using another piece of cardboard if necessary to keep soil from falling out of container. (See Figure 3.)
5. After four more days turn container right side up. (See Figure 4.)
6. More advanced students might want to experiment with turning the box on its side and even upside down.
7. Movements may be repeated as many times as necessary.
8. Remove cardboard and observe at each turning.
9. Replace cardboard after each observation.

D. Result:

The roots will grow downward regardless of the position of the container or plant.

E. Basic Facts and Supplemental Information:

1. The course of growth for all roots, regardless of the position of the plant, is generally downward.
2. The direction of the main root is the one of primary concern. Many smaller root fibers often travel away and in all directions from the main root.
3. The predisposition of roots to always travel downward is called "geotropism" or "gravitropism."

F. Thought Questions for Class Discussions:

1. What would happen to root growth if rocks were placed in its path?
2. What would happen to root paths if after several turnings of container the cardboards were left off?
3. Do all plant roots follow the same general path?

G. Related Ideas for Further Inquiry:

1. Study the growth of roots on hillsides. In which direction do they grow?
2. Study Activity III-E-1, "How do roots absorb water?"
3. Study Activity III-E-4, "How does water move in stems?"
4. Study Activity III-E-6, "What is photosynthesis?"
5. Study Activity III-C-2, "Are some soils better than others for holding water?"
6. Study Section VII-D, "Gravity."

H. Vocabulary Builders—Spelling Words:

1) **geotropism** 2) **gravitropism** 3) **container** 4) **soil** 5) **roots** 6) **cardboard** 7) **downward** 8) **humus** 9) **repeat** 10) **rectangular**

I. Thought for Today:

"Saying it with flowers doesn't mean throwing bouquets at yourself."

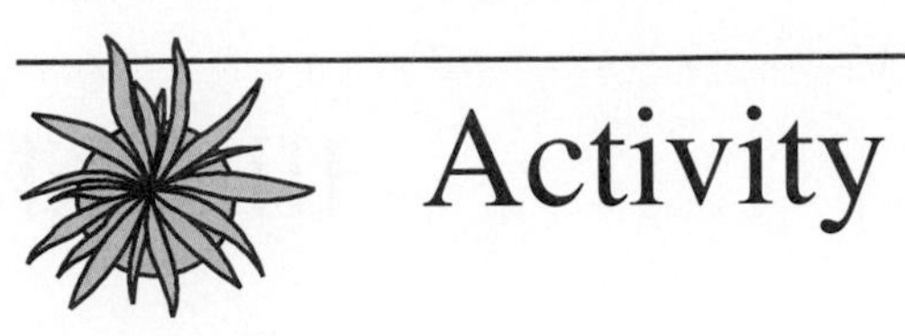

Activity III E 3

A. Problem: *How Do Stems of Plants Differ?*

B. Materials Needed:

Pictures or specimens of:

1. Tree stem (horizontal cut)
2. Celery stalk
3. Weed stem
4. Flower stalk

C. Procedure:

1. Show the different kinds of stems.
   a. Woody
      1) hard
      2) tall
      3) evergreens
      4) have bark
   b. Herbaceous
      1) soft
      2) green
      3) clumps
2. Discuss the two major types of stems.
3. Discuss the functions of stems:
   a. support
   b. if green, make food
   c. transportation system for food and water
   d. storage for food and water
4. Study stem growth in plants around the school campus and classroom.
5. Study the different kinds of seeds.
6. If time permits, make soil boxes to plant seeds and study developing stems.

D. Results:

1. Plants will grow.
2. Most stem growth occurs near the tip.

E. Basic Facts and Supplemental Information:

1. Stems grow in rings from inside to out.
2. Large plants show green colors of rings in spring, and brown during summer.
3. Older students can study more in detail about the xylem (pronounced "zi-lem") and phloem (pronounced "flome").
4. Stems conduct food from the leaves to the roots.

F. Thought Questions for Class Discussions:

1. Which foods do we eat that are basically the stems of plants?
2. What are some uses of plant bark?
3. From what part of the plants do natural ropes come?
4. From what part of plants do we get our lumber?

G. Related Ideas for Further Inquiry:

1. Examine different types of lumber.
2. Cut a piece of celery horizontally and observe the vascular tubes (small vertical cylinders).
3. Study all Activities in this Section.

H. Vocabulary Builders—Spelling Words:

1) **woody** 2) **herbaceous** 3) **bark** 4) **xylem** 5) **phloem** 6) **stem** 7) **stalk** 8) **transportation**

I. Thought for Today:

"All parents believe in heredity until their children start bringing home report cards."

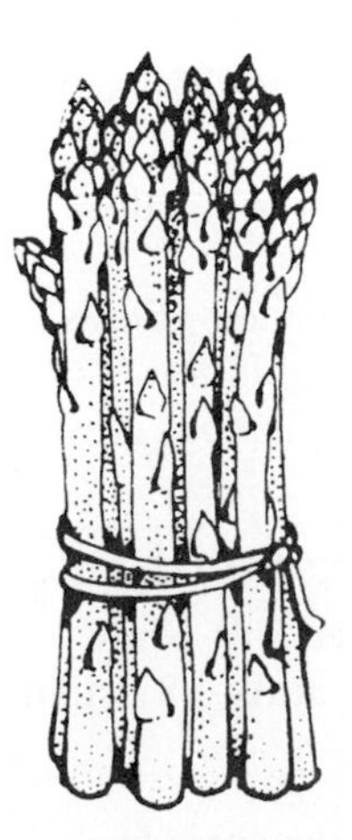

Asparagus

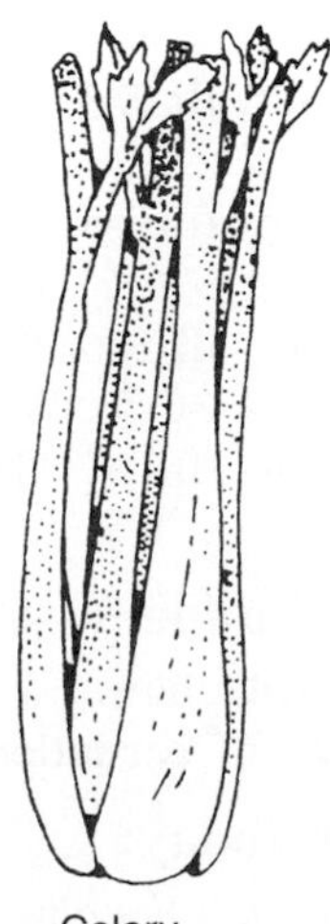

Celery

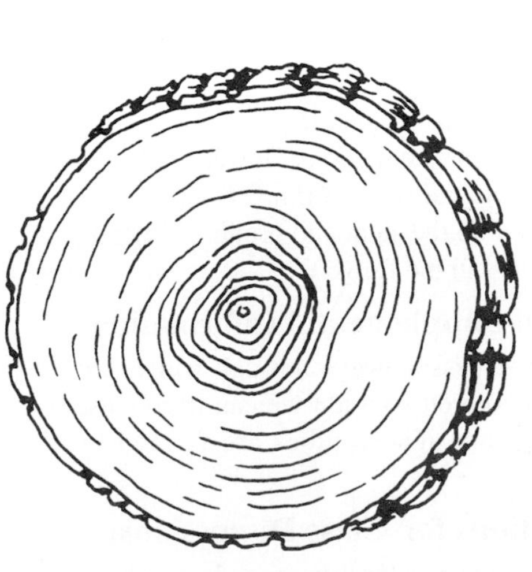

Tree rings (annual)

Corn stalk

Activity III E 4

A. Problem: *How Does Water Move in Stems?*

B. Materials Needed, Procedure One:

1. Carrots, celery, or flowers
2. Calla lilies or white carnations
3. Ink or food coloring
4. Tall water glass or clear plastic container
5. Eyedropper
6. Water

Materials Needed, Procedure Two:

1. Three tall water glasses or clear plastic containers
2. Calla lily or white carnation
3. Water
4. Three different colors of ink or food coloring

C. Procedure One:

1. Fill glass two-thirds full of water.
2. Color water with ink or food coloring.
3. Let carrot, celery, or flower stand in solution for one hour.
4. Remove and make crosscuts to show colored streaks.
5. Leave some calla lilies or white carnations in colored liquid for several hours and note results.

Procedure Two:

1. Split the stem of a calla lily or white carnation in three parts. (See drawing.)
2. Fill the liquid containers about two-thirds full of water.
3. Add different color food coloring to each container.
4. Place one of the cut stalks in each of the containers.

D. Results:

1. In Procedure One, the colored fluid travels upward, coloring the stem and/or flower.
2. In Procedure Two, the colored fluids from all containers travel up the stem and produce a blend of all three colors in the flower.

E. Basic Facts and Supplemental Information:

Plants have well-defined passageways through which liquids travel. By using a colored solution we can trace these channels through the plant. These tubes are formed by xylem cells in the plants.

F. Thought Questions for Class Discussions:

1. Do tall trees get their water through xylem cells?
2. What functions do you think the stems and stalks have other than transporting water?

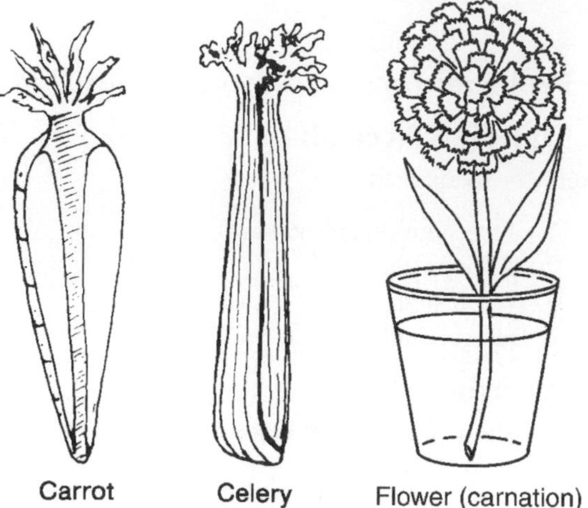

3. What happens to plants during dry seasons and/or summertime?

G. Related Ideas for Further Inquiry:

1. Study Activity III-E-1, "How do roots absorb water?"
2. Study Activity III-E-3, "How do stems of plants differ?"
3. Study Activity III-E-5, "Do stems always grow upward?"
4. Study Activity III-E-6, "What is photosynthesis?"
5. Study Activity I-C-5, "What is 'capillarity'?"
6. Study Activity III-D-7, "How do clippings grow into plants?"

H. Vocabulary Builders—Spelling Words:

1) **xylem** 2) **calla lilies** 3) **colored** 4) **knife** 5) **eyedropper** 6) **carnations** 7) **stalk** 8) **stem**

I. Thought for Today:

"Facility of speech is not always accompanied by fertility of thought."

A. Problem: *Do Stems Always Grow Upward?*

B. Materials Needed:

1. Six small flowerpots
2. Six plant cuttings (lima beans, geraniums, ivy, etc. all work well)
3. Rich, humus soil
4. Water
5. Fine mesh wire screen
6. String to secure wire screen

C. Procedure:

1. Study plants in general.
2. Discuss the function of plant leaves.
3. Ask which direction plant leaves grow.
4. Tell class that you are going to try to fool the plant.
5. Plant your cuttings in all of the flowerpots.
6. Water carefully.
7. Set the flowerpots in an upright position.
8. Place in area of the classroom where they will receive some sunlight.
9. When plants are firmly established (usually takes 4 to 7 days) lay four of the flowerpots on their sides, leaving two in their original upright position.
10. After another equal period of time, place fine wire screen over two of the cuttings that were laying on their sides and invert them so that they will be facing downward. (See drawing.)
11. Observe for several weeks.
12. Discuss the results of these tests.

D. Results:

1. The two cuttings that remained in an upright position will have stems that grow upward.
2. The two cuttings that were rotated and left on their side started to grow sideways, but after they remained in a horizontal position, the stems started to grow upward again.
3. The two cuttings that were rotated on their sides and then turned upside down had their stems grow upward on both occasions.

E. Basic Facts and Supplemental Information:

1. This attribute of stems always seeking to grow upward is called "phototropism."
2. This means that plants grow toward light.
3. Roots have the opposite tendency. They always seek to grow downward. This attribute is called "geotropism."
4. This means that roots tend to grow toward the center of the Earth, and stems tend to grow away from the center, toward light.

Two flowerpots remain upright.

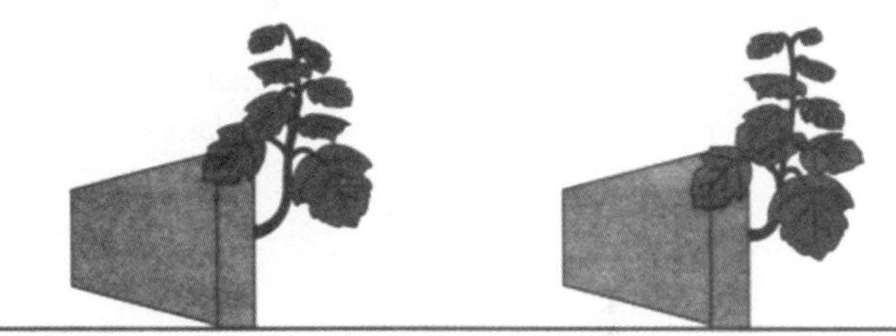

Two flowerpots are rotated once 90°.

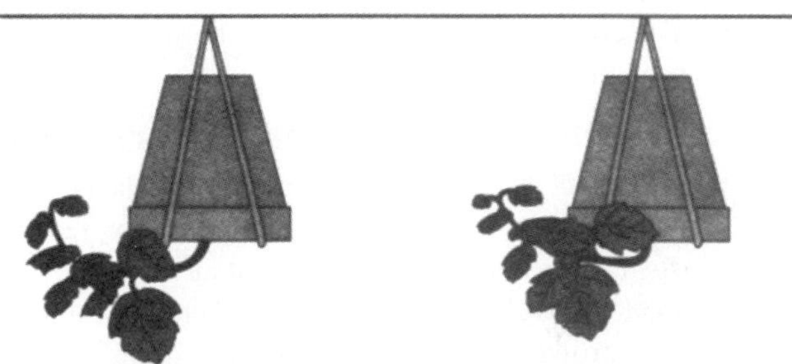

Two flowerpots are rotated twice.

F. Thought Questions for Class Discussions:

1. What factors affect plant growth?
2. Do plants have the same needs as animals?
3. How do leaves vary in different plants?

G. Related Ideas for Further Inquiry:

1. Study all Activities in this Section III-E "Roots, Stems, and Leaves."
2. Study also Activities in Section III-D, "Growth."
3. Study also Activities in Section III-F, "Fun with Plants."

H. Vocabulary Builders—Spelling Words:

1) **phototropism** 2) **geotropism** 3) **rotation** 4) **humus** 5) **loam** 6) **screen** 7) **upward**

I. Thought for Today:

"All the flowers of all the tomorrows are in the seeds of today."

Activity III E 6

A. Problem: *What Is Photosynthesis?*

B. Materials Needed:

1. Two flowerpots, plastic cups or cans filled with soil (humus)
2. Bean seeds
3. Opaque paper bag or dark area

C. Procedure:

1. Soak bean seeds overnight to speed germination.
2. Plant seeds and allow plants to break through the soil. This may take one to two weeks.
3. If you don't want to take time to plant seeds, obtain two plants of similar physical condition.
4. Cover one other pot with a paper bag or place in a dark area. (Figure 1.)
5. Keep one pot in direct sunlight. (Figure 2.)

Figure 1

Figure 2

D. Results:

1. The plant which has received sunlight will be hearty and green.
2. The covered or shaded plant will be stunted in growth and light in color.

E. Basic Facts and Supplemental Information:

1. Photosynthesis is the process whereby plants convert water and carbon dioxide in the presence of sunlight to plant food. Without any of these three factors, plants cannot manufacture food for their growth and development. The simplified formula for photosynthesis is:

   Carbon dioxide + water + sunlight (produces) (yields) sugar (food) + oxygen

   This is usually stated, "Carbon dioxide and water in the presence of sunlight produces sugar (food) and oxygen."
2. The sunlight provides the energy for this reaction to take place.
3. The sugar produced is glucose.

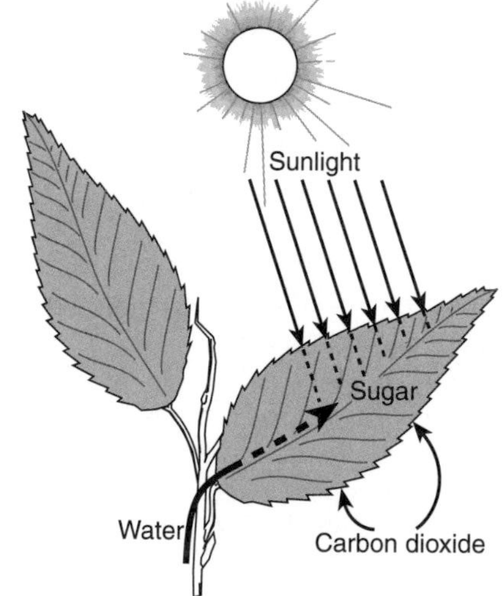

Figure 3

F. Thought Questions for Class Discussions:

1. What would happen if the paper bag were switched in the middle of the test period?
2. What would happen if a heavy, clear cellophane bag were placed over one plant instead of an opaque paper bag?
3. Is there any difference during the first few days when both plants break through the soil?

G. Related Ideas for Further Inquiry:

1. Repeat test, only expose to electric lights instead of sunlight.
2. Study Activity III-D-2, "Do plants grow toward light?"
3. Study Activity III-D-5, "Do plants give off carbon dioxide in darkness?"
4. Study Activity III-E-4, "How does water move in stems?"
5. Study Activity III-E-5, "Do stems always grow upward?"

H. Vocabulary Builders—Spelling Words:

1) **photosynthesis** 2) **sunlight** 3) **carbon dioxide** 4) **oxygen** 5) **sugar** 6) **presence** 7) **produces**

I. Thought for Today:

"When your work speaks for itself, don't interrupt."

SECTION F: FUN WITH PLANTS

Activity

III F 1

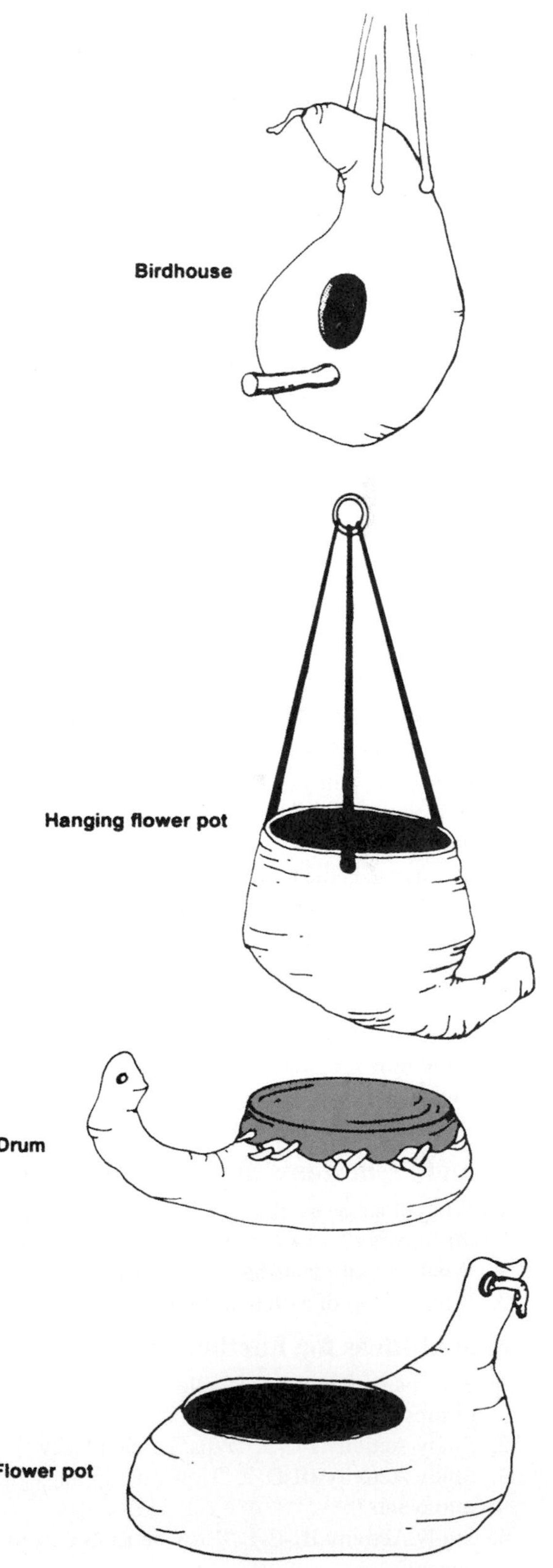

A. Problem: *What Can We Make with Gourds?*

(Gourds are the hard-shelled fruit of certain vines. They are related to cucumbers, squash, pumpkins, and muskmelons. The hard shells of gourds can be used for many things.)

B. Materials Needed:

1. Dry gourd rinds
2. String
3. Yarn
4. Supporting device
5. Dowels or branch for bird feeder
6. Heavy balloon or heavy plastic sheet tube
7. String or heavy rubber band

C. Procedure:

1. Cut holes in top half of gourd and suspend for making a bird feeder.
2. Cut gourds in half and suspend for hanging planters.
3. Stretch the balloon or heavy plastic over the top of a cut half of a gourd to make a drum.
4. Secure with string or heavy rubber band.
5. For table planters, may make legs for support.

D. Results:

Creative projects can be made.

E. Basic Facts and Supplemental Information:

1. Gourds can be obtained in many grocery stores.
2. Gourds can be kept for many years.
3. Even though "gourd" is the name of the whole fruit, most people refer to the rinds as gourds.

F. Thought Questions for Class Discussions:

1. What other items can you create with gourds?
2. Would gourds make good liquid containers?
3. Could other musical instruments be made from gourds?

G. Related Ideas for Further Inquiry:

1. Plan some plants that might be placed in the gourds.
2. Gourds can be painted for artistic activities.
3. Plan other uses for gourd containers.
4. Study all Activities in this Section.

H. Vocabulary Builders—Spelling Words:

1) **gourd** 2) **planters** 3) **hinged** 4) **support** 5) **suspend** 6) **yarn** 7) **string** 8) **hanging**

I. Thought for Today:

"An open mind collects more riches than an open purse."

Activity III F 2

A. Problem: *How Can We Make a Carrot Basket?*

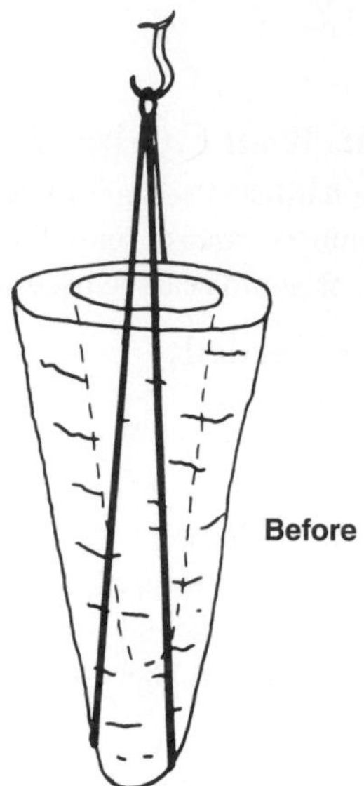

Carrot basket

B. Materials Needed:

1. Fresh, large carrot
2. Apple corer
3. String
4. Supporting device
5. Water
6. Knife

C. Procedure:

1. Wash the carrot carefully.
2. Cut the carrot in half horizontally.
3. Using the lower half, carefully hollow out the central core of the carrot about halfway down.
4. Make a sling to support the carrot. (See drawing.)
5. Hang on supporting device.
6. Keep hollowed-out portion full of water.

D. Results:

1. Roots will sprout from the bottom.
2. The roots will continue to grow until food from the carrot is gone.

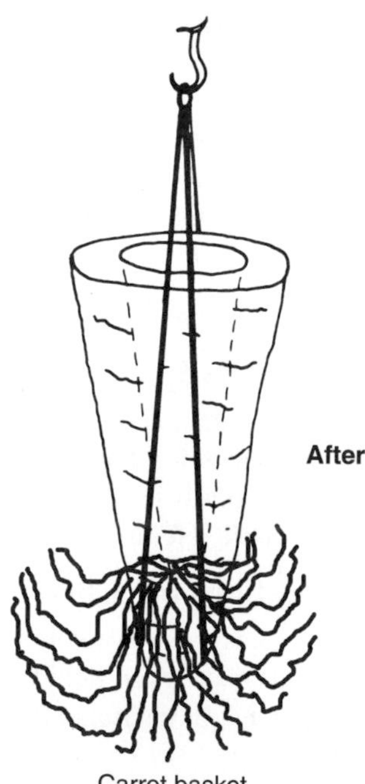

Carrot basket

E. Basic Facts and Supplemental Information:

1. Carrot must be kept watered or plant will die. (This is a plant.)
2. It is always a good idea to make several of these and compare.
3. The carrot is the food for the plant.
4. The leaves of the carrot which develop are necessary for photosynthesis.
5. Photosynthesis is the ability of a plant to absorb sunlight and convert carbon dioxide from the air and water from the ground into plant food (glucose).
6. In this Activity, the water must be supplied so that the carrot plant can continue to grow.

F. Thought Questions for Class Discussions:

1. What other types of vegetables could be grown in this manner?
2. What type of plants have similar food storages?
3. What part(s) of a plant are shown in this Activity?

G. Related Ideas for Further Inquiry:

1. Try this with other vegetables such as onions, turnips, and beets.
2. Study Activity I-C-5, "What is 'capillarity'?"
3. Study Activity III-D-7, "How do clippings grow into plants?"
4. Study Activity III-E-1, "How do roots absorb water?"
5. Study Activity III-E-4, "How does water move in stems?"
6. Study all other Activities in this Section.

H. Vocabulary Builders—Spelling Words:

1) **carrot** 2) **basket** 3) **supporting** 4) **string** 5) **suspend** 6) **horizontally** 7) **apple corer**

I. Thought for Today:

"The biggest thing college prepares young people for is the knowledge of what it's like to be broke."

Activity

III F 3

A. Problem: *How Can We Make a "Spray Print"?*

B. Materials Needed:

1. White or colored construction paper, size 9″ × 12″
2. Spray paint of contrasting color
3. Large leaf with a distinctive outside edge
4. Pins (enough to fasten leaf points)
5. Newspapers

C. Procedure:

1. Place several thicknesses of newspaper on a working surface.
2. Place construction paper on newspaper.
3. Place the leaf on top of the construction paper.
4. Pin the leaf points to keep leaf from moving.
5. Test spray paint on old newspaper to be sure that the proper effect will be achieved when spraying on the leaf.
6. Stand a little in front of the leaf; begin spraying gently and carefully over the leaf.
7. Cover as much of the surface of the leaf as you wish, making sure that the edges are well defined.
8. Several practice attempts usually need to be made to keep the leaf and background material free from blobs.
9. After the paint has dried, remove the leaf from the paper.
10. The print should be labeled with:
    a. type of leaf (oak, elm, etc.)
    b. name of collector
    c. date of collection
11. Prints can be framed.
12. The best specimens can be mounted on the classroom bulletin board.

D. Results:

1. Beautifully colored silhouettes of the leaves will have been created.
2. A lot of enjoyment will have been realized as a result of combining this science and art Activity.

E. Basic Facts and Supplemental Information:

1. Leaves can be collected around the school campus, in local areas on field trips, and around the home.
2. Leaves are very important to us. They collect energy from the sun, which is then available to us; they supply us with needed oxygen.

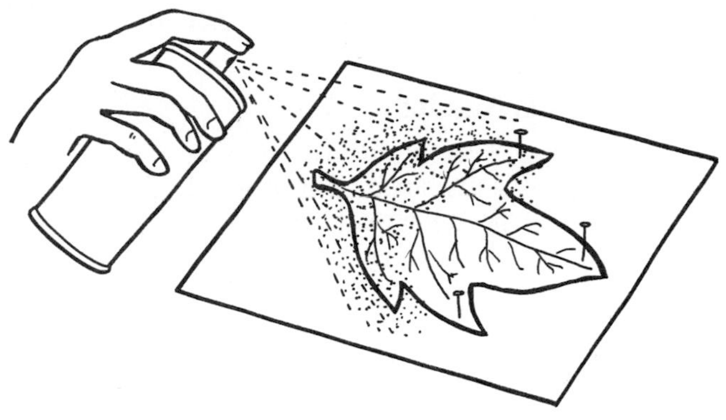

3. Many other materials have been used to make spray or splatter prints: toothbrushes, old knives, wire screens, shaving brushes, flat sticks, etc.

F. Thought Questions for Class Discussions:

1. What would be some good colors to use as background for green leaves?
2. What other objects might use this technique for outlining them?
3. What other methods could be used for making silhouettes?

G. Related Ideas for Further Inquiry:

1. Make hearts for Valentine's Day, pumpkins for Halloween, turkeys for Thanksgiving, etc.
2. Study Activity III-A-4, "What kinds of trees are found in our neighborhood?"
3. Study Activity III-C-4, "What is composting?"
4. Study Activity III-D-6, "How can plants be transplanted?"
5. Study Activity III-E-6, "What is photosynthesis?"
6. Study Activity VI-D-6, "How can we protect our recreational areas?"
7. Study all the Activities in this Section.

H. Vocabulary Builders—Spelling Words:

1) **spray** 2) **print** 3) **colored** 4) **edges** 5) **construction** 6) **harmony** 7) **knife** 8) **newspaper** 9) **contrasting** 10) **leaves**

I. Thought for Today:

"The only thing most people do better than anyone else is read their own handwriting."

Activity III F 4

A. Problem: *How Can We Make Blueprints of Leaves?*

B. Materials Needed:

1. Piece of window glass, 4" × 6"
2. Piece of stiff cardboard or plywood, 4″ × 6″
3. Wide adhesive or masking tape
4. Blueprint paper (cut desired size)
5. Pan of water
6. Leaf or fern frond

C. Procedure:

1. Place the glass on the piece of stiff cardboard or plywood.
2. Fasten these together at the top with a piece of adhesive or masking tape. This is your printing frame.
3. Lift up the glass cover and place a piece of blueprint paper face up on the cardboard.
4. Lay the leaf (or fern) to be printed on top of the blueprint paper.
5. Cover all with the glass top.
6. Expose the frame to the sun for a few minutes.
7. Remove blueprint paper and soak print in a pan of water.

D. Result:

The last step brings out the blue color of the print and makes it permanent. The strength of the sunlight will determine the length of exposure. It will be necessary to experiment several times to obtain best results.

E. Basic Facts and Supplemental Information:

1. Blueprints are used extensively in the construction business for building plans, etc.
2. The value of blueprints is the ease with which they can be used.
3. Any opaque flat object can be used to copy its size and outline.
4. Newer plans for plumbers, electricians, carpenters, etc. are primarily pencil or heavy ink drawings on vellum paper.
5. Plans are usually filed away and can be used again for new projects or as references for other projects.

F. Thought Questions for Class Discussions:

1. What other methods can be used to duplicate plans, drawings, or small, flat objects?
2. What other plant parts can be shown in blueprints?
3. Are there any ways that leaves can be duplicated and magnified by some graphic means?

G. Related Ideas for Further Inquiry:

1. Study Activity III-A-4, "What kinds of trees are found in our neighborhood?"
2. Study Activity III-A-2, "What are the main parts of a flower?"
3. Study Activity III-D-2, "Do plants grow toward light?"
4. Study Activity III-E-6, "What is photosynthesis?"
5. Study Activity III-F-3, "How can we make a 'spray print'?"
6. Study Activity III-F-5, "How can we make mounts for plants?"
7. Study Activity III-F-8, "How can we make a simple plant terrarium?"

H. Vocabulary Builders—Spelling Words:

1) **blueprint** 2) **window** 3) **leaf** 4) **fern** 5) **frond** 6) **masking** 7) **permanent** 8) **sunlight**

I. Thought for Today:

"It's what guests say as they swing out of the driveway that really counts."

Activity

A. Problem: *How Can We Make Mounts for Plants?*

B. Materials Needed:

1. Shallow cardboard box of any desired dimensions
2. Piece of glass, clear plastic, or heavy cellophane to fit under cover of cardboard box (If glass is used, an adult should cut it to fit the box cover.)
3. Cotton
4. Razor blade or knife
5. Adhesive tape, masking tape, or glue
6. Dry plant or artificial flower or plant

C. Procedure:

1. Draw one-half inch margin along all sides of cover.
2. Cut out along these lines with razor blade or knife. (Be very careful.)
3. Fit glass, plastic, or cellophane cover taping or gluing it to the bottom side of box cover.
4. Place enough cotton in box to nearly fill it.
5. Arrange the specimen, and label it. (See E-4, below.)
6. Replace cover.
7. Paint box if desired.

D. Result:

An attractive Riker-type box for storing a plant is made.

E. Basic Facts and Supplemental Information:

1. An inexpensive Riker-type box for mounting leaves, pressed flowers, branches or stems, butterflies, or other insects, shells, etc., for display is easily made.
2. Attractive and durable display boxes can be made from inexpensive or discarded materials.
3. Only a minimum of time and work is needed to make the boxes.
4. Label should contain:
   a. scientific name of specimen
   b. common name of specimen
   c. where found
   d. date
   e. collector's name
5. A "specimen" is a part of an object or an item that is typical of a group.
6. This type of box can also be used for small animals or animal specimens.
7. A similar box with a heavier base, and omitting the cotton, can be used for mounting insects.
8. Students enjoy collecting things and teachers should take advantage of this.

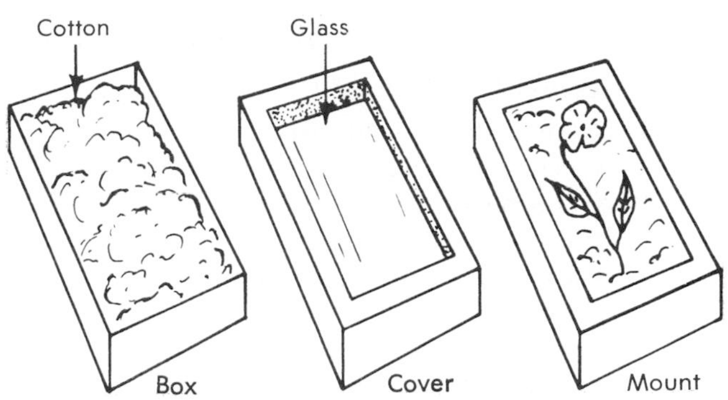

9. In this Activity "intrinsic motivation" is self-evident.

F. Thought Questions for Class Discussions:

1. What kind of plant specimens could be placed in these mounts?
2. What animal specimens could be placed in this type of mount?
3. What would cause spoilage of specimens in this Riker mount? What could be done to help eliminate this source or sources of trouble? (Answer: mothballs or mothflakes.)
4. Could a similar type of box be used for preserving other objects?

G. Related Ideas for Further Inquiry:

1. Moths and butterflies make beautiful displays using these boxes.
2. Many games and contests can be held using these mounts from identification to unusual characteristics.
3. Study Activity IV-C-3, "How can we collect insects and spiders?"
4. Study Activity IV-C-5, "How can we preserve insects or start a butterfly collection?"
5. Study Activity III-F-3, "How can we make a 'spray print'?"
6. Study Activity III-F-6, "Let's go on a wildflower hunt."
7. Study other Activities in this Section.

H. Vocabulary Builders—Spelling Words:

1) **Riker box** 2) **plastic** 3) **specimen**
4) **butterflies** 5) **cellophane** 6) **label**
7) **collection** 8) **insect**

I. Thought for Today:

"Snowflakes are one of nature's most fragile things, but just look at what they can do when they stick together."

Activity

A. Problem: *Let's Go on a Wildflower Hunt*

B. Materials Needed:

1. Reference books on flowers
2. Materials needed to collect wildflowers:
   a. Notebooks
   b. Pens and/or pencils
   c. Plastic folders to hold specimens
   d. Newspapers
   e. Magnifying glasses
3. Appropriate multisensory aids

C. Procedure:

1. First decide whether to make this an individual assignment or a class field trip.
2. If a field trip is planned, make certain that the area visited is:
   a. safe
   b. available
   c. sufficient in numbers and varieties of wildflowers
   d. permit-free
3. Show films, slides, and/or transcriptions about wildflowers.
4. Discuss the wildflowers seen.
5. Identify the wildflowers by common names, not scientific names.
6. Establish class or individual guidelines such as:
   a. approximate number to collect
   b. time allotment
   c. safety precautions
   d. work party (individual, pairs, or small group)
   e. field notes for references for each specimen:
      1) color
      2) size
      3) location
      4) unusual characteristics
      5) date collected
7. Take the field trip.
8. When the field trip is completed, bring the specimens to class and identify as many as possible, using the reference materials at hand.

D. Results:

1. Students enjoy collecting items.
2. Students will learn about wildflowers.
3. They will learn how wildflowers are identified and classified.
4. Students will become junior botanists.

E. Basic Facts and Supplemental Information:

1. Wildflowers are native plants with attractive blooms.
2. Trees and shrubs are not wildflowers.
3. There are over 15,000 species of wildflowers in North America.
4. Wildflowers can best be identified by studying their characteristics:
   a. flowers (single to clusters)
   b. fruits
5. Most wildflowers need an outside agent to transfer pollen. Grasses need winds. Many others need animals that are attracted by color and/or scent.
6. Many wildflowers are used in medicine.
7. Others are used as herbs.
8. Ordinary precautions should be taken when handling wildflowers.

F. Thought Questions for Class Discussions:

1. Are there any major differences between garden flowers and wildflowers?
2. Where have you seen the prettiest flowers?
3. Where did the seeds come from that started the wildflowers?

G. Related Ideas for Further Inquiry:

1. Study Activity III-A-1, "How do we classify living things?"
2. Study Activity III-A-2, "What are the main parts of a flower?"
3. Study Activity III-B-2, "How many different kinds of seeds can we collect?"
4. Study other Activities in this Section.

H. Vocabulary Builders—Spelling Words:

1) **wildflowers** 2) **collecting** 3) **storing**
4) **preserving** 5) **identifying** 6) **reference**

I. Thought for Today:

"The mighty oak was once a little nut that stood its ground."

Activity

A. Problem: *How Can We Measure the Height of Tall Trees?*

B. Materials Needed:

1. Protractor
2. Tape measure
3. Tree
4. Ruler

C. Procedure:

1. Discuss with students how protractors measure angles.
2. Select a tall tree.
3. With protractor as level as possible, walk away from tree until a reading on the protractor shows an angle of 45° to the top of the tree. This can best be accomplished by laying the top of a ruler on the 45° mark and the middle of the base of the protractor and sighting along the top of the ruler.
4. Mark this spot on the ground.
5. Measure or estimate the distance the protractor is above the ground.
6. With measuring tape or walking steps, estimate the distance from the tree to the mark you made on the ground.
7. To this figure, add the height of the protractor.

D. Result:

The distance from the bottom of the tree to the mark on the ground plus the height of the protractor is equal to the height of the tree.

E. Basic Facts and Supplemental Information:

1. Mathematicians can compute the height of many object by knowing the angle to the top of the object.
2. This branch of mathematics is called trigonometry, the study of triangles.
3. Mathematics is a vital part of science that enables us to measure:
   a. distance
   b. speed
   c. volume
   d. weight
   e. time
   f. shape, etc.
4. Mathematics enable us to make predictions.
5. A second method is to take a ruler or pencil, and while holding it in an upright position with arm outstretched, walk away from the tree until the height of the tree is noted on the ruler or pencil. Using this height measurement, turn the ruler or pencil horizontally and align the height of the tree from its base to a perpendicular point on the ground. The distance from the base of the tree to the point noted on the ground is equal to the height of the tree.

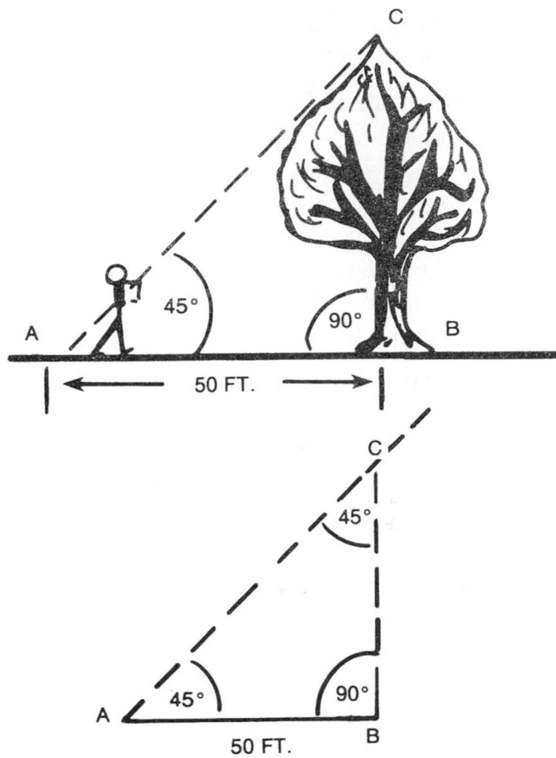

F. Thought Questions for Class Discussions:

1. Why wouldn't the reading be accurate if the distance were measured from the point of the protractor?
2. What do they call the angle between the tree and the ground?
3. What is a triangle?

G. Related Ideas for Further Inquiry:

1. Compute the height of other tall objects.
2. Mark off two 45° angles on the flat surface of a playground to construct a right triangle.
3. Have students construct similar triangles on worksheets in the classroom.
4. Study other Activities in this Section.

H. Vocabulary Builders—Spelling Words:

1) **measure** 2) **triangle** 3) **angle**
4) **protractor** 5) **height** 6) **trigonometry**

I. Thought for Today:

"Everyone is a self-made person but only the successful admit it."

Activity III F 8

A. Problem: *How Can We Make a Simple Plant Terrarium?*

B. Materials Needed:

1. Fish bowl
2. Lid, plastic or glass (doesn't have to fit perfectly)
3. Different small plants
4. Sufficient soil to fill one-third of container
5. Small trowel or tongue depressor
6. Decorative rocks or driftwood
7. Sprinkling can

C. Procedure:

1. Plan with class the interior setting of the terrarium (a wooded area, a desert scene, a farm, or other scene) and the planting arrangement.
2. Put 3 inches of soil in the container.
3. Demonstrate proper method of removing plants from pots. (Gently tap sides and bottom with trowel until soil is loosened enough to lift plant from pot.)
4. Plant the plants in container.
5. Arrange rocks and other decorative material.
6. Lightly sprinkle garden.
7. Place lid to one side on terrarium allowing air to get to plants.

D. Result:

Class will have created an artistic terrarium.

E. Basic Facts and Supplemental Information:

1. A small dish garden or terrarium needs little or no water, as it uses the evaporation which condenses as moisture on the underside of the lid. If the terrarium appears dry, add a slight amount of water.
2. The terrarium should be given sufficient sunlight, and the air should be allowed to reach the plants. The terrarium should last for weeks and can be kept indefinitely by replacing the dead plants with live ones. Students will not only learn how to make a terrarium, but will also enjoy watching the plants develop.
3. Three terms are often confused: "vivarium," "terrarium," and "aquarium."
4. An aquarium is essentially a container with water.
5. A terrarium is essentially a container with sand, or soil(s).
6. A vivarium is essentially a container that contains both water and soil(s).
7. The plural of these terms end in "ia" (aquaria, vivaria, and terraria).

F. Thought Questions for Class Discussions:

1. What are the differences between a terrarium, a vivarium, and an aquarium?
2. Why are some plants more suited to a terrarium than others?
3. What would happen if the terrarium lid were kept on?

G. Related Ideas for Further Inquiry:

1. Collect weeds around the school and plant them in the terrarium.
2. Plant grasses.
3. Plant radish seeds.
4. Study Activity III-C-1, "What can we find in our soil?"
5. Study Activity III-C-2, "Are some soils better than others for holding water?"
6. Study Activity III-C-6, "How can we improve our soils?"
7. Study Activity III-D-1, "How can we improve crop growth?"
8. Study Activity III-D-6, "How can plants be transplanted?"
9. Study Activity III-D-7, "How do clippings grow into plants?"

H. Vocabulary Builders—Spelling Words:

1) **terrarium** 2) **vivarium** 3) **aquarium** 4) **trowel** 5) **decorative** 6) **plants** 7) **scene** 8) **bowl** 9) **lid** 10) **develop**

I. Thought for Today:

"It is by logic that we prove, but by intuition that we discover."

PART IV

ANIMALS

Section A: Classification

Activity IV A 1

A. Problem: *What Are Some Characteristics of All Living Things?*

B. Materials Needed:

1. Classroom plants
2. Classroom animals
3. Pictures or models of other plants and animals including microscopic ones
4. Multisensory materials
5. Reference books

C. Procedure

1. Discuss the different kinds of plants and animals that students know.
2. Discuss where they live.
3. Discuss what they need to survive.
4. List some of the characteristics of living things (** items apply to animals only):
   a. grow
   b. reproduce
   c. respire
   d. eliminate wastes
   e. locomotion**
   f. communication**
   g. digestion
   h. chemical factories
   i. defense mechanisms
   j. specific life cycles
   k. feed (food and water)
   l. energy transfers
   m. care for young**
   n. sensing
5. Discuss the reasons and general principles of classification.
6. Show any available multisensory materials about plants and animals that would be appropriate for this Activity.
7. Have the students research and/or discuss some of the major characteristics of each of the five major kingdoms:
   a. Monera
      1) one-celled
      2) no movement capabilities
      3) consumers and producers
      4) procaryotic (lack nuclear membrane) (cell parts appear clumped)
      5) feed by absorption

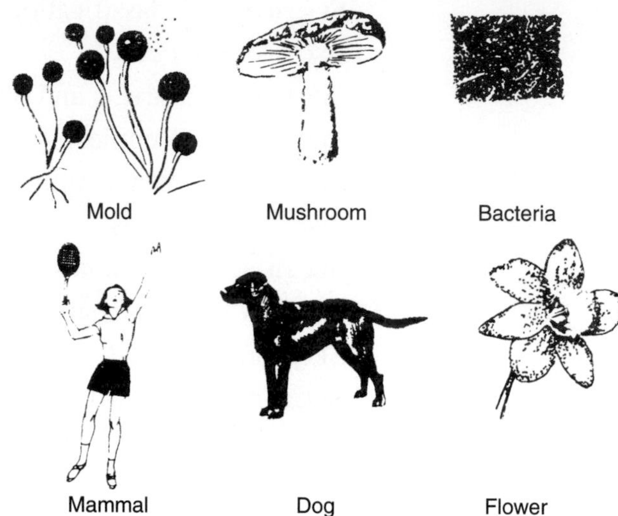

      6) reproduce by fission (splitting)
      7) Organisms include bacteria and blue-green algae.
   b. Protista
      1) one-celled
      2) eucaryotic (have nuclei) (discrete cell parts)
      3) limited movement
      4) Organisms include amoebas, euglena, and diatoms.
   c. Fungi
      1) no movement capabilities
      2) have nuclei
      3) made of cells, tubular
      4) Organisms include molds, mushrooms, yeasts, and mildews.
   d. Plants (Plantae)
      1) multicelled, walled cells
      2) no movement capabilities
      3) specialized parts (roots, stems, leaves)
      4) photosynthesis
      5) producers of food
      6) Members include trees, flowers, and legumes.
   e. Animals (Animalia)
      1) movement capabilities
      2) consumers of food
      3) various sizes

4) Organisms include fish, amphibians, reptiles, birds, mammals, etc.
5) Human beings are mammals.

8. Have the students develop their own organizational scheme for any group of objects. (Study Section G. Related Ideas for Further Inquiry for some suggestions.)
9. Make a list of terms that the students should become familiar with in their study of living things such as:
   a. predator
   b. prey
   c. consumer
   d. producer
   e. habitat
   f. ecosystem
   g. environment

D. Results:

1. Students will learn about the different forms of living things.
2. Students will learn the general principles of classification.
3. Students will become aware of the different characteristics of living things.
4. Students will learn that there are small, even microscopic organisms that are classified besides the Plant and Animal Kingdoms.
5. Students will learn the difference between living things and nonliving things.

E. Basic Facts and Supplemental Information:

1. This classification system was developed by R. H. Whittaker of Cornell University and has generally been accepted by most life scientists.
2. Young students can develop their own classification system which could be based on size, color, shape, function, etc.
3. There are about 3 million species of organisms that are now known.
4. Some scientists predict that there may be 10 to 15 million species of plants and animals on Earth.
5. Every year new organisms are discovered and other organisms become extinct.

F. Thought Questions for Class Discussions:

1. What is the largest animal you know?
2. What is the smallest animal you know?
3. What is the prettiest plant you know?
4. Are most of the foods we eat formerly living things?
5. Should we be concerned about plant and animal extinction?
6. What are some factors that cause changes in the lifestyle of organisms?

G. Related Ideas for Further Inquiry:

1. Study seeds and eggs.
2. Examine buds, flowers, and bulbs.
3. Have each student take off one shoe and put it in a pile in the middle of the room. Have them develop a classification for these, based on size, color, shape, etc.
4. Have students classify other items such as bottles, rocks, automobiles, etc.

H. Vocabulary Builders—Spelling Words:

1) **classify** 2) **nucleus** 3) **consumers**
4) **producers** 5) **photosynthesis** 6) **and of:**
a) The names of the five kingdoms
b) The characteristics of living things

I. Thought for Today:

"A problem is a chance for you to do your best."

Activity IV A 2

A. Problem: *What Is the Triangle of Life?*

B. Materials Needed:

1. Sketch of the "Food Triangle" (See drawing.)
2. Newspaper, magazine accounts of the "Food Triangle" in action
3. Reference materials about the above

C. Procedure:

1. Discuss how all living creatures must have other organisms to eat in order for them to continue to survive.
2. Discuss how fortunate it is that nature provides the "triangle of life" and produces more individuals on the lower end of the triangle so they will continue to exist and provide food for those higher up on the "Food Triangle."
3. Cite the problems that would exist if there were an equal number of all species.

D. Results:

1. Students will gain a new insight into the relationships between each level of the "Food Triangle."
2. Students will learn about "food chains" and "food webs."
3. Students will learn how important the "balance of nature" is. The "Food Triangle" depicts this balance.

E. Basic Facts and Supplemental Information:

1. The "Food Triangle" includes plants as well as animals.
2. "Food chains" are the straight-line interrelationships of individuals in the "Food Triangle." For example: phytoplankton are eaten by small fish; small fish are eaten by larger fish; and larger fish are eaten by people.
3. "Food webs" are the interrelationships among all potential prey-predator possibilities. For example: phytoplankton could be eaten by zooplankton, small fish, or small amphibians; zooplankton could be eaten by small fish, turtles, jellyfish, mussels, etc; and so on up the "Food Triangle." "Food Webs" attempt to describe all possibilities.
4. The size of each level of the "Food Triangle" represents the number of organisms contained therein. The broader the base, the more organisms would be found in that level.

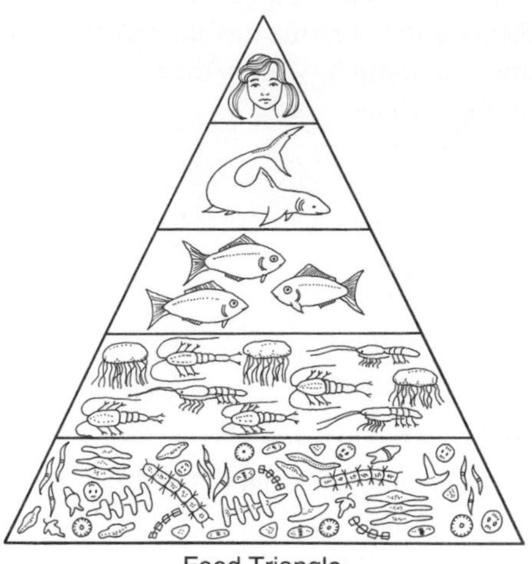

Food Triangle

F. Thought Questions for Class Discussions:

1. Why has the cost of shellfish climbed so rapidly?
2. What causes some animals to become extinct?
3. What causes some plants to become extinct?

G. Related Ideas for Further Inquiry:

1. Study Activity III-A-1, "How do we classify living things?"
2. Study Activity IV-A-1, "What are some characteristics of all living things?"
3. Study Activity IV-A-3, "What are the scientific classification of dogs, cats, and human beings?"
4. Study Activity VI-A-6, "What are Food Chains? Food Webs?"
5. Study Activity VI-A-1, "What is the balance of nature?"
6. Study Activity VI-A-2, "What is 'biological diversity'?"

H. Vocabulary Builders—Spelling Words:

1) **triangle** 2) **food** 3) **chain** 4) **web** 5) **interrelationships** 6) **numbers** 7) **exist**

I. Thought for Today:

"Hereditary is what causes parents of teenagers to look at each other with suspicion."

Activity IV A 3

A. Problem: *What Are the Scientific Classifications of Dogs, Cats, and Human Beings?*

B. Materials Needed:

1. Books, pamphlets, or simple photocopy materials on classification
2. Pictures of various animals, and in particular, dogs, cats, and human beings

C. Procedure:

1. Explain the purposes of classification.
2. Show pictures of various animals.
3. Explain how taxonomists would group them.
4. Ask class if they can find the classification of their pets: dogs, cats, fish, etc.
5. Ask class where they categorize themselves.
6. Classify as many animals as possible in time allotted.

D. Results:

1. Students will be able to classify certain animals.
2. Pupils will be able to see that all animals fall into various categories that depend on similar characteristics.

E. Basic Facts and Supplemental Information:

1. Plants can be classified as well as animals.
2. Some of the characteristics that separate groups of animals are backbones, living areas, means of bearing young, etc.
3. Dogs, cats, and human beings belong to the animal kingdom.
4. Classification of cats:
   a. Kingdom—Animalia
   b. Phylum—Chordata
   c. Subphylum—Vertebrata
   d. Class—Mammalia
   e. Order—Carnivora
   f. Family—Felidae
   g. Genus—Felis
   h. Species—Felis domesticus
5. Classification of dogs:
   a. Kingdom—Animalia
   b. Phylum—Chordata
   c. Subphylum—Vertebrata
   d. Class—Mammalia
   e. Order—Carnivora
   f. Family—Canidae
   g. Genus—Canis
   h. Species—Canis familiaris
6. Classification of human beings:
   a. Kingdom—Animalia
   b. Phylum—Chordata
   c. Subphylum—Vertebrata
   d. Class—Mammalia
   e. Order—Primates
   f. Family —Hominidae
   g. Genus—Homo
   h. Species—Homo sapiens

F. Thought Questions for Class Discussions

1. Could you make up your own system of animal classification using your own subdivisions?
2. Are lions closely related to house cats?
3. Are plant classifications similar to animal classifications?

G. Related Ideas for Further Inquiry:

1. Study Activities in Part III, "Plants."
2. Study Activities in Part IV, "Animals."
3. Study Activities in Part V, "Health."
4. Study Activity III-A-1, "How do we classify living things?"
5. Study Activity IV-A-2, "What is the Triangle of Life?"
6. Study Activity IV-A-6, "Which animals are helpful? Harmful? Just a nuisance?"
7. Study Activity VI-A-I, "What is the balance of nature?"
8. Study Activity VI-A-2, "What is 'biological diversity'?"

H. Vocabulary Builders—Spelling Words:

Use the terms in Classification E-4, E-5, and E-6 of this Activity.

I. Thought for Today:

"Man is the only animal that blushes and the only one that needs to."

Activity IV A 4

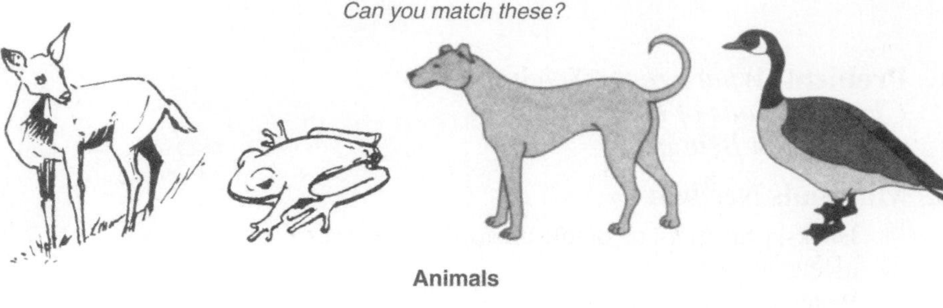

Their footprints

A. Problem: *What Do Animal Tracks Tell Us?*

B. Materials Needed:

1. Pictures of various animals
2. Drawings of a wide variety of animals' footprints (See drawings.)
3. Newspapers
4. Large white sheets of paper
5. Cellophane tape
6. Poster paint
7. Clean cloths
8. Water
9. Student volunteer

C. Procedure:

1. Discuss how early Indians, colonial hunters, and trappers studied the footprints of animals.
2. Ask for a student volunteer.
3. Lay out the newspapers in a long line about 10 feet long.
4. Lay the large white sheets on the newspapers so that they are touching.
5. Tape them together so they will not move or slip.
6. Paint the bottom of the volunteer student's feet with water-soluble poster paint.
7. Have the student walk on the papers the full length of the paper trail.
8. Wash the volunteer student's feet thoroughly.
9. Have the class study the footprints and play detective by gaining as much information as they can from the clues left by the student.
10. Discuss with students any animal tracks they have seen.

D. Results

1. Students will learn that footprints tell many things such as:
   a. kind of animal
   b. size of animal
   c. direction animal is/was going
   d. whether animal was standing still, walking, or running
   e. if animal was alone or with other animals
   f. if the print was freshly made
2. Students will become more observant of animal trails.

E. Basic Facts and Supplemental Information:

1. Each species of animal has its own distinctive footprint.
2. Knowing the footprint, the geography, and the habits of animals, enables us to come close to identifying the animal whose footprints we observe.
3. Footprints can also tell us if the animal has claws and if it is a predator.
4. If the animal is a bird, we can tell its lifestyle by its footprint: curved claws—percher, eats seeds and insects; sharp, long claws—predator, eats small ground animals; and webbed feet—wader and swimmer, feeds on water plants and small water creatures.

F. Thought Questions for Class Discussions:

1. Where would you look for animal tracks?
2. What animal tracks would you prefer not to see?
3. Do snails and slugs leave animal tracks?
4. What kind of animals have footpads?

G. Related Ideas for Further Inquiry:

1. Assign students the task of looking for animal tracks around their home and the school campus.
2. Have students match the pictures and footprints in the drawings above.
3. Study Activity IV-F-4, "How do we classify common birds?"
4. Study Activity III-A-1, "How do we classify living things?"
5. Study Activity IV-A-2, "What is the Triangle of Life?"
6. Study Activity IV-A-1, "What are some characteristics of all living things?"

H. Vocabulary Builders—Spelling Words:

1) **tracks** 2) **prints** 3) **identify** 4) **confirm** 5) **compare** 6) **footpads** 7) **toes** 8) **webbed**

I. Thought for Today:

"One is never wrong in obeying the Laws of Nature."

Activity IV A 5

A. Problem: *What Are Some Animals That Live in the Oceans?*

B. Materials Needed:

1. Pictures of sea animals
2. Reference books on ocean life
3. Multisensory aids on sea life

C. Procedure:

1. Discuss oceans in general:
   a. size
   b. importance
   c. students' experiences
2. Show any available multisensory aids about sea life.
3. Contrast sea life and land life.
4. Separate class into groups and have each group study one of the classifications cited in Section E, "Basic Facts and Supplemental Information."
5. Have each group give a report on its findings.
6. Compare the different forms of animal life found in the oceans.

D. Results:

1. Students will realize that there are many animal species other than fishes that live in the oceans.
2. Students will become more environmentally concerned with the care and use of the oceans.

E. Basic Facts and Supplemental Information:

1. Sponges:
   a. live on the seabed
   b. have a central cavity on the bottom and a hole on the top through which water passes and food is extracted
2. Coral and Jellyfish:
   a. have single cavity where food is assimilated
   b. catch prey by use of their stinging tentacles
3. Sea worms
4. Flat worms:
   a. Most glide on the bottom of the sea.
   b. Some are parasites and live in other animals.
5. Mollusks:
   a. 80,000 species
   b. single coiled shells
   c. paired shelled: clams, mussels
   d. internal or nonshelled: octopuses, squid
6. Crustaceans:
   a. crabs, lobsters
   b. shrimp

Common dolphin

7. Fish:
   a. vertebras
   b. gills to obtain oxygen
8. Amphibians:
   a. frogs, toads, newts, and salamanders
   b. primarily land animals but lay their eggs in water
9. Mammals:
   a. streamlined shapes
   b. pointed teeth
   c. dolphins, whales, sea lions, gray seal

F. Thought Questions for Class Discussions:

1. How does ocean life differ from land life?
2. What are zooplankton?
3. Are most ocean animals warm-blooded or cold-blooded?
4. Do all ocean animals need oxygen to breathe?

G. Related Ideas for Further Inquiry:

1. Have students report on their visits to oceans and describe any ocean life they might have seen.
2. If any students have visited oceanariums, have them discuss the ocean life they have seen with class.
3. If any students have gone ocean fishing, have them give a report on sea creatures.

H. Vocabulary Builders—Spelling Words:

1) **animals** 2) **oceans** 3) **contrast**

Use also the animal species mentioned in Section E. Basic Facts and Supplemental Information.

I. Thought for Today:

"Nothing makes a fish bigger than almost being caught."

Activity IV A 6

A. Problem: *Which Animals Are Helpful? Harmful? Just a Nuisance?*

B. Materials Needed:

1. Pictures of animals
2. Other multisensory materials on animals
3. Newspaper accounts of animals
4. Bulletin board
5. Reference materials about animals

C. Procedure:

1. Tell class that we are going to try to group specific animals in one of the three categories cited in the "Problem."
2. Pictures can be posted on the bulletin board.
3. Newspaper accounts can also be posted on the bulletin board.
4. Multisensory materials can be shown if available and appropriate.
5. Have each student make a chart listing 5 to 10 animals that would fall into each category.
6. When the students have finished, develop a class chart showing the various animals in each category.
7. Have students discuss their experiences with animals that would fall into each category.

D. Results:

1. Each student will develop his/her own chart on animal classification.
2. A class chart will be developed on these animal classifications.
3. Students will realize that not all animals can be easily classified in these areas. Many animals will fall into several or all three classifications.

E. Basic Facts and Supplemental Information:

1. Students' judgments are based on past experiences.
2. Some feelings have been influenced by parents, friends, or other acquaintances reciting their experiences or attitudes about specific animals.
3. Most attitudes are based on:
   a. heresay
   b. misinformation
   c. actual experiences
   d. unsubstantiated or substantiated facts
   e. lack of knowledge, etc.
4. All animals are involved in ecosystems.

5. Many animals are becoming endangered because of lack of concern by people.
6. We could not survive without animals.

F. Thought Questions for Class Discussions:

1. Which is your favorite animal? Why?
2. Which animal do you dislike the most? Why?
3. Do you think ALL animals should be protected? Some? Which ones?
4. Are you afraid of any animals? Why?
5. What do animals need to survive?

G. Related Ideas for Further Inquiry:

1. Have students make a study of animals that are:
   a. threatened
   b. endangered
   c. extinct
2. Have students study the quotation "Survival of the Fittest" as to its meaning and significance.
3. How are people helpful or harmful to animals?

H. Vocabulary Builders—Spelling Words:

1) **helpful** 2) **harmful** 3) **nuisance** 4) **category** 5) **classifications** 6) **threatened** 7) **endangered** 8) **extinct**

I. Thought for Today:

"Bad officials are elected by people who don't vote."

Activity IV A 7

A. Problem: *How Do Animals Communicate?*

B. Materials Needed:

Pictures of many animals

C. Procedure:

1. Discuss animal characteristics.
2. Discuss the need of animals to communicate to other members of their species.
3. Discuss how many animals are "social" animals.
4. Discuss the various means animals use to communicate such as:
   a. touching
   b. making sounds
   c. lighting (night lights)
   d. pheromones (chemical substances)
      1) lay trails to food
      2) alarms
      3) mating attractants
   e. movements
5. All students have seen dogs associating with each other. Discuss how dogs "communicate":
   a. fear
   b. anger
   c. friendliness
   d. attention-seeking
   e. possessiveness, etc.
6. Pair students and assign one of them the task of "communicating" such activities as:
   a. inviting one to go to a movie
   b. having a hamburger at a "fast-food" restaurant, etc.
   c. playing tennis after school

D. Result:

Students learn that animals communicate in many ways.

E. Basic Facts and Supplemental Information:

1. Animals need to protect themselves and to protect other members of their species.
2. Since animals prey on other animals, warnings are a vital part of the survival of those preyed upon.
3. Some animals communicate by running away.
4. Some communication is highly technical, such as bees communicating with other bees telling them the direction and distance where food has been located.
5. Cats, dogs, and other household pets communicate with people in many ways.

F. Thought Questions for Class Discussions:

1. In what ways do people communicate that are similar to the ways animals communicate?
2. In what ways do people communicate that are different from the ways animals communicate?
3. What are the main reasons people communicate?
4. In what ways do animals communicate with people?
5. In what ways do people communicate with animals?

G. Related Ideas for Further Inquiry:

1. Study people's gestures. Do they mean different things to different people?
2. Study how transportation is related to communication with people.
3. Study gestures and/or hand signals used by people in training pets.
4. Study Section IV-B, "Pets."
5. Study Activity IV-A-1, "What are some characteristics of all living things?"
6. Study Activity IV-A-2, "What is the Triangle of Life?"
7. Study Activity IV-A-3, "What are the scientific classifications of dogs, cats, and human beings?"
8. Study Activity IV-A-11, "Are any animals threatened with extinction?"

H. Vocabulary Builders—Spelling Words:

1) **touching** 2) **sounds** 3) **attractants**
4) **pheromones** 5) **alarm** 6) **protection**

I. Thought for Today:

"The first thing children learn when they get a drum is that they will never get another one."

Ants "communicate" showing the location of a dead milkweed butterfly caterpillar.

Activity IV A 8

A. Problem: *How Do Animals Reproduce?*

B. Materials Needed:

1. Reference books on animals
2. Multisensory materials on animal behaviors
3. Pictures or drawings of the anatomy of the male and female of selected species

C. Procedure:

1. A good starting point is the discussion of how flowers reproduce by pollen grains impregnating the ovule. Study Activity III-A-3, "How do plants reproduce?"
2. Compare flower "parts" with "animal organs."
3. Describe in general the "mating game" of animals:
   a. Finding a mate (courting):
      1) Sometimes it is a convenient geographical location.
      2) Some species advertise with "mating calls."
      3) Some species try to attract a mate with "dance rituals."
      4) Some species use body color and unusual body distortions to attract the opposite sex.
      5) Many animals use scents; males are attracted to these scents not only to locate the female but also to know when the females are ready to mate.

   b. Accepting a mate:
      1) Courtship is important so that the male and female will become friendly toward each other rather than display normal early aggressiveness.
      2) Fighting among some males over females or "territories" during breeding season is very common, especially among mammals.

   c. Mating of male and female:
      1) This act essentially involves the male injecting his sperm into the entrance leading to the ovary, where fertilization takes place.
      2) There are millions of sperm but normally one or a few ova to accept only one sperm each.

   d. Gestation Period:
      1) The gestation period is the time from fertilization of the ovum to the birth(s) of the offspring(s).
      2) Each species reproduces only its own kind.
      3) The gestation period varies among species from weeks to years.
      4) The gestation period in human beings is 9 months.

   e. Caring for the young:
      1) There is a wide range of parental treatment of animals for their young, from complete abandonment to a lifelong family life.
      2) The higher the animal on the evolutionary ladder, the longer the family stays together.

D. Results:

1. Students will realize that reproduction is a normal and natural function of all animals.
2. Students will learn that there is more to reproduction than just the sex act.

E. Basic Facts and Supplemental Information:

This information was contained in Procedure.

F. Thought Questions for Class Discussions:

1. Do you think movies overplay sex?
2. Is abstinence the best way to prevent venereal diseases?

G. Related Ideas for Further Inquiry:

Study all Activities on plants and animals.

H. Vocabulary Builders—Spelling Words:

1) **reproduction** 2) **courtship** 3) **species** 4) **sperm** 5) **ova** 6) **fertilization** 7) **gestation** 8) **caring**

I. Thought for Today:

"The most important job of parents is the education of their children."

Activity IV A 9

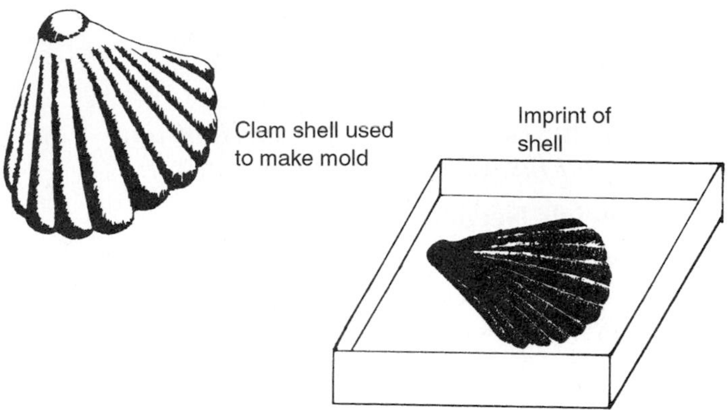

A. Problem: *What Are Fossils?*

B. Materials Needed:

1. Cardboard box
2. Clam or scallop shell
3. Clay (soft, any kind)
4. Plaster of Paris
5. Vinegar or salt
6. Fossils if obtainable

C. Procedure:

1. Mix enough clay to cover the bottom of the box one or more inches deep.
2. Press the shell (curved side down) deeply into clay.
3. Carefully lift the shell out so that a clear imprint is made.
4. Make a thick paste of plaster of Paris, adding a little salt or vinegar to prevent its hardening too quickly.
5. Pour plaster of Paris into the shell imprint.
6. When the plaster of Paris hardens, remove the cast carefully from the mold.
7. If no fossils are brought in by the students, the teacher may be able to borrow some fine specimens from a local museum or university science department.
8. After discussion by the class, the demonstration can be done by the students.
9. There is no feasible way to demonstrate actual fossilization by petrification or settlement, so the teacher should have several examples of each of these types to display.
10. As the activity progresses, relate the similarity between these materials and what they represent.
    a. The clay represents the mud on the ocean bottom.
    b. The plaster of Paris represents the minerals held in solution by the sea water.
    c. The fossil cast was formed when the shell made a print of itself, then decayed, leaving a space which was ultimately filled with a hard mineral material making a perfect replica of the original shell.
    d. The cast, represented by the plaster of Paris, was dissolved by some other mineral, leaving only a hollow or mold of the shell.

D. Results:

1. This demonstration shows how some fossils are formed.
2. Students will gain a basic understanding of fossils.

E. Basic Facts and Supplemental Information:

By understanding how fossils are formed we can make a more accurate study of plants and animals of the past.

F. Thought Questions for Class Discussions:

1. What would be some clues in determining the age of a fossil?
2. What animals do you know about that do not exist any longer?
3. Do you know anything about carbon dating?

G. Related Ideas for Further Inquiry:

1. Study plants and animals of the past.
2. Take a field trip to a natural history museum.
3. Collect stories of ancient findings and discoveries.
4. Study Activity III-A-1, "How do we classify living things?"
5. Study Activity IV-A-2, "What is the Triangle of Life?"
6. Study Activity IV-A-5, "What are some animals that live in the ocean?"

H. Vocabulary Builders—Spelling Words:

1) **fossil** 2) **minerals** 3) **plaster of Paris** 4) **vinegar** 5) **clam shell** 6) **dissolved**

I. Thought for Today:

"One motivation is worth ten threats, two pressures, and six reminders."

SECTION B: PETS

Activity IV B 1

A. Problem: *How Do We Care for Hamsters, Guinea Pigs, Gerbils, and/or Mice?*

B. Materials Needed:

1. Male animal
2. Female animal of same species
3. Two wire mesh pens, about 3′ × 2′ in area, with sides at least 16″ high
4. Four pans for food and water

C. Procedure:

1. Select students for specific duties, such as feeding the animals, cleaning the pens, or recording observations.
2. If desired, place two animals of the opposite sex in the same pen and in time they will mate. Do not cage two males of the same species together because they are apt to fight.
3. Feed the animals a good commercial food product (well-balanced).
4. Keep fresh water in the pen at all times.

D. Results:

1. Students will learn about the care and feeding of animals.
2. Students will discover some of the responsibilities of breeding and caring for young animals.

E. Basic Facts and Supplemental Information:

1. All life comes from life, and each species reproduces its own kind of living organism.
2. Life is dependent upon certain materials and conditions.
3. Most animals need food, water, exercise, fresh air, and sunshine.
4. Use caution in handling the females for a short time preceding and following the birth of a litter.
5. Mice and hamsters are usually the most available rodents.
6. Mice and white rats make good pets and they are a lot of fun to watch.
   a. They are nearsighted and timid.
   b. They are nocturnal and love to explore.
   c. They can produce up to 17 litters a year with 6 to 12 young in each litter.

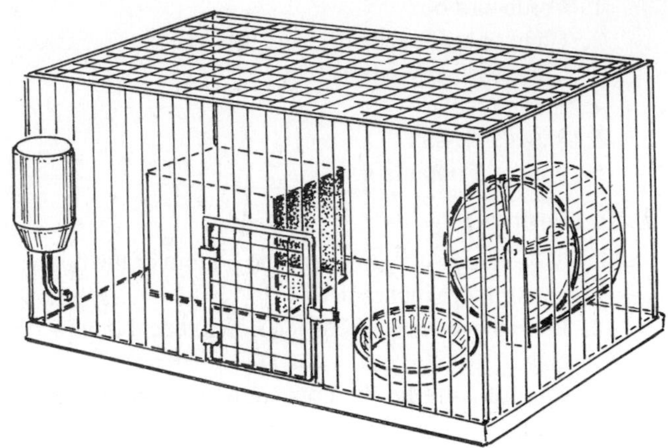

   d. They eat about 2 ounces of food a day, which should include seeds, nuts, dry dog food, bread, cheese, and green vegetables.
   e. Mice should have a litter box, which needs to be cleaned every 2 days.
7. Responsibilities must always be assigned to students so that the pets do not suffer from lack of food, water, exercise, or physical comfort.

F. Thought Questions for Class Discussions:

1. What are some common characteristics of pets?
2. What are the natural habitats of these animals?
3. How do these animals differ from dogs and cats?
4. Should animals be raised for fur coats and/or scientific research?

G. Related Topics for Further Inquiry:

1. Stories can be collected about pets.
2. Students can write creative stories about pets.
3. Students can relate their art work to these activities.
4. Study other Activities in this Section.

H. Vocabulary Builders—Spelling Words:

1) **hamster** 2) **guinea pigs** 3) **gerbils** 4) **mice** 5) **rodents** 6) **exercise** 7) **sunshine** 8) **cleaning**

I. Thought for Today:

"Strolling through the back alley the seventy-four pound mouse cried, 'Here Kitty, Kitty, Kitty.' "

Activity IV B 2

A. Problem: *Do Turtles Make Good Classroom Pets?*

B. Materials Needed:

1. Two or three baby turtles
2. Large bowl or small aquarium
3. Small rocks
4. Water
5. Food (insects, worms, plants)
6. Reference materials about turtles

C. Procedure:

1. Set bowl or aquarium away from direct sunlight.
2. Place rocks in center of aquarium so turtles can get out of the water.
3. Put water in aquarium or bowl but do not cover the rocks.
4. Feed turtles daily.
5. Observe their mannerisms and characteristics.
6. Do some research on turtle life.
7. Compare turtles with other reptiles.

D. Results:

1. Students will learn that turtles make good classroom pets.
2. Students will learn how to take care of turtles.

E. Basic Facts and Supplemental Information:

1. Turtles are well protected by their shells.
2. Turtles are reptiles as are snakes, lizards, alligators, and crocodiles.
3. They hatch from eggs.
4. Some live in fresh water; some in salt water.
5. Land turtles are called tortoises.
6. Fresh-water turtles are called terrapins.
7. Turtles vary in size from several inches to 8 feet long and can weigh up to 1,000 pounds.
8. Turtles have no teeth.
9. Turtles are cold-blooded.
10. The shells of turtles correspond to the ribs and scales of other reptiles.
11. Land turtles are slow-moving plant eaters.
12. Sea turtles and fresh-water turtles are good swimmers and good hunters.
13. Sea turtles and fresh-water turtles must surface to breathe.

Turtle

F. Thought Questions for Class Discussions:

1. What would be an advantage and disadvantage of being a turtle?
2. Do turtles ever know their parents?
3. Do many sea turtles survive to adulthood?
4. Scientists say that turtles are the oldest species of reptiles. How could they determine this?
5. One of the biggest problems facing turtles is their possible extinction. Poachers are killing them. Encroaching populations are threatening them. Should we be concerned about these problems?

G. Related Topics for Further Inquiry:

1. Compare turtles with other pets.
2. Study the life cycle of turtles.
3. Visit a pet store. Acquire all the information you can about the care and feeding of turtles and then decide whether you or the class should have a turtle as a pet.
4. Study other Activities in this Section.

H. Vocabulary Builders—Spelling Words:

1) **turtle** 2) **tortoise** 3) **terrapin**
4) **aquarium** 5) **reptiles** 6) **threatened**

I. Thought for Today:

"Turtles don't make any progress until they stick their necks out."

Activity IV B 3

A. Problem: *Do White Rats Make Good Classroom Pets?*

B. Materials Needed:

1. Four to six white rats
2. Adequate cage (multipurpose wire)
3. Exercise wheel
4. Food trays
5. Water source
6. Printed materials on care and feeding of classroom pets

C. Procedure:

1. Discuss the care and feeding of white rats.
2. If any of the students have these pets in their homes, let them discuss some of the problems and joys of having them.
3. Have students study the feasibility of caring for these animals.
4. Have the class decide whether they want these pets in the classroom.
5. After studying the pros and cons of accepting white rats for their classroom pets, definite plans should be established for their care and feeding.

D. Results:

1. Students will probably decide in favor of keeping white rats as classroom pets.
2. Many students will overcome their fear of these animals.
3. Students will learn that the care and feeding of any animal requires constant attention.

E. Basic Facts and Supplemental Information:

1. White rats usually make fine classroom pets.
2. Students can pick them up.
3. They are less apt to bite than hamsters.
4. It takes about three weeks for their gestation period (21 to 22 days).
5. Their eyes open in about 16 to 18 days.
6. They should be kept with their mother for about 21 to 24 days.
7. Adult rats need bread, milk, lettuce, carrots, sunflower seeds.
8. If rats are handled carefully and slowly, there usually are no problems.
9. Newspaper strips and cloth pieces help female rats at nesting time.

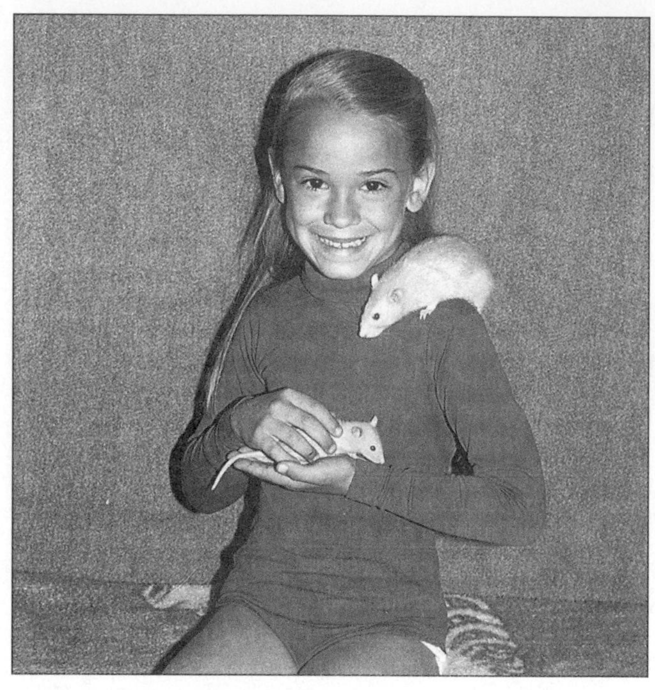

F. Thought Questions for Class Discussions:

1. To what family do white rats belong?
2. Are mice related to rats?
3. What animals prey on rats?

G. Related Topics for Further Inquiry:

1. Study all other Activities in this Section.
2. Study Section IV-G, "Mammals," then compare rats to other mammals.
3. Rats make excellent specimens for carefully controlled experiments involving nutrition. The most important thing to do in these tests is to be sure to "rescue" the weaker rat(s) after the experiment has been run for a short period of time. The weaker rat(s) can then be nourished back to full health.
4. Study Activity IV-A-8, "How do animals reproduce?"

H. Vocabulary Builders—Spelling Words:

1) **rodents** 2) **mammals** 3) **nutrition**
4) **gestations** 5) **white rats** 6) **experiments**

I. Thought for Today:

"Heads, hearts, and hands could settle the world's problems better than arms."

Activity IV B 4

A. Problem: *What Are Some Unusual Pets That We Could Keep in Our Classroom?*

B. Materials Needed:

Pictures, articles, books, and pamphlets on:

1. Lizards
2. Snakes
3. Birds
4. Fish
5. Snails
6. Rabbits
7. Other animals as suggested by the students

C. Procedure:

1. Study the list of unusual pets and do a little research to determine which might be fun and practical to have in the classroom.
2. If possible, obtain one of these.
3. If not, students can tell stories about them, write about them, and/or draw pictures of them.

D. Result:

Students will learn about some unusual pets.

E. Basic Facts and Supplemental Information:

1. All pets need constant care, feeding, and protection.
2. Some animals make good pets when young, but are not so good as adults: raccoons, skunks, woodchucks, etc. Consult with:
   a. pet store personnel
   b. veterinarians
   c. local zoo personnel
   d. forest rangers, etc., for advice and recommendations.

F. Thought Questions for Class Discussions:

1. What is the most unusual characteristic of each unusual pet studied?
2. Is the pet essentially a "prey," a "predator," or both?
3. How is the pet going to be cared for during vacation periods?
4. Should animals be removed from their native habitats just to make them "classroom pets"?
5. What precautions should be taken in acquiring a pet from a pet store?

G. Related Topics for Further Inquiry:

1. Study the feasibility of having a pet show.
2. Compare a potential pet's habitat with the classroom environment.
3. Compare the classroom environment with a home environment.
4. Study Part VI, "Ecology."
5. Study other Activities in this Section.

H. Vocabulary Builders—Spelling Words:

1) **lizard** 2) **snake** 3) **snail** 4) **rabbit** 5) **unusual** 6) **different** 7) **strange**

I. Thought for Today:

"It's real nice for children to have pets until the pets start having 'children.' "

Section C: Insects and Spiders

Activity IV C 1

A. Problem: *How Do We Study Common Insects?*

B. Materials Needed:

1. Collections of insects that are common in your locality
2. Reference materials that show the characteristics of the more common order of insects
3. Magnifying glasses

C. Procedure:

1. Students should carefully examine all the insects that are available. The common characteristics to look for are:
   a. six legs
   b. whether the insect has wings
   c. shape of the body
   d. kind of head
   e. special characteristics or features of insects:
      1) outside skeleton (exoskeleton)
      2) bilateral symmetry
      3) three body parts:
         (a) head
         (b) thorax
         (c) abdomen
2. Using the supplemental information included in this Activity, the students should try to classify the insects they collected or acquired.
3. Locate an area of moist soil on campus. Have students count the number of insects in a specified area using their naked eyes and then using magnifying glasses.

D. Results:

1. Students will learn the common characteristics of insects.
2. Students may want to make insect collections. The label on each specimen should include the name of the collector, common name of the insect, date, and location of find. Older students may want to include the scientific name of the specimen.

E. Basic Facts and Supplemental Information:

1. Insects make up the largest group of animals.
2. Insects include bees, ants, wasps, butterflies, moths, cockroaches, ladybugs, fireflies, termites, crickets, houseflies, dragonflies, mosquitoes, grasshoppers, lice, fleas, etc.
3. This is a highly motivating activity for individuals or groups.
4. Some insects undergo complete metamorphosis and others undergo incomplete metamorphosis.
5. Complete metamorphosis is the changing states of an insect and includes:
   a. egg (could have one or up to 10,000)
   b. larva (when eggs hatch, they look like worms)
   c. Pupa (full growth, larva hibernates and encases itself in a "shell" or "cocoon")
   d. adult (when full grown, it emerges from the pupa)
6. Incomplete metamorphosis is also changing states but includes:
   a. egg (could have one or many)
   b. early stage nymph (resembles adult; those that will have wings, still not developed)
   c. late stage nymph (skin begins to molt [shed]; wings begin to develop)
   d. adult (insect now fully grown)
7. Some insects are harmful to people and carry diseases.
8. Some insects are helpful because they feed on plants and other animals that are harmful to people.
9. Over 850,000 different species of insects have been named by scientists.
10. Spiders are not insects; they have eight legs. Spiders are in the "class" of Arachnids.
11. There are 25 groups (orders) of insects.
12. Characteristics of the more common insect orders and selected representatives are:
    a. *Coleoptera*—sheath wings: beetles
       two pairs wings; outer hard covering, membranous hind wings, complete metamorphosis, biting mouthparts
    b. *Hemiptera*—half or no wings: true bugs, aphids, and scale insects
       Three types:
       1) forewings thickened at base, thin ends overlap
       2) forewings thickened throughout, roof-shaped over back
       3) no wings at all
       Metamorphosis incomplete, sucking mouthparts
    c. *Lepidoptera*—scale wings: butterflies and moths; two pair wings—often showy—covered with scales (spicules); complete metamorphosis, adult mouthparts sucking

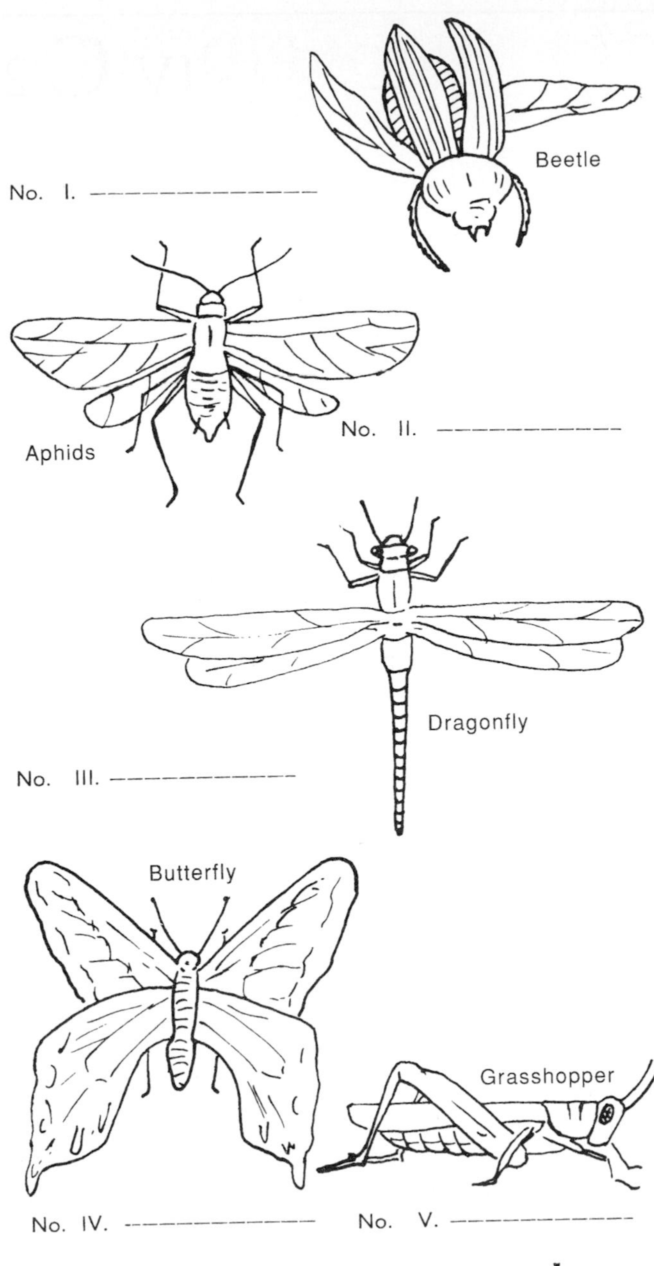

d. *Hymenoptera*—membrane wings: bees, wasps, ants. etc.;
two pairs of wings, membranous wings, sometimes hooked together; metamorphosis complete, mouthparts biting, sometimes modified

e. *Diptera*—two wings: true flies, flies, mosquitoes, midges;
one pair membranous wings, complete metamorphosis; mouthparts biting or sucking

f. *Neuroptera*—nerve wings: equal numerous cross-veins: aphis lions, mayflies; both complete and incomplete metamorphosis, biting mouthparts

g. *Orthoptera*—straight wings: grasshoppers, crickets, etc.
Two pairs wings, outer straight over; back, somewhat thickened; hind wings for flight, folded under forewings metamorphosis incomplete, mouthparts biting

13. Collecting equipment includes:
    a. insect nets
    b. killing jar (carbon tetrachloride)
    c. spreading board
    d. mounts
    e. collecting cages
    f. display cages
    g. ant colony

F. Thought Questions for Class Discussions:

1. What are some common insects found around our homes? our school? our community?
2. What are the main characteristics of insects?
3. Are spiders insects?
4. How do insects help us? hurt us?

G. Related Topics for Further Inquiry:

1. Younger students can describe the more obvious differences in insects.
2. Older students may make collections of insects.
3. Study metamorphosis.
4. Study Activity III-A-1, "How do we classify living things?"
5. Study Activity IV-C-2, "How do bees communicate?"
6. Study Activity IV-C-3, "How can we collect insects and spiders?"
7. Study Activity IV-C-4, "Do caterpillars change to butterflies? Do larvae change to moths?"
8. Study Activity IV-C-5, "How can we preserve insects or start a butterfly collection?"

H. Vocabulary Builders—Spelling Words:

1) **beetle** 2) **aphid** 3) **dragonfly**
4) **grasshopper** 5) **butterfly**
6) (**other insects by name**)

I. Thought for Today:

"Ants and mosquitoes know in advance if it is going to rain. That's why they never miss a picnic."

Activity IV C 2

A. Problem: *How Do Bees Communicate?*

B. Materials Needed:

1. Pictures of bees
2. Charts of bee dance patterns similar to those in sketches
3. Reference materials on bees

C. Procedure:

1. Study insects.
2. Study bees in particular.
3. Display charts of bee dance patterns.
4. Tell students that bees can really communicate to other bees the direction and distance of flowers.

D. Results:

1. Students will learn that bees do communicate.
2. Students will realize that animals communicate in various ways.

E. Basic Facts and Supplemental Information:

1. Scientists have studied the behavior patterns of bees and they realized that bees perform a ritualistic dance.
2. In further study they learned that these dance performances were associated with certain flowers.
3. They realized that the bees were actually pointing to the direction of the flowers by "dancing" in adjacent half circles with the common midline, the "arrow," pointing to the location of the flowers. (See top drawing.)
4. The speed of the rotation of the bees coincides with the distance to the flowers. The slower the dance is performed, the farther away the flower is.

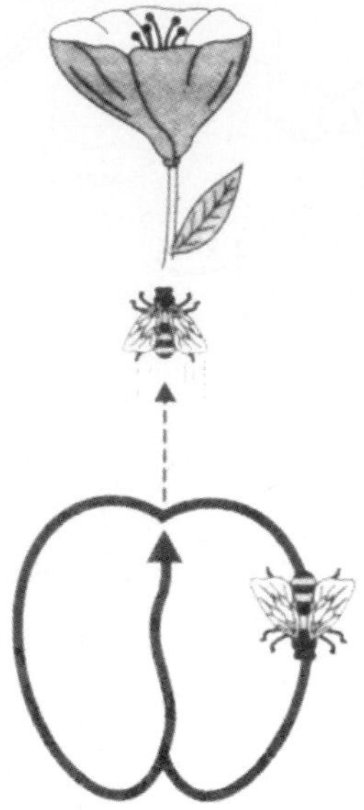

The dance of the bee is done in half circles.

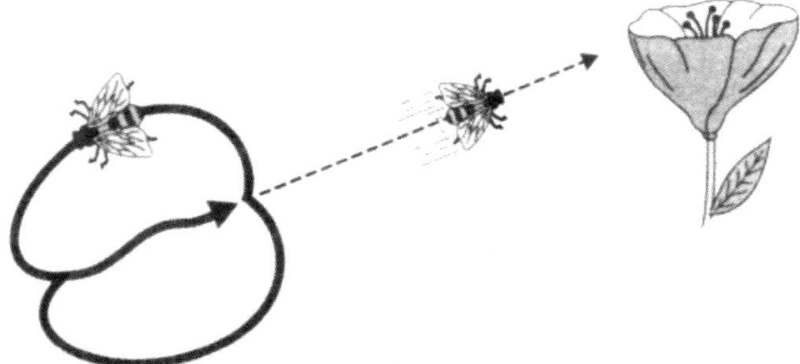

Speed of rotation determines distance.

F. Thought Questions for Class Discussions:

1. How do other animals communicate?
2. In what ways do people communicate?
3. Is television a form of communication?
4. What problems would develop if bees and other insects did not aid in the pollination of flowers?
5. Why does honey have different flavors?

G. Related Topics for Further Inquiry:

1. Study Activity V-B-1, "What senses do we use to communicate with each other?"
2. Study Activity V-B-13, "How do we use our sense of smell?"
3. Study Activity VI-A-2, "What is 'biological diversity'?"
4. Study all other Activities in this Section.

H. Vocabulary Builders—Spelling Words:

1) **communicate** 2) **bees** 3) **flowers** 4) **direction** 5) **distance** 6) **ritual** 7) **dance**

I. Thought for Today:

"Bees can't make honey and sting at the same time."

Activity

A. Problem: *How Can We Collect Insects and Spiders?*

B. Materials Needed:

1. Butterfly net
2. Killing jar and cover
3. Carbon tetrachloride, ethyl acetate, or acetone
4. Cotton
5. Envelopes, small
6. Magnifying glass or lens (10 power)
7. Cardboard box, siding
8. Dowels (12″–18″)
9. Kitchen sieve (for water insects)
10. Reference materials for identifying insects and spiders

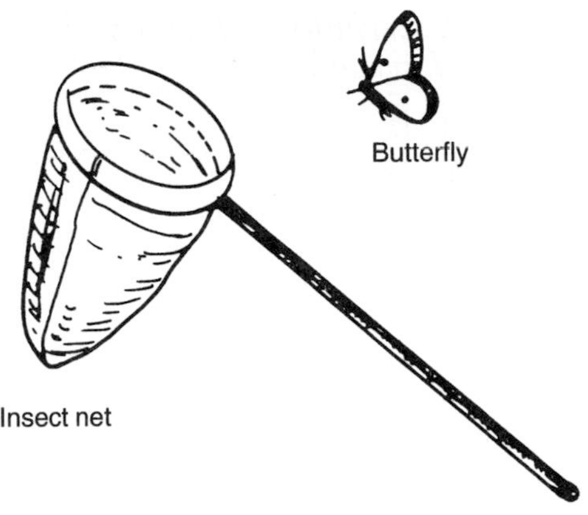

C. Procedure:

1. Have students take a walk around the school campus to look for insects and spiders.
2. Bring all equipment listed under Materials Needed.
3. Watch for flying insects.
4. Use net to entrap.
5. Use net to scoop along grasses and wooded areas.
6. Work specimens to small end of net.
7. Place killing jar with liquid next to specimen.
8. Have some students select a bush.
9. Specimens will be found in the bush.
10. Have one or two students hold a side of a cardboard box slightly bent in the middle next to bush or under part of it while others use dowels to tap lightly on the bush. Insects will fall onto the cardboard.
11. Also look under rocks and dead wood carefully.
12. If water is nearby use kitchen sieve to collect specimens.
13. After the insects have been killed, place in envelopes for classifying and mounting.

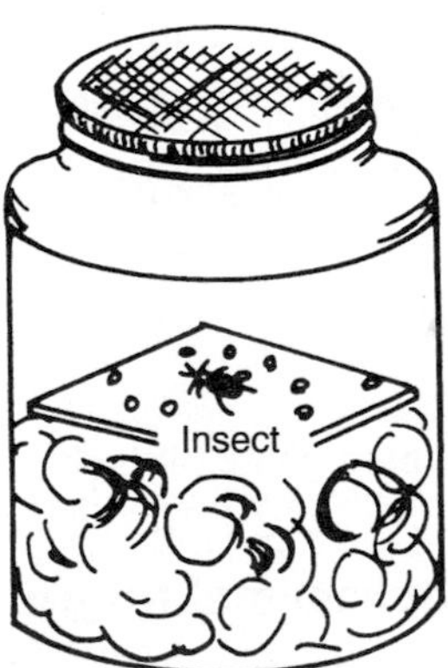

D. Results:

1. A school campus walk will be planned.
2. Insects and spiders will be collected.
3. Most specimens will be identified.

E. Basic Facts and Supplemental Information:

1. Students will enjoy this activity.
2. Usually, besides insects and spiders, other animals will be seen and can be identified.

F. Thought Questions for Class Discussions:

1. Where else might insects be found?
2. How do farmers protect their fruits and vegetables from unwanted insects?
3. How is food in the home protected from insects?

G. Related Topics for Further Inquiry:

1. Take field trips to study other plants and animals.
2. Turn on porch light at night and collect flying insects.
3. Study other Activities in this Section.

H. Vocabulary Builders—Spelling Words:

1) **killing jar** 2) **poison** 3) **sieve** 4) **envelope** 5) **insects** 6) **spiders** 7) **cotton**

I. Thought for Today:

"Be thankful if you have a job a little harder than you like. A razor cannot be sharpened on a piece of velvet."

Activity IV C 4

A. Problems: *Do Caterpillars Change to Butterflies? Do Larvae Change to Moths?*

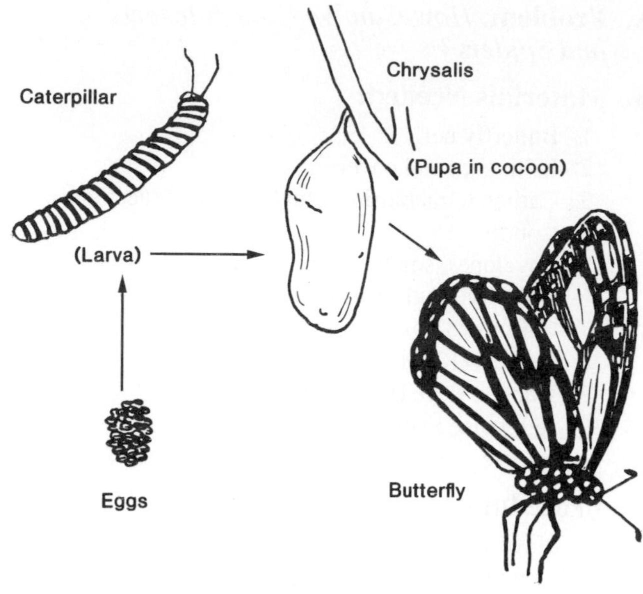

B. Materials Needed:

1. Live caterpillars
2. Pictures of moths and butterflies
3. Reference books
4. Live moths
5. Mounted moths and/or butterflies

C. Procedure:

1. Have a brief, general discussion about caterpillars and butterflies.
2. Have the students who are interested form a study committee.
3. The committee should find live caterpillars and plan how they will care for them.
4. As the caterpillars pass through the different stages, the members of the committee can report to the class by showing the stages and telling what they have observed.
5. If live caterpillars are unavailable, the class can study about the life cycles of butterflies and moths from reference books.

D. Result:

The students will learn about each phase of the life cycle of a butterfly and/or a moth.

E. Basic Facts and Supplemental Information:

1. Caterpillars eat specific types of food. If you are not sure about the food to feed the caterpillars, use the leaves or grass from where they were found.
2. Caterpillars and moths pass through four stages in their life cycles:
   a. First—eggs (adults lay them)
   b. Second—larvae (caterpillars)
   c. Third—chrysalis (pupae in cocoons)
   d. Fourth—butterflies or moths (adults)
3. The larvae of the gypsy moth are one of the worst pests of humans. They devour the leaves of the apple, oak, gray birch, alder, willow, and many other deciduous trees.
4. Butterflies are the most beautiful of all insects, and students enjoy collecting and mounting them.

F. Thought Questions for Class Discussions:

1. How does the life cycle of a butterfly compare with the life cycles of other animals?
2. How are the caterpillars going to be kept in class to ensure their health and safety?
3. What are the differences between a moth and a butterfly?

G. Related Topics for Further Inquiry:

1. Study the differences between moths and butterflies.
   a. Butterflies have thin bodies; moths are thicker.
   b. Butterflies fly during the day; moths fly at night.
   c. Butterflies' antennae are knobby; moths' antennae are feathery.
   d. Both migrate; some, long distances.
   e. We get silk from a silkworm moth's cocoon.
2. It is fun to search for these creatures.
3. Start a collection of butterflies and/or moths. They are beautiful.
4. Study especially Activities IV-C-1, "How do we study common insects?" and IV-C-5, "How can we preserve insects or start a butterfly collection?"

H. Vocabulary Builders—Spelling Words:

1) **eggs** 2) **larvae** 3) **chrysalis** 4) **butterfly** 5) **moth** 6) **metamorphosis** 7) **pupae**

I. Thought for Today:

"To know what is right and not do it is the worst form of cowardice."

Activity

A. Problem: *How Can We Preserve Insects or Start a Butterfly Collection?*

B. Materials Needed:

1. Insects collected on a field trip
2. Insect pins (size 2 or 3) or common pins
3. Forceps
4. Cardboard insect boxes (See Activity III-F-5 on constructing Riker-type mounts.)
5. Glue
6. White index card
7. Fine point pen
8. Spreading board, sheet of cork, or cardboard
9. Relaxing jar
10. Formalin (or fingernail polish remover, which contains acetone)
11. Sand, moist

C. Procedure:

1. Mount insects with insect pins or common pins.
2. Place previously collected specimens in a relaxing jar, a widemouth jar with wet sand on the bottom.
3. Add to this a few drops of formalin or acetone.
4. To soften the insect specimens for easier handling, place the insect on the moist sand in the jar and close the jar tightly. In a few days it will be ready to use. A small dish with moist sand may be substituted. (Cover to keep moist.)
5. Hold the specimen between the fingers of one hand while putting the pin in vertically with the fingers of the other hand. Push the specimen up toward the head of the pin 3/8 of an inch for grasping the pin with the fingers. Forceps may be used for pushing the insects on the pins.
6. Put the pin through the center of the stoutest part of the body, but never through a joint that lies between two parts of the insect.
7. Beetles must be pinned through one of the hard shell wings, just to the right of the midline down through where the two wings meet on the body.
8. True bugs will need to be pinned through the small, triangular piece that is attached to the hind end of the thorax off the midline.
9. Keep specimen in most natural position. Place those with slender abdomens low on the pin.
10. Spread out legs and antennae and let dry, then push to proper place on the pin.
11. Some insects should have wings spread in mounting. Sometimes only one wing is spread to save room in the insect box. A spreading board is best to use, but a sheet of cork can also be used.

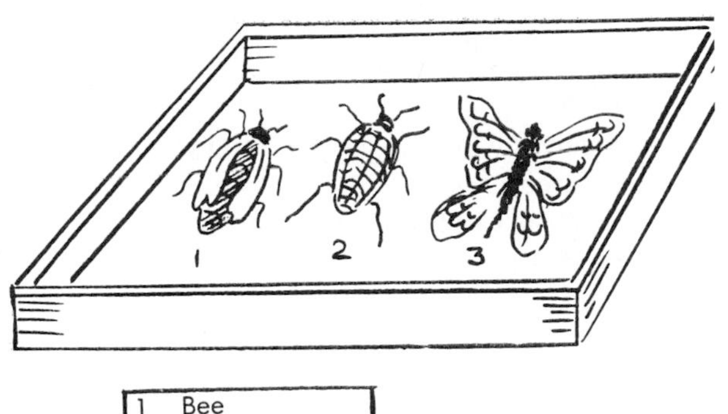

1	Bee
2	Beetle
3	Butterfly

Pin mounting for small insects

12. Insects too small to pin are best glued to the tips of points on small cards. Use a card as thick as an index card. Cut it into strips about 3/8″ in width. Then make crosscuts across the strip at slight angles to make slender triangular points 3/8″ long and about 1/8 ″ wide at the base. These points can be made more quickly with a punch secured from an entomological supply house.
13. Now lay out the small insects on a clean sheet of paper so they rest on their right sides with their wings extending to your left, and with their heads toward you. This position could be reversed. Other positions tend to hinder proper viewing.
14. Put glue on the paper and pick up a cardboard point with the forceps, touch its smaller tip to the glue, and touch the point to the uppermost side of the insect. The insect will be fastened to the point with the right side up and its head away from you, when it is turned over. Put pin through the base of triangular point, letting the specimen extend to the left of the pin.
15. When labeling the specimens put a number on every insect pin. Make a label as small as it can possibly be made and still contain as much data as possible. Too many insect collections contain more paper labels than insects. Try making the labels as small as 1/2″ × 5/16″.

16. Each specimen should be labeled with the locality, town and state, date, month, day and year (written 3.9.01 rather than March 9, 2001) and name of the collector. Add any other information you can as to the area in which the insect was found, what it was doing, etc.
17. Add mothballs or mothflakes for best preservation.

D. Results:

1. Students will learn common and scientific names of insects.
2. Students will learn how to collect insect specimens.
3. Students will learn proper insect mounting techniques.

E. Basic Facts and Supplemental Information:

1. Specimens could be preserved in an airtight box (called a Schmitt box) if you hope to keep certain small beetles called "museum pests" from getting in and eating them up. You may want to keep a few specimens in a plastic box or some other similar container, but you will surely be disappointed if you try to keep them for any length of time. If the school has Schmitt boxes for its collections, they will probably appreciate any gifts you care to make them, and students for years to come will profit from your skill and care in mounting these specimens.
2. If these steps are used for mounting and preserving these specimens which have been collected, you will have a collection which you will be proud of and may keep safely for many years.

F. Thought Questions for Class Discussions:

1. Where would be the best locations to look for insects?
2. Is there a best time of day or season to try to collect insects?
3. What materials are needed to catch insects?

G. Related Topics for Further Inquiry:

1. Students enjoy collecting things, and insect specimens make beautiful collections.
2. Study Activity IV-C-1, "How do we study common insects?"
3. Study Activity IV-C-3, "How can we collect insects and spiders?"
4. Study Activity VI-A-1, "What is the balance of nature?"
5. Study Activity VI-A-2, "What is 'biological diversity'?"
6. Study Activity VI-A-6, "What are food chains? food webs?"

H. Vocabulary Builders—Spelling Words:

1) **preserve** 2) **forceps** 3) **spreading board**
4) **relaxing jar** 5) **abdomen** 6) **thorax**
7) **points**

I. Thought for Today:

"The butterfly counts not months but moments and has time enough."

Activity IV C 6

A. Problem: *How Do Spiders Differ from Insects?*

B. Materials Needed:

Specimens or pictures of spiders

C. Procedure:

1. Collect specimens and pictures of as many spiders as possible.
2. Study the body parts of each of them.
3. Note that the main difference between spiders and insects is the number of legs. Insects have 6 legs; spiders have 8 legs.
4. Also, most insects have 3 main body parts, whereas spiders have only 2.

D. Results:

1. Students will learn about the main characteristics of spiders.
2. They will learn about spiders' homes.

E. Basic Facts and Supplemental Information:

1. Arachnids include spiders, scorpions, ticks, mites, horseshoe crabs, and king crabs.
2. One of the master engineering jobs is accomplished by the spider in spinning its web with silk-like fibers.
3. Webs are sticky so spiders can catch their prey.
4. The spiders feel a "catch" when the web vibrates.
5. Each spider then paralyzes its prey.
6. Later the spider feeds upon the prey.
7. Spiders do not sting; some bite.
8. Some spiders are nomadic, that is they have no webs or homes.
9. Insects have wings; spiders have none.
10. The head and thorax, usually separate in insects, are combined in the spider to form a cephalothorax, which is separate from the abdomen.

F. Thought Questions for Class Discussions:

1. What kinds of spiders have you seen?
2. Where have you seen them?
3. Do spiders fight among themselves?

Spiders

Spiders differ in residences.

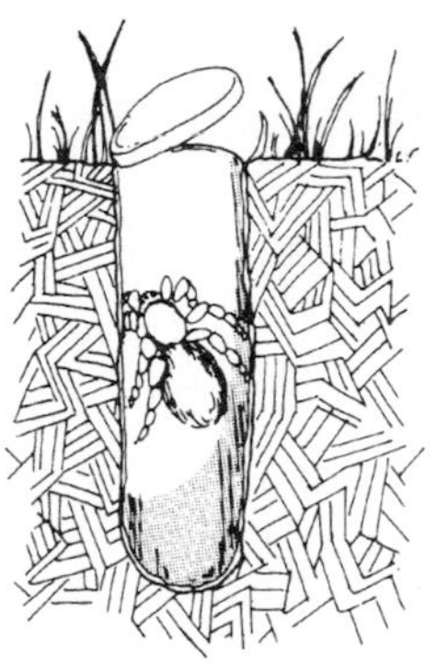

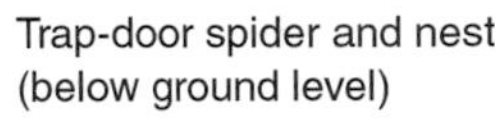

Trap-door spider and nest (below ground level)

Turret spider and nest (partially below ground level)

Spiders differ in web design.

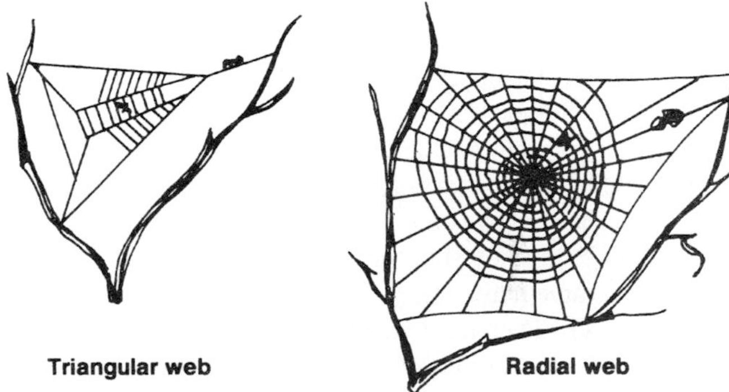

G. Related Topics for Further Inquiry:

1. Make collections or copies of spiders' webs.
2. Make a spider vivarium.
3. Study other Activities in this Section.

H. Vocabulary Builders—Spelling Words:

1) **spiders** 2) **cobweb** 3) **radial** 4) **triangular** 5) **trapdoor** 6) **insects**

I. Thought for Today:

"If it weren't for the last minute, a lot of things wouldn't get done."

SECTION D: REPTILES

Activity IV D 1

A. Problem: *What Are Reptiles?*

B. Materials Needed:

1. Models, specimens, or pictures of:
   a. snakes
   b. lizards
   c. turtles
   d. crocodiles
   e. alligators
   f. other reptiles
2. Reference materials on reptiles

C. Procedure:

1. Discuss with students their experiences with snakes, lizards, turtles, and other reptiles.
2. Discuss the characteristics of common reptiles:
   a. lay eggs on land
   b. have leathery skin or shell
   c. ectothermic—body temperature varies with external temperature (cold-blooded)
   d. have two pairs of legs (except snakes)
   e. have claws on their toes
   f. have scaly skin for body covering
   g. three main groups:
      1) squamates (snakes and lizards)
      2) crocodilians (crocodiles, alligators, caimans, and gavials)
      3) chelonians (tortoises, turtles, and terrapins)
3. Study local reptiles.
4. Relate any unusual characteristics found in reference materials such as:
   a. About 6,500 species of reptiles exist today.
   b. Dinosaurs were reptiles that dominated the Earth for millions of years.
   c. Snakes can spring only half of their body length.
   d. Very few snakes are poisonous.
   e. Lizards and snakes shed their skin from time to time so they can grow.
   f. A few species of crocodiles can reach almost 30 feet in length.
   g. Fertilization takes place inside the body.

D. Results:

1. Students will acquire some basic information about reptiles.
2. Students will learn that most snakes are not poisonous and that they help keep the rodent population in balance.

E. Basic Facts and Supplemental Information:

1. Reptiles are a "class" of animals.
2. They are found primarily in warm climates, especially in the tropics.
3. The Anaconda snake can reach 30 feet in length.
4. The "Marine Leatherback" turtle weighs up to 1,500 pounds.
5. Except for snakes, reptiles have four limbs which project from the sides.
6. Reptile hides are valued in the making of shoes, purses, etc. In some parts of the world reptiles are hunted for food.

F. Thought Questions for Class Discussions:

1. Would Canada, Alaska, or Siberia have many reptiles?
2. How do reptiles differ from mammals?
3. How do crocodiles differ from alligators?

G. Related Topics for Further Inquiry:

1. Study reptiles in local zoos.
2. Study the rise and fall of dinosaurs.
3. Study Activity IV-D-2, "Are all snakes poisonous?"
4. Study Activity IV-D-4, "What do we know about dinosaurs?"

H. Vocabulary Builders—Spelling Words:

1) **snakes** 2) **lizards** 3) **turtles** 4) **tortoises** 5) **crocodiles** 6) **alligators** 7) **reptiles**

I. Thought for Today:

"He swam up the Nile as far as the first crocodile."

Activity IV D 2

A. Problem: *Are All Snakes Poisonous?*

B. Materials Needed:

1. Pictures of snakes (king, gopher, garter, bull, coral, and rattle)
2. Plaster specimens (may be borrowed from local museums, colleges, or universities)
3. Reference materials about snakes

C. Procedure:

1. Discuss animals in general.
2. Discuss reptiles.
3. Have students relate their experiences with snakes.
4. Have students study the pictures of snakes and ask if they look familiar.
5. Have students study snakes and discuss their research.

D. Results:

1. Students will learn that most snakes are not poisonous or dangerous.
2. Students will learn that there are over 3,000 species of snakes, very few are poisonous to humans, and some make very fine pets.
3. Students will gain a better understanding of snakes, which will help them to correct misconceptions, will result in less fear of snakes, and will encourage them to protect useful snakes.

E. Basic Facts and Supplemental Information:

1. Snakes only attack humans if they think they are endangered.
2. Snakes tend to shun humans.
3. Snakes can only strike one-half their body length.
4. Snakes are helpful to people. They eat rodents and insects.
5. Although snakes have no legs, they move freely, can swim, and climb trees.
6. The four poisonous snakes found in the United States are the coral snake, rattlesnake, copperhead, and water moccasin.
7. Coral snakes are found only in the southern part of the United States.
8. Rattlesnakes are found in most of this country.
9. Copperheads are found in the Eastern United States.
10. Water moccasins live in the southeast part of the United States.
11. First aid measures to take in case of snakebite:
    a. Call a doctor.
    b. Tie a tourniquet around the limb above the bite.
    c. Cut an X across the bite to help the bleeding and let the venom out.
12. Do not try to collect poisonous snakes; leave them to the professionals.

Rattlesnake

Copperhead snake

F. Thought Questions for Class Discussions:

1. How do snakes differ from other reptiles?
2. How can a snake swallow something larger than its head size?
3. Are snakes warm-blooded or cold-blooded?

G. Related Topics for Further Inquiry:

1. Study other Activities in this Section.
2. Study other Activities in Part IV, "Animals."
3. Develop a snake terrarium.

H. Vocabulary Builders—Spelling Words:

1) **reptiles** 2) **snakes** 3) **rattlesnakes** 4) **poisonous** 5) **dangerous** 6) **venom**

I. Thought for Today:

"Many of the most firmly held beliefs are those based solidly on ignorance."

Activity IV D 3

Alligator — blunt nose

Crocodile — pointed nose

A. Problem: *What Are the Differences between an Alligator and a Crocodile?*

B. Materials Needed:

1. Pictures of crocodiles
2. Pictures of alligators
3. Other multisensory materials on alligators and crocodiles

C. Procedure:

1. Ask students if they have ever seen a live alligator or crocodile. If so, have them explain the circumstances.
2. Show the pictures of the alligators and crocodiles.
3. Show the other multisensory materials about these reptiles.
4. Discuss selected items from Basic Facts and Supplemental Information, below.

D. Results:

1. Students will learn the differences between alligators and crocodiles.
2. Students will learn that reptiles have lived on the Earth for a long time.

E. Basic Facts and Supplemental Information:

1. Alligators and crocodiles are "armored animals."
2. Reptiles have existed on the Earth for over 200,000,000 years.
3. Dinosaurs were reptiles and were related to alligators and crocodiles.
4. Alligators and crocodiles have four legs.
5. Crocodiles live in Africa, Asia, North America, and South America.
6. Alligators live in China and the Southern United States.
7. Both crocodiles and alligators are egg-bearers.
8. Females lay between 20 to 90 eggs per clutch.
9. Their eggshells are tough, but nature has provided newborns with a tough egg tooth to break birth shells. After birth, this tooth drops off.
10. Both species love to sun themselves along river banks.
11. Their tails are very powerful and can be used as weapons of defense.
12. They have air flaps which prevent water from entering their lungs when submerged. They can submerge for hours at a time.
13. The most obvious difference between them is the shape of the nose. The crocodile has a narrow, tapering snout while the alligator has a broad, blunt snout.
14. Alligators are usually between 8 and 10 feet long with some lengths to 19 feet.
15. Crocodiles are larger, usually between 10 and 12 feet, with some species as large as 23 feet long.
16. Crocodiles are man-eaters.
17. Alligators are not man-eaters; you can swim in the same water with them.

F. Thought Questions for Class Discussions:

1. Do you think we should buy alligator shoes and purses?
2. Would you rather be tossed in a pool with crocodiles or alligators?
3. Do you know any other kind of reptile?

G. Related Topics for Further Inquiry:

1. Compare alligators and crocodiles to turtles, amphibians, and dinosaurs.
2. Study Activity IV-D-1, "What are reptiles?"
3. Study Activity VI-A-1, "What is the balance of nature?"
4. Study Activity VI-A-2, "What is 'biological diversity'?"

H. Vocabulary Builders—Spelling Words:

1) **alligator** 2) **crocodile** 3) **armour** 4) **reptile** 5) **snout** 6) **submerge** 7) **clutch**

I. Thought for Today:

"If you love the good that you see in another, make it your own."

Activity IV D 4

Tyrannosaurus Rex
"King of the Dinosaurs"

A. Problem: *What Do We Know about Dinosaurs?*

B. Materials Needed:

1. Pictures of dinosaurs
2. Models of dinosaurs
3. Other multisensory materials about dinosaurs
4. Reference materials on dinosaurs

C. Procedure:

1. Ask students if they have ever heard of dinosaurs.
2. Have them relate these experiences.
3. Show pictures and models of dinosaurs.
4. Tell the class dinosaurs existed a long time ago—about 200 million years ago.
5. Discuss appropriate items cited below in Basic Facts and Supplemental Information.

D. Results:

1. Students will learn that dinosaurs really existed.
2. Students will learn that changes in the environment can cause great changes in animal life.

E. Basic Facts and Supplemental Information:

1. Dinosaurs were:
   a. reptiles.
   b. cold-blooded (body temperature changed with outside air temperature).
   c. land animals.
   d. mostly plant eaters.
2. Dinosaurs had:
   a. four legs; most had two large hind legs and two small front legs.
   b. small heads and small brains.
   c. short, flat teeth.
3. Dinosaurs:
   a. walked on their hind legs.
   b. varied in appearance: some looked like lizards, others like turkeys, turtles, or elephants.
   c. lived in marshy, swampy lands.
   d. varied in size. The largest was Brontosaurus who ranged up to 80 feet long and weighed up to 40 tons (80,000 pounds)–(36,000 kilograms).
   e. were oviparous (hatched from eggs).
4. Many dinosaurs were able to live in the water.
5. The Earth's climate became colder and drier about 60 million years ago, and the swamps and marshes dried up. A lot of their vegetation was lost, and the dinosaurs became extinct.
6. We know dinosaurs existed because we have found a lot of their fossil remains.
7. The word "dinosaur" means "terrible lizard."
8. A flying dinosaur was the Pterodactyl (actually it glided or soared rather than flew).
9. Tyrannosaurus Rex was the most ferocious, and the name means "King of the Lizards."
10. The dinosaurs lived in the Mesozoic era, which lasted from 230 to 65 million years ago.

F. Thought Questions for Class Discussions:

1. What animals today do you think are the most closely related to dinosaurs?
2. Do all animals "like" the same kind of temperature?
3. What could cause changes in the Earth's temperature?

G. Related Topics for Further Inquiry:

1. Study Activity VI-C-4, "What is the ozone problem?"
2. Study Activity VI-C-6, "What is global warming (the 'greenhouse effect')?"
3. Study Activity VI-C-7, "What is global cooling (the 'icehouse effect')?"
4. Study Part VI, "Ecology."
6. Students can make models of dinosaurs with clay or papier-maché.
7. Students can make dioramas of habitats of dinosaurs. (Dioramas are three-dimensional scenes, usually in a box.)

H. Vocabulary Builders—Spelling Words:

1) **dinosaurs** 2) **swamps** 3) **marshes**
4) **oviparous** 5) **reptiles** 6) **extinct**

I. Thought for Today:

"The turtle lays thousands of eggs without anyone knowing, but when the hen lays one egg, the whole country is informed."

Section E: Water Animals (Fish and Amphibians)

Activity IV E 1

A. Problem: *How Do Fish Differ from Other Animals?*

B. Materials Needed:

1. Reference materials about fish
2. Pictures, stories, specimens of fish

C. Procedure:

1. Discuss how we classify living things. See Activity III-A-1.
2. Discuss the characteristics of living things. See Activity IV-A-1.
3. Discuss students' experiences with fish and fishing.
4. Discuss different kinds of fish such as bass, trout, carp, perch, blue gill, etc.
5. Ask students how fish differ:
   a. markings
   b. size
   c. color
   d. shape
   e. fins
   f. scales, etc.
6. Tell students (or have them research) to find that fish are:
   a. cold-blooded
   b. water-dwelling
   c. hatched from eggs (few are live-bearers) and have:
      1) backbones
      2) gills to breathe
      3) fins to move
7. Discuss where fish live in the water.
8. Discuss feeding habits.
9. Discuss ways to catch fish.
10. Discuss the problem of reduced fish populations.

D. Results:

1. Students will learn about many animals.
2. They will learn about fish and fishing.
3. They will learn how fish differ from other animals.

E. Basic Facts and Supplemental Information:

1. Fish is not just "brain food" as many people think its nutrients go to all parts of the body.
2. Fish breathe because they need oxygen.

Trout

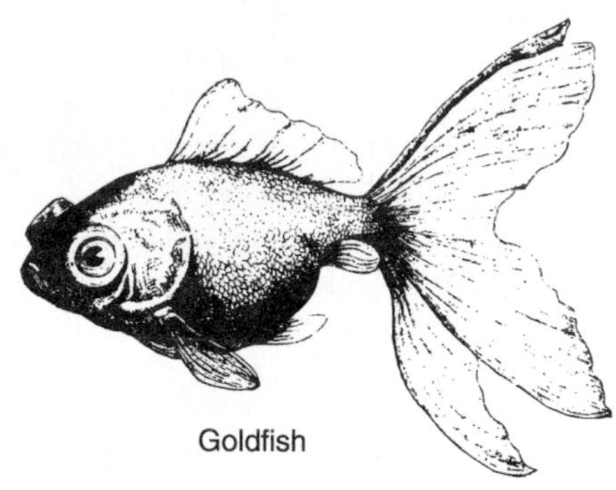

Goldfish

3. The oxygen in the water is absorbed by gills (fleshy filaments), which also release carbon dioxide.
4. Gills are very efficient; they absorb up to 75% of the available oxygen.
5. Fish sleep with their eyes open. (Actually it is more like a deep rest.)
6. Students will realize that we are overfishing many species.
7. As the world's population expands, we will need more fish for proteins to feed a hungry world.

F. Thought Questions for Class Discussions:

1. Do most fish live in fresh or salt water?
2. How do fish protect themselves?
3. Are dolphins and whales classified as fish?

G. Related Topics for Further Inquiry:

1. Start a classroom aquarium.
2. Discuss a balanced aquarium.
3. Study other Activities in this Section.

H. Vocabulary Builders—Spelling Words:

1) **cold-blooded** 2) **fish** 3) **backbone** 4) **gills** 5) **scales** 6) **fins** 7) **breathe**

I. Thought for Today:

"Decision is like a sharp knife that cuts clean and straight. Indecision is a dull one that hacks and tears and leaves ragged edges behind."

Activity IV E 2

A. Problem: *How Do We Care for a Fresh-Water Aquarium?*

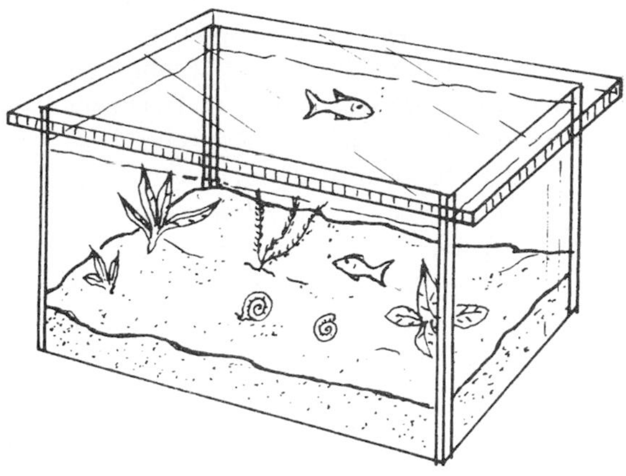

B. Materials Needed:

1. Glass tank and cover
2. Sand
3. Plants (water)
4. Thermometer (aquarium)
5. Fish (start with inexpensive tropical fish)
6. Water
7. Sprinkling can
8. Snails
9. Air pump

C. Procedure:

1. Place the tank in its permanent position. (Moving the aquarium after it is filled with water may cause a leak.) The tank should be placed in a position that ensures a liberal supply of diffused light. This will result in the active process of photosynthesis.
2. Disinfect plants by putting them in a salt solution (4 ounces of salt per gallon of water) for one minute, then washing them in fresh water. All plants, native or purchased, should be disinfected. Use plants sparingly. Too many plants will shut out the light. Too much light encourages the growth of algae and weeds which crowd out cultivated plants. A balance is needed. Floating plants may be added later if desired.
3. Wash glass tank thoroughly. A tank with a rectangular metal frame and a slate or glass bottom is most satisfactory. A tank 10″ × 10″ × 16″ or more is advisable, as it is difficult to keep a smaller tank properly balanced biologically.
4. Wash sand till water is clear. Coarse sand is best for the aquarium.
5. Place a 2-inch layer of sand at the bottom of the aquarium. Large pebbles and rocks, as well as ornamental castles, seashells, and the like should never be placed in the aquarium as they encourage algae growth.
6. Put plants in sand. Roots should be spread and well covered with sand. Plants of like species are best grouped together. A plan should be made on paper before the actual planting.
7. Temperature is important. Cold-water fish, including goldfish, thrive at temperatures from 59° to 65° F. Tropical fish require temperatures of 70° to 80° F.
8. Pour water from a sprinkling can into the tank, taking care to disturb the sand as little as possible. The slow pouring of water from a sprinkling can allows it to become aerated.
9. When tap water is used, the tank should be allowed to stand at least 24 hours before putting the fish in it. This allows the water to clear and become thoroughly oxygenated, the plants to take root, and any unwanted gases to dissipate. An air pump should be attached and utilized to continue proper oxygenation of aquarium.
10. Place fish and snails in the aquarium. The water in the aquarium should be approximately the same temperature as that from which the fish are taken. The fish should not be touched with the hands or dropped into the water, as this may injure their scales and lead to development of a fungus disease. They should be allowed to swim out of the container into the tank.
11. After fish have been placed in the aquarium, cover the aquarium with glass in order to prevent evaporation and the collecting of dust.
12. Fresh-water snails are, for all purposes, the best scavengers. Certain small fish such as the "weather fish" and catfish also are good scavengers.
13. Feed fish sparingly. It is well to remember that prepared fish food is highly concentrated. Fish should be given only what they can eat within 15 minutes. If food remains at the bottom, too much has been given. Uneaten food should be removed.
14. Feedings should be regular, twice a week is usually sufficient in cold weather, three times a week in warm seasons. Prepared food can be obtained at aquarium supply stores, pet stores, and

food markets. This may be supplemented by occasional fresh foods such as tiny scraps of raw beef and chopped lettuce. Live food such as Artemia is also satisfactory.

15. Remove immediately any fish showing signs of illness. Overfeeding, insufficient oxygen, and sudden changes in temperature are the chief causes of sickness in fish. Spotty reddish fins, white fungus on the body, or wobbly body movement are signs of illness. Treatment with salt water has been found best for general use. For a weak bath, one teaspoonful of salt to a gallon of water is recommended. For a strong bath, use one tablespoon of salt to a gallon of water. A sick fish should be left in the weak bath for 24 hours. This treatment should be continued with a new solution until the fish becomes healthy. Salt water treatment is not effective in all types of illness. Consult a book on aquarium care or a knowledgeable person at an aquarium or a tropical fish store if illness persists.
16. Gasping of fish at the top of the water may be due to an excess of carbon dioxide in the water or a lack of oxygen. If the water is oversaturated or undersaturated with oxygen, the excess or lack is quickly adjusted by exposure to the air above the water. However, since carbon dioxide passes from water to air and air to water very slowly, it takes much longer for an excess of carbon dioxide to pass off. It has been found that fish cannot take in oxygen through the gills if too much carbon dioxide is in the water. For this reason, fish can suffocate even when plenty of oxygen is present.

D. Results:

1. The aquarium will continue to provide material for discussion and research into the coexistence of various kinds of aquatic life and also what is required to support that life in various circumstances.
2. The students become aware of the interrelationship between plants and animals. The oxygen needed by the animals is provided by plants, and the carbon dioxide needed by the plants is provided by animals. When the oxygen-carbon dioxide relationship is well-balanced, it is unnecessary to change the water in the aquarium. If a glass aquarium isn't available, a clear plastic box can be utilized.
3. This is an excellent example of an ecosystem even though it is relatively small.

E. Basic Facts and Supplemental Information:

1. The experience of making an aquarium and caring for live animals in the classroom is both interesting and educational. The types of tank, sand, fish, scavengers, and plants selected are all factors to be considered.
2. In the newly planted aquarium, algae may develop and fresh water may become cloudy because of uneaten fish food.

F. Thought Questions for Class Discussions:

1. What are the little dots that form on the sides of the aquarium that look as if they were covered with thin cellophane? (snail eggs)
2. Which type of green plants survive best?
3. What are the advantages of bushy type plants?

G. Related Topics for Further Inquiry:

1. Raise guppies. They are easy to raise and quite prolific.
2. Construct and stock a salt-water aquarium. (Find specific directions. Salt-water fish are more varied and more beautiful.)
3. Study Activity II-A-1, "How do we classify living things?"
4. Study Activity IV-A-1, "What are some characteristics of all living things?"
5. Study Activity IV-A-2, "What is the Triangle of Life?"
6. Study Activity IV-E-1, "How do fish differ from other animals?"
7. Study Activity VI-A-1, "What is the balance of nature?"

H. Vocabulary Builders—Spelling Words:

1) **aquarium** 2) **sprinkling** 3) **snails** 4) **coarse** 5) **decay** 6) **algae** 7) **oxygen** 8) **carbon dioxide** 9) **ecosystem**

I. Thought for Today:

"This would be a fine world if people showed as much patience as they do when waiting for fish to bite."

Activity

A. Problem: *What Are Amphibians?*

B. Materials Needed:

1. Models or specimens of:
   a. frogs
   b. toads
   c. newts
   d. salamanders
   e. caecilians or other Apoda
2. Reference materials on amphibians

C. Procedure:

1. Discuss with class members their experiences with frogs, toads, newts, or salamanders. (Caecilians are aquatic or burrowing animals that live in the tropics. They are a wormlike kind of lizard, almost blind, of the classification order Apoda. Caecilians are like frogs but they have no legs.)
2. Discuss the characteristics of common amphibians.
   a. Adults lay eggs.
   b. Fertilization takes place outside the body.
   c. Eggs develop into larvae.
   d. Larvae grow into adults.
   e. All amphibians are ectothermic (cold-blooded).
   f. There are about 4,000 species of amphibians.
   g. Most amphibians live on land but return to the water to breed.
   h. Frogs have thin skins that must be kept moist.
   i. Toads have dry, bumpy skins.
   j. On land, frogs usually hop while toads tend to walk.
3. Study local amphibians.

D. Results:

1. Students will acquire some basic information about amphibians.
2. Students will learn that amphibians are animals that live in and around the water as well as on land.

E. Basic Facts and Supplemental Information:

1. Tadpoles breathe in oxygen in their mouths and out of their gills. They eventually lose their gills and develop lungs.
2. Amphibians start out in the water and end up on wet land.
3. Amphibians were the first vertebrates to move from a water environment to a land environment.

One common amphibian — a frog

4. Amphibians are the ancestors of reptiles, birds, and mammals.
5. Some amphibian fossils are over 400 million years old.
6. Most amphibians are found in tropical areas.
7. Studying animals that reside in foreign habitats creates an awareness that living organisms live almost everywhere and varying climatic conditions.

F. Thought Questions for Class Discussions:

1. Why do amphibians prefer warm climates?
2. What are the basic differences between a frog and a toad?
3. What is "metamorphosis"?

G. Related Topics for Further Inquiry:

1. Collect tadpoles.
2. Study the interrelationships of humans and amphibians.
3. Study Activity IV-E-2, "How do we care for a fresh-water aquarium?"
4. Study Activity IV-E-4, "Do tadpoles become frogs?"

H. Vocabulary Builders—Spelling Words:

1) **amphibians** 2) **frogs** 3) **toads** 4) **newts** 5) **salamanders** 6) **cold-blooded** 7) **fossils**

I. Thought for Today:

"Don't lay too specific plans for the future; it's like planting toads and expecting to raise toadstools."

Activity

A. Problem: *Do Tadpoles Become Frogs?*

B. Materials Needed:

1. Frog in jar or vivarium
2. Tadpoles in class aquarium
3. Drawings of different stages of frog's development on chalkboard
4. Books with pictures of frog's development
5. Literature (booklets, pamphlets, etc.)

C. Procedure:

1. Let students observe tadpoles and frogs in the science corner.
2. Have students study books and drawings about frogs.
3. Have a question and answer period and pose such questions as:
   a. How far can a frog jump? (20 times its length)
   b. How many kinds of frogs are there? (1,700 species)
   c. How long do they live? (Up to 30 years)
   d. What are the differences between frogs and toads:
      1) *Frogs:* skin: soft, moist, smooth
      teeth: small
      movement: fast
      habitat: mostly in water
      2) *Toads:* skin: tough, dry with bumps (bumps give off a secretion which is harmful to animals)
      teeth: none
      habitat: on land and water
4. Have students observe the changes that occur in the tadpoles and draw sketches of the four main steps in metamorphosis. As a culmination, the teacher and students might cooperate in the making of a chart entitled: "What we have learned about frogs and toads." Frogs and toads are helpful to people in the following ways:
   a. They eat insects.
   b. They are used by scientists in laboratories because their bodies work like ours do.

D. Results:

1. Students gain firsthand experience observing the various phases of metamorphosis.
2. Students learn the characteristics of frogs and toads and the differences between them.

E. Basic Facts and Supplemental Information:

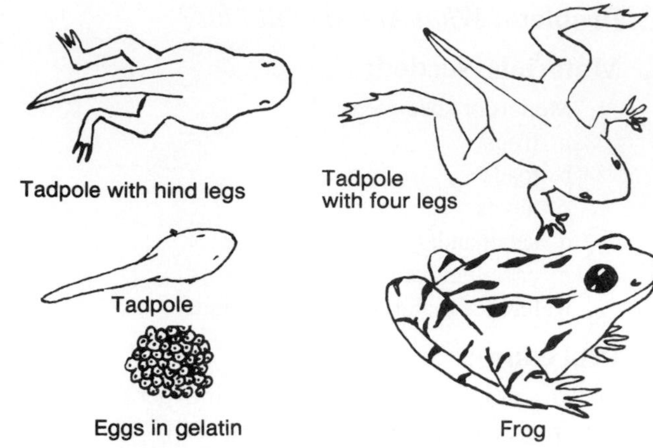

1. Frogs are amphibians. They breathe through their skin under water. When the aquarium is first set up, let the water stand for 24 hours before placing tadpoles in it. If aquarium is kept in the classroom, be sure to change water frequently or the tadpoles will die. Add water plants that have been found in nearby ponds, lakes, or streams. Tadpoles can be fed fish food, lettuce, and bits of hard-boiled eggs. Frogs should be fed worms, mealworms, and flies. Frogs should be fed live insects.
2. The best time to collect the eggs and tadpoles of frogs and toads is during the early summer. Eggs can be found floating on or near the surface of water among plants, particularly in shallow ponds and marshy places close to shore. Toads' eggs look like strings of jelly attached to plants, whereas frogs' eggs look like a mass of jelly.

F. Thought Questions for Class Discussions:

1. How do scientists classify (group) animals?
2. Where would be a good spot to place a "tadpole aquarium" in your classroom?
3. What other animals live near the habitats of frogs and toads?

G. Related Topics for Further Inquiry:

1. Visit a pond or lake.
2. Study the differences between frogs and toads.
3. Study Activity IV-E-2, "How do we care for a fresh-water aquarium?"
4. Study Activity IV-E-3, "What are amphibians?"

H. Vocabulary Builders—Spelling Words:

1) **eggs** 2) **gelatin** 3) **tadpoles** 4) **frogs** 5) **toads** 6) **metamorphosis** 7) **amphibians**

I. Thought for Today:

"When you are in deep water, it's a good idea to keep your mouth shut."

SECTION F: BIRDS

Activity IV F 1

Since birds can fly, they can go anywhere in the world.

A. Problem: *How Can Birds Fly?*

B. Materials Needed:

1. Pictures of various birds
2. Reference books on birds
3. Other multisensory aids on birds
4. Bulletin board

C. Procedure:

1. Place selected pictures of birds on the bulletin board.
2. A good motivating technique for studying birds is to have the class walk around the campus and note how many different kinds of birds they see.
3. Have students draw simple sketches of the birds they see, noting size, color, general shape, and any unusual characteristics.
4. Show any multisensory aids that are available.
5. Discuss how birds differ from other animals.
6. Discuss the characteristics that enable birds to fly:
   a. Many of the bones are hollow and light.
   b. Breastbone is deep with plenty of room for wing-muscle attachment.
   c. Very little muscle is on the wing itself (keeps wings lighter).
   d. Wings have long flight feathers.
   e. Wings are shaped like airplane's wings to provide "lift."
   f. They are endothermic (warm-blooded).
   g. Bodies are well-insulated with down feathers.
   h. Birds have well-developed brains.
   i. They have no teeth; gizzards help them digest their massive food intake.
   j. Birds are able to acquire and expend approximately 20 times the energy of comparable land animals.

D. Results:

1. Students will learn that birds have bodies that are well-developed for flight.
2. Students will learn that birds fly for:
   a. food
   b. warmth
   c. protection
   d. seek mates
   e. lay eggs

E. Basic Facts and Supplemental Information:

1. Ornithologists, scientists who study bird life, have found that birds migrate and navigate by the:
   a. sun
   b. landmarks
   c. semi-magnetic compasses in their heads
2. Birds fly fast to get air moving over their wings to give them "lift" like that of airplane wings.
3. There are about 9,000 species of birds.

F. Thought Questions for Class Discussions:

1. How do birds help us?
2. How do birds harm us?
3. How can birds migrate over hundreds of miles over the oceans?

G. Related Topics for Further Inquiry:

1. Compare a bird in flight to an airplane in flight.
2. Study the paths of some patterns of migration for specific birds. They are very interesting because some birds travel thousands of miles when migrating.

H. Vocabulary Builders—Spelling Words:

1) **feathers** 2) **wings** 3) **weight** 4) **bones** 5) **flight** 6) **hollow** 7) **lightweight**

I. Thought for Today:

"Man has learned how to fly like a bird and swim like a fish; now he has to learn how to walk on the Earth like a man."

Activity IV F 2

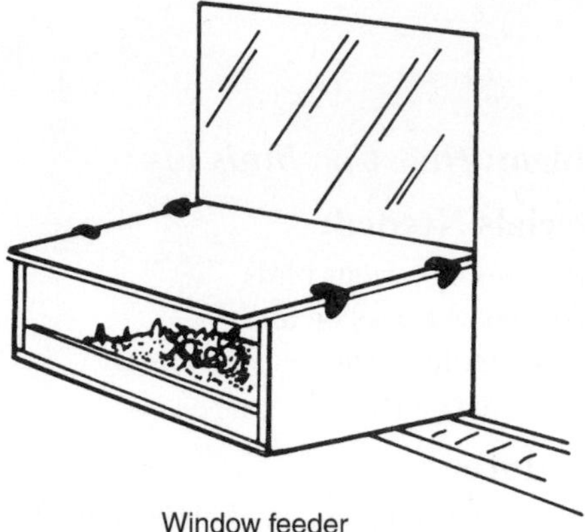

Window feeder

Fence feeder

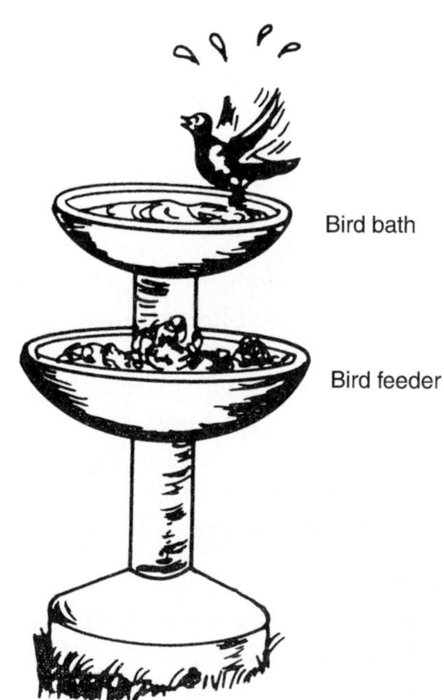

A. Problem: *How Can We Build a Bird Feeder?*

B. Materials Needed:

1. Wood
2. Nails
3. Screws
4. Hinges
5. Brackets
6. Wire
7. Support devices
8. Trays
9. Water
10. Bird book

C. Procedure:

1. Decide on the location of the feeder box.
2. Decide on the style of the feeder. Three examples are shown in the drawings. Build one or create one of your own design.
3. Hinges should be used to provide easy access to inside for cleaning and restocking.
4. Preformed boxes or heavy cardboard can substitute for individual wood parts.
5. Window feeders are excellent for observing birds.
6. Put wild bird seed in the feeder.
7. It is a good idea to have a water supply nearby.
8. When birds come to the feeder to eat, have students look in bird book and identify them.

D. Results:

1. Students will build a bird feeder.
2. Students will be able to identify many bird species that visit the feeder.

E. Basic Facts and Supplemental Information:

1. Bird feeders can be made from coffee cans, coconut shells, small boxes, etc.
2. Bird feeders provide hours of pleasure for bird watchers.
3. Many birds visit during different seasons so that bird identification is a year-round Activity.

F. Thought Questions for Class Discussions:

1. Can you identify all birds that use the feeder?
2. Do the species change from season to season?
3. Do birds eat more in the morning or late afternoon, or do they eat constantly all day long?

G. Related Ideas for Further Inquiry:

1. Vary the feed to determine if different birds eat different foods.
2. Design other kinds of bird feeders: suspended, placed in trees or bushes, etc.
3. Study other Activities in this Section.

H. Vocabulary Builders—Spelling Words:

1) **feeders** 2) **birdhouse** 3) **species**
4) **suspended** 5) **window** 6) **identify**

I. Thought for Today:

"If the cost of education continues to rise, education will become as expensive as ignorance."

Activity

A. Problem: *How Can We Build a Birdhouse?*

B. Materials Needed:

1. Scrap lumber
2. Hammer
3. Nails
4. Dowel
5. Drill or saw
6. Leather or rubber scrap (for hinge)
7. Reference book on bird identification

C. Procedure:

1. Decide on location for birdhouse.
2. Decide on species of birds to be attracted.
3. Look in bird book for suggestions for birdhouses (nesting houses).
4. Lay out construction plans.
5. Build birdhouse.
6. A typical birdhouse is shown in drawing.

D. Result:

A beautiful, functional birdhouse will be constructed.

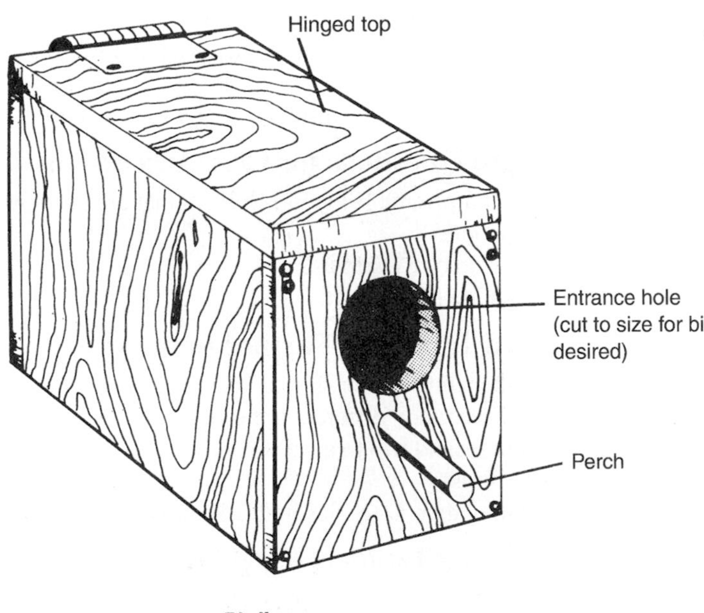

Birdhouse

E. Basic Facts and Supplemental Information:

1. The size of the front hole is very important as it keeps larger birds out.
2. A canopy over the whole birdhouse can be included.
3. To make a birdhouse more attractive to birds, place nesting materials nearby such as:
   a. lint from clothing or clothes dryer
   b. pieces of string
   c. fine twigs
   d. soft paper
   e. bird seed, etc.
4. Birds are slow to move into birdhouses because of scent, traffic, location, season, etc.
5. Birdhouses should be placed in as natural an environment as possible.

F. Thought Questions for Class Discussions:

1. What dangers might be encountered by birds in birdhouses?
2. What could you do to make a birdhouse more inviting?
3. How do birds make their own birdhouses (nests)?

G. Related Ideas for Further Inquiry:

1. Have different groups of students design birdhouses.
2. Create a cat-guard for your birdhouse.
3. Study each species' beaks and feet and then play detective to find the nature of the bird:
   a. birds of prey?
   b. waders?
   c. swimmers?
   d. perchers?
4. Study some unusual birds such as ostriches, pelicans, penguins, hummingbirds, owls, woodpeckers, etc.

H. Vocabulary Builders—Spelling Words:

1) **batten** 2) **hinges** 3) **entrance** 4) **drainages** 5) **underneath** 6) **birdhouse**

I. Thought for Today:

"The opportunities of humans are limited only by the imagination. But so few have imagination that there are ten thousand fiddlers to one composer."
—Charles F. Kettering

Activity IV F 4

A. Problem: *How Do We Classify Common Birds?*

B. Materials Needed:

1. Notebook
2. Pencil
3. Bird identification book(s)

C. Procedure:

1. Quickly peruse bird identification book(s).
2. Have students take a field trip near or around the school campus, taking notes on each different bird species they can see.
3. In their notebooks, have the students fill in the following data on each different species of bird seen. Compare the number after each bird part with the drawing.

   General (common name) ....
   Location ....
   Date ....
   Color(s) ....
   Beak (1) ....
   Throat (2) ....
   Nape (3) ....
   Crown (4) ....
   Eye color (5) ....
   Back (6) ....
   Rump (7) ....
   Belly (8) ....
   Breast (9) ....
   Tail (10) ....
   Wings (11) ....
   Legs (12) ....
   Feet (13) ....

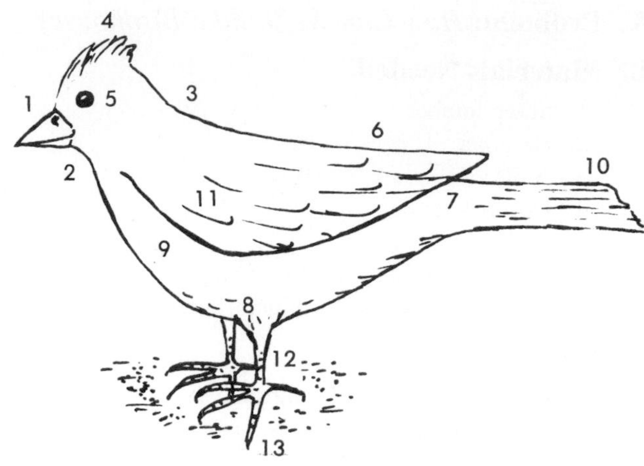

4. Other characteristics which could be included are:
   a. Movements on the ground
   b. Flight patterns (soaring, gliding, undulating, etc.)
   c. Position of wings in flight
   d. Nesting habits
   e. Migration patterns

D. Results:

1. Students will learn about and be able to identify the common birds in their locality.
2. Students will learn how to record field observations.

E. Basic Facts and Supplemental Information:

1. Many birds can be recognized by their flight patterns.
2. Adult birds protect their eggs and their young after they are hatched.
3. Song patterns identify species and are significant in communication among or between birds.
4. Other characteristics which could be included are:
   a. Movements on the ground
   b. Flight patterns (soaring, gliding, undulating, etc.)
   c. Position of wings in flight
   d. Nesting habits
   e. Migration patterns
5. There are more birds than people.
6. Birds have lightweight feathers and hollow bones to make flight easier.
7. Birds have big hearts and strong wing muscles.

F. Thought Questions for Class Discussions:

1. What are some behaviors of birds that are harmful to people?
2. How do birds help us?
3. What do birds eat?

G. Related Topics for Further Inquiry:

1. Make a bird feeder. If you keep it stocked, you will see many different kinds of birds.
2. Take a field trip to a nearby wooded area and look for birds.
3. Study other Activities in this Section.

H. Vocabulary Builder—Spelling Words:

1) **feathers** 2) **bills** 3) **wings** 4) **beaks** 5) **nest** 6) **breast** 7) **nape** 8) **rump**

I. Thought for Today:

"Even the woodpecker owes its success to the fact that it uses its head and keeps pecking away until it finishes the job it starts."

Activity IV F 5

A. Problem: *How Can We Hatch Chicken Eggs?*

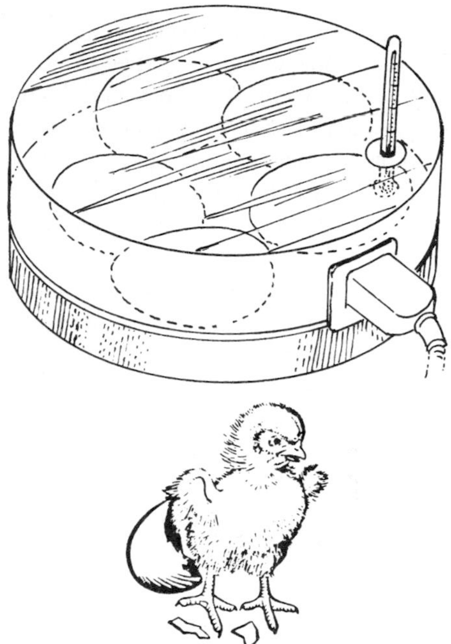

B. Materials Needed:

1. Fresh eggs from store (one for every four students)
2. 6 to 10 fertilized eggs from a farm or store (Store eggs will be labeled "fertilized.")
3. Chicken incubator
4. Saucers
5. Thermometer
6. Pencil and/or crayons
7. Paper
8. Calendar
9. Slide projector
10. Book, pamphlets on egg-hatching
11. Light
12. Thermostat
13. Sponge

C. Procedure:

1. Study what chicken embryos need for full development (food, water, air, and protection).
2. Carefully, have students break one fresh egg per group of four and examine it for its main parts: shell, yolk, albumen, air sac, and membranes.
3. Study the function of each part:
   a. shell—protection
   b. yolk—food
   c. albumen—water
   d. air sac—air
   e. membranes—separate parts
4. Discuss what an egg must have from its environment in order to hatch. Discuss how these needs are met using an incubator.

Needs:	*How met in incubator:*
a. moisture______	pan of water with sponge
b. warmth ______	light (temperature should be about 100°F.)
c. protection ____	container
d. rotation ______	personal handling (twice a day)

5. Place fertilized eggs in incubator.
6. Place a small pan of water with wet sponge inside incubator to keep eggs moist and to prevent newly hatched chickens from drowning.
7. Mark eggs lightly with pencil or crayon showing the date of insertion. These marks will also serve as a guide for their rotational position changes.
8. Turn the incubator on.
9. Regulate temperature to about 100° F. (38° C.).
10. Rotate eggs daily about one-third of the way around.
11. Check temperature and moisture daily.
12. Between the 7th and 10th day, eggs can be "candled." (Candling is observing the inside of eggs with the aid of a strong light.) Use the slide projector with a strong light in a darkened room to look for eye spots, heart, and spinal column.
13. Study the eggs carefully. Discard any that are cracked or infertile.
14. Draw sketches of observations.
15. Between the 17th and 20th day, eggs should be candled again. Discard any dead embryos and juicy eggs.
16. Study the eggs. Look especially for blood vessels.
17. Draw sketches of observations. Check books and pamphlets for corroborating evidence.
18. Around the 21st day, the eggs will hatch at various intervals of time.
19. The chicks will peck their way through the egg shells. Some chicks may need help the next day if they cannot break their shells themselves.

D. Results:

1. Students will learn the parts of an egg.
2. Students will learn the functions of the various parts of an egg.
3. Students will learn that many life forms develop from eggs.
4. Students will learn how baby chicks break out of their shells.

E. Basic Facts and Supplemental Information:

1. This is one of the most exciting activities in which students can become involved. Teachers can compare hen eggs to other animal eggs. The motivation from this Activity will carry over to many related activities in science and other disciplines.
2. There is much controversy over the problem of eggs—whether they are good to eat because of their food value or bad to eat because of their high cholesterol content. A recent report from the health center of a large medical university recommends that "dietary guidelines" limit the intake of eggs to two or three a week. Yolks contain a high concentration of cholesterol.
3. The incubation period of different birds varies: ducks, turkeys, and geese require 20 to 30 days; pheasants, 24 days; and ostriches 41 days.
4. Many animals are oviparous (egg-bearing). All amphibians (frogs, toads), alligators, crocodiles, and most fish, and birds hatch their young from eggs. Animals that produce live births are called "viviparous." All live births begin with a fertilized egg, internally, in the female of the species.

F. Thought Questions for Class Discussion:

1. Are all eggs fertilized?
2. Do all eggs have the same incubation period?
3. Do all animals produce eggs?

G. Related Ideas for Further Inquiry:

1. Compare chickens with other animals that hatch from eggs.
2. Study Section IV-D, "Reptiles."
3. If any farmer in your locality raises chickens, you might have him/her discuss incubation, care, and feeding of chickens with the class, or have several students interview the farmer about these problems.

H. Vocabulary Builders—Spelling Words:

1) **incubator** 2) **fertilized** 3) **thermostat** 4) **candling** 5) **moisture** 6) **sponge** 7) **infertile**

I. Thought for Today:

"A scientist recently crossed a carrier pigeon with a woodpecker. The bird not only carries messages, but also knocks on the door."

Section G: Mammals

Activity IV G 1

A. Problem: *What Are Mammals?*

B. Materials Needed:

1. Pictures of mammals
2. Books about mammals
3. Filmstrips or motion pictures about mammals

C. Procedure:

1. Review Activity III-A-1, "How do we classify living things?"
2. Discuss mammals. Mammals are members of the Phylum Chordota (animals with backbones).
3. Discuss the common characteristics of mammals such as:
   a. large
   b. hairy
   c. warm-blooded
   d. backbones
   e. large brains
   f. born alive (few rare exceptions are born from eggs)
   g. suckle milk from milk glands
4. Have class describe what pets they have that are classified as "mammals."
5. Have class make a list of other animals that are in this classification.
6. Describe or show pictures of other animals that are mammals. These might include:
   a. platypus
   b. anteater
   c. wallaby
   d. shrew
   e. lemur
   f. bat
   g. sloth
   h. gorilla
   i. rabbit
   j. whale
   k. walrus
   l. aardvark
   m. elephant
   n. warthog
   o. tiger
   p. man
7. View accessible filmstrips, slides, or movies about mammals.
8. Discuss the fact that some mammals are meat eaters while others are primarily vegetarians. Meat eaters must be strong, swift, and smart. Vegetarian animals spend a lot of time searching for leaves, twigs, and tender plant shoots.
9. Discuss the wide range of habitats of mammals: equator to poles, land to water, low to high elevations, etc.
10. If possible, plan a trip to the zoo.

D. Result:

Students will learn about mammals and that people are included in this animal classification.

E. Basic Facts and Supplemental Information:

1. Other major characteristics of mammals are that:
   a. They run fast.
   b. They think fast.
   c. Their body parts consist of head, trunk, and appendages.
   d. The mother's milk has all the fat, proteins, water, sugar, vitamins, and minerals their young need.
2. There are many sources where information can be obtained about mammals:
   a. pet stores
   b. veterinarians
   c. medical researchers
   d. zookeepers
   e. farmers
   f. feed stores

F. Thought Questions for Class Discussions:

1. How do mammals differ from other animals?
2. How are mammals similar to other animals?
3. What mammals are very important to people? Why?
4. Is the bat a mammal? (Yes!)

G. Related Ideas for Further Inquiry:

1. Compare mammals with other members of the Phylum Chordota.
2. Have each student research or report on one particular species in this phylum.
3. Study other Activities in this Section.

H. Vocabulary Builders—Spelling Words:

Use the animal names listed in Procedure.

I. Thought for Today:

"Frustration is not having anyone else to blame but yourself."

Activity IV G 2

A. Problem: *How Do Mammals Adapt to a Changing Environment?*

B. Materials Needed:

1. Toy models of animals
2. World globe
3. Pictures of harsh weather conditions
4. Pictures of mammals
5. Reference books on mammals

C. Procedure

1. Study Section VI-A, "Ecosystems" to find out some of the changes in our environment.
2. Study Activity VI-B-7, "How can we conserve our wildlife?"
3. Study Section VIII-C, "Earth's Crust."
4. Discuss and summarize some of the major changes that have occurred on the Earth that have affected the environment of wildlife. These would be natural changes like climate, earthquakes, fires, etc., as well as man-made modification such as residences, businesses, highways, etc.
5. Discuss selected mammals with class; ask how those animals could cope with the natural changes discussed above.

D. Results:

1. Students will realize that environmental conditions are constantly changing locally and globally.
2. Students will learn that mammals and all other animals have to adapt to these changing conditions.

E. Basic Facts and Supplemental Information:

1. Animals have to move to new territories to survive.
2. They move to find food and a place to live.
3. Fish swim, snakes slither, land mammals use their legs and feet (paws).
4. There are millions of types of plants and animals that live together in an ecosystem. When any factor of the environment changes, all organisms must adapt to these changes.

F. Thought Questions for Class Discussions:

1. What will become of pandas whose main food is bamboo if the bamboo supply is reduced or eliminated?

2. Can animals adapt quickly to changes?
3. Mammals and other animals that cannot adapt become extinct.
4. How does the "predator-prey" relationship affect "adaptation"?
5. It is very important to remember that plants, animals, and the physical environment are interrelated.

G. Related Ideas for Further Inquiry:

1. Research the problems the dinosaurs had with adapting to changes in their environment.
2. Study how we humans are adapting to our changing environment.
3. Study the ongoing "war" between humans and other mammals: humans are encroaching on animals' territories, and animals (deer, bears, coyotes, mountain lions, etc.) are encroaching on humans' territories.

H. Vocabulary Builders—Spelling Words:

1) **adapt** 2) **environment** 3) **mammals**
4) **changing** 5) **ecosystem** 6) **habitat**

I. Thought for Today:

"In Columbus's day few believed the world was round. These days the question is: 'How long will it be around'?"

Activity

A. Problem: *How Does Man, a Homo Sapiens, Differ from Other Mammals?*

B. Materials Needed:

1. Books, pamphlets, charts about humans
2. Pictures of humans
3. Multisensory aids about humans

C. Procedure:

Discuss Homo sapiens, including the fact that of all mammals, humans have:

1. the most intelligence
2. been the most successful
3. best adapted to existing environments (surviving on all parts of planet Earth and, for short periods, in space)
4. built their own environments:
   a. cleared forests
   b. drained swamps
   c. irrigated deserts
   d. built villages and cities:
      1) homes
      2) schools
      3) churches
      4) businesses
      5) roads
5. mastered and/or domesticated most animals
6. utilizes the physical environment:
   a. water
   b. air
   c. minerals
   d. soils
7. three very complex anatomical differences from other animals:
   a. complex brain
   b. voice box
   c. prehensile hands
8. body chemicals that include:
   a. 20 odd chemical elements
   b. 75% to 80% water
   c. 10% to 20% proteins and fats (lipids)
   d. about 5% inorganic salts
9. two nucleic acids that differ from other animals:
   a. DNA—master plan for building the body
   b. RNA—permits body to carry out this plan

D. Result:

Students will learn that humans are the most complex and most adaptive of all mammals.

E. Basic Facts and Supplemental Information: (Your body is like a city.)

1. dynamic
2. highly organized
3. carefully designed
4. integrated
5. living
6. self-constructing
7. developing
8. reacting
9. self-regulating
10. self-repairing

F. Thought Questions for Class Discussions:

1. What should you know about your body?
2. How should you take care of your body?
3. Why should you avoid drugs?
4. Is your body like a machine?
5. What roles do your senses play?

G. Related Ideas for Further Inquiry:

1. Study the history of Homo sapiens.
2. Predict the future of Homo sapiens.
3. Study the environmental factors necessary for survival.
4. What dangers do Homo sapiens cause that are harmful to their own existence?
5. Study Activities in Section V-C, "Nutrition."
6. Study Activities in Section V-F, "First Aid."
7. Study other Activities in this Section.

H. Vocabulary Builders—Spelling Words:

1) **Homo sapiens** 2) **intelligent** 3) **creative** 4) **resourceful** 5) **irrigated** 6) **domesticated**

I. Thought for Today:

"A student will learn more if you pull a few cords: the television, the telephone, etc."

Activity IV G 4

A. Problem: *What Are Primates?*

B. Materials Needed:

1. Pictures of primates
2. Multisensory materials about primates

C. Procedure:

1. Discuss animals in general and how they are classified.
2. Discuss the family of animals called "primates."
3. Show pictures and other multisensory aids that highlight primates.
4. Point out that humans fall into this classification.
5. Cite the other important members of the primate family:
   a. lemurs
   b. monkeys
   c. apes
   d. marmosets
   e. gorillas
6. Discuss some of the common characteristics of primates, such as:
   a. big, hairy, and warm-blooded
   b. eat a variety of foods
   c. very social
   d. establish social hierarchies
   e. basic communication by using facial expressions and body gestures
   f. They have 2 or 4 legs for basic, fast movement.
   g. Their eyes are forward-facing.
   h. They have 5 digits (fingers or toes) on each hand or foot.

D. Result:

Students will learn about primates and that the primates are an "Order" in animal classification.

E. Basic Facts and Supplemental Information:

1. Most primates are decreasing in numbers as human population increases.
2. Most primates are arboreal (living in or adapted to living in trees).
3. Primates have prehensile hands (thumb in opposition to other fingers).
4. There are 11 families of primates.
5. Primates are warm-blooded, which enables them to live in a variety of climates.
6. Primates have the largest brains among the vertebrates.
7. There are over 4,000 species of mammals; 181 of them are primates.

Langur (monkey of South Asia)

8. Primates vary in their courting, mating, and family life habits.
9. Courtship to attract prospective mates involves particular behaviors, such as displaying colors, using scents, fighting, establishing territories, organizing "pecking orders," vocal communication, facial expression, and gestures.
10. Family life varies from mother–child only relationships to complex family life. Even the duration of family life varies.

F. Thought Questions for Class Discussions:

1. Why do you think most primates live in wooded areas?
2. How do humans differ from other primates?
3. How do humans reduce the number of primates?

G. Related Ideas for Further Inquiry:

1. Have an outside speaker from some environmental group talk to the class (Sierra Club, Conservation Foundation, etc.).
2. Visit a zoo. There are many primates that can be studied there.
3. Study other Activities in this Section.

H. Vocabulary Builders—Spelling Words:

Use the names of the animals listed in Procedure.

I. Thought for Today:

"The reason many people don't see things in the right perspective is that they are always looking for a new angle."

SECTION H: HIBERNATION

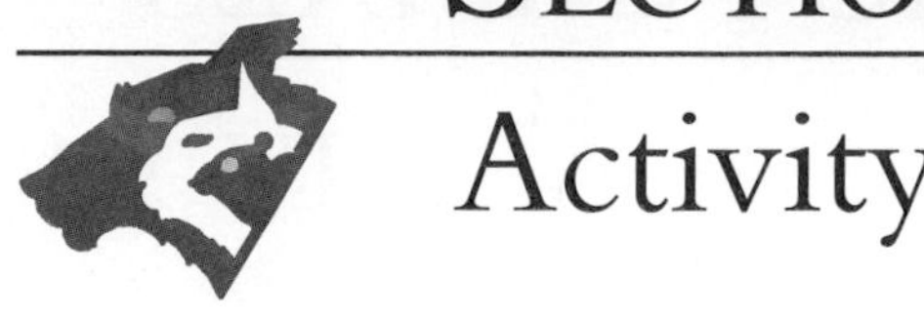

Activity IV H 1

A. Problem: *What Is Hibernation?*

B. Materials Needed:

Books, pictures, pamphlets about hibernating animals

C. Procedure:

1. Discuss animals.
2. Discuss animal classification.
3. List or show pictures of animals that hibernate and ask class what they have in common.
4. Students can study the habits of hibernating animals either as a class or in small groups.

D. Results:

1. Students will learn that some animals hibernate but most do not.
2. Students will learn that the following animals hibernate:
   a. ground squirrels
   b. bears
   c. woodchucks
   d. bats
   e. hedgehogs
   f. frogs, toads
   g. earthworms
   h. reptiles (turtles, snakes, etc.)
   i. some birds
   j. some fish
   k. some insects
   l. opossums
   m. raccoons
   n. chipmunks
   o. groundhogs

E. Basic Facts and Supplemental Information:

1. During harsh winter conditions, warm-blooded animals seek refuge. Most birds migrate to warmer climates. Many animals dig caves or build burrows for hibernating.
2. Hibernation is a sleeplike state during which:
   a. heart rate slows (almost stops)
   b. respiration becomes very shallow
   c. body temperature drops
   d. less energy is needed
   e. energy needed comes from stored fat which they live on during the hibernation period
3. Some animals hibernate for up to 5 months.
4. Frogs and toads hibernate in mud to keep their bodies moist.

A hibernating groundhog

5. Animals vary in the depth and duration of hibernation. In some it is really a semihibernation because they come out frequently to search for food.
6. Some birds like nighthawks and swifts hibernate.
7. Some animals go underground to avoid harsh summer conditions. This is called aestivation (estivation). This is more common around ponds and lakes when the water gets very warm and some animals dig into the shallow or dried-up mud waiting for the water to become cool again.

F. Thought Questions for Class Discussions:

1. Which animals do not hibernate?
2. Why do animals hibernate?
3. Do people ever hibernate?

G. Related Ideas for Further Inquiry:

1. Learn which animals near your community hibernate.
2. Talk to zookeepers or museum workers and ask about animals that hibernate.
3. Study Sections IV-D, "Reptiles," IV-F, "Birds," and IV-G, "Mammals."

H. Vocabulary Builders—Spelling Words:

1) **cold-blooded** 2) **warm-blooded** 3) **hibernate** 4) **classification** 5) **family** 6) **underground** 7) **(animal names listed in Results)**

I. Thought for Today:

"Not everyone repeats gossip. Some improve it."

Section I: Microscopic Animals

Activity IV I 1

A. Problem: *How Can We Collect Microscopic Animals?*

B. Materials Needed:

1. Water from pond or small lake (or see Section E-1 below)
2. Mud (from bottom of pond or lake)
3. Collecting jars
4. Medicine dropper
5. Hard lenses, magnifying glasses, or microscopes
6. Watch glass or glass slide
7. Reference books about microscopic animals

C. Procedure:

1. Gather some water from sources cited above including a little mud if possible.
2. Let the water settle.
3. After several days, stir the water without stirring the mud.
4. Fill the medicine dropper with this water.
5. Place a few drops on a watch glass or glass slide.
6. Using lenses, magnifying glass, or microscope, observe results.

D. Result:

Students will see some protozoa (large, one-celled animals). One type is the paramecium which can be identified by comparing it to reference pictures.

E. Basic Facts and Supplemental Information:

1. To cultivate protozoa, place dry grass, hay, or leaves in a widemouthed jar about 3/4 full of tap water that has been allowed to stand for several days. (This allows the chlorine to evaporate.)
2. Cover the jar and place it in a well-lighted place but not in direct sunlight. Protozoa will multiply for several weeks. Take samples and observe daily.
3. Protozoa move rapidly by body hairs called "cilia."
4. There are 15,000 species of protozoa.
5. One species of protozoa causes malaria.
6. One species of protozoa causes sleeping sickness.
7. Amoebae may also be seen, but they move much more slowly. Check reference books for identification.
8. One unusual characteristic of planaria is its ability to regenerate if dissected. The head generates a new tail and the tail generates a new head.
9. Regeneration is a form of asexual reproduction.

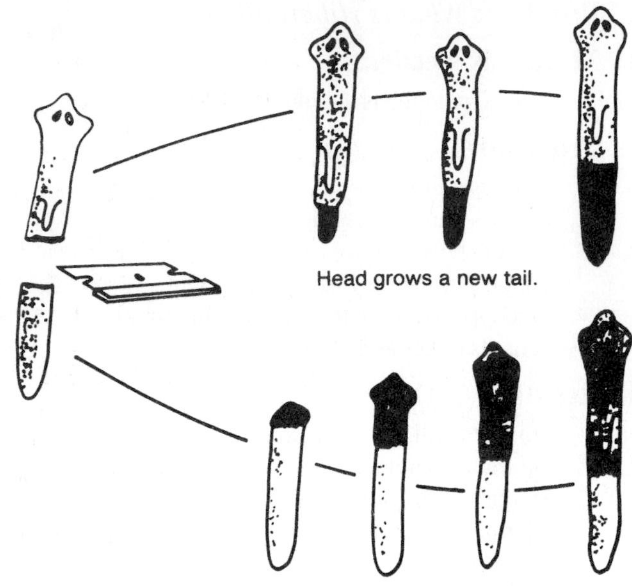

Regeneration of each half of a planaria if cut in half

10. Planaria are flat animals about one quarter of an inch in length. (one-third centimeter)

F. Thought Questions for Class Discussions:

1. Do microscopic animals help us or hurt us?
2. How can we see animals if they are too small to be seen with the naked eye?
3. Do whales eat microscopic animals?

G. Related Ideas for Further Inquiry:

1. Compare microscopic animals with microscopic plants.
2. Compare microscopic animals with macroscopic animals.
3. Field trips to small watering spots are highly recommended for this Activity.

H. Vocabulary Builders—Spelling Words:

1) **protozoa** 2) **paramecium** 3) **amoeba** 4) **microscopic** 5) **lenses** 6) **dissect**

I. Thought for Today:

"If you realize that you aren't as wise today as you thought you were yesterday, you're wiser today."

Section J: Collecting, Storing, and Caring for Animals

Activity IV J 1

A. Problem: *How Can We Trap Small Animals?*

B. Materials Needed:

1. Box cover
2. Stick or dowel
3. Heavy string or cord
4. Scrap lumber
5. Hook and eye
6. Pin
7. Wire screening
8. Bait
9. Hammer
10. Small nails
11. Cheesecloth to wrap bait

C. Procedure:

1. Construct a trap as shown in drawing or purchase a trap like the one shown. (It's more fun to build your own.)
2. Study the habits of the animal you wish to trap.
3. Use appropriate bait.
4. Be sure that traps do not kill or harm animals.
5. The only tricky part is balancing the gate so that it falls easily when the bait is disturbed. The cord releases the "hook" from the "hook and eye."

D. Results:

1. Students will learn how to trap small animals without hurting them.
2. Students will learn to develop patience.

E. Basic Facts and Supplemental Information:

1. Be sure that the tripping mechanism works properly.
2. Have a cage ready to move the animal into so that it won't get hurt in the trap.
3. Proper food and care are essential for caged animals.
4. Many teachers prefer to keep captured animals for only a short time and then release them. This provides ample time to study them, and the students will have had an enjoyable learning experience.

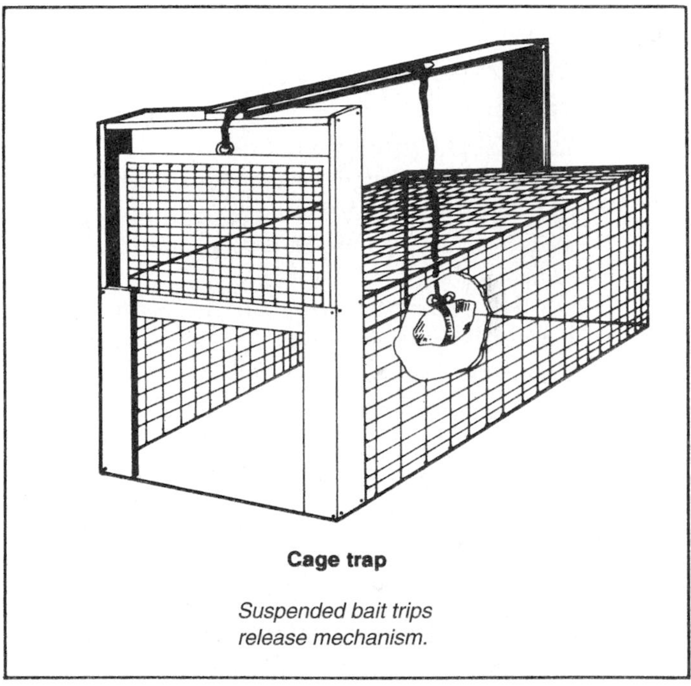

Cage trap

Suspended bait trips release mechanism.

F. Thought Questions for Class Discussions:

1. What care must be taken not to hurt the animals?
2. Are some small animals dangerous?
3. What are the main reasons you want to trap an animal?

G. Related Ideas for Further Inquiry:

1. Visit pet stores, animal shelters, and veterinarians to investigate different small animals that could be used for classroom pets.
2. Study Activity IV-B-1, "How do we care for hamsters, guinea pigs, gerbils, and/or mice?"
3. Study Activity IV-J-2, "How can we trap medium-sized animals?"
4. Study Activity IV-J-4, "What should we feed captured animals?"

H. Vocabulary Builders—Spelling Words:

1) **trapping** 2) **cages** 3) **animals** 4) **bait** 5) **cheesecloth** 6) **suspended** 7) **capture**

I. Thought for Today:

"One who turns the other cheek too far gets it in the neck."

Activity IV J 2

A. Problem: *How Can We Trap Medium-Sized Animals?*

B. Materials Needed:

1. Heavy wire screen
2. Wire cutters
3. Pliers
4. Bait

C. Procedure:

1. Plan the size of your trap.
2. *Carefully* cut the four sides and back so that there are enough wire ends to secure them to adjacent pieces by wrapping the ends around the adjoining sections.
3. Plan your gate so that it hinges on top, is a tight fit on the sides, and is longer on the bottom so that it does not close all the way but will swing in but not out. (See drawing.)

D. Results:

1. An inexpensive, strong, durable trap will be constructed.
2. Students will learn what problems are involved with catching animals for study.

E. Basic Facts and Supplemental Information:

1. Masonite or plywood could be substituted for wire screen.
2. Traps can be baited with whole grains, nuts, raisins, peanut butter, and/or bacon fat; all are very effective.
3. Traps should be checked frequently to reduce exposure of captured animals to the elements.
4. Devise some marking system for locating traps. Sometimes students forget where the traps are placed.
5. Care should be taken in removing the animal and placing it in a proper classroom cage or other storage.

F. Thought Questions for Class Discussions:

1. What kinds of animals would you expect to catch in this type of trap?
2. What safety precautions should be taken for the safety of the students and the animals?
3. Can you devise other traps for catching animals?

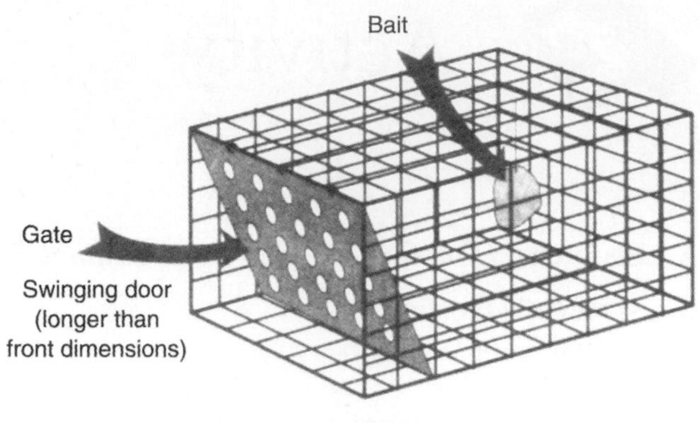

Heavy wire trap

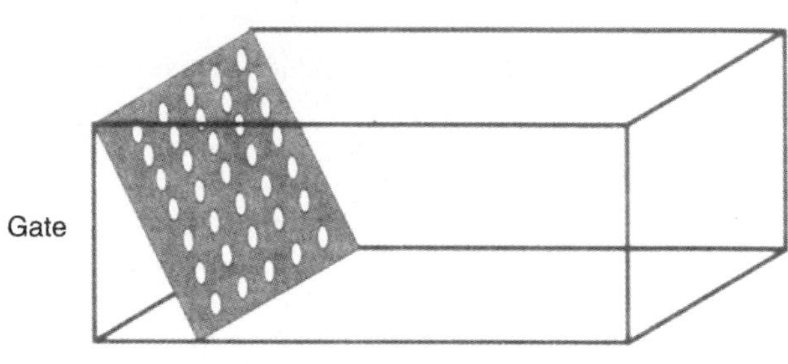

Swinging door

4. Should the animals be rotated so that no one animal is retained for a long period of time?

G. Related Ideas for Further Inquiry:

1. Study Activity IV-J-4, "What should we feed captured animals?"
2. Study Activity IV-J-1, "How can we trap small animals?"
3. Study Activity VI-A-1, "What is the balance of nature?"
4. Study Activity VI-A-2, "What is 'biological diversity'?"

H. Vocabulary Builders—Spelling Words:

1) **medium** 2) **trapping** 3) **swinging** 4) **precautions** 5) **bait** 6) **capture**

I. Thought for Today:

"The noblest of all animals is the dog, and the noblest of all dogs is the hotdog. It feeds the hand that bites it."

Activity

A. Problem: *What Is Good Housing for Tadpoles?*

B. Materials Needed:

1. Five-gallon water container
2. Little sand, mud, or silt
3. Water plants
4. Dowel
5. Water
6. Tadpoles

C. Procedure:

1. Discuss frogs and toads.
2. Discuss tadpoles.
3. Collect tadpoles.
4. Place mud, silt, or sand in bottom of container.
5. Add either fresh water or bottled water after it has been left standing for several days.
6. Fill to about 3 inches from the top.
7. Place water plants in container using the long dowel and pushing them into bottom material.
8. Let water settle.
9. Add specimens to container.

D. Result:

A beautiful, functional tadpole home will be created.

E. Basic Facts and Supplemental Information:

1. Best time to collect tadpoles is in the spring and summer.
2. Tadpoles can be found swimming in ponds and along lake shores among the land plants close to shore.
3. Use nets, scoop quickly, and place tadpoles in collecting jars immediately.
4. A large rock or twig protruding above the water line is excellent for their development in the container.
5. Tadpoles feed on algae and small bits of lettuce.
6. Frog eggs are found in clusters, while toad eggs are found in long strings.
7. If eggs are collected, they should be stored at the same water temperature from which they were taken (usually cool).
8. When tadpoles reach the length of about one-half inch they can be safely placed in this aquarium.
9. They can be fed scraps of lettuce, liver, and pieces of hard-boiled egg yolks.

F. Thought Questions for Class Discussions:

1. Chlorine is frequently added to tap water. What is its purpose?
2. Is chlorine used in pools for the same reason?
3. Do you think chlorine would harm tadpoles?

G. Related Ideas for Further Inquiry:

1. Study Section IV-E, "Water Animals (Fish and Amphibians)."
2. Study Activity III-A-1, "How do we classify living things?"
3. Study Activity VI-A-1, "What is the balance of nature?"
4. Study Activity VI-A-2, "What is 'biological diversity'?"

H. Vocabulary Builders—Spelling Words:

1) **gallon** 2) **silt** 3) **tadpole** 4) **dowel** 5) **specimens** 6) **aquarium** 7) **container**

I. Thought for Today:

"There is no way to unring a bell."

Activity IV J 4

A. Problem: *What Should We Feed Captured Animals?*

B. Materials Needed:

1. Appropriate food for animal(s) as cited below
2. Natural food

C. Procedure:

1. Identify the animal(s).
2. Look up appropriate food for it (them).

D. Result:

Animals will be fed appropriate diets.

E. Basic Facts and Supplemental Information:

1. Animals should be kept in an environment as similar to their natural environment as possible.
2. The temperature range must be considered for each species.
3. Animals should have adequate ventilation.
4. Sunlight should be as close to their natural environment as possible.
5. *Animal(s):* *Suggested Menus:*

a. Ants . . . . grated dry dog food, dead insects and spiders, food scraps, especially products sweetened with sugar or honey

b. Birds. . . . . wild bird seed, breadstuffs, pieces of raw vegetables and fruits, hard-boiled eggs, vegetable greens

c. Butterflies. . . . . . . honey, thick sugar solution, nectar

d. Caterpillars. . . . . . leaves of plants where animals were found

e. Chickens. . . . . scrap meat, grit, bird seed, corn

f. Earthworms . . . . . finely ground leaves, grasses, and meat

g. Frogs and Toads. . soft-bodied insects, worms, caterpillars

h. Gerbils . . . . dry dog food, seeds, lettuce, carrots, grasses

i. Goldfish . . . . commercial goldfish food, ground dry dog food, oatmeal

j. Grasshoppers . . . . leaves were animals were found, celery, lettuce

k. Guinea pigs . . . . . dog or rabbit food, lettuce, celery, carrots

l. Guppies . . . . commercially prepared tropical food; babies require tiny portions

Carrots

Commercially prepared foods

Lettuce

Celery

m. Hamsters . . . . grains, dog biscuits, common vegetables, nuts

n. Lizards . . . . soft-bodied insects, flies, mealworms

o. Mice . . . . grated dry dog food, bread, meat leftovers, cheese

p. Rabbits . . . . commercial foods, most common vegetables

q. Snails . . . . most soft, green vegetables and leaves

r. Snakes . . . . soft-bodied insects, earthworms, small pieces of meat (irregular eaters—may go days without food)

s. Tadpoles . . . . fine guppy food, water plants, finely ground meat in small quantities

t. Turtles . . . . soft-bodied insects, commercial foods, earthworms, lettuce, hard-boiled eggs

6. Larger animals can be fed canned dog and/or cat food available at super markets, pet feed stores, and veterinarian clinics.

F. Thought Questions for Class Discussions:

1. Why is natural food best for all animals?
2. Is water just as important as food in caring for animals?
3. Who is going to be responsible for taking care of classroom animals over extended weekends or vacation periods?
4. Have you seen any motion pictures that have had small animals in them that could be used for classroom pets? Were the animals real or animated?

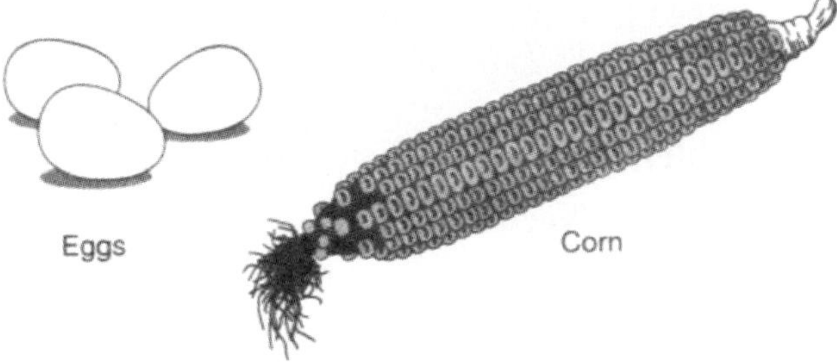

G. Related Ideas for Further Inquiry:

1. There are many potentially highly scientific Activities that can be observed on the local school campus:
   a. identifying animals
   b. watching their behaviors
   c. determining how they acquire their food
   d. analyzing prey-predator relationships
2. Field trips can be taken to surrounding areas, local parks, and zoos to study the care, feeding, and problems of small animals.
3. There are many resource personnel in most communities that can provide information about the care and feeding of small animals:
   a. pet shops
   b. local farmers
   c. veterinarians
   d. zoo keepers
   e. animal trainers
   f. other teachers in different schools and at different grade levels
4. Study Activity IV-A-1, "What are some characteristics of all living things?"
5. Study Activity IV-A-2, "What is the triangle of life?"
6. Study Activity IV-B-3, "Do white rats make good classroom pets?"
7. Study Part III, "Plants."
8. Study Activity III-A-1, "How do we classify living things?"
9. Study Activity IV-B-4, "What are some unusual pets that we could keep in our classroom?"
10. Study Activity IV-B-1, "How do we care for hamsters, guinea pigs, gerbils and/or mice?"
11. Study Activity IV-D-1, "What are reptiles?"
12. Study Activity IV-D-2, "Are all snakes poisonous?"
13. Study Activity IV-E-2, "How do we care for a fresh-water aquarium?"

H. Vocabulary Builders—Spelling Words:

1) **ants** 2) **birds** 3) **butterflies** 4) **caterpillars** 5) **chickens** 6) **earthworms** 7) **frogs** 8) **turtles**

I. Thought for Today:

"To teach is to learn twice."

SECTION K: RESOURCES

Activity IV K 1

A. Problem: *How Do Animals Help People?*

B. Materials Needed:

Pictures of:

1. Elephants
2. Fish
3. Dogs
4. Rabbits
5. Sheep
6. Camels
7. Horses
8. Cows
9. Other animals

C. Procedure:

1. Discuss animals in general
2. Show pictures of animals listed in Materials Needed.
3. Discuss how each specific animal species helps us by one or more of the following:
   a. labor-saving
   b. transportation
   c. food
   d. pleasure
   e. research
   f. companionship
   g. clothing
   h. medicine

D. Result:

Students will learn that many animals help us directly and indirectly by providing us with comfort, recreation, companionship, protection, and food.

E. Basic Facts and Supplemental Information:

1. The list of animals could be greatly expanded with other animals such as: shellfish, frogs, silkworms, etc.
2. As human population has increased, the animal population has decreased.
3. Many animals have been used in research testing, which eventually leads to healthier lives for humans. The use of animals in medical and cosmetic research has become a highly controversial issue.
4. Many people have dogs for protection and security.
5. There are many products made from animals:
   a. buttons for clothing
   b. leather for shoes, wallets, purses
   c. costume jewelry
6. Medical science has used animal organs for human replacement parts. The heart valves of pigs have been highly successful replacements for damaged human heart valves.

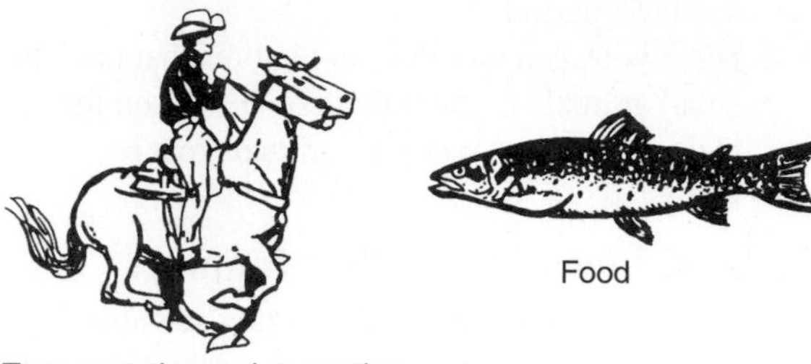

Transportation and recreation

Food

Clothing

Companionship

F. Thought Questions for Class Discussions:

1. How do plants help people?
2. Do plants help other animals?
3. Do some animals harm people?

G. Related Ideas for Further Inquiry:

1. Select an item listed in Procedure and cite as many animals as possible that would be included in this category.
2. Repeat for other items in Procedure.
3. Study Part IV, "Animals."
4. Study Activity III-A-1, "How do we classify living things?"
5. Study other Activities in this Section.

H. Vocabulary Builders—Spelling Words:

Use the animal names listed in Materials Needed.

I. Thought for Today:

"Remember when kids brought teachers apples, instead of driving them bananas?"

Activity IV K 2

A. Problem: *Why Do We Hunt and Fish for Certain Animals?*

B. Materials Needed:

1. Pictures of animals
2. Books about animals
3. Newspaper accounts of animals
4. Other multisensory aids about animals
5. Chalkboard
6. Chalk
7. Class or group notebook(s)

C. Procedure:

1. Ask students if any of them has ever gone fishing. Have them relate their experiences.
2. Ask students if any of them has ever gone hunting. Have them relate their experiences.
3. Have students make a list of all the animals they know that have been hunted or fished for, for specific reasons.
4. Divide the students into groups or have them work individually and do research on each specific animal listed.

D. Results:

A sample list might start like this:

1. deer—food
2. elephants—ivory, work
3. trout—food
4. tropical fish—recreation
5. mink—fur (clothing)
6. birds—food, companionship
7. abalone—buttons and other items, food
8. monkeys—research
9. dolphins—recreation
10 fish—food, recreation etc.

E. Basic Facts and Supplemental Information:

1. Many animal species have become endangered and some have become extinct because of people's activities.
2. We must learn to balance our needs with animals' needs.
3. Many animals have been killed by oil spills, pesticides, and water contamination.
4. Many animals have been fished or hunted for recreational purposes. Some animals have become endangered and others extinct because of excessive fishing and hunting.
5. Animals are needed to provide the basic proteins for the diets of many people.

F. Thought Questions for Class Discussions:

1. What problems will we have as a result of expanding people population and decreasing animal population?
2. How can we protect our animals?
3. What part do you think greed plays in the loss of some of our animals?

G. Related Ideas for Further Inquiry:

1. Study other activities in Part IV, "Animals."
2. Study other activities in Part VI, "Ecology."
3. This is an excellent Activity to combine art and science. Students can draw pictures of their recreational experiences.

H. Vocabulary Builders—Spelling Words:

1) **recreation** 2) **clothing** 3) **endangered** 4) **extinct** 5) **population** 6) **threatened**

I. Thought for Today:

"A racehorse is an animal that can take several thousand people for a ride at the same time."

Activity IV K 3

A. Problem: *Should Animals Be Protected?*

B. Materials Needed:

1. Newspaper and journal accounts of animals that are threatened with extinction
2. Pictures of threatened animals
3. Multimedia aids if available

C. Procedure:

1. Discuss animals that are in danger of extinction.
2. Discuss animals that are being domesticated by people.
3. Discuss the balance of nature. (See Activity VI-A-1, "What is the balance of nature?")
4. Discuss whether animals are worth the expense of protection.

D. Results:

1. Students will place a higher priority on protecting animals.
2. Students will realize that animals are vital in our food web.

E. Basic Facts and Supplemental Information:

1. By selective breeding of nearly extinct animals, scientists hope to increase their populations and return them to their natural environment.
2. There are increasing attempts to overcome the great reduction of numbers of species:
   a. Native condors were captured for breeding. Several pairs have already been released.
   b. The black-footed ferrets are nearing extinction.
   c. The whooping crane is being bred in captivity. The red wolf is also being bred in zoos.
   d. The coho salmon are being protected by new federal and state laws.
   e. Two international conservation groups recently announced that nearly 5,205 animals are near extinction. This includes:
      1) 25% of the world's mammals
      2) 11% of the world's birds
      3) 20% of the world's reptiles
      4) 25% of the world's amphibians
      5) 34% of the world's fish
   f. All animals have some affect on our lives either directly or indirectly.

F. Thought Questions for Class Discussions:

1. Should we have concerns about protecting animals outside of the United States?

Elk

Bison

2. Do plants need protection from extinction?
3. Do people need protection from extinction?

G. Related Ideas for Further Inquiry:

1. Study Activity III-A-1, "How do we classify living things?"
2. Study Activity VI-A-1, "What is the balance of nature?"
3. Study Activity VI-A-2, "What is 'biological diversity'?"
4. Study Activity VI-A-11, "Are any animals threatened with extinction?"

H. Vocabulary Builders—Spelling Words:

1) **protection** 2) **survival** 3) **extinct** 4) **condor** 5) **balance** 6) **nature** 7) **world**

I. Thought for Today:

"Success is a journey, not a destination."

PART V

HEALTH

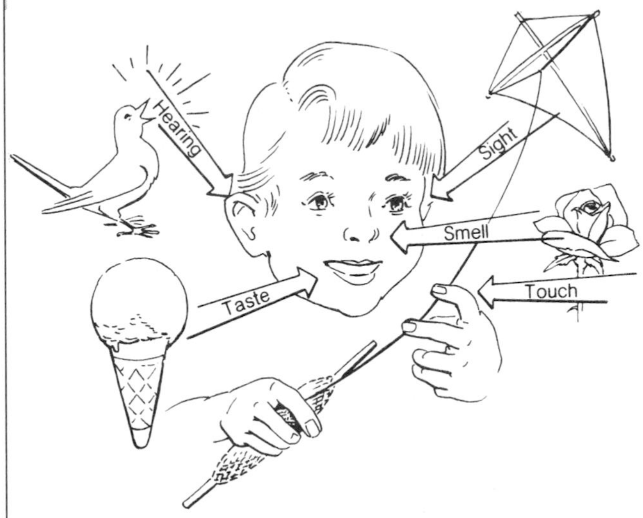

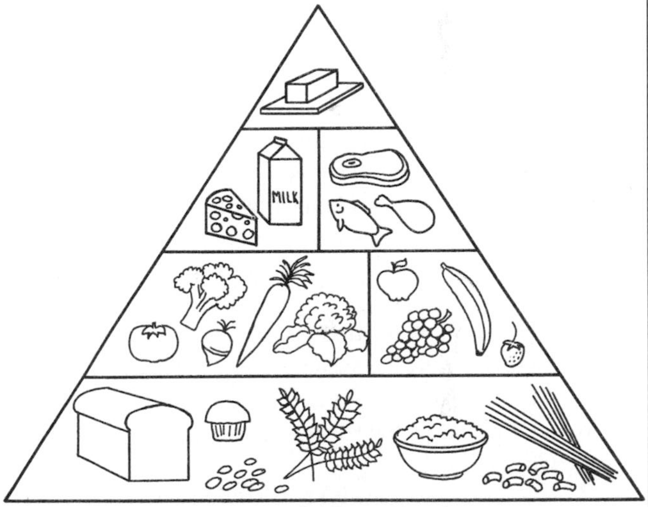

The Food Pyramid

SECTION A: BODY STRUCTURE AND FUNCTION

Activity V A 1

A. Problem: *What Are Cells, Tissues, and Organs?*

B. Materials Needed:

1. Onion
2. Strip of bacon, raw
3. Picture of heart, liver, and/or spleen
4. Microscope or magnifying glass
5. Pictures of mouth, windpipe, lungs (cross-sectional if possible)
6. Tongue depressors

C. Procedure:

1. Discuss how a body is like an automobile or a house. Each is a complete unit but made up of smaller and smaller parts or sections.
   a. Automobile has chassis, tires, motor, etc.; each of these has component parts.
   b. House has rooms; each room has component parts: windows, floors, walls, ceilings, etc.
2. Discuss the body as a whole entity.
3. Describe how the body is composed of systems.
4. Describe how the systems contain organs.
5. Describe how the organs are composed of tissues.
6. Describe how the tissues are composed of many cells.
7. In other words, the body is composed of:
   a. cells—which form
   b. tissue—which form
   c. organs—which are part of
   d. systems—which form the
   e. whole body
8. Cut an onion and slice one layer of it very thin.
9. Look at this one layer under a microscope or magnifying glass.
10. *Carefully* scrape inside the cheek for cheek cells with the tongue depressor.
11. Examine these under a microscope.
12. Examine the strip of bacon under the microscope.

D. Results:

1. Students will see cells under the microscope.
2. Students will learn that the body is composed of many parts all working in unison.

E. Basic Facts and Supplemental Information:

1. The body is composed of trillions of cells.
2. While no one has counted them, the human body at birth is estimated to contain 3 trillion (3,000,000,000,000) cells.

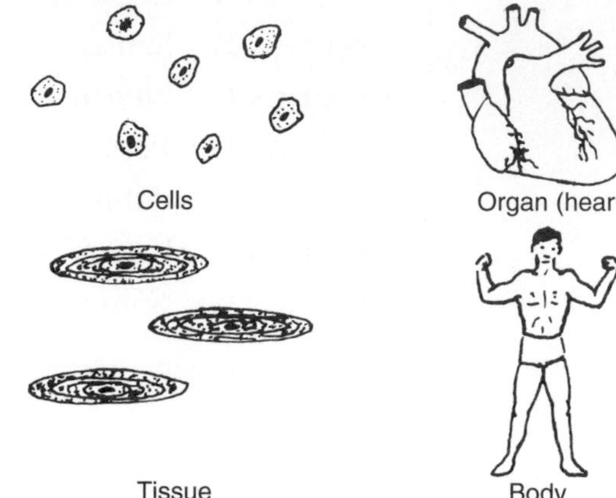

3. The most remarkable fact is that each human being started out as one cell.
4. Vitamins and minerals must be supplied by the mother to convert proteins, carbohydrates, and fats into living cells.
5. The main kinds of tissue are muscle, skin, and organ.
6. The main organs of the body are heart, spleen, liver, kidneys, reproductive organs, pancreas, stomach, lungs, and skin.
7. The main systems of the body are the muscular, reproductive, circulatory, lymphatic, digestive, respiratory, and nervous.

F. Thought Questions for Class Discussions:

1. Which systems are involuntary and which are voluntary? (Voluntary are those which individuals can control consciously.)
2. Do all animals have the same kinds of systems?
3. Do plants have the same kinds of systems?

G. Related Ideas for Further Inquiry:

1. Study the main purpose of each body group.
2. Study how the structures of humans differ from the structures of other animals.
3. Study the parts of an individual body cell.
4. Study other Activities in this Section.

H. Vocabulary Builders—Spelling Words:

1) **cells** 2) **tissue** 3) **organs** 4) **systems** 5) **heart** 6) **spleen** 7) **liver** 8) **lungs**

I. Thought for Today:

"One learns much from one's teachers, more from one's colleagues, and most from one's pupils."

Activity V A 2

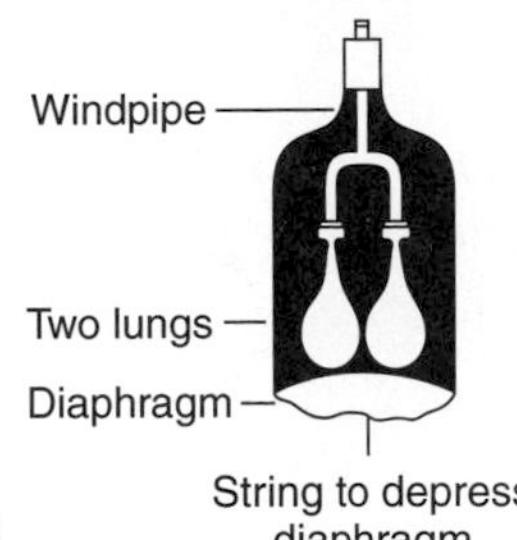

Diaphragm moves up and down

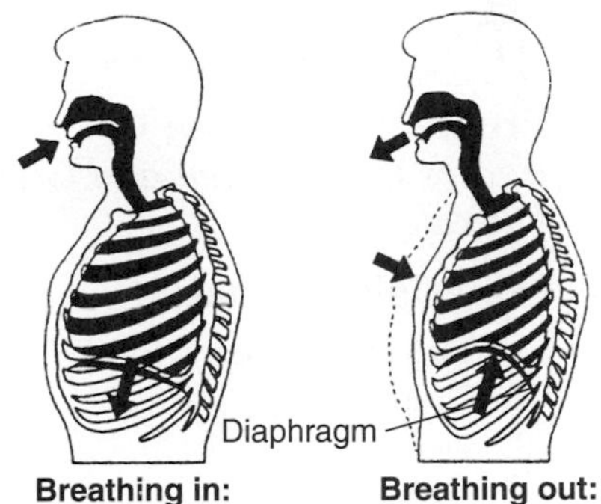

Breathing in: diaphragm contracts

Breathing out: diaphragm relaxes

A. Problem: *How Do Our Lungs Work?*

B. Materials Needed:

1. Gallon jar with bottom removed. (Teacher can prepare by tying a string around the base, soaking it in alcohol, lighting it, and as soon as the flame stops, quickly dip in water.)
2. A one-hole stopper
3. Glass tubing branched at one end
4. Two small rubber balloons
5. Large piece of rubber balloon to fit over the open end (bottom) of gallon jar. This represents the diaphragm.
6. Heavy rubber band or string

C. Procedure:

1. Blow up the balloons to stretch them, and then release the air.
2. Attach the small rubber balloons to the two ends of the glass tubing.
3. Put the single end of the glass "Y" tubing through the stopper and secure to the top of the jar. Wet the glass tubing before insertion into the rubber stopper.
4. Tie the string to the center of the rubber "diaphragm" and put it over the large opening of the jar, securing it with the heavy rubber band.
5. To demonstrate, push the rubber diaphragm in, making the chamber inside the jar smaller, and then pull the rubber diaphragm down with the string, making the chamber inside the glass jar larger. Note what happens to the rubber balloons on the ends of the glass tubing.
6. Compare the apparatus demonstrated to actual lungs.
7. Relate breathing rate to exercise and rest.

D. Results:

1. As the diaphragm is pushed in, the balloons will deflate (expiration).
2. As the diaphragm is pulled down, the balloons will inflate (inhalation).
3. Students will learn about breathing and how exercise influences the rate of breathing.

E. Basic Facts and Supplemental Information:

1. The rubber balloons on the ends of the glass tubing represent the lungs, and the large glass jar represents the thoracic cavity. The rubber shape on the large open end represents the diaphragm at the bottom of the thoracic cavity. This apparatus illustrates exactly what happens when we breathe.
2. The surface area of adult lungs is about 1,000 square feet which is 20 times greater than the surface area of your skin.
3. Oxygen drawn in when we breathe passes through the nose and/or mouth to the pharynx, larynx, trachea, and bronchi to the lungs. It is absorbed by the red blood cells as blood passes through the lungs.
4. Carbon dioxide is delivered to the lungs by the red blood cells in the blood and is expired during expiration (exhaling).
5. The lungs hold about 0.7 gallons (2.5 liters) of air.
6. A normal breath is about 15 ounces (500 milliliters) of air.

F. Thought Questions for Class Discussions:

1. What will happen if there is a hole in the rubber diaphragm?
2. What will happen if the opening in the end of the glass tubing is plugged up with a cork or with the finger?
3. Why does the breathing rate speed up during exercise?

G. Related Ideas for Further Inquiry:

1. Relate this activity to the heart and exercise.
2. Discuss how smokers destroy some lung tissue and then can't perform as well due to a decrease in the supply of oxygen and food to every cell in the body.
3. Study other Activities in this Section.

H. Vocabulary Builders—Spelling Words:

1) **breath** 2) **breathe** 3) **diaphragm** 4) **lungs** 5) **cavity** 6) **larynx** 7) **thoracic** 8) **oxygen**

I. Thought for Today:

"The greatest bankruptcy is the mind that has lost its enthusiasm."

Activity

V A 3

A. Problem: *How Can We Show That Our Bodies Use Oxygen and Give Off Carbon Dioxide?*

B. Materials Needed:

1. Two quart jars
2. Plastic tubing
3. Two candles
4. Large, clear bowl
5. Matches
6. Tap water
7. Four 1/2" bolts
8. Limewater
9. Temporary lid for jar (index card)

C. Procedure One:

1. Fill bowl with water.
2. Fill one jar with tap water. Cover open end of jar with temporary lid, invert jar, and place in vertical position in the bowl of water. (See drawing.)
3. Place the four bolts under neck of jar for support so tubing can be inserted.
4. Insert one end of plastic tubing into the jar of water.
5. Holding top of jar so it will not shake, blow air through tube into jar until the water has been replaced with *exhaled* air. (Do not inhale through tube.)
6. Remove jar; quickly and gently set it upside down on the table.
7. Light two candles side-by-side.
8. Place the jar filled with exhaled air over one candle. At same time, place the jar filled with ordinary air over the other candle.

Procedure Two:

1. Repeat Procedure One except that instead of placing jars over the candles, test the jars (one "exhaled air" and one "ordinary air") with limewater.
2. Testing for carbon dioxide with limewater is best done by pouring 2 or 3 ounces of limewater into each jar, capping the jar, and shaking briskly. The jar with *exhaled* air should have the limewater added and be capped quickly.

D. Results:

1. In Procedure One, the candle which is covered with the jar of exhaled air will go out first; it does not contain as much oxygen as the bottle of ordinary air.
2. In Procedure Two, the exhaled air when tested for carbon dioxide will turn slightly milky.

E. Basic Facts and Supplemental Information:

The body requires oxygen. Exhaled air has less oxygen than inhaled air. The body uses about 5% of each inhalation of oxygen. Normal exhalations will produce better results than forced blowing into the tube. (See previous Activity.)

F. Thought Questions for Class Discussions:

1. Where did the oxygen go that was lost from the air?
2. How does the body use oxygen? Why not nitrogen?
3. Do plants use oxygen and carbon dioxide?

G. Related Ideas for Further Inquiry:

1. Test your lung capacity by taking a full breath and blowing it into an inverted gallon container filled with water as described in Procedure One.
2. Count the times students breathe normally in a minute and compare this with the number of times the students breathe after exercise.
3. Study other Activities in this Section.

H. Vocabulary Builders—Spelling Words:

1) **oxygen** 2) **carbon dioxide** 3) **inhale**
4) **exhale** 5) **inhalation** 6) **exhalation**
7) **candles** 8) **breathing** 9) **limewater**
10) **blowing**

I. Thought for Today:

"Sometimes the person of action is the one who just got both feet into hot water."

Activity

A. Problem: *How Does The Heart Work?*

B. Materials Needed:

1. Model of heart
2. Pictures, posters, and/or charts showing the chambers of thc heart and the circulatory system

C. Procedure:

1. Discuss the four chambers of the heart:
   a. Left Ventricle—starts the blood moving to all parts of the body
   b. Right Atrium—receives blood from all parts of the body
   c. Right Ventricle—starts blood moving to the lungs to be oxygenated
   d. Left Atrium—receives oxygenated blood from the lungs
2. Have the students make a simple drawing of where the blood circulates and the main blood vessels the body has to transport the blood.
3. Describe the pumping action of the heart.
4. Define the terms:
   a. Systolic—how hard the heart works (contracting)
   b. Diastolic—blood pressure when the heart relaxes (dilating)
5. Blood pressure is usually reported by citing the systolic pressure (upper reading) followed by the diastolic (lower reading). Thus a reading of 120/80 (one twenty over eighty) are the pressures in millimeters of mercury of the systolic and diastolic systems, respectively.

D. Result:

Students can better understand how a four-chambered human heart circulates blood throughout the body.

E. Basic Facts and Supplemental Information:

1. Blood circulates to the lungs to give off carbon dioxide and to get oxygen. It then returns to the heart to be pumped to all parts of the body.
2. The heart pumps about 100,000 times a day and pumps about 3,000 gallons of blood through 60,000 miles of arteries, veins, and capillaries. In an average lifetime it pumps about 73,000,000 gallons of blood.
3. The blood is composed of serum (the liquid part) and white cells, red cells, and platelets (the solid parts). The white cells fight infection, the red cells distribute oxygen and pick up carbon dioxide, and the platelets help in blood clotting.

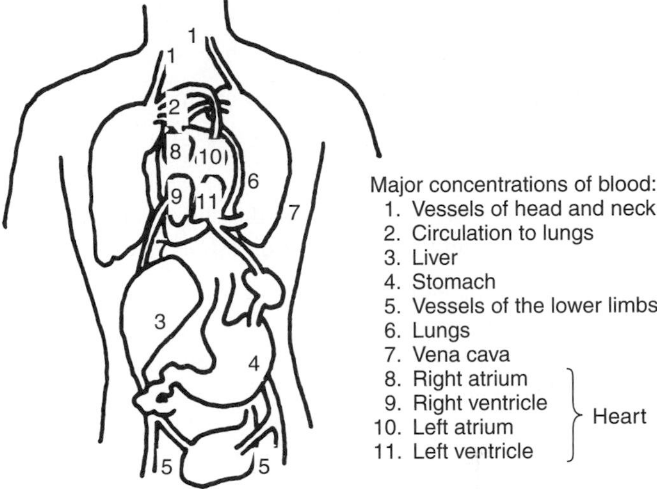

4. There are four types of blood: Types A, B, AB, and O. These must be matched in blood transfusions.
5. There is also an "Rh" factor that concerns blood clotting (agglutinogen). The blood of a person who has it is called "Rh positive;" if not, it is called "Rh negative."
6. The heart is about the size of a closed fist and weighs about 12 ounces in men and 9 ounces in women. There are valves which control the flow of blood during pumping motions.
7. The blood starts from the heart in large arteries and ends up in capillaries smaller than the diameter of a human hair.
8. The blood delivers food to every cell in the human body.

F. Thought Questions for Class Discussions:

1. What is heart disease?
2. How serious is heart disease?
3. Is there such a thing as "athlete's heart"?
4. How can we take better care of our hearts?

G. Related Ideas for Further Inquiry:

1. Discuss what happens during accidents which result in bleeding.
2. Study Section V-F, "First Aid."
3. Study other Activities in this Section.

H. Vocabulary Builders—Spelling Words:

1) **artery** 2) **vein** 3) **capillary** 4) **atrium** 5) **ventricle** 6) **platelets** 7) **circulation** 8) **heart**

I. Thought for Today:

"The heart is happiest when it beats for others."

Activity V A 5

A. Problem: *How Do We Digest Food?*

B. Materials Needed:

Enlarged charts for each student such as those shown in sketch below.

C. Procedure:

Have students number their charts as the class notes how a piece of apple pie moves through the digestive system:

1. entering the mouth cavity
2. chewing with teeth
3. mixing with salivary gland fluid (saliva)
4. swallowing
5. moving down the throat (esophagus) by peristolic action (squeezing and releasing)
6. entering the stomach
7. mixing with enzymes, gastric juices, and hydrochloric acid for several hours. (This changes most of the food to a semiliquid form and kills bacteria which might be in the food.) Carbohydrates move through quickly, but meats take up to 4 hours.
8. entering the small intestine where most of the digestion takes place and the digested food is absorbed by the blood
9. entering the large intestine
10. exiting at the rectum

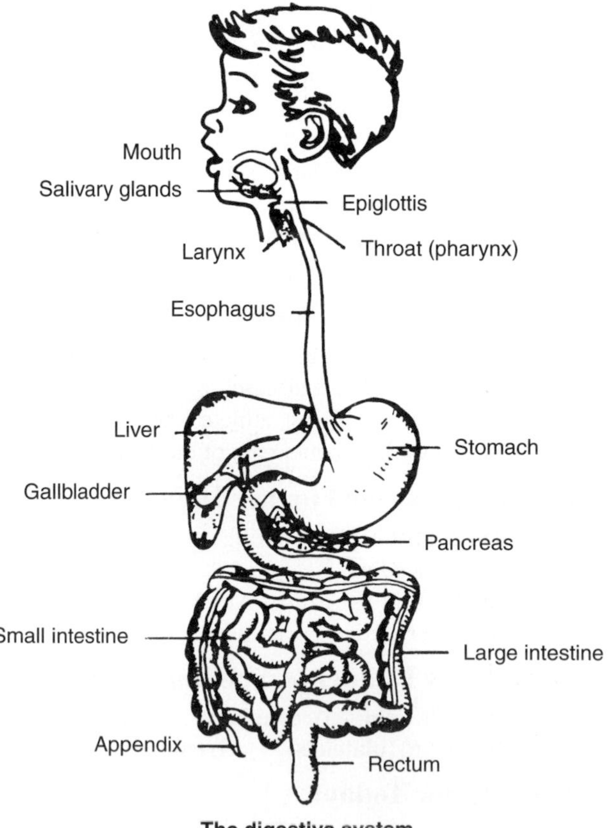

The digestive system

D. Result:

Students will learn about the many bodily functions involved in the digestion of food.

E. Basic Facts and Supplemental Information:

1. Our stomachs do not digest food; they change the contents to a liquid form and the small intestine does the actual job of digesting. All unabsorbed liquids and solids are eliminated.
2. The digestive tract is about 30 feet long. The small intestine is about 24 feet long, and the large intestine is about 6 feet long.
3. The salivary glands, pancreas, liver, and gallbladder all add digestive fluids during the process.
4. Single additives in foods might be all right, but mixing additives can cause severe digestive problems.
5. Intestines have villi (projections) which increase the surface area to aid absorption of foods.

F. Thought Questions for Class Discussions:

1. What is the purpose of the tongue?
2. Why do we have different kinds of tastes in food?
3. Would it be better for the digestive system if we ate only one kind of food at a time?
4. Could we call the digestive system a chemical factory?

G. Related Ideas for Further Inquiry:

1. Compare the different sizes and shapes of teeth.
2. Check food labels for food additives.
3. Study food preservation including irradiation.
4. Study Activity V-C-1, "What would be a perfect menu for a day?"
5. Study Activity V-C-2, "What is the 'Food Pyramid'?"

H. Vocabulary Builders—Spelling Words:

1) **digestion** 2) **salivary** 3) **esophagus**
4) **stomach** 5) **pancreas** 6) **intestine**

I. Thought for Today:

"Education is not a vessel to be filled but a fire to be kindled."

Activity

V A 6

A. Problem: *How Does Our Nervous System Help Us?*

B. Materials Needed:

1. Books about the nervous system
2. Pamphlets about the nervous system
3. Multisensory aids on the nervous system

C. Procedure:

1. Explain that:
   a. The nervous system is really a communication system with nerves (the wires) running to all parts of the body.
   b. It tells us that we are alive.
   c. It enables us to sense our environment.
   d. Its voluntary and involuntary actions control our being.
   e. The base of the nervous system is the brain.
   f. The brain has two hemispheres or halves:
      1) The right half controls emotions, intuitions, values, and that is the creative half.
      2) The left half controls the rational factors: logic, analysis, etc.
   g. The nerves are not joined physically but transfer messages at the nerve junctions.
   h. Nerves transmit messages to the muscles and glands.
   i. Nerve impulses travel about 350 feet per second.
2. Follow a simple movement of the body, such as drinking a glass of milk, showing nerve communication.
   a. Nerves see it.
   b. Nerves move hand toward it.
   c. Nerves tell us contact is made.
   d. Nerves tell us to lift glass.
   e. Nerves tell us exact position.
   f. Nerves tell us it touched our lips.
   g. Nerves give us our sense of heat, flavor, etc.
   h. Nerves give us the sensation of swallowing.
   i. Reverse actions for putting empty glass down.

D. Result:

Students will learn about their nervous system.

E. Basic Facts and Supplemental Information:

1. Most parts of the body will regenerate, but not nerve cells. Once they are destroyed, they are never replaced.
2. Accidents that sever nerve pathways lead to paralysis.
3. Our brain has about ten billion (10,000,000,000) brain cells.

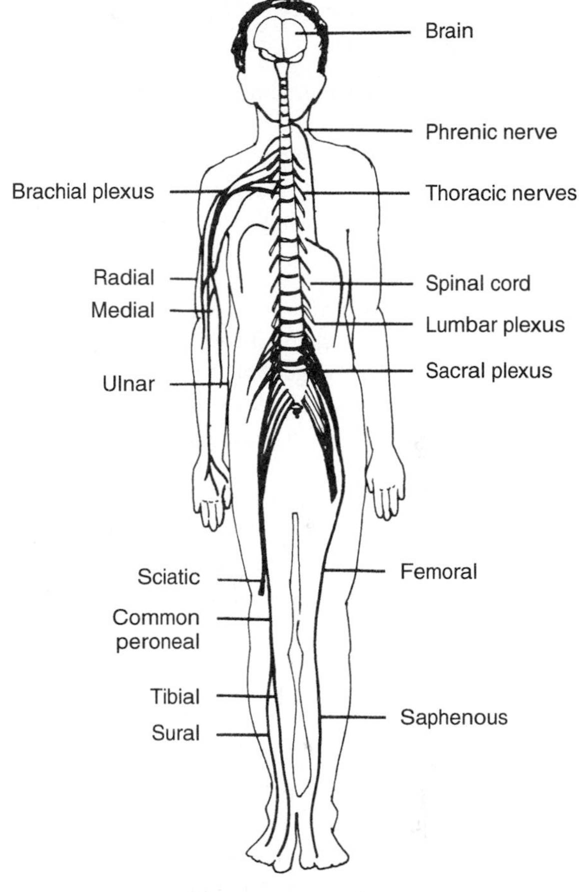

The nervous system

F. Thought Questions for Class Discussions:

1. What is "reaction time"?
2. Is "reaction time" important in emergencies?
3. Is "nervousness" a nerve defect?

G. Related Ideas for Further Inquiry:

1. Study especially Activity V-A-7, "What are hormones?"
2. Study especially Activity V-F-4, "What is CPR (cardiopulmonary resuscitation)?"
3. Study reaction times.
4. Study other Activities in this Section.

H. Vocabulary Builders—Spelling Words:

1) **nerve** 2) **impulse** 3) **hemisphere**
4) **cranium** 5) **brain** 6) **transmit**

I. Thought for Today:

"A person's intellect is judged by his/her ability to disagree without being disagreeable."

Activity V A 7

A. Problem: *What Are Hormones?*

B. Materials Needed:

1. Books about hormones and their purpose in the body
2. Pamphlets about hormones
3. Multisensory aids on vital glands
4. Study chart (see drawing.) (one for each student)

C. Procedure:

1. Pass out the study charts.
2. While students are perusing the charts, discuss the endocrine system in general, the specific glands, and the hormones they secrete.
3. Point out that the main glands secreting hormones are:
   a. Pituitary gland (size of a pea)
      1) Anterior part—sex hormone
      2) Posterior part—growth and development
   b. Pancreas—secretes insulin; digests food, regulates sugar
   c. Thyroid—regulates calcium
   d. Parathyroids—emotional tone; growth roles
   e. Adrenals—regulates fluids, minerals, glucose, sex hormone, blood pressure
   f. Gonads—testes in males: sex development; ovaries in females: reproduction, controls menstrual cycle
   g. Thymus—white cell production; fights disease
   h. Hypothalamus—controls hunger, thirst, body temperature, sexual behavior
   i. Pineal—regulates body growth rate

D. Result:

Students will learn that our bodies are chemical factories and have many glands that control most of the body's functions.

E. Basic Facts and Supplemental Information:

1. The endocrine system is a complex system of glands.
2. These glands secrete chemicals into the bloodstream which send messages throughout the body.
3. These chemicals are called "hormones."
4. Endocrine glands are ductless glands which discharge their secretions directly into the bloodstream.
5. Hormones play a vital role in growth, reproduction, digestion, emotional balance, etc.

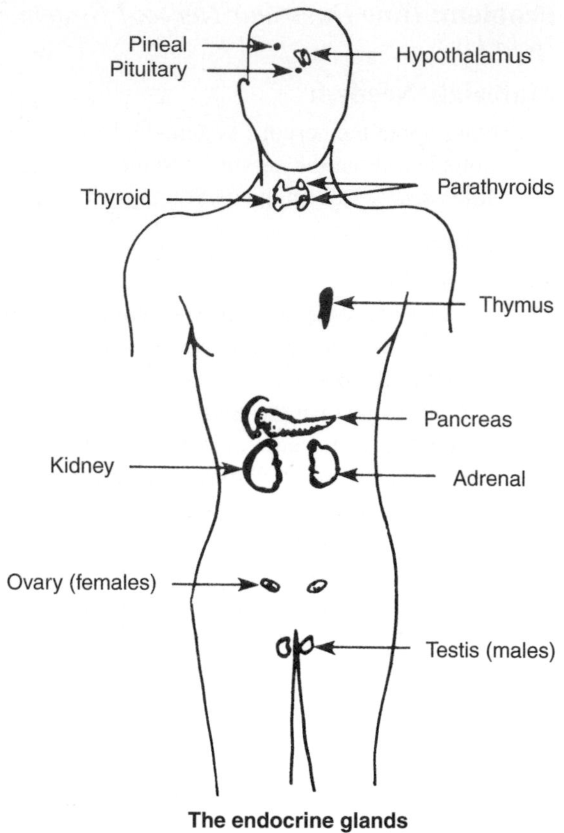

The endocrine glands

6. Disorders of the endocrine system can cause physical, mental, and emotional problems.

F. Thought Questions for Class Discussions:

1. Are there male hormones? female hormones?
2. Do you think hormones determine our temperament?

G. Related Ideas for Further Inquiry:

1. Study V-A-8, "How do our bodies fight disease?"
2. Study Activity V-A-9, "What is the reproductive system?"
3. Study other Activities in Part V, "Health."

H. Vocabulary Builders—Spelling Words:

Use the gland names listed in Procedure.

I. Thought for Today:

"Keep your head and your heart going in the right direction and you'll not have to worry about your feet."

Activity

A. Problem: *How Do Our Bodies Fight Disease?*

B. Materials Needed:

1. Books about the immune system and circulatory system
2. Pamphlets about the lymphatic system
3. Multisensory aids about lymph glands

C. Procedure:

1. Ask students to discuss various illnesses they have had.
2. Have them relate which ones required medical attention and medication.
3. Ask them to discuss any illnesses they had that did not require medical attention or medication.
4. Explain the main facts about the lymphatic system, such as:
   a. It is a circulatory system without a pump.
   b. Movement of lymph fluids is caused by muscle contractions and other body movements.
   c. It has white blood cells that feed, provide fluids, and actually bathe individual cells.
   d. These fluids collect in tiny ducts and flow around the skin, muscles, bones, and organs.
   e. The major lymphatic ducts empty into the veins near the heart.
   f. The lymph nodes are filled with white blood cells that are vital in fighting infection.
   g. The lymphatic system can be considered a filtering system.
   h. Lymphocytes are white cells.
5. Various health assignments can be made depending on the teacher's discretion and resources available.

D. Results:

1. Students will learn about their bodies' immune system.
2. Students will realize that a healthy body requires constant care.

E. Basic Facts and Supplemental Information:

1. Doctors can diagnose diseases by a swelling of the lymph glands.
2. The main lymph glands are located under the jaw, in the armpits, and in the groin area.
3. The immune system does not attack everything foreign that enters the body. Most of the food, liquid, and medicinal drugs that we ingest do not trigger an immune response.

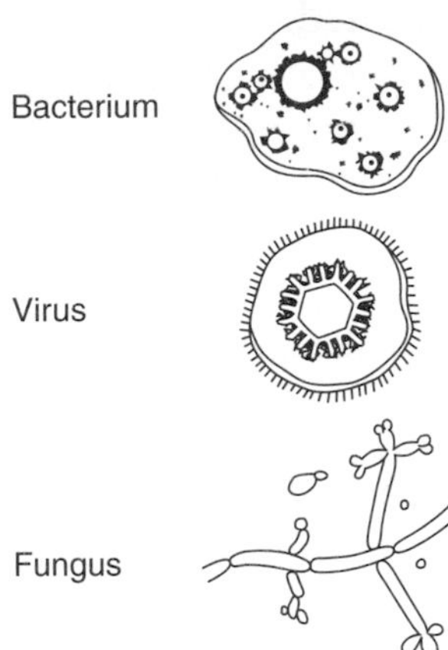

4. The immune system does respond to agents such as germs, viruses, and other invaders that cause disease.
5. Our bodies' defense system includes:
   a. first—the skin
   b. second—the gastrointestinal tract
   c. third—the immune system, including:
      1) B cells which produce antibodies that destroy antigens (foreign invaders)
      2) T cells which rid the body of antigens by engulfing or dissolving them

F. Thought Questions for Class Discussions:

1. What would happen if the lymphatic system did not function?
2. What can we do to better protect our environment from disease agents?
3. Is the disease AIDS related to the function of the lymphatic system?

G. Related Ideas for Further Inquiry:

1. Study about the disease AIDS.
2. Compare the circulation of the blood and the lymph.
3. If possible, examine blood cells under a microscope.
4. Study other Activities in this Section.

H. Vocabulary Builders—Spelling Words:

1) **lymph** 2) **nodes** 3) **lymphocytes** 4) **infection** 5) **lymphatic** 6) **antibodies**

I. Thought for Today:

"The credit card has created another American first—instant debt."

Activity

V A 9

A. Problem: *What Is the Reproductive System?*

B. Materials Needed:

1. Books and pamphlets about the reproductive system of humans
2. Multisensory aids about human babies

C. Procedure:

First, decide whether you want to become involved in this teaching area. If you feel uncomfortable or that it is inappropriate depending on the maturity of your students, then avoid it. If you decide to teach it then:

1. Discuss and talk about the reproductive system as you would any other system of the body, being very factual and open-minded.
2. Discuss the anatomy of females concerned with reproduction:
   a. heart and blood vessels
   b. womb (vagina, uterus)
   c. fallopian tubes
   d. ovaries
3. Discuss the anatomy of males concerned with reproduction:
   a. scrotum
   b. testes (produce sperm)
   c. penis
   d. seminal vesicles
   e. prostate
   f. semen (sperm and secretions)
4. Discuss the needs of every child:
   a. mother
   b. father
   c. food
   d. home
   e. clothing
   f. education
   g. play time (recreation)
   h. care
   i. protection
   j. supervision
   k. financial support (average cost is about $60,000 to rear a child)
   l. loving parents
   m. security, etc.

D. Results

1. Students will learn the basic anatomical structures of reproduction.
2. Students will learn that there are many responsibilities and financial costs involved in rearing a child.

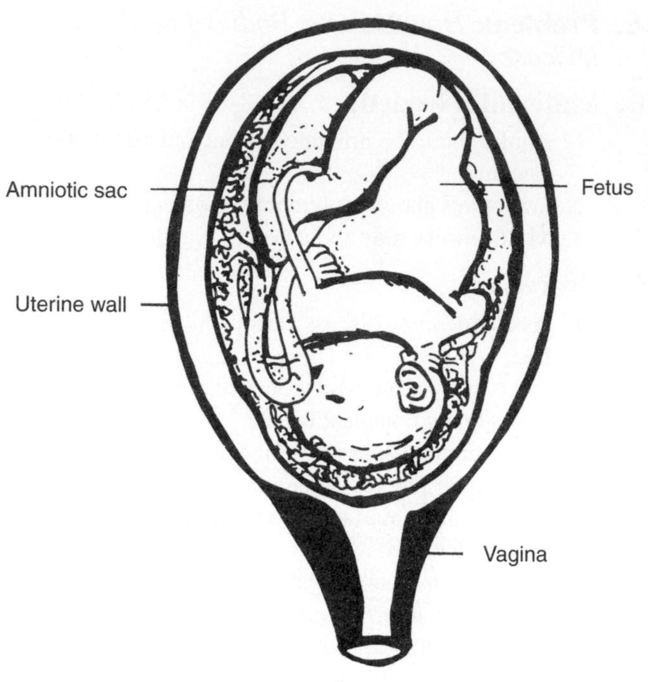

Mother's womb

E. Basic Facts and Supplemental Information:

1. Birth shock and a sense of security are two main factors in personality development.
2. The fertilized egg is a living cell, and each day the fetus multiplies and develops more fully.
3. Over 1,000,000 unmarried teenagers become pregnant every year.
4. Sex education can't be started too early.
5. There is a big difference between sex and love.

F. Thought Questions for Class Discussions:

1. Why are so many children born out of wedlock?
2. Do children of divorced parents get a "fair break" in life?
3. Why is our divorce rate so high in the United States?

G. Related Ideas for Further Inquiry:

1. Study plants and their reproduction.
2. Study animals and their reproduction.
3. Study other Activities in this Section.

H. Vocabulary Builders—Spelling Words:

Use appropriate terms cited in Procedure (C-2 and C-3).

I. Thought for Today:

"What reproduction and nutrition are to biological life, education is to social life."

Activity

V A 10

A. Problem: *What Characteristics Do We Inherit from Our Parents?*

B. Materials Needed:

1. Pictures of people with diverse physical characteristics
2. Pictures of students and their parents
3. Pictures of students' grandparents

C. Procedure:

1. Describe how babies of one animal look like their parents:
   a. Bears have cubs and the cubs look like bears, not elephants.
   b. Dogs have pups and the pups look like dogs, not giraffes.
   c. Cats have kittens and the kittens look like cats, not spiders.
   d. All living things reproduce and look like their parents, not some other creature.
2. People have children. (Homo sapiens have Homo sapiens.)
3. Discuss the fact that some of our physical features come from our father and some come from our mother.
4. Our parents got their looks (appearances) from their parents.
5. Discuss with students that the study of inherited traits is called "genetics."
6. Scientists have found that certain traits tend to be more dominant, and certain others are more recessive. The dominant ones are likely to be passed on to the children. The recessive ones are usually carried or hidden and may come out in later generations.
7. The chart shows some traits that belong to each category.
8. Have students develop a genealogy chart with pictures of their grandparents, their parents, and finally, themselves.
9. Have students compare the likenesses and differences of the three generations.

HEREDITARY CHARACTERISTICS

Dominant:	*Recessive:*
Curly Hair	Straight Hair
Dark Hair	Light Hair
Non-red Hair	Red Hair
Normal Skin Pigmentation	Albinism
Brown Eyes	Blue or Gray Eyes
Near or Farsightedness	Normal Vision
Broad Lips	Thin Lips
Large Eyes	Small Eyes
Nervous Temperament	Calm Temperament
A or B Blood Type	O Blood Type
Rh-Positive	Rh-Negative

If both parents have a dominant characteristic, it is passed on to their offspring.
If one parent has a dominant characteristic, and one parent has a recessive characteristic, the dominant characteristic prevails.
If both parents have a recessive characteristic, it is passed on to their offspring.

D. Results:

1. Students will become more aware of hereditary characteristics.
2. Pupils will realize that many individual differences are a result of heredity.

E. Basic Facts and Supplemental Information:

1. Every organism has a line of ancestors.
2. Each generation resembles its parents in some ways.
3. Individuals in families usually resemble one another because physical characteristics are determined by the genes received from their parents.
4. There is no way to determine the results of heredity. It is governed by the laws of chance and probability. Chromosomes determine our hereditary characteristics. A human egg may be fertilized by a sperm containing an X chromosome and become a female embryo or a sperm containing a Y chromosome and become a male embryo; either could happen.

F. Thought Questions for Class Discussions:

1. Would you expect two curly-haired parents to have a straight-haired child?
2. Why are pygmies always short?
3. Is temperament an inherited characteristic?

G. Related Ideas for Further Inquiry:

1. There have been many studies about heredity that are worth exploring:
   a. Gregor Mendel—study of peas
   b. Francis Galton—study of twins and the effects of heredity and environment
2. Study DNA (dioxyribonucleic acid)

H. Vocabulary Builders—Spelling Words:

1) **heredity** 2) **dominant** 3) **recessive**
4) **inherited** 5) **genetics** 6) **characteristics**

I. Thought for Today:

"Insanity is inherited—you can get it from your children."

Activity

V A 11

A. Problem: *What Human Body Parts Can Be Replaced?*

B. Materials Needed:

Chart like that shown in drawing

C. Procedure:

1. Discuss the differences between people and automobiles, e.g., fuel needed, parts, etc.
2. Discuss what automobile parts can be replaced.
3. Discuss bionic people (Frankenstein, etc.).
4. Discuss what body parts can be replaced.

D. Result:

Students will learn that many body parts can now be replaced.

E. Basic Facts and Supplemental Information:

1. Blood vessel replacements made using flexible polyurethane or Dacron.
2. Skin replacements made using animal collagen and silicon film.
3. Cochlear implants help restore hearing.
4. An artificial eye is close to reproducing images by a grid of electrodes implanted in the brain.
5. Tissue, cartilage, and bone replacements are now common operations.
6. Some body parts can be stored in banks but most require recent transfer to new patients.
7. There are about 1,000,000 body replacement operations every year in the United States.
8. Adult livers have been cut to size and transplanted in children; recently, several adults have had liver transplants.
9. Lasers can now be used for bloodless operations when performing body transplants.
10. We should consider the pig a very good friend. We can use pig heart valves in humans; pigskin could be used for human replacement; pig tissue is the nearest to human tissue of all animals.

F. Thought Questions for Class Discussions:

1. What would be some problems in transplant operations?
2. Do you think they will ever be able to transplant a brain?
3. Do replacement parts work as well as the original ones?

G. Related Ideas for Further Inquiry:

1. Compare an old automobile with a new part to an old person with a new part.
2. Study "cloning" of animals.

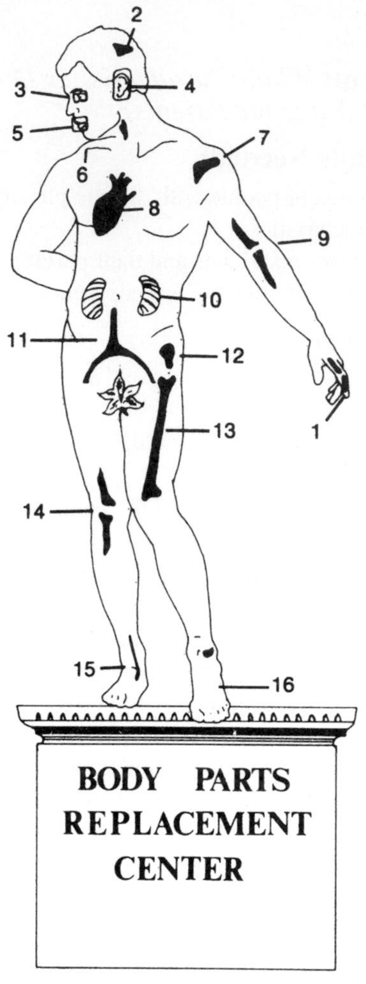

What do you need?

1. Fingers
2. Skull plate
3. Vision (camera eye and brain cortex stimulation
4. Hearing (cochlear transplants)
5. Dentures
6. Speech assistance device
7. Shoulder joint
8. Heart valves and vessels
9. Elbow
10. Kidney (artificial and transplant)
11. Arteries (Dacron and replacements)
12. Hip joint (or parts)
13. Thigh bone
14. Knee joint
15. Tendon
16. Ankle

3. Study Activity V-A-1, "What are cells, tissues, and organs?"

H. Vocabulary Builders—Spelling Words:

1) **body** 2) **replacement** 3) **operations** 4) **bionic** 5) **collagen** 6) **cloning**

I. Thought for Today:

"It is better to debate a question without settling it than to settle a question without debating it."

Activity V A 12

A. Problem: *What Can We Learn About Our Muscles?*

B. Materials Needed:

1. Pictures about muscles
2. Books about anatomy
3. Multisensory items about muscles
4. Drawings showing muscles, and muscles at work
5. Pictures of athletes in motion

C. Procedure:

1. Ask students to flex their biceps.
2. Ask students to turn their heads, stand up, wiggle their toes, jog in place, open and close their eyes, rub their arms, etc.
3. Discuss the heart muscle.
4. Discuss meat that is purchased in meat markets. (Meat is the main part of the muscular system.)
5. Have students do some research on muscles.

D. Result:

Students will learn about their muscles, i.e., the different muscles involved in different movements.

E. Basic Facts and Supplemental Information:

1. People have about 600 muscles.
2. All the muscles working together could lift about 25 tons or 50,000 pounds.
3. Some muscles are voluntary (can be controlled): biceps, triceps, etc.
4. Some muscles are involuntary (cannot be controlled): heart, diaphragm, etc.
5. Muscles are usually joined to tendons and tendons to bones.
6. About 40% of men's body weight and 30% of women's body weight is muscle.
7. The largest muscle is the latissimus dorsi (lies across the back).
8. Many muscles work in opposition to other muscles. Example: one group of muscles flex (bend) the knee and another group extends (straightens) it.
9. Muscles are stimulated by nerves.
10. Good posture depends on good muscle development.
11. Good posture promotes good health.
12. Good nutrition is a prerequisite for good muscular development.

F. Thought Questions for Class Discussions:

1. Does gravity affect our movements?
2. How can we develop our muscles (make them grow larger and stronger)?
3. How do athletes protect their muscles?

G. Related Ideas for Further Inquiry:

1. Study how animals use their muscles for movement and survival.
2. Some students might want to study great athletes.
3. Study what sports require the use of many muscles.
4. Study what sports require very strong muscles.
5. Study other Activities in this Section.

H. Vocabulary Builders—Spelling Words:

1) **muscles** 2) **movement** 3) **posture** 4) **latissimus dorsi** 5) **strength** 6) **nutrition**

I. Thought for Today:

"When your outgo exceeds your income that's when your upkeep becomes your downfall."

SECTION B: SENSES

Activity V B 1

A. Problem: *What Senses Do We Use to Communicate with Each Other?*

B. Materials Needed:

Pictures or objects showing:

1. Newspapers
2. Magazines
3. Radio
4. Television
5. Letters (notes)
6. Telephone
7. Voice (speaking)
8. Gestures
9. Books
10. Pamphlets
11. Records and transcriptions
12. Cassettes
13. Video disks
14. Motion pictures
15. Still pictures
16. Telegraph
17. Flags
18. Hands and fingers (Sign Language)
19. Computers (Internet)
20. Signals (smoke, lights, sounds)
21. Fax
22. Other forms of communication

C. Procedure:

1. Discuss how animals communicate.
2. Discuss the different sounds animals make.
3. Discuss the difference between communication and noise.
4. Describe how important it is that we communicate with other people.
5. Have students cite all the ways by which they can get information.
6. Ask if they can learn anything by themselves with just direct, firsthand experiences.

D. Results:

1. Students will learn that there are many ways to gain knowledge and information.
2. Students will learn the importance of communication.

E. Basic Facts and Supplemental Information:

1. People can store information outside of their bodies; animals cannot.
2. Communication is vital to learning.
3. If there were no communication we would have to learn everything as a new firsthand experience.

F. Thought Questions for Class Discussions:

1. What are our best sources of information?
2. How can we best learn about historical happenings?
3. Is knowledge more important today than it ever was before?
4. How did people communicate in ancient times?
5. What are hieroglyphics?
6. How important is communication in court trials?
7. How important is communication in our classroom?

G. Related Ideas for Further Inquiry:

1. Have each student study, in detail, one form of communication.
2. Can communication ever be misleading?
3. Study other Activities in this Section.

H. Vocabulary Builders—Spelling Words:

Use the words listed under Materials Needed.

I. Thought for Today:

"You really can't judge a person until you've met his dog."

Activity

A. Problem: *How Well Do We See?*

B. Materials Needed:

1. Snellen chart (lettering chart)
2. Astigmatic test chart
3. Color-blind chart

Snellen chart

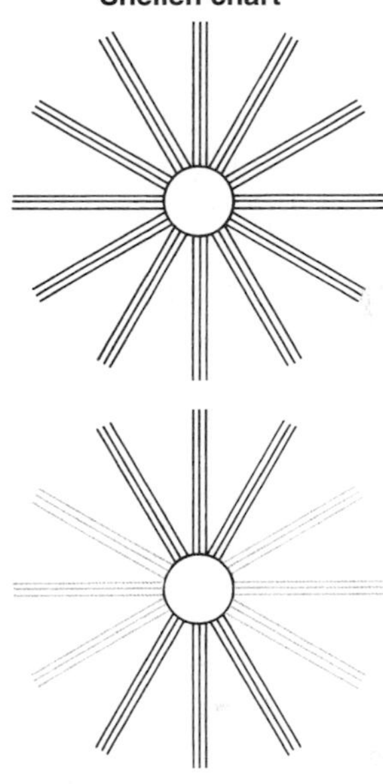

C. Procedure:

1. Discuss the fact that our eyes are among our most important possessions.
2. Discuss how people differ in their ability to see just as they differ in their ability to hear or in their sense of smell.
3. Test each of the students using the above charts to determine how well each can see. (In most cases, the school nurse or a doctor would be happy to administer and discuss eye tests. If not, see a local optometrist or ophthalmologist.)

D. Results:

1. Some students will be found to have astigmatism.
2. Some students will be found to have visual problems in reading the letters at various distances.
3. Some students will be found to be color-blind.

E. Basic Facts and Supplemental Information:

1. We do not see with our eyes, but with our brain and nervous system.
2. Some people use one eye more than the other and turn their head to see better.
3. About 25% of all students have some visual difficulties, and about 10% should be wearing glasses or contact lenses to see properly to do their classwork.
4. Glasses or contact lenses correct most visual problems.
5. Don't take your eyes for granted. Be sure your sight is right; have frequent checkups.
6. No one should watch television from a distance closer than 8 feet.
7. Healthy eyes can distinguish almost 5,000,000 differences in color.

F. Thought Questions for Class Discussions:

1. What are some ways that we can protect our eyes?
2. If red-green color blindness is most common, should our traffic lights be red and green?
3. Since good sight is related to good health, should we try to keep as healthy as possible so that we can see better and keep our eyes free from disease?
4. Should the light from the classroom windows come from the back, sides, or front of the room?

G. Related Ideas for Further Inquiry:

1. Study Activity V-B-3, "How do we see motion?"
2. Study Activity V-B-5, "Are there blind spots in our eyes?"
3. Study Activity V-B-7, "Are our eyes like a camera?"
4. Study Activity V-B-8, "Are you right-eyed or left-eyed?"

H. Vocabulary Builders—Spelling Words:

1) **Snellen** 2) **astigmatism** 3) **color blindness** 4) **focus** 5) **problems** 6) **contact lenses** 7) **eyes** 8) **ophthalmologist** 9) **seeing** 10) **visual**

I. Thought for Today:

"Motivation is the pulse of good teaching."

Activity V B 3

A. Problem: *How Do We See Motion?*

B. Materials Needed:

1. Heavy white or light-colored cardboard, 2 1/2" x 3"
2. Fine string, 36" long
3. India ink or black paint
4. One-hole punch
5. Marking pen
6. Scissors

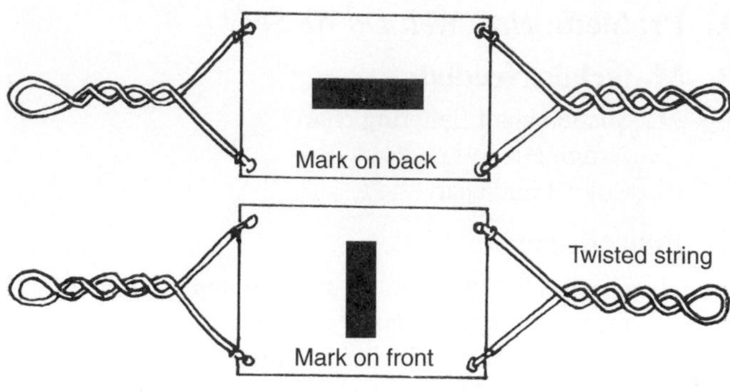

C. Procedure:

1. Punch four holes in the card as shown in the drawing.
2. Cut string in half.
3. Thread each string through two holes on both sides of card, securing ends well. (See drawing.)
4. Use black ink to make a heavy vertical line on one side of the card.
5. Use black ink to make a heavy horizontal line on the opposite side of the card.
6. Wind up the string and card by rotating card 20 to 30 times.
7. Spin the card rapidly by pulling the two loops outwardly.

D. Result:

The two marks will appear to blend, forming a cross.

E. Basic Facts and Supplemental Information:

1. We may conclude that vision persists for a short time in the eye after the object is gone from view. This phenomenon is called "visual persistency."
2. This characteristic is used in motion pictures and television.
3. We receive light sensations with our eyes and interpret these sensations with our brain.

F. Thought Questions for Class Discussions:

1. Could you design a test to determine how long a vision persists?
2. What percent of our population has visual handicaps?
3. What percent of our population should be wearing glasses or contact lenses?
4. Do motion pictures move?

G. Related Ideas for Further Inquiry:

1. Study the actual film of a motion picture.
2. Try other designs and combinations like those illustrated in the drawings.
3. Study Activity II-C-1, "What is light?"
4. Study Activity II-C-6, "What is an image?"
5. Study Activity II-C-7, "What causes an image to change shape, size, and/or position?"
6. Study Activity V-B-2, "How well do we see?"
7. Study Activity V-B-4, "Do our eyes get tired?"
8. Study Activity V-B-6, "Do our eyes ever deceive us?"

H. Vocabulary Builders—Spelling Words:

1) **visual** 2) **persistency** 3) **vertical**
4) **horizontal** 5) **cardboard** 6) **spin**
7) **strong** 8) **wind** 9) **eyes** 10) **brain**

I. Thought for Today:

"Few people ever get dizzy from doing too many good turns."

Activity V B 4

A. Problem: *Do Our Eyes Get Tired?*

B. Materials Needed:

1. Flashlight or slide projector
2. White surface (wall or screen)
3. Red sheet of paper
4. Blue circular cutout

C. Procedure:

1. Place the red sheet of paper over the white surface.
2. Place the blue cutout in the middle of the red sheet.
3. Darken the room.
4. Have the students face the display.
5. Flash the light on the blue design.
6. Have the students stare at the design for 1 minute.
7. After 1 minute, remove the red sheet of paper and blue cutout, revealing only the white surface.

D. Result:

The students will see a yellow dot on a green background instead of the original colors.

E. Basic Facts and Supplemental Information:

1. The eyes do get tired by steady gazing intently at one color.
2. The complementary color replaces the original color seen.
3. The term "complementary colors" means those two colors which when mixed together produce white. Tired eyes in this experiment could no longer see the red rays in the white light, so they saw the complementary color, green, and similarly, the dot appeared as "yellow."
4. White light is a mixture of all of the colors of the rainbow.
5. If we see a red dress, it is because white light strikes the dress. The dress absorbs all the colors except red, so the color of the dress is really the complementary color of red, which is green.
6. Laser beams are beams of intense light.

F. Thought Questions for Class Discussions:

1. Can all people see red and green?
2. What is color blindness?
3. Can all animals see colors?

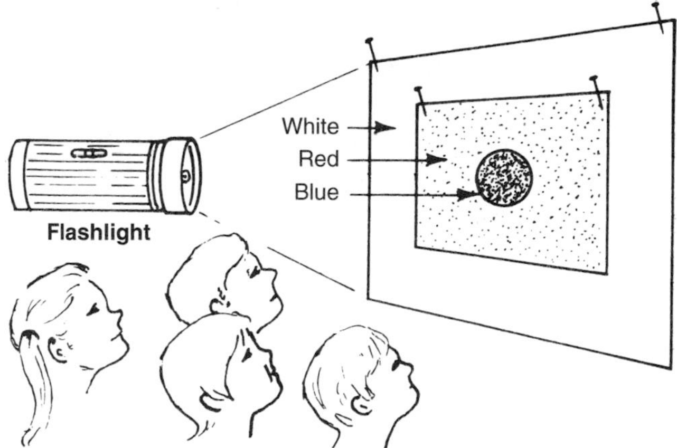

4. Do you think it is good to stare at television for long periods of time? (The average child watches about 25,000 hours of television before graduating from high school. Students spend about 20,000 hours in school during this same time period.)
5. Why does the ocean appear blue when white light from the sun strikes the water?

G. Related Ideas for Further Inquiry:

1. Try other combinations of colors using this Procedure.
2. Test light passing through a prism.
3. Try passing each primary color through a prism. Hint: What does "primary color" mean?
4. Place different colored cloths in the sun. Which feels warmer? cooler?
5. Study Activity II-C-1, "What is light?"
6. Study Activity II-C-2, "Is light a form of energy?"
7. Study Activity II-C-5, "How can we project a rainbow on the ceiling?"
8. Study Activity V-B-2, "How well do we see?"
9. Study Activity V-B-5, "Are there blind spots in our eyes?"
10. Study Activity V-B-7, "Are our eyes like a camera?"

H. Vocabulary Builders—Spelling Words:

1) **complimentary** 2) **complementary** 3) **mixed** 4) **color blindness** 5) **circular** 6) **experiment**

I. Thought for Today:

"Few people have good enough eyesight to see their own faults."

Activity

A. Problem: *Are There Blind Spots in Our Eyes?*

B. Materials Needed:

1. 3″ × 5″ cards, plain (one for each student)
2. Pencils
3. Rulers

C. Procedure:

1. Have each student reproduce the card in the sketch using a dark pencil.
2. Have each student hold the card at arm's length with the right hand.
3. Have each student close his/her left eye or cover it with his/her hand.
4. Have each student stare at the cross and slowly move his/her hand holding the card toward his/her right eye.

D. Result:

When the card is about halfway toward the right eye, if the student has followed the procedures carefully, the dot will disappear.

E. Basic Facts and Supplemental Information:

1. This blind spot is where the image of the object seen would focus on the retina (optic nerve). Since there are no light sensitive cells there, the eye blanks out.
2. In normal viewing, the right eye sees the "blind spot" of the left eye and vice versa.
3. In the middle drawings there are two sketches which have double perceptions. What do you see?
4. In the bottom drawing is an illustration on how our brain "sees" for us. We can "see" an equilateral triangle, but in reality, our eyes perceive only three angles—no triangle!
5. You can use the drawing in the book in lieu of a card if you wish. The results will be the same.

F. Thought Questions for Class Discussions:

1. How large a dot can each student make disappear? This can be tested by gradually increasing the size of the dot with a pencil.
2. Why don't we see the blind spot when we are using both eyes?
3. How many times do we blink our eyes in one minute?

G. Related Ideas for Further Inquiry:

1. Collect other optical illusions.
2. Study a model of the eye.
3. Study Activity V-B-6, "Do our eyes ever deceive us?"
4. Study other Activities in this Section.

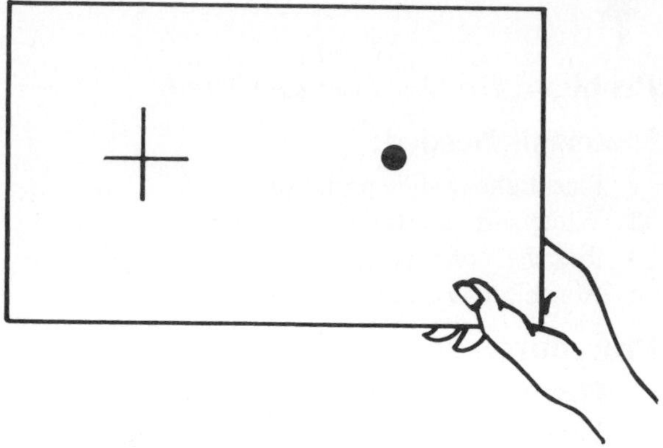

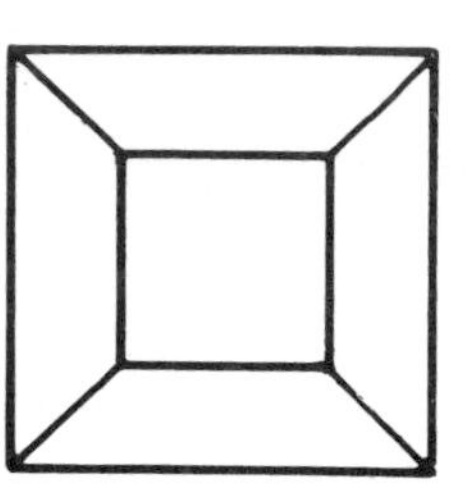

The inner square appears to be first in the back, then in front.

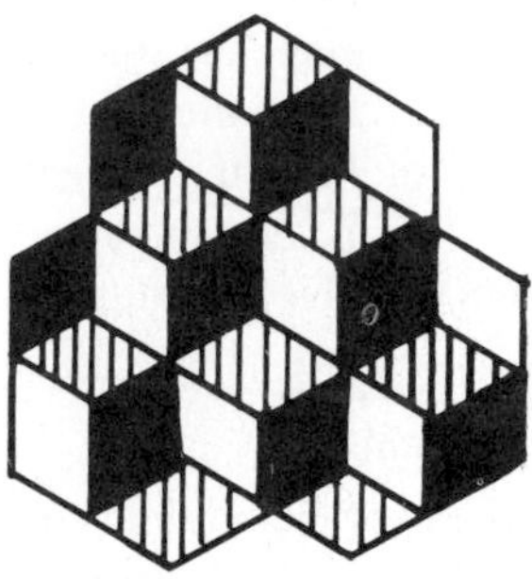

How many blocks do you see? Six or seven?

One triangle or two?

H. Vocabulary Builders—Spelling Words:

1) **blind spot** 2) **length** 3) **cover** 4) **cross** 5) **outwardly** 6) **stare** 7) **illusion** 8) **perspective**

I. Thought for Today:

"If at first you don't succeed, you're running about average."

Activity

V B 6

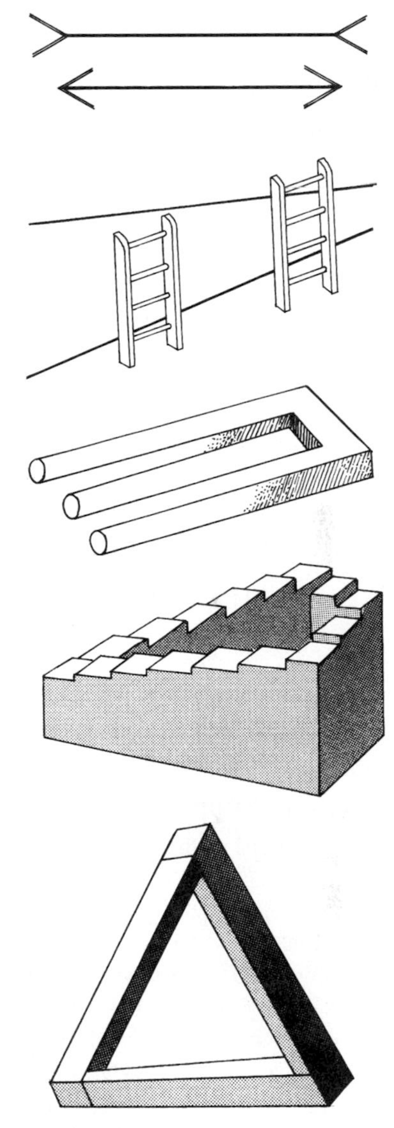

A. Problem: *Do Our Eyes Ever Deceive Us?*

B. Materials Needed:

Drawings of the illustrations depicted and other optical illusions

C. Procedure

1. Briefly describe how our eyes see. (Our eyes receive light and the light impulses travel to the brain via our optic nerves. The brain interprets these impulses and sometimes is confused.)
2. Have the students look at the drawings and report what they see.
3. In the top drawing, which line is longer?
4. In the second drawing, which ladder is taller?
5. In the third drawing, is the middle tube attached?
6. In the fourth drawing, can all the stairs be ascending?
7. Discuss the problems of interpreting three-dimensional objects on a two-dimensional plane.

D. Result:

Students will enjoy these optical illusions, but more important, they will realize why the drawings can be interpreted in several ways.

E. Basic Facts and Supplemental Information:

Start a collection of optical illusions. They are always good for a rainy day.

F. Thought Questions for Class Discussions:

1. Discuss how two people can see the same thing but interpret it differently.
2. Are witnesses to accidents always able to describe the facts accurately?
3. How important is the brain in seeing?

G. Related Ideas for Further Inquiry:

1. Study the cause of optical illusions.
2. Run other tests about the eyes and seeing.
3. Study Activity V-B-4, "Do our eyes get tired?"
4. Study Activity V-B-5, "Are there blind spots in our eyes?"
5. Study Activity V-B-7, "Are our eyes like a camera?"
6. Study other Activities in this Section.

H. Vocabulary Builders—Spelling Words:

1) **optical** 2) **illusion** 3) **interpreting**
4) **brain** 5) **problems** 6) **viewing** 7) **seeing**
8) **deceive** 9) **optic** 10) **nerve**

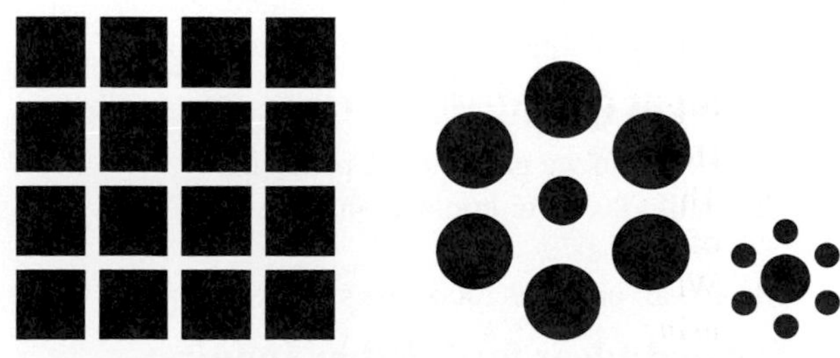

Are there any tiny gray squares at the intersections?

Which center dot is larger?

I. Thought for Today:

"Heredity determines the color of a child's eyes, but it is the environment that lights them up."

Activity V B 7

A. Problem: *Are Our Eyes Like a Camera?*

B. Materials Needed:

1. Camera
2. Chart, picture, or schematic drawing of the eye
3. Chart, picture, or schematic drawing of a camera

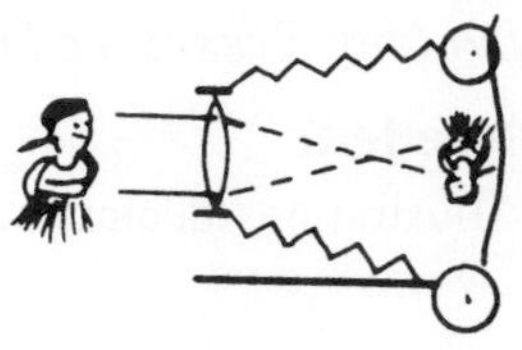

Lens inverts image.

C. Procedure:

1. Describe the main parts of a camera pointing out specific parts and functions, such as: shutter, lens, film, film speed, positioning, etc.
2. Describe the main parts of the human eye: lens, eyelids, pupils, iris, cornea, sclera, muscles, optic nerve, retina, etc.
3. Compare and contrast the parts.

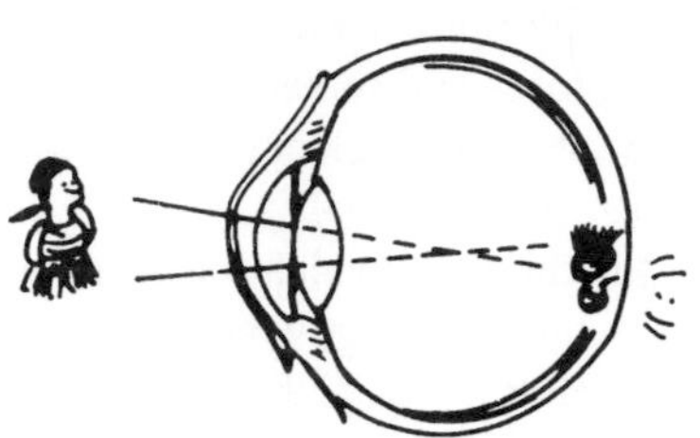

Lens of eye inverts image.

D. Results:

1. Our eyes and a photographic camera have many things in common and operate similarly in many ways.
2. The students will learn that the images (pictures) they see are upside down as they strike the retina, but they are inverted by the brain.

E. Basic Facts and Supplemental Information:

1. We have two eyes so that we can judge distances by triangulation.
2. The iris, the colored part of our eyes, does not affect our images.
3. Some people have trouble with their vision. If they see things clearly close up but not in the distance, they are called myopic or nearsighted.
4. If people can see things clearly in the distance but not close up, they are hyperopic or farsighted.
5. Glasses or contact lenses will usually correct these conditions.
6. Our eyes weaken with use, abuse, and age.

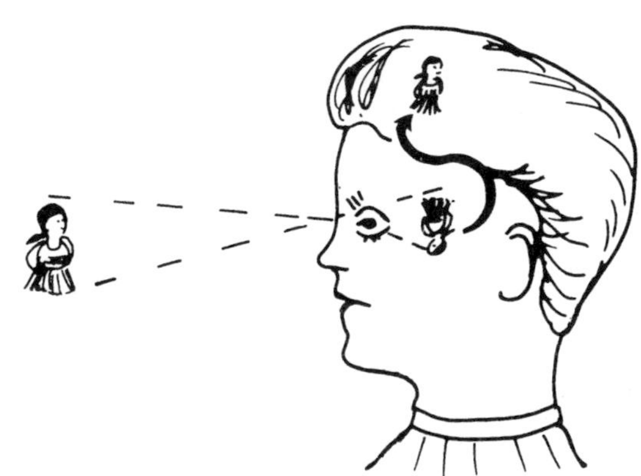

Eye inverts image; brain re-inverts it.

F. Thought Questions for Class Discussions:

1. How can we prevent eye problems?
2. Will glasses or contact lenses cure all eye problems?
3. Do all cameras focus the same way?

G. Related Ideas for Further Inquiry:

1. Study eyeglasses.
2. Have an optometrist or ophthalmologist talk to the class about eyes.
3. Study Activity V-B-2, "How well do we see?"
4. Study Activity V-B-3, "How do we see motion?"
5. Study Activity V-B-5, "Are there blind spots in our eyes?"
6. Study other Activities in this Section.

H. Vocabulary Builders—Spelling Words:

1) **camera** 2) **cornea** 3) **pupil** 4) **lens** 5) **iris** 6) **optic** 7) **retina** 8) **myopic** 9) **hyperopic** 10) **shutter** 11) **optic nerve**

I. Thought for Today:

"The world really isn't any worse. It's just that the news coverage is so much better."

Activity

V B 8

A. Problem: *Are You Right-Eyed or Left-Eyed?*

B. Materials Needed:

1. White or light-colored background
2. Forefingers

C. Procedure:

1. Discuss general characteristics of the eyes.
2. Discuss right-handedness and left-handedness.
3. Select a white (or light) background in the room.
4. Have students place one forefinger in an upright position at nose height and about one-half arm's length out from the body.
5. Have students stare at the wall looking "through" the finger.
6. Have them describe what they see.
7. Have students close one eye, or have them cover one eye and stare at the white or light background, again looking "through" the forefinger.
8. Have them note what they see.
9. Without moving their forefinger, have them close or cover the other eye and stare at the white or light background "through" their forefinger.

D. Result:

The forefinger will appear to move when the students look through the eye which is less dominant, and students will know if they are right-eyed or left-eyed.

E. Basic Facts and Supplemental Information:

1. Eyes are very complex but very important because the bulk of our knowledge about our surroundings comes to us through our sense of sight.
2. Since they are so important, we must take very good care of our eyes.

F. Thought Questions for Class Discussions:

1. Should a person aiming a bow and arrow use his/her dominant eye?
2. Are both eyes ever equal in dominance?
3. Are both eyes ever equal in recessiveness (neither one dominating)?

G. Related Ideas for Further Inquiry:

1. Try putting the bird in the cage by putting an envelope on the line separating the bird and the cage and bring your head closer to the envelope.
2. Try putting both forefingers about an inch apart pointing at each other and about 8 inches from your eyes. Look "through" them by staring at a wall and moving the tips slightly. (A third finger resembling a small hot dog will appear between the two fingers.) Wiggle your fingers.
3. Study other Activities in this Section.

Which eye is stronger? (Dominating)

Can you put the bird in the cage without changing the picture?

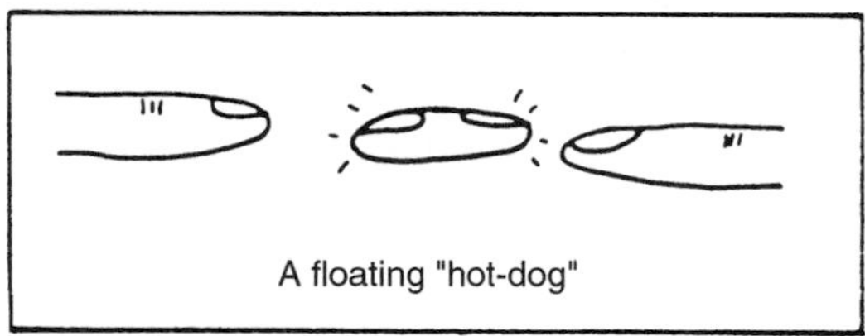

A floating "hot-dog"

H. Vocabulary Builders—Spelling Words:

1) **right-eyed** 2) **left-eyed** 3) **dominant** 4) **recessive** 5) **secondary** 6) **stronger**

I. Thought for Today:

"The world is filled with willing people; some willing to work; the rest willing to let them."—Robert Frost

Activity V B 9

A. Problem: *Do You Have X-ray Vision?*

B. Materials Needed:

Paper or cardboard cylinder:

1. Empty center rolls from paper towels and/or
2. Cylinders made from plain paper secured with cellophane tape

C. Procedure:

1. Have each student obtain or make a paper cylinder.
2. Tell students to keep both of their eyes open and to hold the cylinder up to one eye and stare at a distant wall in the classroom.
3. Then have each student pick up a book with the other hand and slowly move it horizontally from shoulder level to halfway in front of the cylinder, and then withdraw it.
4. Repeat this process, except that instead of holding a book or notebook, use your hand in an upright position.
5. If one eye is stronger than the other, the best results are obtained when the stronger eye is used to look through the cylinder.

D. Results:

1. Part of the book will seem to disappear and it will seem that you are looking right through the book.
2. The same illusion will be realized when the hand is used instead of the book.

E. Basic Facts and Supplemental Information:

1. This is not a true X-ray.
2. We really see with our brains, not our eyes.
3. Our eyes receive the light stimuli and our brain interprets these.
4. Since our brain "interprets" the view of the wall, it omits the part of the book or hand since by staring at the wall, the book or hand is not in clear focus.
5. X-rays were an accidental discovery when some radioactive material was left on a film.
6. Medical and dental X-rays are much less powerful than formerly because the newer film is much more sensitive.
7. MRI (Magnetic Resonance Imaging) is another method of diagnosing medical problems. Its use can help doctors detect small tumors, blocked blood vessels, damaged vertebral disks, etc. The MRI process does not involve radiation; it is noninvasive and nonionizing.

F. Thought Questions for Class Discussions:

1. What does a real X-ray do?
2. Why do doctors use X-rays?
3. Have you ever had any X-rays taken?
4. Has anyone in the class ever had an MRI? Discuss the procedure noise involved?

G. Related Ideas for Further Inquiry:

1. See Section II-C, "Light and Color."
2. See Activity V-D-12, "Are X-rays harmful?"
3. Study Activity V-B-2, "How well do we see?"
4. Study Activity V-B-3, "How do we see motion?"
5. Study Activity V-B-4, "Do our eyes get tired?"
6. Study Activity V-B-5, "Are there blind spots in our eyes?"
7. Study Activity V-B-6, "Do our eyes ever deceive us?"
8. Study Activity V-B-7, "Are our eyes like a camera?"
9. Study Activity V-B-8, "Are you right-eyed or left-eyed?"

H. Vocabulary Builders—Spelling Words:

1) **X-rays** 2) **illusion** 3) **cylinder**
4) **cardboard** 5) **horizontal** 6) **magnetic**
7) **resonance** 8) **imaging** 9) **tumors**

I. Thought for Today:

"A sure way to stop a red hot argument is to add a few cold facts to it."

Activity

V B 10

A. Problem: *How Do We Use a Microscope?*

B. Materials Needed:

1. Microscope
2. Glass slides
3. Cover slides
4. Onion skin
5. Leaves
6. Carrot
7. Water samples from various sources

C. Procedure:

1. Place a microscope where the outside light will hit the mirror of the microscope.
2. Be sure that slides are thoroughly washed; they must be clean.
3. Place material to be examined on the slide.
4. Place slide cover on slide.
5. Focus lens by lowering slowly and carefully until it almost hits the cover slide, and then focus sharply by raising the lens. It is very important for first focusing to be adjusted upward to prevent breakage of slide and cover and for the viewer to be confident that no major problem will arise.
6. When slide is focused (sharp and clear) have student(s) study it carefully.
7. It is always a good idea to have student(s) draw what they see and write down a few commentaries to help them remember their findings.
8. After this is done, remove the original slide and replace it with the next slide to be studied.
9. Repeat process with each slide.
10. When all slides have been studied, findings should be summarized for all students.

D. Results:

1. A whole new world will be realized by students.
2. Microscopic techniques will be learned.

E. Basic Facts and Supplemental Information:

1. The lens is the most expensive part of the microscope and it should be treated with extreme care.
2. More advanced students can study blood circulation by using a goldfish carefully wrapped in wet cotton, and while holding it very gently, placing its tail under the microscope. This can be done for very short periods of time without harming the goldfish.
3. An overhead projector can also be used if a microscope is not available.

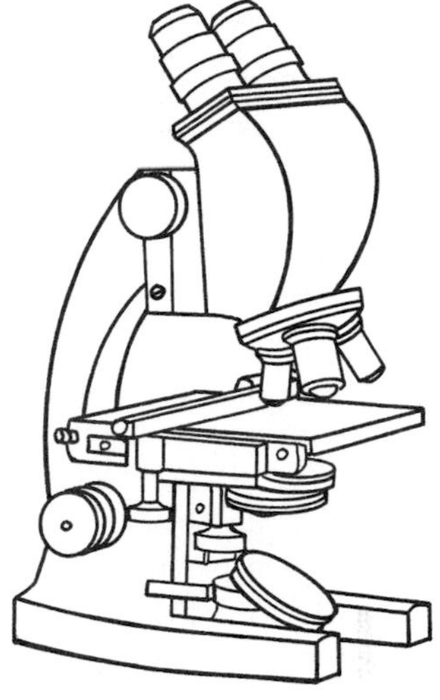

F. Thought Questions for Class Discussions:

1. Why do doctors use microscopes?
2. How can microscopically small things live?
3. What are some essentials for all living things?
4. Why do laboratory technicians use microscopes?

G. Related Ideas for Further Inquiry:

1. Compare what can be seen with a magnifying glass and a microscope.
2. Compare a microscope and a telescope.
3. Study Activity IV-A-1, "What are some characteristics of all living things?"
4. Study Activity III-A-1, "How do we classify living things?"
5. Study Activity IV-C-1, "How do we study common insects?"
6. Study Activity V-B-2, "How well do we see?"
7. Study Activity V-B-4, "Do our eyes get tired?"
8. Study Activity V-B-6, "Do our eyes ever deceive us?"
9. Study other Activities in this Section.

H. Vocabulary Builders—Spelling Words:

1) **microscope** 2) **slides** 3) **cover** 4) **focusing** 5) **lowering** 6) **onion** 7) **leaves** 8) **samples**

I. Thought for Today:

"We should all be concerned about the future because we have to spend the rest of our lives there."
—Charles Kettering

Activity V B 11

A. Problem: *How Well Do We Hear?*

B. Materials Needed:

1. Measuring tape (25–50 feet)
2. List of words to be used
3. Clock

C. Procedure One:

1. Have a student measure a distance of 20 feet by drawing a chalk line on the floor.
2. Have the student come to the front of the room to be tested. Explain carefully what you are going to do.
3. The student is to turn his/her back and repeat after you the words whispered at a distance of 20 feet. Care should be taken to whisper in a natural voice, not a forced whisper.

Procedure Two:

1. Have the student hold his/her hand over the right ear.
2. Have another student hold a clock to the left ear and then move slightly away from him/her.
3. When the student being tested can no longer hear the ticking of the clock, he/she is to call, "Stop."
4. Have another student measure the distance between the tested student's ear and the clock.
5. Double check by walking toward the student to see when he/she begins to hear the ticking.
6. Repeat for right ear.

D. Result:

In most cases, the degree of hearing varies between the left and right ear. The distance at which the student hears words and the ticking of the clock determines relative hearing ability.

E. Basic Facts and Supplemental Information:

1. If the average student hears the clock or whisper at 20 feet, then hearing and correctly repeating the words scores 20–20. The first number represents the hearing distance, the second, the actual distance.
2. If the student cannot hear at 20 feet, the tester moves forward until he/she can hear, and the hearing is rated accordingly, i.e., 10–20, etc.
3. Let students place their hands on their throats to discover vibrations of whispered words.
4. Our sense of balance is accomplished by nerves within the inner ear.
5. There are essentially two major types of hearing loss:
   a. "Nerve deafness" means there is a problem with nerve stimulation.
   b. "Bone deafness" means there is some problem with the conduction of sound in the bones of the middle ear.

6. We are able to detect the source of sounds because of the "triangulation" sensed by our ears.

F. Thought Questions for Class Discussions:

1. How well do hearing aids re-establish "natural" hearing?
2. What percentage of the students have hearing losses? (about 10%)
3. What percentage of the students require hearing aids to hear adequately at school? (about 3%)
4. What is the most beautiful sound you have ever heard?

G. Related Ideas for Further Inquiry:

1. Discuss ways that our hearing can be impaired (sudden loud blasts, loud rock music, etc.).
2. What can we do to protect our ears from loud noises?
3. Have students close their eyes for several minutes being very quiet, and then report on noises they have heard.
4. Study Activity V-B-12, "What makes our ears 'pop' when we go up or down a steep hill?"
5. Study Activity V-B-1, "What senses do we use to communicate with each other?"
6. Study other Activities in this Section.

H. Vocabulary Builders—Spelling Words:

1) **measure** 2) **distance** 3) **whisper** 4) **ticking** 5) **clock** 6) **hearing aids** 7) **nerves**

I. Thought for Today:

"Mother nature is wonderful. Years ago she didn't know we were going to wear glasses, yet look at the way she placed our ears."

Activity V B 12

A. Problem: *What Makes Our Ears "Pop" When We Go Up or Down a Steep Hill?*

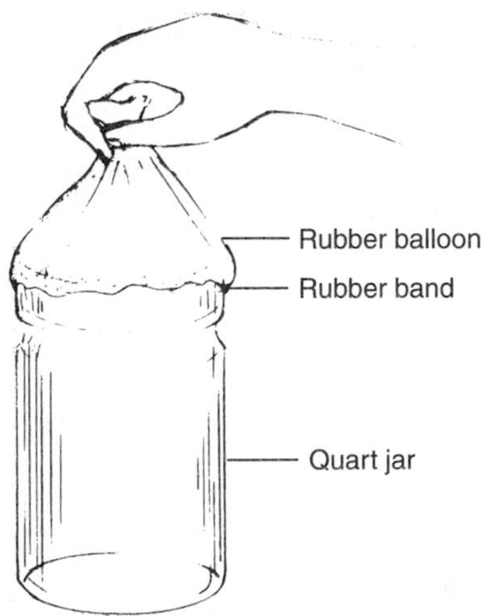

B. Materials Needed:

1. Quart jar (wide mouth)
2. Rubber balloon
3. String or rubber bands

C. Procedure:

1. Ask students if they ever experienced their ears "popping" when they have been in a car travelling up or down high hills or mountains.
2. Have them recount their sensations in these situations and ask if they know why their ears "popped."
3. Cut the rubber balloon to get a large enough area to cover the mouth of the jar and still have enough left over to be able to grasp a section to be raised. (See drawing.)
4. Place the balloon over the mouth of the jar.
5. Secure the balloon to the jar with string or rubber bands.
6. Raise the center of the balloon and release.

D. Result:

Students will hear a pop.

E. Basic Facts and Supplemental Information:

1. The pop that is heard is the equalization of air pressure when the air moves from one area of concentration to another.
2. A drum makes a sound in the same way. The drumstick compresses the air within the drum suddenly. This makes a sound or pop.
3. In back of the eardrum lies the Eustachian tube which is filled with air. This opens up in the pharynx.
4. Sudden changes in air pressure, either higher or lower, on the eardrum will cause the eardrum to move suddenly and make the eardrum pop like a drum. To avoid eardrums from popping, one can swallow air frequently, yawn, or yell. This opens the Eustachian tube and equalizes the air pressure on the eardrum.
5. When we blow our nose, we should gently close one nostril to prevent the building up of air pressure, then repeat with the other nostril.
6. Anytime there is a quick change in air pressure to our ears, we may hear (feel) a "pop." This might happen in airplanes or even in elevators.

F. Thought Questions for Class Discussions:

1. Are all sounds really small "pops"?
2. How can we protect our hearing?
3. Can an excessively loud noise actually break an eardrum as a very hard beat would break the drum skin?
4. Why don't passengers on airline flights complain of their ears popping?
5. Is sound a form of energy?

G. Related Ideas for Further Inquiry:

1. Discuss loud music and how it leads to hearing loss.
2. Study Activity V-A-1, "What are cells, tissues, and organs?"
3. Study Activity V-A-6, "How does our nervous system help us?"
4. Study Activity V-B-1, "What senses do we use to communicate with each other?"
5. Study Activity V-B-11, "How well do we hear?"
6. Study other Activities in this Section.

H. Vocabulary Builders—Spelling Words:

1) **Eustachian tube** 2) **eardrum** 3) **pharynx** 4) **noise** 5) **swallow** 6) **yawn** 7) **ears** 8) **pressure** 9) **sounds** 10) **balloon**

I. Thought for Today:

"To entertain some people all you have to do is listen."

Activity

V B 13

A. Problem: *How Do We Use Our Sense of Smell?*

B. Materials Needed:

1. Air freshener or deodorizer in spray can
2. Soap
3. Cinnamon
4. Coffee
5. Onion
6. Cloves
7. Vanilla
8. Mint
9. Garlic
10. Lemon extract
11. Sage
12. Fresh flowers
13. Chart paper

C. Procedure:

1. Have students close their eyes.
2. Spray a small amount of air freshener or deodorizer around the room.
3. Tell them to raise their hands quietly if they can smell anything different.
4. Check the distance that fragrance can be detected.
5. Ask students if fragrance can be detected in areas where spray was not seen.
6. Have several volunteers close their eyes and see if they can identify different substances by their smell, such as:
   a. soap
   b. cinnamon
   c. coffee
   d. onion
7. Record their findings.

D. Results

1. Very, very small parts of air freshener or deodorizer which we call molecules moved about the room.
2. These small parts (molecules) will be detected by the students' sense of smell.
3. The tiny molecules of soap, cinnamon, coffee, and onion will be detected as they circulate within the room because of air currents.

E. Basic Facts and Supplemental Information:

1. A molecule is the smallest part of a substance that retains the properties of that substance.
2. We detect odors when molecules of certain substances reach nerve receptors inside our nose.
3. Our sense of taste comes essentially from our sense of smell.
4. We can recognize about ten thousand different kinds of scents and/or odors.
5. If you burn a piece of toast you can smell it all over the room.
6. An odor is added to the gas used in our homes to warn and protect us in case of gas leaks.
7. This Activity can also be used to detect air movement.

F. Thought Questions for Class Discussions:

1. Can you tell what is cooking on the stove at home without looking?
2. Can you detect two odors at the same time?
3. Can you smell anything if it is in a closed container?

G. Related Ideas for Further Inquiry:

1. Discuss smoke detectors (molecules in movement during fires).
2. There are many other odors that can be detected when our eyes are closed: garlic, herbs, ammonia, etc.
3. Discuss how air smells different after a rain.
4. Study Activity V-A-1, "What are cells, tissues, and organs?"
5. Study Activity V-A-6, "How does our nervous system help us?"
6. Study Activity V-B-1, "What senses do we use to communicate with each other?"
7. Study other Activities in this Section.

H. Vocabulary Builders—Spelling Words:

Use the words listed in Materials Needed.

I. Thought for Today:

"Experience is a hard teacher because she gives the test first; the lessons come afterwards."

SECTION C: NUTRITION

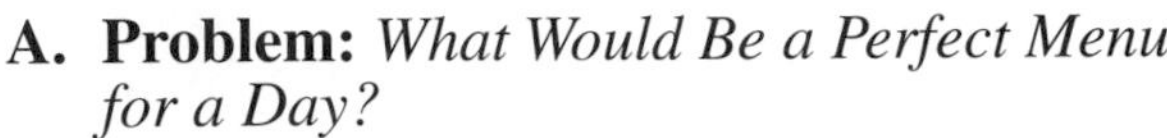

Activity V C 1

A. Problem: *What Would Be a Perfect Menu for a Day?*

B. Materials Needed:

Books, pamphlets, pictures, charts, and/or multisensory aids on nutrition

C. Procedure:

1. Several days beforehand, have the students keep track of the food they consumed for one day including all meals and snacks.
2. When this is completed, tell the students that you want to plan a "perfect" menu for a day for a typical student in their age-group.
3. Discuss the value of a healthy body.
4. Discuss the concept of "we are what we eat."
5. Ask the students to help you plan a perfect menu for one day.
6. List the four basic food groups:
   a. milk
   b. meat
   c. bread-cereal
   d. vegetable-fruit
7. List the items that should be included in a perfect diet:
   a. carbohydrates
   b. fats
   c. proteins
   d. minerals
   e. vitamins
   f. water
8. Discuss an ideal day's food intake that would consist of about:
   a. 65%—carbohydrates
   b. 15%—fats
   c. 20%—proteins
9. Discuss what good servings of each group would be:
   a. Milk group—about 4 servings a day for children.
   b. Meat group—2 servings (includes beans, peas, and nuts)
   c. Bread-Cereal group—4 servings
   d. Vegetable-Fruit group—4 servings
10. Check with class on vitamins and minerals. Study also Activity V-C-3, "How many calories should we have each day?"
11. Plan an ideal diet that includes:
    a. sufficient calories
    b. items from each basic food group
    c. the approximate percentages as listed for carbohydrates, fats, and proteins
    d. number of servings from each of the basic food groups
    e. all vitamins
    f. all minerals

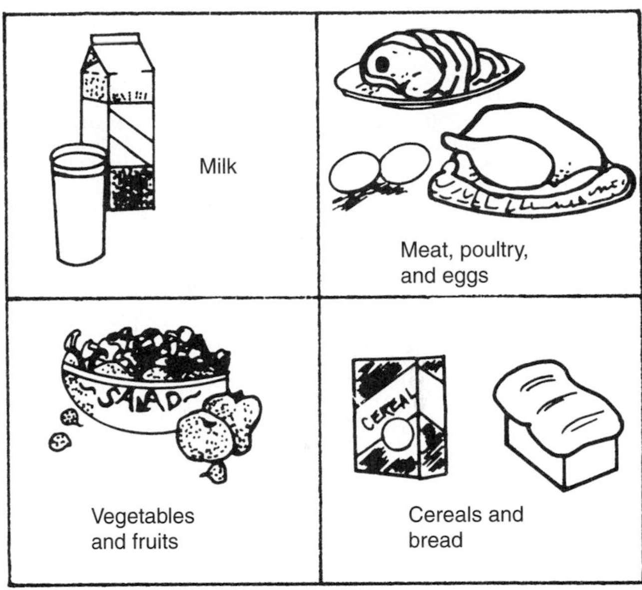

12. Compare the students' menus with the ideal class menu.

D. Results:

1. Class will plan an ideal diet for one day.
2. Class will realize that planning a perfect diet takes a lot of care and effort.

E. Basic Facts and Supplemental Information:

1. There is no one perfect diet that will be best for everybody.
2. Diets vary with people depending on age, sex, size, weight, type of work, etc.
3. Excessive amounts of one type of food, vitamins, or minerals can cause problems.
4. One calorie is the heat required to raise one cubic centimeter of water one degree Celsius (Centigrade). (See chart, next pages.)
5. The "Calorie" that nutritionists use is 1,000 times larger than the regular "calorie." It is really a kilocalorie. It's still referred to as a calorie.
6. Natural foods are better than processed foods.
7. "Living foods" (raw or sprouted) are better for us than "dead foods."
8. Fruits are better than juices.
9. The more additives in food, the greater the chance of harm to the body.

F. Thought Questions for Class Discussions:

1. Do you think your diet is close to a perfect diet?
2. Is taste a good judge of what we should eat?
3. Should children eat the same foods as their parents but only in smaller quantities?

G. Related Ideas for Further Inquiry:

1. Plan a diet for a professional football player.
2. Plan a diet for an office secretary.
3. Study other Activities in this Section.

H. Vocabulary Builders—Spelling Words:

1) **calorie** 2) **grain** 3) **bread** 4) **cereal** 5) **vegetable** 6) **fruit** 7) **meat** 8) **poultry**

I. Thought for Today:

"Appetizers are those little bits you eat until you lose your appetite."

FOOD CHART SHOWING AMOUNTS, CALORIES, PROTEINS, FATS, AND CARBOHYDRATES

Food values or nutrients are more important than we ever realized previously. The following table shows the calories (food), and the grams of proteins, fats, and carbohydrates of the following foods. In physics one calorie is the amount of heat required to raise one cubic centimeter of water one degree centigrade. In foods, nutritionists use the large calorie,which is 1,000 times larger. Many texts use a small "c" for a physics calorie and a capital "C" for a food calorie. In discussing foods, a calorie is always a large calorie whether a small "c" or a capital "C" is used.

FOOD:	*AMOUNT:*	*Calories*	*Proteins (g)*	*Fat (g)*	*Carbohydrates (g)*
Almonds, chopped	Cup	775	24	70	25
Apple, raw	Medium	76	.4	6.5	19.7
Apricots	3	55	1	T	14
Asparagus	Cup	30	3.6	.3	3.6
Avocado	1	370	5	37	13
Bacon, slices	2	85	4	8	1
Bagel	1	165	6	2	28
Banana	1	100	1	T	26
Barbecue sauce	Cup	230	4	17	20
Beans, green	Cup	30	2	T	7
Beans, lima	Cup	260	16	1	49
Beef, hamburger	3 oz.	235	20	17	0
Beef, roast (lean)	3 oz.	210	25	12	0
Beef, steak, broiled	3 oz.	220	24	13	0
Beer	12 oz.	150	1	0	14
Beets	Cup	55	2	T	12
Blackberries	Cup	85	2	1	19
Bologna	2 slices	170	6	16	1
Bouillon cube	1	5	1	T	T
Bread					
White	1 slice	70	2	1	13
Wheat or rye	1 slice	60	2	T	21
Breakfast cereals:					
Bran flakes	Cup	105	4	1	28
Corn flakes	Cup	95	2	T	21
Oatmeal	Cup	130	5	2	23
Shredded wheat	1 piece	90	0	1	20
Broccoli	Cup	40	5	T	0
Butter	1 pat	25	T	4	T
Cabbage, raw	Cup	15	1	T	4
Candy					
Chocolate, milk	1 oz.	145	2	9	16
Gum drops	1 oz.	100	T	T	25
Marshmallows	1 oz.	90	1	T	23
Cakes					
Angel food	1 piece	135	3	T	32
Devil's food	1 piece	235	3	8	40
Cantaloupe, half	Medium	40	1	.4	7
Carrots, average	1	30	1	T	7
Cashews	Cup	785	24	64	41
Cauliflower, cooked	Cup	31	3	T	6
Celery, raw, diced	Cup	20	1	T	5
Cheese:					
American	1 oz.	105	6	9	T
Blue or Roquefort	1 oz.	105	6	8	1
Cheddar	1 oz.	115	7	9	1
Cottage	Cup	235	28	10	6
Cherries, canned	Cup	105	2	T	26
Chicken, fried	¼ bird	232	25	14	3
Chicken, roasted	1 slice	79	11	3	0
Chocolate, baking	1 oz.	145	3	15	8
Cocoa	Cup	245	10	12	27
Corn, fresh	1 ear	70	2	1	16
Crackers, saltine	4	50	1	1	8
Cream or half-and-half	1 tbsp.	20	T	2	1
Cucumbers	1	20	1	T	5

FOOD:	AMOUNT:	Calories	Proteins (g)	Fat (g)	Carbohydrates (g)
Dates, pitted	Cup	490	4	1	130
Doughnut	1	205	3	11	16
Egg, boiled	1	80	6	6	T
Fish and shellfish:					
Clams, raw	3 oz.	65	11	1	2
Haddock, fried	3 oz.	140	17	5	5
Halibut	5 oz.	205	21	12	0
Oysters	Cup	160	20	4	8
Salmon, canned	3 oz.	120	17	5	0
Tuna, canned	3 oz.	170	25	7	0
Fudge	1 oz.	120	1	3	24
Grapefruit	1/2	72	1	T	25
Grapes	Cup	70	1	1	16
Ham	3 oz.	185	25	8	0
Hamburger on bun	Medium	335	17	22	15
Honey	1 tbsp.	65	T	0	17
Hot dog	2 oz.	170	7	16	1
Ice cream	Cup	270	5	14	32
Jams	1 tbsp.	55	T	T	14
Jellies	1 tbsp.	50	T	T	13
Lamb chop	3 oz.	350	18	32	0
Lamb, leg	3 oz.	235	22	16	0
Lemonade	Cup	105	5	T	28
Lettuce, iceberg	Head	70	5	T	16
Liquors (gin, vodka, whiskey)	1 1/2 oz.	110	0	0	T
Liver, beef	3 oz.	195	22	9	5
Liverwurst	2 oz.	170	8	15	2
Lobster, tail	4 oz.	195	21	2	T
Macaroni	4 oz.	111	4	T	39
Margarine	1 tbsp.	100	T	11	0
Mayonnaise	1 tbsp.	90	10	10	T
Milk:					
Whole	Cup	170	9	10	8
Low fat (2%)	Cup	120	8	5	12
Nonfat	Cup	85	9	T	13
Milkshake	Reg.	350	8	11	52
MSG (mono sodium glutamate)	1 tsp.	0	0	0	0
Muffin	1	120	3	4	17
Mushrooms	Cup	20	2	T	3
Nectarines	1	40	1	T	12
Noodles	Cup	200	7	2	37
Oils	1 tbsp.	120	0	14	0
Olive	1	15	T	2	T
Onions, green	1	40	2	T	10
Orange	1	70	2	T	17
Orange juice	6 oz.	80	2	1	20
Pancake with butter, syrup	4 in.	60	2	2	9
Peach	1	40	1	T	10
Peanut butter	1 tbsp.	95	4	8	3
Peanuts, roasted	Cup	840	38	72	27
Pear	1	100	1	1	25
Peas, fresh	Cup	110	3	T	10
Peas, canned	Cup	150	8	1	29
Peppers	1 pod	15	1	T	4
Pineapple, canned	Cup	190	1	T	49

FOOD:	AMOUNT:	Calories	Proteins (g)	Fat (g)	Carbohydrates (g)
Pineapple juice	Cup	140	1	T	34
Pies (1/7 of 9"):					
Apple	1	345	3	15	51
Pecan	1	495	6	27	61
Lemon meringue	1	305	4	12	45
Pumpkin	1	275	5	15	32
Pizza	1 slice	145	.6	4	22
Plum	1	30	T	T	8
Popcorn, plain	Cup	25	1	T	5
Potato, white	1	145	4	T	33
Potato chips	10	115	1	8	10
Potatoes (french fries)	10 pieces	155	2	7	20
Prunes, dried	4	100	2	1	T
Pudding, rice	Cup	330	8	6	60
Pudding, tapioca	Cup	220	8	8	28
Radishes	10	135	T	T	4
Raisins	Cup	480	4	T	110
Rice, brown	Cup	160	4	2	34
Rice, white	Cup	225	4	T	50
Roll, hot dog	1	120	3	2	21
Salad dressings:					
Blue Chesse	1 tbsp.	75	1	8	1
French	1 tbsp.	65	T	6	3
Mayonnaise	1 tbsp.	100	T	11	T
Thousand Island	1 tbsp.	80	T	8	2
Salt	1 tsp.	0	0	0	0
Sandwiches:					
Bologna	1	365	10	24	27
Cheeseburger	1	540	28	37	22
Ham	1	265	11	12	28
Lettuce and tomato	1	200	6	22	31
Tuna	1	390	22	21	28
Turkey	1	325	25	8	38
Sausage	4 oz.	425	21	37	2
Shortening	1 tbsp.	125	0	14	0
Soft drinks, diet (ave.)	12 oz.	1	0	0	T
Soft drinks regular (ave.)	12 oz.	140	0	0	35
Soups:					
Bean	Cup	170	8	6	22
Clam Chowder	Cup	90	2	4	7
Tomato	Cup	90	2	3	16
Vegetable	Cup	80	5	2	10
Spaghetti	Cup	155	5	1	32
Spinach	Cup	40	5	T	6
Strawberries	Cup	55	1	1	12
Sugar, brown	Cup	410	0	0	105
Sugar, granulated	Cup	700	0	0	165
Syrups (ave.)	1 tbsp.	50	T	T	12
Tea	Cup	2	T	T	T
Tomato	1	30	2	1	6
Tomato juice	Cup	42	2	T	10
Walnuts	Cup	785	26	74	19
Watermelon (4" x 8 ")	Wedge	110	2	1	27
Wine, table	4 oz.	100	T	0	6
Yogurt	Cup	140	8	7	11

Activity

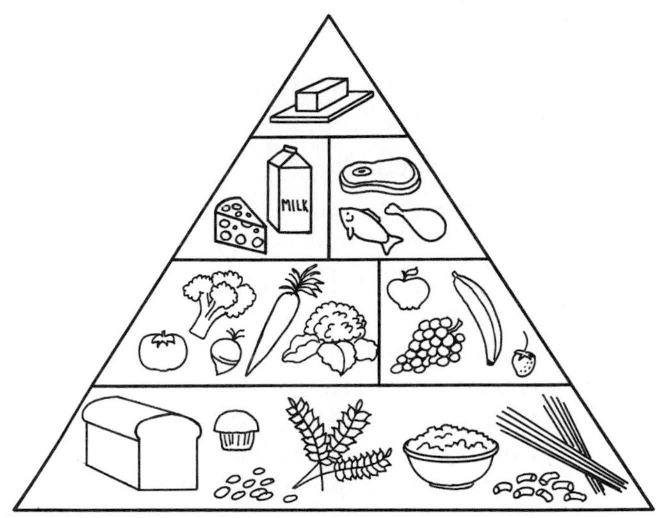

The food pyramid
Four levels—six groups

A. Problem: *What Is the "Food Pyramid"?*

B. Materials Needed:

1. Samples, empty cartons or cans, or pictures of the six food groups (See drawing.)
2. Reference materials on the above items

C. Procedure:

1. Discuss the need for healthy foods:
   a. growth
   b. energy
   c. disease prevention
2. Discuss what foods contain in general:
   a. carbohydrates (starches and sugars)
   b. proteins
   c. fats
   d. water
   e. vitamins
   f. minerals
3. Discuss calories.
4. Discuss what a pyramid is.
5. Describe the purpose of the Food Pyramid.
   a. Cite the kinds of foods we should eat.
   b. Show the proportions of each food group that we should eat.
6. With the items cited in Materials Needed describe each food level and the number of recommended servings of each per day.
   a. *Lower level:*
      grains (bread, cereals, rice, pasta, etc.), servings: 6 to 11
   b. *Second level:*
      1) vegetables (carrots, broccoli, lettuce, etc.), servings: 3 to 5
      2) fruits (oranges, apples, bananas, etc.), servings: 2 to 4
   c. *Third level:*
      1) dairy (milk, cheese, yogurt, etc.), servings: 2 to 4
      2) meats and proteins (beef, chicken, fish eggs, beans, etc.), servings: 2 to 3
   d. *Top level:*
      1) fats and oils (salad oils, salad dressings), servings: use sparingly
      2) sugars (candy, jams, jellies, etc.), servings: use sparingly
7. The amount of food that counts as "one serving" is often less than the average person's serving.

D. Results:

1. Students will learn about a balanced diet.
2. Students will realize that it takes a lot of time to plan a healthy diet.

E. Basic Facts and Supplemental Information:

1. The "Food Pyramid" was designed by the U.S. Department of Agriculture.
2. The "Food Pyramid" is designed to:
   a. reduce saturated fats
   b. increase the amount of fiber
   c. vary the proportions of the main basic food groups
   d. coincide with the latest medical findings on health and nutrition

F. Thought Questions for Class Discussions:

1. What food organizations might find fault with this new idea?
2. Are there any bad foods? bad diets?
3. What could you do to change your diet to make it more healthy according to the "Food Pyramid"?

G. Related Ideas for Further Inquiry:

1. Study Activity V-C-1, "What would be a perfect menu for a day?"
2. Study Activity V-C-3, "How many calories should we have each day?"
3. Study Activity V-C-4, "What are good sources of vitamins and minerals?"

H. Vocabulary Builders—Spelling Words:

1) **grains** 2) **vegetables** 3) **fruit** 4) **meats** 5) **milk** 6) **cheese** 7) **oils** 8) **fats** 9) **sugars**

I. Thought for Today:

"A young boy with a weekly allowance told his mother after reading a food label: 'Look, even the USDA recommends daily allowances.' "

Activity V C 3

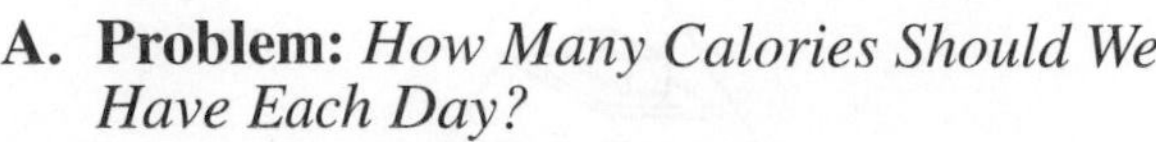

A. Problem: *How Many Calories Should We Have Each Day?*

B. Materials Needed:

1. Calorie booklet
2. List of foods students ate the previous day, including amounts

C. Procedure:

1. For homework have students make a list of a typical day's food intake.
2. With calorie booklet, have students count the number of calories in each item.
3. Have them total the calories for their daily intake.

D. Results:

1. Students will produce an estimated total count of daily calories.
2. Students will learn that they are consuming too many, too few, or the proper number of calories per day for optimum health.

E. Basic Facts and Supplemental Information:

1. Daily calorie chart for boys and girls:
   a. Boys and girls 4, 5, 6 1,500–1,700 calories
   b. Boys, ages 7, 8, 9 2,200 calories
   c. Girls, ages 7, 8, 9 1,800 calories
   d. Boys, ages 10, 11, 12 2,500 calories
   e. Girls, ages 10, 11, 12 2,300 calories
   f. Boys, ages 13, 14, 15 3,200 calories
   g. Girls, ages 13, 14, 15 2,500 calories
2. More important than calories is a balanced diet. Some youngsters metabolize foods faster than others and thus they burn up more calories. Other youngsters burn up calories more slowly. The source of calories is very important.
3. A "calorie" is the amount of heat (energy) required to raise one gram of water 1° Celsius (Centigrade).
4. A Calorie (large "C" Calorie) is 1,000 times larger than the calorie (small "c" calorie).
5. Large "C" calories are the ones used in Physics and Nutrition.
6. Many writers still interchange the small "c" and the large "C" in discussing food Calories, as was done in E-1 above.

F. Thought Questions for Class Discussions:

1. What might be the cause of being overweight?
2. What might be the cause of being underweight?
3. What foods are high in calories?
4. What foods are low in calories?

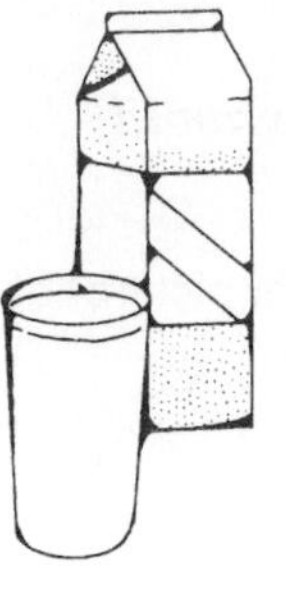

Milk

Eggs

Snack (bread and jam)

Corn

Banana

Dessert (ice cream)

G. Related Ideas for Further Inquiry:

1. See Part III, "Plants."
2. See Part IV, "Animals."
3. Study Activity V-C-1, "What would be a perfect menu for a day?"
4. Study Activity V-C-2, "What is the 'Food Pyramid'?"
5. Study Activity V-C-4, "What are good sources of vitamins and minerals?"
6. Study Activity V-C-6, "What foods contain carbohydrates (sugars and starches)?"
7. Study Activity V-C-8, "Are food additives good for us?"

H. Vocabulary Builders—Spelling Words:

1) **calorie** 2) **balanced** 3) **overweight** 4) **underweight** 5) **daily** 6) **energy**

I. Thought for Today:

"Calories don't count; they multiply."

Activity V C 4

A. Problem: *What Are Good Sources of Vitamins and Minerals?*

Milk

Meat

Oranges

Sun

B. Materials Needed:

1. Empty vitamin bottles
2. Pictures of different foods cited in the charts on the following pages
3. Paper and pencils—to plan a perfect diet

C. Procedure:

1. Discuss the value of vitamins and minerals.
2. Describe how the foods we are eating are gradually losing some of the essential vitamins and minerals that we need for good health.
3. Students can make a collection of articles, newspaper accounts, and advertisements about vitamins and minerals.
4. Have students develop a vitamin and mineral chart showing "Sources" and "Essential For" categories. (See the following two pages.)
5. Have class plan a perfect diet that will provide all necessary vitamins and minerals without taking supplements.
6. Discuss the value of taking vitamin and mineral supplements.

D. Result:

Students will develop an understanding of mineral and vitamin requirements for optimum health.

E. Basic Facts and Supplemental Information:

1. The charts on the following pages show body requirements, and sources of vitamins and minerals.
2. "Organic" means containing carbon (i.e., made from living material).
3. "Natural" means not artificial (not manufactured).
4. There are 13 well-known vitamins.
5. Vitamins A, D, E, K, and beta carotene are fat-soluble. The body stores these in the liver and fatty tissues for months.
6. The B and C vitamins are water-soluble; consequently, these vitamins should be taken daily.
7. The body does not manufacture vitamins per se, but does synthesize vitamins K, D, and B-12.
8. Most people do not need a daily multivitamin and mineral supplement. The safest procedure is to get the advice of a doctor and then follow his/her instructions carefully.
9. A vitamin pill a day won't change a poor diet into a healthy one.
10. Some vitamins are toxic in large doses.
11. Vitamins and minerals help regulate body functions.
12. Our bodies need only small amounts of vitamins and minerals.
13. Vitamins help the body process proteins, carbohydrates, and fats.
14. Certain vitamins also contribute to the production of blood cells, hormones, genetic material, and chemicals that help our nervous system.
15. Minerals such as calcium, magnesium, potassium, and sodium are essential parts of the human diet.
16. Calcium, phosphorus, and magnesium are important for bones and teeth.
17. Potassium is a major component for our muscles.
18. Sodium helps regulate the fluids in our bodies.

F. Thought Questions for Class Discussions:

1. What is the difference between being underfed and being undernourished?
2. How many people throughout the world starve to death each year? (millions!)
3. Are people on strict diets usually undernourished?

G. Related Ideas for Further Inquiry:

1. Discuss different body shapes and sizes.
2. Discuss which foods are best: natural or processed.
3. Study Activity V-C-1, "What would be a perfect menu for a day?"
4. Study Activity V-C-2, "What is the 'Food Pyramid'?"
5. Study Activity V-C-6, "What foods contain carbohydrates (sugars and starches)?"
6. Study Activity V-C-8, "Are food additives good for us?"

H. Vocabulary Builders—Spelling Words:

1) **vitamins** 2) **minerals** 3) **deficiency** 4) **sources** 5) **essential** 6) **organic** 7) **natural**

I. Thought for Today:

"Food cures hunger; study cures ignorance."

VITAMINS

VITAMIN:	BEST SOURCES:	ESSENTIAL FOR:	SUPPLEMENTATION:*
A	Liver, Dark green vegetables Deep yellow fruits and vegetables	Bone growth Night vision Healthy skin	Not recommended Toxic in high doses
B-1 (Thiamine)	Milk, nuts Seafood Whole grains	Healthy nerves Aids digestion Organ functions	Not necessary, Not recommended
B-2 (Riboflavin)	Meat, eggs Soybeans Green vegetables	Clear vision Healthy skin Healthy mouth	Not necessary Not recommended
B-3 (Niacin)	Meat, fowl Fish, tomatoes Leafy vegetables	Skin Digestion Mental health	Doctors may subscribe megadose to lower cholesterol
B-6 (Pyroxidine)	Whole grains, Bananas, meats, Beans, wheat germ	Chemical reactions of proteins, amino acids, brain function	Megadose can cause numbness and neurological disorders
B-12	Liver, meats, Eggs, milk, cheese, Yogurt, shellfish	Red blood cells Normal functioning of nervous system	Vegetarians need supplements, No benefits from megadoses
Folacin (A B Vitamin)	Leafy vegetables, Wheat germ, liver, Citrus fruits	Synthesis of DNA, Protein metabolism Reduces birth defects	400 mcg for pregnant women, helps prevent birth defects
Biotin	Eggs, milk, liver, Mushrooms, whole grains	Metabolism of protein, fats and carbohydrates	Not necessary, Not recommended
Pantothenic Acid (B-5)	Whole grains, Beans, milk, Eggs, liver	Metabolism of food, production of body chemicals	Not necessary, Not recommended
Beta Carotene (Not a vitamin but converted to Vitamin A in body)	Carrots, sweet potatoes, leafy vegetables, broccoli	Antioxident; may reduce risk of some cancers	10,000–25,000 IU for anyone not consuming carotene rich fruits and vegetables
C (Ascorbic Acid)	Citrus fruits Tomatoes Leafy vegetables	Healthy gums Healing wounds Cement body cells	Recommended 250–500 mg/day for non-eaters of fruits and vegetables rich in Vitamin C
D	Sunlight Fish liver oil Fortified milk	Bone growth Strong teeth	400 IU for anyone who does not drink milk or receive sun exposure; toxic in high doses
E	Leafy greens, nuts, Wheat germ, olives, Asparagus, margarine	Red blood cells Antioxident, helps with Vitamin K	200–800 IU advised for everybody, especially low-fat dieters
K	Leafy vegetables, Cauliflower Broccoli, beets	Blood clotting	Not necessary, Not recommended

*Suggestions from a School of Public Health in a Major University

MINERALS

MINERAL:	BEST SOURCES:	ESSENTIAL FOR:	SUPPLEMENTATION:
Calcium	Asparagus Beans, milk Cauliflower	Bones Teeth Blood clotting	Doctors should be consulted for possible needs and amounts of "minerals"
Chlorine	Bread Eggs Table salt	Osmosis Enzymes Hydrochloric acid	
Cobalt	Liver Seafood Sweetbreads	Appetite Growth Muscle tone	
Copper	Bran, cocoa Liver Oysters	Hemoglobin Tissues Repair	
Flourine	Sunflower seeds, Oats, almonds	Bones Teeth	
Iodine	Shrimp Broccoli, fish, Iodized salt	Forms thyroxin Regulates body metabolism	
Iron	Almonds, egg yolk Meat Soybeans	Hemoglobin (carries oxygen to all cells)	
Magnesium	Beans, bran, Corn, chocolate Peanuts	Muscular activity Enzyme activity	
Manganese	Brown rice Green, leafy vegetables	Activates various enzymes	
Molybdenum	Whole cereals Brewer's yeast	Carbohydrate metabolism	
Phosphorus	Beans, cheese, Oatmeal, peas	Teeth, bones Buffers in blood Muscles	
Potassium	Beans, bran, Molasses, olives Potatoes, spinach	Growth, osmosis Buffers, regulates heartbeat	
Sodium	Beef, bread, Cheese, oysters Wheat germ	Regulates osmosis Buffers prevent water loss	
Sulphur	Beans, bran Cheese, cocoa Fish, eggs	Formation of proteins	
Zinc	Beans, cress, Lentils, liver Peas	Growth, tissue	

Activity V C 5

A. Problem: *What Is the Importance of Fiber in Our Diet?*

B. Materials Needed:

1. Slice of white bread
2. Slice of whole wheat bread
3. Nuts
4. Whole grain cereal
5. Popcorn
6. Seeds, edible

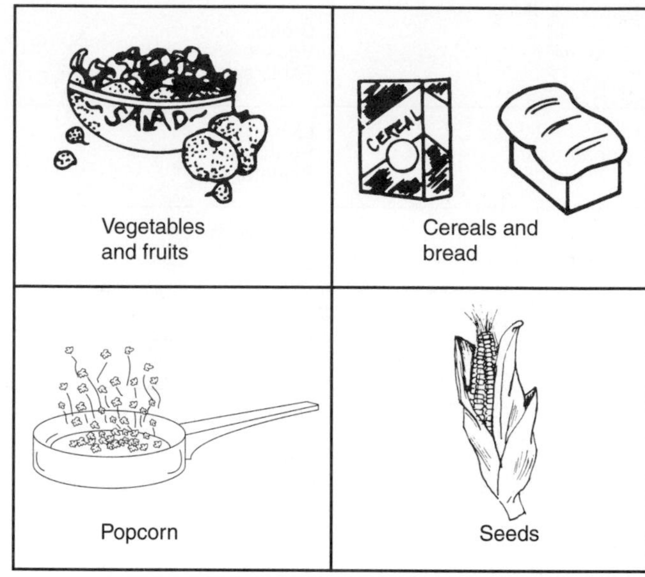

Vegetables and fruits
Cereals and bread
Popcorn
Seeds

C. Procedure:

1. Ask students what should be included in an adequate diet.
2. Ask the students if they know what food fibers are.
3. Briefly explain what a balanced diet would be, including food fibers.
4. Briefly describe food fibers.
5. Have students examine the samples of food listed in Materials Needed.
6. Discuss the value of food fibers.

D. Results:

1. Students will become aware of food fibers and what this term means.
2. Students will learn the value of fiber in their diets.

E. Basic Facts and Supplemental Information:

1. High-fiber foods, often referred to as "bulk" or "roughage," include whole grain products, fruit, vegetables, and legumes.
2. Fiber is not affected by the digestive process (digestive enzymes).
3. To check the fiber in bread, read the label and make sure that the word "whole" is used in the first ingredient listed.
4. Fiber can decrease the risk of colon cancer.
5. Fiber promotes bowel regularity.
6. Some evidence points out that fiber may be effective in lowering the cholesterol level.
7. Fiber should be taken as a food, not a supplement.
8. For snacks, good high-fiber foods include nuts, seeds, popcorn, fruits, and whole grain crackers.
9. Processed foods contain a minimum of fiber.

F. Thought Questions for Class Discussions:

1. What are high-fiber foods?
2. How does fiber help digestion?
3. What foods should you eat for your school lunch?
4. Would a fast-food hamburger sandwich contain much fiber?
5. Should we study the labels on food products for fiber content?

G. Related Ideas for Further Inquiry:

1. Develop two lists:
   a. high-fiber foods
   b. low-fiber foods
2. Study the value of water in the diet.
3. Study Activity V-C-1, "What would be a perfect menu for a day?"
4. Study Activity V-C-2, "What is the 'Food Pyramid'?"
5. Study Activity V-C-4, "What are good sources of vitamins and minerals?"
6. Study Activity V-C-8, "Are food additives good for us?"

H. Vocabulary Builders—Spelling Words:

1) **fiber** 2) **digestion** 3) **roughage**
4) **whole wheat** 5) **popcorn** 6) **bulk**

I. Thought for Today:

"Most kids think of a balanced diet as having a hamburger in each hand."

Activity

A. Problem: *What Foods Contain Carbohydrates (Starches and Sugars)?*

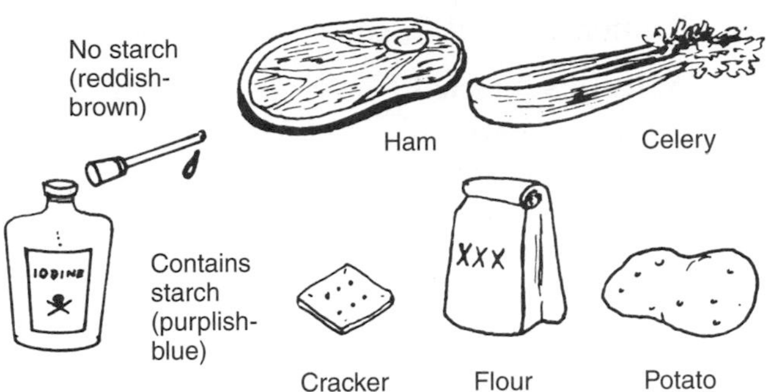

B. Materials Needed:

1. Several 2″ × 4″ pieces of wax paper
2. One 4″ × 6″ piece of white paper for each kind of food to be tested
3. Iodine, tincture (diluted)
4. Foods to be tested: piece of ham, bread, potato, flour, crackers, corn, celery, sugar, candy, etc.
5. 12 test tubes or small plastic cups
6. Benedict's solution

C. Procedure One:

1. Place each food to be tested on a piece of wax paper or double thickness of regular paper (to prevent possible leakage).
2. Label each food to be tested.
3. Place 2 drops of iodine on each foodstuff.
4. Observe results.

Procedure Two:

1. Place each item to be tested in a test tube or cup.
2. Label each test tube or cup with the name of the item to be tested.
3. Add several drops of Benedict's solution to each.
4. Record any visible changes.

D. Results:

1. When iodine is placed on the corn, flour, potatoes, crackers, and bread, the touched areas turn purplish-blue. This color indicates the presence of starch. The ham and celery remain a reddish-brown color, showing no starch.
2. Benedict's solution turns a dark blue-green color in the presence of foods containing sugar.

E. Basic Facts and Supplemental Information:

1. If Benedict's solution is unavailable, Clinitest tablets are available at your local pharmacy. They are used by diabetics to indicate if starch is converted to sugar in the body.
2. Starches and sugars are excellent sources of heat, energy, and calories.
3. Carbohydrates are found in the lower level of the "Food Pyramid."
4. Carbohydrates are starches and sugars found mainly in breads and cereals.
5. Carbohydrates are also found in fruits and vegetables.
6. Starches are complex carbohydrates.
7. Sugars are simple carbohydrates easily digested and found mainly in cane and beet sugar (sucrose) and corn syrup (fructose).
8. When studying ingredients, remember that sugars end in "ose": glucose, sucrose, fructose, etc.
9. The healthiest forms of starches are found in natural, unprocessed foods.

F. Thought Questions for Class Discussions:

1. What other foods contain starch?
2. Where do most starches come from?
3. How much starch should a person consume daily?

G. Related Ideas for Further Inquiry:

1. Make a list of common food items that contain starch.
2. Make a list of common food items that contain sugar.
3. Study the different kinds of popular diets. Are they "balanced"?
4. Study the labels on selected foods. Evaluate the ingredients.
5. Study Part III, "Plants."
6. Study Activity V-C-1, "What would be a perfect menu for a day?"
7. Study Activity V-C-2, "What is the 'Food Pyramid'?"
8. Study Activity V-C-8, "Are food additives good for us?"
9. Study Activity V-C-7, "Which foods contain proteins?"

H. Vocabulary Builders—Spelling Words:

1) **sugar** 2) **starch** 3) **carbohydrates** 4) **iodine** 5) **Benedict's solution** 6) **test** 7) **drops** 8) **glucose** 9) **fructose** 10) **sucrose**

I. Thought for Today:

"Minds are like parachutes; they only function when they are open."

Activity V C 7

A. Problem: *Which Foods Contain Proteins?*

B. Materials Needed:

1. Copper sulfate
2. Lime powder
3. Water
4. Measuring cup
5. Stirring rods
6. Medicine droppers
7. Two plastic cups
8. Paper towels
9. Foods to be tested:
   a. meat
   b. butter
   c. egg
   d. cheese
   e. yogurt
   f. flour
   g. sugar
   h. table salt
   i. piece of fruit, etc.

C. Procedure:

1. Ask the students if they know what constitutes a healthy diet.
2. Review Activities V-C-1, "What would be a perfect menu for a day?" and V-C-2, "What is the 'Food Pyramid'?"
3. Describe the three main food constituents:
   a. carbohydrates (starches and sugars)
   b. fats
   c. proteins
4. Briefly review the tests for carbohydrates (Activity V-C-6) and fats (rubbing the test item on paper to see if a translucent spot appears).
5. Tell the students that foods can also be tested for proteins. If the students are mature enough, you may guide them through the following procedure or you may demonstrate the test:
   a. Place 2 tablespoonfuls of water in each of the 2 plastic cups.
   b. Add lime powder to one cup until it is fully saturated.
   c. Add copper sulfate to the second cup until it becomes fully saturated.
   d. Put a medicine dropper in each cup.
   e. Place the food to be tested on several thicknesses of paper towels.
   f. Put two or three drops of limewater on the test item.
   g. Add 2 or 3 drops of copper sulfate to the same spot on the test item.
   h. Note the color of the test spot.
   i. Repeat the test with each food item.

Test items

D. Results:

1. Proteins will turn the test spot a violet color.
2. Foods with a high protein content will turn a darker violet.
3. Foods with no proteins will show no violet color whatsoever.

E. Basic Facts and Supplemental Information:

1. Proteins are composed of building blocks called amino acids.
2. The body produces some amino acids; some needed amino acids must be supplied by the foods we eat.
3. Those that must be obtained from the diet are called "essential amino acids."
4. Essential amino acids are readily obtained from milk, eggs, meat, and cheese.
5. With the exception of soybeans, proteins from vegetable sources do not provide an optimum amount of amino acids.
6. Vegetarian diets can provide ample amino acids if properly planned. Basically these must include cereals, legumes, and vitamin B-12 which is found in milk.

F. Thought Questions for Class Discussions:

1. Should a vegetarian consult a doctor for nutritional advice?
2. What would be some advantages of being a vegetarian? some disadvantages?
3. Are most protein foods high or low in calories?

G. Related Ideas for Further Inquiry:

Study Activities V-C-1, V-C-2, V-C-3, V-C-4, and V-C-9.

H. Vocabulary Builders—Spelling Words:

1) **proteins** 2) **amino acids** 3) **essential**
4) **vegetarian** 5) **cereals** 6) **legumes**

I. Thought for Today:

"Scientists tell us we are what we eat. Nuts must be more common in diets than we thought."

Activity

A. Problem: *Are Food Additives Good for Us?*

B. Materials Needed:

Labels from various food cans and packages that contain additives

C. Procedure

1. Discuss health and nutrition.
2. Distribute labels.
3. Have students list all the additives.
4. Discuss the purposes of additives.
5. Read material about food additives.

D. Results:

1. Students will learn to be cautious about food additives.
2. Students will be alerted to read labels when shopping for food.

E. Basic Facts and Supplemental Information:

1. Additives are added for many reasons:
   a. Preserve the food
   b. Keep its color
   c. Bleach it
   d. Antioxidants
   e. Add flavor
   f. Anti-foaming
   g. Anti-caking
   h. Enrich the food
   i. Flavor dispersant
   j. Stabilizer
   k. Anti-sticking
   l. Neutralizer
   m. Bactericide
   n. Peeling agent
   o. Firming agent
   p. Drying agent
   q. Thickening agent
   r. Conditioner
   s. Binder
   (This is only a partial list.)
2. Many food advertisers claim their product is "organic." Technically, this means that the product contains "carbon." Its common definition also refers to organic farming methods which use no chemicals in the growing or the processing.
3. Some people have allergic reactions to certain chemicals, and some of these chemicals can be found in food additives.

4. It is always a good idea to minimize the amount of additives you consume and eat the most natural foods you can.

F. Thought Questions for Class Discussions:

1. Are natural foods better for us than foods containing additives?
2. Do you think chemicals added to foods could possibly harm us?
3. Could two chemicals, each harmless, react to form a harmful substance in our bodies?

G. Related Ideas for Further Inquiry?

1. Discuss with doctors or nutritionists the value of additives.
2. Older students could check with the U.S. Food and Drug Administration regarding specific additives.
3. Study Activity V-C-1, "What would be a perfect menu for a day?"
4. Study Activity V-C-2, "What is the 'Food Pyramid'?"
5. Study Activity V-C-4, "What are good sources of vitamins and minerals?"
6. Study Activity V-D-3, "How can we protect our heart?"
7. Study Activity V-D-4, "How can I get more pep?"

H. Vocabulary Builders—Spelling Words:

1) **preservatives** 2) **additives** 3) **antioxidants**
4) **natural** 5) **organic** 6) **allergies**

I. Thought for Today:

"A shopper to a friend at a supermarket: 'There's a lot more food mixed with the additives in this product.' "

Activity

V C 9

A. Problem: *What Is Food Irradiation?*

B. Materials Needed:

1. Picture of irradiating processing plants, if available
2. Pictures or sketches of radioactivity (Cobalt-60 or Cesium-137)
3. Pictures of foods labeled with the irradiated food symbol, if available (or labels)

C. Procedure:

1. Discuss food irradiation. Irradiation is a technique in which gamma rays or X-rays are passed through food after it is harvested or slaughtered. This is done to kill insects and bacteria, to prevent sprouting, and to slow ripening by altering the chemical structure of these organisms.
2. Discuss atomic fission and its by-products.
3. Discuss how the by-products of atomic fission are used to irradiate certain foods.
4. Discuss the need for food irradiation:
   a. Some foods spoil quickly.
   b. People would starve if they did not receive food.
   c. Insects are killed that would otherwise damage food.
   d. Bacteria and viruses are killed during the food irradiation processes.
5. Discuss the arguments against food irradiation:
   a. Carcinogenic (cancer causing or stimulating)
   b. Reduces the Vitamin B content
   c. Reduces the Vitamin E content
   d. Reduces important amino acids
   e. Reduces proteins in milk
   f. Some fats are destroyed
   g. Some enzymes are destroyed
6. When foods are irradiated, exposure to a high dose of gamma radiation kills insects, parasites, and microorganisms that cause gastrointestinal diseases and spoilage of processed foods.
7. Irradiation also slows spoilage in fresh produce.
8. The FDA has approved irradiation for potatoes, spices, pork, fruits, vegetables, and poultry.
9. The World Health Organization has also approved irradiation.
10. Most health experts now agree that fears of irradiation of foods are groundless. Radiation is not left in the foods.

D. Results:

1. Students will learn that radiation is being used to preserve some foods.
2. Students will realize that science doesn't have all the answers to methods of food preservation.

Symbol used when food is irradiated. (Need not be used if only additives are irradiated.)

E. Basic Facts and Supplemental Information:

1. Food irradiation facilities use radioactive isotopes, Cobalt-60, Cesium-137, or X-ray generators which produce irradiation.
2. The problem with irradiating foods is that there is not sufficient evidence to make wise decisions regarding the effectiveness of this process.

F. Thought Questions for Class Discussions:

1. Should we eat irradiated foods?
2. What is the role of the U.S. Food and Drug Administration in this regard?
3. Should people be informed if irradiation is used in any food or any of its ingredients?
4. Should we wait for further testing before allowing more foods to be irradiated?

G. Related Ideas for Further Inquiry:

1. Discuss nuclear radiation.
2. Discuss the problems of millions of people starving and suffering from malnutrition, particularly in parts of Africa.
3. Keep track of food irradiation bills in Congress.
4. Study other Activities in this Section.

H. Vocabulary Builders—Spelling Words:

1) **irradiation** 2) **carcinogen** 3) **cobalt**
4) **cesium** 5) **preservation** 6) **gamma rays**
7) **X-rays** 8) **radioactive** 9) **evidence**

I. Thought for Today:

"Facts do not cease to exist because they are ignored."

SECTION D: PERSONAL HEALTH

Activity

V D 1

A. Problem: *How Does the Body Protect Itself?*

B. Materials Needed:

Pictures of healthy children, men, and women

C. Procedure:

1. Discuss all the ways the body resists, reduces, or prevents sickness, accidents, or other bodily harm.
   a. Blood circulation
   b. Blood clotting
   c. Lymphatic system
   d. Skin
   e. Perspiration
   f. Muscles (run from danger)
   g. Eyesight
   h. Hearing
   i. Tears
   j. Hair
   k. Nails
   l. Teeth
2. Demonstrate and discuss how we can help strengthen our bodies through proper exercise.
   a. Medical exam before starting exercise program
   b. Begin with simple exercises
   c. Slowly increase muscle work (progressive)
   d. Balanced program involving heart, lungs, muscles
   e. Exercise in fresh air
      1) Relative humidity of about 60% is best for health and comfort
      2) Ideal temperature is between 68° and 72° Fahrenheit
3. Stress appropriate cleanliness.
   a. Daily shower or bath; wash hands frequently
   b. Use mild soap (harsh soaps irritate the skin)
   c. Wear clean clothing
   d. Brush teeth after meals and at bedtime
   e. Floss teeth daily
4. Discuss ways that the common cold can be prevented or reduced in numbers and severity.
   a. Stay away from people with colds.
   b. Keep up your body strength.
   c. Get plenty of rest.
   d. Drink 6 to 8 glasses of water daily.
   e. Eat nutritious foods.

D. Results:

1. Students will learn that the body has many defense mechanisms.
2. Students will learn what to do to attain and maintain a healthy body.

E. Basic Facts and Supplemental Information:

1. You can't see germs but they are in the air you breathe, the food you eat, and on everything you touch.
2. Germs cause illness.
3. Many people used to die of infections resulting from simple injuries, e.g., cuts, wounds, and from infected gums. Now doctors and dentists treat once-deadly infections with lifesaving antiseptics, antibiotics, and other appropriate treatments.
4. Modern medical science has increased our average life expectancy.
5. In order for the body to properly defend itself it must be supplied with nutritious food, rest, and exercise.
6. Parts of the body are growing and being renewed all the time.
7. People who solve their problems rationally remain mentally healthy.

F. Thought Questions for Class Discussions:

1. What would happen to us if any one of our defense mechanisms or protective devices failed?
2. Can you think of any way that you might better protect yourself from disease or injury?
3. How are our protective mechanisms the same as those of other animals? How are they different?

G. Related Ideas for Further Inquiry:

1. Discuss good health practices.
2. Clip out articles on health from newspapers and magazines.
3. Find out which germs cause which disease.
4. Study other Activities in this Section.

H. Vocabulary Builders—Spelling Words:

1) **sickness** 2) **accident** 3) **perspiration** 4) **exercise** 5) **cleanliness** 6) **rest** 7) **doctor** 8) **disease**

I. Thought for Today:

"One who has health has hope and one who has hope has everything."

Activity V D 2

A. Problem: *Why Should We Wash Our Hands Frequently?*

B. Materials Needed:

1. 8 potatoes
2. Paring knives
3. 8 glass jars that can be sterilized and sealed
4. Heating device to sterilize jars

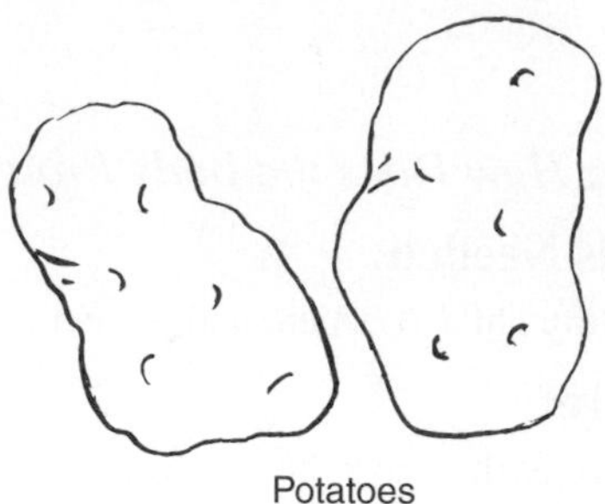

Potatoes

C. Procedure:

1. Sterilize the jars by heating them to 140° F. for 5 to 10 minutes.
2. Have 8 students volunteer to help with the experiment.
3. Send 4 students to the restroom to wash their hands thoroughly.
4. Leave the other 4 students with their hands unwashed.
5. Have each of the 8 students peel a potato and place it in a sterile jar.
6. Label the jars with either "Hands washed" or "Hands unwashed" as the case may be.
7. Place the jars on the science table and observe from day-to-day to note if any changes occur.

D. Results:

1. In about 3 to 5 days the jars labeled "Hands unwashed" will show mold growth on the potatoes.
2. The other jars labeled "Hands washed" will show little or no growth.

E. Basic Facts and Supplemental Information:

1. Our hands come in contact with our environment constantly.
2. Germs are plentiful in our environment.
3. Germs thrive in and on unclean objects.
4. To reduce the germs that contact our bodies we should wash our hands frequently.
5. We should also try to keep our environment clean (our rooms, toys, clothing, playthings, etc.).

F. Thought Questions for Class Discussions:

1. What are some sources of germs?
2. How do people help keep their food clean?
3. How do people preserve their food?
4. Should hands be washed before, after, or before and after going to the restroom?

G. Related Ideas for Further Inquiry:

1. Discover why doctors scrub before operations.
2. Discuss cleanliness at school and at home.
3. If microscopes are available, many experiments on "dirtiness versus cleanliness" can be devised.
4. Examine your fingernails after a full day of work and/or play.
5. Study Activity III-A-1, "How do we classify living things?"
6. Study Activity V-A-1, "What are cells, tissues, and organs?"
7. Study Section V-C, "Nutrition."
8. Study Activity V-D-1, "How does the body protect itself?"
9. Study Activity III-A-6, "How fast do bacteria grow?"
10. Study Activity IV-A-1, "What are some characteristics of all living things?"
11. Study Activity V-A-8; "How do our bodies fight disease?"

H. Vocabulary Builders—Spelling Words:

1) **washed** 2) **unwashed** 3) **sterile** 4) **germs** 5) **volunteer** 6) **disease** 7) **potato** 8) **clean**

I. Thought for Today:

"Instruction ends in the classroom, but education ends with life."

Activity

V D 3

A. Problem: *How Can We Protect Our Hearts?*

B. Materials Needed:

1. Pictures or models of the heart
2. Pictures or charts of blood circulation
3. Pictures of children at play

C. Procedure:

1. Discuss the anatomy of the heart and circulation (heart has two pumps).
2. Compare the heart to the engine of a car:
   a. Both make the "object" move.
   b. Both can be damaged.
   c. Both, with proper care, can last a long time.
3. Cite exercises and activities that can help the heart.
4. Discuss apathy. If the heart doesn't change exercise patterns, it will act like an old engine.
5. Discuss diseases of young children that can hurt the heart:
   a. Anemia—insufficient red blood cells or lack of hemoglobin in the blood (lack of oxygen in the blood)
   b. Leukemia—rise in the number of white cells (cells that fight infection)
   c. Purpura—unusual, frequent, free bleeding
   d. Hemophilia—blood fails to clot or clots very slowly
6. Discuss rules for a healthy heart:
   a. Proper food, rest, and exercise (a healthy body means a healthy heart).
   b. Keep your weight about right. (Extra weight is extra baggage to carry, which puts strain on the heart.)

D. Result:

Students will learn the basics of the anatomy of the heart, and methods to keep the heart healthy.

E. Basic Facts and Supplemental Information:

1. Labor-saving devices have made our lives more pleasurable but have robbed us of former natural, regular exercises that we need for optimum health.
2. Youngsters who spend hours in passive "activities" in front of television sets or operating computers are not developing their heart muscles, thus denying them the extra strength and stamina that would come naturally from a regular exercise program.
3. Everyone, young and old, should have an exercise program to keep their heart in top condition.

4. Vigorous exercise requires more oxygen so the heart must pump harder and faster to pump blood to the muscles. This will eventually make the heart stronger and more resilient.
5. Any new exercise program should be started after a checkup and approval by a doctor.

F. Thought Questions for Class Discussions:

1. What specific recommendations would you make to friends to keep their hearts healthy?
2. Can hearts be replaced?
3. How successful have heart operations been?

G. Related Ideas for Further Inquiry:

1. Consult the school nurse or doctor to help develop a good exercise program that will strengthen the heart.
2. Study blood under a microscope. Make drawings. Label items.
3. Discuss heart operations (bypasses, valve corrections, replacements, etc.).

H. Vocabulary Builders—Spelling Words:

1) **heart** 2) **auricle** 3) **ventricle** 4) **valves**
5) **aorta** 6) **exercise** 7) **stamina** 8) **strength**

I. Thought for Today:

"Most of us would enjoy living the simple life if the way back to it weren't so complicated."

Activity

A. Problem: *How Can I Get More Pep?*

B. Materials Needed:

Books, pamphlets, pictures, charts, and/or multisensory aids on athletes and/or nutritious food

C. Procedure:

1. Discuss health, pep, and good athletes.
2. Discuss nutritious diets:
   a. Generous in good carbohydrates
   b. Moderate in proteins
   c. Low in fats
3. Relate how meals should be:
   a. Heavier in the morning
   b. Lighter in the evening
4. Discuss the recommended percentages of daily food intake for meals:
   a. Breakfast—40%
   b. Lunch—30%
   c. Dinner—30%
5. Some nutritionists are now recommending 5 small meals a day including mid-morning and mid-afternoon.
6. Discuss how we get energy from food:
   a. glucose from carbohydrates and proteins
   b. fatty acids from fats (Fats are a poor source of quick energy because they take a long time to digest.)
   c. carbohydrates (sugars and starches) Starches are the highest efficiency foods; they are found in breads, cereals, grains, pastas, and rice. Sugars give a quick burst of energy but are short-lived. Sugars lead to tooth decay.
   d. The best plan is a balanced diet.
7. Relate how exercise is essential. Almost everyone should have at least 20 minutes of continued exercise each day, when the heart is beating above its normal rate.

D. Results:

1. Students will become more aware of their nutritional needs.
2. Students will realize the value of exercise for a healthy body.

E. Basic Facts and Supplemental Information:

1. Cut down on fats.
2. Add a mid-morning and a mid-afternoon snack.
3. At breakfast and midmorning, the focus should be on carbohydrates, proteins, and fruit.
4. Lunches should be focused on vegetables and proteins.

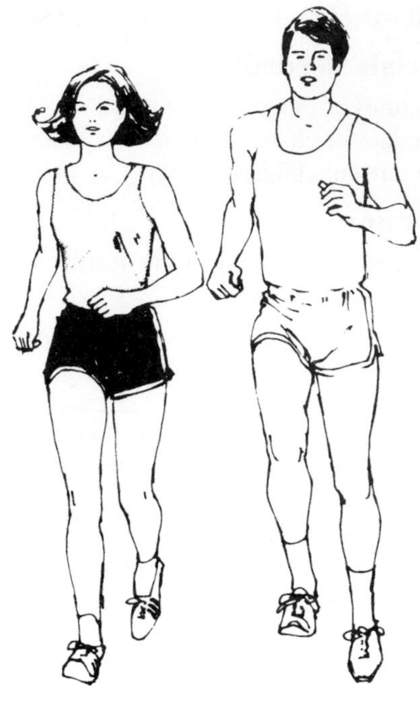

5. Dinners should be lighter with a small amount of proteins.
6. Lack of pep can be due to:
   a. Thyroid deficiency
   b. Depression and worry
   c. Medications
   d. Poor eating habits
   e. Boredom
   f. Too little activity
   g. Drugs
   h. Alcoholic beverages

F. Thought Questions for Class Discussions:

1. What should you do to become peppier?
2. Why are stimulants of any kind harmful?
3. Do some people burn calories faster than others?

G. Related Ideas for Further Inquiry:

1. Study Section V-C, "Nutrition."
2. Plan an exercise program.
3. Study other Activities in this Section.

H. Vocabulary Builders—Spelling Words:

1) **athlete** 2) **athletics** 3) **moderate**
4) **breakfast** 5) **depression** 6) **worry**
7) **boredom** 8) **exercise** 9) **program**

I. Thought for Today:

"Human history is a race between education and catastrophe."—H. G. Wells

Activity

V D 5

Motherhood is a lifetime of responsibilities

A. Problem: *What Should We Know About Sex?*

B. Materials Needed:

1. Reference materials on the reproductive systems
2. Multisensory aids on sex education
3. Local media reports on problems concerning children, such as child abuse, child molestation, kidnapping, teenage pregnancies, etc.

C. Procedure:

1. Many problems concerning sex arise frequently for children, and when they do, this is an opportune time to address these problems and do some teaching on this delicate subject.
2. Some of the problems that you might want to discuss are:
   a. Teenage pregnancies occur on all social levels—not only in ghettos.
   b. One out of every ten teenage girls becomes pregnant every year.
   c. Thirty thousand pregnancies occur annually in girls under the age of 15.
   d. Fifty percent of pregnant teenagers never finish their high school education.
   e. One recent study of TV programs in one year's time found that over 9,000 scenes suggested sexual intercourse.
   f. Another recent study reported that the vast majority of parents of elementary-age children have never discussed sex, venereal disease, or birth control with their children.
   g. One out of every seven teenage girls contracts a venereal disease every year.
   h. Sexual thoughts, wishes, and dreams are normal but should not be "acted out."
   i. About 250 million new cases of STDs (sexually transmitted diseases) occur every year (report of World Health Organization).

D. Results:

1. Students will learn something about sex and the consequences for promiscuous behavior.
2. Students will be hearing about sex in a healthy classroom atmosphere from a teacher who is concerned about their safety and well-being.
3. Students can discuss problems they have in this delicate area, openly, without restraints and without peer pressure.

E. Basic Facts and Supplemental Information:

1. We should start sex education with students at the earliest possible grade level because of the deadly health hazards that can result without this indoctrination.
2. Daily statistics of American children:
   a. 1,900 girls have abortions
   b. 30 die from poverty
   c. 225 are arrested for drug abuse
   d. 450 are arrested for drinking
   e. 2,000 are abused or neglected
   f. 3,000 run away from home
   g. 2,500 are born out of wedlock

F. Thought Questions for Class Discussions:

1. Do you think television, computer programs, and movies play a role in corrupting our youth?
2. Do you think the lyrics in some "popular" songs contribute to juvenile crime?
3. Why do children run away from home?
4. Do one-parent families have more problems than families with both parents living in the home?

G. Related Ideas for Further Inquiry:

1. Study plant and animal reproduction.
2. Study problems between parents and children in the home.
3. Study Activities V-D-1, V-D-6, V-D-8, and V-D-11.

H. Vocabulary Builders—Spelling Words:

1) **education** 2) **abuse** 3) **sex** 4) **pregnant** 5) **disease** 6) **smoking** 7) **drinking** 8) **drugs**

I. Thought for Today:

"When children are doing nothing, they are doing mischief."

Activity V D 6

A. Problem: *Is Smoking Bad for Our Health?*

B. Materials Needed:

1. Flexible, widemouthed plastic bottle (quart or half-gallon size)
2. Cotton
3. 3 or 4 cigarettes
4. Matches
5. Insect or small rodent
6. Small electric fan

C. Procedure:

NOTE: This Activity should be done in a well-ventilated classroom. Open a window so smoke will not be breathed in by teacher or students. The fan should be set to blow the smoke toward the open window.

1. Explain to students that this bottle filled with air is similar to lungs.
2. Wrap a cigarette with cotton so that it fits snugly into the top of the container. As much of the cigarette as possible should be extended in the air.
3. Place the apparatus where all the students can view it clearly.
4. Light the cigarette.
5. Squeeze the container and release in a pumping motion.
6. Repeat this procedure a number of times.
7. When this cigarette is lighted and pumped, the apparatus will "smoke" the cigarette.
8. Remove the cotton and cigarette butt quickly, insert the insect or small rodent in the jar and let it stay there for a while.
9. Observe the changes in the air.
10. Observe what happens to the insect or the small rodent.

D. Result:

If the insect or rodent is not removed in a short time, it will die. If you do not want it to die, you should remove it from the jar as soon as it becomes groggy, and quickly expose it to fresh air; it will revive.

E. Basic Facts and Supplemental Information:

1. What happens to the insect or rodent is quite extreme because the concentration of the cigarette smoke in the bottle is greater than would be found in a smoke-filled room.
2. The fact that cigarette smoke is detrimental to health, both in the lungs and the circulatory system, has been demonstrated so conclusively that there is no doubt whatever about the harmful effects of cigarette smoke.

3. Secondhand smoke (passive smoking) is far more damaging to nonsmokers than previously thought. One out of ten cases of lung cancer occurs in nonsmokers who have been exposed to firsthand smoking over a period of time.
4. Cigarette smoke contains over 4,600 chemicals whether firsthand or secondhand. The chemicals in smoke that doctors are most concerned about are:
   a. Nicotine
   b. Carbon monoxide
   c. Arsenic
   d. Alcohol
   e. Ammonia
   f. Hydrocyanic acid
   g. Other acids (11 different kinds)
   h. Pyridine
   i. Phenols
   j. Aldehydes
   k. Aromatic hydrocarbons
   l. Benzo-pyrene
5. It is estimated that over $100 billion is spent each year for health costs and loss of productive work because of smoking.
6. Each year smoking kills more than 400,000 Americans. This is more than were killed in World War II and Vietnam combined.
7. In America 25% of people over the age of 20 are still smoking and 70% of these know that smoking is addictive. Nicotine can be as addictive as alcohol or cocaine.
8. Fifty million Americans consume 80 million packs of cigarettes every day.
9. Smoking is the largest preventable cause of death and disability in this country.

10. One in five deaths in this country is attributable to smoking.
11. Tobacco companies spend almost $5 billion a year in advertising and promotion to entice youngsters, and a few oldsters, to take up this health-impairing habit.
12. Specifically cigarette smoking:
    a. Impairs the sense of taste
    b. Impairs the sense of smell
    c. Causes bad breath ("smoker's breath")
    d. Slows down circulation by constricting blood vessels so the heart has to pump harder, which causes a rise in blood pressure
    e. Robs the body of 10% of its oxygen-carrying capacity
    f. Contains tars (like paving material used on streets and highways) which are carcinogens
    g. Contains over 15 known carcinogens
    h. Has 3 deadly agents: 1) nicotine, 2) tars, and 3) carbon monoxide
    i. Causes carbon monoxide to replace oxygen in the blood (hemoglobin)
    j. Causes stomach to secrete acids, producing ulcers
    k. Causes 300,000 premature deaths every year
    l. Causes 52,000 new cases of lung cancer each year
    m. Has impaired the lungs of 50,000,000 people in the United States
    n. Entices 1,000,000 new teenagers to start smoking every year
    o. Harms tissue in the mouth, throat, larynx, trachea, and lungs
    p. Leads to the use of other drugs
    q. Is responsible for the sales of 585,000,000,000 cigarettes a year in the United States
    r. Contains enough nicotine in one pack of cigarettes to kill a person if all the nicotine were in a single dose
    s. Produces a hacker's cough
    t. Leads to emphysema
    u. Leads to heart disease
    v. Leads to chronic bronchitis
    w. Corrodes the membranes of the lips and palate
    x. Stains teeth
    y. Leaves nicotine odor in clothing, hair, drapes, upholstered furniture, etc.
    z. Shortens lifespan
13. The U.S. Centers for Disease Control and Prevention reports that:
    a. One thousand lives are lost each week because of secondhand smoke.
    b. Secondhand smoke is the third leading cause of preventable death; it follows active smoking and alcohol use.
14. One of six cases of children's lung cancer has definitively been traced to parental smoking in the home.
15. Of all the people who are alive today, fully 500 million will die from tobacco-related diseases, according to estimates from the World Health Organization.
16. Peer pressure is the number one reason why young teenagers take up smoking. Parental example is the number two reason.

F. Thought Questions for Class Discussions:

1. Do you think the federal government should declare nicotine "addictive?" The Food and Drug Administration is seriously considering this at the present time.
2. Is nicotine the only harmful ingredient in cigarette smoke?
3. Have you ever been in close quarters with people who are smoking? How did you feel about it? What do you think about it?

G. Related Ideas for Further Inquiry:

1. List the many disadvantages of smoking: health impairment, monetary cost, odor, etc.
2. List the advantages (if any) of smoking.
3. Compare lists.
4. Have a smoker take a big drag on a cigarette and exhale it on a clean white handkerchief. (A big, brown stain will appear.) Ask students if they would like to have a lot of this in their lungs.
5. Open a cigarette filter to examine its contents.
6. Have students discuss any experiences they have had in a smoked-filled room.
7. Estimate the cost of smoking over a period of several years.
8. Discuss with doctors and nurses the experiences they have had with smokers.
9. Interview ex-smokers on why they decided to quit.
10. Interview smokers on why they are continuing to smoke when all the negative evidence is well-known.
11. Study Activity V-D-1, "How does our body protect itself?"
12. Study Activity V-D-3, "How can we protect our heart?"
13. Study Activity V-D-7, "Is smoking marijuana bad for our health?"
14. Study other Activities in this Section.

H. Vocabulary Builders—Spelling Words:

1) **nicotine** 2) **smoking** 3) **cigarette** 4) **tar** 5) **carcinogen** 6) **emphysema** 7) **habit** 8) **cough** 9) **peer pressure** 10) **expensive** 11) **deadly**

I. Thought for Today:

"The most incredible creation in the universe is your body. Don't destroy it with cigarette smoking and drugs."

Activity

A. Problem: *Is Smoking Marijuana Bad for Our Health?*

B. Materials Needed:

1. Simulated marijuana cigarette (Roll your own "make-believe" cigarette.)
2. Crushed alfalfa

C. Procedure:

1. The most impressive method would be to have an outside speaker, i.e., a medical doctor, police officer, or narcotics officer.
2. If unable to get an expert resource person, discuss the perils of smoking marijuana ("pot") such as:
   a. Causes birth defects, impairs reproductive capability, increases miscarriages.
   b. Interferes with cell division and can cause cellular abnormalities.
   c. Leads to genetic mutations by interfering with chromosome development. (Chromosomes carry our hereditary characteristics.)
   d. The more "pot" that is used, the more addictive it becomes. It is a hallucinogen; its effects can last for many hours. Withdrawal leads to personality problems. The main point to drive home is that "pot" users have altered perceptions.
   e. Marijuana smokers have about a 40% reduction in white blood cells. This lessens the body's ability to fight disease.
   f. Causes more cancer than regular cigarette smoking.
   g. There were about 10,000,000 pounds of marijuana smoked in the United States last year.
3. The odor of crushed alfalfa is similar to that of marijuana.
4. Show the class the "make-believe" cigarette, citing the abnormal appearance because it is produced illegally.

D. Results:

1. Students will learn that the use of "pot" leads to the use of other deadly drugs.
2. Almost all heroin addicts start with smoking tobacco, then marijuana, then heroin.

E. Basic Facts and Supplemental Information:

1. Marijuana can be an expensive, long-term, and potentially life-threatening addiction that is extremely difficult to overcome.
2. Two-thirds of all teenagers have tried marijuana before they have graduated from high school.
3. Smoking marijuana prevents rational thinking and decision making. This leads to poor grades in school, conflicts at home, and sexual promiscuity.
4. Marijuana is the most popular illegal drug in the United States.
5. There are over 400 different chemicals in marijuana, including THC, a psychoactive drug that reduces physical coordination and mental functions.
6. Cannabis is the dried part of the hemp plant from which marijuana is derived.
7. Marijuana use is increasing and younger children are smoking it.
8. Drug use is primarily a health and social problem which has also become a police problem.
9. We must make the outside world more attractive to our youth so they won't turn to drugs for security.

F. Thought Questions for Class Discussions:

1. Should you abuse the only body that you will ever have?
2. Why do you think people smoke, drink alcoholic beverages, and take mood-altering pills?
3. Have you ever been in close quarters with people who are smoking? How did you feel? What did you think?
4. Would you like to lose control of your body?
5. Would you like to lose control of your mind?

G. Related Ideas for Further Inquiry:

1. See especially Activity, V-D-6, "Is smoking bad for our health?"
2. Study other illicit drugs and their harmful effects.
3. Study other Activities in this Section.

H. Vocabulary Builders—Spelling Words:

1) **marijuana** 2) **heroin** 3) **psychic** 4) **perception** 5) **dependency** 6) **abnormalities** 7) **hallucinogen**

I. Thought for Today:

"Freedom is the right to be wrong, not the right to do wrong."—John G. Diefenbach

Activity

A. Problem: *Is Alcohol Bad for Our Health?*

B. Materials Needed:

1. Empty beer can
2. Empty wine bottle
3. Empty whiskey bottle
4. Rubbing alcohol
5. Earthworm
6. Saucer

C. Procedure:

1. Have students relate experiences they have observed with alcoholic beverages without citing names or relationships.
2. Discuss why some young people drink:
   a. they think they are "grown-up"
   b. to show off
   c. to escape from reality
   d. peer pressure
3. Describe some beverages that contain alcohol.
4. Tell the students that it is not what you drink but how much alcohol you consume that affects you and can make you drunk or cause your death.
5. Place some alcohol in saucer.
6. Place earthworm in the saucer.
7. Observe results.

D. Results:

1. The earthworm will die.
2. Students will learn about the harmful effects of drinking alcoholic beverages.

E. Basic Facts and Supplemental Information:

1. Many people who drink liquor can limit their intake; this causes no health or social problems.
2. Millions of people drink liquor to excess.
3. Alcoholism is a serious major health problem in the United States.
4. Beer contains 2% to 5% alcohol; wines, 8% to 17% alcohol.
5. Whiskey, gin, vodka, and rum contain 40% to 50% alcohol.
6. Alcohol is a depressant, not a stimulant.
7. Alcohol dulls the nerve centers in the brain.
8. Muscular coordination is affected and visual acuity is reduced.
9. Forty percent of all automobile fatalities are caused by drinking drivers.
10. Drinking by drivers and pedestrians is reported to cause 30,000 highway deaths a year in the United States.
11. Alcohol causes brain damage—usually to delirium tremens (horrifying hallucinations).
12. Seventy percent of adults drink.
13. There are 13,000,000 alcoholics in the United States (compulsive drinkers).
14. All alcoholic drinks contain ethyl alcohol (C_2H_5OH).
15. Ninety percent of alcohol consumed gets into the bloodstream in one hour.
16. If a 150 pound person drinks two beers, the alcohol level in his/her blood = 0.05%.
    .10% affects motor activity.
    .20% affects the midbrain (sleep).
    .50% could produce death from respiratory failure.
17. Alcohol causes cirrhosis of the liver.
18. Alcohol is involved in 31% of the homicides and 36% of the suicides in the United States.
19. Half of all the crimes in the United States are committed by people under the influence of alcohol.
20. "Don't let peer pressure lead to beer pressure."

F. Thought Questions for Class Discussions:

1. Are there any good arguments for drinking alcoholic beverages?
2. Do you think some people drink for social reasons?
3. Do you think some people drink because they are persuaded or influenced by friends? advertisements? peers?

G. Related Ideas for Further Inquiry:

1. Visit a food market and observe the size of the liquor section.
2. Have the school nurse discuss the problems with alcohol.
3. Have a lecture from a recovering alcoholic.
4. Study Activity V-D-6 "Is smoking bad for our health?"
5. Study Activity V-D-7 "Is smoking marijuana bad for our health?"
6. Study Activity V-D-9, "Are illicit drugs bad for our health?"

H. Vocabulary Builders—Spelling Words:

1) **alcohol** 2) **drinking** 3) **beer** 4) **wine** 5) **whiskey** 6) **earthworm** 7) **depressant**

I. Thought for Today:

"If you drink like a fish, swim, don't drive."

Activity VD9

A. Problem: *Are Illicit Drugs Bad for Our Health?*

B. Materials Needed:

1. Simulated pills
   a. Empty capsules from pharmacy
   b. Food coloring added to salt, sugar
2. Pictures of pills and capsules
3. Pictures of drugged individuals
4. Newspaper and magazine articles about drugs

C. Procedure:

1. Discuss the rise of the use of drugs among young people.
2. Discuss why the drugs are used:
   a. Profit
   b. Peer pressure
   c. Taking a dare
   d. False sense of reality
   e. Escape from problems
3. Show students the simulated pills and briefly describe each:
   a. Stimulants (uppers) amphetamines, cocaine
      1) deaden body's normal warning systems
      2) methedrine (speed) can cause brain damage, paranoia
         (a) person becomes jittery
         (b) false sense of bravado
   b. Depressants (downers) barbiturates
      1) overdose can paralyze breathing center
      2) drowsiness or escape (false)
      3) defective judgment can lead to falls, accidents, etc.
   c. Hallucinogens
      1) altered perceptions
      2) impaired judgment
   d. Narcotics (opium, morphine, heroin, etc.)
      1) loss of appetite
      2) painful withdrawal symptoms
      3) temporary impotency or sterility
4. Stress the fact that most information from peers regarding drugs is very misleading.

D. Results:

1. Students will learn correct information about illicit drugs from their teacher rather than from peers.
2. Pupils will realize the serious problems associated with the use of any or all drugs.

E. Basic Facts and Supplemental Information:

1. Drug use is becoming more prevalent among our young children.
2. If students don't get honest and accurate information in their homes and schools, they will believe their peers.

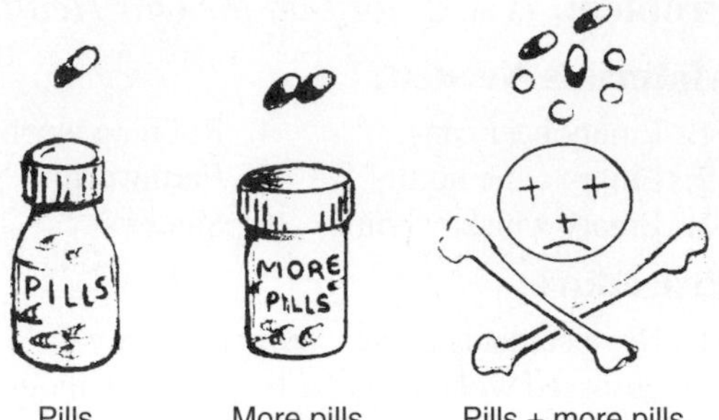

Pills More pills Pills + more pills

3. Over half of the amphetamines find their way to illegal markets.
4. Many students who take pep pills to cram for exams lack the coordination to take the exam.
5. Over 3,000 deaths per year in the U.S. result from the use of barbiturates.
6. Don't let street names fool you—all illicit drugs are potentially killers.
7. Drug use is primarily a health and social problem, but it has also become a police problem.
8. Most people take drugs to relieve anxieties. They're not pursuing pleasure, only less pain.
9. The solution is education, not prisons.
10. Drug users can be detected by:
    a. change in behavior
    b. new questionable friends
    c. drowsiness
    d. callousness
    e. lack of concentration
    f. falling grades at school

F. Thought Questions for Class Discussions:

1. If you know anybody who is on drugs, why do you think she/he is taking them?
2. Do you think youngsters take drugs for kicks, curiosity, rebellion—or what?
3. Why are potent legal drugs prescribed only by medical doctors?

G. Related Ideas for Further Inquiry:

1. Compare alcohol to drugs.
2. It is effective to have a former drug addict talk to the class.

H. Vocabulary Builders—Spelling Words:

1) **illicit** 2) **drugs** 3) **hallucinogens** 4) **killers** 5) **stimulants** 6) **depressants** 7) **narcotics**

I. Thought for Today:

"Dare to say NO to drugs."

Activity V D 10

A. Problem: *Is Caffeine Bad for Us?*

B. Materials Needed:

1. Coffee cup
2. Teapot
3. Soft drink bottle or can
4. Chocolate candy
5. Pill bottle

C. Procedure:

Discuss caffeine citing some key points such as:

1. Mild stimulant
2. One of the most widely used drugs
3. Is in coffee, tea, and chocolate
4. Gives a psychological lift
5. Improves alertness
6. Possible link to birth defects
7. Contained in many over-the-counter drugs, including some headache relievers
8. Increases heartbeat
9. Increases basic metabolism rate
10. Mildly addictive
11. Many soft drinks contain caffeine

D. Result:

Students will learn about the effects of caffeine on their bodies and, in particular, that many soft drinks contain caffeine.

E. Basic Facts and Supplemental Information:

1. Most decaffeinated coffee has 97% of the caffeine removed.
2. Most of the caffeine taken out of coffee is sold to the soft drink industry.
3. Soft drinks have replaced coffee as the number one drink.
4. A teaspoon of tea leaves contains more of the stimulant drug caffeine than a teaspoon of ground coffee, but the caffeine in tea is usually more diluted when served (50% to 70%).
5. There is a lot of discussion about the effects of caffeine.
6. Unfortunately, there is no definitive answer as to whether it is harmful or how much is too much because the research is incomplete.
7. We associate caffeine with coffee, but there are many other sources including: tea, chocolate, colas, cocoa, and many nonprescription drugs for colds and allergies.
8. Most common medical advice states that about two 6-ounce cups of regular coffee or 20 ounces of decaffeinated coffee per day is relatively safe for the average person.
9. If a person has any stomach problems, intestinal upset, heart palpitations, anxiety manifestations, insomnia, depression, muscle twitching, etc., caffeine should be avoided in any form.

F. Thought Questions for Class Discussions:

1. Do you think it is wise to drink beverages which contain caffeine?
2. Is chocolate a good food?
3. Should tired automobile and truck drivers use caffeine to stay awake?

G. Related Ideas for Further Inquiry:

1. Study decaffeinated coffee and determine whether it is good or bad.
2. Study anti-sleeping pills to see if they contain caffeine.
3. Study other Activities in this Section.

H. Vocabulary Builders—Spelling Words:

1) **caffeine** 2) **coffee** 3) **chocolate** 4) **tea** 5) **stimulant** 6) **addictive** 7) **drug**

I. Thought for Today:

"A person wrapped up in himself makes a pretty small bundle."

Activity V D 11

A. Problem: *How Can I Keep Mentally Healthy?*

B. Materials Needed:

1. Pictures of people involved in sports activities, projects, etc.
2. Multisensory materials of the above
3. Reference materials on mental health

C. Procedure:

1. Discuss physical health. See Activity V-D-1, "How does our body protect itself?"
2. Show pictures of people per Materials Needed, Item 1 above, and discuss the benefits of these experiences.
3. If multisensory materials are available, show slides, motion pictures, sound filmstrips, etc., of activities that promote mental health.

D. Results:

1. Students will learn that there are many activities they can share which lead to good mental health.
2. Students will compare their lifestyles with other students, friends, and peers.

E. Basic Facts and Supplemental Information:

1. A good mental health program involves time and planning. It should include:
   a. time for dreaming—setting goals
   b. time for working—leads to success
   c. time for thinking—source of power
   d. time for playing—relaxation; secret of youth
   e. time for reading—foundation of knowledge
   f. time for worship—philosophy of life
   g. time for friends—source of happiness
   h. time for love—heart of life
   i. time to laugh—life's enjoyment
   j. time for beauty—everywhere in nature
   k. time for health—treasure of life
   l. time for family—builds security
   m. time to rest—recharging oneself
2. Mental health is vital to a person's well-being.
3. More people are in beds for the mentally ill than the physically ill.
4. One person out of ten will spend time in a mental hospital, and many more should.
5. Mental illness occurs when we can't solve our problems.
6. The Menninger Clinic reports that there are four ways to solve one's problems. They are the "Four F's:"
   a. Forget it (The problem is still there.)
   b. Fight it (Never really solves the problem.)
   c. Flee it (Run away from it. Problem remains.)
   d. Face it (Only mentally healthy way) Many problems are solved by "constructive compromises."

F. Thought Questions for Class Discussions:

1. What are fears? phobias?
2. Why do some people act "strangely"?
3. Are accidents related to mental health?
4. Are mental health, emotional health, and physical health interrelated?
5. Is watching television or playing computer games for long periods of time harmful to mental health?

G. Related Ideas for Further Inquiry:

1. Have a school psychologist speak to the class about mental health.
2. If a school counselor is available, ask him/her to discuss the problems of mental health with the class.
3. See Activities V-A-6, V-B-1, and V-D-13.

H. Vocabulary Builders—Spelling Words:

1) **mentally** 2) **healthy** 3) **planning** 4) **goals** 5) **work** 6) **read** 7) **friends**

I. Thought for Today:

"If you want to be the picture of good health, you'd better have a happy frame of mind."

Activity V D 12

A. Problem: *Are X-rays Harmful?*

B. Materials Needed:

1. Books, pamphlets, pictures, and/or multisensory aids on X-rays
2. Chart on light radiation

C. Procedure:

1. Discuss radiation chart. (See lower drawing.)
2. Discuss concerns of people when they need X-rays:
   a. financial?
   b. harmful?
   c. necessary?
3. Describe X-rays:
   a. electrical and magnetic energy that travels in waves
   b. penetrates many materials including bones and skin
   c. exposes film
   d. picture is a "radiograph"
4. Doctors and dentists can use them for:
   a. detection
   b. diagnosis
   c. treatment
5. Advantages of using X-rays:
   a. early detection of disease
   b. saves time
   c. saves money
   d. saves discomforture
   e. locates fractures and other problems
6. Disadvantages of using X-rays:
   a. possible tissue damage
   b. radiation allowance is cumulative

D. Result:

Students will learn that X-ray examinations have both positive and negative aspects and that doctors and dentists should be consulted about the consequences of its use.

E. Basic Facts and Supplemental Information:

1. People are exposed to natural radiation all the time from cosmic radiation (sun) and from some rocks.
2. No radiation remains in your body after an X-ray.
3. Faster films have reduced the amounts of radiation that were formerly needed.
4. You actually receive less radiation from a chest X-ray than you would receive from cosmic radiation by flying from New York to Los Angeles.

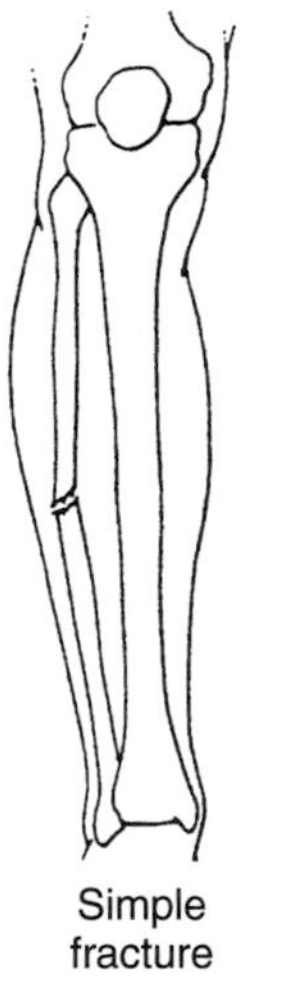

Simple fracture

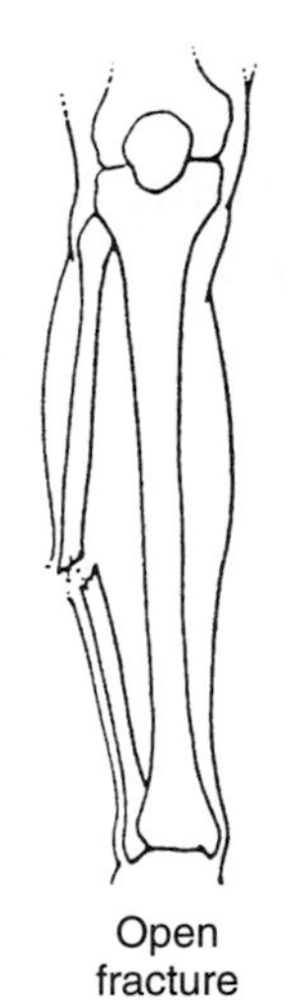

Open fracture (skin broken)

Outer space 8%
Rocks and soil 8%
Inside our bodies 11%
X-rays 11%
Miscellaneous sources 7%
Radon 55%

Sources of radiation

F. Thought Questions for Class Discussions:

1. Do you think X-rays are helpful or harmful?
2. How do you think doctors and dentists feel about the use of X-rays?
3. Do you think early detection of disease outweighs disadvantages of using X-rays?

G. Related Ideas for Further Inquiry:

1. Compare light waves and X-rays.
2. Compare ultraviolet light and X-rays.
3. Study other Activities in this Section.
4. Invite a doctor, dentist, or radiologist to discuss X-rays.

H. Vocabulary Builders—Spelling Words:

1) **X-ray** 2) **detection** 3) **diagnosis**
4) **treatment** 5) **therapy** 6) **risks**

I. Thought for Today:

"Life can only be understood by looking backward, but it must be lived by looking forward."

Activity V D 13

A. Problem: *What Is Personality?*

B. Materials Needed:

Pictures of many people expressing a number of different kinds of emotion

C. Procedure:

1. Discuss people in general.
   a. different jobs
   b. different interests
   c. different activities
2. Discuss the characteristics of the 10 best-liked students (no names) in school outside of your class.
3. List these traits on the board.
4. Discuss physical traits that are acquired from heredity such as:
   a. facial features
   b. body build
   c. skin pigmentation
   d. hair color and texture
   e. certain visual defects
   f. certain hearing defects
   g. blood type
   h. color of eyes
5. Discuss other traits that can be acquired by choice such as:
   a. habits
   b. attitudes
   c. mannerisms
   d. posture
   e. skills for potential abilities
   f. grooming
   g. initiative
   h. behaviors (friendly, shy, etc.)

D. Results:

1. Students will learn about individual differences.
2. Pupils will learn what traits they inherited and which were acquired.
3. Students will learn some ways to improve their personalities.

E. Basic Facts and Supplemental Information:

1. We know about physical illness and that the best way to stay physically healthy is with good food, proper rest, and exercise.
2. We should be equally concerned with our mental health and personality development.

3. Doctors estimate that 30% to 50% of their patients are ill because of personality problems.
4. Your whole future is determined by your personality, so begin now to develop a personality just as you would work to develop a healthy body.
5. Personality can be developed like a physical muscle; it must be conscientiously worked on to produce the best results.

F. Thought Questions for Class Discussions:

1. What personality traits do you admire?
2. Which traits do you dislike?
3. What are your primary goals in life?

G. Related Ideas for Further Inquiry:

1. Have the school psychologist talk to the class about personality.
2. Have students outline a program for their personality development.
3. Study other Activities in this Section.

H. Vocabulary Builders—Spelling Words:

1) **personality** 2) **character** 3) **traits** 4) **inherited** 5) **acquired** 6) **behavior**

I. Thought for Today:

"It's easy to spot someone with a lot of personality—they remind you so much of yourself."

Activity V D 14

A. Problem: *Is One Student Stronger Than Three? (Fun Activity)*

B. Materials Needed:

Four student volunteers (one to portray a "weak" person and three to portray "strong" individuals)

C. Procedure:

1. Discuss strengths and weaknesses of people—athletes versus nonathletes.
2. Cite how many nonathletes are strong.
3. Have the "weak" student stand facing the wall with hands outstretched and touching wall.
4. Have the three "strong" students line up in back of the "weak" student, with each in position to push on the shoulders of the one in front.
5. Instruct the students to push steadily (no jerking) to see if they can get the "weak" student to collapse his or her arms.
6. Have them try.
7. May want to repeat, substituting students.

D. Result:

"Strong" students will be unable to collapse the arms of the "weak" student.

E. Basic Facts and Supplemental Information:

The reason they can't collapse the "weak" student's arms is because of Newton's Third Law of Motion: For every action there is an equal and opposite reaction. When the "strong" students push forward their bodies exert an equal and opposite force back; consequently, there are as many forces acting back from the wall as there are acting toward the wall.

F. Thought Questions for Class Discussions:

1. Can you think of any other activities that involve Newton's Third Law of Motion?
2. When you are walking and pushing against the ground, is the ground pushing back against you?
3. Is it Newton's Third Law of Motion that enables rockets to move in space?

G. Related Ideas for Further Inquiry:

1. Study Activity II-F-1, "What are Newton's laws of motion?"
2. Study Activity II-F-4, "What is the conservation of energy?"
3. Study Activity II-F-7, "Are there forces acting without movement of objects?"
4. What forces are involved in:
   a. running?
   b. bicycling?
   c. in-line skating?
   d. skateboarding?
5. Study other Activities in this Section.

H. Vocabulary Builders—Spelling Words:

1) **strength** 2) **weakness** 3) **motion**
4) **equal** 5) **opposite** 6) **Newton**

I. Thought for Today:

"In making a living today, many no longer leave room for life."

Section E: Public Health

Activity V E 1

Rain doesn't cause illness — it cleans the air.

A. Problem: *How Does Our Environment Affect Our Health?*

B. Materials Needed:

1. Pictures of air pollution
2. Toy automobile
3. Picture of air conditioner
4. Picture of heater
5. Thermometer
6. Pictures of businesses
7. Pictures of industries
8. Empty containers of insecticides, pesticides, and herbicides
9. Pictures of microorganisms
10. Pictures of garbage, wastes, etc.

C. Procedure:

Using the multisensory aids listed above, discuss how these environmental agents or conditions affect our health, such as:

1. polluted air (from business, industry, automobiles, trucks, etc.)
2. unsafe water
3. tainted food
4. poison plants
5. unsanitary conditions
6. smoke (and smoking)
7. electric power plants
8. sun (ultraviolet radiation) (sunburn)
9. microorganisms

D. Result:

Students will learn that almost all of our unhealthy conditions are due to environmental conditions.

E. Basic Facts and Supplemental Information:

1. Oxygen is a vital necessity for life, but we are:
   a. using it up by burning trees and shrubs for energy
   b. cutting down trees to make room for our population explosion
   c. slowly destroying the phytoplankton along the coastal waters that also supply us with oxygen
2. Fresh water is a vital necessity for life as found in rivers, ponds, wetlands, aquifers, wells, etc., but we are:
   a. dumping wastes into it
   b. adding pesticides to it
   c. wasting it
3. Land and soils so critically needed for food sources are:
   a. being lost by the building of residences, businesses, highways, etc.
   b. being lost by erosion
   c. being used as dumping grounds for our garbage and wastes
   d. saturated with pesticides and herbicides
4. Millions of people all over the world are starving to death every year which is certainly a major health problem.

F. Thought Questions for Class Discussions:

1. How can our local school environments be improved?
2. How can our community's environment be improved?
3. How can our home environments be improved?
4. Should smoking be banned on all planes?
5. Should smoking be banned in all restaurants?
6. Should government play a larger role in improving our environment?

G. Related Ideas for Further Inquiry:

1. Study especially Section V-G, "Safety."
2. Study Part VI, "Ecology."
3. Study other Activities in this Section.

H. Vocabulary Builders—Spelling Words:

1) **environment** 2) **pollution** 3) **thermometer** 4) **tainted** 5) **unsanitary** 6) **necessities**

I. Thought for Today:

"The most difficult thing to open is a closed mind."

Activity

V E 2

A. Problem: *How Is Water Purified?*

B. Materials Needed:

1. Large jar (See drawing.)
2. Stopper with center hole
3. Three-inch piece of glass tubing to fit bottom stopper
4. Clean gravel
5. Coarse clean sand
6. Very fine sand
7. Charcoal paste (carbon and water)
8. Glass bowl
9. Dirty water
10. Supporting device for jar

C. Procedure:

1. Insert glass tube into center of stopper, wetting stopper and twisting tubing slowly and carefully.
2. Put stopper with tube in the small open end of jar.
3. Fill the jar with the following layers in this order:
   a. two inches of clean gravel (A)
   b. two inches coarse, clean sand (B)
   c. one-half inch fine sand (C)
   d. one-half inch charcoal paste (D)
4. Support jar firmly, and gently pour some dirty water solution into jar. Save some for comparison.

D. Result:

The dirty water drains through the filters, capturing the foreign particles and yielding clean water in the glass bowl below.

E. Basic Facts and Supplemental Information:

1. Impurities have been held back by the sharp edges of the ingredients as the water seeped through each layer, thus giving us filtered water.
2. Filtration is part of the procedure used in purifying water. Unclean drinking water can carry many diseases. Among the most common are dysentary, cholera, and bacterial infections.
3. It is estimated that 60 million Americans are now drinking water of questionable standards.
4. In the event of a natural disaster water should be boiled for at least 5 minutes.
5. Many people are now buying bottled water or using tap water with a filter added.

F. Thought Questions for Class Discussions:

1. What other methods do we use to keep our water clean?

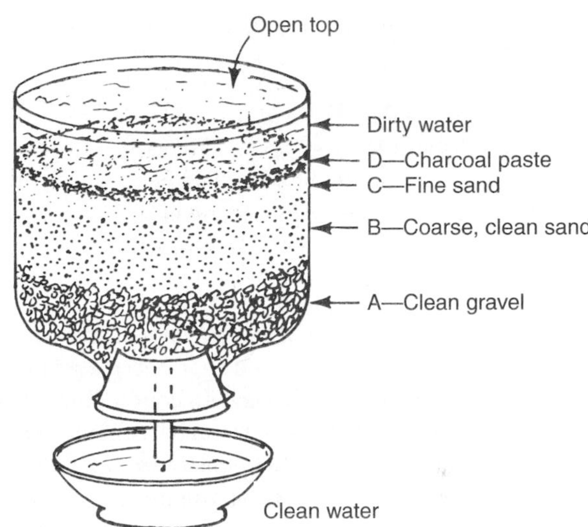

2. What are some possible contaminants?
3. Is it possible to get fresh water from the sea?

G. Related Ideas for Further Inquiry:

1. Check with the local health department on the status of your community's water purity.
2. Check with the same department on the effectiveness of home water filtering systems.
3. See Section I-C, "Water."
4. Study Activity VI-B-3, "How can we conserve our fresh water?"
5. Study Activity VI-C-1, "What are the main environmental problems?"
6. Study Activity VI-A-1, "What is the balance of nature?"
7. Study Activity VI-D-1, "How can we help solve some of the pollution problems?"
8. Study Activity VI-D-3, "What is recycling? salvaging? reusing?"
9. Study other Activities in this Section.

H. Vocabulary Builders—Spelling Words:

1) **purified** 2) **gravel** 3) **charcoal** 4) **filter** 5) **impurities** 6) **ingredients** 7) **disease** 8) **contaminants** 9) **prevention**

I. Thought for Today:

"If you don't think cooperation is necessary, watch what happens to a wagon if one wheel comes off."

Activity V E 3

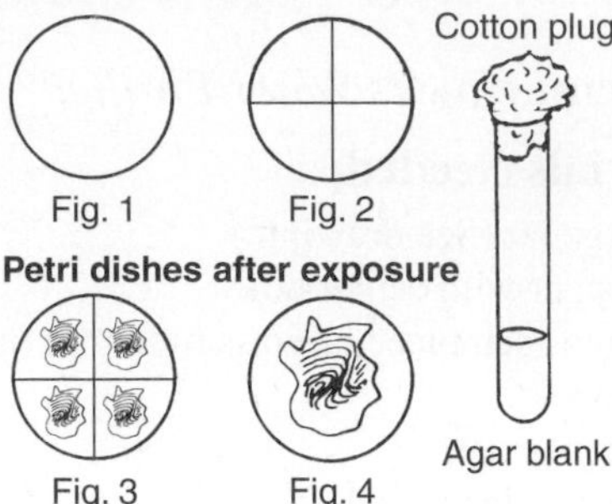

A. Problem: *How Can We Test for Microorganisms?*

B. Materials Needed:

1. Petri dishes (4)
2. Test tube
3. Cotton
4. Heating device
5. Water
6. Pencil
7. Agar

C. Procedure:

1. For older students, or a teacher demonstration, obtain four Petri dishes and agar. Place agar in the test tube and then cap tube with cotton plug. (See drawing.) Hold tube in hot water to soften agar.
2. Pour agar into Petri dishes and cover quickly, taking care not to expose agar to the air.
3. Allow agar to set.
4. Divide agar in one dish into quarters by making grooves with a point of pencil. (See Figure 2.)
5. Taking care not to expose to air longer than necessary, have four students place the tips of their fingers in each of the four quarters. Cover the dish immediately. (See Figure 3.)
6. Have one student cough into the second Petri dish. Cover immediately. (See Figure 4.)
7. Leave the agar in the third Petri dish unexposed. (See Figure 1.)
8. Plan your own test with the fourth Petri dish.
9. Incubate all Petri dishes at 37° C. for 24 hours.

D. Results:

1. Students will learn some diagnostic tests for microorganisms.
2. Bacteria will grow in the Petri dish that has been touched by the students.
3. Bacteria will grow in the Petri dish that has been coughed in by a student.
4. The unexposed Petri dish should show no evidence of microorganisms.

E. Basic Facts and Supplemental Information:

1. Bacteria are microorganisms.
2. Microorganisms are individually too small to be seen with the naked eye.
3. Colonies of microorganisms can be seen with the naked eye.
4. Microorganisms grow in unsanitary conditions.
5. Since the nutrient agar plates were sterile before the exposures, then any bacteria growth observed will be due to the fact that bacteria were present on the fingers and in the expired air of the cough. This should demonstrate the necessity for keeping the hands clean and for covering the mouth when coughing.
6. All communicable diseases are caused by microorganisms.
7. There are many species of microorganisms.
8. Some bacteria are helpful to people; others cause disease.
9. Most fungi, like bacteria, are tiny plants; some are helpful and some are harmful.
10. Yeast is a type of fungi; so are molds.
11. Viruses are another kind of microorganism which cause colds, chicken pox, measles, etc., and are so small that they can live inside bacteria.
12. All microorganisms must enter the body some way to cause disease (mouth, nose, cuts, bites).
13. Some diseases are spread through air, water, and food.

F. Thought Questions for Class Discussions:

1. What tests do doctors use to detect the causes of illness?
2. Where else are bacteria likely to be?
3. Are all bacteria bad?
4. Why is bacteria added to certain milk products?
5. Are there bacteria in the air?

G. Related Ideas for Further Inquiry:

1. Study Activity V-D-1, “How does our body protect itself?”
2. Study Activity V-D-2, “Why should we wash our hands frequently?”
3. Study Activity V-C-9, “What is food irradiation?”
4. Study Activity III-A-1, “How do we classify living things?”
5. Study other Activities in this Section.

H. Vocabulary Builders—Spelling Words:

1) **Petri dish** 2) **agar** 3) **sterile** 4) **bacteria** 5) **sanitary** 6) **disease** 7) **clean** 8) **unhealthy**

I. Thought for Today:

“One way to keep your health is to eat what you don’t want, drink what you don’t like, and do what you’d rather not.”—Mark Twain

Activity

V E 4

A. Problem: *What Is AIDS?*

B. Materials Needed:

1. Pictures of AIDS victims
2. Newspaper accounts of AIDS
3. Reference materials on AIDS

C. Procedure:

1. Discuss what is presently known about AIDS. (Information to be given depends on the maturity of the students and the willingness of the teacher to discuss AIDS with the students.)
   a. It is a disease caused by a virus.
   b. It stands for Acquired Immune Deficiency Syndrome.
   c. It is almost always fatal.
   d. It is increasing in the number of victims.
   e. It has been contracted through anal sex contacts.
   f. It has been contracted through unsterile blood transfusions.
   g. It has been contracted through dirty-needle injections of drugs.
   h. There is no known cure for it.
   i. There are many experimental drugs being tested with some giving slight delaying actions.
   j. AIDS is a very prevalent disease in Africa, and is rapidly increasing in China, India, Brazil, and France.
   k. AIDS is not an easy disease to contract.
   l. AIDS is not contracted by air or clothing.
   m. AIDS can be contracted by coming in contact with the body fluids of an infected person.
   n. High-risk groups are:
      1) gay and bisexual men
      2) intravenous drug users
      3) hemophiliacs
      4) blood transfusion recipients
      5) sexual partners of the above groups
   o. AIDS has been contracted by babies born to AIDS-infected mothers. Ordinary contact with AIDS victims is safe with proper precautions.
2. Discuss other viral diseases: small pox, polio, influenza, rabies, measles, and the common cold.

D. Result:

Students will learn that AIDS is a serious, often fatal disease that is acquired by coming in contact with the body fluids of a person with AIDS or a person who carries the virus that produces AIDS.

AIDS
Acquired Immune Deficiency Syndrome

E. Basic Facts and Supplemental Information:

1. Many people carry the AIDS virus without any symptoms of AIDS.
2. AIDS is spreading but it is far from being an epidemic. It is pandemic.
3. Education and proper precautions could reduce the number of AIDS victims.
4. AIDS reduces the body's immune system and consequently, even slight infections of any kind can be fatal.
5. AIDS strikes multiple systems of the body, not just one organ or area.
6. Body fluids such as tears, sweat, and saliva do not carry significant amounts of HIV and therefore, are not considered to be a means of transportation.
7. Only when the virus is transmitted across normal barriers and enters into the bloodstream does infection occur.
8. HIV can be contracted through sexual contact with an infected person.

F. Thought Questions for Class Discussions:

1. How do you feel about children with AIDS?
2. How can we help AIDS victims?
3. Why do you think AIDS is spreading?

G. Related Ideas for Further Inquiry:

1. A doctor's talk to the class is the best authoritative education.
2. Ask school nurse to speak to the class about AIDS.
3. Study all Activities in Part V, "Health."

H. Vocabulary Builders—Spelling Words:

1) **AIDS** 2) **acquired** 3) **immune** 4) **deficiency** 5) **syndrome** 6) **fluids**

I. Thought for Today:

"Some people should be in the Olympics the way they jump to conclusions."

Activity

A. Problem: *What Are Venereal Diseases?*

B. Materials Needed:

Books, pamphlets, pictures, charts, and/or multisensory aids about venereal diseases

C. Procedure:

The teacher must use professional judgment in presenting whatever factual material he/she feels is suitable for the levels and the maturity of the students. If he/she feels uncomfortable with this subject, perhaps the school nurse could present appropriate information to the class.

1. Relate the following information:
   a. Venereal diseases have to do with the genitals (reproductive organs) and are contracted through sexual intercourse.
   b. Syphilis is caused by bacteria called *Spirochetes.*
   c. Genital herpes is a viral disease that has infected about 20,000,000 Americans. There is no known cure!
   d. Gonorrhea is a bacterial infection. It can cause sterility, arthritis, and heart problems. It has infected about 2,000,000 persons. Penicillin has been effective in treatment, but new strains of this bacteria are building up a resistance to it.
   e. Chlamydia is also a bacterial infection and is the most prevalent of all sexually transmitted diseases (STDs).
   f. Papilloma, another STD, appears as warts in the genital area. Papilloma is also called "venereal warts."
   9. AIDS also must be included as a venereal disease because it can be transmitted through sexual contact with an infected person.
   h. There are many ways that people try to prevent pregnancies but all involve risks of pregnancies and/or diseases.
2. Have the students study printed materials about venereal diseases.
3. If multisensory aids are available, use them with discrimination.

D. Result:

Students will learn about venereal diseases; they are transmitted sexually, and they can be deadly.

E. Basic Facts and Supplemental Information:

1. It is estimated that 10% of our population suffers from venereal diseases. They are the second most common communicable diseases.

2. Venereal diseases are all very serious diseases.
3. The most common age group for venereal diseases is between 14 and 30.

F. Thought Questions for Class Discussions:

1. Do you think the risk involved of contracting a serious venereal disease is worth taking?
2. Do you think if people knew the truth about venereal diseases that so many of them would take the risk of becoming infected?
3. When you get married, wouldn't you like to know that your spouse has never been infected with a venereal disease?

G. Related Ideas for Further Inquiry:

1. Ask a doctor to talk to the class about venereal diseases. This is too important an area not to educate our young people with some basic information.
2. Show visual aids or drawings of the bacteria and viruses which cause venereal diseases.
3. Study Activity III-A-1, "How do we classify living things?"
4. Study Activity V-E-3, "How can we test for microorganisms?"
5. Study Activity V-E-4, "What is AIDS?"

H. Vocabulary Builders—Spelling Words:

1) **syphilis** 2) **herpes** 3) **gonorrhea**
4) **chlamydia** 5) **contracted** 6) **venereal**

I. Thought for Today:

"A dollar sign has been described as a capital S which has been double-crossed."

SECTION F: FIRST AID

Activity V F 1

A. Problem: *What Are the Main Procedures for Treating Injuries and/or Accidents?*

B. Materials Needed:

1. Compresses
2. Tourniquets
3. Vaseline
4. Bactine
5. Disinfectant
6. *The American National Red Cross First Aid Book*
7. Adhesive tape
8. Soap
9. Band-Aids
10. Cotton swabs
11. Roller bandages
12. First aid kit

C. Procedure:

The teacher, doctor, school nurse, or a qualified first aid instructor could:

1. Have students list the ways that they have seen people injured.
2. Discuss what was done in each of these cases.
3. Demonstrate the proper kind of first aid in each instance using the items cited in Materials Needed.
4. Discuss other injuries and discomforts that people have suffered.
5. Discuss the order of treating patients with multiple first aid problems.

D. Results:

1. Students should learn what steps to take until help arrives in cases of:
   a. foreign object in the eye
   b. fainting
   c. convulsions
   d. overdose of medication
   e. burns
   f. poisons
   g. drowning
   h. insect bites
   i. scratches, cuts, wounds
   j. bruises
   k. epileptic seizures
   l. nosebleed
   m. bleeding
   n. choking
2. Students will develop skills in treating minor injuries.

E. Basic Facts and Supplemental Information:

1. Stress the fact that first aid is only a temporary treatment until professional medical help is available.

How would you help a person who has fainted?

2. In case of drowning and loss of breathing, mouth-to-mouth resuscitation should be taught. A plastic square with a hole cut in the center can be used to teach this technique.
3. Encourage students to take a course in first aid. A local Red Cross chapter could furnish information about these classes. *First aid training can save lives!*
4. Students should learn the Heimlich maneuver for choking accidents.
5. CPR (cardiopulmonary resuscitation) should be in everyone's repertoire.

F. Thought Questions for Class Discussions:

1. Which of the problems listed in Results is most serious and should be administered to first?
2. Can fire and police personnel help in administering first aid?
3. What is the role of paramedics?

G. Related Ideas for Further Inquiry:

1. Ask a member of the fire department or local paramedic unit to discuss first aid procedures.
2. Take a field trip with selected students to visit a hospital's emergency facility.
3. Study Activity V-F-2, "How can breathing be restored in drowning or shock?"
4. Study Activity V-F-3, "How can severe bleeding be stopped?"
5. Study Activity V-F-4, "What is CPR (cardiopulmonary resuscitation)?"
6. Study other Activities in this Section.

H. Vocabulary Builders—Spelling Words:

1) **first aid** 2) **compresses** 3) **tourniquet** 4) **sterile** 5) **fainting** 6) **burns** 7) **abrasions** 8) **(other terms in Results)**

I. Thought for Today:

"The life of the party may be death on the highway."

Activity V F 2

A. Problem: *How Can Breathing Be Restored in Case of Drowning or Shock?*

B. Materials Needed:

1. Student volunteers
2. Handkerchiefs
3. Plastic squares
4. *The American National Red Cross First Aid Book*

C. Procedure:

The teacher, doctor, school nurse, and/or members of the fire department rescue squad could conduct the following activity:

1. Discuss ways that breathing might be stopped or impaired: drowning, poisonous gases, shock, choking, etc.
2. Discuss different ways that artificial respiration has been done in the past (rolling over logs, holding legs up, etc.). Death comes quickly if air doesn't get into the lungs.
3. Demonstrate mouth-to-mouth resuscitation as the preferred method.
   a. Start as quickly as possible.
   b. Bend neck back, keeping one hand under the neck.
   c. Pinch nose and keep it closed.
   d. Cover mouth with handkerchief or plastic square with hole in it. (In real cases, must use mouth directly if no cover is available.)
   e. Take a deep breath and blow into victim's mouth. (If you cannot, blow into victim's nose.)
   f. On a small child, blow into both nose and mouth.
   g. After blowing in, remove your mouth and listen for air exhalation.
   h. Repeat about 12 times a minute for adults, 20 times a minute for children.
   i. Keep respiration going until breathing is restored or there is no possibility of recovery.

D. Results:

1. Students will learn how to do mouth-to-mouth resuscitation.
2. Students will gain confidence in the effectiveness of this procedure.

E. Basic Facts and Supplemental Information:

1. A doctor, fire department personnel, or paramedics should be summoned as quickly as possible in an emergency.

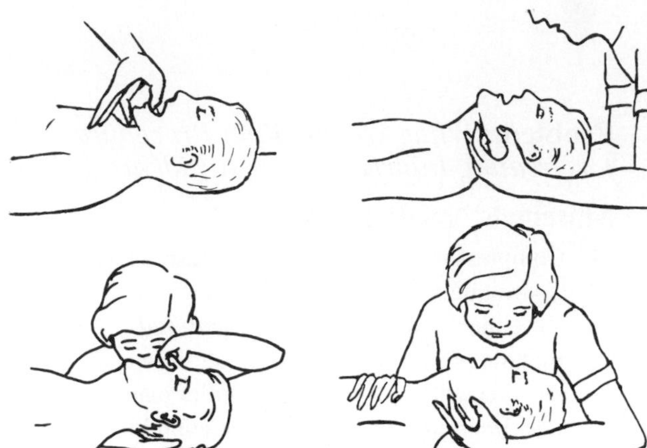

2. Cardiopulmonary resuscitation (CPR) should also be taught to older students. Everyone should learn this technique.
3. Many needless deaths occur because no one has administered artificial respiration or CPR effectively and soon enough.

F. Thought Questions for Class Discussions:

1. Should anyone ever swim alone?
2. What would cause someone to be in a state of shock?
3. If a person is not breathing and is bleeding, which of these symptoms should be taken care of first?

G. Related Ideas for Further Inquiry:

1. Doctors, nurses, and paramedics can present this Activity effectively.
2. Check with the Red Cross for appropriate pamphlets.
3. Study Activity V-A-2, "How do our lungs work?"
4. Study Activity V-F-4, "What is CPR (cardiopulmonary resuscitation)?"
5. Study Activity V-F-6, "What can you do if a person is choking?"
6. Study other Activities in this Section.

H. Vocabulary Builders—Spelling Words:

1) **breathing** 2) **drowning** 3) **resuscitation** 4) **artificial** 5) **victim** 6) **mouth-to-mouth**

I. Thought for Today:

"A young person is a theory; an old person is a fact."—Ed Howe

Activity

V F 3

A. Problem: *How Can Severe Bleeding Be Stopped?*

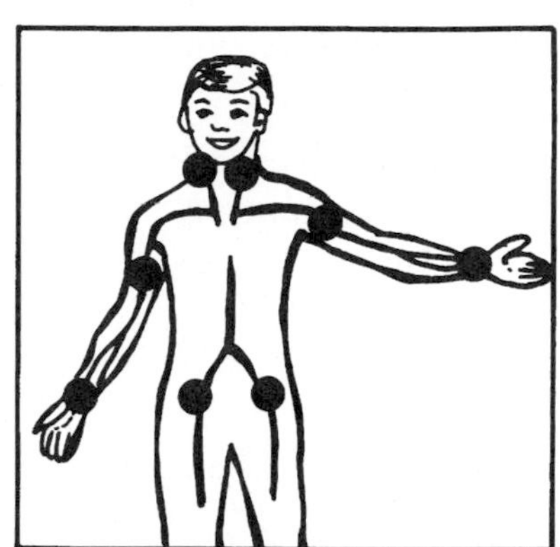

Pressure points to help stop severe bleeding (areas where blood vessels are close to skin)

B. Materials Needed:

1. Sterile bandages
2. Ruler or stick
3. Reference materials on bleeding
4. Multisensory aids about first aid

C. Procedure:

1. Cite a hypothetical injury and ask students what they would do to help the victim.
2. Instruct them how to make and use a tourniquet and how to apply sterile compresses to stop severe bleeding. (A tourniquet is a bandage twisted with a stick to stop bleeding.)
3. Teach them the following key points:
   a. Arterial blood will spurt; venous blood will ooze or run steadily.
   b. Tourniquets are used primarily for severe arterial wounds on arms or legs and applied between the heart and the wound. If a tourniquet is applied, care by a doctor is imperative.
   c. Sterile compresses are used for all other types of bleeding.
   d. It is important to keep bandages from sticking to wounds.
   e. A puncture wound should be allowed to bleed to cleanse the wound, if the bleeding is not excessive.
   f. Cleanliness is extremely important.
4. Discuss the nature of blood flow and the reasons why blood will clot.
5. Students should be given the opportunity to use tourniquets and compresses. *Caution:* Do not allow tourniquet to stop flow of blood to any area for more than a very brief time. See item 3.b. above.

D. Result:

Students will learn the correct methods of stopping bleeding.

E. Basic Facts and Supplemental Information:

1. Stopping loss of blood when excessive bleeding occurs may save a life.
2. Almost all areas of the body can be self-treated in an emergency.

F. Thought Questions for Class Discussions:

1. What are pressure points?
2. Why should compresses be sterile?
3. Should tourniquets be placed above or below the wound for arterial bleeding? For venous bleeding? Why? How can you tell the difference?

G. Related Ideas for Further Inquiry:

1. Visit a pharmacy for possible first aid supplies.
2. Talk to doctors about first aid.
3. Study Activity V-A-4, "How does the heart work?"

H. Vocabulary Builders—Spelling Words:

1) **bleeding** 2) **compresses** 3) **tourniquet**
4) **vein** 5) **artery** 6) **sterile** 7) **bandages**

I. Thought for Today:

"I seldom think of the future; it comes soon enough."

Activity V F 4

A. Problem: *What Is CPR (Cardiopulmonary Resuscitation)?*

B. Materials Needed:

1. Handouts on CPR
2. Mats
3. Blankets
4. Gauze
5. Bandages
6. Adhesive tape
7. Scissors
8. Soap

C. Procedure:

A doctor, nurse or qualified teacher is best able to present this lesson.

1. Under what conditions is CPR necessary?
2. Handout materials on CPR (Red Cross has great materials.)
3. Discuss with class the important steps to take before administering CPR.
   a. check for injuries
   b. immobilize injured parts immediately
   c. get victim to safe place
   d. send for help
4. Demonstrate CPR
   a. Place the heel of the hand on the lower half of the sternum (breastbone).
   b. Put the other hand on top of the first.
   c. Compress the lungs and sternum with 15 hard pushes about one every second, quickly followed by 2 quick lung inflations by mouth-to-mouth resuscitation.
   d. If you have a partner, give 5 heart compressions and then let your assistant follow with one deep lung inflation.
   e. Repeat these until normal breathing is restored or until medical examiner pronounces victim dead.
5. If time permits, demonstrate other first aid procedures that might be needed to accompany the cause of CPR administrations: wounds, shock, bruises, etc.

D. Result:

Students will learn how to apply cardiopulmonary resuscitation.

E. Basic Facts and Supplemental Information:

Remember A.B.C.

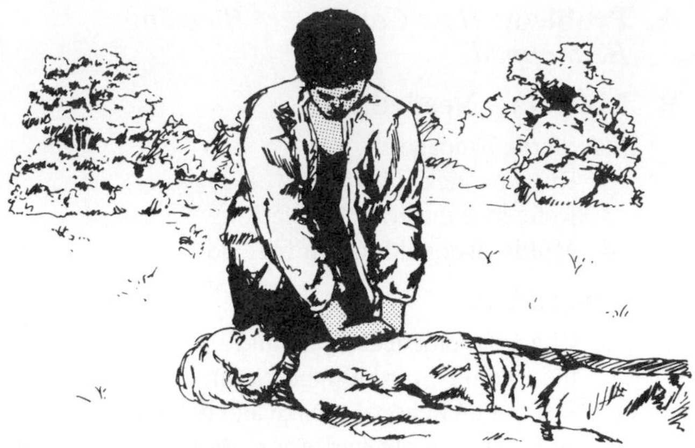

1. A Airways Clear airways of obstructions (false teeth, tongue, blood, vomit, etc.).
2. B Breathing Start mouth-to-mouth resuscitation. Breathe into victim's mouth every 5 seconds.
3. C Circulation Check pulse to see if CPR is needed.
4. This lifesaving technique is used for a wide range of emergencies such as cardiac arrest, drowning, choking, etc.
5. The two main symptoms indicating the need for CPR are that the person is unconscious or has stopped breathing. It could be both.
6. Treatment must begin immediately. Irreparable brain damage will occur in a few minutes, and death can happen in 8 to 10 minutes.
7. The most vital maneuver is to tilt the head back with the chin raised high to ensure an open airway.
8. On an infant, breathe into the child's mouth and nose while alternating compression of the chest.

F. Thought Questions for Class Discussions:

1. How many lifesaving techniques do you know?
2. How important is time in starting breathing?
3. Which is more important, to start the breathing or to stop the bleeding?

G. Related Ideas for Further Inquiry:

1. Have students do research on CPR.
2. Have the pupils practice CPR frequently; the timing is easily forgotten.
3. Study other Activities in this Section.

H. Vocabulary Builders—Spelling Words:

1) **cardiopulmonary** 2) **resuscitation** 3) **victim** 4) **sternum** 5) **palms** 6) **rhythm** 7) **damage**

I. Thought for Today:

"An apology is a good way to have the last word."

Activity V F 5

A. Problem: *Why Do We Use Medicines and Pills?*

B. Materials Needed:

1. Empty medicine bottles
2. Empty pill containers
3. Samples of first aid supplies

C. Procedure:

1. Discuss reasons why medicines, drugs, and pills are prescribed by doctors.
2. Review common accidents that require some medicinal aid.
3. Discuss common diseases that require appropriate medical help such as infections from:
   a. bacteria (cocci, staphylococci, streptococci)
   b. fungi (yeast, molds, etc.)
   c. protozoans, etc.
   d. viruses: Common viral infections include the common cold, influenza, herpes, and shingles.
4. Tell the students about some over-the-counter medications and pills (those that do not require prescriptions) that could be misused and cause harmful effects.
5. Review Activity V-E-3, "How can we test for microorganisms?"
6. Show the class some simple first aid procedures in which nonprescription medicines can be used:
   a. simple cuts
   b. small splinters or slivers
   c. cold sores

D. Results:

1. Students will learn that only doctors can prescribe potent medicines and pills for serious accidents and major diseases.
2. Students will begin to recognize the differences between serious and nonserious health problems.

E. Basic Facts and Supplemental Information:

1. On the skin, there are many bacteria that grow and multiply.
2. Wounds should be disinfected to kill bacteria which otherwise would enter the wound and cause infection.
3. It is wise to avoid using medication unless prescribed by your doctor.
4. Some pills do more harm than good.

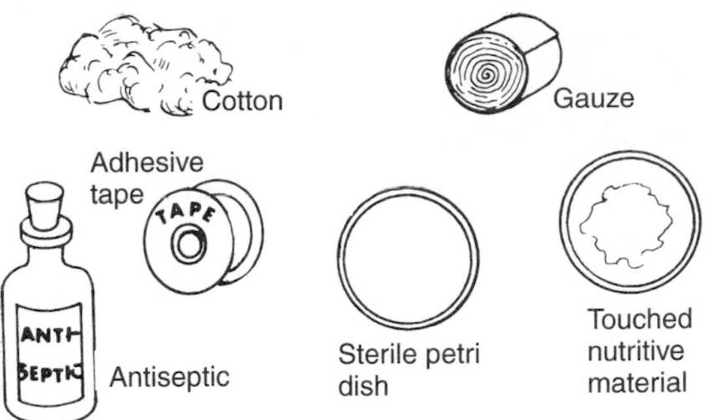

5. Some pills are addictive or cause problems.
   a. Aspirin—can cause ulcers and also bleeding in sensitive people
   b. Codeine
   c. Some nasal sprays
6. Frequent use of mouthwash may kill good as well as bad bacteria. The good bacteria are our first line of defense against infection.
7. Most diet pills don't work. They reduce the water content of the body, thus giving people a psychological lift because of water weight loss.
8. There are over 100,000 over-the-counter drugs and pills. No one knows for sure how they will interact with other body chemicals.

F. Thought Questions for Class Discussions:

1. What would happen if your finger were touched to a Petri dish and an antiseptic was added over the touched area of the Petri dish?
2. What are some good antiseptic agents?
3. What are bacteria? Are they all bad?

G. Related Ideas for Further Inquiry:

1. Have the school doctor, school nurse, or local pharmacist speak to the class about prescription drugs and medicines.
2. Study Activity V-D-9, "Are illicit drugs bad for our health?"
3. Study other Activities in this Section.

H. Vocabulary Builders—Spelling Words:

1) **medicine** 2) **drugs** 3) **pills** 4) **bacteria** 5) **antiseptic** 6) **sterilize** 7) **Petri dish** 8) **viruses**

I. Thought for Today:

"Trying to squash a rumor is like trying to unring a bell."

Activity V F 6

The "Heimlich Maneuver"

A. Problem: *What Can You Do If a Person Is Choking?*

B. Materials Needed:

Pictures of the Heimlich maneuver

C. Procedure:

1. Discuss foods, eating, and proper chewing of foods.
2. Ask students if anyone has ever had any food caught in his or her throat.
3. Have them describe the incident.
4. Teach students the Heimlich maneuver for removing food caught in someone's throat by showing them the procedures and then having them practice on each other.
5. Teach them the following steps:
   a. First, have the victim try to cough.
   b. Second, strike the victim firmly between the shoulder blades with the heel of your hand 4 times. This usually eliminates the problem before the maneuver is used.
   c. If unsuccessful, then use the Heimlich maneuver:
      1) Stand in back of victim, both facing the same direction.
      2) Grasp victim *firmly* with both hands over the diaphragm (just above the navel).
      3) Pull back and up *firmly* several times.
      4) Repeat if necessary.
      5) Don't worry about hurting the person; if food particle is not dislodged immediately, he/she can suffocate within minutes.
      6) If the victim is a very young child, hold the child upside down by the ankles. Open the child's mouth and pull the victim's tongue forward. Strike the child *firmly* between the shoulder blades.
      7) If breathing is restored but the food particle is not dislodged, get the child to a doctor immediately. The particle may have settled in the lungs.
      8) Call 911 (local emergency number).

D. Results:

1. Students will learn some emergency techniques for choking relief.
2. Students will also learn that choking could be a death-producing accident.

E. Basic Facts and Supplemental Information:

1. In the Heimlich maneuver, each thrust should be made as if you are trying to lift the victim *off the ground.*
2. If you are alone and choking, you can use the following procedure:
   a. Place your fist above your navel.
   b. Give a quick upward thrust, or bounce the front of your body over the back of a chair.
3. With a pregnant woman or a very flabby person, lay the person down, face up, place your hands below the rib cage, and make upward thrusts.

F. Thought Questions for Class Discussions:

1. Do you think that lying on the bed or with head near the floor would help? (old technique)
2. Is time an important factor in administering these first aid techniques?
3. In serious cases, after dislodging the obstruction, do you think a doctor should be consulted?

G. Related Ideas for Further Inquiry:

1. Study Activity V-A-5, "How do we digest food?"
2. Study Activity V-C-1, "What would be a perfect menu for a day?"
3. Study Activity V-F-4, "What is CPR (cardiopulmonary resuscitation)?"
4. Study other Activities in this Section.

H. Vocabulary Builders—Spelling Words:

1) **Heimlich** 2) **maneuver** 3) **choking** 4) **firmly** 5) **diaphragm** 6) **thrust** 7) **dislodge**

I. Thought for Today:

"I can prove anything by statistics except the truth."

Activity V F 7

A. Problem: *What Should You Do If Someone Has Taken a Poisonous Substance Internally?*

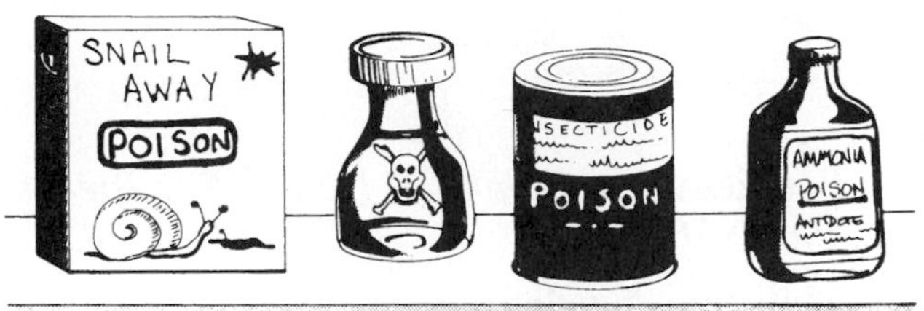

B. Materials Needed:

1. Pictures of common poisons
2. Empty containers of poisonous substances (insect sprays, tainted foods, household cleaners, etc.)

C. Procedure:

1. Discuss potential poisons found around the home: kitchen, garage, bathroom, etc.
2. Discuss some effects of taking poisonous substances internally.
3. Discuss procedures to be used in various cases such as:
   a. If poison is known, give antidote. (Many bottles are labeled and prescribe antidote.)
   b. If poison is known, call doctor (or Poison Control Center) and tell what poison has been taken.
   c. If medical aid is unavailable, or if the poison and the antidote are not known, give the victim several glasses of milk or water to dilute the poison, and *do not induce vomiting.*
   d. Also, *do not induce vomiting* if the victim has swallowed lighter fluid, drain cleaner, paint thinner, or other corrosive substances. If possible, have the victim swallow some olive oil or a glass of warm water, and rush the victim to nearest doctor or hospital for emergency treatment.
   e. If the poison taken is not acid, alkali, or a petroleum product (gasoline, etc.) then vomiting is encouraged.
   f. To induce vomiting, insert finger down throat (back of tongue) or drink salt water (one teaspoonful in one-half glass of water).
   g. If victim goes into shock (slowing of the flow of blood around the body, peripheral circulation):
      1) Have victim lie down.
      2) Lower victim's head to get blood to the brain.
      3) Keep victim warm.

D. Result:

Students will learn about poisons and their antidotes and treatment.

E. Basic Facts and Supplemental Information:

1. Acids should be neutralized with baking soda in a glass of water or milk of magnesia.
2. Alkalines should be neutralized with several teaspoonfuls of lemon juice, teas, or vinegar, followed with milk or four egg whites.
3. One way of preventing accidents by poisons would be to keep them out of the house and out of the reach of small children.
4. Certain medicines or drugs may be seriously harmful or lethal if taken in too large doses.

F. Thought Questions for Class Discussions:

1. How can we protect ourselves from poisonous substances?
2. Do you think "dilute and wash out" are two cardinal rules for first aid in accidents with poison?
3. Should poisonous substances be used to get rid of unwanted animals? insects? spiders? rodents?

G. Related Ideas for Further Inquiry:

1. Study about carbon monoxide, a very poisonous gas.
2. Have a person from the local Poison Control Center address the class.
3. Study Section I-B, "Air."
4. Study Section V-G, "Safety."
5. Study other Activities in this Section.

H. Vocabulary Builders—Spelling Words:

1) **poison** 2) **vomit** 3) **induce**
4) **potential** 5) **shock** 6) **precautions**

I. Thought for Today:

"The person who knows how will always have a job. The person who knows why will be the boss."

Section G: Safety

Activity V G 1

A. Problem: *What Should I Do If a Fire Breaks Out in My Home?*

B. Materials Needed:

1. Pictures of fires
2. Newspaper accounts of fires

C. Procedures:

1. Ask students if any of them has ever been in a fire.
2. Ask them for details.
3. Describe some precautions you should take in case a fire breaks out in your home.
   a. Leave the room immediately.
   b. Close the door behind you (prevents smoke and fire from spreading quickly).
   c. Alert parents and everyone else in the home.
   d. If fire is large, leave home, call the telephone operator and report the fire. Most areas have a 911 emergency number. Check your locality for its emergency number. All students should know this number by heart.
4. If student lives in a condo or upstairs apartment:
   a. Roll out of bed (if at night).
   b. Contact parents and others in the building.
   c. Phone for help if needed and unreported.
   d. Get out quickly.
   e. If hallway is blocked:
      1) Hang sheet out of window:
         a) quick sign of trouble inside
         b) if secured to a stationary object, can be used as an emergency "rope."
      2) Turn on exhaust fan.
      3) Fill bathtub with water.
      4) Get fresh air (open outside windows).

D. Result:

Students will learn some emergency fire procedures.

E. Basic Facts and Supplemental Information:

1. Students should know:
   a. all the escape routes from their residence
   b. emergency telephone numbers
2. More people are lost in fires because they panic.
3. There is always a chance for survival if people stay calm and *think.*
4. All homes should be equipped with fire and smoke alarms and these should be routinely checked to be sure that they are in good working condition.

F. Thought Questions for Class Discussions:

1. Where is the freshest air in a smoke-filled room?
2. Where should fire and smoke alarms be placed?
3. What good does an exhaust fan do?
4. Is the fire department's phone number easily accessible?

G. Related Ideas for Further Inquiry:

1. Have a firefighter talk to class.
2. Make a fire prevention inspection of your home.
3. Study Part II-B, "Fire and Heat."
4. Study other Activities in this Section.

H. Vocabulary Builders—Spelling Words:

1) **fire** 2) **emergency** 3) **panic** 4) **survival** 5) **parents** 6) **escape** 7) **alarm** 8) **equipped**

I. Thought for Today:

"A real home is more than just a roof over your head—it's a foundation under your feet."

Activity

V G 2

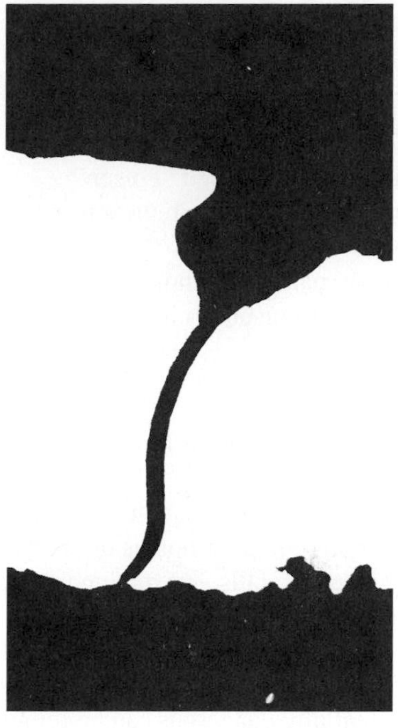

A. Problem: *What Should I Do in Case of an Earthquake or Tornado?*

B. Materials:

1. Pictures of damages done by earthquakes and tornados
2. Newspaper accounts of such damage
3. Demonstration materials

C. Procedure:

(Select items appropriate for age level.)

1. Stress the scout motto, "Be Prepared."
2. Teach students things they should know before an emergency, such as:
   a. how to turn off gas, water, and electricity
   b. first aid
   c. plans for reuniting family in case of separation
3. Have students compile a list of emergency (survival) items to keep on hand such as:
   a. flashlight
   b. portable radio
   c. extra batteries
   d. first aid book
   e. fire extinguisher
   f. emergency phone list
   g. tools for turning off utilities
   h. emergency food and water supplies
   i. nonelectric can opener
4. Teach the students what to do after an emergency strikes, such as:
   a. try to locate all family members
   b. check for injuries
   c. provide first aid if necessary
   d. check utilities for possible damage
   e. turn on radio to get information and instructions
   f. use telephone for emergency use only (others may need it desperately)
5. Discuss with students what they should be doing during the emergency:
   a. for earthquakes:
      1) Stay calm.
      2) If inside, stand in doorway or get under a table or desk away from the windows.
      3) If outside, stay away from buildings, tall trees, utility lines.
   b. for tornados:
      1) Stay calm.
      2) If inside, go into basement if you have one; otherwise, get under a desk, table, or sturdy object away from windows.
      3) If outside, stay low, keep away from anything that might be uprooted or moved.

D. Result:

Students will be prepared for any emergency caused by an earthquake or tornado.

E. Basic Facts and Supplemental Information:

Gas leaks are the most dangerous aftereffects. If gas has been shut off, don't restart unless positive that no problem exists.

F. Thought Questions for Class Discussions:

1. What government workers could help in case of one of these emergencies?
2. What dangerous items might be overlooked in an emergency?
3. Are most earthquakes centered on the surface of the Earth?

G. Related Ideas for Further Inquiry:

1. Study Activity VII-C-3, "What causes earthquakes?"
2. Have people who have been through an emergency talk to the students.
3. Have someone from the Red Cross talk to the students about emergencies.
4. Study other Activities in this Section.

H. Vocabulary Builders—Spelling Words:

1) **earthquake** 2) **survival** 3) **injuries**
4) **precautions** 5) **first aid** 6) **tornado**

I. Thought for Today:

"Nothing makes it easier to resist temptation than a proper bringing up, a sound set of values—and witnesses."

Activity VG3

A. Problem: *How Safe Are Our Homes?*

B. Materials Needed:

1. Empty bottles labeled "Poison"
2. Empty miscellaneous bottles from the medicine cabinet
3. Cooking pan with handle
4. Pictures of poisonous insect spray cans
5. Oily rags, etc.

C. Procedure:

1. Have students discuss how they have been hurt around the house.
2. Have students discuss how others have been injured around their homes by such accidents as burns, scalds, falls, fire, taking unprescribed medicines, etc.
3. Have each student become a "Home Health and Safety Inspector" for a day to see if anything that is potentially dangerous can be found.
4. Discuss the possible results of carelessness around the home.
5. Discuss the benefit of smoke and heat detector alarms in the home.
6. Discuss ways that homes can be made safe from burglars: alarm systems, watch dogs, dead bolts, precautions you would take when leaving for a vacation, etc.

D. Result:

Students will become more aware of hazards around the home and the consequences if left uncorrected.

E. Basic Facts and Supplemental Information:

1. Accidents around the home are one of the leading causes of deaths and severe injuries of young children.
2. There are many potentially dangerous practices around the home:
   a. cooking pots with handles not turned toward center of burners.
   b. medicines, sprays, insecticides within easy reach of children.
   c. anywhere there are fires or heat is a potential danger area: fireplace, stove, kerosene-type heater, water heater, furnace, etc.
3. Unfortunately, crime is on the increase, and students should be made aware of not only crime prevention but also what they might do to help prevent such incidents.

F. Thought Questions for Class Discussions:

1. How can our homes be made safer?
2. How can our homes be made healthier?
3. What are other potentially dangerous areas in our homes? garages? cars? yards?

G. Related Ideas for Further Inquiry:

1. Have students make a list of items in the home that can be used for emergencies such as:
   a. first aid kit
   b. fire extinguisher
   c. flashlight
   d. portable radio
   e. shut-off valves
   f. circuit breakers
   g. food and water supply
2. Have students discuss how their homes are prepared for emergencies such as fire, floods, hurricanes, earthquakes, tornadoes, etc.
3. Ask students what they would do immediately following each of the above disasters.
4. Have each student make a list of phone numbers to be used in an emergency, including 911 if that is an emergency number in your area.

H. Vocabulary Builders—Spelling Words:

1) **safety** 2) **inspector** 3) **health** 4) **poison** 5) **alarm** 6) **drinking** 7) **scalds** 8) **accidents**

I. Thought for Today:

"Some of our schools have gone modern. The kids who once cleaned erasers now dust the computers."

Activity

A. Problem: *How Can I Be Safe in the Water If I Get Tired?*

B. Materials Needed:

1. Glass aquarium
2. Inexpensive flexible doll

C. Procedure:

1. Discuss some of the dangers of:
   a. boating
   b. swimming
   c. wading
   d. surfing
   e. undertows
   f. scuba diving
2. Discuss the human body in a water environment:
   a. buoyancy
   b. motion
   c. relaxation
   d. breathing
3. Survey the class to find out how many can swim and how far.
4. Fill the aquarium with water.
5. With the flexible doll, demonstrate the Survival Floating Technique:
   a. Try to get lungs full of air.
   b. Place head in water and let feet and arms and head hang down.
   c. When air is needed, push hands down and raise head above water.
   d. When air is obtained, return to initial position.
6. Have students stand up and go through motions.

D. Results:

1. Students will learn this survival technique.
2. Students will become aware of some of the dangers in pools, lakes, coastal waters, etc.

E. Basic Facts and Supplemental Information:

1. Most drownings involve young children who cannot swim.
2. This technique could save thousands of lives each year if children knew how to keep afloat until help arrives.
3. The Red Cross has printed material about this technique. See or obtain their Swimming and Water Safety manual.
4. Younger children who don't know how to swim should be encouraged to learn how to swim using proper breathing procedures.
5. Older children and teenagers should be encouraged to learn some basic water lifesaving techniques.

F. Thought Questions for Class Discussions:

1. How long can a person live without air?
2. What factors determine how long a person could live in water: salt, temperature, etc.?
3. What are some ways to prevent drownings?
4. Do you think the "buddy system" is a good idea for playing in and around swimming areas?

G. Related Ideas for Further Inquiry:

1. Have students discuss accidents they know of which happened in a pool, lake, river, or ocean.
2. If possible, have a lifeguard speak to the class about his/her experiences in saving lives.
3. Discuss safety around the pool: jumping or diving in too close to others, playing on diving boards, running around the pool.
4. Teach artificial respiration.
5. Study Activity V-F-1, "What are the main procedures for treating injuries and/or accidents?"
6. Study other Activities in this Section.

H. Vocabulary Builders—Spelling Words:

1) **survival** 2) **buoyancy** 3) **breathing**
4) **relaxation** 5) **technique** 6) **swimming**
7) **safety** 8) **precautions** 9) **lifesaving**

I. Thought for Today:

"When I see a child, he inspires me in two sentiments: tenderness for what he is, and respect for what he may become."—Louis Pasteur

PART VI
ECOLOGY

SECTION A: ECOSYSTEMS

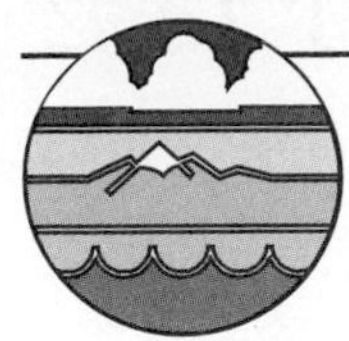

Activity VI A 1

A. Problem: *What Is the Balance of Nature?*

B. Materials Needed: (on Ecology)

1. Books
2. Magazines
3. Newspaper accounts
4. Pictures
5. Animal cut-outs
6. Drawing supplies

C. Procedure:

1. Discuss ecosystems (biotic communities and their environments).
2. Describe several biotic communities (the interrelationships of all living things).
3. Discuss some of the ecosystems that include humans.
4. Describe some of the limitations of environments:
   a. temperature
   b. food supplies
   c. oxygen
   d. water
   e. land types, soil
5. Discuss the possible outlook when all animal life would be drastically reduced and human populations would double.
6. Discuss the terms "food chain" and "food web."
   a. Food chain—consists of a direct line of energy transfer from the:
      1) sun to plant (producer) to
      2) herbivore to
      3) primary consumer to
      4) secondary consumer to
      5) tertiary or final consumer.
   b. Food web—consists of all the possibilities of food sources and their interrelationships.
7. Students should draw charts of food chains and food webs that they have studied either at school or at home.

D. Results:

1. Students will learn about biotic communities and ecosystems.
2. Students will discover that as animal populations expand, plant foods decrease.

E. Basic Facts and Supplemental Information:

1. Ecosystems are "balanced" when the numbers of plants and animals remain about the same and the physical environment is relatively stable.
2. Most plants and animals can adapt to minor changes in the physical environment.
3. Many species of animals have become extinct because their ecosystems were dramatically changed in one way or another.

Plants, animals, and the physical environment

4. Many more species are in danger of becoming extinct.
5. The two terms, "biotic community" and "ecosystem," are going to become increasingly important in the language of all people especially with the pressure of growing populations and the corresponding reductions of food supplies per person is realized.

F. Thought Questions for Class Discussions:

1. Do we change ecosystems when we spray with strong insecticides?
2. Are there any animals that are 100% bad?
3. What changes will there be in the food web if our human population doubles?

G. Related Ideas for Further Inquiry:

1. Study your local school community as an "ecosystem."
2. Study Activity VI-A-2, "What is 'biological diversity'?"
3. Study Activity VI-A-3, "Do we belong to an ecosystem?"
4. Study Activity VI-A-6, "What are food chains? food webs?"
5. Study Activity VI-A-10, "What are wetlands?"
6. Study Activity VI-A-11, "Are any animals threatened with extinction?"

H. Vocabulary Builders—Spelling Words:

1) **biological** 2) **balance** 3) **nature** 4) **ecosystem** 5) **herbivores** 6) **consumers** 7) **food** 8) **web**

I. Thought for Today:

"When we were in school the hard stuff meant algebra."

Activity VI A 2

A. Problem: *What Is "Biological Diversity"?*

B. Materials Needed:

1. Small planted area around the school campus
2. Reference materials on small animals
3. Notebooks
4. Drawing materials (pencils, paper, rulers, etc.)

C. Procedure:

1. Select a "plot" of land at or near school.
2. Have students make a rough drawing of the area.
3. Have students study the area for all forms of living organisms, such as:

a. insects	h. grasses
b. spiders	i. weeds
c. worms	j. flowers
d. bees	k. trees
e. flies	l. bushes
f. beetles	m. mosses
g. lizard(s)	n. butterflies

4. In their drawing, have students indicate where each organism was seen.
5. Have students look up the scientific name and/or common name of each.
6. Have students draw lines from one organism to another in which there was any kind of relationship. These might include:
   a. spider—fly (food)
   b. insect—grass (hiding) protection
   c. bees—flowers (pollenating)
7. Discuss other items of "biological diversity" and "interrelationships" of organisms.

D. Results:

1. Students will learn that there are many organisms that live within a very small area.
2. Students will become familiar with reference materials on classification.
3. Students will learn that all organisms have many interrelationships.

E. Basic Facts and Supplemental Information:

1. Taxonomists' estimates of the number of plant and animal species that exist on Earth vary from 3 million to 30 million.
2. Biological diversity (biodiversity) is the total variety of life on Earth.
3. Humans are the dominant species.
4. All the plants and animals that live together make up an ecosystem.

A variety of plants and animals

5. To be healthy, an ecosystem has to have many different kinds of species.
6. Species of plant and animal life are rapidly dwindling in the United States and the rest of the world.
7. Life is very complicated, interrelated, and mutually dependent.

F. Thought Questions for Class Discussions:

1. On what species are people very dependent?
2. What role does the physical environment play in maintaining organisms?
3. How have people disturbed other organisms?

G. Related Ideas for Further Inquiry:

1. Study Part III, "Plants."
2. Study Part IV "Animals."
3. Study the "biological diversity" that exists within:
   a. tundras
   b. savannahs
   c. grasslands
   d. deserts
   e. oceans
   f. temperate rain forests
   g. tropical rain forests
   h. wetlands
   i. arctic icepacks
   j. cities, etc.

H. Vocabulary Builders—Spelling Words:

1) **biological** 2) **diversity** 3) **species**
4) **interdependent** 5) **organisms** 6) **taxonomy**

I. Thought for Today:

"A mule makes no headway while he is kicking; neither does a person."

Activity VI A 3

A. Problem: *Do We Belong to an Ecosystem?*

B. Materials Needed:

1. Notebook paper
2. Pens
3. Pencils
4. Compasses (for drawing)

C. Procedure:

1. Describe what an ecosystem is: living and nonliving interrelationships.
2. Give several examples of ecosystems:
   a. lake or pond community
   b. farm community
   c. forest community
   d. desert community
3. Ask the class if they think they are part of an ecosystem now.
4. Have them draw four large concentric circles.
5. Label them from inside out:
   a. Classroom
   b. School Building
   c. School Grounds
   d. School Community
6. Ask them to fill in all elements that they can in each of these areas as shown in the drawing.

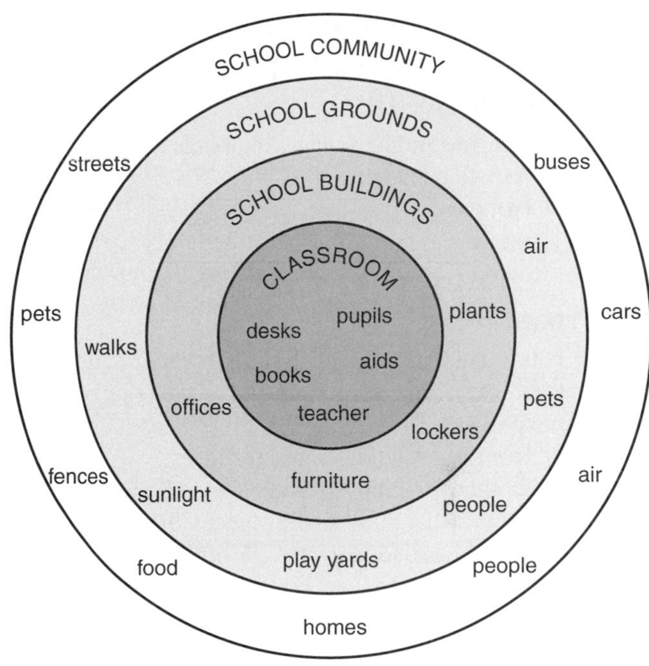

D. Results:

1. Students will realize that they are a part of many ecosystems.
2. They will realize that ecosystems consist of animals, plants, and things.

E. Basic Facts and Supplemental Information:

1. Individuals are one element in a complex web of living things in natural surroundings.
2. Every element that affects an individual whether living or nonliving is part of that individual's ecosystem.
3. No living organism lives in complete isolation from all others.
4. Plants and animals that live in the same habitat share the same air, water, ground, and climate as all others.
5. Without plants and animals, no human being can survive.
6. An "ecosystem" includes all plants and animals and the physical environment.
7. A "biological community" focuses only on the interrelationships of plants and animals.
8. This is an excellent activity for each student to begin to realize his/her place in nature and the interrelationships of all living and nonliving things.

F. Thought Questions for Class Discussions:

1. Can our homes be considered an ecosystem?
2. Can our planet be considered an ecosystem?
3. What is the difference between an ecosystem and a biological community?
4. Are the oxygen, nitrogen, water, and carbon cycles part of our ecosystem?
5. Are the sun, moon, and stars part of our ecosystem?

G. Related Ideas for Further Inquiry:

1. Have each student study the ecosystem of his/her home and local community.
2. Study Part III, "Plants," Part IV, "Animals," and Section VII-C, "Earth's Crust."
3. Study Activity VI-A-1, "What is the balance of nature?"
4. Study Activity VI-A-2, "What is 'biological diversity'?"

H. Vocabulary Builders—Spelling Words:

1) **ecosystem** 2) **biotic** 3) **community**
4) **nonliving** 5) **concentric** 6) **environment**

I. Thought for Today:

"Most of us would be better off financially if it weren't for the extravagances of our neighbors."

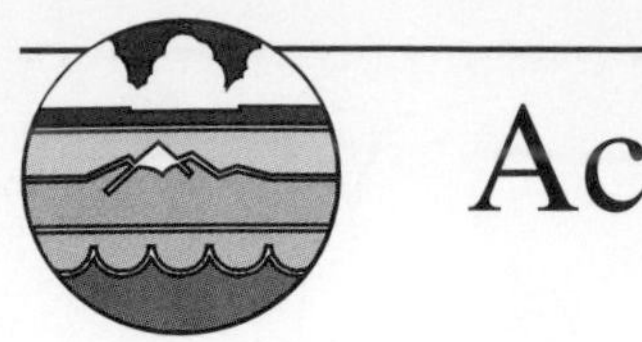

Activity VI A 4

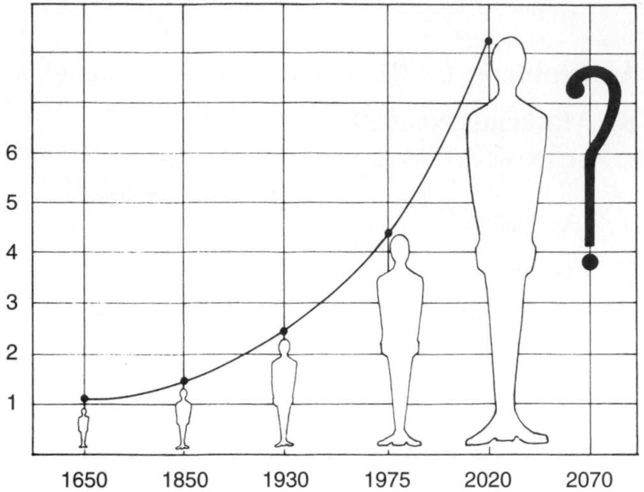

A. Problem: *Is the World's Population Growing Too Fast?*

B. Materials Needed:

1. Magazine and newspaper clippings about population statistics
2. Chart paper
3. Pencils
4. Rulers

C. Procedure:

1. Have students look at all the evidence, statistics, etc., they can collect in regard to the population explosion.
2. Chart these findings for the world.
3. Chart these findings for the United States.
4. Discuss what these findings mean in regard to medical care, food, water, power, schools, smog, pollution, wastes, etc.

D. Results:

1. Students will see that there is a fast and steady rise in population in the United States and throughout the world.
2. Students will realize that this added growth will create many new problems, particularly in the areas of food, fresh water, health care, education, and housing. Feeding more people with less farmland will be the number one problem in the future.

E. Basic Facts and Supplemental Information:

1. The world's population in 1975 was 4 billion.
2. The world's population is expected to reach 8 billion in the year 2020. It is now about 6 billion.
3. The United States is adding 2.4 million people to its population every year.
4. The world is adding 90 million more people to its population every year.
5. Since 1995 the amount of food per person has dropped, and more and more shortages are predicted as our population increases.
6. Vital Statistics world-wide:

Year	*Population*	*Time to Double*
6,000 B.C.	5,000,000	Doubled @
1650 A.D.	500,000,000	1200 yrs.
1850	1 billion	200 yrs.
1930	2 billion	80 yrs.
1975	4 billion	45 yrs.
2020	8 billion	45 yrs.
2900	100 people/sq. yd.	(estimated)

7. Even though the U.S. birthrate has dropped, there are still more women of childbearing age than old people; consequently, we are recording more births than deaths.
8. More people will produce more:
   a. dirty air
   b. fresh-water contamination
   c. urban sprawl
   d. loss of wildlife
   e. loss of farmland
   f. traffic congestion
   g. waste disposal problems, etc.

F. Thought Questions for Class Discussions:

1. Will there be enough food, water, and clean air for everyone in 2020?
2. Will there be beautiful rivers, forests, and wildlife in 2020?
3. Do you think there is enough space for all the people, world-wide?
4. Do we act the same in crowded areas as we do where there is plenty of space?

G. Related Ideas for Further Inquiry:

1. Study Activity VI-A-1, "What is the balance of nature?"
2. Study Activity VI-A-2, "What is 'biological diversity'?"
3. Study Activity VI-A-6, "What are food chains? food webs?"
4. Study other Activities in this Section.

H. Vocabulary Builders—Spelling Words:

1) **population** 2) **explosion** 3) **evidence** 4) **statistics** 5) **graph** 6) **starvation** 7) **double**

I. Thought for Today:

"The glory of young people is their strength; of old people, their experience."

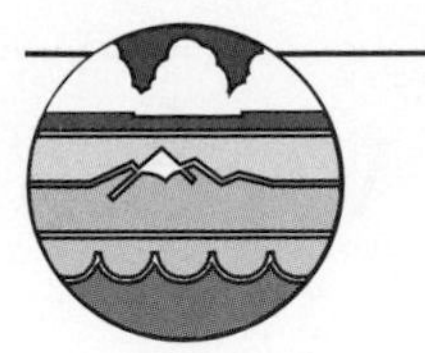

Activity VI A 5

A. Problem: *Is There Enough Food to Feed All the People in the World?*

B. Materials Needed:

1. Loaf of bread
2. Can of vegetables
3. Carton of milk
4. 10 dolls (or paper cutouts)

C. Procedure:

1. Set the food on the desk or table.
2. Set the 10 dolls in a row in front of the food.
3. Point out that the world is suffering from a food shortage problem and that 2 out of every 10 individuals will die of starvation. (Take away 2 dolls.)
4. Discuss some of the problems of producing, transporting, and distributing food to all peoples of the world.
5. Discuss the problems of being underfed and/or undernourished.
6. Point out that half of the people of the world do not get enough food or food of the right kind. (Many lack adequate protein.) Take away 5 of the remaining dolls.

D. Results:

1. Students will visualize dramatically that many people in the world are starving.
2. Many more people in the world are underfed and undernourished.
3. Students will begin to realize how lucky they are to be living in a country with no major food problems.

E. Basic Facts and Supplemental Information:

1. Every year about 18 million people starve to death or die because of poor health related to a lack of adequate food and related diseases. The average world-wide life expectancy is about 50 years. During any 50-year period, about one billion people will die from these causes. This amounts to one person in five or 20%. Consequently the removal of two dolls.
2. About two-thirds of the people of the world are barely existing as far as food is concerned.
3. At the present time there is enough food to feed the people of the world, but we are unable to provide adequate means for its distribution; consequently, many people are now suffering from undernourishment and malnutrition.
4. In the future, the food shortage problem will be increased because production of food will not increase as fast as the need of the world's increasing population.
5. While some teachers may feel this is too sensitive an activity to discuss, these are hard facts and the food problems are going to get worse. Hiding from facts is like the proverbial ostrich that buried its head in the sand. The maturity of the students should be the major criterion for the teacher in utilizing this activity.
6. Our supply of fresh water is becoming a real problem as well. There is a limited supply of fresh water, and if the population doubles within three or four decades, each person's water allotment will be halved. To make the situation even more alarming, we are contaminating much of our fresh-water supplies with sewage, agricultural wastes, and industrial runoffs. We can obtain fresh water by desalinization of ocean water, but it is a very expensive process.

F. Thought Questions for Class Discussions:

1. What will happen to our resources 45 years from now when the world's population is calculated to double?
2. What would you do to help people in poor countries who are starving to death? going hungry?
3. Should we be concerned about food shortages in other countries?
4. Should the United States help feed people in poor countries around the world?

G. Related Ideas for Further Inquiry:

1. Study Section V-C, "Nutrition."
2. Study Activity VI-A-1, "What is the balance of nature?"
3. Study other Activities in this Section.

H. Vocabulary Builders—Spelling Words:

1) **food** 2) **dolls** 3) **undernourishment**
4) **underfed** 5) **starvation** 6) **distributing**
7) **producing** 8) **transporting**

I. Thought for Today:

"Good manners are made up of petty sacrifices."

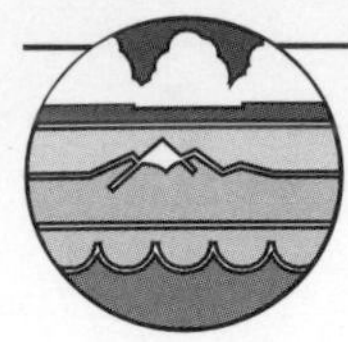

Activity VI A 6

A. Problem: *What Are Food Chains? Food Webs?*

B. Materials Needed:

1. Pictures of various edible plants
2. Pictures of various animals depicted in drawings
3. Reference books
4. Bulletin board or chalkboard

C. Procedure

1. Have students define the word "chain."
2. Have students describe what a "web" is.
3. Mount two sets of pictures on the bulletin board similar to those shown in drawings.
4. Define "food chain."
   A food chain is a series of living things linked together with each being food for the next. Two examples are:
   a. carrot—rabbit—wolf
   b. grass—cow—man
5. Define "food web."
   A food web consists of many organisms interrelated with many food sources and many possible eaters. The normal sequence is:
   a. producers (plants)
   b. herbivores (plant eaters)
   c. carnivores (animal eaters)
6. Have the students list as many examples of "food chains" and "food webs" as they can.

D. Results:

1. Students will be able to distinguish between the two terms "food chains" and "food webs."
2. Students will realize that all organisms depend on other organisms for food, with the exception of plants which are the "starting blocks."

E. Basic Facts and Supplemental Information:

1. All of our food and all of our energy originates from the sun.
2. All animals depend on plants for their source of food.
3. Transfer of food is really a transfer of energy.
4. Carnivores eat other animals that have eaten plants.

Food chain

Beavers	Bears	Otters
Frogs	Fish	Shrimp
Insects	Mollusks	Animal Plankton
Larvae	Plants	Plant Plankton

SIMPLE FOOD WEB

Any in higher level can feed on any in lower level.

F. Thought Questions for Class Discussions:

1. Where do human beings get their energy?
2. What is photosynthesis?
3. What role does oxygen play in food chains and food webs?

G. Related Ideas for Further Inquiry:

1. Have each student design a food chain in which he/she is involved.
2. Have each student design a food web in which he/she is involved.
3. Have each student try to list the longest food chain he/she can (the one with the most links).
4. Study Activity VI-A-1, "What is the balance of nature?"
5. Study Activity VI-A-2, "What is 'biological diversity'?"

H. Vocabulary Builders—Spelling Words:

1) **food chain** 2) **food web** 3) **links**
4) **organism** 5) **energy** 6) **edible**

I. Thought for Today:

"All of the animals except man know that the principal business of life is to enjoy it."

Activity VI A 7

A. Problem: *What Is the Water Cycle?*

B. Materials Needed:

Large sketch as shown in drawing

C. Procedure:

1. Discuss water:
   a. covers two-thirds of the Earth
   b. vital to life
   c. two-thirds of the human body is water
2. Discuss:
   a. water cycle (See C-3 below.)
   b. oxygen cycle
   c. carbon cycle
3. Discuss the details of the water cycle:
   a. evaporation from surface water
   b. collects on particles in the air
   c. condenses in air by cooling
   d. falls on land and water surfaces
   e. on land, picked up by plants and animals
   f. on water, evaporates to start another cycle
   g. some plant food (with water) eaten by animals and is involved in the carbon cycle

D. Result:

Students learn about and should be able to sketch a water cycle (also called the "hydrological cycle").

E. Basic Facts and Supplemental Information:

1. Heat speeds water evaporation.
2. Humidity is water in the air.
3. Relative humidity is the amount of water in the air compared to the amount it could hold for that temperature. It is recorded in percents.
4. Wind speeds evaporation.
5. Dew and frost are forms of water that have condensed from the air.
6. Hail is frozen raindrops.
7. Snow is frozen water crystals that fall to the Earth in soft, white flakes and spread upon the ground as a white layer.
8. We have a limited supply of fresh water.
9. We could get fresh water from the ocean but desalinization is relatively expensive.

F. Thought Questions for Class Discussions:

1. What forms of water leave the air as frozen particles?
2. What is the difference between precipitation and condensation?
3. What factors affect the water cycle?
4. What is the difference between rain, snow, sleet, and hail?

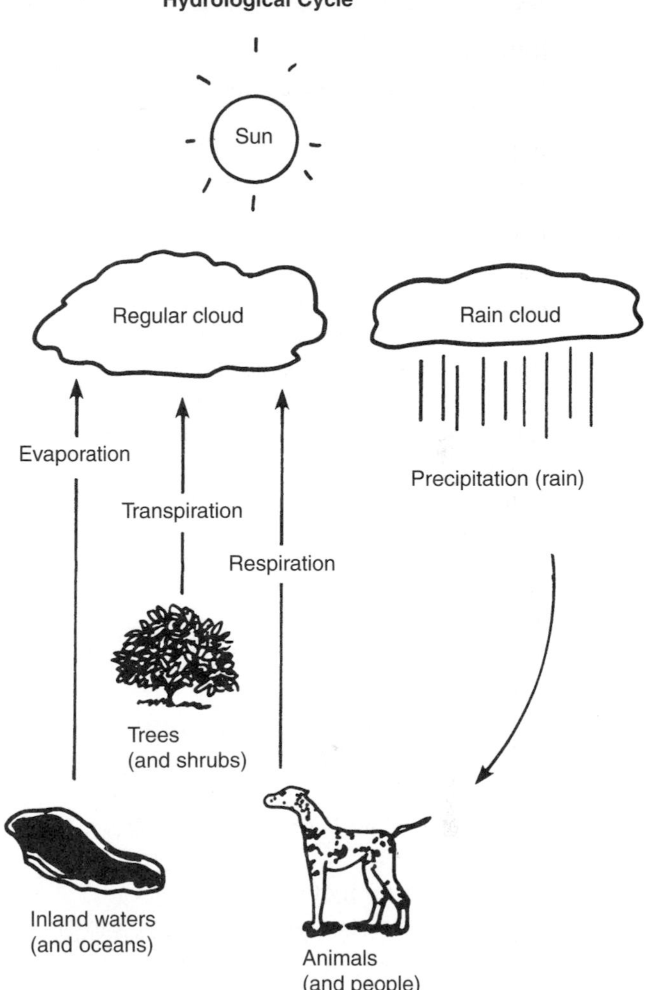

G. Related Ideas for Further Inquiry:

1. Study how we can preserve our fresh-water supplies.
2. Research the value of aquifers.
3. Study Activity VII-E-7, "Where do clouds come from?"
4. Study Activity VI-A-1, "What is the balance of nature?"
5. Study Activity VI-A-6, "What are food chains? food webs?"
6. Study Activity VI-A-10, "What are wetlands?"

H. Vocabulary Builders—Spelling Words:

1) **water** 2) **cycle** 3) **precipitation** 4) **hydrological** 5) **condensation** 6) **oceans** 7) **transpiration**

I. Thought for Today:

"I believe in getting into hot water; it keeps me clean."

Activity VI A 8

A. Problem: *What Is the Oxygen Cycle?*

B. Materials Needed:

Large drawing as shown in this Activity.

C. Procedure:

1. Discuss oxygen:
   a. basic element
   b. required for living
   c. chemically very active
   d. vital element in photosynthesis
   e. required in burning
   f. Our main supply of oxygen comes from phytoplankton in oceans and lakes.
   g. Our second main source of oxygen is from trees.
   h. Most plants consume as much oxygen as they produce.
2. Discuss the complete oxygen cycles.

D. Result:

Students will learn about and be able to sketch the oxygen cycle.

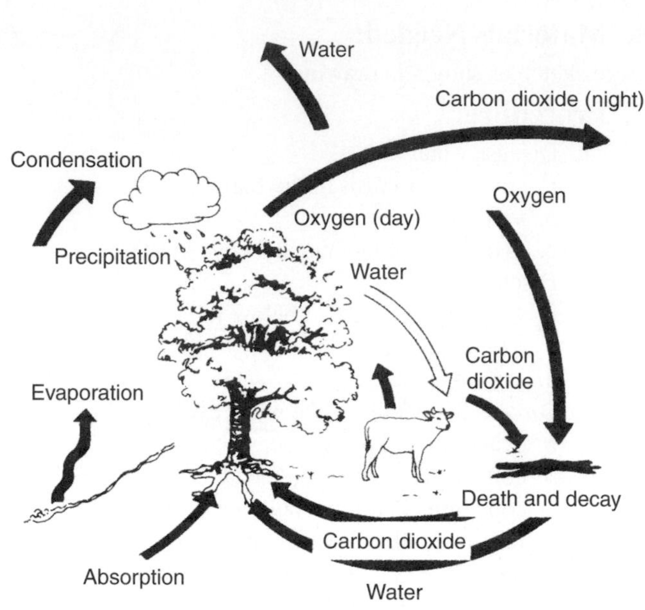

E. Basic Facts and Supplemental Information:

1. Half the weight of elements that make up the Earth's crust is oxygen.
2. Sixty-five percent of our body weight is composed of oxygen.
3. Twenty-one percent of the air is oxygen.
4. Animals breathe in oxygen and give out carbon dioxide day and night.
5. Plants take in carbon dioxide and give out oxygen using photosynthesis during the daytime.
6. Plants take in oxygen and give out carbon dioxide at night.
7. Fish, lobsters, clams, and other forms of aquatic life get their oxygen from the air dissolved in the water.
8. Phytoplankton, microscopic plants that live primarily near coastal waters, are our main source of oxygen. Unfortunately, we are polluting and contaminating many of these waters by dumping sewage, industrial runoffs, and agricultural wastes along our coastlines; consequently, we are reducing the number of phytoplankton and their effectiveness.

F. Thought Questions for Class Discussions:

1. What would happen to our oxygen supply if phytoplankton were destroyed or weakened?
2. What is photosynthesis?
3. Could fires be extinguished by eliminating their supply of oxygen?
4. How do human beings disturb the oxygen cycle?
5. What effects do raising farm animals have on our oxygen supplies?

G. Related Ideas for Further Inquiry:

1. A very provocative area that should be studied is "phytoplankton."
2. Ozone, an isotope of oxygen, is another problem area. Two areas that should be researched are "ground level ozone" and the "ozone layer" in our atmosphere.
3. Study Part III, "Plants."
4. Study Part IV, "Animals."
5. Study Activity VI-A-1, "What is the balance of nature?"
6. Study Activity VI-A-6, "What are food chains? food webs?"
7. Study Activity VI-A-7, "What is the water cycle?"
8. Study Activity VI-A-9, "What is the carbon cycle?"

H. Vocabulary Builders—Spelling Words:

1) **oxygen** 2) **carbon** 3) **dioxide** 4) **element** 5) **photosynthesis** 6) **phytoplankton**

I. Thought for Today:

"Most of us would rather risk catastrophe than read directions."

A. Problem: *What Is the Carbon Cycle?*

B. Materials Needed:

Large drawing as shown in this Activity

C. Procedures:

1. Discuss carbon:
   a. a basic element
   b. found in coal, lead pencils, and diamond rings
2. Discuss the three cycles vital to all living things:
   a. carbon cycle
   b. water cycle
   c. oxygen cycle
3. Discuss the carbon cycle(s):
   a. Slow cycle (millions of years):
      1) Carbon is found in seashells, rocks, and organic fossils in the form of oil, oil shale, and coal.
      2) These erode and change slowly over millions of years.
   b. Fast cycle (hundreds of years):
      1) Carbon dioxide is in air.
      2) It is absorbed by plants.
      3) It is then eaten by animals.
      4) It gets back to soil via death or elimination.
      5) It is then picked up by plants and insects or returned to atmosphere.

D. Result:

Students will learn about and be able to draw the carbon cycle.

E. Basic Facts and Supplemental Information:

1. All living things have carbon as part of their components. It is the basis of life.
2. When we burn gasoline, oil, coal, or wood, we release a lot of carbon dioxide into the atmosphere. This forms a "porous blanket" that allows the shortwave radiation from the sun to pass through, but most of the long-wave radiation from the Earth is diverted back to Earth. This extra heating produces "global warming." Study Activity VI-C-6, "What is global warming (the Greenhouse Effect)?"
3. Decomposers, mainly bacteria and fungi, break down dead organic materials and return them to the soil so that nothing is lost. Carbon is a vital element in this process.
4. Carbon dioxide is used to make carbonated soda water.
5. Dry ice is the solid state of carbon dioxide.

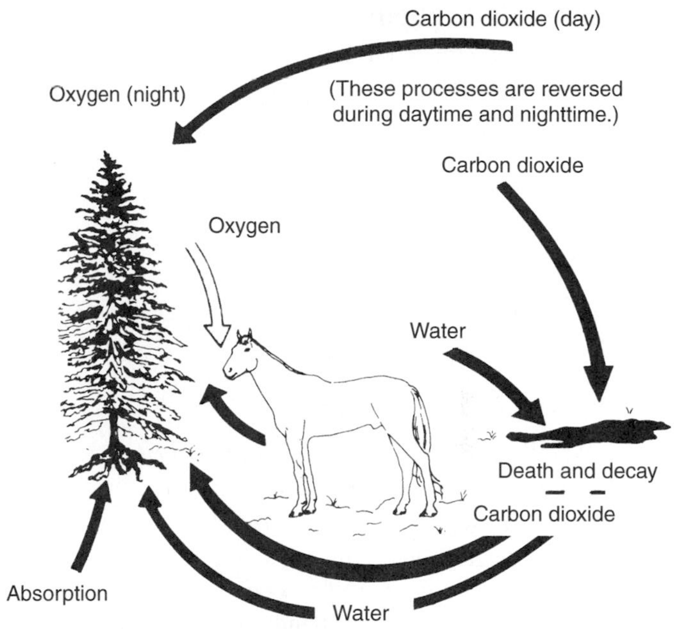

F. Thought Questions for Class Discussions:

1. What would happen if plants stopped making carbon dioxide?
2. Why do they use carbon dioxide in fire extinguishers?
3. How does the decaying process produce carbon dioxide?

G. Related Ideas for Further Inquiry:

1. Study Activity VI-A-7, "What is the water cycle?"
2. Study Activity VI-A-8, "What is the oxygen cycle?"
3. Study Activity VI-A-1, "What is the balance of nature?"
4. Study Activity VI-A-6, "What are food chains? food webs?"

H. Vocabulary Builders—Spelling Words:

1) **carbon** 2) **dioxide** 3) **cycle** 4) **decomposers** 5) **decay** 6) **organic** 7) **fossils** 8) **absorption**

I. Thought for Today:

"Retirement, we understand, is great if you are busy, rich, and healthy. But then, under those conditions, work is great, too."

Activity VI A 10

A. Problem: *What Are Wetlands?*

B. Materials Needed:

1. Reference materials on:
   a. swamps
   b. bogs
   c. marshes
   d. estuaries, etc.
2. Two sponges (same size)
3. Water
4. Pictures of wetlands
5. Maps of wetlands (if available)
6. Bulletin board
7. Large tray
8. Book (to support tray)
9. Desk or tabletop

C. Procedure:

1. Define "wetlands."
   Wetlands are lands that are saturated with surface or ground water for all or a good portion of time.
2. Display pictures of wetlands on the bulletin board.
3. With student help, set up the tray on desk or tabletop.
4. Place one dry sponge to one side of the tray.
5. Wet a second sponge and squeeze it very carefully so that it is not dripping but is still wet.
6. Place this sponge next to first sponge.
7. Raise one end of the tray with book.
8. Add equal amounts of water to both.
9. Observe results.
10. Add vital information about wetlands. (See Basic Facts and Supplemental Information.)

D. Results:

1. Students will be able to define "wetlands."
2. They will learn the value of wetlands.
3. The wet sponge will absorb water more quickly than the dry sponge.

E. Basic Facts and Supplemental Information:

1. Wetlands form vital ecosystems for plants and animals.
2. One-third of our endangered plants and one-third of our endangered animals are dependent on wetlands.
3. The United States originally had about 220 million acres of wetlands. Today there are only about 100 million acres left. The United States is losing 117,000 acres of wetlands per year.
4. California, Iowa, Indiana, and Missouri have lost over 87% of their wetlands. Connecticut has lost over 50% of its coastal wetlands, and Florida has lost over 50% of its everglades.
5. Wetlands are valuable because they:
   a. provide food for wildlife
   b. provide water for wildlife
   c. help control floods
   d. filter water naturally
   e. provide homes for wildlife
   f. are naturally beautiful
6. Wetlands have been altered or destroyed by cities, roads, industries, and farms.

F. Thought Questions for Class Discussions:

1. Should wetlands be protected?
2. How important is it to save our wetlands?
3. Should we reclaim some of our wetlands?
4. What governmental policies should we establish in regard to our wetlands?

G. Related Ideas for Further Inquiry:

1. Study any wetlands in or near your community.
2. Study the different kinds of wetlands.
3. Study Activity VI-A-1, "What is the balance of nature?"
4. Study Activity VI-A-2, "What is 'biological diversity'?"
5. Study Activity VI-A-11, "Are any animals threatened with extinction?"

H. Vocabulary Builders—Spelling Words:

1) **wetlands** 2) **marshes** 3) **swamps** 4) **bogs** 5) **estuaries** 6) **lagoons** 7) **wildlife**

I. Thought for Today:

"A shallow thinker seldom makes a deep impression."

A. Problem: *Are Any Animals Threatened with Extinction?*

B. Materials Needed:

Pictures and accounts of as many of the following as possible:

1. Eastern elk
2. Passenger pigeon
3. American alligator
4. Southern bald eagle
5. Columbian white-tailed deer
6. Utah prairie dog
7. Ivory-billed woodpecker
8. Whooping crane
9. Wolves
10. Sea otter
11. Giant panda
12. Hawk
13. Pine martin
14. Polar bears
15. Leopards (five species)
16. Black-footed ferret
17. Sea turtles
18. Whales
19. Condors
20. Peregrine falcon
21. Masked bobwhite
22. Kirtland's warbler
23. Mountain gorilla
24. Siberian tiger
25. Florida panther
26. Coho salmon, etc.

C. Procedure:

1. Have students study the general characteristics of each of the major species in which these animals are found (elk, pigeons, eagles, etc.).
2. Emphasize the interrelationships of these animals to other animals in their species.
3. Describe how these endangered animals are interrelated with resident plants.
4. Research animal species that have been classified as "threatened," "endangered," or extinct."

D. Results:

1. The students will learn that the first two animals listed are now extinct.
2. The rest of the animals and many others are being threatened with extinction.

E. Basic Facts and Supplemental Information:

1. *Worldwatch* magazine reported that 70% of the biologists believe that the world is in the midst of the fastest mass extinction of living things in the 4.5 billion year history of planet Earth.
2. Scientists have rated biodiversity loss as a more serious problem than the depletion of the ozone layer, global warming, or pollution and contamination.
3. Defenders of Wildlife claim that there are 1,900 animal species nearing extinction.
4. Hawaii, thought to be isolated, is an example of what has happened:
   a. Outside predators have been introduced.

Alligator　　Passenger pigeon

   b. Humans have entered the scene.
   c. Both have reduced fresh-water fish, land mullusks, and birds by over 36%.
5. Conservationists have helped slow the extinction rate by setting up sanctuaries, refuges, and zoos. These have helped the grizzly bear, bison, African cheetah, condors, turtles, whooping cranes, etc. This represents only a small number of the total threatened animal species.

F. Thought Questions for Class Discussions:

1. Should people wear the furs of animals of endangered species?
2. What happens when the balance of nature is disturbed?
3. If an animal becomes extinct, can it ever be restored?
4. What can you do to keep nature's beautiful plants and animals from being destroyed?
5. What would happen to us if all the animals were to disappear?
6. What would happen to us if all the plants were to disappear?

G. Related Ideas for Further Inquiry:

1. Visit a zoo.
2. Visit a fish hatchery.
3. Visit a game refuge.
4. Study how the government protects some animal species.
5. Study Activity VI-A-1, "What is the balance of nature?"
6. Study Activity VI-A-2, "What is 'biological diversity'?"
7. Study Activity VI-A-6, "What are food chains? food webs?"
8. Study Activity VI-A-10, "What are wetlands?"

H. Vocabulary Builders—Spelling Words:

1) **pigeon** 2) **alligator** 3) **eagle** 4) **woodpecker** 5) **wolves** 6) **bears** 7) **birds** 8) **wildlife**

I. Thought for Today:

"The dictionary is the only place where success comes before work."

SECTION B: CONSERVATION

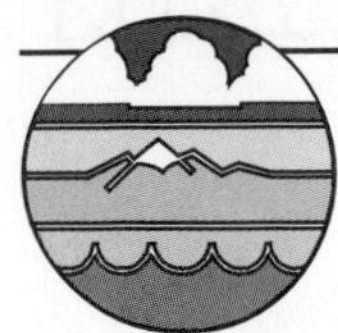

Activity VI B 1

A. Problem: *How Can We Conserve Our Soils and Our Lands?*

B. Materials Needed:

Pictures, models, or sketches of:

1. Terracing
2. Contour farming
3. Wattling process
4. Windbreaks
5. Crop rotation practices
6. Items listed in Procedure 5

C. Procedure:

1. Ask students why our soil is important.
2. Inquire of students if any of them know how farmers keep their soil from being blown away, washed away, or used up.
3. Discuss the major soil conservation practices cited in Results.
4. Compare our soil conservation practices with those of other countries.
5. Describe the problems of our land needs:
   a. homes
   b. farms
   c. businesses
   d. schools
   e. streets
   f. highways
   g. parks
   h. mines
   i. dams
   j. utilities
   k. recreation

D. Results:

1. Students will learn that terracing means leveling and staircasing, and this prevents soil from being washed away.
2. Students will learn that contour farming is a technique in which the land is plowed level around slopes to hold water, soil, and plants.
3. Students will learn that the wattling process is a method of building small dams with branches, twigs, rocks, etc. in gullies so that washed-away soil will build up behind them and prevent further gullying.
4. Students will learn that windbreaks are usually planted trees that grow tall and slow down strong winds, hence preventing soil from being blown away.
5. Students will learn that crop rotation practices are methods which farmers use to balance material in the soil. When one crop depletes one material, another crop is planted that will restore it. There are many techniques used in crop rotation. One example could be:
   a. Year one—plant legumes.
   b. Year two—plant corn.
   c. Year three—plant wheat.
   d. Year four—start the cycle again.
6. Students will realize that as our population increases more land is needed for those items cited in Procedure 5. The best agricultural lands are usually the first ones lost.

E. Basic Facts and Supplemental Information:

1. Write to the United States Soil Conservation Service or contact a local office for additional ideas and activities.
2. Someone once said that a nation could lose its freedom and survive but that if it lost its topsoil it could not exist.
3. Soil is one of our most vital possessions and is eroding faster than we are reclaiming it. Soil is lost by:
   a. overcropping
   b. winds
   c. floods
   d. rains
   e. strip-mining
   f. chemical wastes

F. Thought Questions for Class Discussions:

1. What is soil?
2. Do all plants need the same basic nutrients?
3. How does water help the soil?
4. How do animals help the soil?

G. Related Ideas for Further Inquiry:

1. Study the problem of overgrazing.
2. Study the effectiveness of fertilizers.
3. Study how floods can be prevented.
4. Study Section VII-C, "Earth's Crust."
5. Study other Activities in this Section.

H. Vocabulary Builders—Spelling Words:

1) **conserve** 2) **soil** 3) **terracing** 4) **rotation** 5) **contour** 6) **wattling** 7) **gullying** 8) **recreation**

I. Thought for Today:

"Education is a ladder to gather fruit from the tree of knowledge, not the fruit itself."

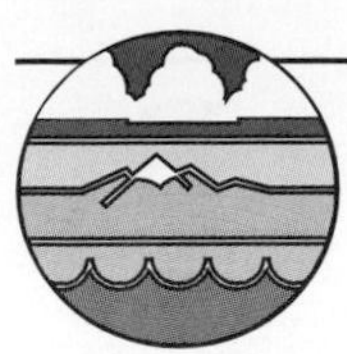

Activity VI B 2

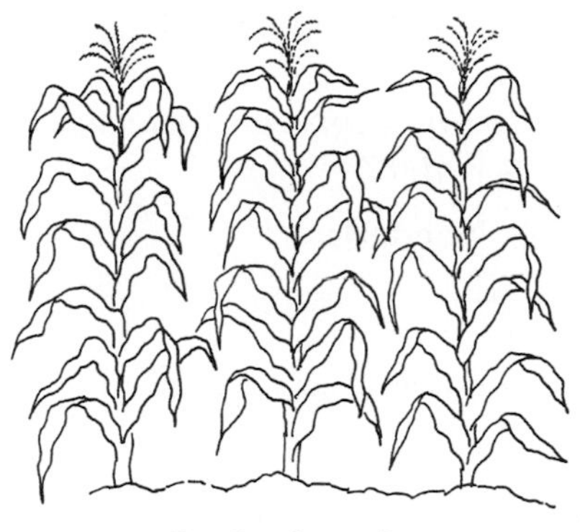

Our food supply

A. Problem: *How Can We Conserve Our Food Sources?*

B. Materials Needed:

1. Cans of food
2. Packages of food
3. Pictures of foods that have short shelf lives
4. Multisensory aids on food shortages
5. Newspaper clippings on food shortages in geographic areas

C. Procedure:

1. Discuss the problems of producing food:
   a. lack of agricultural supplies
   b. weather: rain, frost, drought, etc.
   c. human resources
   d. condition of land:
      1) soil type(s)
      2) pH (acid, neutral, or alkaline)
      3) flat or sloping
   e. water (amount, condition)
   f. fertilizers, nutrients needed
   g. pest control:
      1) chemical
      2) biological
      3) physical (vacuuming)
   h. farming aids:
      1) animals
      2) tractors
      3) other equipment
      4) tools
2. Discuss the problems of transporting food from the grower to the consumer:
   a. means of transportation; refrigeration
   b. laws, regulations, human resources
3. Discuss the amount of food needed for various geographical areas.
4. Discuss ways we can conserve our present food sources:
   a. Conserve our soils
   b. Save our water supplies
   c. Prevent contamination/pollution
   d. Establish local laws to save our agricultural lands
5. It is very important that we don't waste food at home.

D. Results:

1. Students will learn that there are many considerations involved in growing food.
2. Students will learn that all areas have expanding populations which will be requiring more foodstuffs.

E. Basic Facts and Supplemental Information:

1. The most immediate problem is the transportation of foods, not growing foods; that is, getting food to the areas where it is needed.
2. The next problem that must be faced is to prevent farming area loss. As our population increases, the farming areas are the first lost to residential developers.
3. Even though science will be able to help us produce more food per acre and be able to develop new foods, we will still be facing a drastic food shortage situation.
4. Two-thirds of the world's people are now underfed or undernourished (not provided with basic foods, adequate vitamins, and minerals).

F. Thought Questions for Class Discussions:

1. What will happen if our population doubles and our food supplies remain the same?
2. What should have top priority for our land—food? housing? business? recreation?

G. Related Ideas for Further Inquiry:

1. Study Part III, "Plants."
2. Study Part IV, "Animals."
3. Study ways that food can be conserved in your local community.
4. Study Activity VI-A-4, "Is the world's population growing too fast?"
5. Study Activity VI-A-5, "Is there enough food to feed all the people in the world?"

H. Vocabulary Builders—Spelling Words:

1) **soils** 2) **underfed** 3) **undernourished** 4) **agriculture** 5) **farming** 6) **distribution**

I. Thought for Today:

"And then there was the professor who was dieting—he wanted to win the nobelly prize.".

Activity VI B 3

A. Problem: *How Can We Conserve Our Fresh Water?*

B. Materials Needed:

1. Chalkboard
2. Chalk
3. Class-constructed survey form

C. Procedure:

1. Have students list on the chalkboard all the ways water is used around their homes. Parenthetical figures indicate an estimate of the average amount of gallons and/or gallons per unit of time of water used. The list will probably include:
   a. watering garden (60/hr)
   b. bathtub (25)
   c. showers(s) (5/min)
   d. washing machine (40)
   e. dishwasher (25)
   f. toilet (6)
   g. drinking, cooking (5)
   h. refilling aquaria (if any); watering houseplants (2/week)
2. Have the students make a home survey of the amount of water used during a one-week period.
3. Discuss and describe the sources of water for your community.
4. Study the home survey sheets for ways that water can be conserved.
5. If a water bill can be obtained, determine approximately how much money could be saved by conserving water.

D. Results:

1. Students will learn that conservation pays.
2. Parents, too, will become more conservation-minded.

E. Basic Facts and Supplemental Information:

1. As our population grows, more water will be needed.
2. As business and industry grow, more water will be needed.
3. There is no source of fresh water other than rain. Rivers and wells get their water from rain.
4. We can get fresh water from the ocean, but desalinization at the present time is costly.
5. Our wells and aquifers are being drained slowly. Contamination in them is increasing, and some are near the danger zone.

F. Thought Questions for Class Discussions:

1. Will increasing the price of water solve our water shortage problem?
2. Will cloud seeding increase our water supply?
3. Do you think we will ever have to ration water for everybody?
4. Where does your community get its fresh water?

G. Related Ideas for Further Inquiry:

1. If your community had its water supply cut in half, how would you budget your supply?
2. Study Section I-C, "Water."
3. Study Section VII-C, "Earth's Crust."
4. Study Section VII-E, "Weather."
5. Study other Activities in this Section.

H. Vocabulary Builders—Spelling Words:

1) **conserve** 2) **water** 3) **garden** 4) **bathtub** 5) **dishwasher** 6) **showers** 7) **sprinkling** 8) **drinking** 9) **toilet** 10) **cooking**

I. Thought for Today:

"Teachers affect eternity; they can never tell where their influence stops."

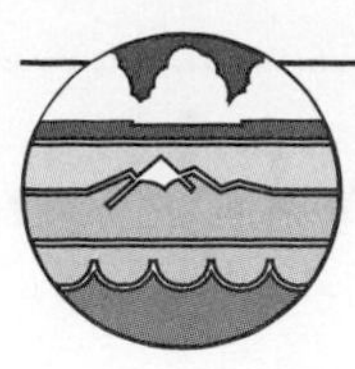

Activity VI B 4

A. Problem: *How Can We Conserve Our Fresh Air?*

B. Materials Needed:

1. Models of:
   a. automobiles
   b. airplanes
   c. motorcycles
   d. motorboats
2. Pictures of:
   a. electrical appliances
   b. gas stove
   c. industrial stack
3. Empty spray can
4. Empty cigarette package

C. Procedure:

1. Place these objects and pictures on the science table and ask the question (preferably on a large sign): "What do these have in common?"
2. Having built up the students' curiosity, if they have not already guessed, tell them that every one of these items is ruining our fresh air.
3. Describe and discuss the effects of each of these:
   a. cars—exhausts
   b. industries—fumes
   c. cigarettes—smoke
   d. airplane—exhaust
   e. motorcycle—exhaust
   f. appliances—burn fossil fuels to produce electricity
   g. gas stove—burns gas
   h. hair spray cans—propellants
4. Discuss ways that harmful gases and particulate matter can be reduced or eliminated.

D. Result:

Students will learn that there are many things that contribute to polluting our fresh air, from turning on lights to riding in automobiles.

E. Basic Facts and Supplemental Information:

1. There is a limited amount of fresh air available to us. There is no new source. (Phytoplankton and trees do produce oxygen, but we are gradually destroying phytoplankton and cutting down too many of our trees.)
2. We live in an ocean of air.
3. Air is composed of many gases.
4. Oxygen is the vital component of air for all of us.
5. Many products we put in the air are very harmful—even deadly. One scientist says that living in our air-polluted cities is like smoking two packs of cigarettes a day.

F. Thought Questions for Class Discussions:

1. What would happen if our oxygen supply were cut in half?
2. What is the best source of oxygen on Earth?
3. Do trees produce much oxygen?

G. Related Ideas for Further Inquiry:

1. Study Activity VI-C-2, "What pollutants are in the air?"
2. Study Activity VI-C-3, "What is smog?"
3. Study other Activities in this Section.

H. Vocabulary Builders—Spelling Words:

1) **business** 2) **industry** 3) **appliance**
4) **exhausts** 5) **fumes** 6) **smoke**
7) **fossil** 8) **automobiles** 9) **sprays**

I. Thought for Today:

"By the time a person realizes that maybe his father was right he usually has a child who thinks he is wrong."

Activity VI B 5

A. Problem: *How Can We Conserve Our Natural Resources?*

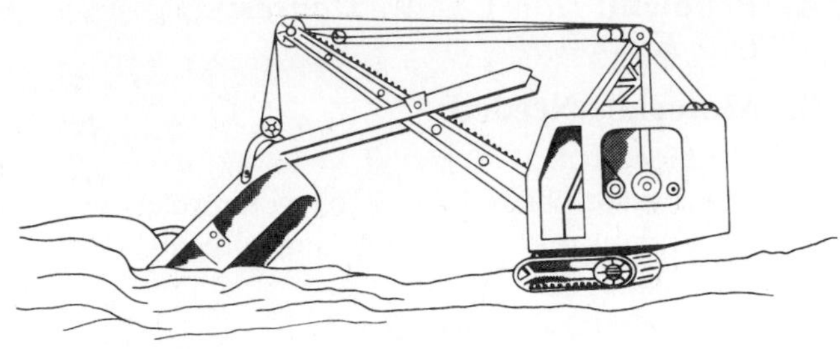

B. Materials Needed:

1. Models or pictures of tractors, excavators
2. Dioramas of land before and after strip-mining
3. Specimens or pictures of our most common natural resources (minerals, chemicals, etc.)

C. Procedure:

1. Describe the problems of food, energy, and recreational needs.
2. Cite the dilemmas we are having and will have over land use. As our population increases, shall our priorities for land use be with residences, nonresident urban uses, farming, or mining? Some of the arguments for farming and mining are cited below:
   a. Farming:
      1) Soil, sun, and rain produce food, fiber, and wood to feed, clothe, and shelter us.
      2) The topsoil must produce more grains, vegetables, and fruits to feed an ever-growing population here and abroad.
      3) Our lands produce the hay and greens for our pasture animals.
      4) Our farmlands must produce millions of bales of cotton to help clothe us.
      5) Our water must be kept clean and flowing to protect the animal life forms that help feed us and to quench our thirst.
      6) Our lands must provide an adequate supply of trees for housing and industry.

   b. Mining:
      1) More and more people are demanding more and more energy and more and more material goods.
      2) Most minerals lie close to the earth's surface.
      3) Coal, our largest nonrenewable source of energy, also lies close to the earth's surface.
      4) We have built bigger and bigger machines to strip the earth of its precious resources, and in so doing, have destroyed trees, flowers, and grasses.

   c. Problem: The lands we use for gathering needed minerals are the same lands that feed, clothe, and shelter us. There is no land to spare.

   d. One of our strip-mining diggers stands nearly 200 feet high, has a boom that is 310 feet long, and scoops up 325 tons of earth with each scoop.

   e. We are losing almost 5,000 acres of topsoil to strip-mining every week.
3. Using models and dioramas, show what strip-mining does to the earth.

D. Result:

This lesson certainly should stimulate student thinking as to what should be done about our natural resources.

E. Basic Facts and Supplemental Information:

1. As of 1999, we have lost over 2.6 million acres of potential agricultural lands to strip-mining.
2. Twenty percent of our best agricultural lands have already been lost to cities and highways.

F. Thought Questions for Class Discussions:

1. Is strip-mining worth the price we are paying? The price we will have to pay?
2. How long does it take to produce an inch of topsoil naturally? (1,000 years)
3. Should we insist on costlier, more dangerous types of mining—namely, underground mining?

G. Related Ideas for Further Inquiry:

1. Study Section III-C, "Soils and Germination."
2. Study Section VII-C, "Earth's Crust."
3. Study Activity VI-B-3, "How can we conserve our fresh water?"
4. Study other Activities in this Section.

H. Vocabulary Builders—Spelling Words:

1) **strip-mining** 2) **survive** 3) **tractors**
4) **excavating** 5) **diorama** 6) **farming**
7) **mining** 8) **natural** 9) **resources**

I. Thought for Today:

"Some get lost in thought because it is such unfamiliar territory."

Activity

A. Problem: *How Can We Conserve Energy?*

B. Materials Needed:

1. Bulletin board
2. Chalkboard
3. Notebooks
4. Pencils
5. Pictures of actual appliances that use electricity in the home:
   a. can opener
   b. toothbrush
   c. frypan
   d. toaster
   e. fan
   f. lamp
   g. television
   h. computer
   i. dishwasher
   j. washing machine
   k. air conditioner
   l. hair dryer, etc.

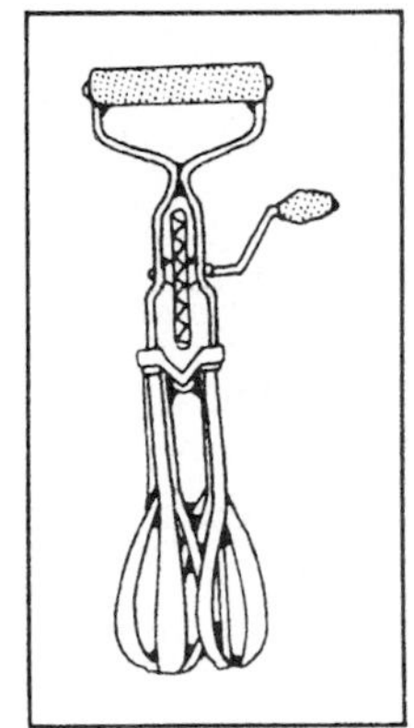

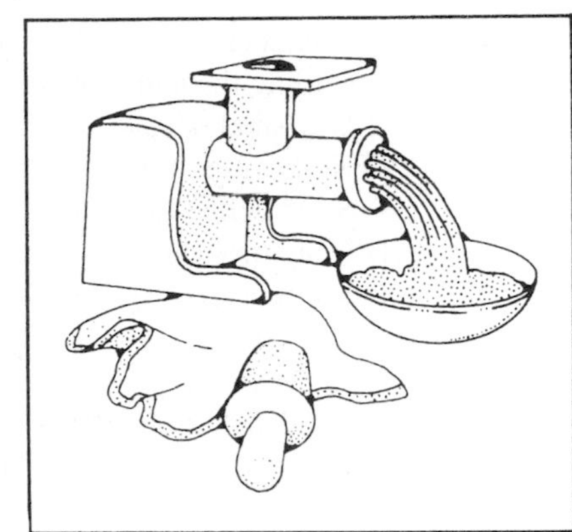

Use nonelectrical appliances whenever possible.

C. Procedure:

1. Have students collect pictures of electrical appliances used in their homes and record these in their notebooks.
2. Ask students to survey parents, friends, and neighbors on how energy can be saved.
3. Have them list items in their notebooks.
4. Allow one week to complete study.
5. Compile results.
6. Discuss how great-grandmother and great-grandfather lived around the year 1900.
7. Describe how (with no electricity in the home) there were no electric lights, electric appliances, TVs, VCRs, microwave ovens, electronic games, etc.
8. Have students list all the electrical appliances they have in their homes, on the chalkboard.
9. Have them go over the list and classify them as:
   a. absolutely essential
   b. desirable, but not essential
   c. could do without
10. Have students go over the list one more time and check to see if each item is used for:
    a. convenience—comfort
    b. health—cleanliness
    c. entertainment—recreation
11. Have students go over the list and cite ways that use of these electric appliances could be reduced.
12. Discuss our sources of power and how every time we use an electrical device we are adding to air pollution through our coal or fuel oil burning power plants, or to water and land pollution if we use atomic power plants.

D. Results:

1. Students will learn about energy conservation.
2. Students will learn that there are many ways we can save energy (and money):
   a. In the home:
      1) Use heavier insulation (6-inch).
      2) Caulk all cracks.
      3) Use fluorescent lighting (more efficient than incandescent bulbs).
      4) Turn off lights when not needed.
      5) Use dimming switches.
      6) Turn hot water down to 120° F.
      7) Keep stove burners clean.
      8) Shut off ovens, gas, stoves before finishing to let appliance's residual heat finish cooking.
      9) Reduce air conditioner time.
      10) Reduce electric home appliance use.
      11) Close windows, drapes, shades at night.
      12) Take more showers, less baths.
      13) Wash dishes by hand.
      14) Preheat oven for 10 minutes before baking.
      15) Reduce lamp wattage.
      16) Use self-igniting gas appliances.
      17) Close heat and air-conditioning ducts in rooms not being used.
      18) Plant trees on south and west side of homes (summer shade).
      19) Dry wash loads consecutively (residual heat).

20) Light colors inside the home saves light.
21) Don't iron unnecessary laundry: sheets, underwear, etc.
22) Keep air filters clean.
23) A humidifier will keep humidity near 55% and will result in more comfort, less heat.
24) Use exhaust fans in summer (keeps cooler, reduces need of air conditioning) etc.

b. Regarding the automobile:
1) Buy smaller cars.
2) Keep motor tuned up.
3) Steel-belted tires have less friction.
4) Keep tires inflated properly.
5) Improve driving habits (no jackrabbit starts, etc.).
6) Drive within posted speed limits (fewer accidents, too).
7) Walk and bicycle short distances.
8) Use car pools, etc.

c. In the community:
1) Eliminate or reduce night advertising.
2) Reduce number of lights in the home.
3) Have all sporting events in the daytime.
4) Encourage thrift of energy users.
5) Increase electric rates on a sliding scale.
6) Advertise energy savers.
7) Reduce population growth through education and abstinence.
8) Avoid or keep to a minimum use of electrical gadgets such as toothbrushes, can openers, knife sharpeners, mixers, etc.

E. Basic Facts and Supplemental Information:

1. Electricity in the homes can be reduced by cutting down on the use of essential items and eliminating the nonessential items. (Different people will hold different views on what is essential and what is not essential.)
2. Learning how to read meters and determine utility costs will make people cost-conscious. See Activity II-G-2, "Reading utility meters."
3. Energy costs are rising and will continue to rise.
4. High energy use items are:
   a. electric ranges
   b. air conditioners
   c. self-cleaning ovens
   d. water heaters
   e. electric clothes dryers
5. A kilowatt-hour of electricity costs about 9¢ = 100 watt light bulb burning for 10 hours—BUT this equals a pound of coal that had to be mined, transported, and burned, or the amount of energy that would have to be expended to lift a 150-pound person to the top of Mt. McKinley.

F. Thought Questions for Class Discussions:

1. If you had to cut back your energy demands by 50% in your home, what items would you cut back or eliminate?
2. Do you think an energy crisis can be avoided?
3. Is conservation of electricity financially worthwhile?
4. Which is more valuable, or important: electric gadgets or clean air?
5. Should power be rationed? or taxed for heavy use?
6. Do you think today's young people would like to "go back" to the days of their great-grandparents in order to have clean air?
7. Would it be possible to return to those times?

G. Related Ideas for Further Inquiry:

1. Have students make specific recommendations on how electricity could be saved in the home, such as:
   a. keep thermostat higher in summer, lower in winter.
   b. close chimney vents when appropriate.
   c. wash clothes in warm water.
   d. use proper ventilation.
   e. close drapes in summer.
   f. install or improve insulation.
   g. turn out lights when not in use.
2. Study Section II-B, "Fire and Heat."
3. Study Section VI-C, "Pollution."
4. Study Section VII-C, "Earth's Crust."
5. Study other Activities in this Section.

H. Vocabulary Builders—Spelling Words:

1) **electricity** 2) **essential** 3) **desirable**
4) **thermostat** 5) **appliances** 6) **conservation**

I. Thought for Today:

"Teaching children to count is not as important as teaching children what counts."

Activity VI B 7

A. Problem: *How Can We Conserve Our Wildlife?*

B. Materials Needed:

1. Classroom pets
2. Bird feeders
3. Classroom plants
4. Pictures of:
   a. zoos
   b. wetlands
   c. refuges
   d. local, state, and national parks
5. Media accounts of the problems of wildlife

C. Procedure:

1. Show the class the classroom pet(s).
2. Show the class a classroom plant.
3. Remove these from the view of students.
4. Ask the students if they would like to have these removed permanently.
5. Tell them this is what is happening to many, many species all over the world. Species are being "removed" permanently for various reasons.
6. Cite these important facts:
   a. Many millions of plant and animal species have become extinct since life began on Earth.
   b. Most of these died out because of natural causes.
   c. In the last three centuries, humans have greatly speeded up the "extinction process" almost 1,000 times by:
      1) overhunting and excessive fishing
      2) destroying habitats
      3) draining wetlands
      4) mining
      5) polluting the environment
      6) collecting
      7) killing for animal parts for unscientific health reasons and body decorations
7. Discuss the interrelationships of various animals.
8. Discuss the interrelationships of plants and animals.
9. Study various ecosystems.
10. Stress the need to protect all wildlife, plants, and animals.
11. Show pictures of the methods used by people to protect wildlife (zoos, refuges, sanctuaries, etc.).

D. Results:

1. Students will learn that a lot of our wildlife is in danger.

Giant panda

2. Students will begin to develop ideas of how they can individually help protect our wildlife.

E. Basic Facts and Supplemental Information:

1. "Extinct" means that a species has disappeared—None is known to exist.
2. "Endangered" refers to a species that is threatened with extinction.
3. "Threatened" signifies that a species has had their numbers severely decreased and could be placed on the "endangered" list.
4. We do not know the exact number of species (plants, animals, etc.) that exist, but estimates vary between 3 and 30 million. Only about 300,000 have been classified.
5. There is no doubt that the numbers are decreasing at faster and faster rates.
6. The primary cause is the human factor—increasing encroachment into the habitats of species.

F. Thought Questions for Class Discussions:

1. How do you think we can slow down the loss of wildlife?
2. Are you in favor of creating more refuges for wildlife?
3. What would happen to us if all other animal life were to become extinct?

G. Related Ideas for Further Inquiry:

1. Study our efforts to stop wildlife extinction of certain species by setting up refuges, breeding endangered animals and returning them to their natural habitats.
2. Study Part III, "Plants."
3. Study Part IV, "Animals."

H. Vocabulary Builders—Spelling Words:

1) **conserve** 2) **wildlife** 3) **extinction**
4) **endangered** 5) **threatened** 6) **species**

I. Thought for Today:

"Do you know how to tune a piano? tuna salad?"

SECTION C: POLLUTION

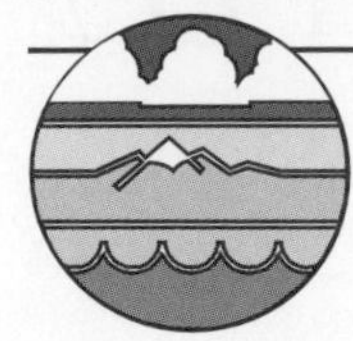

Activity VI C 1

A. Problem: *What Are the Main Environmental Problems?*

B. Materials Needed:

1. Books, pamphlets on ecology
2. Newspaper accounts of environmental problems
3. Multisensory materials that depict environmental problems

C. Procedure:

1. Have students collect pictures, stories, and information about pollution.
2. Discuss each kind of pollution as to its description, cause, and possible ways to eliminate it.

D. Results:

1. Students will learn that there are many kinds of pollution, including:
   a. air
   b. water (oceans, rivers, lakes, etc.)
   c. noise
   d. heat (global warming)
   e. land
2. Students will learn that there are many causes of pollution including:
   a. gases (automobile exhausts, factory emissions)
   b. mine acids
   c. pesticides
   d. herbicides
   e. oil slicks
   f. detergents
   g. raw sewage
   h. thermal materials
   i. garbage and wastes

E. Basic Facts and Supplemental Information:

1. The pollution we allow depends on our values.
   a. Eliminating our wastes is a major concern regarding pollution.
   b. Manufacturing procedures cause a lot of pollution.
2. Raising the temperature of river water by only 5° F. can be disastrous to fish. (Chinook salmon in Washington is a good example. Many salmon become sluggish and cannot find sufficient food.)
3. DDT has proved far more deadly and persistent than anticipated; it has been outlawed.

F. Thought Questions for Class Discussions:

1. Should Americans stop driving gasoline-powered vehicles?
2. Can insects that infest crops be destroyed by biological means?
3. What should we do with our wastes from our homes and factories?
4. Which pollutants are the most harmful?
5. Which would be your first choice of a pollution problem to control or eliminate?
6. Who should pay for pollution cleanups?

G. Related Ideas for Further Inquiry:

1. Study Section I-B, "Air."
2. Study Section I-C, "Water."
3. Study Section VI-A, "Ecosystems."
4. Study especially Activity VI-A-4, "Is the world's population growing too fast?"
5. Study Section VI-B, "Conservation."
6. Study Section VI-D, "Pollution Solutions."
7. Study other Activities in this Section.

H. Vocabulary Builders—Spelling Words:

1) **gases** 2) **pesticides** 3) **herbicides** 4) **detergents** 5) **sewage** 6) **wastes** 7) **ozone** 8) **people** 9) **hazardous** 10) **destruction**

I. Thought for Today:

"Ignorance is a form of environmental pollution."

Activity VI C 2

A. Problem: *What Pollutants Are in the Air?*

B. Materials Needed:

1. Two pint jars with caps
2. Wooden matches
3. Pictures of air pollution (smog, industrial smoke, etc.)

C. Procedure:

1. Take an empty pint jar and cap it. (This jar represents clean air.)
2. Take the other jar; carefully light three matches and drop them into the jar. Cap the jar after a moment or two. The matches will go out because of lack of oxygen. This represents dirty air.
3. Pass the two jars around the class.
4. Ask the students which air they would like to breathe? Why?
5. Discuss what causes the air to become dirty.
6. Have students read about and discuss causes of air pollution.
7. Discuss how cities monitor air pollutants.

D. Results:

1. Students will learn that people contaminate the air.
2. Some of the contaminants are:
   a. oxides of nitrogen
   b. carbon monoxide (results from incomplete burning)
   c. hydrocarbons (burned fuels, industrial wastes)
   d. oxides of sulphur
   e. nitrogen dioxide
   f. agricultural sprays
   g. automobile exhausts
   h. particulates
   i. chlorofluorocarbons

E. Basic Facts and Supplemental Information:

1. The facts are clear—the air is not.
2. Smog can do irreparable physical and psychological damage to people.
3. Smog robs air of vital oxygen, and children need more oxygen than adults, especially when they are active.
4. Smog has been linked to lung cancer, heart disease, brain damage, emphysema, pulmonary problems, respiratory diseases, tissue damage—and even death!
5. Carbon monoxide is the product of incomplete combustion (including smoking) and can cause death. It robs the body of needed oxygen.

Industry Automobile Barbecue

F. Thought Questions for Class Discussions:

1. What will happen if we continue to pollute our air?
2. Can plants reproduce if there is no air?
3. What can we do to get rid of some of our air pollutants?
4. Which do we need more, electricity or clean air?
5. Why do some areas have more air pollutants than others even though their population and industry are about the same?

G. Related Ideas for Further Inquiry:

1. Have students research the air pollutants in their local community.
2. Have students make a list of air pollutants. (Don't be surprised if it becomes very long!)
3. Study Section I-B, "Air."
4. Study Activity VI-C-1, "What are the main environmental problems?"
5. Study Activity VI-C-3, "What is smog?"
6. Study Activity VI-C-5, "What causes acid rain?"
7. Study Activity VI-C-6, "What is global warming (the Greenhouse Effect)?"
8. Study Activity VI-C-7, "What is global cooling (the Icehouse Effect)?"
9. Study Activity VI-A-4, "Is the world's population growing too fast?"

H. Vocabulary Builders—Spelling Words:

1) **pollutants** 2) **smog** 3) **industry**
4) **carbon monoxide** 5) **nitrogen**
6) **sulfur/sulphur (both are correct spellings)**

I. Thought for Today:

"There is a mad scramble to improve everything in the world except people."

Activity VI C 3

A. Problem: *What Is Smog?*

B. Materials Needed:

1. Gallon jug with cap or cover
2. Matches
3. Sulphur
4. Paper

C. Procedure:

1. *Carefully* light some matches, drop in jug, and cover.
2. *Carefully* burn a little sulphur, drop in same jug, and cover.
3. *Carefully* light a little piece of paper, drop in same jug, and cover.
4. Explain inversion. Warm air is normally above cold air, but with inversion, cold air is above warm air and prevents it from rising. (Pollutants are more prevalent in warm air.)
5. Ask the students how they would like to breathe this "smoggy air" continuously in large quantities? smaller quantities? not at all?
6. If possible, ask an expert on smog or smog control to cite what steps have been taken to reduce smog. If not possible, obtain information from newspapers or magazines.

D. Results:

1. The jug will become full of dark, dirty, noxious air.
2. Many of the air pollutants come from burning fossil fuels.
3. Students will learn about smog and smog control.

E. Basic Facts and Supplemental Information:

1. Smog contains:
   a. sulphur dioxide
   b. oxides of nitrogen
   c. hydrocarbons
   d. industrial gases (fumes)
   e. particulates
2. By reducing automobile and industrial combustion we could reduce smog.
3. Smog is caused by the action of *sunlight* on *hydrocarbons* and the *oxides of nitrogen.*
4. Hydrocarbons come mainly from unburned gasoline; oxides of nitrogen are present whenever burning takes place.
5. In Los Angeles, about 70% of smog originates from motor vehicles; the rest comes from stationary sources: power plants, industries, homes, and consumer products.

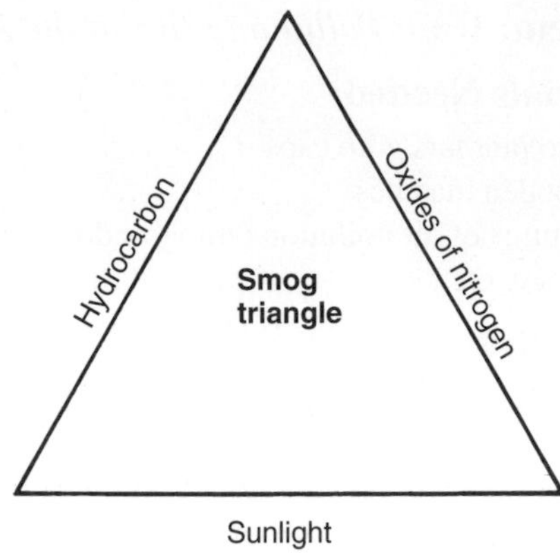

6. Smog is a problem all around the world.
7. The U.S. Environmental Protection Agency lists 450 counties that exceed federal standards for clean air.
8. Most cities that have smog problems have governmental agencies that control emissions that cause smog and air pollution.
9. There are three factors that need to be present for smog:
   a. hydrocarbons
   b. oxides of nitrogen
   c. sunlight
10. These three factors are called the "Smog Triangle."

F. Thought Questions for Class Discussions:

1. How many of these pollutants do you think need to be in the air before people are poisoned?
2. Have we ever had any deaths from smog?
3. Do you think people will voluntarily reduce their automobile driving?

G. Related Ideas for Further Inquiry:

1. Interview a meteorologist about smog.
2. Study Section I-B, "Air."
3. Study Activity VI-C-1, VI-C-2, and VI-C-4.
4. Study Section VII-E, "Weather."

H. Vocabulary Builders—Spelling Words:

1) **smog** 2) **nitrogen** 3) **hydrocarbons**
4) **sunlight** 5) **triangle** 6) **inversion**

I. Thought for Today:

"The smog was so bad this morning that most of the birds woke up coughing."

Activity

VI C 4

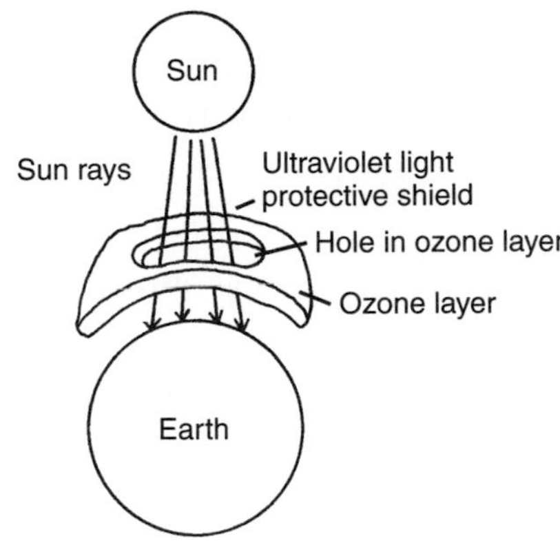

A. Problem: *What Is the Ozone Problem?*

B. Materials Needed:

On ozone:

1. Books
2. Pamphlets
3. Pictures
4. Charts
5. Multisensory aids
6. Newspaper articles

C. Procedure:

1. Describe what ozone is. (A form of oxygen that has three atoms to a molecule; regular oxygen has two.)
2. Tell the students about the ozone layer. It is a layer, like a shield, that protects us from harmful ultraviolet radiation. It is about 15 to 30 miles above the Earth.
3. Two "holes" have developed in this layer. The first and largest "ozone hole" is above Antarctica in the Southern Hemisphere. This hole has reached the size of the continental United States.
4. A second and smaller hole has developed in the Northern Hemisphere.
5. The holes vary in size depending on the latitude and the seasons.
6. Other findings show that:
   a. Chlorofluorocarbon (frequently abbreviated CFC) propellants do damage to the ozone layer.
   b. From 1957 to 1975 there was no apparent change in the ozone layer. Since 1975 the ozone hole has slowly increased in size.
   c. Ozone thinning leads to skin cancer.
   d. Increased ozone would lead to a decrease in Vitamin D and would harm bone development.
   e. Actually there are no "holes" per se, only a great thinning.

D. Results:

Students will learn that:

1. Ozone is a form of oxygen. The ozone layer protects us from dangerous ultraviolet radiation from the sun.
2. The thickness of the ozone layer appears to be diminishing every year.

E. Basic Facts and Supplemental Information:

1. CFCs are catalysts that break down ozone into oxygen. Since catalysts remain unchanged, CFCs continue to act and break down more ozone, causing the "ozone hole."
2. Refrigerators and aerosol sprays containing CFCs are slowly being replaced with carbon dioxide and hydrocarbons which do not destroy the ozone layer.
3. While the United States and a few other countries have stopped using CFC propellants, some countries have not, and so the holes in the ozone layers have continued to grow.
4. CFCs release chlorine, which destroys ozone.
5. Other suspicious factors of ozone depletion might be from soils from tree cutting or atmospheric winds.
6. If CFCs continue to be used, in 50 years the ozone layer will be reduced by 5% to 10%. This would cause an additional 40,000,000 skin cancer cases and 800,000 deaths.
7. The most recent findings have indicated that the ozone layer is also thinning over parts of Canada and the United States.

F. Thought Questions for Class Discussions:

1. Do you think we are still polluting our environment?
2. Are you concerned about the ozone problem?
3. Do you think exhausts from jet planes might be part of the problem? (Most scientists think so.)

G. Related Ideas for Further Inquiry:

1. Study Section I-B, "Air."
2. Study Section I-C, "Water."
3. Study other Activities in this Section.

H. Vocabulary Builders—Spelling Words:

1) **ozone** 2) **layer** 3) **chlorofluorocarbons** 4) **antarctic** 5) **arctic** 6) **protective**

I. Thought for Today:

"A hole is nothing at all but you can break your neck in it."

Activity VI C 5

A. Problem: *What Causes Acid Rain?*

B. Materials Needed:

1. Bulletin board
2. Newspaper and magazine articles about acid rain

C. Procedure:

1. Post accounts of acid rain on the bulletin board.
2. Study these accounts—most are very shocking.
3. Discuss what acid rain is. (Mostly sulphur oxides and nitrogen oxides [gases] which dissolve in water droplets in the air.)

D. Results:

Students will learn that:

1. Acid rain is damaging U.S. and Canadian lakes.
2. There have been problems between the two countries about who is producing acid rain and who should be responsible to work on its elimination.
3. Emissions from oil fields contain acids that are almost 100 times stronger than the acids in acid rain.
4. Nitrogen fertilizers probably cause more soil acidification than acid rain.

E. Basic Facts and Supplemental Information:

1. Acid rain is slowly destroying small organisms, killing fish, interfering with the food pyramid, and deteriorating buildings; it is, therefore, a detriment to our health.
2. Canada claims that acid rain has wiped out fish in 147 lakes in Ontario and 7 salmon streams in Nova Scotia.
3. The Brookhaven National Laboratory indicates that acid rain may play a key role in the fatal illnesses of 50,000 Americans.
4. The cost of restricting air pollutants would cost American industry $200,000,000,000 over the next 30 years to correct.
5. The estimated cost of acid rain damage to American farmers is between $3 billion and $4 billion per year.

F. Thought Questions for Class Discussions:

1. Does acid rain damage statues, buildings, paint, etc.? (Yes!)
2. How could we eliminate acid rain?
3. Does acid rain damage our lungs?

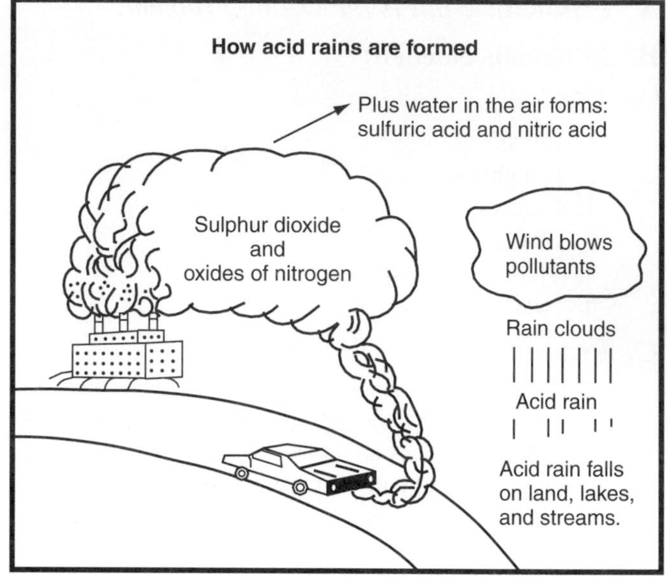

G. Related Ideas for Further Inquiry:

1. Interview a meteorologist about acid rain.
2. Interview a chemist about acid rain.
3. Study Activity VI-C-1, "What are the main environmental problems?"
4. Study Activity VI-C-2, "What pollutants are in the air?"
5. Study Activity VI-C-3, "What is smog?"
6. Study Activity VI-C-4, "What is the ozone problem?"
7. Study Activity VI-C-6, "What is global warming (the Greenhouse Effect)?"
8. Study Activity VI-C-7, "What is global cooling (the Icehouse Effect)?"
9. Study Activity VI-C-8, "How does pollution affect food chains and food webs?"
10. Study Activity VI-A-4, "Is the world's population growing too fast?"

H. Vocabulary Builders—Spelling Words:

1) **sulfur (or sulphur)** 2) **nitrogen** 3) **oxides** 4) **droplets** 5) **emissions** 6) **automobiles**

I. Thought for Today:

"Orators used to say history is at the crossroads—now we're at a cloverleaf."

Activity VI C 6

A. Problem: *What Is Global Warming (the Greenhouse Effect)?*

B. Materials Needed:

1. Flannel board
2. Large orange, flannel semicircle
3. Smaller, dark-colored flannel circle
4. Tiny circles of flannel (any color)
5. Many thin, white or orange flannel strips

C. Procedure:

1. Place large semicircle at top of flannel board. This is the sun.
2. Place the smaller circle at the bottom of flannel board. This is the Earth.
3. Place tiny circles at random between the "sun" and the "Earth." These are "air pollutants." Air pollutants consist of particulate matter, carbon dioxide gas, and other gases.
4. Place thin strips of flannel as shown in drawing. These are rays of the sun.
5. Discuss what a "greenhouse" is, what it does.
6. Discuss how the air is full of particles such as:
   a. smoke
   b. soot
   c. industrial gases
   d. automobile exhausts
   e. aerosprays
   f. salt particles
   g. ashes, etc.
7. Using the flannel board, show how the sun's rays strike the Earth, bounce back to hit the particles, and bounce back to the Earth again.
8. Explain that this "double warming" raises the temperature of the Earth's surface. This is called the "Greenhouse Effect."
9. Also tell the class that some of the rays that are reflected back from the Earth to the air miss the particles and return to space.

D. Result:

Students will learn, by visualization, a very difficult concept, the "Greenhouse Effect."

E. Basic Facts and Supplemental Information:

1. If the Greenhouse Effect were the only additional factor affecting the Earth's atmospheric temperature, our Earth would gradually warm up and cause some or all of the polar caps to melt.
2. If the polar caps melt this would increase the water level all over Earth up to 20 feet, flooding many of our coastal cities and lowlands. The latest predictions by meteorologists are that the ocean water levels will rise only 10 feet (3 meters) in the next 100 years if the current trend continues.

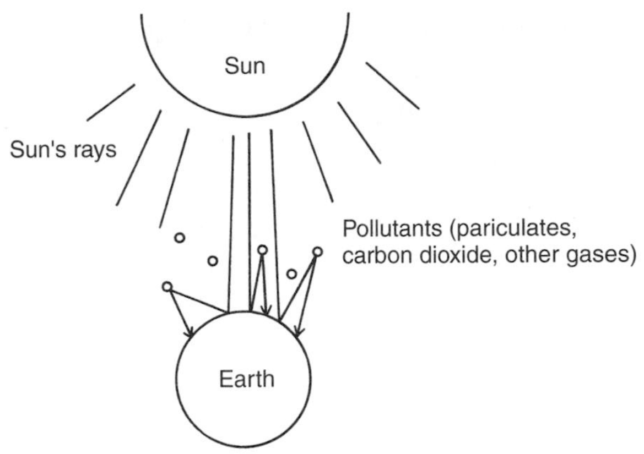

3. When we burn oil, coal, or wood we release a lot of carbon dioxide into the atmosphere.
4. Global warming is caused by people producing too much carbon dioxide and other pollutant gases.
5. These gases act as a blanket and retain the heat that would normally escape into the atmosphere.
6. This blanket permits the sun's short-wave radiation to pass through but reflects the Earth's long-wave heat radiation that tries to escape.

F. Thought Questions for Class Discussions:

1. Would this effect decrease the Earth's land area?
2. What would this do to our present harbors?
3. How would this affect people who live or work along the coast?

G. Related Ideas for Further Inquiry:

1. Study Section VII-C, "Earth's Crust."
2. Study Section VII-E, "Weather."
3. Study other Activities in this Section.

H. Vocabulary Builders—Spelling Words:

1) **Greenhouse Effect** 2) **particles** 3) **rays** 4) **pollutants** 5) **global** 6) **warming**

I. Thought for Today:

"He's the kind of a person that adds more heat than light to a discussion."

Activity

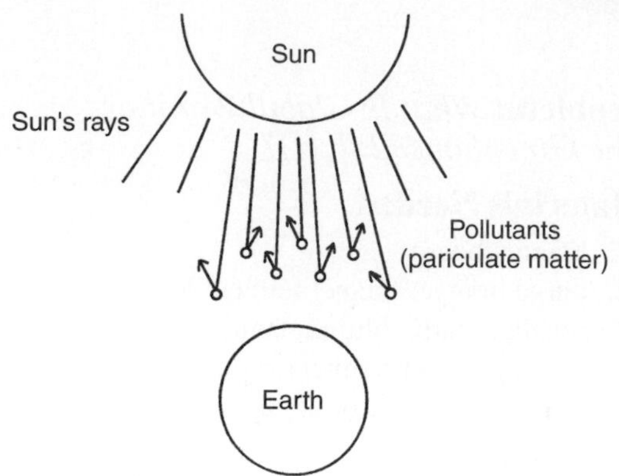

A. Problem: *What Is Global Cooling (the Icehouse Effect)?*

B. Materials Needed:

1. Flannel board
2. Large orange, flannel semicircle
3. Smaller dark-colored flannel circle
4. Tiny circles of flannel (any color)
5. Many thin, white or orange flannel strips

C. Procedure:

1. Place large semicircle at top of flannel board. This is the sun.
2. Place small circle at bottom of flannel board. This is the Earth.
3. Place tiny circles at random between the "Sun" and the "Earth." These are "air pollutants."
4. Place thin strips of flannel as shown in drawing.
5. Discuss with class what an icehouse is. It is (or was) a building for storing ice. At one time it was the only cold place for keeping large quantities of meats and foods from spoiling.
6. Discuss how the air contains pollutants, most of which are initiated by people:
   a. smoke
   b. soot
   c. industrial gases
   d. automobile exhausts
   e. aerosprays
   f. salt particles
   g. ashes, etc.
7. Using flannel board, show how the "Sun's" rays strike the particles and are reflected back into space.
8. Explain how this prevents the Earth from receiving its normal heat and consequently, reduces the temperature of the Earth's surface. This is called the "Icehouse Effect."

D. Result:

Students will learn, by visualization, a very difficult concept: global cooling (the Icehouse Effect).

E. Basic Facts and Supplemental Information:

1. If the Icehouse Effect were the only additional factor affecting the Earth's atmospheric temperature, our Earth would gradually cool, causing our polar icecaps to increase in size; this would cause our glaciers to start to move again.
2. This would have the opposite effect of the Greenhouse Effect. It would drop our ocean water levels and increase the ice-covered land areas.
3. Mt. Pinatubo in the Philippines erupted in June 1991, spewing 20 million tons of sulphur dioxide and an unknown amount of ash into the stratosphere. The National Oceanic and Atmospheric Administration reported that the average global temperature dropped 1° F. after the first year, no doubt because of the excess pollutants in the air.

F. Thought Questions for Class Discussions:

1. Would the Icehouse Effect increase our land area?
2. What would this do to our present harbors? marinas?
3. How would this affect people who live or work along the coast?

G. Related Ideas for Further Inquiry:

1. Study Section I-B, "Air."
2. Study Section VII-C, "Earth's Crust."
3. Study Section VII-E, "Weather."
4. Study Activity VI-C-1, "What are the main environmental problems?"
5. Study Activity VI-C-2, "What pollutants are in the air?"
6. Study Activity VI-C-3, "What is smog?"
7. Study Activity VI-C-4, "What is the ozone problem?"
8. Study Activity VI-C-5, "What causes acid rain?"
9. Study Activity VI-C-6, "What is global warming (the Greenhouse Effect)?"
10. Study Activity VI-C-8, "How does pollution affect food chains and food webs?"

H. Vocabulary Builders—Spelling Words:

1) **Icehouse Effect** 2) **particles** 3) **rays**
4) **reflection** 5) **pollutants** 6) **cooling**

I. Thought for Today:

"The biggest liar in the world is 'They say.' "

Activity

VI C 8

A. Problem: *How Does Pollution Affect Food Chains and Food Webs?*

B. Materials Needed:

Pictures or models of:

1. Plants
2. Herbivores (plant-eating animals)
3. First-level carnivore (meat-eating animals)
4. Second-level carnivore (larger carnivores that eat first-level carnivores)
5. Flannel board and flannel cutouts (optional)

C. Procedure:

1. Describe several food chains:
   a. carrot, rabbit, people
   b. kelp, fish, tuna, people
   c. grass, cow, people
   d. kelp, small fish, large fish, people
2. Discuss ways pollution affects each of these:
   a. grass—harmed by air pollutants
   b. animals—harmed by insecticides
   c. people—harmed by increased irritants from all sources
3. If desired, these processes can be effectively shown on a flannel board adding one step in the food chain at a time.
4. If desired, food webs can also be explained in a similar way except that instead of a straight-line chain pattern, a circular pattern can be shown with several alternative food sources for each higher-level organism.

D. Results:

1. Students will learn about food chains and food webs.
2. Students will learn that some poisons become more concentrated as they move up the food chain, and the more concentrated they are, the more damaging they are to the organisms involved. Poisoning organisms destroys the natural food chains and food webs.
3. Students will learn that pollution anywhere affects our food supply.

E. Basic Facts and Supplemental Information:

1. Poisons build up in organisms.
2. Poisons tend to stay in the organism that eats them.
3. For example, if a phytoplankton picks up one unit of mercury (a poison) it will have one unit of mercury in its body.

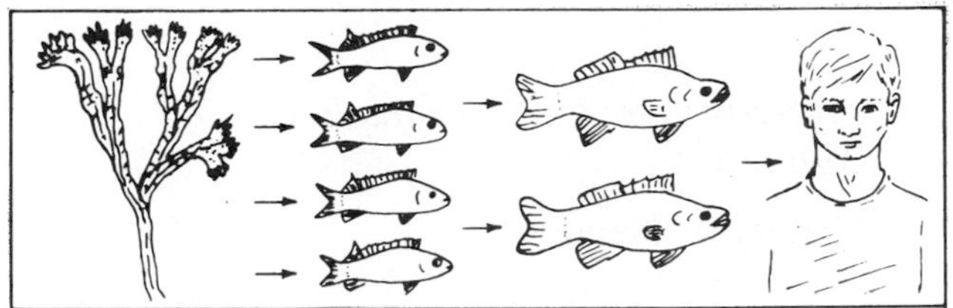

A food chain

4. If a small fish eats 1,000 phytoplankton, it will ingest 1,000 units of mercury.
5. If a large fish eats 50 small fish, it will ingest 50 times 1,000 or 50,000 units of mercury.
6. If a large mammal or a person eats two large fish, then 2 times 50,000 or 100,000 units of mercury will be ingested.
7. Large mammals and people can become very seriously ill because of this buildup of mercury.
8. Japanese individuals who ate a lot of fish that were contaminated developed very deformed bodies—a symptom of mercury poisoning.
9. Other toxic materials act in a similar fashion.
10. Phytoplankton are important because they supply us with about 75% of our oxygen supply.

F. Thought Questions for Class Discussions:

1. How can people avoid poisoning themselves (regarding pollution)?
2. Do you think people should go back to living like they did 100 years ago? What would be the advantages? the disadvantages?
3. What is the difference between a food chain and a food web?

G. Related Ideas for Further Inquiry:

1. Study Section IV-E, "Water Animals (Fish and Amphibians)."
2. Study Section IV-G, "Mammals."
3. Study Section V-C, "Nutrition."
4. Study Activity VI-A-2, "What is 'biological diversity'?"
5. Study Activity VI-C-1, "What are the main environmental problems?"
6. Study Activity VI-C-9, "Are our oceans becoming polluted?"

H. Vocabulary Builders—Spelling Words:

1) **plants** 2) **herbivores** 3) **carnivores**
4) **insecticides** 5) **mercury** 6) **phytoplankton**

I. Thought for Today:

"A little learning is a dangerous thing—just ask any kid who comes home with a bad report card."

Activity VI C 9

A. Problem: *Are Our Oceans Becoming Polluted?*

B. Materials Needed:

1. Scraps of paper
2. Empty cans
3. Oil
4. Pan
5. Water
6. Hot plate
7. Large bucket or sink
8. Pieces of glass (handle carefully)
9. Food coloring (for chemicals)

C. Procedure:

1. Tell students that the bucket or sink will represent the ocean.
2. Heat a pan of water on the hot plate.
3. While water is heating, throw paper scraps in the bucket (or sink). Tell students this represents everything from cardboard boxes to sandwich wrappers which people throw in streams, rivers, lakes, and oceans.
4. Toss in empty cans and pieces of glass. This represents broken bottles, dishes, and beer and soft drink cans people throw in all our waters. (Handle glass and cans carefully.)
5. Add food coloring. This represents industrial chemicals, sewage disposal, etc.
6. Add the hot water. This represents atomic wastes.
7. Ask students if they would like to swim in this "ocean," "lake," etc.
8. Ask students if they think that fish can live in this "ocean."

D. Results:

1. The water in the bucket (or sink) becomes dirtier and dirtier and more and more polluted.
2. Students will realize that everyone contributes to polluted waters.

E. Basic Facts and Supplemental Information:

1. Jacques Cousteau said that unless ocean pollution is abated, it will destroy the seas within 50 years.
2. All types of pollution originating on land and air, wind up in the oceans.
3. Many of our shorelines and beaches are being polluted and reducing our phytoplankton.
4. All oceans and land areas have seasons, and each one has its own food web.
5. We get about 55,000,000 tons of food from the oceans now; this will be decreased significantly unless we stop polluting and overfishing.

6. Areas where the streams enter into the oceans are becoming deadly and killing many shellfish that live in these areas. Shellfish provide food for many large fish.

F. Thought Questions for Class Discussions:

1. Do you think our fish should be harvested like other crops?
2. Should we have some international controls over the oceans fishing?
3. How can we stop polluting the oceans?

G. Related Ideas for Further Inquiry:

1. Study Section I-C, "Water."
2. Interview ocean travelers, sailors, and/or fishermen about ocean pollution.
3. Study Section VII-C, "Earth's Crust."
4. Study other Activities in this Section.

H. Vocabulary Builders—Spelling Words:

1) **oceans** 2) **pollution** 3) **chemicals**
4) **streams** 5) **shellfish** 6) **disastrous**

I. Thought for Today:

"Seventy-five years ago the only water pollution people knew anything about was the Saturday night bath."

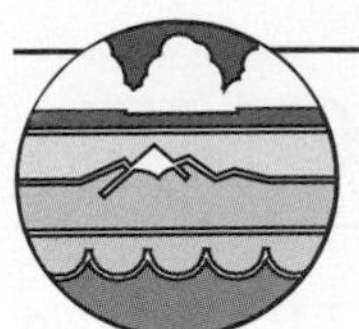

Activity VI C 10

A. Problem: *What Is Soil Erosion?*

B. Materials Needed:

1. Large clear glass or clear plastic jar
2. Small rocks
3. Pebbles
4. Sand
5. Small leaves
6. Twigs
7. Dirt
8. Reference books about soil erosion

C. Procedure:

1. Place the items (2 through 7) listed in Materials Needed in layers in the jar in the order listed.
2. Ask students if they have had any experiences with planting or growing agricultural products.
3. Discuss the values of our topsoil.
4. Cite how our topsoils are slowly becoming eroded.
5. Discuss how soils are formed.

D. Results:

1. Students will realize that soils are a very precious resource and must be used judiciously.
2. Students will learn that soils take a long time to develop.

E. Basic Facts and Supplemental Information:

1. Much of our food and clothing originates from topsoil.
2. Topsoil is partially made up of the plants that grow in it.
3. It contains organic material from animals.
4. Soil contains nutrients with compounds containing nitrogen, sulphur, phosphorus, potassium, calcium, magnesium, and many other substances that are essential for plant and animal life.
5. We must safeguard our soils and maintain their fertility.
6. When crops are grown, most of the nutrients are gradually withdrawn from the soil.
7. If these are not put back into the soil, the plants will become dwarfed because the soil will be less fertile.
8. If this happens, animals (including people) that eat the plants will become increasingly unhealthy.
9. Erosion does more damage to the soil than the growing of crops.
10. Erosion, carrying away the soil, is caused by winds and rains after:
    a. clearing away brush and forests
    b. removing ground cover
    c. overgrazing by farm animals
    d. using heavy farm equipment
11. When erosion occurs, the soil is left barren and the winds and the rains wash the soils into rivers and streams, silting the water, and killing most of the aquatic life.

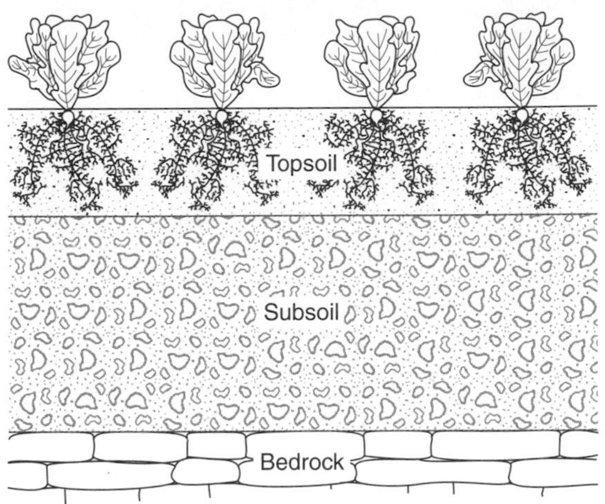

12. Soil conservation is a science. The following are some very important techniques to prevent soil erosion:
    a. adding soil nutrients
    b. crop rotation
    c. contour farming
    d. wind breaks
    e. plowing land and leaving it unseeded for a growing season or two (fallowing)

F. Thought Questions for Class Discussions:

1. Is there any soil erosion in your community?
2. Will our increasing population cause more soil erosion?
3. How can we feed more people if our soil becomes increasingly eroded?

G. Related Ideas for Further Inquiry:

1. Study the soil conservation procedures in your community.
2. Discuss with the school gardener how the soil on campus is protected.
3. Study Section VII-C, "Earth's Crust."
4. Study Section VII-E, "Weather."
5. Study the effects and consequences of using pesticides, herbicides, and fertilizers on our agricultural lands.
6. Study "gulleying."

H. Vocabulary Builders—Spelling Words:

1) **erosion** 2) **crops** 3) **weathering**
4) **rotation** 5) **terracing** 6) **minerals**
7) **fertilizers** 8) **pesticides**

I. Thought for Today:

"Soil erosion occurs when a ten-year-old boy washes his hands."

Activity

VI D 1

A. Problem: *How Can We Help Solve Some of the Pollution Problems?*

B. Materials Needed:

1. Colored paper towels or tissue
2. Wire clothes hanger
3. Glass bottle
4. Newspaper
5. Lunch box
6. Pictures of litter, strip-mined lands, hovels, automobile junkyards, etc.

C. Procedure:

1. Discuss the problems of pollution.
2. Students can do research on or students can discuss ways in which they can personally help with the pollution solutions.
3. Discuss how America is made up of states: states have counties, counties have cities, cities have schools, and schools have classrooms.
4. To make and keep America beautiful, the students should start with their own rooms at home and their own classroom.
5. After the classroom is neat, initiate a clean-campus campaign.
6. After the campus is cleaned up, the class or school might make a list of ways in which they all can help solve our pollution problems such as:
   a. Have students make a list of actions that they can do individually or collectively that will help our environment.
   b. Discuss with students what each is doing to save our planet.
   c. Post items on the bulletin board describing environmental problems and activities that can alleviate them.

D. Results:

Students will learn that they should:

1. Use only white paper towels, paper napkins, or tissue. (Dyes pollute water.)
2. Use cloth towels instead of paper towels *when possible.*
3. Use a lunch box rather than paper bags.
4. Reduce the amount of electricity consumed in their homes, particularly electric appliances. (Electricity requires generating plants which produce pollution.)

5. Save newspapers and magazines. (One ton of recycled paper saves 17 trees.)
6. Use both sides of writing paper at home and at school.
7. Walk and bicycle when possible rather than asking parent(s) or other adult(s) to drive automobiles.
8. Compost or bury garbage (especially vegetable trimmings).
9. Return wire coat hangers to the cleaners.
10. Use containers that disintegrate easily (paper or cardboard).
11. Plant trees and vegetable gardens.
12. Stop littering.
13. Avoid wasting water.
14. Avoid buying products or clothes made from endangered species.
15. Use reusable shopping bags (cloth and net types).
16. Avoid suntan lotions when swimming in a lake, river, or ocean.
17. Use biodegradable soap and cleaning products.
18. Refuse to buy overpackaged items.
19. Initiate rummage sales.
20. Recycle paper, plastic, glass, and metal products.
21. Ride in car pools.
22. Promote wildlife.
23. Practice soil conservation.
24. Discourage everyone from using off-road vehicles that scar the environment.
25. Choose biodegradable products marked "cruelty free" or "not tested on animals."
26. Take more showers, less baths.
27. Use rechargeable batteries.
28. Properly dispose of toxic substances.
29. Remember the 5 Rs in helping our environment:
    recycle — repair
    reuse — refuse (excess packaging, wasting)
    reduce
30. Talk about and practice ecology.

E. Basic Facts and Supplemental Information:

1. Students will learn that cleanliness is everybody's responsibility.
2. With everyone helping a little, a great deal can be accomplished.
3. There are many activities that adults can do to protect our environment:
   a. conserving
   b. recycling
   c. salvaging
   d. reducing electric consumption
   e. composting
   f. reducing oil use
   g. using biological controls of pests
   h. reusing materials
   i. rotating crops
   j. terracing
   k. contour farming
   l. reducing watershed contamination
   m. reducing noise pollution
   n. preventing littering
   o. reducing radiation
   p. halting the destruction of our forests and especially our rain forests
   q. protecting wild life
   r. promoting health
   s. educating everyone about environmental problems and solutions

F. Thought Questions for Class Discussions:

1. Why should we keep America clean?
2. Who should be responsible for keeping America clean?
3. How can vandalism be stopped?
4. Who owns the forests, parks, highway roadsides, beaches, etc.?
5. What will happen if we don't think ecologically?
6. Is pollution everybody's responsibility or just the government's?

G. Related Ideas for Further Inquiry:

1. Have students check their homes for ways they can improve the environment.
2. Have students add other activities to the list cited in Results to help our planet.
3. Study Section VI-A, "Ecosystems."
4. Study Section VI-C, "Pollution."
5. Study Activity VI-D-2, "What is 'sustainability'?"
6. Study Activity VI-D-3, "What is recycling? salvaging? reusing?"
7. Study Activity VI-D-6, "How can we protect our recreational areas?"

H. Vocabulary Builders—Spelling Words:

1) **pollution** 2) **solution** 3) **recycle**
4) **reuse** 5) **reduce** 6) **repair**
7) **refuse** 8) **research**

I. Thought for Today:

"Thanks to the miles of superhighways under construction, America will soon be a wonderful place to drive—if you don't have to stop."

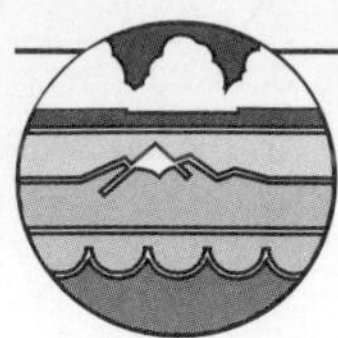

Activity VI D 2

A. Problem: *What Is "Sustainability"?*

B. Materials:

1. Several cans of food
2. Several cans of oil
3. Bottle of water
4. Empty milk carton
5. Pictures of:
   a. trees, shrubs, and other plants
   b. wildlife
   c. atmosphere

C. Procedure:

1. Explain to students that we are all passengers on a great spaceship—Planet Earth.
2. Tell the students that each spaceship must carry its own supplies. There is no other place where we can stop and replenish them.
3. Our spaceship cannot use up or destroy more resources than it can subsequently develop. This is called "SUSTAINABILITY." It is the key to our survival.
4. Ask students what they would do if there were no more of the items listed in Materials Needed (B-5).
5. Challenge them to propose alternatives for our food, water, oil, etc., if these items were to become scarce, nonexistent, or unfit for human consumption.

D. Results:

1. Students will begin to realize that our planet has limited resources.
2. Students will learn that if life on our planet is to survive, we must use our resources more intelligently and not waste or destroy them.
3. They will learn that "sustainability" should be the main criterion for the use of many of our earthly supplies.

E. Basic Facts and Supplemental Information:

1. Our air is becoming more polluted.
2. Our population is expected to double in the next century.
3. Doubling the planet's population will double the need for water, living space, food, energy, and all the other basic resources we need.
4. Our agricultural lands are being diminished as new residences, streets, buildings, etc., are developed.
5. Our wildlife is being depleted.
6. Fresh-water supplies are not evenly distributed throughout the world, and as populations increase, water will become a premium commodity.

F. Thought Questions for Class Discussions:

1. Can the world support twice as many people? ten times as many?
2. How can we prevent millions of people from starving to death every year?
3. Should we continue to bury our garbage in landfills and dump our wastes in the oceans?
4. Do you think "sustainability" is a good idea?
5. If we double the number of people in the world, will we double the amount of air pollution? water pollution?
6. Will there be enough food, water, and natural resources for future generations?

G. Related Ideas for Further Inquiry:

1. Study the difference between "renewable" and "nonrenewable" sources of energy.
2. Study the problems of soil erosion.
3. Study the causes of droughts.
4. Study Activity VI-D-1, "How can we help solve some of the pollution problems?"
5. Study Activity VI-D-3, "What is recycling? salvaging? reusing?"
6. Study Activity VI-D-4, "What is the best way to dispose of our garbage and wastes?"
7. Study Activity VI-D-5, "Can we use solar energy to reduce pollution?"
8. Study Activity VI-D-6, "How can we protect our recreational areas?"
9. Study Section VII-C, "Earth's Crust."

H. Vocabulary Builders—Spelling Words:

1) **sustainability** 2) **conserve** 3) **recycle** 4) **reuse** 5) **sewage** 6) **wastes** 7) **wildlife**

I. Thought for Today:

"One of our biggest problems is heir pollution."

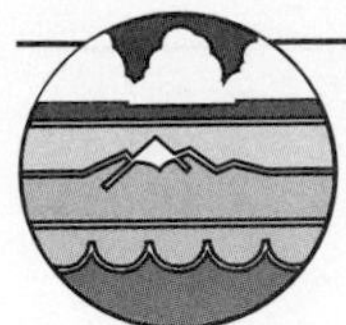

Activity

A. Problem: *What Is Recycling? Salvaging? Reusing?*

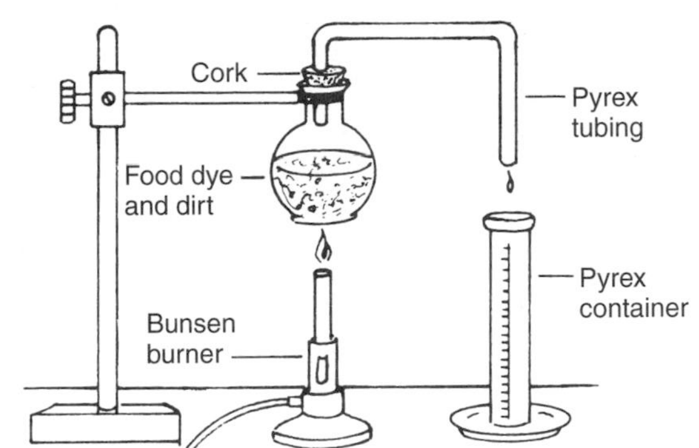

This symbol tells you that the product can be recycled. It does not mean that the product is made of recycled materials.

This symbol tells you that the product has been made with a minimum of 50% recycled materials.

B. Materials Needed:

1. Florence flask
2. Single-hole stopper
3. Stand and clamps
4. Heating device
5. Pyrex jar
6. Pyrex tubing
7. Piece of toweling
8. Dirt
9. Leaves
10. Salt
11. Food dye
12. Gloves
13. Wet rag

C. Procedure:

1. Discuss with students the necessity of recycling and salvaging. (If we used things only once, we would soon run out of things to use.)
2. Discuss biodegradable (naturally decomposable) items.
3. Discuss how we now recycle, salvage, and reuse some materials that we have on hand.
4. Place some dirt, leaves, salt, and colored water in a Florence flask.
5. Place glass tubing connections in rubber or cork stopper and fit on flask. (Tubing can be bent by gently warming over heating device and carefully rotating and bending as tubing gets hotter. Use gloves as a safety precaution against burns.)
6. Heat contents with Bunsen burner, hot plate, or Sterno.
7. Place wet rag around tubing to cool liquid.
8. Clear water will come out the condensed side.
9. Have students name other items that have been recycled or salvaged; paper, cars, metals, glass, etc.

D. Results:

1. The water has been recycled.
2. Pure water has been salvaged.
3. Recycled water is pure and can be reused.
4. Students will learn about using materials over and over again.

E. Basic Facts and Supplemental Information:

1. Many discarded items made of paper, glass, metals, tires, plastic, cloth, etc., can be returned to industry for new products or energy. Recycling of this sort requires a major focus involving careful planning.
2. Even unusable garbage can be used for some landfills.
3. Some items can be burned, and if complete burning takes place the only products will be water and carbon dioxide. Incomplete burning will produce carbon monoxide, smoke, sulphur dioxide, nitrous oxides, etc.
4. Our landfills are rapidly filling up; most large cities have a shortage of landfill areas.
5. Discarded furniture, clothing, and household items have been recycled in America for over 75 years by collecting agencies.

F. Thought Questions for Class Discussions:

1. Should we worry about salvaging and recycling, or should we let the next generation worry about itself?
2. Are some solid items biodegradable? (It takes glass about 100 years, aluminum about 1,000 years, and plastics many thousands of years to disintegrate.)
3. Should we separate our garbage into salvageable and nonsalvageable items?

G. Related Ideas for Further Inquiry:

1. Make a collection of items that could be recycled. *Look for symbols on packaging.* (See drawings.)
2. Make two lists of disposable items: one that is recyclable and one that is biodegradable.
3. List items that would make good compost (plant enrichment).
4. Students might want to develop a compost site for a school garden. A school gardener can make some good suggestions.
5. Study other Activities in this Section.

H. Vocabulary Builders—Spelling Words:

1) **recycle** 2) **salvage** 3) **compost** 4) **reusable** 5) **biodegradable** 6) **landfills** 7) **Pyrex**

I. Thought for Today:

"Nothing is more confusing than people who give good advice but set bad examples."

Activity

VI D 4

A. Problem: *What Is the Best Way to Dispose of Our Garbage and Wastes?*

B. Materials Needed:

1. Newspaper accounts of:
   a. landfills
   b. wastes collection
   c. other waste disposal methods
2. Pictures of garbage
3. Pictures of nonhazardous waste items:
   a. empty cans
   b. old newspapers
   c. glass, plastic, and metal containers
   d. miscellaneous junk

C. Procedure:

1. Discuss some of the ways that we presently get rid of our garbage and wastes:
   a. bury (landfills)
   b. burn
   c. dump in ocean
   d. recycle
   e. litter
2. Discuss whether these are good or bad practices.
3. Have students make a study of the disposable items that they must get rid of from their own homes. Show or describe samples.
4. Have students study where these items are eventually "stored" or "eliminated."
5. Collect data on landfills. Cite the fact that the average person disposes of about one ton of garbage and wastes each year and this must be disposed of in some safe way.
6. Discuss the problems of landfills.
   a. Many are filling up fast and hundreds have already been closed.
   b. When new dumpsites are proposed, the vast majority of people have the "NIMBY" attitude (*N*ot *I*n *M*y *B*ackyard).
7. Discuss the problems of hazardous and nuclear wastes, especially long-term radioactivity from nuclear energy production.

D. Results:

1. Students will learn that the problem of wastes is a serious problem and that it is getting worse all the time as more and more people use more and more materials which must be disposed of.
2. Students will realize that the disposal of hazardous and nuclear wastes is of great concern.

E. Basic Facts and Supplemental Information:

1. Many materials can be reclaimed or recycled.
2. Glass can be broken into many small pieces and used as a base for roadbeds.
3. Meltable products can be reclaimed.
4. Some materials can be burned with a minimum of air pollution, while others produce highly toxic pollutants.
5. Newspapers can be recycled.
6. Last year, people threw out more than 100 million tires, 30 billion bottles, 60 billion cans, 9 million automobiles, 4 million tons of plastics, 1 million television sets, and uncounted millions of other appliances.

F. Thought Questions for Class Discussions:

1. Can you think of any constructive ways to get rid of our waste products?
2. Do you think we should levy a tax on disposable items?
3. Should we pass laws to prevent throw-away packaging for one-way containers?

G. Related Ideas for Further Inquiry:

1. Study Section VII-C, "Earth's Crust."
2. Study Section VI-C, "Pollution."
3. Study other Activities in this Section.

H. Vocabulary Builders—Spelling Words:

1) **solids** 2) **wastes** 3) **litter** 4) **recycle** 5) **landfills** 6) **reuse** 7) **nontoxic**

I. Thought for Today:

"The mind is a wonderful thing. It starts working the minute you're born and never stops until you get up to speak in public."

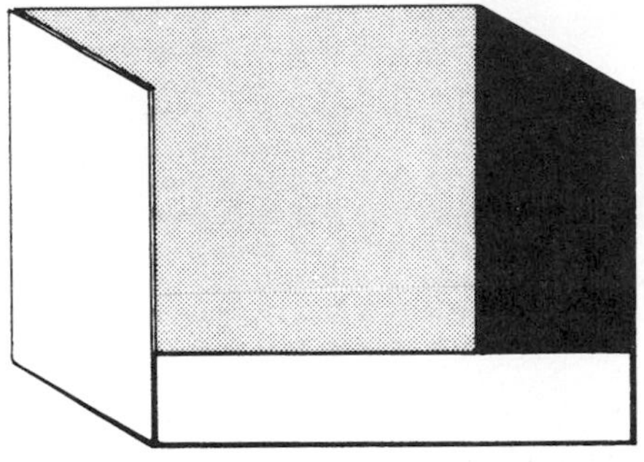
Cutout box

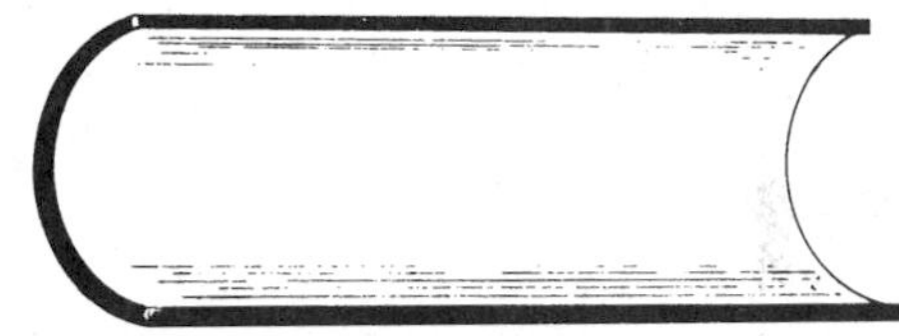
Half-cylindrical reflector

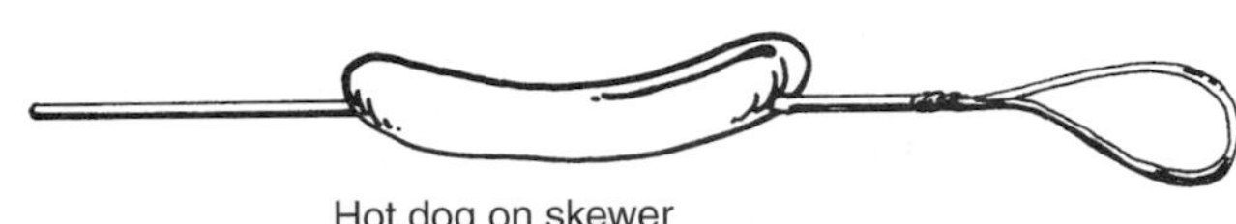
Hot dog on skewer

A. Problem: *Can We Use Solar Energy to Reduce Pollution?*

B. Materials Needed:

1. Hot dog, raw
2. Cardboard box, large
3. Filament tape
4. Aluminum foil
5. Coat hanger
6. Scissors
7. Black spray paint
8. Awl (or pointed scissors)

C. Procedure:

1. Construction Procedure:
   a. Cut the top and three-fourths of one large side off one large cardboard box. (See top drawing.)
   b. Spray black paint on all insides including inside bottom.
   c. Using the top of the original box curve it to make a reflector. (See middle drawing.)
   d. Cover this reflector with aluminum foil.
   e. Secure this to back of box with filament tape and face the opening toward the sun when completed.
   f. With awl or pointed scissors, carefully punch holes on two sides of the box.
2. Teaching Procedure:
   a. Discuss forms of energy.
   b. Discuss solar energy.
   c. Discuss personal uses of solar energy: pool heaters, home water heating, etc.
   d. Demonstrate how a magnifying glass concentrates the sun's rays to produce heat and fire.
   e. On a hot day, tell the class that we're going to see if we can use solar energy to cook a hot dog.
   f. Start skewer through one side of box, impale the hot dog, then insert through hole on other side.
   g. For best results, rotate the hot dog after 5 minutes.

D. Results:

1. On a hot day with direct sunlight, the hot dog will cook in about 45 minutes.
2. Students will realize that solar energy can be a practical source of energy.

E. Basic Facts and Supplemental Information:

1. Don't place hot dog too close to curved surface. Ideally it should be at the focal point of the curved backing (4 to 6 inches from the back).
2. Keep turning the box toward the sun if more time is needed.
3. White reflects light; black absorbs light.
4. Eventually, solar energy is going to be a necessity for all people everywhere.

F. Thought Questions for Class Discussions:

1. Why is black the best color to use?
2. Was there any pollution in this Activity?
3. What other uses of solar energy might be used?

G. Related Ideas for Further Inquiry:

1. Study Section II-B, "Fire and Heat."
2. Study Section V-C, "Nutrition."
3. Study Section VII-B, "Solar System."
4. Study other Activities in this Section.

H. Vocabulary Builders—Spelling Words:

1) **solar** 2) **energy** 3) **pollution**
4) **cardboard** 5) **cooker** 6) **aluminum**

I. Thought for Today:

"To be born a gentleman or gentlewoman is an accident; to die one, an achievement."

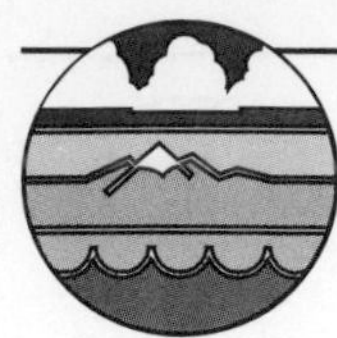

Activity VI D 6

A. Problem: *How Can We Protect Our Recreational Areas?*

B. Materials Needed:

1. Litterbag
2. Aerosol spray can
3. Shovel
4. Pick
5. Trash can, bucket
6. Newspaper accounts of forest fires, vandalism, etc.

C. Procedure:

1. Discuss where students take their vacations.
2. Ask how many have been to our forests? parks?
3. Discuss what they have seen people do that caused harm to the attractiveness or usefulness of these resources.
4. Discuss what they could have done to keep these resources beautiful.
5. Show some of the materials that could be used to keep our public resources clean and beautiful, and discuss some of the procedures that could help save our natural resources. These might include:
   a. Carry a litterbag in your car and always use it.
   b. Don't paint on rocks, trees, or fences. Let the natural beauty show.
   c. Clean up a trail, stream, or campsite.
   d. Picnic areas, beaches, parks, and roadsides do not provide maid service. Help keep these areas clean.
   e. Keep volume on your radio, tape deck, or CD set at moderate level.
   f. Have an effective muffler on your car, truck, or motorcycle.
   g. Sound your horn only when safety dictates.
   h. Help fight vandalism and graffiti that detract from the outdoor environment.
   i. Start an Ecology Club or environmental improvement committee in your school or community.
   j. Be sure your community participates in environmental beautification programs.

D. Results:

1. Students will realize that the beauty of natural resources is everyone's responsibility.
2. Students will learn that as our population increases there will be increasing demands to replace our recreational areas with homes, businesses, and other community projects.

E. Basic Facts and Supplemental Information:

1. Our natural resources are beautiful—let's keep them that way.
2. Our forests and parks are important not only to us but also to many species of plant and animal life.
3. It takes 500,000 trees to produce the Sunday newspapers read in the United States each week.
4. Many of our present and potential medicines and drugs come from our trees. We must protect them carefully.
5. Many fruits, nuts, and berries come from our forests.
6. The enemies of our forests and parks are fire, disease, insects, natural elements, and people.

F. Thought Questions for Class Discussions:

1. Why should we take care of our forests and public parks?
2. Who should have prime responsibility for their upkeep?
3. What should we do about the vandalism in our public areas?
4. Who owns the public forests and parks?

G. Related Ideas for Further Inquiry:

1. Study Section VII-C, "Earth's Crust."
2. Study Section II-B, "Fire and Heat."
3. Study Section VI-C, "Pollution."
4. Study Part IV, "Animals."
5. Study other Activities in this Section.

H. Vocabulary Builders—Spelling Words:

1) **litter** 2) **litterbag** 3) **ecology**
4) **responsibility** 5) **resources** 6) **beaches**
7) **forests** 8) **parks**

I. Thought for Today:

"Personal liberty ends where public safety begins."

Activity

A. Problem: *How Can We Help Prevent Forest Fires?*

B. Materials:

1. Picture of Smokey Bear
2. Matches
3. Dry grass
4. Metal tray
5. Pitcher of water
6. Widemouthed quart jar
7. Heat protective pad
8. Desk or tabletop

C. Procedure:

1. Explain the "Fire Triangle" (See Activity II-B-1.) Tell the students that if all three of the following elements are present, fire will occur:
   a. burnable material
   b. oxygen
   c. heat (kindling point)
2. Tell the students how the elimination of one of these elements will stop any fire.
3. Place the protective pad on desk or tabletop.
4. Place the tray on the pad.
5. Place a few blades of dry grass on the metal tray.
6. *Carefully* ignite them with a match.
7. Cover with a quart jar (eliminates oxygen).
8. Place a few more blades of dry grass on the metal tray.
9. *Carefully* ignite them with a match.
10. Pour cold water on burning grass (reduces temperature or heat).
11. *Carefully* light match on tray. Nothing else on the tray is burnable (except the match).

D. Results:

1. Fire will be extinguished when oxygen is removed.
2. Fire will be extinguished when heat is reduced below the kindling point.
3. Fire will not take place if no burnable material is present.

E. Basic Facts and Supplemental Information:

1. Many fires are started without matches if the three major elements of the fire triangle are present.
2. For older students, heat can be applied to the tray and a wooden match on top will be ignited from the heat. Be sure heat protection pad is under the tray.

F. Thought Questions for Class Discussions:

1. How are forest fires started?
2. What can be done to prevent forest fires? Smokey advises us to:
   a. Extinguish the flame on the match, then break the match in two.
   b. Drown all campfire ashes and drown again.
   c. REMEMBER, ONLY YOU CAN PREVENT FOREST FIRES.

G. Related Ideas for Further Inquiry:

1. Study Section II-B, "Fire and Heat."
2. Study Activity V-F-1, "What are the main procedures for treating injuries and/or accidents?"
3. Study Activity V-G-3, "How safe are our homes?"
4. Study Activity VI-D-6, "How can we protect our recreational areas?"
5. See other Activities in this Section.

H. Vocabulary Builders—Spelling Words:

1) **Smokey** 2) **burnable** 3) **material** 4) **triangle** 5) **oxygen** 6) **kindling** 7) **matches** 8) **extinguish**

I. Thought for Today:

"One tree can make a million matches. One match can destroy a million trees."

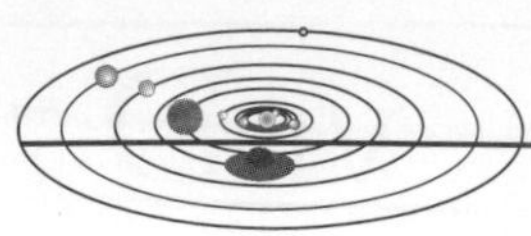

PART VII

EARTH AND SPACE

Section A: Universe

Activity VII A 1

A. Problem: *What Kinds of Heavenly Bodies Are There?*

B. Materials Needed:

1. Astronomy charts
2. Model spaceships
3. Books and pictures on space

C. Procedure:

1. Discuss travel by planes.
2. Discuss the difference between plane travel and space travel (leaving Earth's atmosphere).
3. Ask students to list all the different kinds of heavenly bodies that they know about outside the Earth's atmosphere.
4. Have them read books and pamphlets about space and space travel.

D. Results:

1. Students will learn that there are many kinds of heavenly bodies.
2. They will realize that space is vast.

E. Basic Facts and Supplemental Information:

1. All heavenly bodies are contained in the universe.
2. No one knows whether our universe is finite or infinite, how it got started, or exactly how old it is.
3. Many astronomers believe that the universe was created 12 to 13.4 billion years ago from a great explosion called the "Big Bang."
4. Only about 10% of the cosmic material is known.
5. Known heavenly bodies consist of galaxies, superclusters, star clusters, constellations, supernovas, novas, stars, and quasars that emit light.
6. Planets, asteroids, meteors, satellites, and comets do not emit light.
7. The balance of known objects in space consists of gas, radiation, and dust and includes nebulae, and rays (gamma, X-rays, ultraviolet, and infrared).
8. Black holes (recently confirmed objects in space) are highly dense. Their gravity is so strong that they pull in everything around them—even light. Since they do not emit any light, they are black and consequently, they are called "black holes."
9. The Van Allen Radiation Belts lie within our atmosphere and protect us from strong ultraviolet radiations.

10. In 1993, our spacecraft Galileo photographed a tiny satellite, a moon ("Dactyl") one mile wide, encircling the 34-mile-long asteroid, "Ida."

F. Thought Questions for Class Discussions:

1. Would you like to take a space trip to another galaxy? (Even if it took 25 to 50 years?)
2. What would be some of the problems you might encounter on such a trip?
3. Do you think there could be other planets like the Earth where conditions would be similar and life could exist? (Scientists estimate that there could be about 10,000,000 planets like the Earth in our universe.)

G. Related Ideas for Further Inquiry:

1. Visit an observatory.
2. Study Section I-A, "Matter."
3. Study Part II, "Energy."
4. Study Activity VII-A-2, "How far away are the stars?"
5. Study Activity VII-A-3, "How big is the universe?"
6. Study Activity VII-A-4, "How can we locate a given star or constellation? How can we build an astrolabe?"

H. Vocabulary Builders—Spelling Words:

Use the heavenly bodies cited in Basic Facts and Supplemental Information.

I. Thought for Today:

"An eminent scientist has announced that, in his opinion, intelligent life is possible on several planets—including the Earth!"

Activity VII A 2

A. Problem: *How Far Away Are the Stars?*

B. Materials Needed:

1. Pictures of stars
2. Astronomy books
3. Star charts

C. Procedure:

1. Have as many references available as possible.
2. Ask students how we measure distances on land.
   a. Direct—use ruler, tape measure, odometer, etc.
   b. Indirect—use trigonometry, the study of triangles.
3. Ask the class: "How can we tell how far the moon is from us? the sun?"
4. Tell students we can measure star distances by trigonometry and other methods.
5. We have found that the closest star to us is Alpha Centauri, which is 4.3 light-years away (26 trillion miles). Driving at 55 miles per hour it would take 193 years to reach our sun, but 52 million years to reach Alpha Centauri. This is equal to about 135 round trips to the sun.
6. The brightest star in the sky is Sirius in the Constellation of Orion. It is 8.6 light-years away from Earth.
7. All the stars vary in distances from us even though they all seem to be the same distance away.

D. Results:

1. Students will learn that all the stars are very, very far away.
2. Students will realize that space is vast and distances are measured in light-years, the distance light travels in one year. (Light travels at 186,282 miles per second, 300,000 kilometers per second. We normally round off the number and state that light travels at 186,000 miles per second.)

E. Basic Facts and Supplemental Information:

1. Our galaxy, the Milky Way, has about 200 billion (200,000,000,000) stars in it.
2. We can see about 3,000 stars with the naked eye.
3. One light-year equals 5.88 trillion (5,880,000,000,000) miles.
4. We can locate any celestial body by knowing its azimuth and altitude. The azimuth is measured in degrees west or east of the "Prime Meridian," which is an imaginary vertical circle running through Greenwich, England. The altitude is the height of the object measured in degrees from the horizon (plane around the equator) toward the zenith (point above the North Pole).

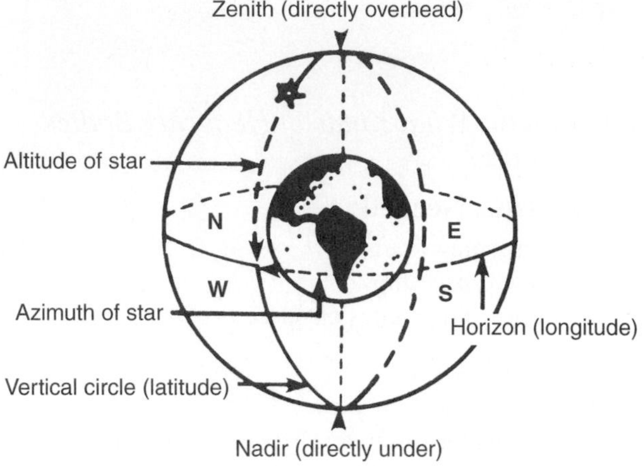

F. Thought Questions for Class Discussions:

1. Do you think a person will ever be able to reach a star?
2. Are all stars really suns? (yes)
3. Why do stars twinkle? (pollutants in the air)

G. Related Ideas for Further Inquiry:

1. See Section II-C, "Light and Color."
2. With a star chart, locate the North Star, Polaris.
3. Go out at night and observe the stars.
4. Visit an observatory.
5. Look at star charts and see if you can locate constellations.
6. Study Activity VII-A-1, "What kinds of heavenly bodies are there?"
7. Study Activity VII-A-3, "How big is the universe?"
8. Study Activity VII-A-4, "How can we locate a given star or constellation? How can we build an astrolabe?"

H. Vocabulary Builders—Spelling Words:

1) **star** 2) **sun** 3) **distance** 4) **light-year** 5) **twinkle** 6) **trigonometry** 7) **astronomy**

I. Thought for Today:

"There would be more parents kissing their children goodnight if the children would come home at a reasonable hour."

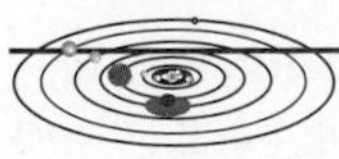

Activity

A. Problem: *How Big Is the Universe?*

B. Materials Needed:

1. Sketches and drawings about the universe
2. Books about astronomy
3. Multisensory aids on the universe
4. Diagrams as shown in drawings

C. Procedure:

1. Have the students look up at the sky at night and have them report on what they have seen.
2. Ask them how far they can see in the night sky.
3. Ask them what is up in the sky.
4. Tell them that we use the term "universe" to include everything that exists in space:
   a. stars
   b. sun (another star)
   c. moon
   d. planets (like our Earth)
   e. "shooting stars"
   f. and many other "things"
5. Explain the diagrams:
   (The "dot" represents one object; the circle, a much larger object.)
   a. Top Drawings:
      1) You are a student in the school.
      2) The school is in the community.
      3) The community is in the nation.
      4) The nation is on Earth.
   b. Bottom Drawings:
      1) The Earth is in the solar system.
      2) The solar system is in our galaxy, the Milky Way.
      3) The Milky Way is in the Supercluster, a large group of galaxies.
      4) Our supercluster is part of the universe.
      5) There are millions of superclusters in the universe.
      6) Explain that measuring the universe is an impossible concept even for scientists. No one can grasp the vastness of space.
6. Select additional information from the items below depending on the age, ability, and interest of your class.
   a. Begin with known distances: miles from home to school, miles to grandma's and grandpa's house, or the farthest students have traveled from their homes.
   b. Ask them how long it took to get there.
   c. Compare this to the distance to the moon—240,000 miles.

A student is part of the Earth.

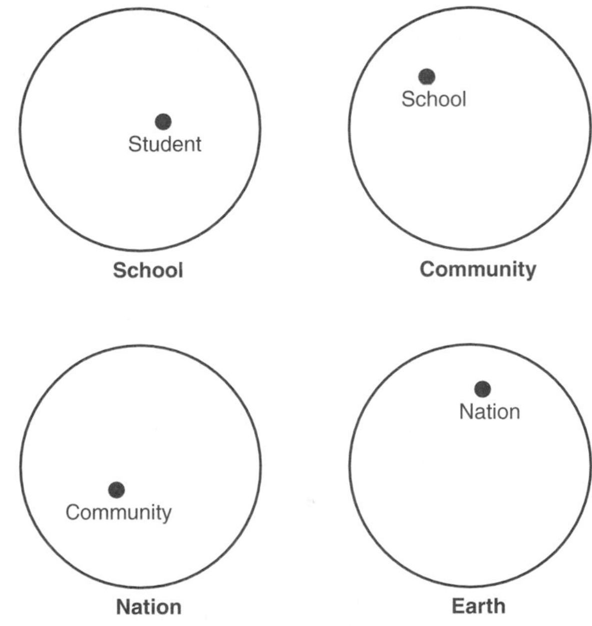

The Earth is part of the Universe.

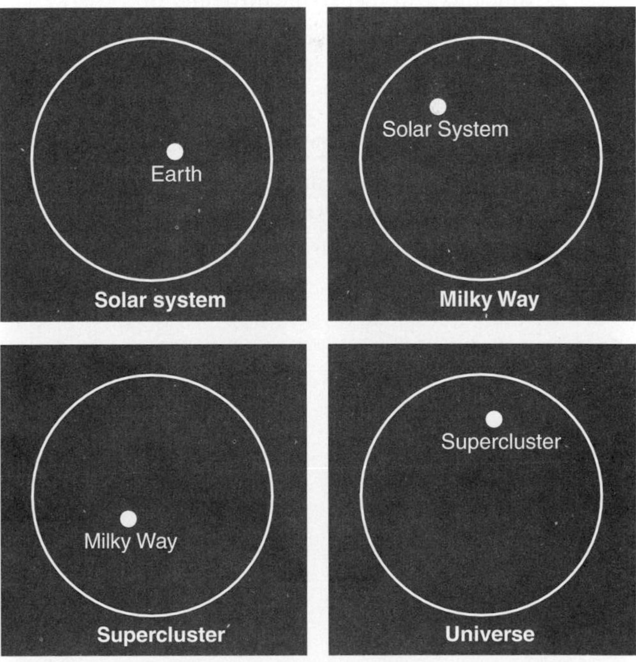

   d. Compute time to get to the moon if driving a spaceship at the speed of a car traveling 60 miles per hour (240,000 divided by 60, with the answer in hours). (This would take 167 days.)
   e. Compare this to traveling to the sun, which is 93,000,000 miles away. A person traveling at

60 miles per hour would require 178 years to get there.

f. Relate the following statistics even though they are mind-boggling:
   1) The diameter of the Earth is 7,926 miles.
   2) The diameter of the sun is 865,400 miles.
   3) The diameter of our solar system is 7,340,000,000 miles.
   4) The diameter of the solar system can also be measured in light-years. A light-year is the distance light travels in a year. Light travels at 186,200 miles per second. A light-year equals 5.88 trillion miles (5,880,000,000,000).
   5) Our solar system measures a little over .001 light-years across.
   6) The diameter of the Milky Way is 100,000 light-years. It contains about 200 billion stars.
   7) The diameter of our supercluster is 40 million light-years. It contains about 2,500 galaxies.
   8) The diameter of the known universe has been estimated to be from 12 to 13.4 billion light-years in diameter. It contains millions of superclusters.

D. Results:

1. Students will be aware of the vastness of space.
2. Students will realize the difficulty of comprehending large numbers.
3. Students will begin to realize how small each person is in the large universe.

E. Basic Facts and Supplemental Information:

1. All celestial bodies are in motion.
2. It takes our solar system 200 million years to make one revolution around our galaxy, the Milky Way.
3. The most recent studies of time and distances in the universe tend to support the "Big Bang" theory because all celestial bodies are moving away just as lettering does on an expanded balloon (also a good Activity).
4. The Earth is near the center of our solar system.
5. Our solar system is near the edge of the Milky Way.
6. The Milky Way is between the center and the edge of our supercluster.
7. We're really not sure of the relative position of our supercluster in the universe.

F. Thought Questions for Class Discussions:

1. Does our planet seem very large to you now?
2. Is our sun far away?
3. Is a week very long?

G. Related Ideas for Further Inquiry:

1. Construct a bulletin board full of news items that pertain to objects in the universe.
2. Take a field trip to an observatory.
3. Discuss the universe with astronomers and/or cosmologists.
4. Study Activity VII-A-1, "What kinds of heavenly bodies are there?"
5. Study Activity VII-A-2, "How far away are the stars?"
6. Study Activity VII-A-5, "What are 'black holes'?"
7. Study Activity VI-C-4, "What is the ozone problem?"

H. Vocabulary Builders—Spelling Words:

1) **light-year** 2) **solar system** 3) **Milky Way** 4) **supercluster** 5) **universe** 6) **vast**

I. Thought for Today:

"To love the world is no problem. It's the person next door that is the problem."

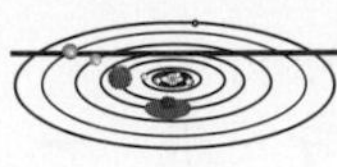

Activity VII A 4

A. Problem: *How Can We Locate a Given Star or Constellation? How Can We Build an Astrolabe?*

B. Materials Needed:

1. Soda straw
2. Protractor
3. Baseboard, approximately 6″ × 6″
4. Wooden upright, approximately 3/4″ × 3/4″ × 8″
5. Compass disk, can be hand-drawn using a protractor (See drawing.)
6. Sealing wax or glue
7. Rubber cement
8. Screwdriver
9. Screw, approximately 1″ long
10. Common pin or thin nail
11. Drill
12. Reference materials on constellations and/or star charts

C. Procedure to Construct:

1. Drill a hole in the center of baseboard to insert screw.
2. Use rubber cement to affix compass disk to baseboard.
3. Screw baseboard to upright.
4. Drill a tiny hole in top of protractor for pin or nail to go through.
5. Mount protractor to top of the wooden upright with sealing wax or glue. (See drawing.)
6. Affix straw with pin or nail to top of protractor so that straw is movable.

Procedure to Teach:

1. Have students study reference materials to become acquainted with stars and constellations.
2. Describe how early sailors used simple materials like this to locate stars and constellations and to help them navigate on the oceans.
3. Mark a point in the classroom which is "true north."
4. Cite the difference between "true north" and "magnetic north."
5. Have the students locate various points around the room using the astrolabe for direction and altitude.

D. Results:

1. Students will construct a simple astrolabe.
2. Students will learn how ancient mariners navigated when out of sight of land.
3. Students will improve their math skills.

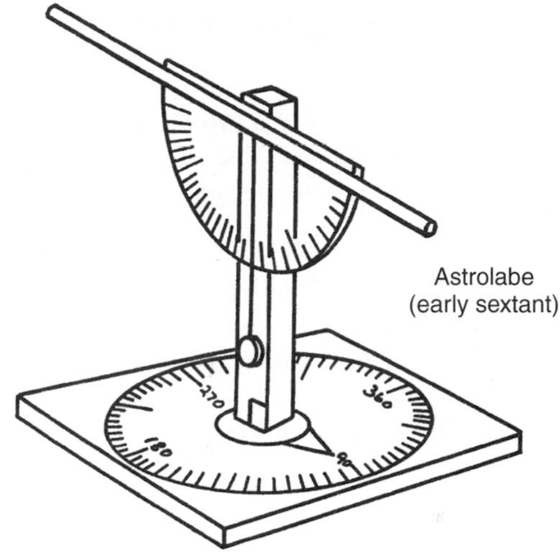

Astrolabe (early sextant)

E. Basic Facts and Supplemental Information:

1. This device is also called a "theodolite."
2. This device can measure the angle of any star or any other object.
3. The upright can be checked for accuracy by dropping a plumb line from its top.
4. Early mariners made many discoveries of new lands by using a simple apparatus like this.

F. Thought Questions for Class Discussions:

1. How does this device differ from a sextant?
2. What is the study of trigonometry?
3. What causes stars to appear to move across the sky at night?
4. Would the angle of the stars change if we viewed them from different locations on the Earth?

G. Related Ideas for Further Inquiry:

1. Study Activity VII-A-1, "What kinds of heavenly bodies are there?"
2. Study Activity VII-A-2, "How far away are the stars?"
3. Study Activity VII-A-3, "How big is the universe?"
4. Study Activity VII-A-5, "What are 'Black Holes'?"

H. Vocabulary Builders—Spelling Words:

1) **astrolabe** 2) **angle** 3) **constellation** 4) **height** 5) **protractor** 6) **baseboard** 7) **altitude**

I. Thought for Today:

"Too many people look up at the stars and then head off in all directions."

Activity VII A 5

A. Problem: *What Are "Black Holes"?*

B. Materials Needed:

1. Small black balls of any size and shape
2. Newspaper accounts of "black holes"
3. Printed materials about the sun and the stars

C. Procedure:

1. Discuss the heavenly bodies that the students are aware of such as sun, moon, comets, etc.
2. Discuss the general makeup of suns (atomic furnaces).
3. Describe the life of a sun (star):
   a. birth
   b. life
   c. death (lost its fuel)
4. Describe what we think we know about black holes.
   a. Physical phenomena
   b. Give off no light
   c. Act like stellar vacuum cleaners
   d. Result of death of star
   e. Hydrogen fuel has been burned up
   f. The star's life span could have lasted thousands of millions of years.
   g. Show the black balls that have been collected.
   h. These are similar to the collapsed stars.
   i. All remaining matter has been drawn into the black holes—even light. That is why, since we can't see them, we can only guess that they exist.
   j. Cosmologists believe that there is far more matter in the universe than we have detected. Their theory is that the rest of it exists in black holes.
   k. Recent studies claim that in the middle of black holes there are extremely violent reactions of exploding stars and broiling gases. Gravity pulls them into the hole.
   l. The most recent studies show that our own Milky Way galaxy has a black hole or some black holes in its core.
   m. Black holes are so dense that they could contain the mass of millions of stars in a mass as small as an atom.
   n. This is one area of science where future scientists will continually study our universe, and they will find out more information about this cosmic reality.
   o. Guesses (hypotheses) regarding unknowns are called theories. We should call black holes a theory for now, even though there is strong evidence that they do exist.

D. Results:

1. Students will become acquainted with the term "black holes" and get a general idea of what they are.
2. Students will realize that there are still a lot of unknowns in the universe.

E. Basic Facts and Supplemental Information:

1. Scientists believe black holes emit electromagnetic waves as they are collapsing, and cosmologists have detected some of these waves but don't know for sure what their origins are.
2. Possibly in the future we will be able to detect certain types of radiation which might prove the existence of black holes.

F. Thought Questions for Class Discussions:

1. Do you know any other theories in science?
2. What is the "Big Bang" theory?
3. What dangers are there for space travelers?

G. Related Ideas for Further Inquiry:

1. Look up "pulsars" and "quasars."
2. Study Section VIII-C, "Space Travel."
3. Study Activity VII-A-1, "What kinds of heavenly bodies are there?"
4. Study Activity VII-A-2, "How far away are the stars?"

H. Vocabulary Builders—Spelling Words:

1) **black holes** 2) **atomic** 3) **hydrogen**
4) **cosmologist** 5) **theory** 6) **universe**

I. Thought for Today:

"Home is where our feet may leave but never our hearts."

Section B: Solar System

Activity VII B 1

A. Problem: *What Is the Sun Like?*

B. Materials Needed:

1. Flannel board
2. Flannel cutouts (See drawing.)
   a. large orange ball (sun)
   b. medium-sized green ball (Earth)
   c. red irregular sections (solar flares)
3. Red knitting yarn, 15 feet
4. Gray flannel section (Earth's atmosphere)
5. Reference materials about the sun

C. Procedure:

1. Place cutouts on flannel board.
2. Ask students what they know about the sun.
3. Demonstrate and discuss appropriate information cited in Section E, Basic Facts and Supplemental Information.

D. Results:

1. Students will learn that life on Earth depends upon the sun.
2. They will learn that the energy needed to heat the land, oceans, and air are three important factors in creating our weather and climates.

E. Basic Facts and Supplemental Information:

1. **CAUTION:** Never look directly at the sun with your unprotected eyes, through binoculars, or through a telescope.
2. The sun, our primary source of heat, is 93 million miles away.
3. It is a ball of glowing gases.
4. It is an atomic furnace.
5. It bombards the Earth with 126 trillion horsepower every second.
6. The Earth receives only one and one-half of a billionth of the sun's total energy; most of it is lost in space.
7. About 43% of the sun's radiation to our planet is absorbed by the surface, 42% is reflected back into space, and 15% is absorbed by our atmosphere.
8. The sun's energy is transmitted as waves like radio waves.
9. The temperature of the sun at its center is about 25,000,000°F (14,000,000°C).
10. The sun's gases are primarily hydrogen, some helium, and traces of several other elements.

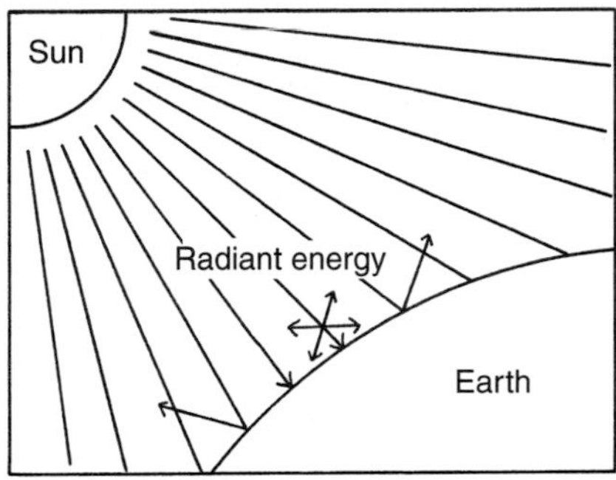

11. It is nuclear fusion which produces the heat and light.
12. The middle part of the sun rotates every 25 days; the top and bottom, about every 30 days.
13. The sun has some sunspots which are cooler areas of the sun, and they individually last for about 11 years.
14. The sun also shoots huge flamelike clouds of gases from its surface. These sometimes extend up to 62,000 miles and can last for several months.
15. The sun also emits ultraviolet light which is invisible to the naked eye.
16. The Earth is protected, in part, by our ozone layer which is located about 15 to 30 miles above the Earth's surface.

F. Thought Questions for Class Discussions:

1. What is the difference between "atomic fission" and "atomic fusion"?
2. How can we protect ourselves from the sun?
3. How important is the sun to the process of "photosynthesis"?

G. Related Ideas for Further Inquiry:

1. Study Activity VII-B-2, "How is the Earth different from other planets?"
2. Study Activity VII-B-3, "How can we tell time by using the sun?"
3. Study also Activities VII-B-4, VII-B-6, and VII-B-10.

H. Vocabulary Builders—Spellings Words:

1) **sun** 2) **solar** 3) **fusion** 4) **waves** 5) **absorb** 6) **radiate** 7) **prominences** 8) **fission** 9) **rays**

I. Thought for Today:

"Wisdom usually consists of knowing what to do next."

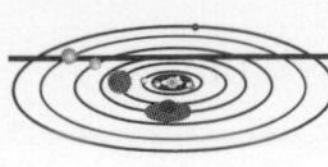

Activity 

A. Problem: *How Is the Earth Different from Other Planets?*

B. Materials Needed:

1. World globe
2. Planisphere (model of the Earth, moon, and sun) if available
3. Reference materials about our planet
4. Bulletin board
5. Multisensory materials

C. Procedure:

1. Read reference materials about the Earth.
2. Show whatever multisensory materials are available.
3. Discuss the pertinent information about the Earth cited in Section E, Basic Facts and Supplemental Information.
4. Construct a bulletin board display comparing the planets.
5. Use the world globe and/or planisphere to show some of the Earth's characteristics.

D. Results:

1. The students will learn that the Earth is a very unique planet in our solar system.
2. Students will learn how to construct a bulletin board display.
3. Students will learn that we are living on a spaceship that needs attention and care.

E. Basic Facts and Supplemental Information:

1. The Earth is one of nine planets in our solar system.
2. The Earth rotates on its axis and is tilted about 23 1/2 degrees from its orbital path.
3. This tilt causes the Northern Hemisphere to have summer when the tilt is toward the sun and winter when the tilt is away from the sun.
4. The Earth orbits around the sun in one year (365-1/4 days).
5. The Earth rotates on its axis once every day (23 hours, 56 minutes).
6. The Earth has one moon which affects our tides.
7. The Earth is the third planet away from the sun (about 93,000,000 miles away).
8. If we were much closer to the sun, we would sizzle; if we were much farther away, we would freeze.

Our planet Earth

9. The Earth has an atmosphere composed primarily of nitrogen (78%), oxygen (21%), and a variety of gases which make up the balance.
10. The troposphere, the lower layer of our atmosphere, is where our weather occurs and makes life possible.
11. The sun sends to the Earth about 99.9% of the energy we need to heat the land, oceans, and air—three important factors in creating our weather and climates.
12. A layer of ozone concentrated about 15 to 30 miles above the Earth protects us from most of the sun's harmful ultraviolet radiation.
13. Air pollution can cause changes in our weather and climate. The burning of fossil fuels and biomass releases carbon dioxide into the atmosphere which forms a "blanket." Therefore, heat that is normally reflected back into space is reflected back to the Earth instead, giving us the "Greenhouse Effect."
14. Water covers 70% of the Earth's surface.
15. The Earth's gravity keeps us and our atmosphere from being lost in space.
16. The Earth is part of the solar system and our solar system is part of the Milky Way galaxy, which is composed of billions of stars.
17. The core of the Earth is a very hot molten mass that ranges from 4,000° F. to 8,000° F. Thanks to our mantle and crust, we are insulated from this extreme heat. Actually our crust is composed of large pieces of land mass which float on the molten core. The shifting of adjacent land masses (tectonic plates) causes earthquakes.

18. Our planet has seven major land masses called continents. They are:
    a. North America
    b. South America
    c. Europe
    d. Asia
    e. Africa
    f. Australia
    g. Antarctica
19. The planet Earth is our spaceship, travelling through space at tremendous speeds.
20. As passengers aboard our spacecraft, we must take good care of it and be careful of its provisions.
    a. There are millions of species of plant and animal life that exist on our planet, but these are being reduced at faster and faster rates as people encroach on their habitats.
    b. Our population is expected to double in the next 35 to 50 years, causing problems in supplying sufficient food and fresh water.
    c. Our rain forests are being depleted. Our wetlands are being dramatically reduced.
    d. Our natural resources are being used up.
    e. Our landfills are being topped.

F. Thought Questions for Class Discussions:

1. How have people changed the surfaces of the Earth?
2. How would life be different if we lived on the moon?
3. What are some dangers to people's existence on our planet?
4. What are we doing to our air?
5. What are we doing to our water?
6. Are we taking good care of our natural resources?

G. Related Ideas for Further Inquiry:

1. Have students try to locate planets in the night skies.
2. Study Activity VII-B-1, "What is the sun like?"
3. Study Activity VII-B-5, "How old is the Earth?"
4. Study Activity VII-B-7, "What is our atmosphere like?"
5. Study Part VI, "Ecology."
6. Study Section VII-C, "Earth's Crust."
7. Study Section VII-E, "Weather."

H. Vocabulary Builders—Spellings Words:

1) **planet** 2) **moon** 3) **axis** 4) **rotation** 5) **revolution** 6) **seasons** 7) **atmosphere**

I. Thought for Today:

"Isn't it amazing that we don't get dizzy on our spinning Earth?"

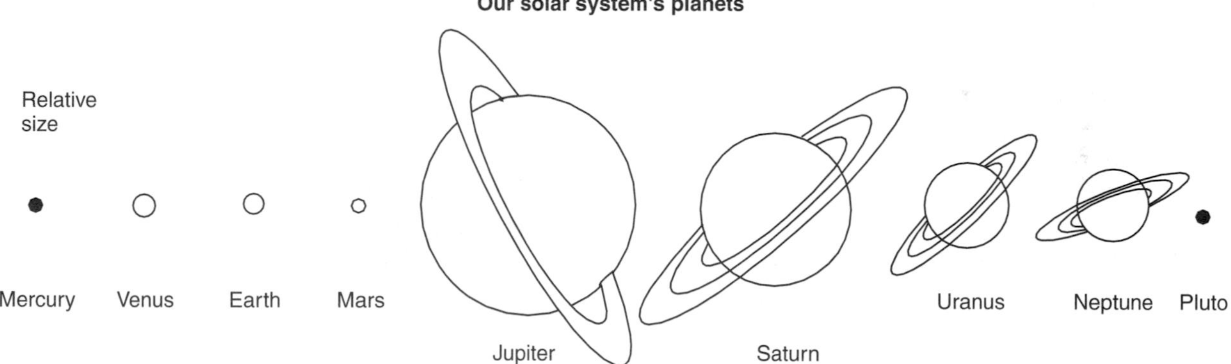

BASIC INFORMATION ABOUT THE PLANETS IN OUR SOLAR SYSTEM

Name:	*Diameter:*	*Miles from Sun:*	*Rotation Time:*	*Revolution Time:*	*Moons:*
Mercury	3,000 miles	36 million	59 days	88 days	0
Venus	7,550 miles	69 million	243 days	225 days	0
Earth	7,926 miles	93 million	24 hours	365-1/4 days	1
Mars	4,200 miles	142 million	25 hours	687 days	2
Jupiter	88,700 miles	434 million	10 hours	12 years	16
Saturn	74,000 miles	891 million	11 hours	29 years	22
Uranus	29,000 miles	1.8 billion	18 hours	84 years	15
Neptune	28,000 miles	2.8 billion	18 hours	165 years	8
Pluto	1,460 miles	3.7 billion (avg.)	6 days	248 years	1
Sun	865,400 miles	0	25–35 days	0	9 (planets)

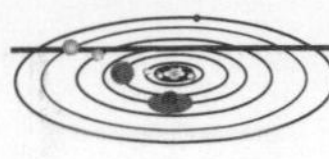

Activity VII B 3

A. Problem: *How Can We Tell Time by Using the Sun?*

CAUTION: Never look directly at the sun. It can damage your eyes permanently.

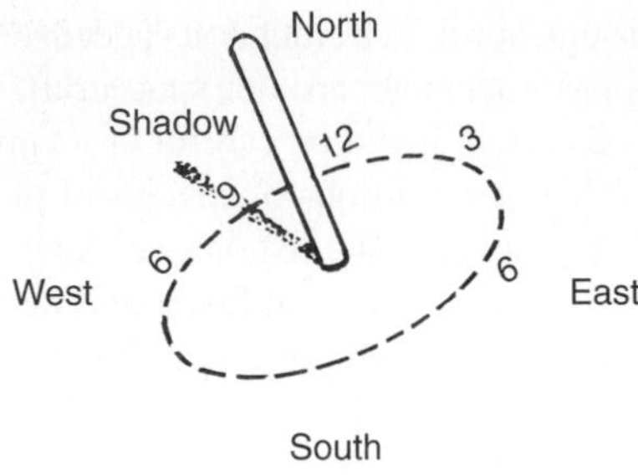

A simple sundial

B. Materials Needed:

1. Sunshine, outside
2. Broom handle
3. Compass
4. Piece of cardboard, or heavy tagboard, about a foot square, for each student
5. Tall nail, or dowel, for each student
6. Thumbtacks
7. Drawing instruments

C. Procedure:

1. Ask students if they can tell time by using the sun.
2. Ask them if they have ever seen a sundial.
3. If so, have them relate their experiences.
4. Take class outside to a paved, open area of campus on a sunny day. Draw a circle about 4 or 5 feet in diameter.
5. Using the compass for directions, number the clock hours as shown on the sundial drawing, beginning with the 6 to the west, 12 to the north, and 6 to the east. (Note: 2 hours of time on the face of a sundial equals one hour on the face of a regular watch.)
6. Secure the broom handle in the center of circle using any convenient means.
7. Note shadow cast by sun and approximate time.
8. While inside, have each student draw a "sundial" clock on his/her cardboard or tagboard with hour markings as shown in the drawing.
9. Tell students to fasten the nails or dowels given to them to the clock face they have drawn.
10. Take the students outside to check their new sundial clock.
11. The 12 on the clock should be pointed north.

D. Results:

1. The sun will cast a shadow which will record the time on the sundial.
2. The students will enjoy making these simple sundials.

E. Basic Facts and Supplemental Information:

1. If your community is on daylight saving time, subtract one hour so that the sundial will indicate standard time.
2. Of course a wrist watch is more accurate; however, the sundial the students could actually make would be useful if a watch were unavailable.
3. The shortest shadow of the broom handle during the day will point to "true south."

F. Thought Questions for Class Discussions:

1. Will daylight saving time affect your readings?
2. Will the sundial work at any season of the year?
3. Why is the shadow longer at some seasons than others?
4. If your broom handle, dowel, or nail is pointed directly to the sun at 12 o'clock noon, so no shadow is cast, what would its angle to the ground represent in terms of your location on the Earth? (its latitude)
5. How do sailors find the exact time by the sun?

G. Related Ideas for Further Inquiry:

1. A more elaborate and permanent sundial can be made by nailing a wooden dowel to a wooden base.
2. Encourage students to make more permanent sundials at home.
3. Study Section VII-E, "Weather."
4. Study Activity VII-B-1, "What is the sun like?"
5. Study Activity VII-B-2, "How is the Earth different from other planets?"
6. Study Activity VII-B-4, "How does the length of day and night change from season to season?"
7. Study Activity VII-B-8, "How can our latitude be determined?"
8. Study Activity VII-B-10, "What causes an eclipse?"

H. Vocabulary Builders—Spelling Words:

1) **time** 2) **direction** 3) **hours** 4) **compass** 5) **sunshine** 6) **shadow** 7) **sundial** 8) **dowel**

I. Thought for Today:

"Thanks to digital watches, students won't have to learn how to tell time."

Activity

A. Problem: *How Does the Length of Day and Night Change from Season to Season?*

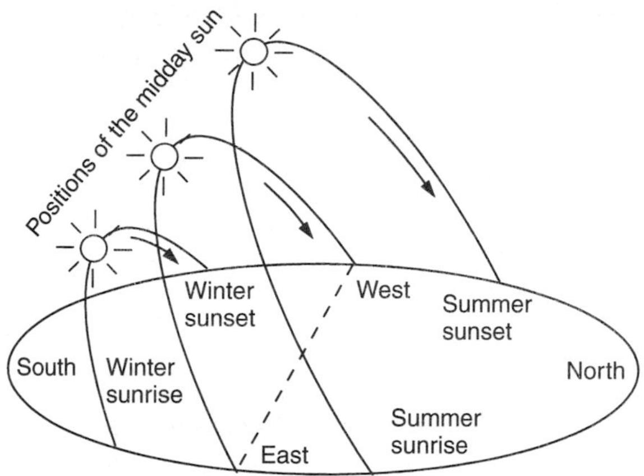

B. Materials Needed:

1. Desk, table, or stand
2. World globe
3. Filmstrip projector (flashlight may be substituted)
4. Compass
5. Chalkboard pointer or yardstick

C. Procedure:

1. Place globe on desk or table.
2. Place filmstrip projector about 15 feet from the globe.
3. Darken the room.
4. Turn the projector on.
5. Shine the light from the projector to the globe. (The light side represents daytime; the dark side, nighttime.)
6. Using compass, tilt the globe northward until the elevation of the axis above the horizontal is the same as the latitude of the school. (If your community is located at 38° North Latitude, then the globe should be tilted 38° from the horizontal position. You can estimate tilt; it doesn't have to be exact.)
7. Slowly rotate the globe on its axis noting the amount of light on the North Pole and the South Pole.
8. Select another point on the globe, and as the globe rotates, determine if it receives no light, all light, more than half or less than half of the light during one rotation.
9. Move the projector to the floor and repeat rotation.
10. Move the projector to a high level and repeat rotation.

D. Results:

1. Students will visualize that the North Pole is opposite the South Pole as to lightness and darkness.
2. Students will learn that lightness and darkness change as the seasons change (moving the projector up and down).

E. Basic Facts and Supplemental Information:

1. In the spring and fall the axis of the Earth is tilted neither toward nor away from the sun, thus providing equal amounts of night and day.
2. In the Northern Hemisphere during the summer, the axis of the Earth is tilted toward the sun. The daylight arc is longer than the nighttime arc; therefore, the days are longer than the nights.
3. In the Northern Hemisphere during winter, the axis of the Earth is tilted away from the sun. The daylight arc is shorter than the nighttime arc; therefore, the days are shorter and the nights are longer.

F. Thought Questions for Class Discussions:

1. If you could live where the daylight was the longest, where would you live in the summer? winter? autumn? spring?
2. Check with the weather bureau and find the average temperature of your locality for a winter month and a summer month. Is there much difference?
3. What is the international date line? Why is it necessary?

G. Related Ideas for Further Inquiry:

1. Design a test to prove that our Earth tilts at 23-1/2 degrees from its orbital plane.
2. Discuss how plants, animals, and people adjust to each season.
3. Study Section VII-E, "Weather."
4. Study all Activities in this Section.

H. Vocabulary Builders—Spelling Words:

1) **length** 2) **day** 3) **night** 4) **season** 5) **orbit** 6) **tilt** 7) **summer** 8) **winter**

I. Thought for Today:

"Winter is the season in which people try to keep the house as warm as it was in the summer when they complained about the heat."

Activity VII B 5

A. Problem: *How Old Is the Earth?*

B. Materials Needed:

1. Classroom clock
2. Watch with luminous dial
3. Calendar
4. Rock (assume to be radioactive)
5. Bar of soap
6. Knife
7. Marking pen

C. Procedure:

1. Discuss with students how we tell time with a classroom clock.
2. Ask students how old they are and when they were born.
3. Ask students how we keep track of time and calendar dates.
4. Ask the students if you can judge the age of people just by looking at them.
5. Ask the students if we can judge the age of rocks just by looking at them.
6. Since we cannot judge the age of rocks just by looking at them, we need to use some other methods.
7. Describe atomic dating by showing the class the luminous watch dial and how the dial can be read because the atoms are splitting and giving off light. By knowing how fast the atoms split, we can determine the kind of material that is giving off radiations.
8. Tell the students you are going to demonstrate time by the half-life method. This means that any radioactive element divides itself into half at a definite amount of time for that element. Then each new half has its own half-life if it has become radioactive.
9. Each radioactive element is continuously breaking down in a slow process, but it will take its half-life time to break down to half its original state. Half of it will maintain its original state and the other half will become a new substance(s). This/these may be entirely new or may be an isotope of the original material.
10. Tell the students that you are going to use a bar of soap to represent a radioactive element and a minute of time to represent half-life.
11. Place the bar of soap where all can see it.
12. Tell the students to watch the clock and record each minute.

Bar of soap is to be cut in halves to show half-lives.

13. After one minute, cut the bar of soap in half.
14. Mark one of the halves with an ink spot. This represents a new, entirely different substance.
15. The other half will remain as the same original material.
16. Cut the unmarked half in half.
17. Mark one of these two halves with an ink spot. This too, represents the new substance.
18. Wait one more minute.
19. Cut the unmarked half in half.
20. Mark one half of this half with an ink spot. The other half remains unmarked.
21. Ask the class how long it took, by figuring out what portion of the total bar is left.
22. Tell the class that we have some radioactive materials that break down naturally, just like the soap has been broken down (split up), only the half-life is in years, rather than minutes.

D. Results:

1. Students will visualize the concept of half-life.
2. Students will learn that by using this half-life method, scientists have computed the age of the Earth to be between 4.5 and 5 billion years old.

E. Basic Facts and Supplemental Information:

1. Following is a list of the half-lives of various radioactive elements:
   a. Radium . . . 1,600 years
   b. Uranium-238 . . . 5 billion years
   c. Cesium-137 . . . 27 years
   d. Strontium-90 . . . 28 years
   e. Carbon-14 . . . 5,568 years
2. See the Geological Time Chart of the Earth on following page.

F. Thought Questions for Class Discussions:

1. Can you tell time by the sun?
2. Can you tell how old a mountain is by its shape?
3. How is an exact year measured?

G. Related Ideas for Further Inquiry:

1. Study Section VII-C, "Earth's Crust."
2. Study Activity VII-B-1, "What is the sun like?"
3. Study Activity VII-B-3, "How can we tell time by using the sun?"
4. Study Activity VII-B-6, "How fast is the Earth moving?"

H. Vocabulary Builders—Spelling Words:

1) **radioactive** 2) **half-life** 3) **luminous** 4) **years** 5) **dates** 6) **time** 7) **radium**

I. Thought for Today:

"A father put a 50 foot cord on the telephone so his teenagers could spend more time outdoors."

EARTH'S GEOLOGICAL TIME PERIODS

APPROX. TIME AGO, YEARS	EON	ERA	PERIOD	EPOCH	CHARACTERISTICS
Present–20,000	Phanterozoic	Cenozoic	Quaternary	Recent	Humans emerge, dominate
2,000,000	Phanterozoic	Cenozoic	Quaternary	Glacial	Humans form societies Large mammals become extinct Four glacial movements
2 to 13 Million	Phanterozoic	Cenozoic	Tertiary	Pliocene	Early Homo species Modern mammals Cooling of land
25 Million	Phanterozoic	Cenozoic	Tertiary	Miocene	Many mammals Widespread grasses Dry and mild climate
36 Million	Phanterozoic	Cenozoic	Tertiary	Oligocene	Modern mammals spread Archaic animals disappear
58 Million	Phanterozoic	Cenozoic	Tertiary	Eocene	Modern birds emerge Modern mammals emerge Climate warms
64 Million	Phanterozoic	Cenozoic	Tertiary	Paleocene	Archaic animals spread Spreading glaciers, colder
135 Million	Phanterozoic	Mesozoic	Cretaceous	Paleocene	Spread of flowering plants Extinction, toothed birds
					Rise of archaic animals Extinction of dinosaurs
180 Million	Phanterozoic	Mesozoic	Jurassic	Paleocene	Toothed birds appear Dinosaurs flourish Spread of great seas
230 Million	Phanterozoic	Mesozoic	Triassic	Paleocene	Dinosaurs appear Reptiles, dominant Climate, dry and cool
280 Million	Phanterozoic	Paleozoic	Permian	Paleocene	Many ancient plants die Many marine animals die Reptiles, increase Climate cold and dry
310 Million	Phanterozoic	Paleozoic	Pennsylvanian	Paleocene	First reptiles appear Large insects abide Many spore plants Warm, humid climate
350 Million	Phanterozoic	Paleozoic	Mississippian	Paleocene	Trilobites almost extinct Many shark-like fish Climate dry; many swamps
400 Million	Phanterozoic	Paleozoic	Devonian	Paleocene	First amphibians First forests Marine life numerous

APPROX. TIME AGO, YEARS	EON	ERA	PERIOD	EPOCH	CHARACTERISTICS
425 Million	Phanterozoic	Paleozoic	Silurian	Paleocene	Land plants appear First air-breathing invertebrates Marine animals dominant Climate generally mild
500 Million	Phanterozoic	Paleozoic	Ordovician	Paleocene	Earliest vertebrates Fresh-water fish increasing 60% N. America under water
625 Million	Phanterozoic	Paleozoic	Cambrian	Paleocene	Crustaceans appear Trilobites are abundant Mild climate
5 Billion	Crypotozoic	Paleozoic	Pre-Cambrian	Paleocene	First living organisms Old life appears like algae Volcanic activity Development of planets

A. Problem: *How Fast Is the Earth Moving?*

B. Materials Needed:

Pictures, charts, or models of:

1. Earth
2. Solar system
3. Milky Way
4. Supercluster
5. Observable universe

C. Procedure:

1. Have students discuss the various celestial bodies.
2. Have students discuss movement of people on Earth in relation to fixed positions; relative to moving objects such as a student's speed on a bicycle in relation to the wind blowing on his/her back or toward his/her face.
3. Discuss the way the Earth moves in relation to the:
   a. moon
   b. sun
   c. our solar system
   d. our galaxy (Milky Way)
   e. supercluster
   f. observable universe
4. Students can further study the relative movements of the Earth by independent research.

D. Results:

1. Students will learn that the Earth and all heavenly bodies are moving at great speeds.
2. Students will comprehend that space is vast.

E. Basic Facts and Supplemental Information:

1. Earth moves approximately 1,300 miles per hour in relation to the moon.
2. Earth moves approximately 66,500 miles per hour around the sun.
3. Earth moves approximately 481,000 miles per hour around its galaxy.
4. Earth moves around the center of the supercluster at approximately 1,350,000 miles per hour.
5. Earth moves with the supercluster at about 360,000 miles per hour.
6. Studies show that the speed of an object is relative to other objects, fixed or moving.
7. Einstein was one of the earliest scientists to study the relationships of moving bodies.

8. It is interesting to note that early residents of our planet thought that the world was flat and that if you ventured out too far you would fall off.
9. There are several other movements of the Earth. For example, the Earth also wobbles on its axis, and thus our North Star has not always been the star closest to the direction in which the Earth's axis points.
10. It takes the solar system, traveling at 418,000 miles per hour, 200 million years to make a single revolution around the axis of the Milky Way.

F. Thought Questions for Class Discussions:

1. Can speed be measured by any one instrument?
2. Can anything travel faster than the speed of light?
3. With the Earth traveling so fast in so many directions, why doesn't our atmosphere dissipate or blow away?

G. Related Ideas for Further Inquiry:

1. See Section II-F, "Movement and Resistance."
2. Devise some relative problems for the students to consider such as:
   "If you were on a train traveling 60 miles per hour and you used a skateboard to skate 10 miles per hour from the back of your railroad car to the front of it, how fast would you be traveling in relation to the ground?"
3. Study Activity VII-B-5, "How old is the Earth?"
4. Study Activity VII-B-7, "What is our atmosphere like?"
5. Study Activity VII-B-9, "What is in the center of the Earth?"

H. Vocabulary Builders—Spelling Words:

1) **Earth** 2) **solar system** 3) **supercluster** 4) **universe** 5) **Milky Way** 6) **relative**

I. Thought for Today:

"If you ask enough people, you can usually find someone who'll advise you to do what you were going to do anyway."

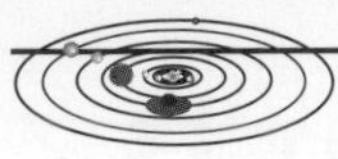

Activity VII B 7

A. Problem: *What Is Our Atmosphere Like?*

B. Materials Needed:

Related to atmosphere:

1. Books
2. Pamphlets
3. Pictures
4. Charts
5. Multisensory aids related to our atmosphere

C. Procedure:

1. Ask the students if they have ever been up in an airplane or up on a high mountain.
2. Ask them if the air is any different up high.
3. Ask class what causes any changes in the condition of our air.
4. Describe our "ocean of air" to the class. (The details and technicalities will depend on the academic level of your students.) (See drawing on next page.)

D. Results:

Students will learn that:

1. There are different layers of our atmosphere even though these blend into each other.
2. For the most part the layers are based on temperature gradients.
3. The heights and distances of the layers vary with the latitude, seasons, and reporting cosmologists.
4. The air is about 78% nitrogen, 21% oxygen, and 1% carbon dioxide, argon, neon, and water vapor.
5. The basic layers of the atmosphere starting at the Earth's surface and moving upward are shown below in miles. Kilometers have been added in parentheses (. . .)
   a. *Troposphere:* 0 to 6 miles up (0 to 10 km.)
      1) Dropping temperatures (25° C. to –60° C.).
      2) Almost all weather takes place here.
      3) Jet stream winds blow up to 200 m.p.h.
      4) Most airplanes fly in this space.
   b. *Stratosphere:* 6 to 30 miles up (10 to 45 km.)
      1) Temperatures fairly constant (–60° C. to –50° C.).
      2) Contains the ozone layer.
   c. *Mesosphere:* 30 to 50 miles up (45 to 80 km.).
      1) Temperature drops from 0°C. to –90°C.
      2) Coldest layer in the atmosphere.
      3) Reflects radio waves back to Earth.
   d. *Thermosphere:* 50 to 310 miles up (500 to 700 km.)
      1) Few air molecules.
      2) Fast moving molecules raise temperatures to 1,000°C.
      3) Sunlight not scattered.
   e. *Exosphere:* 310 miles and up (500 km. and up)
      1) Atmospheric atoms can escape.
      2) Air is thin.
      3) Gravity is weak.
   f. *Ionosphere:* 50 to 300 miles up (80 to 500 km.)
      1) Overlapping layer.
      2) Sun heats air and ionizes molecules.
      3) Produces electrons and ions of nitrogen and oxygen.
      4) Reflects radio waves back to Earth.

E. Basic Facts and Supplemental Information:

1. The Earth's gravity holds the atmosphere to the Earth.
2. The atmosphere exerts pressure in all directions.
3. The temperature decreases about 3 1/2 degrees Fahrenheit for every 1,000 feet rise in elevation.
4. The density of the air decreases the higher up one goes.
5. There are no sharp lines dividing the various layers of the atmosphere. Actually there are gradual emergings on one layer into the next.
6. The greatest concentrations of gases are at the Earth's surface, diminishing rapidly with height.

Percent of Sea Level Pressure at Selected Altitudes:

Altitude (miles):	*Percent of Sea Level Pressure:*
0	100
3.5	50
10.1	10
19.5	1
30.1	.1
40.7	.01
49.5	.001
62.5	.00003

F. Thought Questions for Class Discussions:

1. Does it take more time for a plane to take off at Denver, Colorado (high elevation) than at New York or San Francisco (low elevations)?
2. What layer of the atmosphere contains weather-making substances?
3. Where does rain come from?
4. What keeps satellites up?

G. Related Ideas for Further Inquiry:

1. Study the news media for space news. There are always new discoveries and new theories appearing daily that are very interesting and worthy of consideration.
2. Study Section I-B, "Air."
3. Study Section VI-C, "Pollution."
4. Study Activity VII-B-4, "How does the length of day and night change from season to season?"
5. Study Activity VII-B-5, "How old is the Earth?"
6. Study Activity VII-B-6, "How fast is the Earth moving?"
7. Study Activity VII-B-9, "What is in the center of the Earth?"
8. Study other Activities in this Section.

H. Vocabulary Builders—Spelling Words:

Use words indicating each layer of the atmosphere.

I. Thought for Today:

"A great person, like the tallest mountain, retains majesty and stability during the most severe storm."

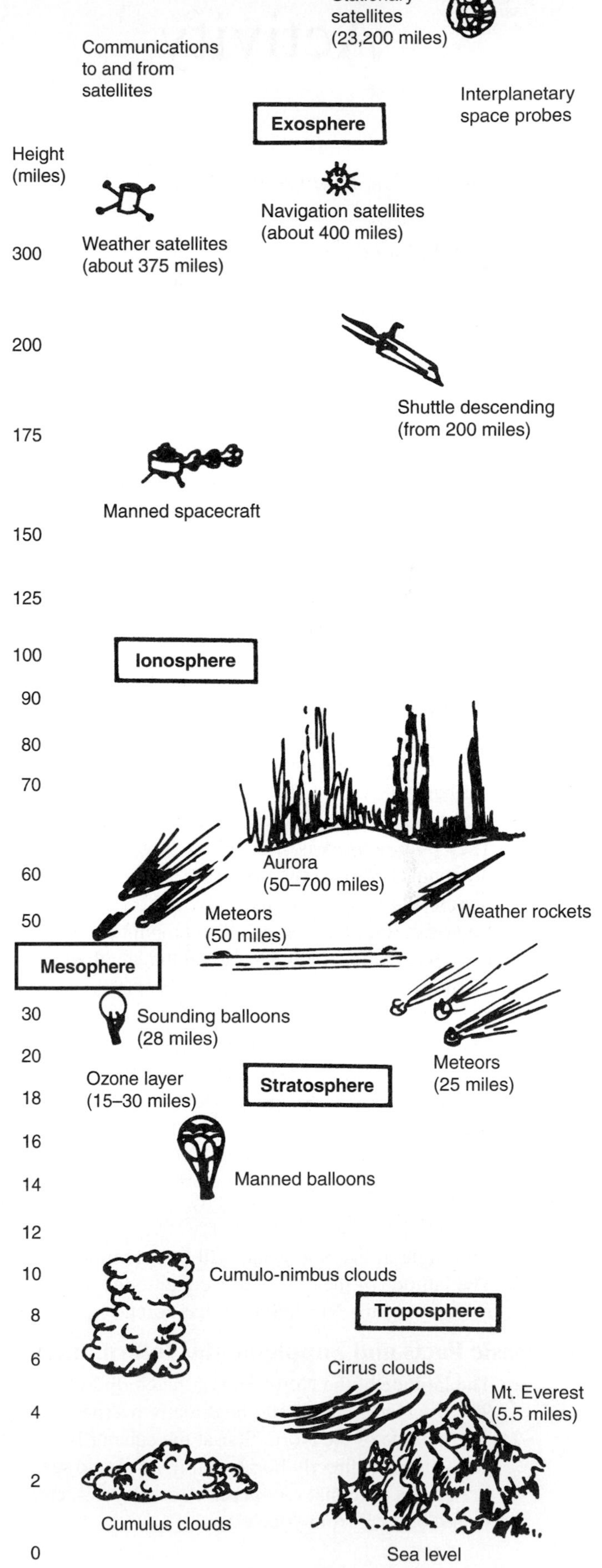

Activity VII B 8

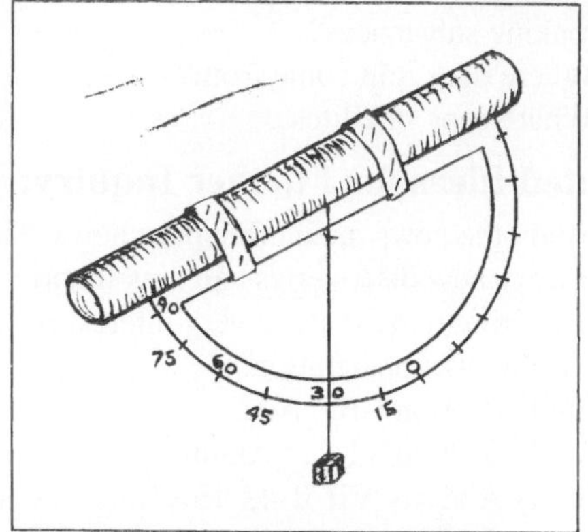

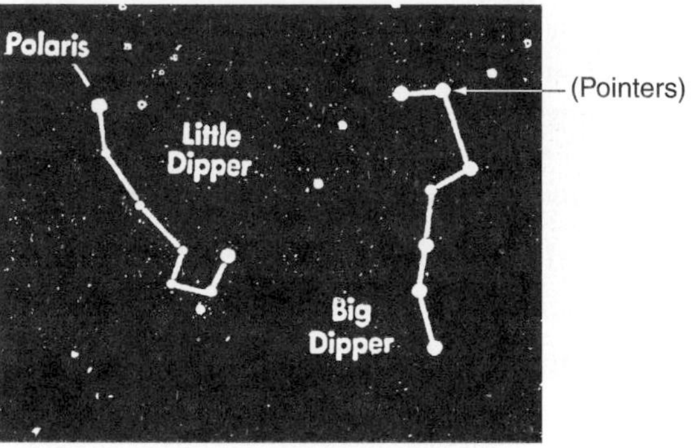

A. Problem: *How Can Our Latitude Be Determined?*

B. Materials Needed:

1. Sheet of paper or piece of thin pipe
2. Protractor
3. Thread
4. Weight
5. Cellophane tape
6. Magnetic compass

C. Procedure:

(Preparation for a night homework assignment.)

1. If you are using paper, roll it up in the shape of a pipe, about one quarter inch in diameter.
2. Tape the protractor to the long part of the pipe or roll. (See drawing.)
3. Convert readings to scale shown in drawing.
4. Fasten the thread to the center of the protractor at its base.
5. Add a weight to the other end of the thread.
6. At night, with magnetic compass, locate the general northerly direction.
7. Look for the constellation of the Big Dipper in the northerly direction. The two stars at the edge of the bowl of the Big Dipper are the "pointers." They point to Polaris, the "North Star." (See drawing.) Polaris's position will remain the same but the Big Dipper will partially revolve around Polaris during one evening. The amount of revolution seen will depend upon the length of nighttime. It takes 24 hours for a complete revolution.
8. Point the roll or pipe at the North Star.
9. When the North Star is centered, hold the thread against the protractor and read the degrees.
10. Repeat several times to be sure that results are accurate.

D. Results:

1. The North Star will be located.
2. The angle of the North Star will be determined.
3. The latitude of the observer is equal to the elevation of the North Star at that point.

E. Basic Facts and Supplemental Information:

1. The latitude of the North Star at the North Pole is 90°; the North Star would be directly overhead.
2. The latitude of the North Star at the equator is 0° and would be directly horizontal if you could see it. (Chances are that mountains, trees, houses, etc. would block it from your view.)

F. Thought Questions for Class Discussions:

1. Could you make a protractor if you didn't have one?
2. Does the North Star appear to move?
3. Does the Big Dipper appear to move?

G. Related Ideas for Further Inquiry:

1. Check the angle of buildings, trees, etc.
2. Show older students math tables to convert angles to heights (study right angles).
3. Study Activity VII-B-2, "How is the Earth different from other planets?"
4. Study Activity VII-B-3, "How can we tell time by using the sun?"
5. Study Activity VII-B-6, "How fast is the Earth moving?"

H. Vocabulary Builders—Spelling Words:

1) **latitude** 2) **protractor** 3) **compass** 4) **north** 5) **direction** 6) **angle** 7) **Polaris** 8) **Big Dipper**

I. Thought for Today:

"Wherever we look upon this Earth, the opportunities take shape within the problems. Point your star in the right direction."

A. Problem: *What Is in the Center of the Earth?"*

B. Materials Needed:

About Earth's core:

1. Books
2. Pamphlets
3. Pictures of geysers, oil wells
4. Charts
5. Model of Earth's core
6. Multisensory aids

C. Procedure:

1. Have students describe the Earth's crust (what they have seen on the surface of the Earth).
2. Discuss the deepest that we have dug or drilled into the Earth.
3. Scientists divide the Earth into three layers:
   a. Crust—mostly granite; 5 to 20 miles thick
   b. Mantle—20 to 1,800 miles thick; mostly rock called basalt
   c. Core—1,800 to 3,000 miles thick; exists in solid and liquid form
4. Relate to the students that the diameter of the Earth is 7,926 miles (12,756 kilometers); the radius is 3,963 miles (6,378 kilometers).
5. Tell the students that by bouncing sound waves toward the center of the Earth, we know about the basic layers of the Earth. Different structures have different sound wave patterns.
6. Tell the students that the center of the Earth is solid because the high pressure surrounding the core squeezes matter together and this causes a temperature rise.

D. Results:

1. Students will learn that the Earth has three main layers.
2. Students will learn that the center of the Earth is very hot.

E. Basic Facts and Supplemental Information:

1. Mine temperatures increase one degree Fahrenheit 1° F.) every 60 feet. Consequently, we estimate the mantle is 3,000° F. (4,800° C.) and the core is 8,000° F. (13,000° C.).
2. The deepest hole ever drilled was in the Kola peninsula in Russia. In 1990 it reached a depth of 7 miles (15 kilometers). Drillers hoped to reach a depth of 9 miles (15 kilometers), but the project was stopped for reasons unknown.

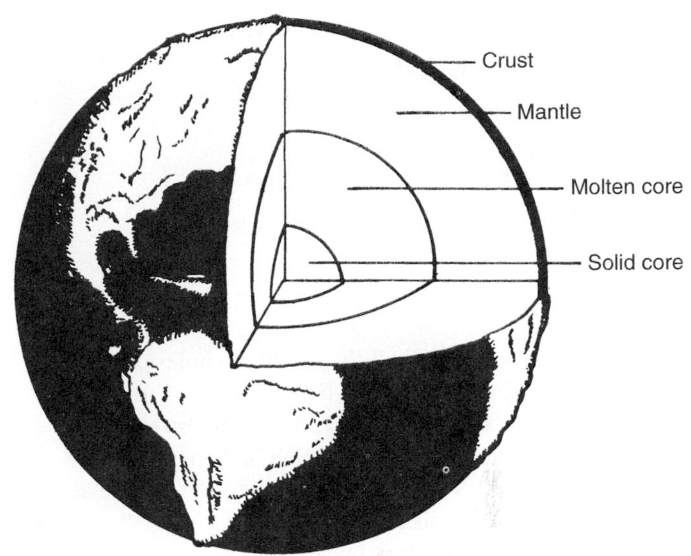

The Earth from the inside out

3. A program called "Project Mohole" is now underway in an attempt to drill through the Earth's mantle below the ocean floor. It is being financed by the United States National Science Foundation.

F. Thought Questions for Class Discussions:

1. What causes heat? cold?
2. What are some problems encountered when digging deep into the Earth?
3. Do you think we could ever reach the center of the Earth?

G. Related Ideas for Further Inquiry:

1. Study Section I-A, "Matter."
2. Study Section II-B, "Fire and Heat."
3. Study Activity VII-B-5, "How old is the Earth?"
4. Study Activity VII-B-6, "How fast is the Earth moving?"
5. Study Activity VII-B-7, "What is our atmosphere like?"
6. Study Section VII-C, "Earth's Crust."

H. Vocabulary Builders—Spelling Words:

1) **core** 2) **mantle** 3) **crust** 4) **outer** 5) **inner** 6) **Fahrenheit** 7) **temperatures**

I. Thought for Today:

"The world is round so that friendship may encircle it."

A. Problem: *What Causes an Eclipse?*

B. Materials Needed:

1. World globe (or large ball)
2. Table or desk
3. Tennis ball (to represent the moon)
4. Ice pick
5. Slide projector
6. Wire

C. Procedure:

1. With ice pick, *carefully* punch two holes on opposite sides of tennis ball.
2. Put wire through holes with loop on top to manipulate it. (Demonstration is more realistic when shadow of your hand is not on the globe as you rotate tennis ball.)
3. Set globe on desk or table.
4. Set up slide projector 10 to 15 feet from globe.
5. Darken room; turn on projector.
6. Revolve tennis ball around the globe so light from projector will cast shadows.
7. Revolve moon (tennis ball) until it falls within the shadow cast by the Earth (lunar eclipse).
8. Revolve the tennis ball close to Earth until it comes between the Earth and the sun, throwing its own shadow over the Earth. This will produce a partial or total eclipse, depending on the observer's position on globe (solar eclipse).

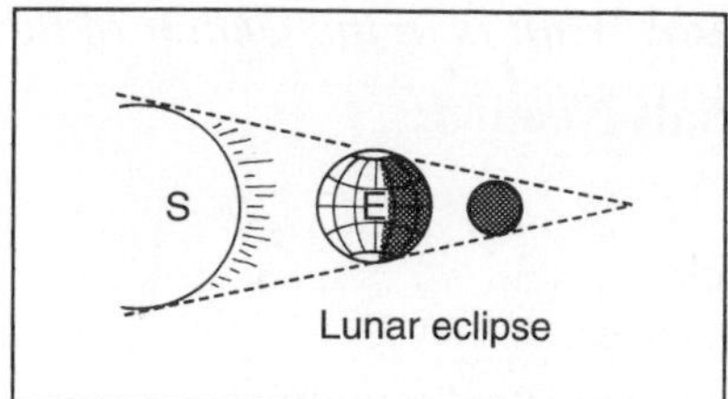

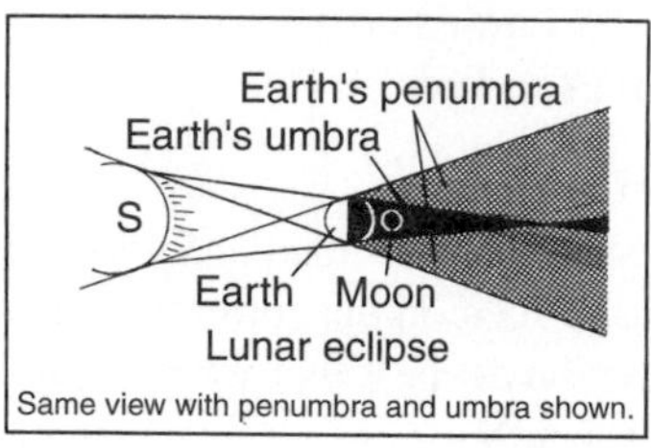

Same view with penumbra and umbra shown.

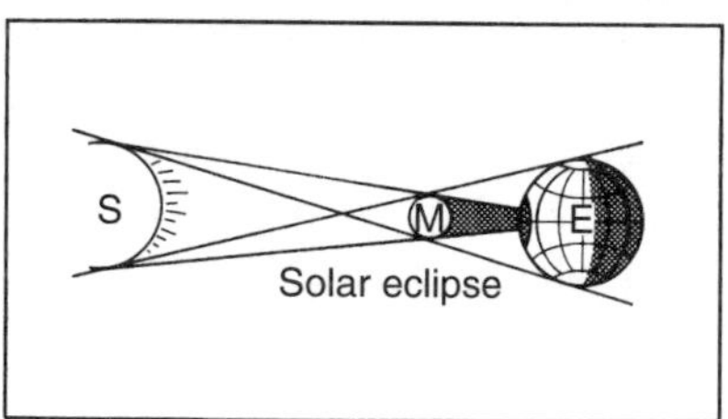

D. Result:

Students learn that the shadows of the Earth and moon are what cause eclipses of the moon and sun. When the moon has light from the sun cut off by the Earth, it is a lunar eclipse (eclipse of the moon). When the Earth has its light cut off by the moon, it is a solar eclipse (eclipse of the sun).

E. Basic Facts and Supplemental Information:

Solar eclipses are visible on limited sections of the Earth because of the relatively small shadow cast by the moon. Lunar eclipses are visible over large areas of the Earth's surface because they are caused by the Earth's casting a shadow on the moon. (The Earth is much larger than the moon.)

F. Thought Questions for Class Discussions:

1. Do we have lunar eclipses every month?
2. Do other planets have moons?
3. Can we see both sides of the moon during one day, one week, or one month? Why or why not? (Hint: It rotates once for every revolution it makes around the Earth.)

G. Related Ideas for Further Inquiry:

1. Discuss what causes the Earth's umbra and penumbra.
2. Discuss what we can learn during an eclipse.
3. Study Activity VII-B-1, "What is the sun like?"
4. Study Activity VII-B-3, "How can we tell time by using the sun?"
5. Study Activity VII-B-6, "How fast is the Earth moving?"
6. Study Activity VII-B-7, "What is our atmosphere like?"
7. Study Activity VII-B-11, "Why does the moon appear to change shape?"
8. Study Section VII-A, "Universe."

H. Vocabulary Builders—Spelling Words:

1) **eclipse** 2) **solar** 3) **lunar** 4) **shadow** 5) **globe** 6) **umbra** 7) **penumbra** 8) **orbits**

I. Thought for Today:

"Science can predict an eclipse of the sun many years in advance, but cannot accurately predict the weather over the weekend."

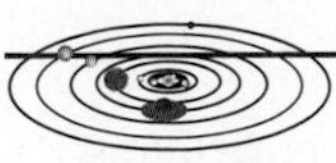

Activity VII B 11

A. Problem: *Why Does the Moon Appear to Change Shape?*

NOTE: This is a very difficult concept and should be undertaken over a month's time. Have the students observe the changes in the moon's appearance during this time.

B. Materials Needed:

1. World globe or large ball
2. Electric lamp
3. Slide projector
4. Bulletin board (preferably covered with light blue construction paper)
5. Flannel board, approximately 24″ × 36″ (preferably light blue color)
6. Colored construction paper: yellow, orange, dark green, light green, black, and white
7. Glue, paste, or cellophane tape
8. Colored yarn

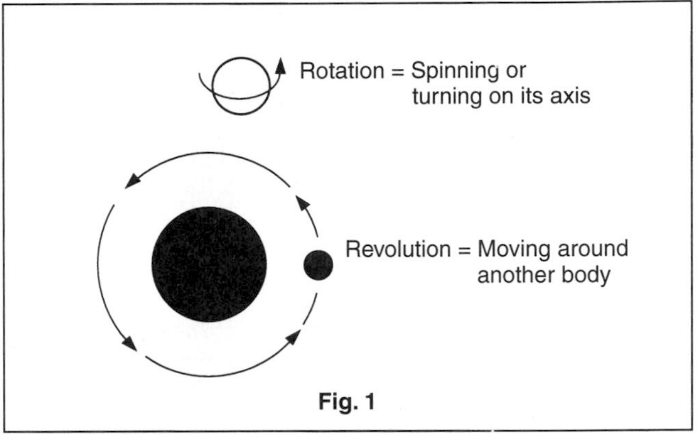

Fig. 1

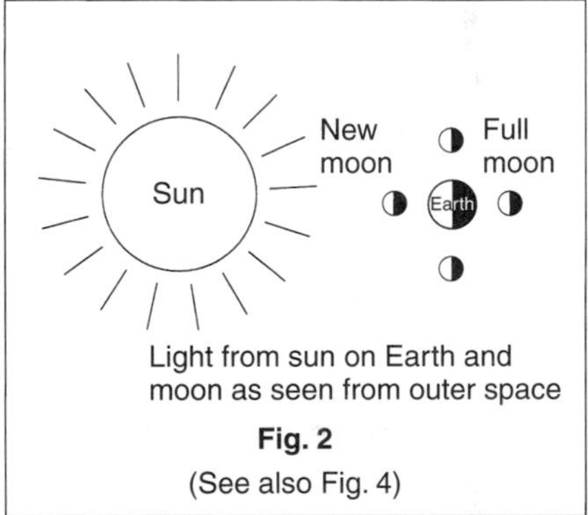

Light from sun on Earth and moon as seen from outer space

Fig. 2

(See also Fig. 4)

C. Procedure One: (See Figure One.)

1. Move chairs and desks to the sides of the room.
2. Set the lamp on a desk in the middle of the room.
3. Turn the lamp on.
4. Darken the room, except for the lamp.
5. Demonstrate the term "rotation" by having one student turn around slowly while staying in one spot. This rotation could be the sun, moon, Earth, or any other celestial body.
6. Demonstrate the term "revolution" by having another student walk around the lamp. This revolution could be any celestial body that moves around another, such as the Earth orbiting the sun, the moon orbiting the Earth, or any celestial body orbiting around another celestial body.
7. Have two students move as the Earth and moon do. The student representing the Earth should walk very, very slowly around the sun (lamp) in a large circle while the second student walks around the first student with his/her face always toward the student who represents the Earth.

Procedure Two: (See Figure Two.)

1. From the construction papers, cut out the following representations:
   a. the sun (approximately 12 inches in diameter) and its rays (yellow or orange). The rays could be represented by colored yarn.
   b. the Earth (approximately 4 inches in diameter). This should be dark green on the half that will be away from the sun, and light green on the half that will be closest to the sun.
   c. four moons, each half white and half black and 2 inches in diameter
2. Place the construction paper "sun" on one side of the flannel board, explaining that the sun gives off light in all directions. (See Figure Two.)
3. Place the construction paper "Earth" about halfway to the side of the flannel board, with the light half facing the "sun."
4. Place the four moons around the "Earth" as shown in Figure Two labeling the positions of the "New Moon" and the "Full Moon." (These show four positions of the moon at different times of the month.)
5. While the light side of the moon always faces the sun, the shape of the moon depends on where we view it from Earth.

Procedure Three: (See Figure Three.)

1. Place a light in a high position (tabletop or desk).
2. Draw an arc on the floor with a piece of chalk to represent 1/13 of the Earth's path around the sun. The arc should be part of a circle about 12 feet in

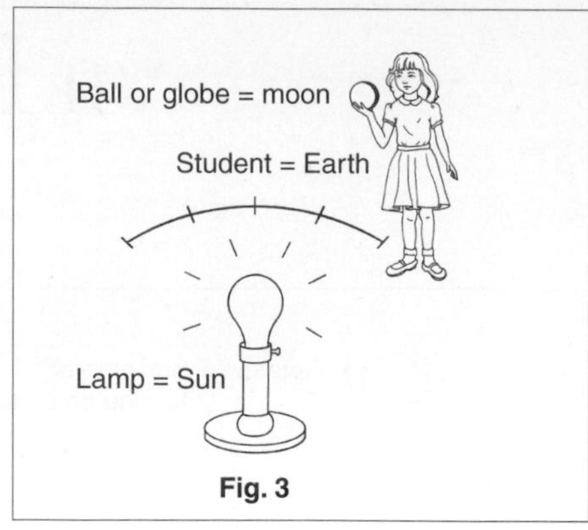

Fig. 3

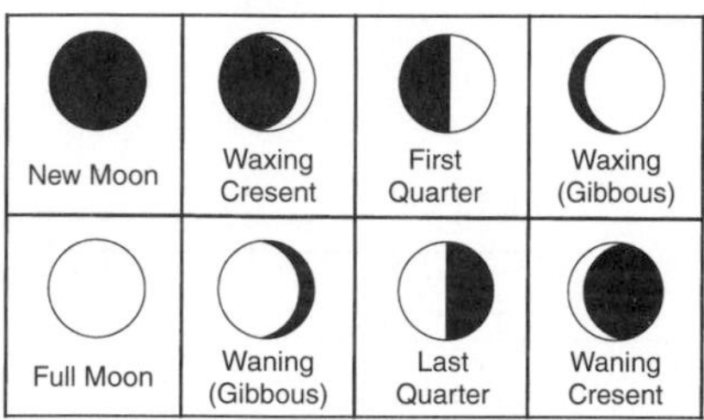

The crescent shape appearances of the moon are due to the light from the sun shining on a ball-shaped moon as seen from Earth.

Fig. 4

diameter. This represents the time the moon orbits the Earth and the Earth's partial orbit around the sun in one month's time.

3. Divide the arc into 4 equal parts and mark them as shown in Figure Three.
4. Darken the room.
5. Have a student hold the globe or ball just over his/her head.
6. Have him/her make one slow rotation in his/her walk along the arc noting the change of the shape of the light on the globe or ball. (See Figure Three.) The student should report viewing changes to class.

Procedure Four: (See Figure Four.)

1. From the construction paper, cut out four white moons and four black moons, each about 10 to 12 inches in diameter.
2. Cut out portions of circles of the opposite color to affix to the moon cutouts, as shown in Figure Four.
3. Glue, paste, or tape these cutouts to the "moons."
4. Mount the "moons" on the bulletin board.
5. Label each phase as shown.
6. Compare this display with the actual observations of the moon during the month.

D. Results:

Major concepts students learn through these procedures:

1. At any one time, half of the Earth and half of the moon are in light.
2. "Rotation" means a body turns on its axis.
3. "Revolution" means a body orbits another body.
4. The moon rotates once for every revolution it makes around the Earth; consequently, we see only one side of the moon.
5. Our perspective of the shape of the moon's lighted side is caused by the sun shining on it.
6. The moon rotates once and revolves around the Earth once every 27.3 days.
7. The moon revolves around the sun about 13 times a year, not once a month.

E. Basic Facts and Supplemental Information:

1. If an orrery is available, be sure to use it to supplement the activities cited.
2. Important facts about the moon:
   a. The moon is a satellite revolving around the Earth.
   b. It is about one-third the size of the Earth; its diameter is about 2,160 miles.
   c. The moon is approximately 240,000 miles from the Earth.
   d. Although continually changing, each phase lasts about 3.4 days.
   e. When there is an increase of light on the moon as seen from the Earth each day, it is "waxing," if decreasing it is "waning."

F. Thought Questions for Class Discussions:

1. How would the Earth appear to change in shape if we were on the moon?
2. If it were possible to view the Earth and moon from the sun, how would they appear to change in shape?
3. What causes an eclipse of the moon? of the sun?

G. Related Ideas for Further Inquiry:

1. Visit an observatory.
2. Study Activity VII-B-1, "What is the sun like?"
3. Study Activity VII-B-10, "What causes an eclipse?"

H. Vocabulary Builders—Spelling Words:

1) **phase** 2) **quarter** 3) **waxing** 4) **waning** 5) **gibbous** 6) **rotation** 7) **revolution**

I. Thought for Today:

"What we learn with pleasure, we never forget."

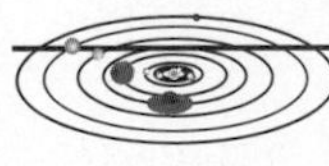

Activity VII B 12

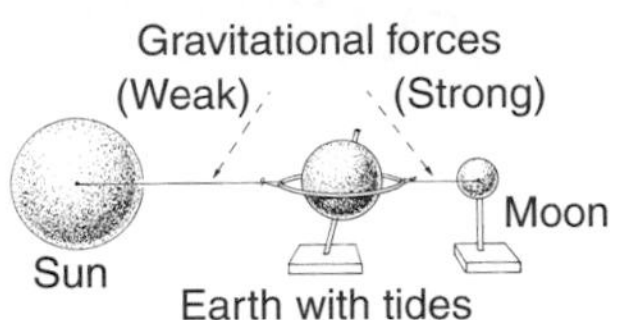

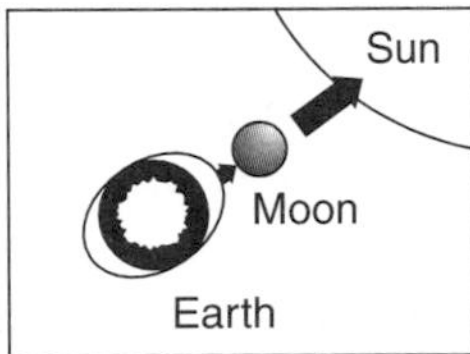

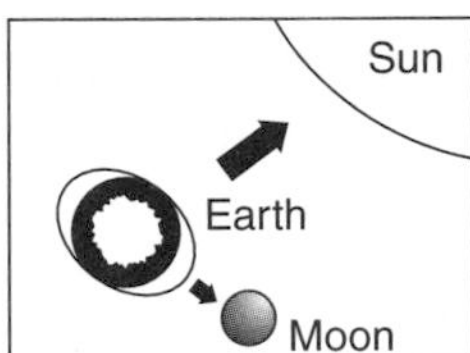

A. Problem: *What Causes Tides?*

B. Materials Needed:

1. Large ball depicting sun
2. Small ball depicting Earth
3. Smaller ball depicting moon (styrofoam balls work well)
4. Wide rubber band
5. Four cup hooks
6. Three supports: one for the sun, one for the Earth, and one for the moon. (The sun's support may be stationary. The Earth's and moon's supports should be movable.)
7. Attach cup hooks and balls to rubber band as shown in drawing.

C. Procedure:

1. Explain that heavenly bodies attract each other. The sun attracts the Earth and the Earth attracts the sun. The Earth attracts the moon and the moon attracts the Earth.
2. Discuss how the moon attracts the Earth and moves the oceans toward the moon.
3. Discuss how the sun attracts the Earth and moves the oceans toward the sun.
4. Explain how the moon exerts a greater pull because it is so much closer to the Earth.
5. By use of the apparatus made, the direction of pull can be demonstrated by the direction of the rubber band. (See drawing.)
6. Move the moon to various positions around the Earth.
7. Explain when the sun, moon, and Earth are in a straight line, the pull is greatest. These tides are called spring tides and occur twice a month. When the moon, Earth, and sun form a right triangle (one week later) the tides are smallest and are called neap tides.
8. Discuss the causes of high and low tides each day. (The Earth's rotation and its relation to the position of the moon.)
9. Discuss the causes of incoming tides. (The oceans are getting closer to the moon.)

D. Results:

1. Students will learn that the sun and moon cause the tides.
2. Students will learn that the moon has a much greater effect on tides than the sun.
3. Students will understand the terms "spring tides," "neap tides," "incoming tides," and "ebb tides."

E. Basic Facts and Supplemental Information:

1. The daily newspapers usually report the time of high tides and low tides each day.
2. Normally there are two bulges of the Earth at the same time—one facing the moon and one on the opposite side.
3. Usually there are two high tides and two low tides every day due to the Earth's rotation.
4. The shape of the seacoast has a great effect on the height and range of tides.
5. "Spring tides" are the tides with the highest waters.
6. "Neap tides" are those tides with the weakest pull of the sun and moon, and the tides are at their lowest level.
7. "Ebb tides" are those periods when the waters are receding.

F. Thought Questions for Class Discussions:

1. In some parts of the world the daily tides are less than 2 feet high, while in other parts of the world they are as great as 70 feet high. Why?
2. How can tides be used to help us?
3. Do you think tides could be used to generate electricity?

G. Related Ideas for Further Inquiry:

1. Students can check the location of the moon at high tide and at low tide.
2. Study Activity VII-B-10, "What causes an eclipse?"
3. Study Activity VII-B-11, "Why does the moon appear to change shape?"
4. Study other Activities in this Section.

H. Vocabulary Builders—Spelling Words:

1) **tide** 2) **gravity** 3) **attract** 4) **spring** 5) **neap** 6) **rotation** 7) **heavenly** 8) **pull**

I. Thought for Today:

"Patience is bitter but its fruit is sweet."

Section C: Earth's Crust

Activity VII C 1

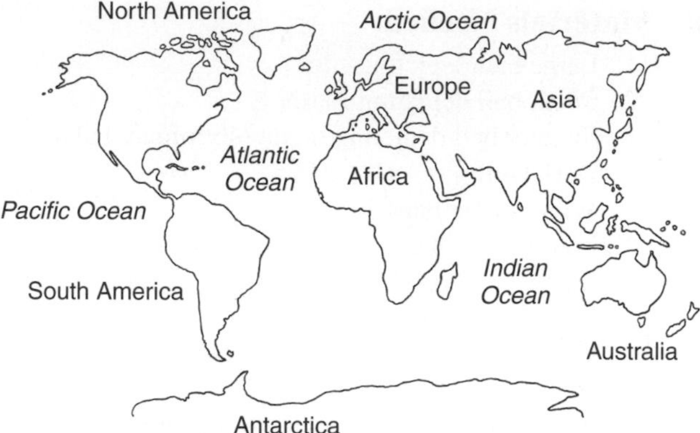

A. Problem: *What Are Continents?*

B. Materials Needed:

1. World globe
2. Maps
3. Reference materials
4. Multisensory aids

C. Procedure:

1. Discuss the features of our planet—the oceans and vast land areas.
2. Define "continents" as very large principal land masses.
3. By convention there are seven continents. From the largest to the smallest they are:
   a. Asia
   b. Africa
   c. North America
   d. South America
   e. Antarctica
   f. Europe
   g. Australia

   Locate these continents on the globe or maps.
4. Have students draw a map of the continents and place it on the bulletin board.
5. Show whatever multisensory aids are available, appropriate, and interesting.
6. Review Section E, Basic Facts and Supplemental Information.

D. Results:

1. Students will learn that there are seven continents and that there are definite physical as well as cultural differences.
2. They will learn that the continents move slowly (as they have been doing for millions of years).

E. Basic Facts and Supplemental Information:

1. North America and Europe are moving away from each other about one inch per year.
2. Continents may split. California could become an island; Africa could split, and other continents could develop.
3. There are three other terms involving continents that are sometimes confusing:
   a. The "Continental Divide" is a line that follows a mountain range—the Rocky Mountains in western North America and the Andes in South America. It is about 3,000 miles long. The river systems of this "divide" empty into different parts of our planet's oceans.
   b. "Continental Drift" is the movement of continents cited earlier. Continents and the seafloor rest on massive rock formations called "plates." The movement and interacting of these is called "plate tectonics."
   c. "Continental shelf" is the name given to the land just under the water along the coastline of each continent. The shelf is really an extension of the continent. Along some of the California coast, the shelf extends only about one-half mile, while in Russia, it extends about 800 miles. Most continental shelves are shallow and teem with sea life.

F. Thought Questions for Class Discussions:

1. What do you think causes the continents to move?
2. What lies in the core of our planet?
3. How do the three main layers of the Earth—the core, the mantle, and the crust—differ?

G. Related Ideas for Further Inquiry:

1. Study Activity VII-C-2, "What is 'plate tectonics'?"
2. Study Activity VII-C-3, "What causes earthquakes?"
3. Study Activity VII-C-5, "What forces change the surface of the Earth?"
4. Study Activity VII-C-8, "What are the different layers of soil?"
5. Study Activity VI-C-9, "Are our oceans becoming polluted?"
6. Study other Activities in this Section.

H. Vocabulary Builders—Spelling Words:

1) **continents** 2) **Asia** 3) **Africa**
4) **North America** 5) **South America**
6) **Antarctica** 7) **Europe** 8) **Australia**

I. Thought for Today:

"Mistakes aren't so bad. Columbus found America by mistake."

Activity

A. Problem: *What Is "Plate Tectonics"?*

B. Materials Needed:

1. Large cookie sheet with raised edges
2. Styrofoam (seven large irregular pieces that will cover about one-third the area of the cookie sheet)
3. Seven small self-stick labels
4. Water
5. Flat working surface

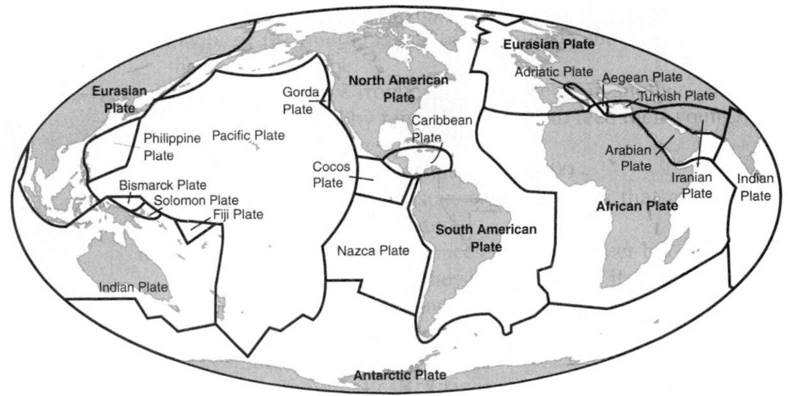

The seven major continental plates and several small ones

C. Procedure:

1. Place the cookie sheet on the flat working surface.
2. Mark each of the labels:
   a. "North American"
   b. "South American"
   c. "African"
   d. "Eurasian"
   e. "Antarctic"
   f. "Pacific"
   g. "Indian-Australian"
3. Affix one of these to each of the pieces of styrofoam.
4. Fill the tray half-full of water.
5. Place the pieces of styrofoam in the relative positions as shown in the drawing.
6. Discuss the information listed in Basic Facts and Supplemental Information.
7. Tell the students that each piece of styrofoam represents a "continental plate."

D. Results:

1. The styrofoam "continental plates" will move about.
2. Students will learn about "plate tectonics," the reshaping of continental plates.

E. Basic Facts and Supplemental Information:

1. In 1912, a German scientist, Alfred Wegener, proposed that continents are not in fixed positions; they move.
2. His theory has proved correct.
3. Recent studies show that these plates move from 2.5 to 5.0 inches (6 to 13 centimeters) per year.
4. In addition to the seven major plates, five smaller plates have been identified:
   a. Cocos Plate (Central America)
   b. Nazca Plate (Central America)
   c. Philippine Plate
   d. Arabian Plate
   e. Iranian Plate
5. Each plate contains land, ocean, and sea floor. The moving part of the Earth that contains these is called the "lithosphere."
6. Each plate is called a "lithosphere plate."
7. When two plates meet, one is "subducted." It slides under the other, causing friction, heating, volcanos, earthquakes, mountains, and/or rifts.

F. Thought Questions for Class Discussions:

1. What causes continental plates to move?
2. What causes earthquakes?
3. How are mountains formed?
4. What causes land faults?

G. Related Ideas for Further Inquiry:

1. Research your area for local land faults.
2. If you are near any mountains or hills that are partially barren, study the layers of land.
3. Study Activity VII-C-1, "What are continents?"
4. Study Activity VII-C-3, "What causes earthquakes?"
5. Study Activity VII-C-8, "What are the different layers of soil?"
6. Study Activity VII-C-5, "What forces change the surface of the Earth?"

H. Vocabulary Builders—Spelling Words:

1) **tectonics** 2) **continental** 3) **plates**
4) **faults** 5) **mountains** 6) **volcanos**

I. Thought for Today:

"Digging for facts is a better exercise than jumping to conclusions."

Activity VII C 3

A. Problem: *What Causes Earthquakes?*

B. Materials Needed:

1. Three samples of carpeting or Three pieces of clay or Three blocks of wood, 2″ × 4″ × 12″
2. Tabletop or desk
3. Desk cover (if clay is used)

C. Procedure:

1. Briefly describe the composition of the Earth:
   a. hot, solid inner core
   b. hot, liquid outer core
   c. warm, variable thick mantle
   d. crust, made up of many layers 5 to 25 miles thick
2. Tell the students that the carpeting, clay, and wood represent the layers of the Earth's crust. The layers can be represented by different pieces of carpeting, different colors of clay, or markings on the wood blocks.
3. Describe the pressures that act on the Earth's surface: hot gases, winds, rains, glaciers, etc.
4. On the Earth's molten core float large land masses called continental drifts or, more commonly, plate tectonics. These plates rub, bump, and move over or under other plates, causing vibrations and cracks (faults). Any of these movements cause earthquakes.
5. If blocks of wood are used, place the three blocks together.
6. Move one block forward and show how the earth has moved along a fault line.
7. Replace the blocks so that the three are again lined up in their original position.
8. Lift two adjoining blocks up, or holding all three, let one move downward.
9. Explain that this is what causes earthquakes—the resettling of the portions of the Earth's crust caused by internal pressures.
10. Explain that the strength of earthquakes is measured by a Richter Scale, measuring from "1" up. Each subsequent number is 10 times greater than the preceding number. Thus, a reading of "3" is 100 times greater than a reading of "1." Most earthquakes are reported in tenths, such as 4.6, 3.5, or 2.8.

D. Results:

1. The movement of the blocks demonstrate earth movements that produce earthquakes.
2. Students will realize that the earth has natural cracks, or "faults," which are in a constant state of stress and sometimes produce earthquakes.

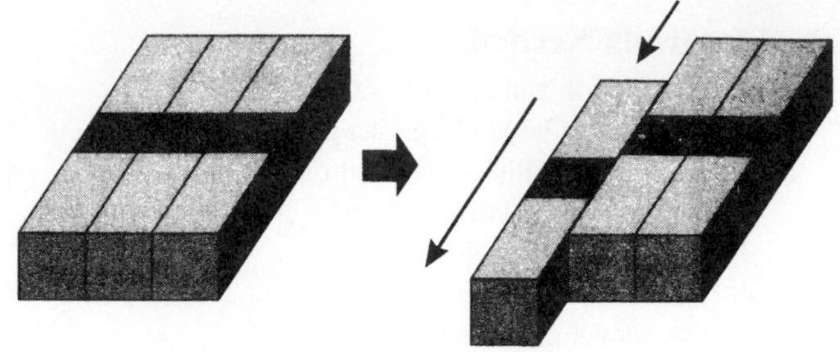

Horizontal movement

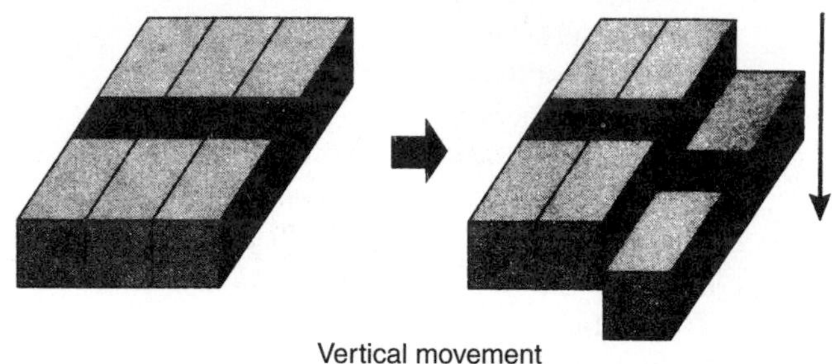

Vertical movement

E. Basic Facts and Supplemental Information:

1. The shifting of the earth as represented by the movement of the blocks usually occurs under the surface of the earth and usually does not break the surface.
2. When an earthquake occurs, its vibrations travel rapidly through the body of the Earth.
3. These vibrations are detected by seismographs.

F. Thought Questions for Class Discussions:

1. What causes the different layers of the Earth?
2. What are fault lines?
3. If an earthquake happened in one area, what are the chances that it can happen in that area again?

G. Related Ideas for Further Inquiry:

1. Have students interview people who have experienced a major earthquake.
2. Study all Activities in this Section.

H. Vocabulary Builders—Spelling Words:

1) **earthquake** 2) **crust** 3) **seismograph**
4) **Richter Scale** 5) **erosion** 6) **pressure**

I. Thought for Today:

"To err is human, but when the eraser wears out before the pencil, you're overdoing it."

Activity VII C 4

A. Problem: *What Causes a Volcano to Erupt?*

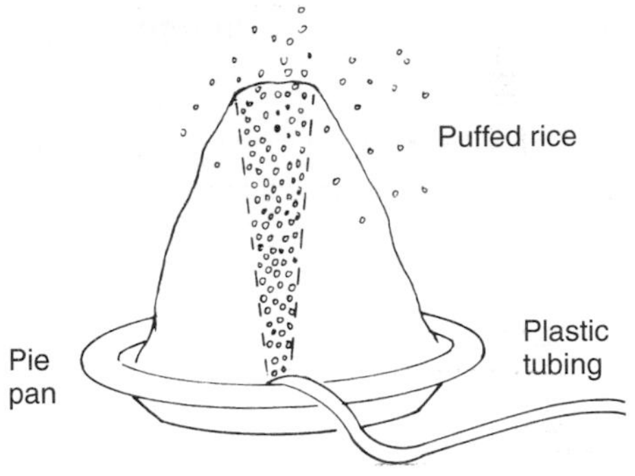

B. Materials Needed:

1. Pie pan
2. Length of plastic tubing, about 15″ long
3. Salt and flour paste
4. Puffed rice (cereal)
5. Dry, ground cereal
6. Tempera paint (brown)
7. Carbonated soft drink in a bottle or can
8. Water

C. Procedure:

1. Have a class committee do the research on the shape, general appearance, and structure of a volcano.
2. Students can make a paste of flour, salt, and water.
3. From this paste, students can make a model of a volcano. A vertical cone-shaped hole should be left in the center. A plastic tube should be connected to the bottom of this hole. (See drawing.)
4. When paste has hardened, paint volcano brown with tempera paint.
5. Place some puffed rice cereal in the cavity.
6. Have a student blow, with great force, into the end of the plastic tube.
7. Open the soft drink bottle or can and notice the bubbles and some liquid droplets escaping.

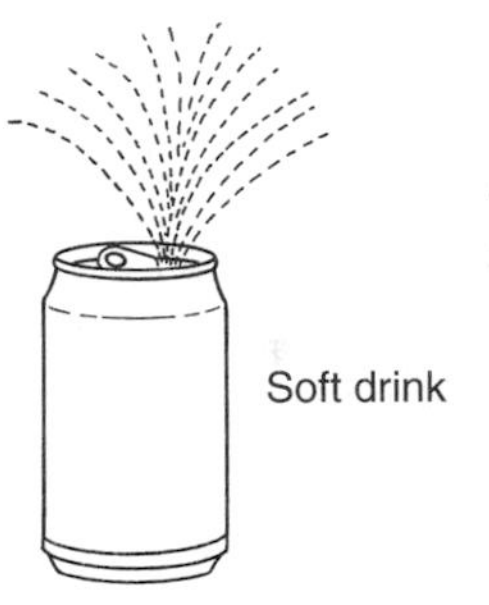

D. Results:

1. The increased air pressure caused by the student blowing into the plastic tube will cause the "puffed rice" volcano to erupt.
2. Gas pressure forces the bubbles to spray out of the bottle or the can.

E. Basic Facts and Supplemental Information:

1. Volcanic eruptions are due to gas pressures that build up from the molten material from the Earth's core and reach the mantle and crust of the Earth.
2. This demonstration could lead to a discussion on the formation of mountains by pressure from the Earth's core.
3. Eruptions from volcanos cause major influences in the atmospheric environment by spewing carbon dioxide, nitrogen dioxide, and particulates into the air.

F. Thought Questions for Class Discussions:

1. In what way is the "erupting" model volcano similar to a real volcano erupting on Earth?
2. What causes the internal pressures within the Earth?
3. What pollutants from volcanos affect the atmosphere the most?

G. Related Ideas for Further Inquiry:

1. Combine this activity with an art project.
2. Study Activity VII-C-1, "What are continents?"
3. Study Activity VII-C-2, "What is 'plate tectonics'?"
4. Study Activity VII-C-3, "What causes earthquakes?"
5. Study Activity VII-C-5, "What forces change the surface of the Earth?"
6. Study Activity VII-C-8, "What are the different layers of soil?"
7. Study other Activities in this Section.

H. Vocabulary Builders—Spelling Words:

1) **volcano** 2) **erupt** 3) **cone** 4) **pressure** 5) **simulate** 6) **puffed rice** 7) **plastic**

I. Thought for Today:

"If you think you have somebody eating out of your hand, it's a good idea to count your fingers."

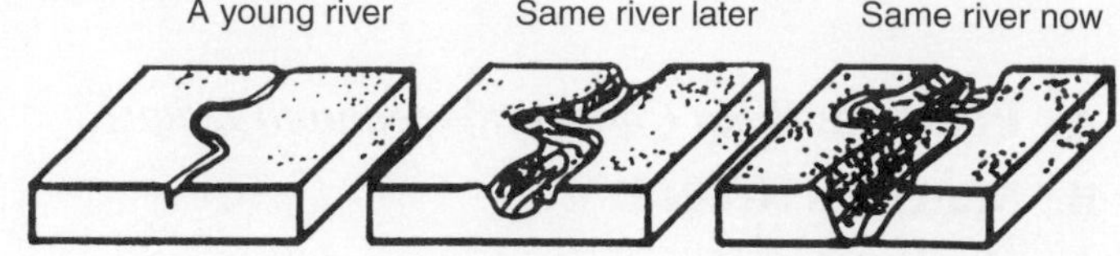

A natural change of the Earth's surface

People change the surface of the Earth by plowing and by constructing buildings, streets, and highways.

A. Problem: *What Forces Change the Surface of the Earth?*

B. Materials Needed:

Multisensory aids about "Earth changers":

1. Books
2. Pamphlets
3. Pictures
4. Charts
5. Newspaper articles
6. Films, film strips, slides, etc.

C. Procedure:

1. Have students collect pictures of anything that will change the surface of the Earth. These will probably include:
   a. oceans
   b. glaciers
   c. rivers
   d. waterfalls
   e. wind
   f. rain
   g. tractors
   h. shovels
   i. earthquake damage
   j. volcanos
   k. geysers
   l. underground water
   m. landslides, etc.
2. Have students mount the pictures on a bulletin board or place on a display table.
3. Assign a student or small committee to report on the affects on our planet of each item listed in C-1 above.
4. You might want to separate Earth's damage into two parts: human and natural.

D. Results:

1. Students will learn that there are natural and human forces that are continually changing the surface of the Earth.
2. Students will realize that change is a part of life.

E. Basic Facts and Supplemental Information:

1. Glaciers are rivers of ice which usually move about 2 feet per day.
2. The glaciers are currently moving poleward, but in time they will reverse themselves and head toward the equator.
3. The continents are on the move.
4. Some earthquakes are caused by opposing movement of sections of the Earth's crust.
5. All the items listed in Procedure (C-1) affect our lives, especially in regard to:
   a. food
   b. shelter
   c. transportation
   d. work
   e. recreation, etc.
6. People change the surfaces of the Earth by building cities, streets, highways, bridges, residences and by planting crops, etc.
7. Plants change the surfaces of the Earth by their growth, development, and spreading.
8. Animals change the surface of the Earth mainly by foraging for food and water.

F. Thought Questions for Class Discussions:

1. What forces have you seen that have changed the Earth's surface?
2. What force do you think changes the Earth's surface most quickly?
3. What force do you think changes the Earth's surface most drastically?
4. What makes gullies?
5. What is erosion?

G. Related Ideas for Further Inquiry:

1. Study your local community for ways that nature has changed the locality.
2. Take a field trip around the area where your school is located and note the ways people have changed the former natural setting.
3. Study Activity VII-C-2, "What is 'plate tectonics'?"
4. Study Activity VII-C-3, "What causes earthquakes?"

H. Vocabulary Builders—Spelling Words:

Use words listed in Procedure 1.

I. Thought for Today:

"The world changes so fast that you couldn't stay wrong all the time if you tried."

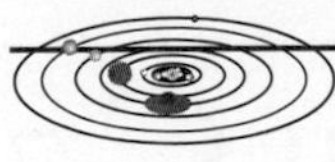

Activity

A. Problem: *How Are Mountains Formed?*

B. Materials Needed:

1. Heavy towel, carpeting, or sheet of clay
2. Waxed paper
3. Table or desk top

C. Procedure:

1. Discuss the elements that change the surface of the Earth. (See Activity VII-C-5.)
2. Discuss the internal structure of the Earth, describing the liquid portion of the core which can cause the crust (surface) to move up and down like the waves on an ocean.
3. Lay a sheet of waxed paper on the table or desk.
4. Lay the heavy towel, carpeting, or sheet of clay on the waxed paper.
5. Tell students that this represents the surface of the Earth and that they are to assume that the inner part is going to exert a force in the middle of the material.
6. Push the material inward and a little bit upward. (See drawing.)

D. Results:

1. A replica of a mountain will be formed.
2. Students will learn that inner pressures of the Earth cause portions of the Earth's surface to rise and form mountains.

E. Basic Facts and Supplemental Information:

1. The main inner pressure causing mountains to form arises when continental plates collide and one subducts under the other. This causes great pressure on the Earth's crust, thus forming mountains.
2. These movements also cause cracks in the Earth's crust, making fault lines.
3. Volcanos are also a result of the movement of colliding continental plates.
4. The relative age of mountains can be determined by looking at them.
   a. Old mountains have tops shaped like triangles that have been worn away by the winds and rains.
   b. New mountains have rounded tops much like the appearance of the material used in this Activity.
5. If different layers of clay are used, a much more realistic appearance is seen.

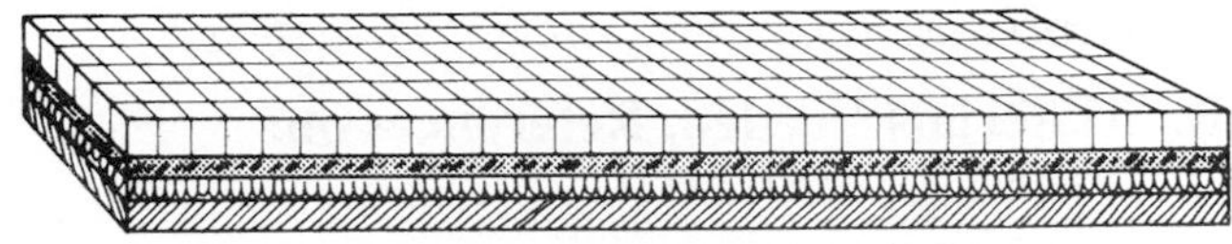

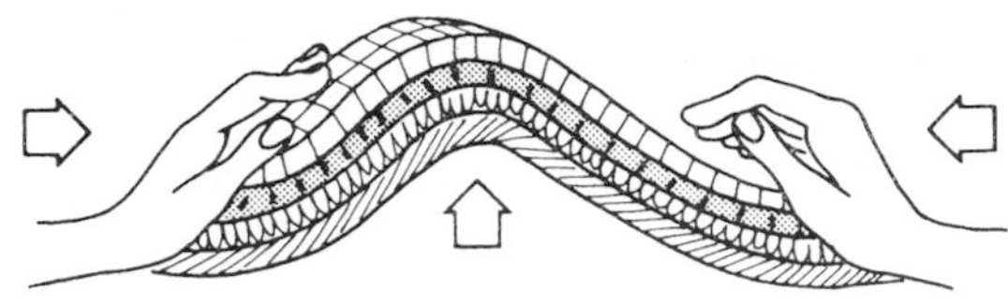

Push slightly downward.

F. Thought Questions for Class Discussions:

1. If there are mountains near the school, are they old or new?
2. Why are some mountains higher than others?
3. What could cause valleys?
4. What kinds of rocks are usually found on the tops of mountains?
5. Where are the highest mountains near your community?

G. Related Ideas for Further Inquiry:

1. If there are mountains near your community, examine them for strata formations. By doing this you can determine where the main thrust was that formed the mountains.
2. Study Activity VII-C-2, "What is 'plate tectonics'?"
3. Study Activity VII-C-3, "What causes earthquakes?"
4. Study Activity VII-C-4, "What causes a volcano to erupt?"
5. Study Activity VII-C-8, "What are the different layers of soil?"
6. Study Activity VII-C-10, "What is soil erosion? What causes losses of our topsoil?"
7. Study Section VII-E, "Weather."

H. Vocabulary Builders—Spelling Words:

1) **mountains** 2) **Earth** 3) **crust** 4) **valleys** 5) **thrust** 6) **continental** 7) **causes**

I. Thought for Today:

"People are funny. They spend money they don't have to buy things they don't need to impress people they don't like."

Activity

A. Problem: *What Are Natural Disasters?*

B. Materials Needed, References on:

1. Floods
2. Earthquakes
3. Typhoons
4. Famines
5. Plagues (diseases)
6. Tsunamis (huge ocean waves produced by earthquakes or undersea volcanic eruptions)

C. Procedure:

1. Ask the class if there are any "disasters" occurring anywhere in the world today?
2. Ask students if they have heard about some of the kinds of major disasters we have had in the past.
3. Discuss the differences between man-made disasters (wars) and natural disasters.
4. Cite some of the world's worst *natural* disasters.
5. Cite which of these disasters could have been avoided or reduced in intensity.
6. List some of the man-made disasters (wars).
7. List the wars in which the United States was involved that cost our country millions of lives and casualties. These include:
   a. Revolutionary War
   b. Civil War
   c. World War I
   d. World War II
   e. Korean War
   f. Vietnam

D. Results:

1. Students will learn that there are natural disasters over which we have no control; only famine and plagues can be reduced.
2. Students will realize that wars can be prevented and that nobody wins a war.

E. Basic Facts and Supplemental Information:

1. Natural disasters can hit anywhere, anytime.
2. If they occur locally, even on a small scale, they are considered disasters.
3. The biggest disasters now occurring are the famines in parts of Africa.

F. Thought Questions for Class Discussions:

1. How can we help people to become more understanding of others so that potential future wars can be prevented?
2. Do you think modern medical science can do anything to prevent plagues?

Krakatoa (Volcano)

1. Off coast of Indonesia in 1883
2. Darkened skies for 150 miles
3. Spewed ash for 950 miles
4. Estimated loudest sound ever

3. What can we do to reduce famine that is so prevalent in many parts of the world?

G. Related Ideas for Further Inquiry:

1. Study Section V-E, "Public Health."
2. Study Section V-C, "Nutrition."
3. Study Section V-F, "First Aid."
4. Study Activity VII-C-1, "What are continents?"
5. Study Activity VII-C-3, "What causes earthquakes?"
6. Study Activity VII-C-5, "What forces change the surface of the Earth?"
7. Study Activity VII-C-8, "What are the different layers of soil?"
8. Study Activity VII-C-9, "What are aquifers?"
9. Study Activity VII-C-10, "What is soil erosion? What causes losses of our topsoil?"

H. Vocabulary Builders—Spelling Words:

1) **floods** 2) **famines** 3) **typhoons**
4) **tsunami** 5) **disease** 6) **natural**

I. Thought for Today:

"Peace has its victories no less than war, but it doesn't have as many monuments."

THE WORLD'S WORST NATURAL DISASTERS

The death tolls given in the following list are based on commonly accepted data but are not definitive.

Deaths	Date	Cause	Place
75,000,000	Mid-14th century	Bubonic plague (Black Death)	Europe and Asia
22,000,000	1918	Influenza	Worldwide
20,000,000	1969–71	Famine	Northern China
10,000,000	1939	Floods/famine	Northern China
9,500,000	1877–78	Famine	China
3,700,000	1931	Flood	Yellow River, China
3,000,000	1669–70	Famine	Bombay/Madras, India
1,500,000	1943–44	Famine	Bengal, India
1,000,000	1201	Earthquake	Syria/Egypt
1,000,000	1846–47	Famine	Ireland
900,000	1887	Flood	Honan Province, China
830,000	1556	Earthquake	Shensi, China
800,000	1838	Famine	Northwestern India
655,000	1976	Earthquake	Tientsin/Tangshan, China
500,000	1970	Typhoon/flood	Bangladesh
300,000	1737	Earthquake	Calcutta, India
300,000	1881	Typhoon	Haiphong, Indochina
300,000	1642	Flood	Yellow River, China
250,000	526 B.C.	Earthquake	Antioch, Syria
215,000	1876	Tsunami	Bay of Bengal, India
200,000	1703	Earthquake	Tokyo, Japan
200,000	856	Earthquake	Persia
180,000	1920	Earthquake	Kansu Province, China
20,000,000 (estimated)	1983–present (annually)	Famine (continuing) Hunger, related diseases	Worldwide, highest in Africa

Source: National Geographic

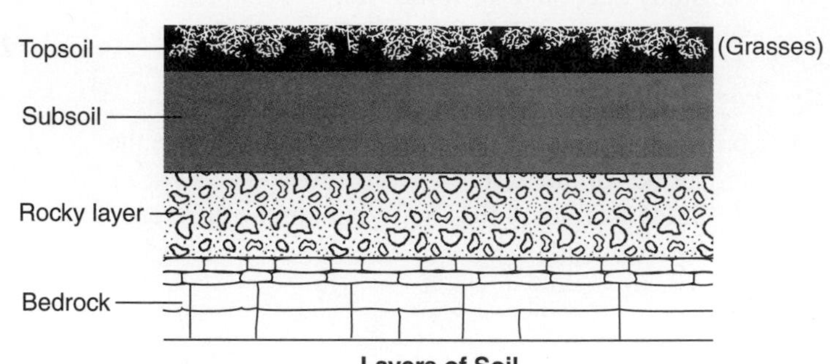

Layers of Soil

A. Problem: *What Are the Different Layers of Soil?*

B. Materials Needed:

1. Tall glass or clear plastic cylinder
2. Solid heavy rock
3. Small rocks
4. Smaller rocks (pebbles)
5. Organic material:
   a. dirt
   b. small pieces of plants, animal remains (e.g., hair, feathers, bones, etc.)
6. Live plants in soil

C. Procedure:

1. Discuss with students the value of soils.
2. Discuss with students the various elements that make up our soils.
3. Discuss how soils are sometimes classified by layers:
   a. bedrock: put the large rock in the bottom of a cylinder.
   b. rocky layer (small rocks): place a layer of small rocks on top of the heavy (large) rock.
   c. subsoil: mix some smaller rocks with dirt and place it on top of the rocky layer.
   d. topsoil: place the dirt with living plants on top of the subsoil.
4. Fill the cylinder with the typical layers shown in the drawing.
5. Discuss additional items in Section E, Basic Facts and Supplemental Information.

D. Results:

1. Students will learn that life is dependent on our soils.
2. Students will learn that there are many types of soils and that soils are usually found in layers.

E. Basic Facts and Supplemental Information:

1. When we look over the Earth's crust, we see many plants.
2. Plants could not exist without soils.
3. Soils are complex mixtures of rocks and decayed (decaying) organic materials.
4. Soils are usually layered as described in Procedure.
5. There are many topsoil types:
   a. humus
   b. loam
   c. silt
   d. sand
   e. clay
   f. peat, etc.
6. Soils vary tremendously in composition depending on weather, physical terrain, water content, etc.
7. Part of the rocky content of soils are minerals. (Study Activity VII-C-11.)
8. One of the most serious problems facing people today is the loss of topsoil.

F. Thought Questions for Class Discussions:

1. If we continue losing our topsoil at the present rate, how will we feed all the people, since the world's population is fast increasing in numbers?
2. What is the predominant soil in your community?
3. Can soil be enriched?
4. What are the most important chemicals needed for plant growth?

G. Related Ideas for Further Inquiry:

1. Study the soil types in your community.
2. Interview nursery workers, farm supply house people, etc. to determine what kinds of crops are best for your area. Also inquire about the kinds of fertilizers they recommend.
3. Study Activity VII-C-3, "What causes earthquakes?"
4. Study Activity VII-C-9, "What are aquifers?"
5. Study Activity VII-C-10, "What is soil erosion? What causes losses of our topsoil?"

H. Vocabulary Builders—Spelling Words:

1) **topsoil** 2) **subsoil** 3) **layers**
(Also use types of soil listed in E-5.)

I. Thought for Today:

"Dirt is just matter in the wrong places."

Activity VII C 9

A. Problem: *What Are Aquifers?*

B. Materials Needed:

1. Empty plastic spray bottle
2. Water
3. Sponge
4. Water glass
5. Plate or shallow bowl

C. Procedure:

1. Discuss the importance of fresh water.
2. Discuss geographical areas that are in critical need of water.
3. Tell the class that an "aquifer" is a large water basin under the ground.
4. Partially fill water glass with water.
5. Place the dry sponge on the plate or in the shallow bowl.
6. Slowly drip water onto the sponge until it is well saturated.
7. Compare this to rain falling on the Earth where the soil absorbs most of the water, but some of it settles down in aquifers and is held in place by hard rock—like a plate or a bowl.
8. Ask students how they would get water if it were hundreds of feet down in the ground.
9. Fill spray bottle half-full of water.
10. Pump the water out of the bottle by using the hand pump.
11. Tell the class that this is the way we get water out of aquifers—by pumping it out.

D. Results:

1. Students will learn what aquifers are.
2. Students will know that water in aquifers can be obtained by pumping it out.

E. Basic Facts and Supplemental Information:

1. Groundwater is exploited where there is little rainfall and few rivers, lakes, etc.
2. The upper level of the underground water is called the "water table."
3. Movement of water to the aquifers is a slow trickle and takes years to fill up.
4. Many aquifers are being pumped out faster than they are filling up.
5. Other aquifers are being contaminated by pesticides and fertilizers that are in the water runoffs from farm areas.

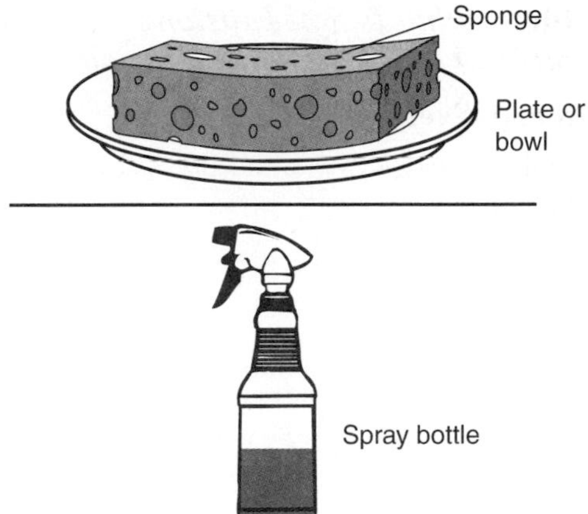

6. It is estimated that 62.5% of all fresh water is in aquifers.
7. Some aquifers are hundreds of miles in diameter.

F. Thought Questions for Class Discussions:

1. What would be the consequence of using up all the water in our aquifers?
2. What other sources of fresh water do we have other than groundwater?
3. Should we eliminate the use of pesticides and fertilizers since some of it gets into our fresh-water supplies?

G. Related Ideas for Further Inquiry:

1. Explore your community sources for fresh water.
2. Interview local personnel in your community's water district for the status and cleanliness of your local water supply.
3. Study Activity VII-C-2, "What is 'plate tectonics'?"
4. Study Activity VII-C-3, "What causes earthquakes?"
5. Study Activity VII-C-5, "What forces change the surface of the Earth?"
6. Study Activity VII-C-8, "What are the different layers of soil?"

H. Vocabulary Builders—Spelling Words:

1) **aquifers** 2) **groundwater** 3) **pumping** 4) **trickle** 5) **absorbs** 6) **saturated**

I. Thought for Today:

"A person with a reservoir of knowledge is not well-educated unless he/she knows when to turn the spigot on and off."

A. Problem: *What Is Soil Erosion? What Causes Losses of Our Topsoil?*

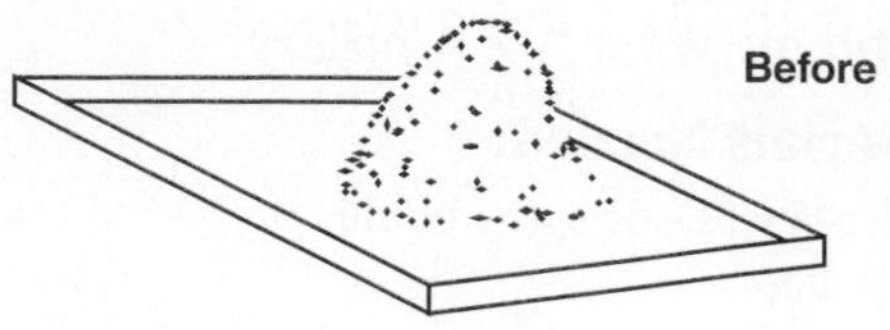

Sand and gravel

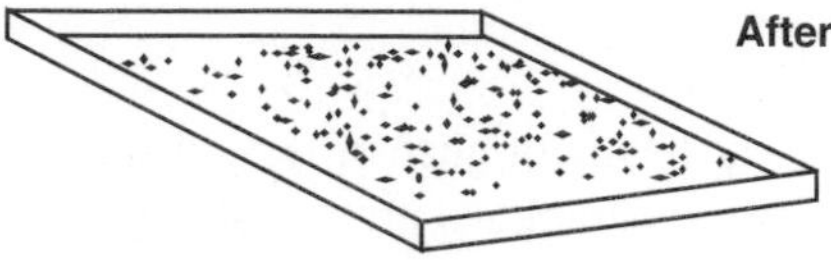

Sand and gravel

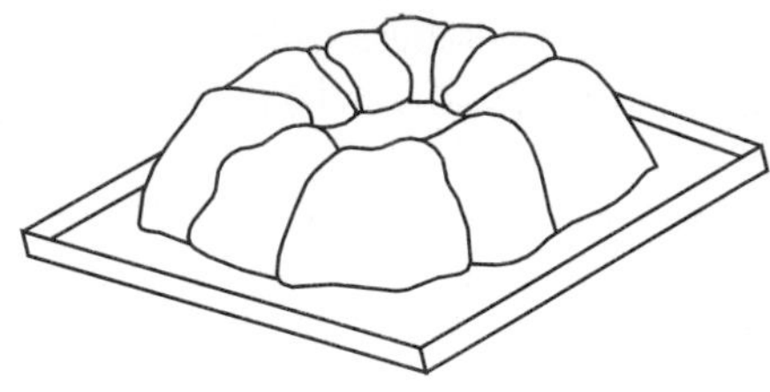
Simulated valley

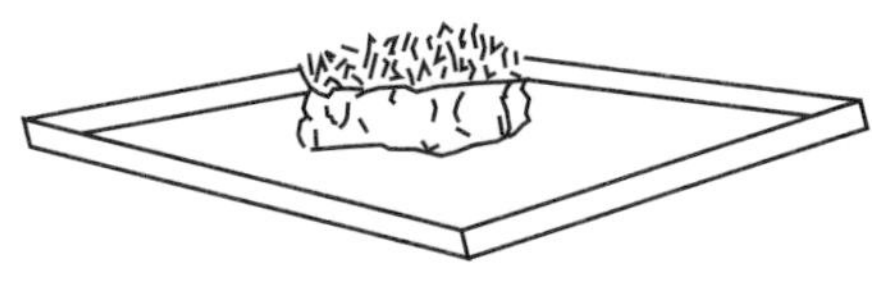
Grass sod

B. Materials Needed:

1. Cookie sheet
2. Sand
3. Grass, square, 6″ × 6″
4. Gravel
5. Water
6. Small-necked pint bottle
7. Newspapers
8. Table or desk
9. Bucket

C. Procedure:

1. Lay the newspapers on the table or desk.
2. Place the cookie sheet on the newspapers.
3. Using a mixture of 2/3 sand and 1/3 gravel, make a mound on the cookie sheet about 6 inches high.
4. Fill the bottle with water.
5. Slowly pour about half the water on top of the sand and gravel mound.
6. Notice the results.
7. Drain the excess water from the cookie sheet into the bucket.
8. Flatten the sand and gravel.
9. Carefully sprinkle more water from the bottle over the whole area of sand and gravel.
10. Notice the results.
11. Drain the excess water from the cookie sheet into the bucket.
12. Shape the sand and gravel into a circular shape with a high ridge and a large depression in the center.
13. Fill the bottle with water again.
14. Pour about half the contents of the bottle into the middle of the depression.
15. Notice the results.
16. Remove all sand and gravel from the cookie sheet.
17. Place the grass square in the middle of the cookie sheet.
18. Pour the remaining half of the water equally over the grass area.
19. Notice the results.

D. Results:

1. In the first trial, some sand and gravel will wash down the sides forming gullies.
2. In the second trial, there is little or no movement of sand and gravel.
3. In the third trial, the water will collect in the "valley" (middle of the depression).
4. In the last trial, the water will have little runoff because of the holding power of the grass sod.

E. Basic Facts and Supplemental Information:

1. Moving water changes the surface of the Earth.
2. Rain and melting snow develop streams and rivers.
3. Overflowing of lakes, ponds, and aquifers also contributes to streams and rivers.
4. All running waters, from little streams to large rivers, produce gulleys which wash away our topsoils by eroding our lands.
5. Our topsoils, which produce our foods, are becoming thinner and thinner due to gulleying, erosion, and poor farming techniques.

6. Many procedures are available to reduce gulleying, erosion, and loss of our precious topsoil. The most frequently used ones are:
   a. crop rotation
   b. terracing
   c. contour farming
   d. "wattling process" (constructing artificial fences across gulleys with tree limbs, branches, stones, etc. so that topsoil washed down the gulleys will collect in back of the fences, forming a series of small terraces)
   e. planting trees to make windbreaks to reduce soil loss caused by strong winds
7. The first attempt to quantify global erosion rates estimated that cropland losses exceeded new soil formation by 25.4 billion tons per year.
8. Another recent study claims that the average depth of our topsoil has been reduced from 9 inches to 6 inches.
9. The "bottom line" is that we are losing our topsoil at a time when our population is increasing, and we need more topsoil to produce more food crops.
10. We can add some chemicals to the soil to enrich it, but we cannot replace all the natural ingredients needed for most crops.
11. Scientists estimate that it takes nature 500 to 1,000 years to produce one inch of topsoil.

F. Thought Questions for Class Discussions:

1. Do you think running water is a powerful force?
2. If you were a farmer, what kind of land surface would you prefer?
3. What techniques could be used to retain topsoil?
4. Can you think of any other ways that would help save our topsoil?

G. Related Ideas for Further Inquiry:

1. If you have farmers in your area, ask them how they conserve the topsoil.
2. Study the different kinds of soil in your area.
3. Study all Activities in Section III-C, "Soils and Germination."
4. Study Activity VII-C-2, "What is 'plate tectonics'?"
5. Study Activity VII-C-3, "What causes earthquakes?"
6. Study Activity VII-C-5, "What forces change the surface of the Earth?"
7. Study Activity VII-C-8, "What are the different layers of soil?"
8. Study Activity VII-C-9, "What are aquifers?"

H. Vocabulary Builders—Spelling Words:

1) **erosion** 2) **gulleys** 3) **conservation** 4) **topsoil** 5) **sprinkle** 6) **valleys** 7) **rotation** 8) **terracing**

I. Thought for Today:

"A country can lose its freedom and regain it, but if it loses its topsoil the country is doomed forever."

A. Problem: *What Are Some Common Uses of Minerals?*

B. Materials Needed:

1. Talcum powder
2. Sandpaper
3. Table salt
4. Rocks
5. Epsom salts
6. Milk of Magnesia
7. Baking soda
8. Baking powder
9. Pictures of precious gems

C. Procedure:

1. Have students bring in one type of mineral found in the home or community.
2. Discuss what the mineral is and how it is used.
3. Describe some of the minerals listed in Materials Needed and show how they are used.

D. Results:

1. Many minerals will be brought in that have practical applications at home and at work.
2. Discuss the difference between minerals, rocks, elements, compounds, salts, etc. (Minerals are considered to be ores found in nature.)

E. Basic Facts and Supplemental Information:

1. Students like to collect rocks. Capitalize on this interest to help them learn more about the uses of minerals.
2. Field trips can be taken to nearby areas to look for rocks and minerals.
3. A mineral is a chemical compound that is found in nature.
4. Minerals have definite crystalline structures.
5. Minerals are classified in four main groups:
   a. silicious (contains silicon): quartz, feldspar, mica, and talc
   b. nonmetallic: rock salt, graphite, sulphur, gypsum
   c. metallic ores: gold, silver, lead, zinc, aluminum, tin, mercury, titanium, and uranium
   d. gems: opal, jade, garnet, topaz, tourmaline, emerald, aquamarine, ruby, amethyst, sapphire, zircon, and diamond
6. Minerals are found in rocks.
7. There are three types of rocks:
   a. Igneous rocks occur as a result of molten mass from the Earth cooling down and becoming solid.
   b. Sedimentary rocks occur when a layer of mud, sand, or other natural materials are compressed and cemented together.
   c. Metamorphic rocks occur as a result of land masses grinding together causing a great deal of pressure and heat, producing some new minerals.
8. Minerals can be tested by:
   a. color (cold and heated)
   b. luster
   c. crystalline form
   d. hardness
   e. weight (specific gravity)
   f. magnetic
   g. fluorescence
   h. radioactivity

F. Thought Questions for Class Discussions:

1. Where does the steel come from that is used in the manufacture of automobiles, stoves, etc.?
2. Is coal a mineral?
3. How many other uses of minerals can you name?

G. Related Ideas for Further Inquiry:

1. Have students make a list of some gems that are found in their home.
2. Make a collection of metallic ores. Be sure to label the specimens.
3. Study Activity VII-C-2, "What is 'plate tectonics'?"
4. Study Activity VII-C-5, "What forces change the surface of the Earth?"
5. Study Activity VII-C-8, "What are the different layers of soil?"
6. Study Activity VII-C-14, "What kinds of rocks are there?"

H. Vocabulary Builders—Spelling Words:

Use the words in Section E-8 of this Activity.

I. Thought for Today:

"If a gem be not polished it will not shine—if a person study not, the person will have no wisdom."—Jitsu go Kiyo

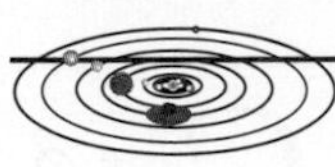

Activity

A. Problem: *How Are Crystals Formed?*

B. Materials Needed:

1. Hot plate or heating apparatus
2. Two one-quart glass jars
3. Three ounces powdered alum (obtain at pharmacy)
4. 1/4 teaspoon food coloring
5. Circle of blotting paper, paper coffee filter, regular filter paper, or cheesecloth
6. Water
7. Saucepan or tea kettle
8. Stirring rod or spoon
9. Cotton ball
10. Pipe cleaners or flexible wires
11. Small basket
12. Pot holders

C. Procedure One:

1. Fill the pan or kettle half-full of water.
2. Add alum and stir thoroughly.
3. Heat to a rolling boil.
4. Boil for several minutes more.
5. Turn off heat.
6. Add a pinch of food coloring and stir.
7. *Carefully* remove from heat source.
8. Secure the filter paper over the top of one of the quart jars.
9. *Carefully* pour the mixture into the jar through the blotting paper, paper coffee filter, regular filter paper, or cheesecloth.
10. Allow to stand for 24 hours. Tap jar occasionally while mixture is cooling to help formation of crystals.

Procedure Two:

1. Repeat the first five steps in Procedure One.
2. While the mixture is heating, suspend a small basket made of pipe cleaners or a ball of cotton as shown in the drawing.
3. *Carefully* pour the mixture into the quart jar through the coffee filter paper.
4. Allow to stand for a day or two.

D. Results:

1. In Procedure One, crystals form in the bottom of the jar.
2. In Procedure Two, crystals will adhere to the basket.

E. Basic Facts and Supplemental Information:

1. Crystals have a variety of shapes and are formed in many different materials.

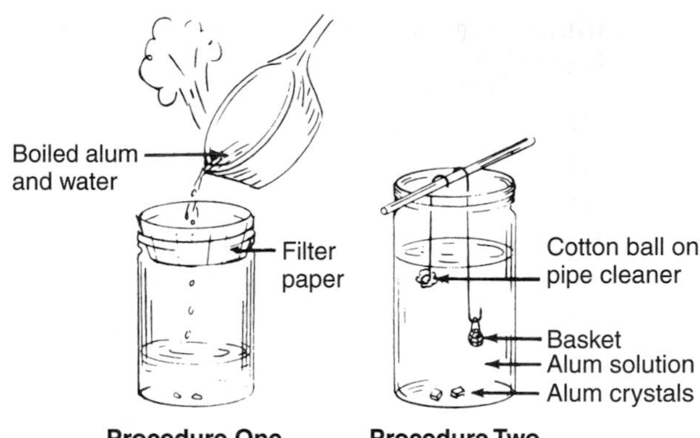

2. To study different formations of crystals, put both alum and salt crystals on a slide under a microscope (low magnification).
3. If a microscope is not available, use a strong magnifying glass.
4. Alum crystals are diamond-shaped.
5. Table salt crystals are cube-shaped.

F. Thought Questions for Class Discussions:

1. Can the same process be done with a saturated salt solution?
2. If an object were immersed in the Great Salt Lake for a few months, would it be covered with salt crystals?
3. Why do the alum crystals form when the saturated liquid is cooled?
4. Can you name any other crystals?

G. Related Ideas for Further Inquiry:

1. Have students research what objects are crystalline in shape?
2. Older students can study the seven basic forms of crystals: 1) rhombic, 2) cubic, 3) hexagonal, 4) tetragonal, 5) monoclinic, 6) triclinic, and 7) trigonal.
3. Study Activity VII-C-13, "What are stalagmites? stalactites?"
4. Study Activity VII-C-11, "What are some common uses of minerals?"
5. Study other Activities in this Section.

H. Vocabulary Builders—Spelling Words:

1) **crystal** 2) **solution** 3) **filter** 4) **ounces** 5) **boiled** 6) **coloring** 7) **alum** 8) **mixture**

I. Thought for Today:

"Interoffice memos increase our work by heaps and mounds."

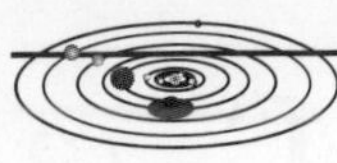

Activity VII C 13

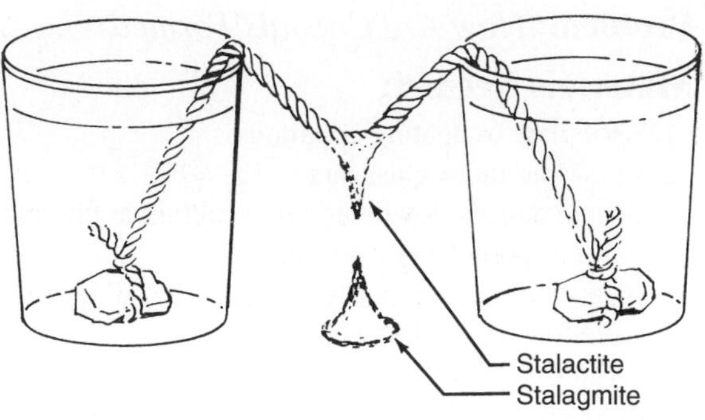

A. Problem: *What Are Stalagmites? Stalactites?*

B. Materials Needed:

1. Tea kettle or saucepan
2. Two one-quart glass jars
3. Yarn, soft, 24″ long
4. Hot plate or heating device
5. Powdered alum, 8 oz. (obtain at pharmacy)
6. Water
7. Two small rocks

C. Procedure:

1. Boil water and fill the two glass jars.
2. Stir in several ounces of powdered alum in both jars.
3. Tie one rock at each end of the yarn.
4. Place one rock in each of the jars.
5. Form a small loop (not shown in drawing) on the yarn between the jars.
6. Place apparatus in a corner where it can be observed.

D. Results:

1. After several days, a small "salt-icicle" will begin to form on the bottom of the loop of yarn, and as the salt water drops on the surface from the loop, a small salt-icicle will begin to rise from the surface.
2. Students will learn patience. This Activity takes awhile to develop.
3. Students will learn the difference between a stalagmite and a stalactite.

E. Basic Facts and Supplemental Information:

1. The salt-icicle forming on the loop is called a stalactite. The salt-icicle forming on the surface and rising is called a stalagmite.
2. In many caves, stalactites and stalagmites are formed by water absorbing salts. When the water evaporates, the salts are left behind in the appearance of icicles.
3. Stalagmites form from the ground up. Stalactites form from the ceiling down.
4. A good way to remember this is that stalagmite has the letter "g" in it, for "ground" and stalactite has the letter "c" in it, for "ceiling."

F. Thought Questions for Class Discussions:

1. Where does the water get its salt?
2. How are water icicles formed similarly to salt icicles?
3. Where does the water come from to form the frost or icicles in a freezer?

G. Related Ideas for Further Inquiry:

1. If students have visited caves and seen stalagmites or stalactites, have them relate their experiences to the class.
2. Study Section I-C, "Water."
3. Study Activity VII-C-5, "What forces change the surface of the Earth?"
4. Study Activity VII-C-8, "What are the different layers of soil?"
5. Study Activity VII-C-10, "What is soil erosion? What causes losses of our topsoil?"
6. Study Activity VII-C-11, "What are some common uses of minerals?"
7. Study Activity VII-C-12, "How are crystals formed?"
8. Study Activity VII-C-14, "What kinds of rocks are there?"
9. Study other Activities in this Section.

H. Vocabulary Builders—Spelling Words:

1) **stalagmites** 2) **stalactites** 3) **yarn** 4) **caves** 5) **evaporation** 6) **icicle** 7) **ceiling** 8) **ground**

I. Thought for Today:

"Modern science is simply wonderful. It would take fifty people twenty years to make the same mistake that a computer can make in two seconds."

Activity

A. Problem: *What Kinds of Rocks Are There?*

B. Materials Needed:

1. Reference books about rocks
2. Tables about rock characteristics (See Tables in this Activity.)
3. Pictures of rocks
4. Rock collections (could be brought in by students)
5. Hammer
6. Vinegar or dilute hydrochloric acid
7. Eyedropper
8. Multisensory aids
9. Test tray

C. Procedure:

1. Discuss rocks using multisensory aids to motivate students' questions.
2. Ask students to collect as many different kinds of rocks as they can.
3. Make a display of the rocks.
4. Using reference books, have students identify as many rocks as possible.
   a. Being careful of fingers, tap the rock sample with the hammer to determine its relative hardness.
   b. The students can use 6 to 8 drops of vinegar to test samples, or the teacher can test with dilute hydrochloric acid. (The students should never be allowed to use acids for these tests.)
5. Have students label rocks and cite characteristics of each type. (See next page.)
6. Plan a field trip to increase the classroom collection.

D. Results:

1. Some rocks when hit will break into small pieces; some will chip, and some will remain in one piece.
2. Some rocks will bubble when vinegar or dilute acid is placed on them showing the presence of carbonates. Most rocks are carbonates or silicates.
3. Students will learn to identify the main types of rock formations.

E. Basic Facts and Supplemental Information:

1. This Activity is always motivating for students.
2. Students are natural collectors, and this Activity makes use of their natural curiosity.
3. With a little persuasion from the teacher, many students will start their own rock collections.
4. Rocks are classified by their color, hardness, cleavage, size, etc.

5. Rocks usually contain a mixture of minerals.
6. It's fun to collect minerals.
7. Minerals are building blocks of rocks.
8. There are over 2,000 known minerals.
9. Twenty of them make up 95% of the Earth's crust.
10. Minerals contain no living or once living material. Silver, gold, and diamonds are minerals (and also elements). Diamonds are pure crystalline carbon.
11. Semiprecious stones such as sapphires, rubies, and emeralds are also minerals.
12. Minerals have definite physical characteristics; rocks do not.
13. Characteristics of minerals to look for:
    a. luster (glossy or dull)
    b. crystalline
    c. appearance when split
    d. color
    e. hardness (See Moh's Scale on next page.)
    f. magnetic or not
    g. Acid test—White vinegar is best for elementary students to use. Many minerals contain calcium carbonate ($CaCO_3$) and will bubble when acid is placed on them.
    h. Advanced students may want to test specimens with a smelting or heat test to determine if sulphur or metals are present.
    i. Advanced students may want to use a flame test. A small sample is heated in a flame. Different substances have different colors when heated. Extreme caution should be taken when heating rocks. Long tongs and gloves should be worn by the students, or, better yet, the instructor should perform this part of the rock test.

14. Rocks are of three major types:
    a. sedimentary—formed by mineral deposits from oceans or rivers.
    b. igneous—formed by cooling of hot lava.
    c. metamorphic—formed by a combination of igneous and sedimentary rocks.

F. Thought Questions for Class Discussions:

1. Why do we need to know anything about rocks?
2. How many ways can you name in which rocks are helpful or harmful to us?
3. How do rocks differ?

G. Related Ideas for Further Inquiry:

1. Make a campus survey to study the different kinds of rocks.
2. Have students make a survey of the different kinds of minerals that are found in homes.
3. Interview a jeweler about his/her work with minerals (and rocks).
4. Study Activity I-A-2, "What are atoms? molecules?"
5. Study Activity I-A-3, "What are elements? compounds? mixtures?"
6. Study Activity I-A-5, "What is the difference between a physical change and a chemical change?"
7. Study Activity VII-C-5, "What forces change the surface of the Earth?"
8. Study Activity VII-C-8, "What are the different layers of soil?"
9. Study Activity VII-C-3, "What causes earthquakes?"
10. Study other Activities in this Section.

H. Vocabulary Builders—Spelling Words:

1) **sapphire** 2) **diamond** 3) **silver** 4) **gold**
5) **crystalline** 6) **carbon** 7) **luster** 8) **scratches**

I. Thought for Today:

"A rolling stone gathers no moss, but it gains a certain polish."

COLOR TABLE

EXTERNAL COLOR	STREAK TEST	EXAMPLE
Blue or white	White	Calcite
Green, purple, white	White	Fluorite
Gray or green	White	Talc
Blue-green	White	Apatite
Gray	Gray	Galena
Pale yellow	Dark green	Pyrite
Orange-yellow	Green-black	Chalcopyrite
Gray; Red-brown	Red-brown	Hematite
Bright green	Pale green	Malachite
Brown	Ochre yellow	Limonite
Black	Black	Magnetite

HARDNESS TABLE (MOH'S SCALE)

HARDNESS NUMBER	HARDNESS TEST	EXAMPLE
1	Scratches easily with a fingernail	Talc
2	Scratches with a fingernail	Gypsum
3	Scratches with a pin or penny	Calcite
4	Scratches easily with a knife	Fluorite
5	Scratches with a knife	Apatite
6	Knife will not scratch rock; rock will not scratch glass	Feldspar
7	Scratches glass easily	Quartz
8	Scratches quartz easily	Topaz
9	Scratches topaz easily	Corundum
10	Scratches all other rocks	Diamond

SIZE TABLE

NAME	SIZE IN INCHES	(METRICS)
Boulder	More than 10 inches across	(25 cm)
Cobble	2-1/2 to 10 inches across	(6–25 cm)
Pebble	1/8 to 2-1/2 inches across	(30 mm–6 cm)
Granules	1/16 to 1/8 inches across	(15–30 mm)
Sand	1/64 to 1/16 inches across	(5–15 mm)
Silt	As fine as scouring powder	(—)
Clay	Particles can only be seen with microscope	(—)

Section D: Gravity

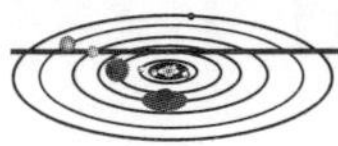

Activity

VII D 1

A. Problem: *How Can You Find the Center of Gravity of Irregularly Shaped Flat Objects?*

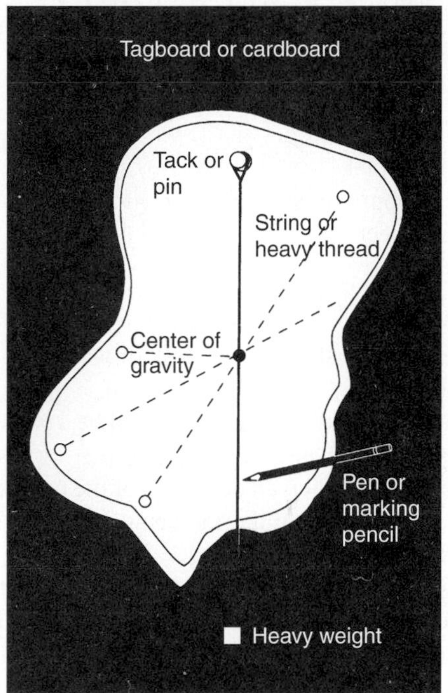

Procedure One

B. Materials Needed, Procedure One:

1. Tagboard or cardboard, approximately 2′ × 3′
2. Thumbtack or large pin
3. String or heavy thread
4. Weight
5. Irregularly shaped cutout, different color than tagboard or cardboard (See drawing, Procedure One.)
6. Pen or marking pencil
7. Punch

Materials Needed, Procedure Two:

1. Ruler
2. Wire
3. Hammer
4. Desk or table

C. Procedure One:

1. Tack or pin the irregularly shaped cutout to the tagboard, with tack or pin near the top.
2. Challenge the students to see if they can find its center of gravity.
3. Punch a hole near one of the edges and place a tack in it.
4. Make a loop with string or thread, place the loop over the tack, and fasten the weight to the other end of the string or thread.
5. Draw a dotted line along the thread.
6. Repeat with other holes along different edges.

Procedure Two:

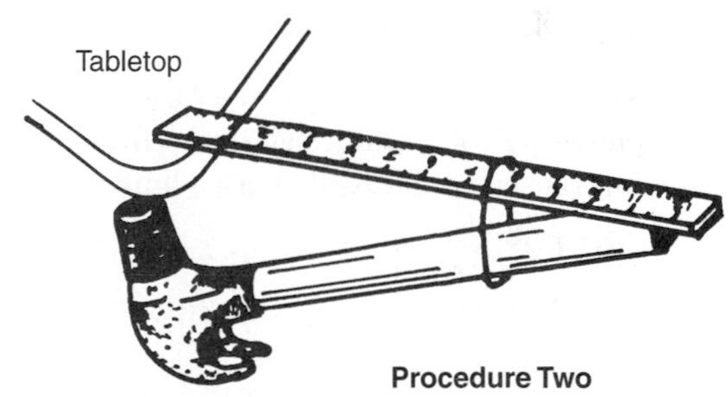

Procedure Two

1. Make a loop of wire and place it in position around the hammer handle and ruler. (See drawing, Procedure Two.)
2. Place the edge of the ruler on the tabletop making sure that the head of the hammer is well under the table or desk top.
3. Release apparatus slowly, checking balance.

D. Results:

1. In Procedure one, the center of gravity will be shown to be the point where all the lines intersect.
2. In Procedure two, the hammer and ruler will balance and not fall.

E. Basic Facts and Supplemental Information:

1. Each object has a center of gravity.
2. If the center of gravity is beyond the edges, the object will fall.

F. Thought Questions for Class Discussions:

1. Do all objects have a center of gravity?
2. What would happen if there were no gravity?

G. Related Ideas for Further Inquiry:

1. How did our moon-walkers make use of gravity?
2. Study other Activities in this Section.

H. Vocabulary Builders—Spelling Words:

1) **hammer** 2) **ruler** 3) **table** 4) **center** 5) **gravity** 6) **stability** 7) **balance** 8) **careful**

I. Thought for Today:

"Neighbor to friend: 'My economic philosophy is middle of the road; I spend money left and right.' "

Activity VII D 2

A. Problem: *If You Burn a Horizontally Balanced Candle at Both Ends, Will Its Center of Gravity Change?*

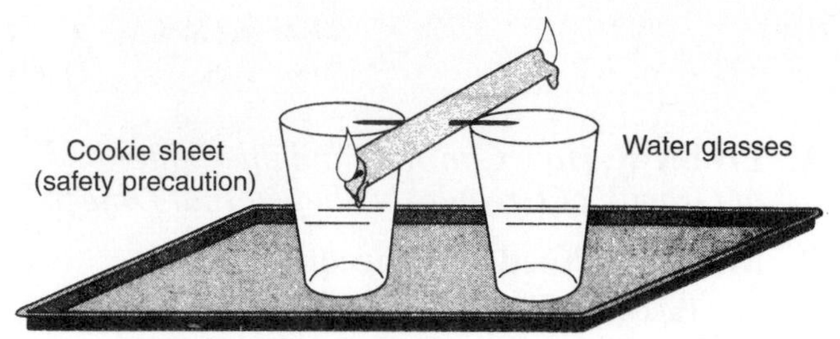

Toothpick-balanced candle

B. Materials Needed:

1. Two water glasses
2. Two toothpicks
3. Candle, approximately 6″ long
4. Cookie sheet
5. Matches

C. Procedure:

1. Place a cookie sheet on the desk or working surface.
2. Prepare the candle so that there will be a wick exposed on both ends.
3. Place one toothpick on each side of the candle, as close to the center of the candle as possible. (See drawing.)
4. Place the two glasses on the sheet so that the tips of the toothpicks will be just over the edges of the glasses.
5. Ask class to hypothesize (guess) what the candle will do if both wicks are lit. Remain stationary or . . . ?
6. After students have made their guesses, carefully light both wicks and watch the results.

D. Results:

1. The candle will usually start out well-balanced.
2. Then one end will usually burn a little faster and become lighter.
3. This half will rise up.
4. When this happens, the down half will then burn faster and soon it will rise up.
5. The candle will continue to "bob" up and down.

E. Basic Facts and Supplemental Information:

1. Since this could possibly be a dangerous Activity because of the flames, it is recommended that it be done as a teacher demonstration.
2. Needles or finishing nails could be substituted for the toothpicks.
3. The center of gravity will move frequently from one side of the candle to the other.
4. The center of gravity is very important in balancing objects, especially if they are irregularly shaped.
5. When people fall down, they have lost (changed) their center of gravity.

F. Thought Questions for Class Discussions:

1. What causes the center of gravity to change?
2. What safety precautions should be observed in this Activity?
3. What would happen if only one of the wicks were lighted?
4. Does gravity affect airplanes in flight?
5. Does air pressure affect gravity?

G. Related Ideas for Further Inquiry:

1. Study kinetic energy and potential energy as it is related to this Activity.
2. Study Section II-B, "Fire and Heat."
3. If you were going to design a new car, how could you make it safer in regard to gravity?
4. Study Activity VII-D-1, "How can you find the center of gravity of irregularly shaped flat objects?"
5. Study Activity VII-D-3, "Do people have a center of gravity?"
6. Study Activity VII-D-5, "Which falls faster, a dropped object or a horizontally propelled object?"
7. Study Activity VII-D-6, "How is gravity related to inertia?"
8. Study other Activities in this Section.

H. Vocabulary Builders—Spelling Words:

1) **candle** 2) **wick** 3) **burning** 4) **center** 5) **gravity** 6) **hypothesize** 7) **kinetic**

I. Thought for Today:

"Thinking is like living and dying: you must do it for yourself."

Activity

A. Problem: *Do People Have a Center of Gravity?*

B. Materials Needed:

1. Books
2. Pencils
3. Two "phony" one dollar bills (play money)
4. Two genuine dollar bills

C. Procedure:

1. Study Activity VII-D-6, "How is gravity related to inertia?"
2. Select two students to come to the front of the classroom.
3. Place a book on the floor in front of each of them and have the students pick up the books without moving their feet, bending their knees, or losing their balance.
4. Place a pencil on the floor in front of each student, and have them pick up the pencils without moving their feet, bending their knees, or losing their balance.
5. Now tell the two students you are going to give them a chance to win a genuine dollar bill if they can pick up a phony dollar bill, with one added stipulation: they must keep their heels against the wall.
6. Show them the genuine dollar bills.
7. Have the two students stand against a wall.
8. Place a phony dollar bill on the floor in front of each of them.
9. Let the students try to pick up the phony dollar bills several times.
10. You might also repeat this test with other students.

D. Results:

1. The students will easily pick up the books and pencils.
2. The students will not be able to pick up the phony dollar bills without moving their feet, bending their knees, or losing their balance, while they keep their heels against a wall.

E. Basic Facts and Supplemental Information:

1. Your genuine dollar bills are safe!
2. Any object will fall over if the center of gravity lines up outside of the boundary of the object.
3. The center of gravity is the key element in determining the stability of any object.
4. When the heels are kept against the wall, the center of gravity of the students prevents them from bending down without falling over.

F. Thought Questions for Class Discussions:

1. Do you think the Leaning Tower of Pisa will ever fall down?
2. Why does any object fall down?
3. What causes gravity?

G. Related Ideas for Further Inquiry:

1. Discuss why cars turn over in accidents.
2. Discuss why some people fall over when riding a bicycle.
3. Study Activity VII-D-4, "Is it easy to become a gymnast?"
4. Study other Activities in this Section.

H. Vocabulary Builders—Spelling Words:

1) **center** 2) **gravity** 3) **conditions**
4) **bending** 5) **moving** 6) **dollar**

I. Thought for Today:

"Despite all our ingenuity and knowhow, science still hasn't found a better or faster way to get firemen downstairs than by sliding down a pole."

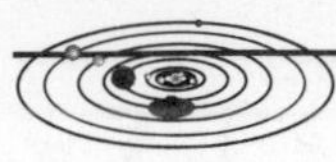

Activity VII D 4

A. Problem: *Is It Easy to Become a Gymnast?*

B. Materials Needed:

1. Tagboard, light cardboard, or heavy paper
2. Cellophane tape
3. Two coins (same weight)
4. Scissors
5. Crayons or tempera paints
6. Pencil
7. Glue
8. Piece of string
9. Attachment devices for string

C. Procedure:

1. Carefully draw an outline of a gymnast of your choice on the tagboard, cardboard, or paper, making sure that his/her nose or chin will be the balancing point. (See drawing.)
2. Draw another gymnast exactly the same size and shape. (This is the reverse side.)
3. With crayons or paints, color your gymnast with bright colors.
4. With cellophane tape attach one coin to each hand (on the reverse side of the gymnast).
5. Glue front and reverse sides of gymnast together. Coins will be hidden and the front and reverse sides of the gymnast will match.
6. Secure the string to the attachment devices.
7. Carefully place your gymnast on the string as shown in drawing. One hand will be in front of the string; one hand will be behind the string.
8. Ask the students why the gymnast doesn't fall off.

D. Results:

1. The gymnast will balance on the string.
2. The students will be amazed.

E. Basic Facts and Supplemental Information:

1. The "trick" of the apparatus is that the "center of gravity" is below the nose or chin of the gymnast, thus preventing it from falling over or down.
2. Gravity is one of the least understood of the major forces that exist in the universe.

F. Thought Questions for Class Discussions:

1. What keeps people in an upright position?
2. How do airplanes overcome gravity?
3. Are astronauts concerned with gravity?
4. Why do tightrope walkers use a long pole?
5. Why is the center of gravity important to gymnasts?

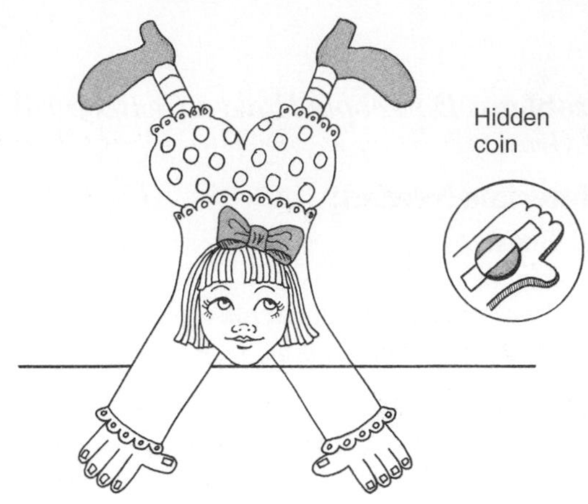

G. Related Ideas for Further Inquiry:

1. Study how the center of gravity is related to:
   a. new bicycle riders
   b. skateboarders
   c. construction workers
   d. athletes
2. Study Section I-A, "Matter."
3. Study Section I-B, "Air."
4. Study Section II-F, "Movement and Resistance."
5. Study Activity VII-D-1, "How can you find the center of gravity of irregularly shaped flat objects?"
6. Study Activity VII-D-3, "Do people have a center of gravity?"
7. Study Activity VII-D-6, "How is gravity related to inertia?"

Here is another amazing balancing Activity.

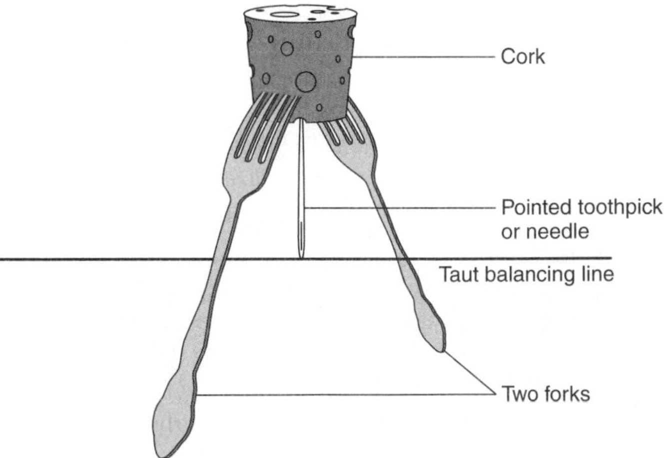

H. Vocabulary Builders—Spelling Words:

1) **gymnast** 2) **gravity** 3) **balance** 4) **string** 5) **coins** 6) **center** 7) **force** 8) **glue**

I. Thought for Today:

"Character is made by what you stand for; reputation, by what you fall for."

Activity VII D 5

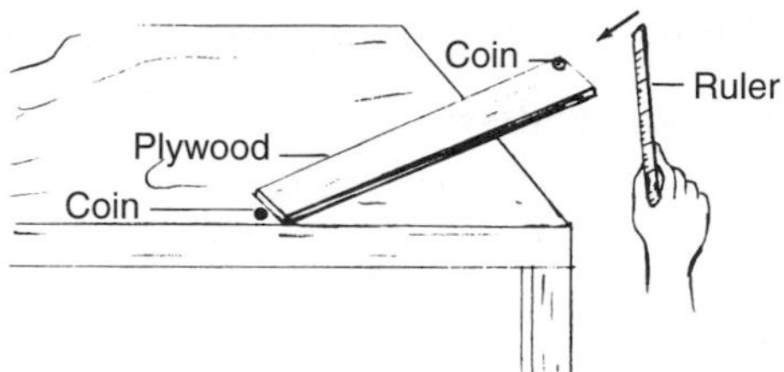

Procedure One

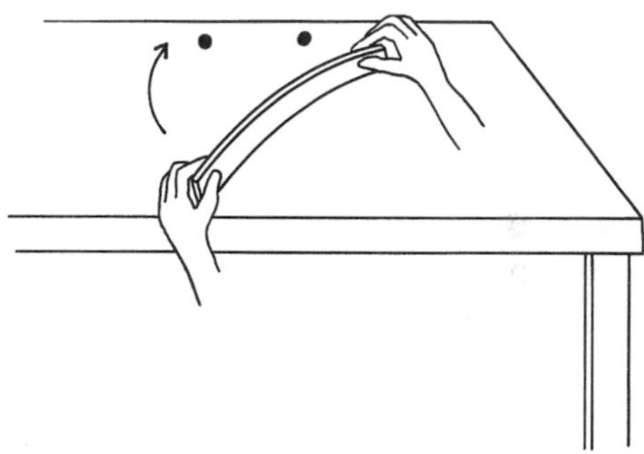
Procedure Two

A. Problem: *Which Falls Faster, a Dropped Object or a Horizontally Propelled Object?*

B. Materials Needed, Procedure One:

1. Table
2. Plywood, 2″ × 15″
3. Two coins
4. Ruler or dowel

Materials Needed, Procedure Two:

1. Table
2. Thin metal band 10″ to 15″ long
3. Two marbles or small balls

C. Procedure One:

1. Place the plywood strip on the table with one end extending over the edge. (See drawing, Procedure One.)
2. Place the coins as shown in the illustration.
3. Tell the students to be extremely quiet and listen for sounds of the coins hitting the floor.
4. With the ruler or dowel, strike the end of the plywood that extends over the table with a sharp blow on the edge opposite the coin on the table.
5. Listen for the sounds of the coins hitting the floor.

Procedure Two:

1. Place the two marbles on the edge of the table. (See drawing.)
2. Holding one edge of the metal band firmly, bend the other end back and release so that both marbles will be hit at the same time but with different force so that one will be propelled farther than the other. Several trials may be necessary to ensure simultaneous striking of marbles.
3. Listen for the sounds of the two objects hitting the floor.

D. Results:

1. The coins will strike the floor at the same time.
2. The marbles will strike the floor at the same time.

E. Basic Facts and Supplemental Information:

1. The only force acting *down* on the objects is gravity.
2. Since gravity is the same, the objects will fall at the same time, regardless of whether there is any propulsion to the side.

F. Thought Questions for Class Discussions:

1. Does the size make any difference in falling objects?
2. Does weight make any difference?
3. Would a bullet fired horizontally hit the ground at the same time as one dropped from the same height?

G. Related Ideas for Further Inquiry:

1. Make a list of the ways gravity is beneficial. Make a list of ways that gravity is a problem.
2. Study Activity VII-D-1, "How can you find the center of gravity of irregularly shaped flat objects?"
3. Study Activity VII-D-3, "Do people have a center of gravity?"
4. Study Activity VII-D-4, "Is it easy to become a gymnast?"
5. Study Activity VII-D-6, "How is gravity related to inertia?"

H. Vocabulary Builders—Spelling Words:

1) **gravity** 2) **horizontal** 3) **propelled** 4) **simultaneous** 5) **dowel** 6) **coins** 7) **marbles**

I. Thought for Today:

"Humanity's capacity for justice makes democracy possible; but humanity's inclination to injustice makes democracy necessary."

Activity VII D 6

A. Problem: *How Is Gravity Related to Inertia?*

B. Materials Needed:

1. Two rocks about the same size
2. Thread (3 pieces, each 3 feet long)
3. Supporting device

C. Procedure:

1. Tie the rocks in the middle of the threads.
2. Tie one end to each of the supporting devices.
3. Ask the class where the thread will break if you pull down on the lower end of the thread.
4. In the first trial, have one student gently pull the end of the thread down slowly.
5. Again ask the students where they think the thread will break if it is done a second time.
6. In the second trial, have another student pull the thread down briskly.
7. Ask the class to explain the difference.
8. Repeat demonstrations as long as necessary.

D. Results:

1. In the first trial, the thread will break above the rock.
2. In the second trial, the thread will break below the rock.

E. Basic Facts and Supplemental Information:

1. In the first trial, the weight of the hand and the rock will cause the thread to break above the rock.
2. In the second trial, jerking the thread causes the rock to remain in its position, thus causing the thread to break below the rock.
3. In the first trial, the rock was more affected by gravity.
4. In the second trial, the rock was more affected by inertia.

F. Thought Questions for Class Discussions:

1. Would it make any difference if the rock were tied to the bottom instead of the middle of the thread?
2. What is inertia? momentum?
3. What are Newton's "Laws of Motion"?

G. Related Ideas for Further Inquiry:

1. Place a card on top of a water glass. Place a coin on the card. Snap the card away. What happens?

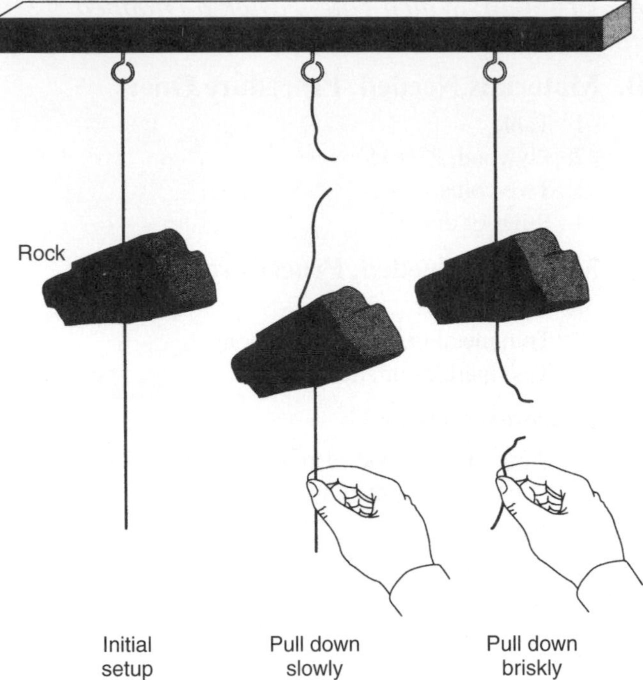

2. Have students describe their movements in an automobile when it starts fast or stops quickly.
3. Discuss why a bicycle doesn't stop instantly when the brakes are applied.
4. Which of Newton's Laws of Motion applies to this Activity?
5. Study Activity II-F-1, "What are Newton's Laws of Motion?"
6. Study Activity VII-D-3, "Do people have a center of gravity?"
7. Study Activity VII-D-4, "Is it easy to become a gymnast?"
8. Study other Activities in this Section.

H. Vocabulary Builders—Spelling Words:

1) **inertia** 2) **momentum** 3) **jerking** 4) **motion** 5) **Newton** 6) **gravity**

I. Thought for Today:

"Nothing makes you feel older than the discovery that your children are studying in history classes what you studied in current events."

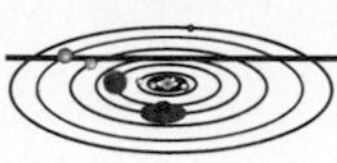

Activity VII D7

A. Problem: *How Can We Make a Simple Scale?*

B. Materials Needed:

1. Heavy tagboard or cardboard
2. Four paper clips
3. Two wide rubber bands
4. Tape
5. String
6. Weights
7. Marking pen
8. Scissors

C. Procedure:

1. Cut tagboard or cardboard to make a rectangle shape about 4″ × 12″.
2. Attach paper clip to the top of tagboard after bending the bottom part out slightly.
3. Attach the wide rubber band to the bottom of this paper clip.
4. Bend the second paper clip so it looks like the one in the drawing. This is the pointer.
5. Attach this to another rubber band.
6. Tape string to the bottom of this, or you may attach string directly to pointer.
7. Slip the string through the paper clip at the bottom of the tagboard.
8. Bend the bottom loop of the paper clip so that the string is free to move.
9. Attach bottom paper clip to the string. Bend so that it will support whatever you wish to weigh.
10. Using known weights, calibrate and mark the scale with the marking pen.

D. Results:

1. A simple measuring device for weighing small objects will be made.
2. Students will learn the art of calibration.
3. Students will gain a little knowledge about elasticity.

E. Basic Facts and Supplemental Information:

1. A rubber band will stretch equally with added weights up to a point and then its original elasticity will be destroyed. This can be determined by the pointer not returning to zero on the scale.
2. This weighing device can be hung on a wall or supported over the edge of a desk or chair.
3. The weight of an object depends on gravity.
4. Gravity on the moon is about 1/6 that of Earth. A person who weighs 120 pounds on Earth would weigh only 20 pounds on the moon.

F. Thought Questions for Class Discussions:

1. Do all rubber bands of the same size and shape possess the same elasticity?

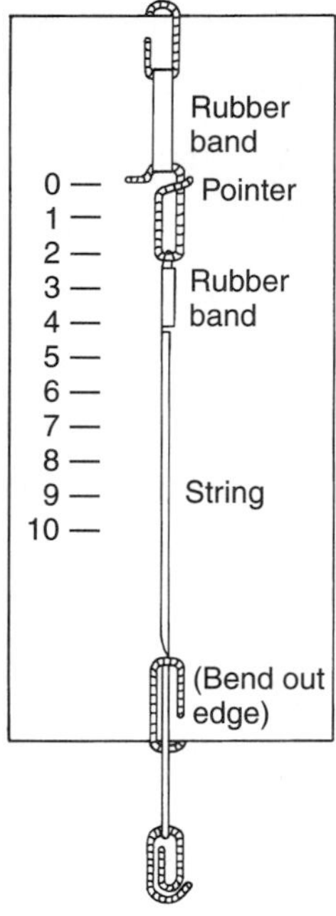

2. What is the main difference between a spring scale and a balance scale?
3. Where have you seen spring scales used?
4. How does the American system of weights and measures compare to the Metric System? Which is better? more practical? easier to use?

G. Related Ideas for Further Inquiry:

1. Weigh various objects to compare weights (rocks, etc.).
2. Study Activity VII-D-1, "How can you find the center of gravity of irregularly shaped flat objects?"
3. Study Activity VII-D-2, "If you burn a horizontally balanced candle at both ends, will its center of gravity change?"
4. Study Activity VII-D-5, "Which falls faster, a dropped object or a horizontally propelled object?"
5. Study Activity VII-D-6, "How is gravity related to inertia?"

H. Vocabulary Builders—Spelling Words:

1) **scale** 2) **simple** 3) **elastic** 4) **calibrate** 5) **rubber** 6) **string** 7) **clip** 8) **stretch**

I. Thought for Today:

"Life has become a struggle to keep our weight down and our spirits up."

Activity VII E 1

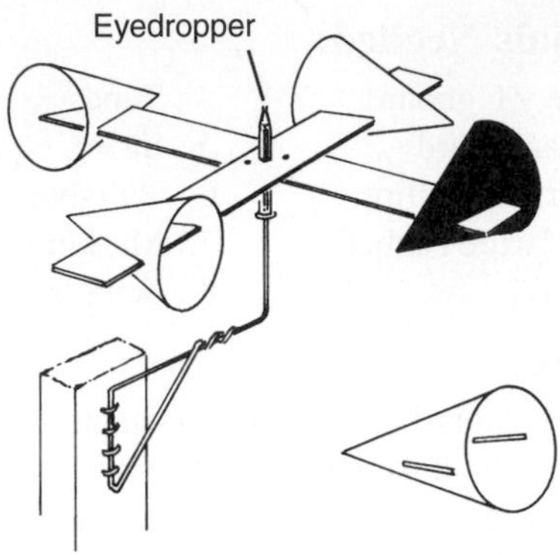

A. Problem: *How Can We Measure Wind Speed?*

B. Materials Needed:

1. Four paper or plastic cones or cups
2. Wire coat hanger
3. Eyedropper (glass part only)
4. Two thin wooden slats, approximately 1″ × 18″
5. Wooden support (See drawing.)
6. Scissors or razor blade
7. Small nails or brads
8. Wire cutter (cutting pliers)
9. Red paint
10. Small paint brush
11. Knife or drill

C. Procedure:

1. Construct anemometer as shown in drawing.
   a. Nail slats together.
   b. Cut hole for eyedropper (glass part).
   c. Cut and shape coat hanger as shown in drawing.
   d. Cut thin slits in cups or cones to ensure a tight fit for wooden slats.
   e. Mount coat hanger on support.
   f. Paint one cup red.
   g. Place cups or cones on slats.
   h. Place eyedropper glass on end of coat hanger.
   i. Mount slats with cups on eyedropper glass.
2. Place anemometer outside where winds can hit it.
3. Count the revolutions per minute by the painted or marked cup.
4. Divide this number by 10 to obtain the approximate speed of the wind in miles per hour.

D. Results:

1. Students will learn how to construct an anemometer.
2. Students will learn how to measure wind speed.
3. Students will learn that wind speed is but one predictor of coming weather conditions.

E. Basic Facts and Supplemental Information:

1. Tennis balls cut in half or styrofoam cups can be substituted in this apparatus.
2. Winds are caused by rotation of the Earth, differences in temperature of air masses, and differences in air pressures of air masses.

BEAUFORT WIND SCALE

Number	Map Symbol	Descriptive Word(s)	Velocity (Miles/Hour)
1	◎	Calm	1–3
2		Light breeze	4–7
3		Gentle breeze	8–12
4		Moderate breeze	13–18
5		Fresh breeze	19–24
6		Strong breeze	25–31
7		Moderate gale	32–38
8		Fresh gale	39–46
9		Strong gale	47–54
10		Full gale	55–63
11		Whole gale	64–75
12		Hurricane or violent storm	above 75

F. Thought Questions for Class Discussions:

1. Does it make any difference which way the wind is blowing in determining wind speed with this anemometer?
2. What occupations would be most concerned with wind speeds?
3. Why is wind speed important to weather forecasters?

G. Related Ideas for Further Inquiry:

1. Study Section I-B, "Air."
2. Study Activity VII-E-3, "What causes changes in the air pressure?"
3. Study Activity VII-E-8, "What are 'cold fronts' and 'warm fronts'?"
4. Study Activity VII-E-15, "How do we read a weather map?"

H. Vocabulary Builders—Spelling Words:

1) **speed** 2) **Beaufort Scale** 3) **anemometer** 4) **hurricane** 5) **modest** 6) **breeze** 7) **calm**

I. Thought for Today:

"If you know all the answers, you haven't asked all the questions."

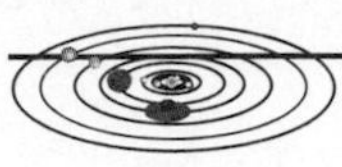

Activity VII E 2

A. Problem: *What Is the "Wind-Chill Factor"?*

B. Materials Needed:

1. Outdoor thermometer
2. Anemometer
3. Wind-chill chart
4. Bulletin board

C. Procedure:

1. When the wind is blowing on a cool day, the time would be excellent to develop the concept of wind chill.
2. Briefly discuss weather conditions.
3. Discuss the extremes of feeling warm or cold when outside.
4. Ask the students if they feel warmer or colder when the wind is blowing.
5. Record the outside temperature.
6. With an anemometer, measure the velocity of the wind. If no anemometer is available, estimate the speed of the wind.
7. Compute the "wind-chill factor" from the chart or estimate it by using the procedure in Section E, Basic Facts and Supplemental Information.
8. Record the data on the bulletin board.

D. Results:

1. Students will learn about the wind-chill factor.
2. Students will know why they feel much colder on a cold day when the wind is blowing.

E. Basic Facts and Supplemental Information:

1. Air temperature is not the only factor that makes people feel cold.
2. The wind plays a prominent role in how one senses coldness, especially in low temperature readings.
3. If a wind-chill chart is not available, one can estimate the wind-chill factor by subtracting one degree Fahrenheit for each one mile per hour of wind speed. If the outside temperature is 50° F. and the wind is blowing at 30 miles per hour, a person will feel just as cold as in a weather condition of 20°F. with no wind blowing.

F. Thought Questions for Class Discussions:

1. What type of clothing is best for very cold days? for very windy, warm days?
2. Does humidity play a role in the wind-chill factor?

G. Related Ideas for Further Inquiry:

1. Study Section I-B, "Air."
2. Study Section II-B, "Fire and Heat."
3. Study Activity VII-E-1, "How can we measure wind speed?"
4. Study Activity VII-E-3, "What causes changes in air pressure?"

H. Vocabulary Builders—Spelling Words:

1) **wind chill** 2) **factor** 3) **anemometer** 4) **thermometer** 5) **weather** 6) **chart** 7) **reading**

I. Thought for Today:

"A cold is both positive and negative; sometimes the Eyes have it; sometimes the Nose."

Thermometer Readings (Fahrenheit)

Wind Speed (mph)																	
0	40	35	30	25	20	15	10	5	0	-5	-10	-15	-20	-25	-30	-35	-40
	EQUIVALENT WIND CHILL TEMPERATURES																
5	35	30	25	20	15	10	5	0	-5	-10	-15	-20	-25	-30	-35	-40	-45
10	30	20	15	10	5	0	-10	-15	-20	-25	-35	-40	-45	-50	-60	-65	-70
15	25	15	10	0	-5	-10	-20	-25	-30	-40	-45	-50	-60	-65	-70	-85	-90
20	20	10	5	0	-10	-15	-25	-30	-35	-45	-50	-60	-65	-75	-80	-85	-95
25	15	10	0	-5	-15	-20	-30	-35	-45	-50	-60	-65	-75	-80	-90	-95	-105
30	10	5	0	-10	-20	-25	-30	-40	-50	-55	-65	-70	-80	-85	-95	-100	-110
35	10	5	-5	-10	-20	-30	-35	-40	-50	-60	-65	-75	-80	-90	-100	-105	-115
40	10	0	-5	-15	-20	-30	-35	-45	-55	-60	-70	-75	-85	-95	-100	-110	-115

Activity VII E 3

A. Problem: *What Causes Changes in Air Pressure?*

B. Materials Needed:

1. Shoe box
2. Cellophane, clear
3. Candle
4. Paper towel
5. Tape (cellophane or filament)
6. Matches
7. Asbestos pad or metal tray
8. Scissors or knife

C. Procedure:

1. Remove the cover of the shoe box.
2. Cover the top with cellophane, securing it in place with cellophane or filament tape.
3. Cut out one end of the box to make a hinged door (to insert candle).
4. Set the box on its side and secure a short candle inside near one end.
5. Cut a hole the size of a quarter directly over the candle and another one the same size in the middle of the far end. (See drawing.)
6. Place the box on the tray.
7. *Carefully* light the candle and close the "door."
8. Dampen a paper towel slightly and carefully set it on fire for a brief moment. Blow out the flame, and the towel will give off smoke.
9. Place on pad or tray near the hole in the door.

D. Result:

As the warm air rises and leaves the box, the cooler, heavier air will rush in and fill the space that was occupied by the lighter, warmer air. Smoke will be drawn in and seen to rise over the candle.

E. Basic Facts and Supplemental Information:

The smoke moving through the box will trace the current of air. Wind is air in motion caused partially by differences in air pressure. This difference sometimes is the result of varying air temperatures. Air currents generally move from high pressures toward low pressures. The rotation of the Earth also has a great effect on causes of winds and the directions they take. In summary winds are caused by:

1. differences in air pressure
2. differences in air temperature
3. rotation of the Earth

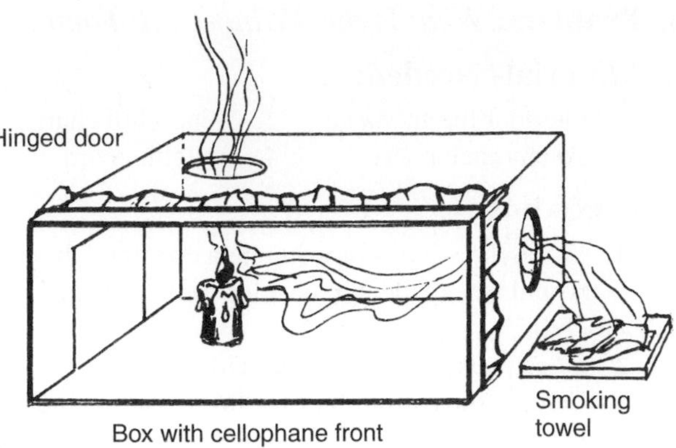

F. Thought Questions for Class Discussions:

1. How is the air on the Earth's surface heated? cooled?
2. Does hot air always rise?
3. Do the winds blow toward the direction of the rising air?
4. What are some other causes of variation in air pressure on the surface of the Earth?

G. Related Ideas for Further Inquiry:

1. Discuss the strength of air pressure when a football, basketball, or soccer ball is inflated.
2. Discuss how automobiles are lifted when they are serviced.
3. Study Activity VII-E-1, "How can we measure wind speed?"
4. Study Activity VII-E-2, "What is the 'wind-chill factor'?"
5. Study Activity VII-E-4, "How can we make a simple barometer?"
6. Study Activity VII-E-8, "What are 'cold fronts' and 'warm fronts'?"
7. Study Activity VII-E-13, "How do we forecast weather?"
8. Study Activity VII-E-15, "How do we read a weather map?"

H. Vocabulary Builders—Spelling Words:

1) **pressure** 2) **cellophane** 3) **candle** 4) **hinged** 5) **dampen** 6) **door** 7) **smoking** 8) **towel** 9) **surface** 10) **circulation**

I. Thought for Today:

"Sign in Iowa munitions factory: 'If you insist on smoking in this building be prepared to leave this world through a hole in the ceiling.' "

Activity VII E 4

A. Problem: *How Can We Make a Simple Barometer?*

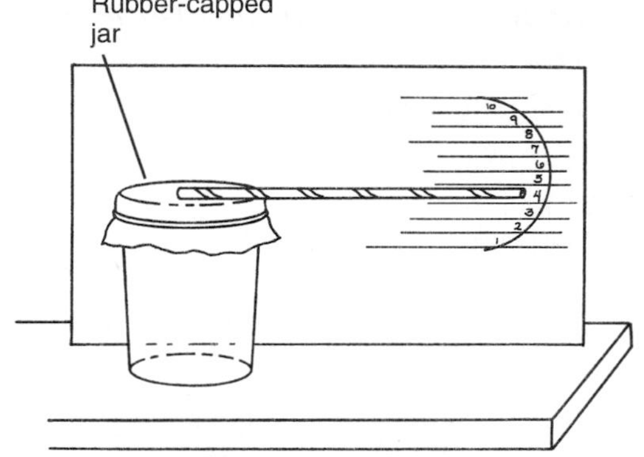

B. Materials Needed:

1. Widemouthed jar
2. Piece of rubber from large balloon
3. Rubber band
4. Drinking straw
5. Glue or rubber cement
6. Chart material
7. Marking pen
8. Wax

C. Procedure:

1. Seal the jar with a piece of rubber from the balloon and a rubber band. A light coating of wax around the lip of the jar will help make an airtight seal.
2. The piece of balloon should not be stretched too tight or it will not respond readily to changes in air pressure.
3. Affix a drinking straw as shown in drawing.
4. Make a simple scale on chart material to which the drinking straw can point.
5. Mount this as shown in drawing.

OUR BAROMETER READINGS:			
Week of ______			
	Morning:	*Afternoon*	*Weather:*
Monday			
Tuesday			
Wednesday			
Thursday			
Friday			

D. Result:

Students will learn that air pressure varies.

E. Basic Facts and Supplemental Information:

1. The straw moves up and down the chart to record changes in air pressure.
2. If the pointer (straw) moves up the scale, the pressure is high; if it moves down the scale, the pressure is low.
3. The up-and-down movement on the scale is caused by the contraction and expansion of air in the jar as a result of changes in atmospheric air pressures.
4. Changes in temperature will also affect the readings, so room temperature should be kept as constant as possible.
5. If air pressure increases, the number that the straw points to on the scale will be higher; this portends good weather.
6. If air pressure decreases, the number that the straw points to on the scale will be lower; this portends bad weather.

F. Thought Questions for Class Discussions:

1. Is this same principle used in regular barometers?
2. How do regular barometers differ from this one?
3. How are pressure changes related to weather?

G. Related Ideas for Further Inquiry:

1. Compare this barometer to a commercially produced one.
2. Keep a record of air pressure for a week as shown on chart.
3. Study Section I-B, "Air."
4. Study Section VII-B, "Solar System."
5. Study Activity VII-E-3, "What causes changes in air pressure?"
6. Study Activity VII-E-15, "How do we read a weather map?"

H. Vocabulary Builders—Spelling Words:

1) **barometer** 2) **scale** 3) **pressure** 4) **varies** 5) **contraction** 6) **expansion** 7) **rising** 8) **falling**

I. Thought for Today:

"Rain is something that, when you carry an umbrella, it doesn't."

Activity VII E 5

A. Problem: *Why Are Summers Warmer than Winters?*

B. Materials Needed:

1. Flashlight
2. Chalk
3. Yardstick

C. Procedure:

1. Make a chalk mark on the floor.
2. Darken the room.
3. Have a student hold a flashlight about one yard above the mark and vertically shine the flashlight on the mark.
4. Have a second student draw a circle with chalk around the spot of light.
5. Moving the flashlight horizontally about one yard from the original spot, shine the light at the same mark on the floor. (The beam will be slightly slanted.)
6. Draw a line on the floor around the spot of the beam of light.
7. Compare the areas of light projection.

D. Result:

The second drawing will be larger than the first.

E. Basic Facts and Supplemental Information:

1. The sun is hotter when directly over us than when it is setting. The same amount of sunlight is given off by the sun in winter as in summer, but the light (heat) is distributed over a wider area, and therefore each small area receives less light (heat). In other words the slanting rays cover a wider area, thus the same amount of energy is not received in winter as it is in the summer at any one point.
2. The second most important factor in determining the Earth's temperature is the length of time the sun shines each day at a given point. Because of the tilt of the Earth, the length of each day is much longer in the summertime than during the wintertime (about 2 hours longer in the midline of the United States).
3. A slide projector could be used instead of a flashlight and the beam could be focused on a wall.
4. We have established four seasons on Earth:
   a. Spring—March 21 to June 21
   b. Summer—June 21 to September 23
   c. Fall—September 23 to December 21
   d. Winter—December 21 to March 21

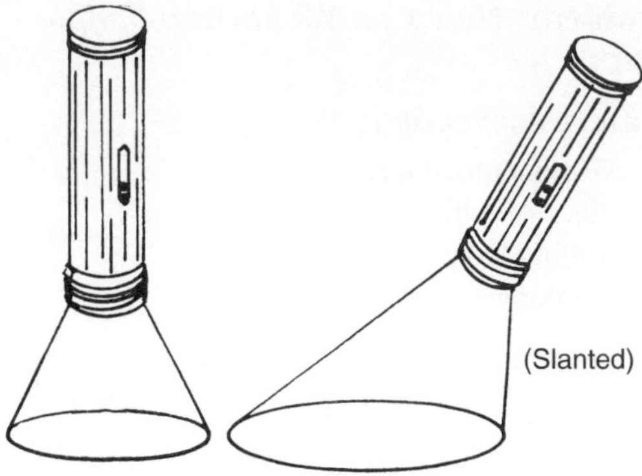

5. "Spring Equinox" occurs on March 21 when the days and nights are equal in length. From this day on the days get longer and the nights get shorter.
6. "Fall Equinox" occurs on September 23 when the days and nights are equal in length. From this day on the days get shorter and the nights get longer.

F. Thought Questions for Class Discussions:

1. What causes the sun's rays to hit any spot on Earth at 90°? slanting less than 90°?
2. Is there any difference in seasons between the Northern Hemisphere and Southern Hemisphere? Why or why not?
3. How do scientists measure light intensity?
4. Is the sun ever directly overhead in your community?

G. Related Ideas for Further Inquiry:

1. Study Part II, "Energy."
2. Study Section II-C, "Light and Color."
3. Study Section VII-B, "Solar System."
4. Study Activity VII-E-7, "Where do clouds come from?"
5. Study Activity VII-E-8, "What are 'cold fronts' and 'warm fronts'?"
6. Study Activity VII-E-13, "How do we forecast weather?"
7. Study Activity VII-E-15, "How do we read a weather map?"

H. Vocabulary Builders—Spelling Words:

1) **summer** 2) **winter** 3) **direct** 4) **slanting** 5) **area** 6) **chalk** 7) **energy** 8) **light**

I. Thought for Today:

"There's one thing to be said for inviting trouble: it usually accepts."

Activity VII E 6

A. Problem: *What Is a "Jet Stream"?*

B. Materials Needed:

1. Weather maps from local newspapers
2. Reference books about meteorology
3. Hair dryer
4. World globe
5. Desk or table

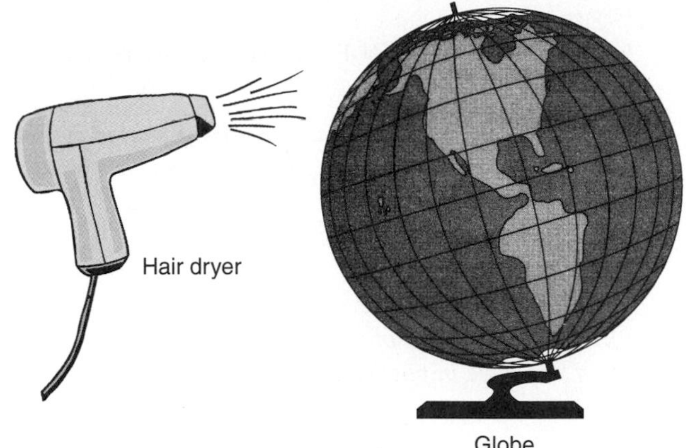

C. Procedure:

1. Discuss local air conditions.
2. Discuss the causes of winds.
3. Study meteorology reference books about the Earth's prevailing winds.
4. Describe the differences between land breezes and sea breezes.
5. Have students look up "doldrums" and find out where they are located.
6. Set the globe on the desk or table.
7. Turn on the hair dryer (low setting) and let the students feel the air stream with their hands.
8. Point the hair dryer at the globe.
9. Ask students what they have heard or know about the jet stream.
10. Cite information given in Section E, Basic Facts and Supplemental Information, that you feel is appropriate for your grade level.

D. Results:

1. Students will learn about jet streams.
2. Students will recognize that jet streams greatly affect our weather.
3. Students will learn that jet streams are like long, wide banners that vary in size, altitude, and direction.

E. Basic Facts and Supplemental Information:

1. A jet stream is a stream of fast-moving air with average speeds of about 120 miles per hour (200 kilometers per hour).
2. There are two jet streams—one north of the equator and one south of the equator.
3. They are found about 6 miles (10 kilometers) above the Earth.
4. Jet streams average about 150 miles (about 260 kilometers) in width.
5. They play a vital role in moving lower-level air masses, consequently, jet streams have a vital effect on our weather.
6. Jet streams vary greatly in force and direction.
7. Jet streams are usually located between the troposphere and the stratosphere.
8. The troposphere is the layer of atmosphere that extends from the Earth to a height of about 10 miles (16 kilometers).
9. The stratosphere is the layer of the atmosphere which lies between 10 and 50 miles (16 to 90 kilometers) above the Earth.
10. Jet streams are caused by the Earth's rotation, which is about 1,000 miles per hour (1,600 kilometers per hour) at the equator.
11. The two main reasons for the fast-flowing jet streams are that the air density and the air pressure are much less at higher elevations than at lower elevations.

F. Thought Questions for Class Discussions:

1. Does the tilt of the Earth affect jet streams?
2. Is cold air denser than warm air?
3. Does air have weight?

G. Related Ideas for Further Inquiry:

1. Study about the air movement in air pumps, automobile lifts, and fans.
2. Study Activity VII-E-1, "How can we measure wind speed?"

3. Study Activity VII-E-3, "What causes changes in air pressure?"
4. Study Activity VII-E-4, "How can we make a simple barometer?"
5. Study Activity VII-E-8, "What are 'cold fronts' and 'warm fronts'?"
6. Study Activity VII-E-13, "How do we forecast weather?"
7. Study Activity VII-E-15, "How do we read a weather map?"

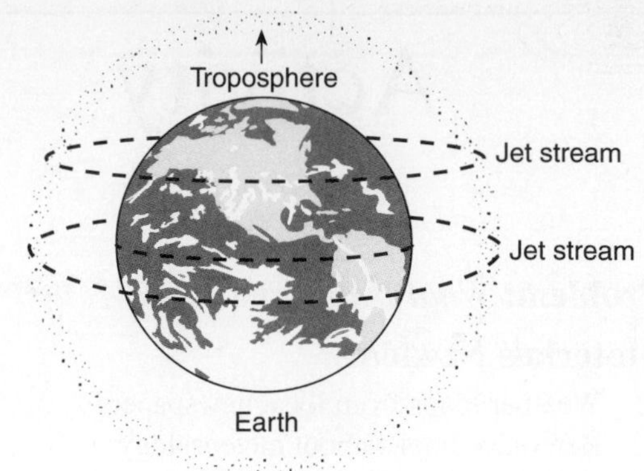

H. Vocabulary Builders—Spelling Words:

1) **jet stream** 2) **pressure** 3) **density**
4) **rotation** 5) **spinning** 6) **barometer**
7) **troposphere** 8) **stratosphere**

I. Thought for Today:

"A meteorologist is one who has more scientific aids than you have in guessing wrong about the weather."

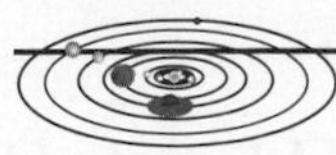

Activity VII E 7

A. Problem: *Where Do Clouds Come from?*

B. Materials Needed:

1. Clean, dry, empty gallon-size glass jug
2. Rubber stopper (with a small hole through the center) that fits the mouth of the jug tightly
3. Tire pump (manual or electric)
4. Rubbing alcohol (one pint)

C. Procedure:

1. Discuss with students their experiences with clouds: sizes, colors, weather conditions, etc.
2. Discuss any clouds in the sky today and then pose the question, "Where do clouds come from?"
3. Pour enough alcohol into the jug to cover the bottom.
4. Place stopper tightly into the mouth of the jug.
5. Place end of hose of the tire pump over the hole in the stopper as tightly as possible, and pump air into the jug.
6. After a few strokes on the pump handle, quickly and simultaneously remove the stopper and air hose.

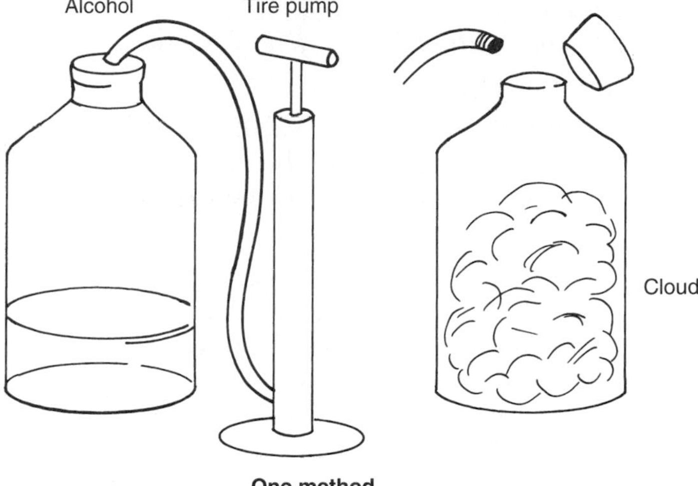

One method

A second method

D. Result:

When the stopper and hose are removed a loud pop will be heard and a cloud will form in the jug.

E. Basic Facts and Supplemental Information:

As a result of the pumping, the air in the jug was compressed and its temperature raised, making it possible for it to hold more moisture, which it picks up from the alcohol. When the stopper was removed, the air immediately expanded and cooled, at which time it could no longer hold as much moisture. Consequently, tiny droplets of moisture collected and formed a cloud inside the jug. Alcohol is used because it condenses at a lower temperature than water.

F. Thought Questions for Class Discussions:

1. What caused the loud noise when the stopper was removed?
2. How do these clouds differ from regular clouds?
3. How do clouds help us?
4. Are clouds ever dangerous?

G. Related Ideas for Further Inquiry:

1. Study Section I-C, "Water."
2. Study Activity VII-E-1, "How can we measure wind speed?"
3. Study Activity VII-E-2, "What is the 'wind-chill factor'?"
4. Study Activity VII-E-6, "What is a 'jet stream'?"
5. Study Activity VII-E-8, "What are 'cold fronts' and 'warm fronts'?"
6. Study Activity VII-E-9, "How can we measure humidity in the air? How can we build a hygrometer?"
7. Study Activity VII-E-10, "What is a simple method for determining relative humidity?"
8. Study Activity VII-E-13, "How do we forecast weather?"
9. Study Activity VII-E-14, "What is 'El Niño'?"
10. Study Activity VII-E-15, "How do we read a weather map?"

H. Vocabulary Builders—Spelling Words:

1) **alcohol** 2) **pump** 3) **gallon** 4) **stroke** 5) **compress** 6) **moisture** 7) **temperature** 8) **droplets** 9) **cloud** 10) **stopper** 11) **expands**

I. Thought for Today:

"A dog has so many friends because he wags his tail instead of his tongue."

Activity VII E 8

A. Problem: *What Are "Cold Fronts" and "Warm Fronts"?*

B. Materials Needed:

1. Newspaper weather maps
2. Books on meteorology
3. Newspaper clippings on weather conditions.

C. Procedure:

1. Have students bring in newspaper articles that concern weather directly or indirectly like an accident, mudslide, postponed parade, etc.
2. Study newspaper weather reports.
3. Discuss different kinds of weather.
4. Review appropriate weather Activities in this Section.
5. Define "fronts" as the boundaries between large air masses.
6. Discuss the characteristics of "weather fronts"
   a. Cold fronts usually form over polar regions.
   b. Warm fronts usually form over tropical waters.
   c. Activity on the fronts depend upon:
      1) temperature
      2) pressure
      3) humidity
      4) wind speed
      5) clouds
      6) jet stream

D. Results:

1. Students will learn how to read weather maps.
2. Students will be able to predict upcoming weather conditions.
3. Students will realize that weather affects our lives in many ways.

E. Basic Facts and Supplemental Information:

1. Fronts may be "occluded" (mixed conditions).
2. If a cold front overtakes a warm front, it causes the warm front to rise because the warm front is less dense.
3. When the warm air is forced up, clouds are pushed up, and as they cool they are less capable of holding moisture, and precipitation results.
4. If a warm front overtakes a cold front, the warm front rides up over it because the warm air is less dense. The clouds in the warm front are pushed up, and as they become colder they can no longer hold their moisture and consequently rain develops.

F. Thought Questions for Class Discussions:

1. What is a cyclone? anticyclone?
2. What weather conditions would probably follow dropping barometer readings? rising barometer readings?

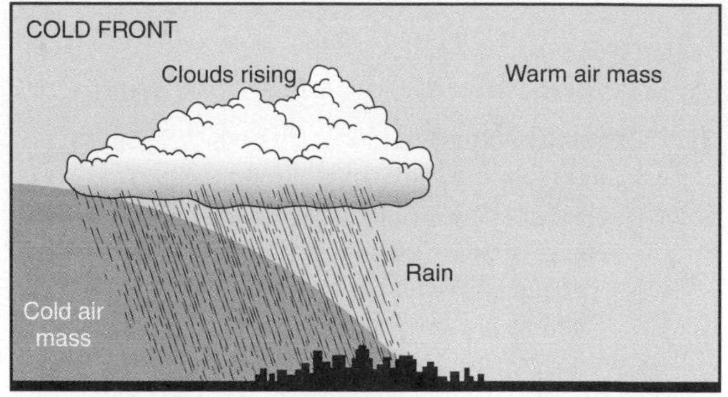

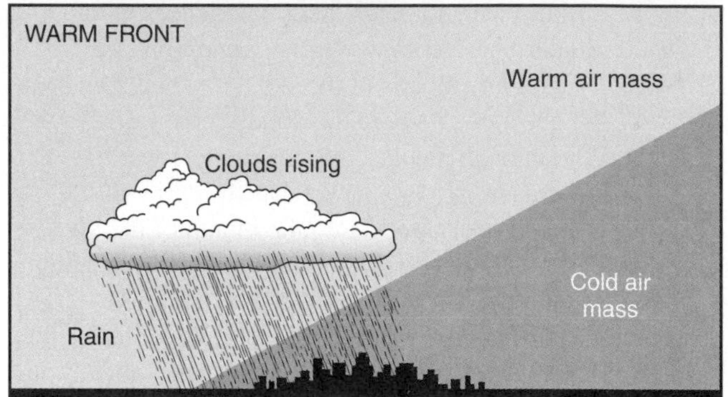

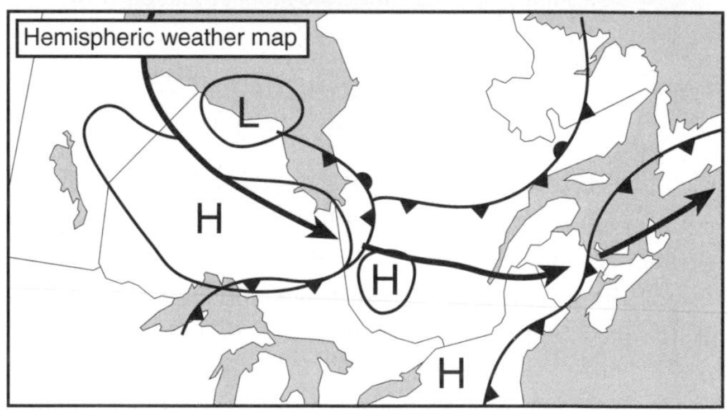

3. What cloud types are associated with good weather? poor weather?

G. Related Ideas for Further Inquiry:

1. Study other Activities in this Section.
2. Develop a weather calendar for your classroom. (Indicate each day's main type of weather.)
3. Develop a class weather station. Predict the weather for your community.

H. Vocabulary Builders—Spelling Words:

1) **warm front** 2) **cold front** 3) **occluded** 4) **precipitation** 5) **barometer** 6) **weather**

I. Thought for Today:

"The sophisticated equipment of today's weatherperson is what enables him/her to explain, in greater detail, why he/she was wrong."

Activity VII E 9

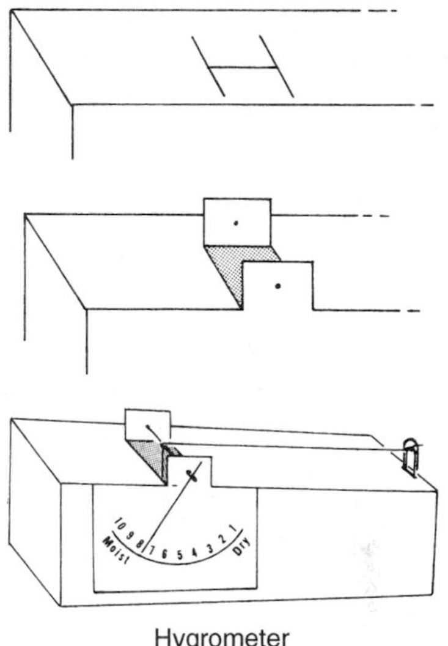
Hygrometer

A. Problem: *How Can We Measure Humidity in the Air? How Can We Build a Hygrometer?*

B. Materials Needed:

1. Single-edge razor blade
2. Quart milk carton
3. Piece of very thin wool yarn or long straight hair
4. Broom fiber
5. Large needle
6. Nail polish
7. Paper clip
8. Soapy water
9. Cellophane tape
10. Penny
11. Basin
12. Sponge
13. Towel
14. Water

C. Procedure:

1. Cut an "H" along one side of the milk carton as shown in the drawing.
2. Bend the two tabs up.
3. If using hair, wash it in soapy water and let dry.
4. Make a hole in each tab with needle so that the needle can turn freely.
5. Cut broom fiber to 3 inches and place in the eye of the needle.
6. Secure fiber to needle with drop of nail polish. (This is the pointer.)
7. Make a scale similar to the one on the front of the carton as shown in the drawing.
8. Tape this to front of milk carton with midpoint of 5 and 6 perpendicular to vertical pointer (down position).
9. Tape paper clip to top of milk carton so that the clip is half exposed. (See drawing.)
10. Affix one end of hair to penny with nail polish.
11. Letting the penny hang halfway down in the carton, wrap the hair or yarn around the needle so that it goes under and around the needle; then secure it to the paper clip.
12. To set hygrometer, place it in a basin with the wet sponge close by, but not touching, and cover with a wet towel. Let stand for 15 minutes. Take off towel and adjust pointer to point at "10." (See drawing.)
13. Place hygrometer in a sheltered place outdoors being careful not to shake it.
14. Take daily readings. Note changes.

D. Results:

1. Students will have constructed a hygrometer.
2. Students will learn that moisture in the air varies from day-to-day, season-to-season.

E. Basic Facts and Supplemental Information:

1. In damp (moist) air the hair or yarn stretches a little. In this case the pointer will move toward the larger numbers.
2. In dry air the hair shrinks a little and the pointer will move toward the smaller numbers.

F. Thought Questions for Class Discussions:

1. How does the weather forecaster use the hygrometer in weather forecasting?
2. What happens to your hair when the weather is damp or raining?
3. Can you think of any other ways that moisture in the air affects people?

G. Related Ideas for Further Inquiry:

1. Study Section I-C, "Water."
2. Study Activity VII-E-4, "How can we make a simple barometer?"
3. Study Activity VII-E-7, "Where do clouds come from?"
4. Study Activity VII-E-10, "What is a simple method for determining relative humidity?"

H. Vocabulary Builders—Spelling Words:

1) **hygrometer** 2) **needle** 3) **perpendicular** 4) **penny** 5) **towel** 6) **pointer** 7) **sponge** 8) **moist** 9) **longer** 10) **shorter**

I. Thought for Today:

"Sign in metropolitan high school, 'Free every Monday through Friday—knowledge. Bring your own containers.' "

Activity

Humidity too high?

A. Problem: *What Is a Simple Method for Determining Relative Humidity?*

B. Materials Needed:

1. Two long, narrow outdoor thermometers
2. Piece of cheesecloth, 2 inches square
3. Rubber band
4. Water

C. Procedure:

1. Fold the piece of cheesecloth and wrap it around the bulb of one of the thermometers. This is the "wet-bulb thermometer."
2. Secure it in place with the rubber band.
3. Dip the wrapped bulb in water.
4. Fan, shake, or spin vertically the wet-bulb thermometer.
5. After doing this for a few moments, compare the reading of the wet-bulb thermometer with the reading on the dry-bulb thermometer.
6. Record the difference in two readings.
7. By checking the reading on the dry-bulb thermometer and the difference in temperatures recorded by the two thermometers, the relative humidity can be determined from the Table on the next page.

D. Results:

1. Students will learn how to read thermometers.
2. Students will learn about relative humidity.

E. Basic Facts and Supplemental Information:

1. "Humidity" is a term that is used to refer to the moisture in the air.
2. Relative humidity is the amount of water that is in the air compared to the maximum amount of water it could hold for each temperature reading. It is reported in percentages. When the air is dry, evaporation takes place much more rapidly. This causes the thermometer bulb to cool. Therefore, the table will give an indication of the relative humidity in the atmosphere.
3. An instrument that contains both a dry-bulb and a wet-bulb thermometer is called a sling psychrometer.
4. The warmer the weather, the greater the amount of water the air can hold.
5. Plants grow well in high humidity.
6. If the humidity is too high, people are very uncomfortable.

F. Thought Questions for Class Discussions:

1. Why is it necessary to have wet cheesecloth around the thermometer in order to determine the wet-bulb reading?
2. Do you feel better when the humidity is very high, very low, or somewhere in between?
3. How is humidity related to weather conditions?

G. Related Ideas for Further Inquiry:

1. Check your local newspapers for reports concerning humidity.
2. On days of very high or very low humidity, discuss with students their general feelings regarding temperature and humidity.
3. Study Activity VII-E-2, "What is the 'wind-chill factor'?"
4. Study Activity VII-E-5, "Why are summers warmer than winters?"
5. Study Activity VII-E-7, "Where do clouds come from?"
6. Study Activity VII-E-8, "What are 'cold fronts' and 'warm fronts'?"
7. Study Activity VII-E-9, "How can we measure humidity in the air? How can we build a hygrometer?"
8. Study Activity VII-E-13, "How do we forecast weather?"
9. Study Activity VII-E-14, "What is El Niño?"
10. Study Activity VII-E-15, "How do we read a weather map?"

H. Vocabulary Builders—Spelling Words:

1) **relative** 2) **humidity** 3) **bulb** 4) **thermometer** 5) **temperature** 6) **percentage** 7) **psychrometer**

I. Thought for Today:

"Some people have the genius to make rain, but often lack enough common sense to come in out of it."

RELATIVE HUMIDITY IN PERCENTAGES

Readings of dry-bulb thermometer	*Difference in Degrees Fahrenheit Between Wet- and Dry-Bulb Thermometers*															
	0	1	2	3	4	5	6	7	8	9	10	11	12	13	14	15
60	100%	94%	89%	84%	78%	73%	68%	63%	58%	53%	49%	44%	40%	35%	31%	27%
61	100	94	89	84	79	74	68	64	59	54	50	45	40	36	32	28
62	100	94	89	84	79	74	69	64	60	55	50	46	41	37	33	29
63	100	95	90	84	79	74	70	65	60	56	51	47	42	38	34	30
64	100	95	90	85	79	75	70	66	61	56	52	48	43	39	35	31
65	100	95	90	85	80	75	70	66	62	57	53	48	44	40	36	32
66	100	95	90	85	80	76	71	66	62	58	53	49	45	41	37	33
67	100	95	90	85	80	76	71	67	62	58	54	50	46	42	38	34
68	100	95	90	85	81	76	72	67	63	59	55	51	47	43	39	35
69	100	95	90	86	81	77	72	68	64	59	55	51	47	44	40	36
70	100	95	90	86	81	77	72	68	64	60	56	52	48	44	40	37
71	100	95	90	86	82	77	73	69	64	60	56	53	49	45	41	38
72	100	95	91	86	82	78	73	69	65	61	57	53	49	46	42	39
73	100	95	91	86	82	78	73	69	65	61	58	54	50	46	43	40
74	100	95	91	86	82	78	74	70	66	62	58	54	51	47	44	40
75	100	96	91	87	83	78	74	70	66	63	59	55	51	48	44	41
76	100	96	91	87	83	78	74	70	67	63	59	55	52	48	45	42
77	100	96	91	87	83	79	75	71	67	63	60	56	52	49	46	42
78	100	96	91	87	83	79	75	71	67	64	60	57	53	50	46	43
79	100	96	91	87	83	79	75	71	68	64	60	57	54	50	47	44
80	100	96	91	87	83	79	76	72	68	64	61	57	54	51	47	44

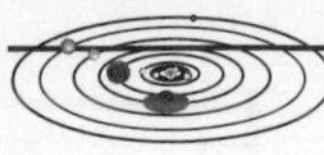

Activity

A. Problem: *What Are Tornadoes?*

B. Materials Needed:

1. Books, pamphlets, charts about weather.
2. Pictures, newspaper clippings, and/or multisensory aids about tornadoes.

C. Procedure:

1. Discuss with class any experiences they might have had with tornadoes.
2. Discuss what they have heard about tornadoes.
3. Use whatever multisensory aids are available.
4. Explain that tornadoes are spiralling columns of wind sometimes formed under special weather conditions when:
   a. Ordinarily cold, heavy air moves under warm, light air.
   b. A layer of cold, dry air is pushed over a layer of warm, moist air; the warm, moist air then quickly forces its way in a spiral movement through the layer of cold air, establishing strong, whirling winds around a center of low pressure.

D. Result:

Students will learn what tornadoes are, that they are very dangerous, and that everyone should take proper safety precautions if there is any danger of one approaching.

E. Basic Facts and Supplemental Information:

1. Tornadoes are sometimes called twisters.
2. A tornado looks like a narrow, funnel-shaped, whirling cloud that is very thick and black.
3. The stem of the funnel sometimes touches the ground as it moves along.
4. The funnel may move up and down as well as moving forward.
5. Tornadoes vary in width from a few hundred feet to a mile.
6. The average speed forward of a tornado is about 30 miles per hour, with normal ranges from 25 to 40 miles per hour.
7. The wind speeds at the top of each tornado reach to hundreds of miles per hour.
8. The average tornado lasts 8 minutes, travels 16 miles, and cuts a swath of about 1,000 feet.
9. In the United States, tornadoes occur most frequently in the Mississippi Valley and the surrounding states: Missouri, Indiana, Illinois, Mississippi, Oklahoma, Texas, Arkansas, Kansas, and Iowa.
10. Tornadoes can occur in any state at any time, but they are most frequently seen (and felt) in the spring and early summer.

11. There are about 200 tornadoes each year in the United States that uproot trees, destroy buildings, toss heavy objects around in the air like feathers in the wind, and cause injury and loss of life to people.
12. Precautions are a must if there is any possibility of a tornado. Get into a storm cellar or basement if available; or get under a table, away from windows. If outside, lie down in a gully or alongside a curb.

F. Thought Questions for Class Discussions:

1. What is the difference between a tornado and a hurricane?
2. What would be some early warning signs of an approaching tornado?
3. What weather conditions cause tornadoes?

G. Related Ideas for Further Inquiry:

1. Study Section I-B, "Air."
2. Study Activity V-G-2, "What should I do in case of an earthquake or tornado?"
3. Study other Activities in this Section.

H. Vocabulary Builders—Spelling Words:

1) **tornado** 2) **twister** 3) **funnel**
4) **uprooted** 5) **spiral** 6) **caution**

I. Thought for Today:

"The world is not interested in the storms you encountered but whether you brought in the ship."

A. Problem: *What Are Hurricanes?*

B. Materials Needed:

1. Books, pamphlets, charts about weather
2. Pictures, newspaper clippings, and/or multisensory aids about hurricanes

C. Procedure:

1. Have students relate any experiences they have had with hurricanes.
2. Discuss what they have heard about hurricanes.
3. Use whatever multisensory aids you have about hurricanes.
4. Explain that hurricanes are low air pressure areas (cyclones) that form in the tropics over the oceans.
5. Discuss other pertinent facts about hurricanes such as:
   a. They form between June and November.
   b. They are caused by the hot summer weather evaporating a large amount of water and from absorbing a lot of energy from the sun.
   c. When cold, heavy air moves over the hot, moist air, the latter rises and a violent, whirling storm develops.
   d. The winds in a hurricane (or cyclone) move in a counterclockwise motion in the Northern Hemisphere and in a clockwise direction in the Southern Hemisphere.

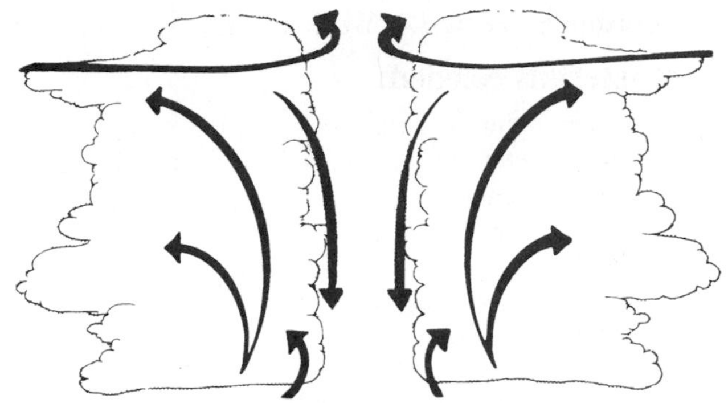

Vertical cross-section of a hurricane showing the eye of the hurricane in the center and the directions of the winds

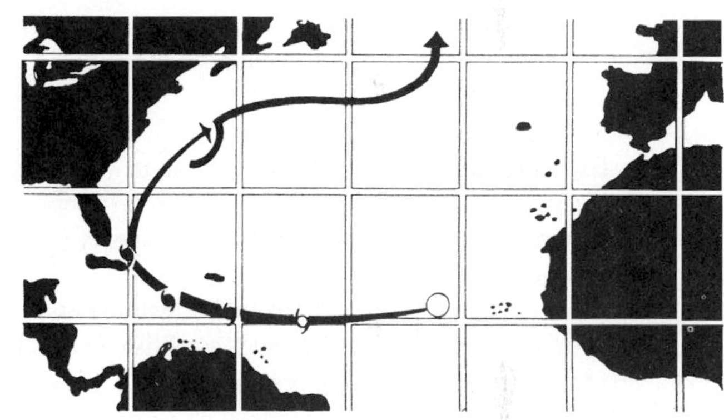

Typical hurricane path from start to finish

D. Result:

Students will learn what hurricanes are, that they are very dangerous, and that everyone should take precautions as they approach.

E. Basic Facts and Supplemental Information:

1. Hurricanes are typhoons.
2. They generate winds up to 150 miles per hour.
3. They average about 400 miles in diameter.
4. The eye of the hurricane is about 12 to 15 miles in diameter and usually is clear and sunny and has no winds.
5. Hurricanes tear up trees, destroy crops, detach roofs from homes, and flatten many small structures.
6. A "Torro Scale" measures the intensity of hurricanes on a scale of 0–12. A 12 rating would seriously damage steel-structured buildings.

F. Thought Questions for Class Discussions:

1. What is the difference between a hurricane and a tornado?
2. What would be some early warning signs of an approaching hurricane?
3. Do hurricane forecasters give people ample warning time?

G. Related Ideas for Further Inquiry:

1. Study Activity VII-E-11, "What are tornadoes?"
2. Study Section I-B, "Air."
3. Study Section V-G, "Safety."
4. Study other Activities in this Section.

H. Vocabulary Builders—Spelling Words:

1) **hurricane** 2) **cyclone** 3) **typical**
4) **eye** 5) **whirling** 6) **dangerous**

I. Thought for Today:

"Red sky at dawning; sailor take warning; Red sky at night, sailors' delight." —old adage

Activity

A. Problem: *How Do We Forecast Weather?*

B. Materials Needed:

1. Thermometer
2. Barometer
3. Hygrometer
4. Wind vane
5. Wind sock
6. Sling psychrometer

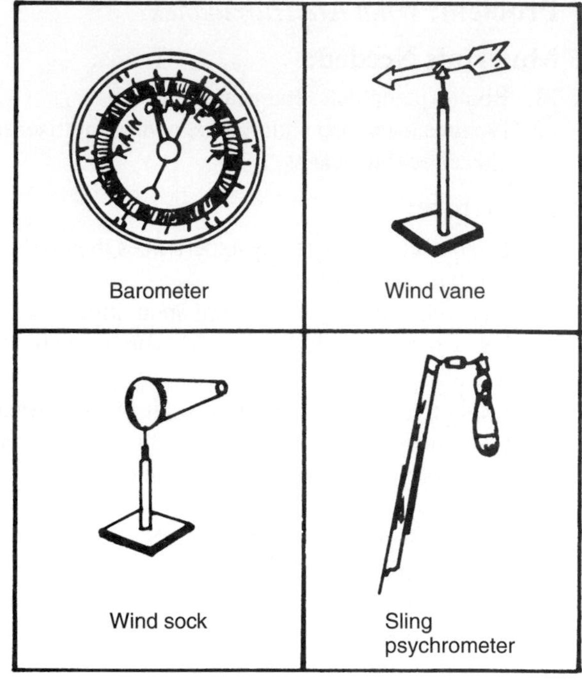

C. Procedure:

1. Ask students if they would like to set up a weather station and predict weather conditions.
2. Tell the class that weather can be predicted by:
   a. type of clouds
   b. air pressure rising or falling (See Activity VII-E-3, "What causes changes in air pressure?")
   c. humidity (moisture in air)
   d. wind direction
3. Explain the weather instruments cited in Materials Needed.
4. Demonstrate how they work and let students practice with them.
5. Have students record data from the instruments.
6. When students are well-trained, establish a period for a complete recording session using all the instruments available.
7. Discuss weather fronts. There are three main types: warm, cold, and occluded. Warm fronts and cold fronts are huge air masses that usually cover several states. Warm fronts have warm air behind them; cold fronts, cold air. Warm fronts bring dry, good weather. Cold fronts push under warm fronts causing the warm, humid air to rise, developing rain clouds and precipitation. An occluded front occurs where the warm and cold fronts meet.
8. Inform the students that the two best indicators of weather are the barometer (rising or falling) and the type of clouds present.
9. Do research on cloud types.

D. Results:

1. Students will gain competency in using weather instruments and recording data from them.
2. Students will become junior weather forecasters.

E. Basic Facts and Supplemental Information:

1. Weather predictions are usually made for a few days or for long-range time frames.
2. Professional weather data is collected from weather stations, automated stations in remote areas, airplanes, ships, and satellites.
3. Study other Activities in this Section for more information on specific weather conditions.
4. Give the students other hints on weather such as:
   a. A ring around the moon is a sign of coming rain or snow.
   b. Heavy dew is a sign of good weather.
   c. Humidity plays a major role in weather and in comfort.

F. Thought Questions for Class Discussions:

1. Can rains cause colds?
2. Can you tell wind direction by looking at trees?
3. Can an airplane pilot fly above the weather?

G. Related Ideas for Further Inquiry:

1. Study Section I-B, "Air."
2. Study Section I-C, "Water."
3. Study Activity VII-E-8, "What are 'cold fronts' and 'warm fronts'?"
4. Study Activity VII-E-15, "How do we read a weather map?"

H. Vocabulary Builders—Spelling Words:

1) **weather** 2) **predicting** 3) **barometer** 4) **front** 5) **clouds** 6) **rising** 7) **falling**

I. Thought for Today:

"Weather forecasting is still a few hours behind arthritis."

A. Problem: *What Is "El Niño"?*

B. Materials Needed:

1. Map of the Pacific Ocean area (or have students reproduce the one shown in drawing)
2. Large, tall, wide-mouthed jar
3. Small jar (to fit inside large jar)
4. Water
5. Food coloring, preferably red
6. Heating element
7. Tissue paper
8. Rubber band
9. Needle or tack
10. Large tray
11. Desk or table
12. Tea kettle or saucepan

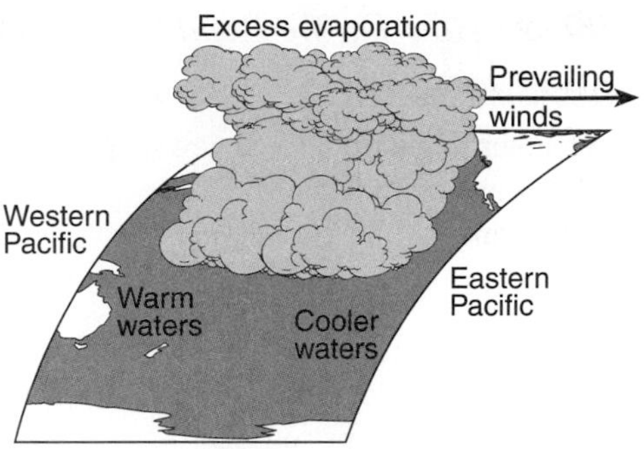

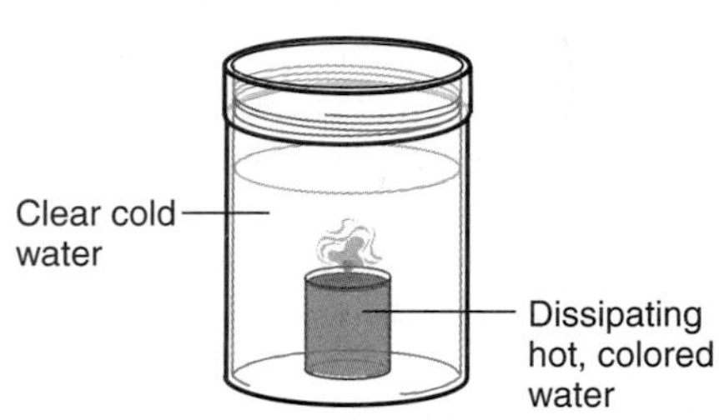

C. Procedure:

1. Set the tray on desk or table.
2. Fill the large jar about half-full of cold water.
3. Boil a small amount of water to put into the small jar.
4. *Carefully* fill the small jar with the boiling water and add the food coloring.
5. Cap the jar with the tissue paper and rubber band.
6. Punch about 6 holes in the tissue paper.
7. Carefully place this jar inside the large jar.
8. Wait and observe results.

D. Results:

1. The colored hot water will slowly dissipate into the cold clear water in the large jar.
2. Students will learn that ocean water is in constant motion and moves into other areas.

E. Basic Facts and Supplemental Information:

1. Ocean water in one area of the Pacific Ocean is heated more than other areas of the same ocean.
2. This excess heat probably originates from the molten portion of the Earth's core that is slightly thinner or closer to the surface of the Earth.
3. There are many effects of this heating:
   a. The warmer the ocean water, the faster the rate of evaporation.
   b. The higher water content in the air, the greater rainfall will be produced in certain affected areas.
   c. While some areas will receive much more rain than normal, other areas will suffer drought conditions.
4. El Niño usually lasts anywhere from only a few weeks to several months. The one in 1998 lasted for many months.
5. El Niño affects not only the amount of rainfall but also has a drastic effect on plant and animal sea life particularly small plants, fish, and birds.
6. El Niño usually occurs every 3 to 7 years.

F. Thought Questions for Class Discussions:

1. How would droughts affect residents?
2. How do people cope with flooding caused by El Niño?
3. How are crops affected by El Niño?

G. Related Ideas for Further Inquiry:

1. Interview a meteorologist.
2. Interview people who live in areas most affected by El Niño.
3. Study Activity VII-E-13, "How do we forecast weather?"
4. Study Activity VII-E-15, "How do we read a weather map?"

H. Vocabulary Builders—Spelling Words:

1) **El Niño** 2) **drought** 3) **warming** 4) **cooling** 5) **periodic** 6) **rainfall**

I. Thought for Today:

"Rain is what makes flowers grow and taxis disappear."

Activity VII E 15

A. Problem: *How Do We Read a Weather Map?*

B. Materials Needed:

1. Weather maps from local newspaper(s)
2. Reference materials on weather
3. Multisensory aids on weather

C. Procedure:

1. Discuss weather conditions in your locality.
2. Encourage students to discuss unusual weather that they have experienced.
3. Show whatever multisensory materials are available about weather.
4. Study weather maps and particularly weather symbols, pointing out:
   a. isotherms—equal temperature lines
   b. weather conditions—fair, rain, snow, thunderstorms, ice
   c. weather fronts—warm, cold, occluded
   d. pressure areas—highs, lows, troughs
   e. jet stream
5. Discuss media reports about weather predictions.

D. Results:

1. Students will learn how to read weather maps.
2. Students will become weather prognosticators.

E. Basic Facts and Supplemental Information:

1. One of the first things we do each morning is to check the weather.
2. The clothes we wear and the activities we engage in are dependent on the weather.
3. Severe weather conditions can have very disruptive effects on our lives.
4. Weather has six main components:
   a. temperature
   b. pressure
   c. wind
   d. humidity
   e. precipitation
   f. cloudiness
5. Some weather predictions also include:
   a. dangers of ultraviolet radiation
   b. data on "particulate matter"
6. Scientists who specialize in studying weather are called "meteorologists."
7. Meteorologists study weather fronts to predict major weather conditions.
8. Warm fronts are indicated by semicircles on the isobars (lines of equal pressure).
9. Cold fronts are indicated by small triangles on the isobars.
10. An occluded front (mixed) would have both semicircles and small triangles on the isobars.
11. The heavy lines with the arrows indicate the flow of the "jet stream."

F. Thought Questions for Class Discussions:

1. How can you predict that a storm is approaching in your area?
2. What weather elements would indicate the approach of good weather conditions?
3. What causes changes in weather?

G. Related Ideas for Further Inquiry:

1. Study jet streams and how they affect weather conditions (Activity VII-E-6).
2. Study other Activities in this section, especially Activities VII-E-8 and VII-E-13.

H. Vocabulary Builders—Spelling Words:

1) **weather** 2) **fronts** 3) **temperature**
4) **pressure** 5) **wind** 6) **humidity**
7) **precipitation** 8) **cloudiness** 9) **warm** 10) **cold**

I. Thought for Today:

"Whether it's cold or whether it's hot, we shall have weather, whether or not."

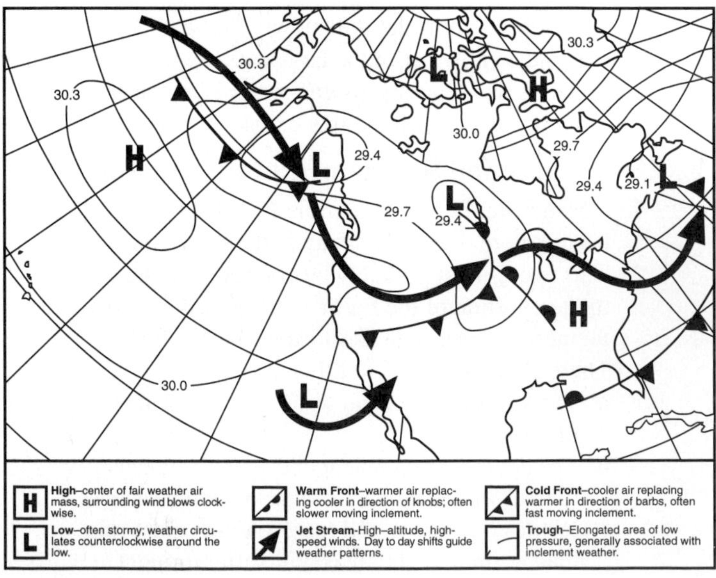

Source: National Weather Service

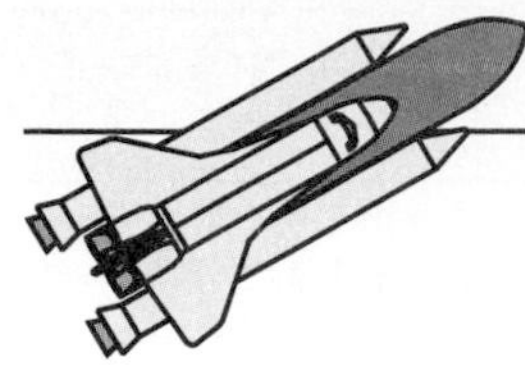

PART VIII

Aviation, Satellites, and Space Travel

SECTION A: AVIATION

Activity VIII A 1

A. Problem: *What Are the Different Kinds of Aircraft?*

B. Materials Needed:

1. Pictures or models of:
   a. Monoplanes
   b. Biplanes
   c. Seaplanes
   d. Amphibians
   e. Helicopters
   f. Gliders
   g. Hang-gliders
   h. Dirigibles
   i. Balloons
   j. Space shuttle
2. Other multisensory aids about aircraft

C. Procedure:

1. Ask students if they have ever flown in an airplane or some other type of aircraft.
2. Have them discuss their experiences.
3. List all the different types of aircraft and explain their functions.
4. With multisensory aids, show appropriate films, slides, transparencies, etc.

D. Results:

Students will realize that there are many different types of aircraft, each with its own special function(s).

E. Basic Facts and Supplemental Information:

1. Aircraft can be divided into two main categories:
   a. Lighter-than-air
   b. Heavier-than-air
2. Most planes built today are monoplanes (one set of wings).
3. Spaceships that carry people cannot be classified as aircraft because they fly above the air.
4. Helicopters have no wings: they have rotating blades.
5. Gliders have no engines or propellers.
6. Hang-gliders are used exclusively for recreation.
7. A new aircraft is now being designed called a "scramjet." It can take off from land and go into orbit and/or be used for space travel.

F. Thought Questions for Class Discussions:

1. How do each of these aircraft stay aloft?
2. How do pilots know in which direction they are flying?
3. How do aircraft bring the people of the world together?

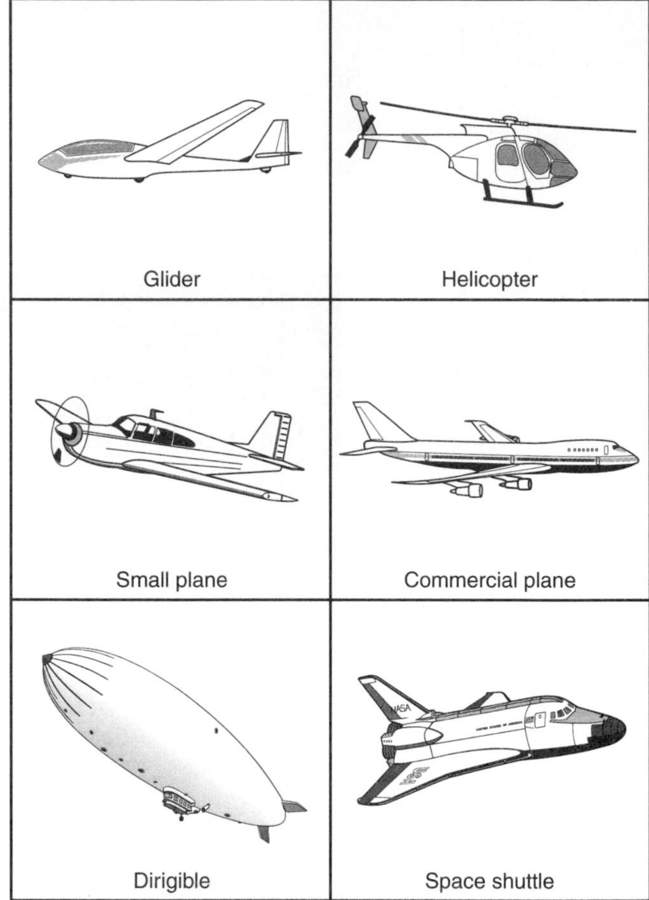

G. Related Ideas for Further Inquiry:

1. Take a field trip to an airport.
2. Devise a teaching unit about the airport or about air transportation.
3. Study Section I-B, "Air."
4. Study Section VII-E, "Weather."
5. Study other Activities in this Section.

H. Vocabulary Builders—Spelling Words:

Use the types of aircraft listed in Materials Needed.

I. Thought for Today:

"Despite all the talk about supersonic transports, no engineer has ever been able to concoct anything that can go faster than a vacation."—Roger Allen

Activity VIII A 2

A. Problem: *How Does an Airplane Get "Lift" From Its Wings?*

B. Materials Needed, Procedure One:

1. Piece of paper, 10″ × 4″
2. Pencil
3. Paste or cellophane tape

Materials Needed, Procedure Two:

1. Strip of writing paper, 3″ × 6″
2. Book

C. Procedure One:

1. Paste or tape ends of paper together.
2. Curve surfaces until it takes the shape of a cross section of an airplane wing.
3. Slip pencil through loop, hold up the wide end for a moment, and blow across the *upper* surface of the paper wing until the wing moves.

Procedure Two:

1. Place one end of the paper in the book (which is standing up) so that the weight of the paper causes it to bend over, away from you. (See drawing.)
2. Blow gently across the surface of the curved paper.

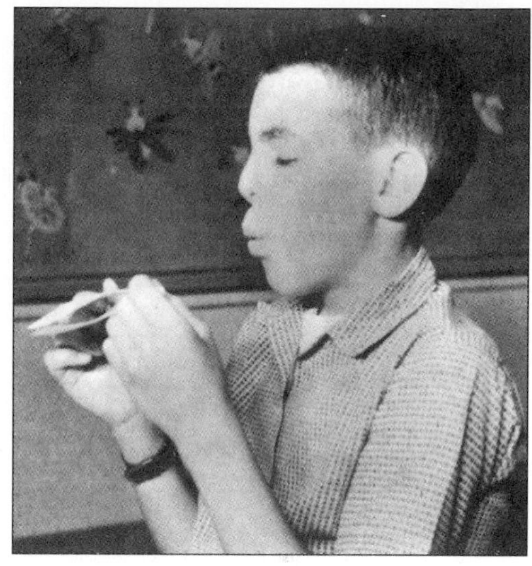

Procedure One

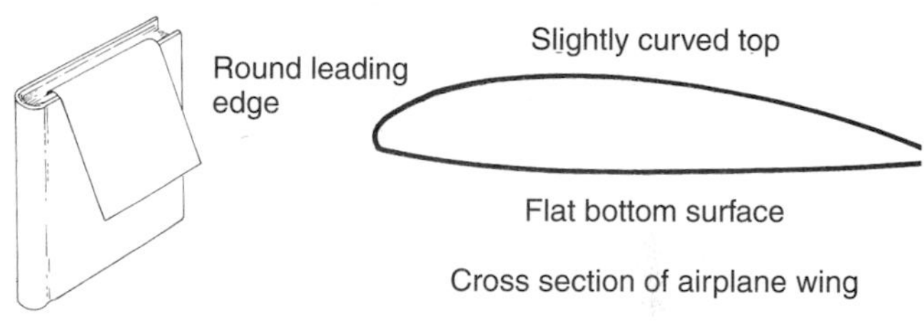

Procedure Two

D. Results:

1. In Procedure One, the paper wing will rise.
2. In Procedure Two, the paper sheet will rise.
3. The students will begin to develop a concept of the effect of "lift" on airplane wings.

E. Basic Facts and Supplemental Information:

1. Air flowing over the wing is less dense on top, and the airplane develops "lift" because there are more molecules below the wing than above the wing. The same is true for the "paper wing." More molecules mean more pressure, and more pressure means more "lift."
2. In an actual plane in flight, more than three-quarters of the entire weight of the plane is held up by the reduced air flow on top of the wings, and only one-quarter by the force of the air on the bottom of the wings.
3. There are four major forces acting on a plane:
   a. Lift—from air flowing over wing(s)
   b. Gravity—attraction to the Earth
   c. Thrust—power from engine(s)
   d. Drag—resistance from the air

F. Thought Questions for Class Discussions:

1. What is Bernoulli's Principle?
2. Is lift a problem in space travel?
3. Is the turning of an airplane accomplished by lift?
4. How does gravity affect lift?

G. Related Ideas for Further Inquiry:

1. If any student has a model airplane, ask him/her to bring it to class and explain how it works.
2. Study Section I-B, "Air."
3. Study Section VII-E, "Weather."
4. Study other Activities in this Section.

H. Vocabulary Builders—Spelling Words:

1) **lift** 2) **curved** 3) **surface** 4) **pressure** 5) **underneath** 6) **gravity** 7) **thrust** 8) **drag**

I. Thought for Today:

"Air travel is wonderful. It allows you to pass motorists at a safe distance."

Activity VIII A 3

A. Problem: *How Does a Pilot Control an Airplane?*

B. Materials Needed:

1. Plyboard for frame
2. Apple crate (if available; if not, use comparable lumber)
3. Scrap lumber
4. Screw eyes
5. Flexible wire
6. Leather for hinges
7. Ball-and-socket device
8. Tools; pliers, handsaw, hammer, screwdriver
9. Books, articles, etc. about the nomenclature of airplanes

C. Procedure:

1. Have students study the main parts of a plane's control system.
2. Define control terms: pedals, stick, ailerons, rudder, and stabilizers.
3. Outline airplane on plyboard frame.
4. Using apple crates and/or scrap lumber, build wings so that controls can be attached.
5. Construct pedals and stick, and attach them to the ailerons, rudder, and stabilizers as shown in drawing.
6. Pedals should be hinged to base with wires going to rudder.
7. Stick should be a ball-and-socket joint or near facsimile at the base so that when the stick is moved from side to side, the aileron on the side toward which the stick is moved rises and the opposite aileron depresses.
8. The stick should also have wires running to the horizontal stabilizers so that when the stick is moved forward the stabilizers depress, and when the stick is pulled back the stabilizers elevate.
9. One apple crate can be used as a pilot's seat.

D. Results:

1. An understanding of an airplane's control system will be learned as the students see and move the pedals and stick.
2. They will begin to realize the effects of air pressure against the various movable parts of the airplane.

E. Basic Facts and Supplemental Information:

1. Students can make the model, thereby gaining experience and knowledge about planes.
2. Two good alternatives to the construction of a whole plane are to build "mock-ups" of the various movable parts or to create a large drawing and explain in detail how the major parts operate.

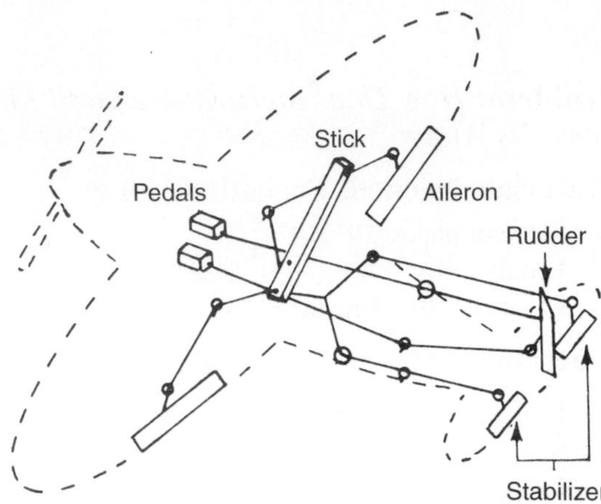

3. Ailerons, rudder, and stabilizers are movable parts controlling the plane and are operated by the pedals and stick.
4. These controls operate like ships' rudders by extending part of the air stream which pushes that part of the plane, thus making the plane change directions.
5. Stabilizers aid the plane in moving up and down. When the stick moves back, the stabilizers move up helping the plane rise.
6. Rudders are used for turning. When the stick moves to the left, the rudder moves toward the left, and the plane moves in that direction.
7. Ailerons are used for banking plane and balance. If one goes up, the other goes down.
8. The aileron that is turned up forces that side of the plane to go down.

F. Thought Questions for Class Discussions:

1. What are trim tabs?
2. How else does a pilot control a plane in flight?
3. What is the function of the propeller?
4. What is "drag?"

G. Related Ideas for Further Inquiry:

1. If any students have model planes, have them bring them to class for study.
2. Study Section I-B, "Air."
3. Study Section VII-E, "Weather."
4. Study other Activities in this Section.

H. Vocabulary Builders—Spelling Words:

1) **pedal** 2) **stick** 3) **rudder** 4) **aileron** 5) **stabilizer** 6) **flight** 7) **maneuver** 8) **thrust**

I. Thought for Today:

"The wife of a pilot is the only woman who is glad to see her husband down and out."

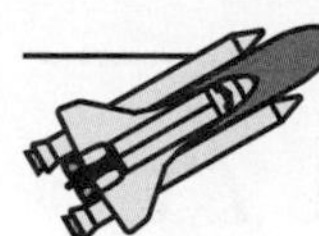

Activity VIII A 4

A. Problem: *How Can Pilots Tell How High They Are? How Can We Make an Altimeter?*

B. Materials Needed:

1. Large Pyrex bottle
2. One-hole rubber stopper to fit bottle
3. Glass tubing, 8 ″ arm, L-shaped
4. White card, 2″ × 4″, scaled as shown in drawing
5. Red food coloring
6. Hot plate
7. Ice cubes
8. Large shallow pan

C. Procedure:

1. Wet rubber stopper and insert glass tubing as shown in drawing.
2. A drop of food coloring can be placed in the tubing by inserting the tubing into the food color bottle. Hold one end closed with your finger and remove. Shake out excess liquid in the tubing until one drop remains. This "indicator" can be positioned by blowing on one end or carefully sucking on the other end of the tubing. Be careful not to swallow any of the food coloring.
3. Carefully insert tubing into jar. Several trials may be necessary to get indicator drop in correct position, as drop will move out because of increased pressure in jar.
4. Attach card to glass tubing. (See drawing.)
5. To simulate flying conditions, warm bottle over hot plate or *carefully* place in hot water to have bottle pressure greater than outside pressure, which would be true if plane were climbing (ascending).
6. At room temperature, place bottle in ice water to simulate plane descending.

D. Results:

1. A simple altimeter will be created.
2. Students will learn how a simple barometer works.

E. Basic Facts and Supplemental Information:

1. An altimeter works like a barometer measuring differences in air pressure.
2. As an airplane climbs to higher altitudes the air pressure decreases; therefore, the air in the jar (altimeter) pushes the red drop (indicator) out toward the open end. As an airplane descends, the air pressure outside increases and the red drop (indicator) moves in, away from the open end.
3. If there are tall buildings or hills nearby, the altimeter can be used and differences in air pressure can be noted.

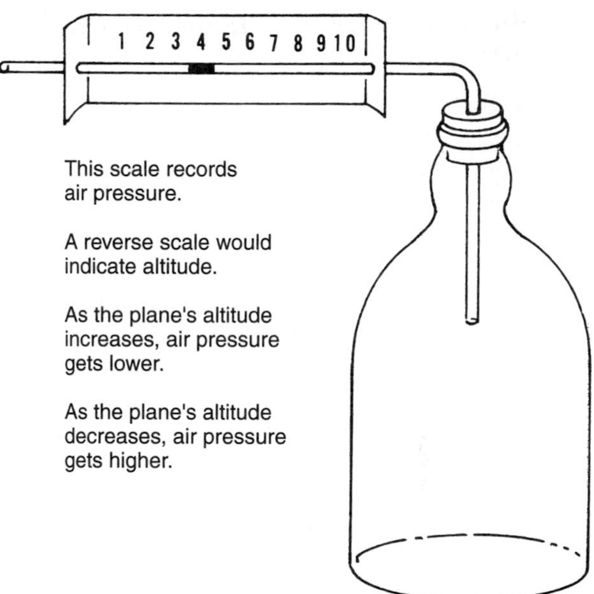

F. Thought Questions for Class Discussions:

1. Why does it take vegetables longer to cook at high altitudes?
2. Is it easier to run at high altitudes or low altitudes? Why?
3. Is it possible to have planes reach an altitude where there is not enough air to have them fly any higher?

G. Related Ideas for Further Inquiry:

1. Study Section I-B, "Air."
2. Study Section VII-E, "Weather."
3. Study especially Activity VIII-A-3, "How does a pilot control an airplane?"
4. Study Activity VIII-A-2, "How does an airplane get 'lift' from its wings?"
5. Study Activity VIII-A-5, "What are the main forces acting on an airplane in flight?"

H. Vocabulary Builders—Spelling Words:

1) **altimeter** 2) **tubing** 3) **ascending**
4) **descending** 5) **indicator** 6) **pressure**
7) **temperature** 8) **colored** 9) **scale**

I. Thought for Today:

"Discussion is the exchange of knowledge; argument is the exchange of ignorance."

Activity VIII A 5

A. Problem: *What Are the Main Forces Acting on an Airplane in Flight?*

B. Materials Needed:

1. Model airplane
2. Drawing of an airplane wing (See drawing.)

C. Procedure:

1. Show the model airplane.
2. Ask students if they know what forces are acting on the plane when it is in flight.
3. Tell them about the ones they don't know about or are not fully aware of.

D. Results:

1. Students will learn that there are many forces acting on an airplane in flight.
2. They will learn about the four main forces:
   a. gravity
   b. lift
   c. thrust
   d. drag

E. Basic Facts and Supplemental Information:

1. *Gravity* is the attraction of two bodies for each other. Since the Earth is bigger than the plane, it has the stronger pull, which forces the plane down.
2. *Lift* is the upward pressure on the aircraft under the wings. While in flight, the number of molecules above the wings are reduced in numbers by the curvature of the wings; this forces the plane upward.
3. *Thrust* is caused by the propeller in prop planes and the exhaust gases in jet planes. This forces the plane forward since there are more molecules behind than in front of the propeller or engine.
4. *Drag* is the resistance of the body of the plane as it moves through the air. This force works in a backward direction when the plane is in flight.
5. A falling object in "free fall" would accelerate at the rate of 32.2 feet (9.8 meters) per second.
6. This increase would last about 14 seconds until it equals the force of gravity. At that time the free fall would remain steady without further acceleration.
7. One more factor must be taken into account: and that is a plane's altitude which changes the amount of thrust, lift, and drag, but not gravity.
8. The final speed of a free-falling object is called its "terminal velocity."

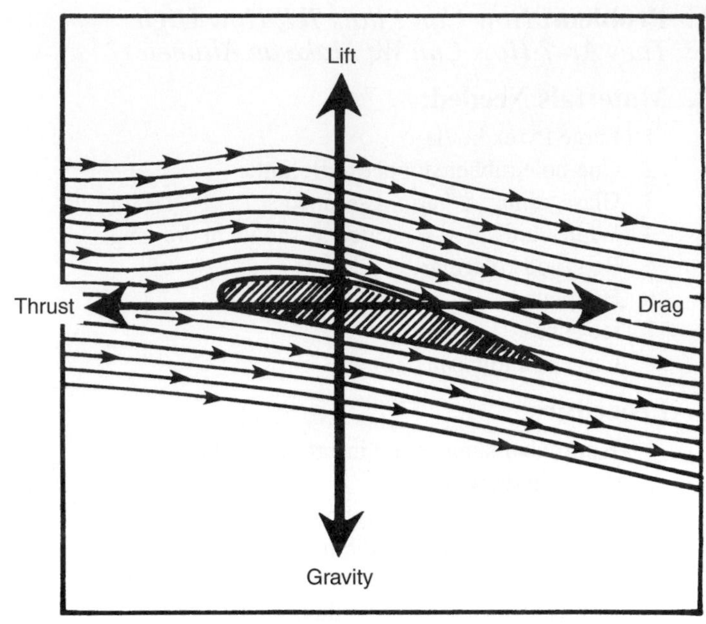

Airplane wing

F. Thought Questions for Class Discussions:

1. What would happen if gravity were stronger than lift?
2. What forces are at work when a pilot lands a plane?
3. Does inertia and/or momentum play any role in keeping an airplane in flight?

G. Related Ideas for Further Inquiry:

1. Study Section I-B, "Air."
2. Study Activity II-F-1, "What are Newton's Laws of Motion?"
3. Study Activity II-F-2, "What is acceleration? deceleration?"
4. Study Section VII-D, "Gravity"
5. Study Section II-F, "Movement and Resistance."
6. Study other Activities in this Section.

H. Vocabulary Builders—Spelling Words:

1) **gravity** 2) **thrust** 3) **lift** 4) **drag** 5) **force** 6) **acceleration** 7) **velocity**

I. Thought for Today:

"First time passenger to pilot, 'Please don't fly faster than sound, we want to talk.' "

SECTION B: SATELLITES

Activity VIII B 1

A. Problem: *What Keeps a Satellite in Orbit?*

B. Materials Needed:

1. Ping-pong ball
2. Filament tape
3. Four or five rubber bands (May use a rubber ball and long rubber line from a paddle ball)
4. Table or desk

C. Procedure

1. Drop the ping-pong ball on the table.
2. Interlock the rubber bands or use the rubber line.
3. Tape the rubber bands to another ping-pong ball.
4. Slowly swing rubber bands, with ball attached, in a circular motion. Note the distance from your hand.
5. Increase the speed of circular swing. Note the distance in this case.
6. Discuss why the ping-pong ball falls to the table and why the distance from the hand increases as the ball revolves at a greater speed.

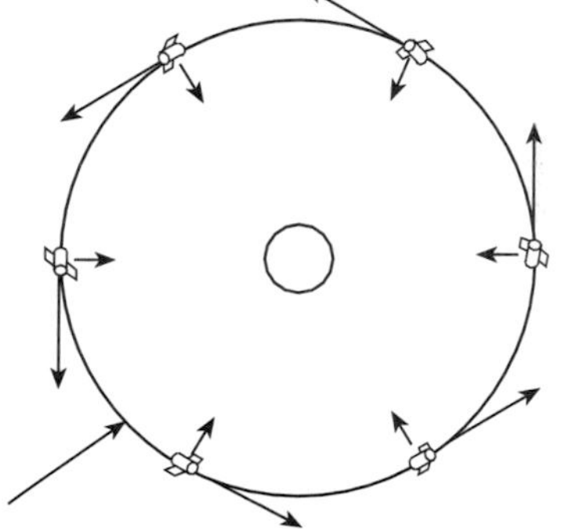

D. Results:

1. The ping-pong ball will fall to the table.
2. In step 4 above, as the ball moves slowly it revolves at a certain distance from the hand.
3. In step 5 above as the speed is increased, the ball moves farther from the hand.

E. Basic Facts and Supplemental Information:

In the first experiment there was one major force acting on the ball and that was gravity, which caused the ball to fall. In the second experiment there were two forces acting on the ball: one was gravity, and the second was centripetal force generated by the muscles of the hand and wrist. Gravity tends to pull the ball to the center of the Earth. The momentum of the ball tends to move it in a straight line perpendicular to the rubber bands, but the centripetal force tends to move the ball toward the hand and wrist. The balancing of gravity and the centripetal force causes the ball to revolve around the hand and wrist. This adds momentum to the ball. As more centripetal force is applied, the ball will move farther away. As centripetal force is decreased, the ball will move closer to the hand. Earth satellites have only two forces acting on them: gravity and centripetal force. Earth satellites are sent high into space and given an initial thrust to start them revolving. Since a body in motion continues to stay in motion, the satellites continue to revolve. Because there is a very light density of air even at high altitudes, these satellites will slow down, come closer to Earth, meet denser air, and slow down still more. This continues until the satellites finally fall to Earth or burn up as they meet denser and denser air.

F. Thought Questions for Class Discussions:

1. What happens to the position of our satellites that maintain an orbit of about 22,300 miles from Earth?
2. Could Earth satellites circle the globe in any direction?
3. What are some potential dangers to our satellites in orbit around the Earth?
4. Are there dangers to us from falling space junk?
5. Have you seen pieces of tires from trucks lying on highways? What causes these pieces to fly off the tires?

G. Related Ideas for Further Inquiry:

1. Study Activity II-F-1, "What are Newton's Laws of Motion?"
2. Study Section VIII-A, "Aviation."
3. Study other Activities in this Section.

H. Vocabulary Builders—Spelling Words:

1) **satellite** 2) **orbit** 3) **circular** 4) **momentum** 5) **distance** 6) **centripetal** 7) **gravity** 8) **inertia**

I. Thought for Today:

"You can't get through this world without making mistakes. The person who makes no mistakes does nothing, and that is a mistake."

Activity VIII B 2

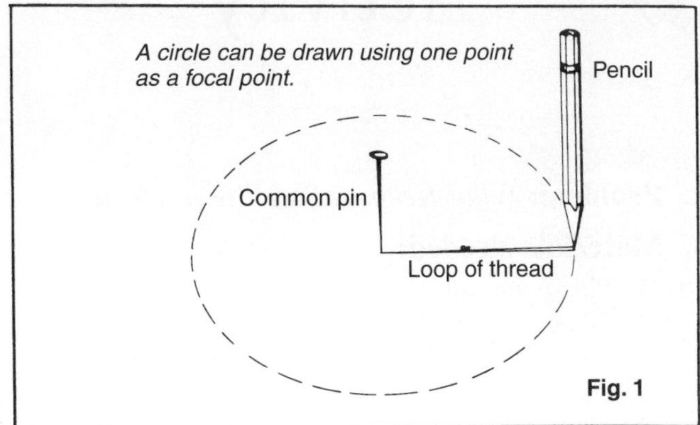

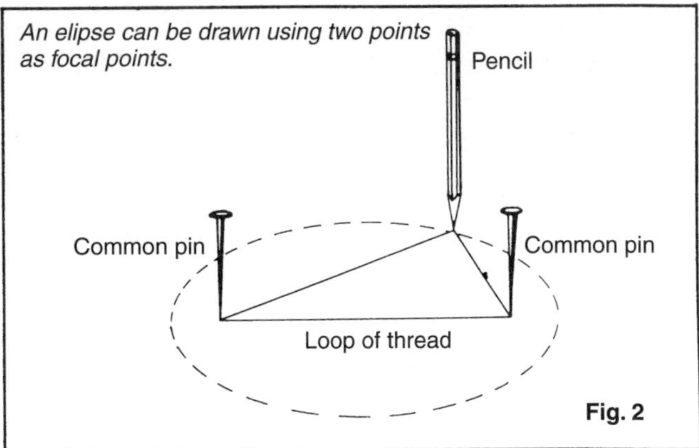

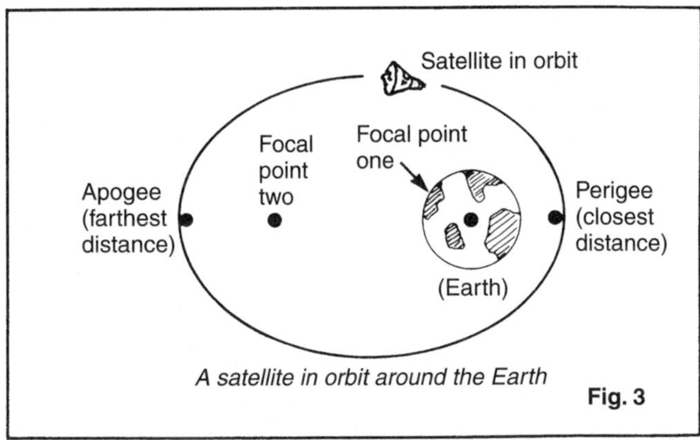

A. Problem: *Is the Path of a Satellite a Perfect Circle?*

B. Materials Needed:

1. Table or desk
2. Tagboard
3. Two common pins
4. Thread
5. Pencil

C. Procedure:

1. Tell the students that we are going to study the path of a satellite around the Earth.
2. Set tagboard on flat surface.
3. Place a pin in the middle of the tagboard.
4. Double the thread but keep doubled thread 10 inches long. Tie ends, making a loop.
5. Place one end of the loop over the pin and the second around the pencil point. (See Figure 1.)
6. Move the pencil around the pin, drawing a circle as it turns.
7. Remove the center pin and place the two pins about 8 inches apart as shown in Figure 2.
8. Loop the thread over the two pins and around the pencil point until the thread is taut.
9. Move the pencil around, drawing its path on the tagboard.

D. Results:

1. In the first case, a perfect circle was drawn.
2. In the second case, an ellipse was drawn.

E. Basic Facts and Supplemental Information:

1. All satellites, including Earth satellites, follow an elliptical path, not a perfect circle.
2. One point (a common pin) shows the position of the Earth.
3. The second point of focus is determined by the position and motion of the satellite when all propulsive thrust stops.
4. The closest point of the satellite's orbit to the Earth is called the "perigee."
5. The farthest point of the satellite's orbit to the Earth is called the "apogee."

F. Thought Questions for Class Discussions:

1. Why do you think satellites follow elliptical orbits?
2. Is the Earth's orbit an ellipse?
3. Is the moon's orbit around the Earth an ellipse?

G. Related Ideas for Further Inquiry:

1. Combine with math activities.
2. Study Section I-B, "Air."
3. Study Section VII-B, "Solar System."
4. Study other Activities in this Section.

H. Vocabulary Builders—Spelling Words:

1) **ellipse** 2) **circle** 3) **orbit**
4) **satellite** 5) **thread** 6) **around**

I. Thought for Today:

"The object of education is to have the children exist without the teachers."

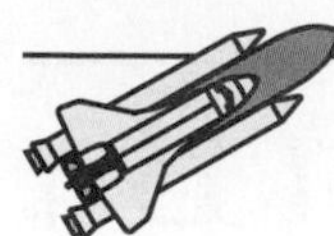

Activity

VIII B 3

A. Problem: *What Is the Difference Between an "Orbit" and a "Revolution"?*

B. Materials Needed:

1. Flannel board
2. Flannel board cutouts representing:
   a. Earth
   b. Two simulated rocket launchers
   c. Satellite
3. Yarn
4. Common pins

C. Procedure:

1. Place the "Earth" on the flannel board.
2. Place one rocket launcher on top of the Earth.
3. Place the yarn in an ellipse around the Earth (about 3 or 4 inches from the Earth).
4. Place the "satellite" over the launcher, just touching the yarn. (See drawing.)
5. Move the "satellite capsule" around the Earth once returning it to its original position.
6. Describe this as an "orbit."
7. Ask students how the Earth is moving while the capsule (satellite) (space shuttle) is in orbit.
8. Tell them that the Earth rotates from east to west, therefore turn the flannel board "Earth" counterclockwise with original launching pad moving also.
9. Inform the class that most orbits take about 1 hour and 45 minutes or about 14 orbits in 1 day.
10. Move the "satellite" around so that it makes one complete orbit; at the same time, you rotate the Earth about 15°.
    Note: the satellite is still behind the original launcher's position in space.
11. Place the second launcher under the satellite showing one complete orbit.
12. Move the satellite over the original launcher explaining that this is one revolution.

D. Results:

1. Students can visualize that an orbit is the path of a satellite from its original launch site to the same position after the Earth has partially rotated.
2. Students will see that a revolution is a path of 360° regardless of the movement of the Earth.
3. The paths of the satellites differ because:
   a. The Earth is moving.
   b. The heights of the satellites vary.
   c. The angle of insertion varies.

Revolution: Distance:		Time:
100 miles	....	90 minutes
1,000 "	....	2 hours
6,000 "	....	5 hours
23,000 "	....	24 hours
240,000 "	....	27.3 days (moon)

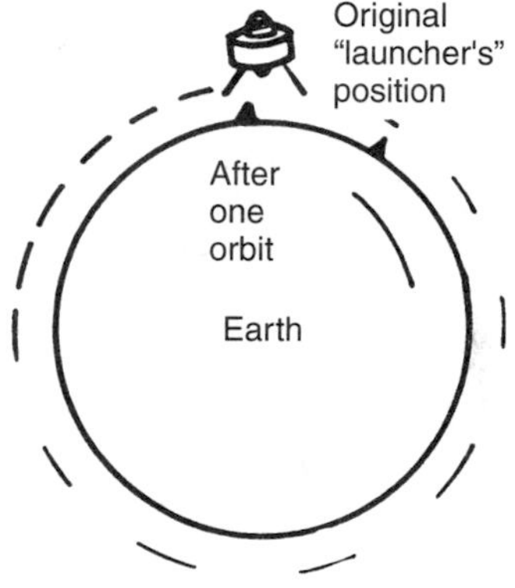

E. Basic Facts and Supplemental Information:

1. Satellites can move in any direction around the Earth: east to west, west to east, over the poles, or any orbits in between.
2. The higher the satellite the longer the revolution time.
3. The paths of satellites differ because the Earth is moving; otherwise, the paths would be identical. (See drawing.)

F. Thought Questions for Class Discussions:

1. Why do we put satellites in orbit?
2. Research the ways that satellites can be maneuvered once they are in orbit.
3. Can the height of a satellite be adjusted while it is in flight?

G. Related Ideas for Further Inquiry:

1. Study Section I-B, "Air."
2. Study Section VII-B, "Solar System."
3. Study other Activities in this Section.

H. Vocabulary Builders—Spelling Words:

1) **orbit** 2) **revolution** 3) **satellite**
4) **capsule** 5) **launch** 6) **maneuver**

I. Thought for Today:

"Those who complain that Americans are going too fast haven't been caught in a traffic jam."

Activity VIII B 4

A. Problem: *What Good Are Artificial Satellites?*

B. Materials Needed:

1. Models or pictures of satellites
2. Pictures of occupations described in Results D-3 below
3. Weather maps
4. Rocks, mineral specimens

C. Procedure:

1. Discuss the development of artificial satellites.
2. Have students find out about the different kinds of satellites.
3. Discuss the purposes of satellites.

D. Results:

Students will learn that:

1. Up to now there have been over a thousand artificial satellites.
2. Most of them have been used for bouncing television pictures and sending messages over long distances, even between continents.
3. Satellites are helping:
   a. farmers—improve farm practices
   b. fishermen—locate water depths, temperatures
   c. foresters—locate best woods (soft, hard, etc.)
   d. industrialists—best location for factories
   e. geologists—locate "faults," shifting glaciers, etc.
   f. hydrologists—identify water movement, pollution, better use
   g. mineralogists—locate deep sources of minerals
   h. mapmakers—up-to-date, more detailed
   i. ecologists—detect water, air pollution
   j. conservationists—locate forest fires early
   k. sailors—report best course for sailing
   l. city planner—up-to-date maps, locate pollution
   m. military—monitoring military installations of other nations
   n. teachers—relay school lessons

E. Basic Facts and Supplemental Information:

1. A space station is an artificial satellite.
2. Russia has a space station, MIR-1, in orbit now. Present plans are to abandon it and let it burn up in the atmosphere unless new funds are found. (Costs are $250,000,000 per year.)
3. The United States and Russia aided by Germany, France, Japan and several other countries are constructing an international space station to be completed early in the next decade.

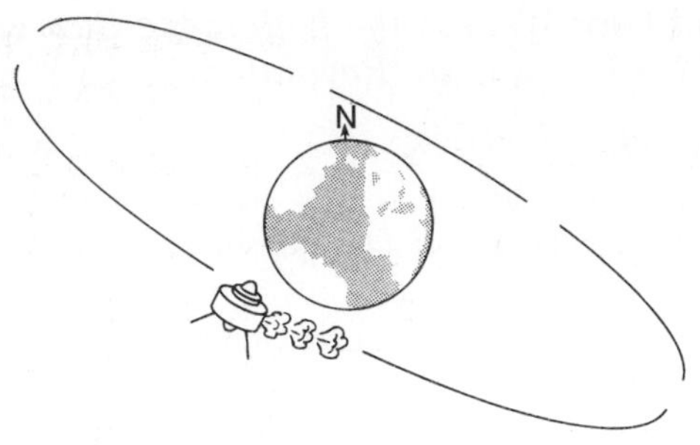

4. Many modern instruments on satellites can see or "feel." These instruments are cameras and remote sensors.
5. Different objects can be detected by the energy patterns that are emitted and/or reflected.
6. We now use cameras with folded optics which increase their seeing power by a series of mirrors within the camera.
7. We also have multiband cameras which can take pictures simultaneously of the visible and infrared portions of the spectrum.
8. Microwave devices, radar, can detect cloud formations and changes of foliage.
9. Magnetometers can locate buried minerals by their magnetic anomalies.

F. Thought Questions for Class Discussions:

1. Can you think up any other uses of Earth satellites?
2. Do you think we should develop a space station where people could work and perform scientific experiments?
3. What would be some problems of people living on a space station?

G. Related Ideas for Further Inquiry:

1. Study Section I-B, "Air."
2. Study Section VII-A, "Universe."
3. Study Activity II-F-1, "What Are Newton's Laws of Motion?"
4. Study other Activities in this Section.

H. Vocabulary Builders—Spelling Words:

Use the occupations cited in Results.

I. Thought for Today:

"One who thinks only of oneself is hopelessly uneducated."

Activity VIII B 5

A. Problem: *What Use Are Space Stations?*

B. Materials Needed:

1. Old refrigerator packing box or other large shipping carton
2. Several smaller cardboard boxes
3. Two small wooden boxes

C. Procedure:

1. Tell the students that we are going to plan a space station and we need volunteers to serve on three committees:
   a. Group 1 will have the responsibility of designing controls, instruments, and equipment.
   b. Group 2 will plan all the services needed.
   c. Group 3 will make a list of supplies needed.
2. Give them ample time to plan their space venture in a space station.
3. Have them construct a mock-up space station in miniature and everything they will need, using materials cited above.
4. Have them cite the potential problems that a space station crew might have that live aboard a space station for a year.

D. Results:

1. Students will have planned and constructed a model space station.
2. They equipped their space station with supplies and equipment.
3. Students will be aware of the many problems and dangers of space ventures.

E. Basic Facts and Supplemental Information:

1. The Soviet Union has a space station in orbit called "Mir," (which means "peace").
2. A Russian astronaut stayed on "Mir," the Russian space station, for 326 days but left in a weakened condition. He did regain full strength.
3. The United States launched a space station, "Skylab," in 1973. It reentered Earth's atmosphere in 1980 and disintegrated.
4. The United States and Russia aided by Germany, France, Japan and several other countries are constructing an international space station to be completed early in the next decade.
5. The values of space stations are:
   a. conduct biological tests
   b. astronomical and astrophysical investigations
   c. manufacture certain products
   d. house camera equipment for Earth and space surveillance
   e. meteorological sensors
   f. communication services
   g. service station for interplanetary spaceships

F. Thought Questions for Class Discussions:

1. What would be some of the benefits of having a permanent space station?
2. Would you like to spend a year in space aboard a space station?
3. What would be some of the major problems of living in space?

G. Related Ideas for Further Inquiry:

1. Study section I-B, "Air."
2. Study section VII-B, "Solar System."
3. Study Section V-D, "Personal Health."
4. Study Section VI-A, "Ecosystems."
5. Study other Activities in this Section.

H. Vocabulary Builders—Spelling Words:

1) **station** 2) **space** 3) **instruments**
4) **supplies** 5) **service** 6) **astronauts**

I. Thought for Today:

"One secret of success is to be able to put your best foot forward without stepping on anybody's toes."

A. Problem: *What Is "Escape Velocity"?*

B. Materials Needed:

1. Flannel board (blue background preferred)
2. Flannel board cutouts of:
   a. first stage rocket
   b. second stage rocket
   c. third stage rocket
   d. nose cone (with satellite)

C. Procedure:

1. Assemble all stages to form one complete spacecraft.
2. Discuss some of the major problems of putting a satellite in orbit.
3. Cite the fact that in order to put a satellite 300 miles in orbit above the Earth requires a speed of 18,000 miles per hour, and to leave the Earth's gravitational pull requires a speed of 25,000 miles per hour.
4. Tell the students that weight is an important hindrance in overcoming gravity.
5. Inform the class that as the fuel to drive the rocket upward is consumed, it is unnecessary to carry the empty fuel containers; therefore, our rockets have been designed in stages so that the containers can be dropped off when emptied.
6. Illustrating with the flannel cutouts, show how the three stages are eliminated one at a time.
7. Explain in detail how this works:
   a. The first stage is ignited and the rocket takes off.
   b. The rocket attains a speed of 4,000 miles per hour and jettisons the first stage. (Remove first stage from flannel board.)
   c. The second stage is ignited. (Since air resistance is now less, we don't need as much fuel, so second container is smaller.)
   d. The rocket attains a speed of 10,000 miles per hour and jettisons the second stage. (Remove second stage from flannel board.)
   e. The third stage is ignited and attains a speed of 25,000 miles per hour, which is the "escape velocity."

D. Results:

Students will be able to visualize how the three stages of rockets (with or without satellites) are ignited, launched into space, and dropped off.

E. Basic Facts and Supplemental Information:

In addition to attaining the correct height and speed, the last stage must also put the rocket on its correct glide path. In order to accomplish this, after the initial stage has been fired straight up, the rocket is programmed to roll toward its final (orbital) path, so in this demonstration, the rollover pattern should also be included.

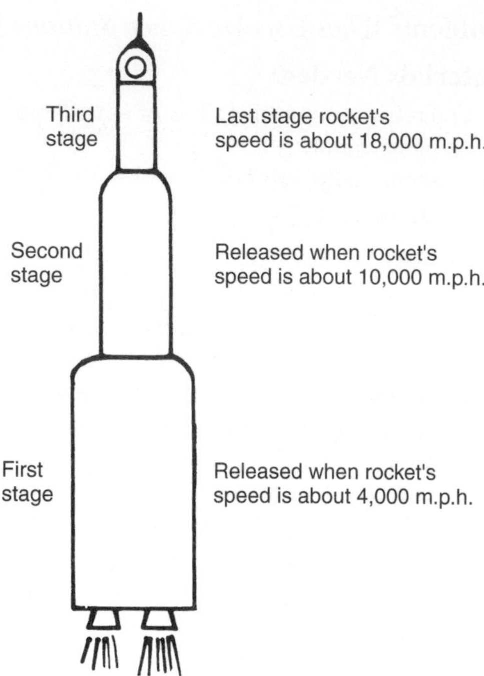

Space rocket with satellite

F. Thought Questions for Class Discussions:

1. What are some of the major problems that might be (and have been) encountered in this program?
2. What additional design problems did we have in landing on and returning from the moon?
3. What happens to the fuel containers?

G. Related Ideas for Further Inquiry:

1. Study Section I-B, "Air."
2. Study Section VII-A, "Universe."
3. Study Section II-F, "Movement and Resistance."
4. Study Section VII-D, "Gravity."
5. Study other Activities in this Section.

H. Vocabulary Builders—Spellings Words:

1) **escape** 2) **velocity** 3) **rollover**
4) **stage** 5) **rocket** 6) **fuel**

I. Thought for Today:

"Sometimes the best helping hand you can get is a good, firm push."

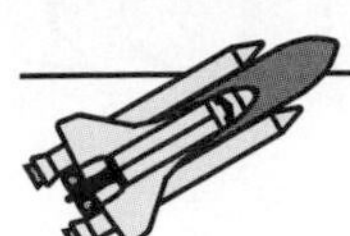

SECTION C: SPACE TRAVEL

Activity

VIII C 1

A. Problem: *How Does a Rocket Work?*

B. Materials Needed:

1. Elongated balloon
2. Monofilament fishline
3. Large paper clips
4. Rubber bands
5. Screw eyes to fasten line to wall

C. Procedure:

1. Fasten screw eyes to opposite walls.
2. Put fishline through screw eyes; tighten line and knot tautly.
3. Bend several paper clips so that they form an eye at one end that goes around the fishlinc.
4. Curve the middle part of the paper clip so that it roughly takes the shape of the balloon.
5. Attach a rubber band to each paper clip making a loop at the other end of the paper clip.
6. Slide the apparatus to one end of the line.
7. Insert balloon between curved part of paper clips and rubber bands. (They make a harness.)
8. Explain Newton's Third Law of Motion. This simply stated is "for every action there is an equal and opposite reaction."
9. Blow up balloon as much as possible; tightly close open end.
10. Release the balloon.

D. Results:

The balloon will shoot across the room with great speed.

E. Basic Facts and Supplemental Information:

1. The air in the balloon, upon being released, will push against the air that was outside of it; this will cause the balloon to move forward.
2. In other words, the "action" of the balloon moving forward is "equal and opposite" to the released air moving backwards.
3. The following are all examples of Newton's Third Law of Motion:
   a. high jumper in a track meet
   b. motorboat speeding
   c. sailboat sailing into the wind
   d. frog jumping off a lily pad
   e. hitting a baseball

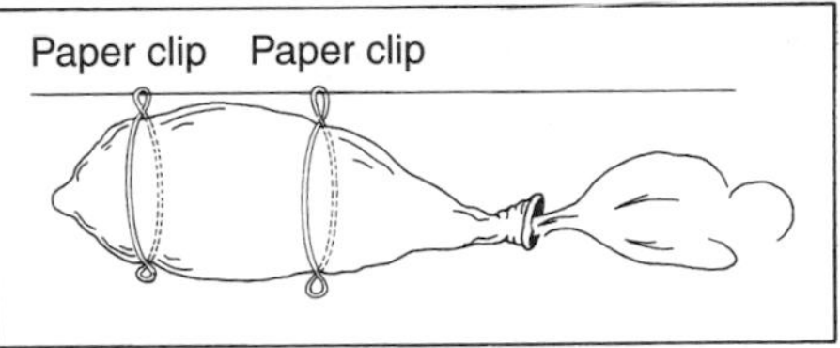

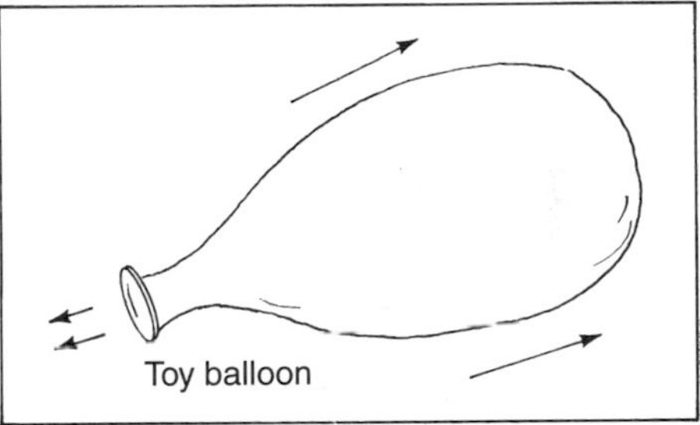

F. Thought Questions for Class Discussions:

1. How many examples of Newton's Third Law of Motion can you name?
2. Does this principle apply to a ball being kicked? or thrown?
3. What are Newton's First and Second Laws of Motion? (Study Activity II-F-1.)
4. How is the movement of the balloon similar to the motion of a jet plane?
5. What makes the balloon stop moving?
6. Would the balloon move if released in outer space?
7. If a student is on roller skates and facing a wall, what will happen if he/she pushes against the wall? Why?

G. Related Ideas for Further Inquiry:

1. An easy alternative activity to demonstrate this principle is to blow up the balloon and release it immediately.
2. Study Section I-B, "Air."
3. Study Section VII-B, "Solar System."
4. Study Section VIII-A, "Aviation."
5. Study other Activities in this Section.

H. Vocabulary Builders—Spelling Words:

1) **rocket** 2) **elongated** 3) **fishline** 4) **Newton** 5) **action** 6) **reaction** 7) **balloon** 8) **released**

I. Thought for Today:

"Don't forget that people will judge you by your actions, not intentions. You may have a heart of gold—but so does a hard-boiled egg."

Activity VIII C 2

A. Problem: *How Is Our Planet (Earth) Like a Spaceship? How Is It Different?*

B. Materials Needed:

1. Pictures and model of Earth
2. Pictures and models of spaceships

C. Procedure:

1. Have students list similarities between our planet travelling in space and a spaceship travelling in space.
2. Have class list differences between our planet traveling in space and a spaceship traveling in space.

D. Results:

1. Students will gain a newer and broader concept of our planet.
2. They will learn that there are no space stations in space for the Earth to take on new supplies.

E. Basic Facts and Supplemental Information:

1. Similarities between Earth and spaceships include:
   a. passengers
   b. oxygen supply
   c. food supply
   d. water resources
   e. mineral resources
   f. livable temperature range
   g. space to move about
   h. communication systems
2. Differences include:
   a. living plants
   b. living animals
   c. waterfalls
   d. caves
   e. buildings
   f. highways
   g. bridges, etc.

F. Thought Questions for Class Discussions:

1. Are we destroying our Earth's oxygen supply?
2. Are we destroying our Earth's water supply?
3. Are people interfering with the Earth's temperature through increased pollution?
4. Are we wasting our Earth's mineral resources?
5. Are we overpopulating the Earth?

Earth traveling through space

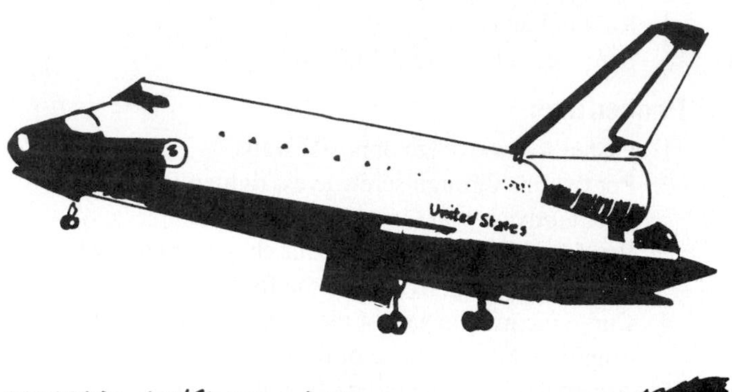

Spaceship (our "shuttle")

G. Related Ideas for Further Inquiry:

1. Study Section VII-B, "Solar System."
2. Study Section V-D, "Personal Health."
3. Study Section VIII-B, "Satellites."
4. Study Activity VIII-C-3, "How do astronauts maneuver a spacecraft?"
5. Study Activity VIII-C-5, "Can you solve this simulated space problem?"

H. Vocabulary Builders—Spelling Words:

1) **passengers** 2) **oxygen** 3) **water** 4) **resources** 5) **temperature** 6) **space**

I. Thought for Today:

"How would you like to be an astronaut just about to be shot into space and realize that the many parts of your spacecraft were all procured from the lowest bidder?"

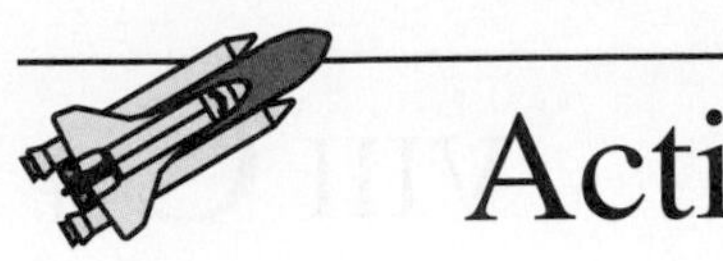

Activity VIII C 3

A. Problem: *How Do Astronauts Maneuver Spacecraft?*

B. Materials Needed:

1. Model of a spacecraft
2. Sketch of a spacecraft on chalkboard (or an overhead transparency)

C. Procedure:

1. Show the students the model or illustration.
2. Discuss space flights in general, including forward thrust.
3. Discuss the terms "rotation" and "axis" to be sure the class understands these terms.
4. Talk to the class about the dangers of the spaceship twisting or turning in launching or maneuvering.
5. Cite the three kinds of maneuvers that might occur or be desired, demonstrating each with the model or illustration:
   a. roll—rotation along the longitudinal axis (length of spaceship)
   b. yaw—rotation along the vertical axis (right and left motion)
   c. pitch—rotation along the short horizontal axis (up and down motion)
6. When students have become proficient in identifying each movement separately, use various combinations of any two maneuvers.
7. For more advanced students you can combine all three maneuvers.
8. Describe to class that there are central mechanisms which work to stop each kind of rotation, like an exhaust thrust. For each mechanism that turns the spaceship one way, there is another that turns it the opposite way (to correct it).
9. If a spacecraft rotates in one direction, by knowing what rotation is involved, the pilot could start a mechanism that would have the opposite affect, thus neutralizing any undesired rotation.

D. Results:

Students will learn that spaceships may twist, turn, and tumble, but there are mechanisms aboard to steady the spacecraft.

E. Basic Facts and Supplemental Information:

1. By use of these mechanisms it is possible to steer a spaceship in any direction in a three-dimensional space.

2. Gyroscopes are used to keep the spaceship in a stabilized position.
3. Using these controls it is possible for one spacecraft to join another spacecraft or a space station.
4. Each spaceship has a redundancy system aboard in case of a failure of one vital part.
5. On a long journey a spacecraft is deliberately rolled to keep the craft from overheating on the side facing the sun.

F. Thought Questions for Class Discussions:

1. What other dangers exist aboard a spaceship?
2. What would happen if one system failed?
3. What is weightlessness?
4. In space, aboard a spacecraft, is there any "up" or "down" or "sides"?

G. Related Ideas for Further Inquiry:

1. Study Section I-B, "Air."
2. Study Section VIII-B, "Satellites."
3. Study Section V-D, "Personal Health."
4. Study Section II-F, "Movement and Resistance."

H. Vocabulary Builders—Spelling Words:

1) **roll** 2) **yaw** 3) **pitch** 4) **rotate**
5) **maneuver** 6) **controls** 7) **redundant**
8) **redundancy** 9) **axis** 10) **rotation**

I. Thought for Today:

"When everything is coming your way, you're probably in the wrong lane."

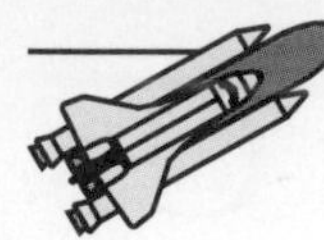

Activity VIII C 4

A. Problem: *What Are the Timing Problems of Landing on the Moon or a Space Station?*

B. Materials Needed:

1. School area large enough to have a 200-foot diameter track or surface in which a circular track can be drawn
2. Tape measure
3. Watch or clock that measures seconds

C. Procedure:

1. Mark off a distance of 200 feet on the school campus and mark the center point.
2. Roughly outline a circle using a 100-foot radius as a guide.
3. Measure a 12-foot diameter circle around the center point. This represents the Earth.
4. Roughly outline a typical path from the circumference of a small circle to intersect with the large circle, as shown in the drawing.
5. Have a student simulating a spacecraft start jogging around the large track (outside circle).
6. Record the time of how long it takes him/her to go around the projected path.
7. Have another student jog very slowly around the small track, inside the large track.
8. Record the time to see how long it takes him/her to follow the spacecraft's path.
9. Estimate point where the paths (joggers) will meet.
10. Estimate the position where the outside jogger must start in order to have the perfect time of intersection.
11. Set up the starting time of both joggers to see how close they can come at the time of intersection.

D. Results:

It will take several experimental joggings and quite accurate timing in order to have the student who is on the inside track intersect the one on the outside track at any exact position. Use the accompanying diagram to help in working out this Activity.

E. Basic Facts and Supplemental Information:

1. When a spaceship is leaving the Earth's gravity, exact calculations must be made so that the spaceship will leave the Earth's force of gravity at the exact time in order to give it the correct direction for intersecting the orbit of the moon.

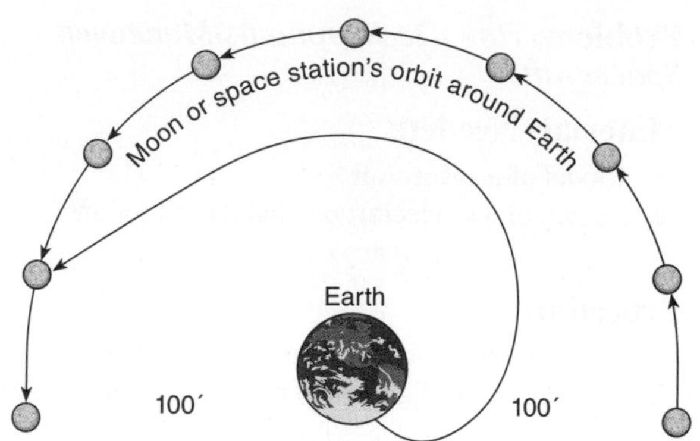

2. A good way to estimate travel time is to time the "Earth jogger" (inner jogger) to the point of anticipated intersection. Then have the "moon jogger" (outer jogger) start from this point and jog in the reverse direction in an equal amount of time. Mark the point where he/she stops. This should be the exact starting point of the "moon jogger."

F. Thought Questions for Class Discussions:

1. What is the speed of the moon?
2. What is the speed of our space ships?
3. If a space crew was off its target course, could they correct their course to reach the moon? How?

G. Related Ideas for Further Inquiry:

1. Study Section I-B, "Air."
2. Study Section VIII-B, "Satellites."
3. Study all Activities concerning "time." (Look up "time" in the Index.)
4. Study Activity VIII-B-3, "How can we tell time by using the sun?"
5. Study Activity VIII-B-1, "What keeps a satellite in orbit?"
6. Study Activity VIII-C-3, "How do astronauts maneuver a spacecraft?"
7. Integrate this Activity with math problems.
8. Study other Activities in this Section.

H. Vocabulary Builders—Spelling Words:

1) **timing** 2) **diameter** 3) **path** 4) **measure** 5) **area** 6) **orbit** 7) **Earth** 8) **moon** 9) **path**

I. Thought for Today:

"What was most significant about the lunar voyage, was not that people set foot on the moon but they set eye on Earth."—Norman Cousins

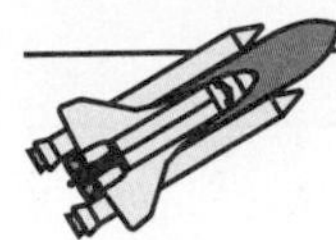

Activity

VIII C 5

A. Problem: *Can You Solve This Simulated Space Problem?*

B. Materials Needed:

Duplicated copies of test (See next page.)

C. Procedure:

1. Describe the problem cited on next page to your students.
2. Read and describe each of the test items.
3. Have each student mark answers.
4. Break into small groups. Have each group rank items.
5. Have the whole class ("Large Group") rank items.
6. Compare the three rankings.

D. Results:

Students will have fun with this game and learn a lot about problems which might be encountered in space exploration.

E. Basic Facts and Supplemental Information:

1. The original test included choices for the individual, small groups, and the total large group.
2. The columns on the chart represent:
   Yours = students' rankings
   A. = Accurate answer (bottom next page)
   D. = Absolute difference between "Yours" and "A"
   S.G. = Small Group Consensus
   S.G.D. = Small Group Difference
   L.G. = Large Group
   L.G.D. = Large Group Difference
3. The differences can be totaled and divided by 15 for the average differences.
4. Usually the small group has a lower total score and difference score than the individual, and the large group has a lower total score and difference score than the small group. This supports the concept that the more people involved in the solution of a problem, the better the results that will be obtained (democracy in action).

F. Thought Questions for Class Discussions:

1. What would be some other problems confronting space explorers on the moon?
2. What would be some problems confronting space explorers on Mars?
3. If you had to explore 200 miles on the moon, leaving your spacecraft, what supplies and equipment would you take?

G. Related Ideas for Further Inquiry:

1. Study Section I-B, "Air."
2. Study Section VII-B, "Solar System."
3. Study Section V-D, "Personal Health."
4. Study other Activities in this Section.

H. Vocabulary Builders—Spelling Words:

Use the items listed in "Astronaut Test."

I. Thought for Today:

"Prejudice is being down on something you're not up on."

ASTRONAUT TEST

Instructions: You are a member of a space crew originally scheduled to rendezvous with a mother ship on the lighted surface of the moon. Due to mechanical difficulties, however, your ship was forced to land at a spot some 200 miles from the rendezvous point. During re-entry and landing, much of the equipment aboard was damaged and, since survival depends on reaching the mother ship, the most critical items available must be chosen for the 200-mile trip. Below are listed the 15 items left intact and undamaged after landing. Your task is to rank order them in terms of their importance for your crew in allowing them to reach the rendezvous point. Place the number 1 by the most important item, the number 2 by the second most important, and so on through number 15, the least important.

	YOURS	A.	D.	S.G.	S.G.D.	L.G.	L.G.D.
Box of matches							
Food concentrate							
50 feet of nylon rope							
Parachute silk							
Portable heating unit							
Two .45 caliber pistols							
One case of dehydrated milk							
Two 100-pound tanks of oxygen							
Stellar map of the moon							
Life raft							
Magnetic compass							
Five gallons of water							
Signal flares							
First-aid kit containing injection needles							
Solar-powered FM receiver-transmitter							
TOTAL							
DIVIDE BY 15							

Courtesy NASA (Modified by author)
(Answers and reasons are found on next page.)

ANSWERS TO "ASTRONAUT TEST"

ITEM:	RANKING:	REASON FOR RANKING:
Box of matches	15	Little or no use on the moon
Food concentrate	4	Supplies Daily Food
50 feet of nylon rope	6	Use in tying the injured, helps when climbing
Parachute silk	8	Shelter against sun's rays
Portable heating unit	13	Useful only if party landed on dark side
Two .45 caliber pistols	11	Self-propulsion devices could be made from them
One case of dehydrated milk	12	Food; mixed with water for drinking
Two 100-pound tanks of oxygen	1	Fills respiration requirements
Stellar map of the moon	3	One of the principal means of finding direction
Life Raft	9	Its carbon dioxide bottles could assist in self-propulsion across chasms and the like
Magnetic compass	14	Probably no magnetic Poles, thus useless
Five gallons of water	2	Replenishes water loss; e.g., sweating
Signal flares	10	Distress call within line of sight
First-aid kit containing injection needles	7	Oral pills or injection medicine valuable
Solar-powered FM receiver-transmitter	5	Distress signal transmitter, possible communication with mother ship

GLOSSARY

Science words and expressions, as well as other words needing explanation, are included in this Glossary. Words are broken down into their basic syllables.

ab a lo ne: large, univalve shellfish.
a bra sion: scraping or wearing away, usually skin damage.
ab so lute zer o: the lowest possible temperature (0° K., –459.67° F, or –273.15° C.).
ab sorb: to take in, or suck up, liquids.
ac cel er a tion: the capacity to gain speed.
ac id: a substance, sour to taste, which dissolves in water. In chemical tests acids turn blue, litmus red.
ac id rain: rain from the burning of fossil fuels, particularly sulphur dioxide and nitrogen dioxide.
a corn: the nut, or fruit, of an oak tree.
ac tion: the act or process of doing.
ad ap ta tion: a change in structure, form or habits to fit different conditions.
ad di tive: any substance added to food or drink to enhance its flavor, color, or life span.
AIDS: disease affecting the immune system, usually fatal.
ai ler on: hinged surface on the trailing edge of an airplane's wing to aid in banking and turning.
air craft: machine for flying in the air; either lighter or heavier than air.
al co hol: usually means *ethyl,* or *grain,* alcohol, a colorless liquid with a strong odor formed by the action of organisms on sugar. Alcohol has many uses in science and industry.
al gae: group of plants that have chlorophyll but do not have true roots, stems, or leaves.
al ka line: water soluble substance with hydroxide ions (OH^-).
al li ga tor: a large reptile with a long body, four short legs, a thick skin, and a long tail. Alligators live in rivers and marshes in warm parts of America.
al ni co mag net: a very strong permanent magnet made of aluminum, nickel, cobalt, and iron.
al tim e ter: instrument for measuring heights; most frequently used in planes for determining altitude.
a lu mi num: a silvery, metallic metal, used for its lightness.
am mo nia: a solution in water of a gas obtained by distilling organic bodies containing nitrogen.
am phet a mine: drug to overcome fatigue, mental depression; also used in diets.
am phib i an: usually refers to members of the class Amphibia, which includes frogs, toads, and salamanders. The young of these animals are hatched and develop in water, but the adults of many species emerge from the water to live on land.
am pli tude: the size of vibration or the height of a wave.
a nat o my: the science of body structure in plants and animals.
a nem i a: reduction in red blood cells or hemoglobin in the blood.
an e mom e ter: instrument that measures wind speed.
an i mal: any living organism that has senses and can move.
an nu als: plants that live for about one year.
an ode: positive pole on a battery.
an ten nae: feelers on the head of an insect.
an thrax: a contagious disease, attended by fever, of human beings and animals.
an ther: top of the stamen in plants.
an thra cite: hard coal which gives much heat and little smoke.
an ti dote: something that hinders or removes the effects of poison or disease.
an ti sep tic: a solution which will check or prevent the growth of bacteria; a disinfectant.
an ti tox in: a substance produced in living tissues of plant or animal to check or hinder or make neutral a bacterial poison that produced it.
ap o gee: point that is the greatest distance from the Earth of orbiting objects.
ap pa ra tus: the equipment, tools, device, or appliance by which a process of work or play is carried on.
a quar i um: tank or bowl in which water plants and water animals are kept.
a rach nid: any of a large group of small arthropods including spiders, scorpions, mites, etc. An arachnid is air-breathing, has four pairs of walking legs, and no antennae; the body is usually divided into two regions.
Ar chi me des: early Greek who invented the screw to raise water.
Ar chi me des' Prin ci ple: a floating object displaces the weight of water equal to its own weight.
ar ter y: any of the blood vessels that carry blood away from the heart.
ar thro pod: one of a large group of invertebrate animals having segmented (jointed) bodies and legs. Insects, arachnids, and crustaceans are arthropods.
ar ti fi cial: made or contrived by human labor; not natural.
as cend: move upward, climb.
a scor bic ac id: vitamin C.
as ter oid: any one of the very small bodies revolving around the sun between the orbit of Mars and the orbit of Jupiter.
a stig ma tism: defect of the eye, or lens of the eye, that makes objects look indistinct or gives imperfect images.
as tro naut: person trained to fly in space.
as tron o mer: a scientist who studies the earth's relation to the sun, moon, stars, and other heavenly bodies.
a stron o my: study of stars, planets, and other space objects.
at mos phere: the air that surrounds the Earth.
atom: the smallest particle of an element that can exist. Atoms are the very small particles that make up molecules.
a tom ic: pertaining to an atom or atoms.
a tom ic en er gy: energy from the nucleus of the atom.
at tract: to draw to oneself as a magnet draws iron filings toward itself.
au to mat ic: able to move or act without help from another source.
ax is: an imaginary line around which a body rotates.

back bone: the bony column tht extends along the middle of the back in man, mammals, birds, reptiles, and fishes; the spine. The backbone consists of many separate bones, called vertebrae, held together by muscles and tendons and separated by pads of cartilage. The backbone protects the spinal cord, which it encloses.
bac te ria: a group of plant organisms, too small to be seen without a microscope.
bak ing so da: sodium carbonate; used in baking as leavening agent.
bal ance: an apparatus for weighing.
Bal ance of Nature: ample food supply for all organisms.

ball-and-sock et joint: a flexible skeletal joint formed by a ball or knob of one bone fitted into the cupped end of another bone. The shoulder and hip are ball-and-socket joints. As such they permit some motion in every direction.
bar bi tu rate: drug used as a sedative or pain deadener.
bas es: chemicals that react opposite to acids; contain hydroxyl ions.
ba sic: in chemistry, an alkaline, having the properties of a base.
beak: bill or nib of a bird.
bea ver: amphibious animal, found in lakes and ponds; builds underwater homes.
Ben e dicts So lu tion: a chemical solution used to test for sugar(s).
Ber nouil li's Prin ci ple: a fast moving fluid has less pressure sideways than it does forward.
bi cus pid: a double-pointed tooth; human adults have eight such teeth.
bi o de grad a ble: easily decomposable, especially biologically.
bi o tic com mun i ty: area where living things are mutually dependent.
bite: seizing by teeth or mouth.
blind spot: a round spot on the retina of the eye not sensitive to light.
blood ves sel: any of many tubes in the body through which blood flows. The three types of blood vessels are arteries, veins, and capillaries.
blow hole: hole for breathing located in the top of the head of whales and some other air-breathing animals. The blowhole usually has a flap of skin that keeps water out of the animal's lungs.
boil er: a container for heating liquids.
boil ing point: point where a liquid changes to a gas.
brain: the part of the nervous system enclosed in the skull.
breed ing: process of developing or propagating plants or animals.
burns: injury due to excessive heat.
buoy an cy: quality of floating on the surface of a liquid such as water.
butter milk the slightly acid liquid left after churning butter.

caf feine: the stimulant found in coffee and tea.
cal ci um: silver-white chemical element found in limestone.
cal o rie: unit of heat. Heat required to raise one gram of water one degree centigrade.
Cal o rie: (Big "C" calorie): Unit of heat, a thousand times that of "small c calorie." This unit is used in evaluating foods.
cam ou flage: disguise, change appearance.
cap il lar y: a small blood vessel with very thin walls. A network of capillaries joins the arteries and veins.
car bo hy drates: sugars and starches.
car bon: chemical element found in diamonds, graphite, and organic compounds.
car bon cy cle: sequence of states that the element passes through.
car bon di ox ide: a heavy, colorless, odorless gas present in the air. Green plants use carbon dioxide to make food.
car bon mon ox ide: a deadly gas, usually the product of incomplete combustion.
car di o pul mon a ry re sus ci ta tion: a method of restoring breathing and/or heartbeat to a victim.
car ni vore: flesh-eating animal.
car te sion di ver: A floating device that can be made to rise or sink.
car ti lage: the firm, tough, flexible substance that forms parts of the skeleton of vertebrates; gristle.
Cas si o pe ia: a northern constellation between Andromeda and Cepheus.
cath ode: negative pole on a battery.
ce les ti al: having to do with space, sky.
cell: the unit of living matter, usually microscopic, of which all plants and animals are made. Cells vary in form according to their use.
Cel si us: scale for measuring heat with water freezing at zero degrees and water boiling at one hundred degrees.
cen ti grade: same as Celsius.
cen trif u gal: apparent force moving away from center.
cen trip e tal: moving toward the center.
chain re ac tion: chemical reactions where each step is initiated by former step.
char ac ter is tic: a special quality or feature.
chem i cal: a substance obtained when two or more substances act upon one another to cause permanent change.
chem is try: the study of elements and compounds and the reactions they undergo.
chlam y di a: most common, severe venereal disease.
chlo rine: a heavy poisonous gas used in liquid form as a disinfectant.
chlo ro fluor o car bons: chemicals used in sprays destroying ozone.
chlo ro phyll: the green-colored material in the cells of green plants.
chol er a: an acute disease of the stomach and intestines.
cho les ter ol: a substance contained in all animal fats.
chrys a lis: a form of an insect when it is encased in a pupa, cocoon.
cir cuit: a complete path made of conductors through which an electric current can flow from the source of electrical energy and back again.
cir cu late: move around, move through a closed system as the blood moves through the blood vessels, or as air moves through a hot-air heating system.
cir cum fer ence: boundary line of a circle, every point in circumference of a circle is at the same distance from the center.
cit rus: relating to fruits such as the orange, lemon, lime, and grapefruit.
clas si fy: to arrange in groups, usually according to certain structures or functions.
clay: fine-grained earth, usually silicates.
clock wise: moving in the direction of the hands on a clock.
cloud: a visible mass of condensed watery vapor in the atmosphere.
coal: combustible solid mineral used for burning and heating.
co caine: drug, narcotic, local anesthetic, addictive.
cold-blood ed: having blood that is about the same temperature as the air or water around the animal; having blood that changes its temperature as the temperature of the surroundings changes.
com bus tion: the act of burning.
com et: a bright heavenly body with a starlike center and often with a cloudy tail of light.
com mu ni ca ble: that which can be spread or communicated from person to person or place to place, as a disease.
com mu ni ca tion: imparting knowledge, opinions, or facts.
com pare: to find out or point out how things are alike and how they differ.
com pass: an instrument for showing directions; it consists of a free-turning magnetic needle; an instrument for drawing a circle.
com pli men tar y: two or more things that enrich other(s).
com pound: to put together.
com press: a pad of folded cloth.
com pres sion: the act of pushing together or bunching up.
con cave: lens shallower in the center.
con clu sion: final decision.
con den sa tion: change of a gas or vapor into a liquid.

con dense: to change from a gas to a liquid.
con duc tion: the passing of heat from one particle to another. The particles vibrate but do not move from one place to another.
cones: the seed-bearing part of pine, cedar, fir, and other evergreen trees, light receptive cells in the eyes.
con ser va tion: preservation; avoidance of waste.
con stel la tion: a group of stars that seems to form a picture in the sky.
con ta gious: that which is communicable, catching, as a disease; can be spread from person to person.
con tam i nate: to spoil or make impure by contact with waste matter or impurities.
con test ing: competing with others for something, fighting; struggling.
con ti nen tal code: scheme of dots and dashes used in telegraphy.
con tin ent: one of the seven large land masses of Earth.
con tour far ming: following natural ridges and furrows to avoid soil erosion.
con tract: to draw together or to make shorter; to shrink or become smaller.
con vection: the movement of particles of a liquid or a gas from a cold place to a warmer one. The movement is somewhat circular, the colder material pushing the warmer material sideways and upward.
con vex: lens thicker in the center.
core: inner part as the Earth's core.
cor ne a: the transparent part of the outer coat of the eyeball. It covers the iris and the pupil.
coun ter clock wise: moving in the opposite direction of the hands on a clock.
CPR: See cardiopulmonary resuscitation.
cray fish: a freshwater animal of the class Crustacea that looks like a small lobster; a similar but larger saltwater shellfish.
croc o dile: large, amphibious lizard, rounded nose.
crus ta cean: any of a group of water animals having tough shells, jointed bodies and legs, and gills for breathing. Crabs, lobsters, and shrimps are crustaceans.
crys tal: a solid substance with a regular shape.
cu ta ne ous: pertaining to the skin.

dam: a framework to obstruct water.
DDT: potent, persistent, pesticide; contaminates food, causes many birds to lay eggs with too thin shells.
de cay: to rot; also, material that has rotted, as tooth decay.
dec i bel: a unit for measuring the volume of sound.
de cid u ous: a tree or bush that sheds its leaves annually.
de com po si tion: to separate into simpler elements.
de flate: to let the air or gas out of an inflated object.
de ger mi nat ed: that grain from which the germ has been removed.
de gree: a step in the scale; a stage in a process; a unit for measuring temperature.
de hy dra tion: the process of removing water from food and other substances; drying.
del ta: the deposit of earth and sand that collects at the mouth of some rivers. A delta is usually three-sided.
den si ty: the mass per unit volume of a substance.
den tin: the hard material of which the main part of the tooth is composed.
de press ant: a substance that pulls down, or lowers.
der ma tol o gist: medical doctor who specializes in the study of the skin.
de sa li ni za tion: removal of salt from sea water.
de scend: move downward.
des ert: dry, barren land.
de ter gent: a cleansing substance.
dew: condensed water from the air.
di ag no sis: the identification of a disease by its symptoms.
di a phragm: the partitions or walls of tissues, sinew, or muscle, for the purpose of separating and protecting adjoining parts in the body or in instruments.
di a stol ic: the pressure of the heart when it is in a state of relaxation.
di et: the kind and amount of food and drink that a person or animal usually eats.
di gest: to change (food) within the stomach and intestines so that it can be absorbed by the body.
di ges tive juice: a juice produced by the body for use in the digestion of food.
di late: to make wider or larger.
di no saur: an extinct reptile of the Mesozoic era.
dir ig i ble: a balloon type airship.
dis ease: an illness or weakened condition of health.
dis in fec tant: something that destroys bacteria and/or viruses.
dis solve: to make liquid; to become liquid, especially by putting or being put into a liquid. When a solid has dissolved completely, it cannot be separated from the liquid by filtering.
dis til la tion: a process where liquids are separated into their component parts by heating and condensing.
do mains: small, jumbled parts of a piece of iron or steel and when aligned become a magnet.
down ers: slang term for drugs that are depressing.
drag: in air travel, the resistance of the gaseous medium on the airship.
drone: nonworking male of most bee species.
drought: a long period with no rain.
drug: prescribed medicine, narcotic, habit-forming; also illegal medicines.
dry ice: solid carbon dioxide, refrigerant.
dys en ter y: a painful disease of the intestines.

earth quake: undulating movement of the earth's crust.
e clipse: a darkening of the sun or the moon.
e col o gist: a scientist who studies the relation of living things to their community and to each other.
ec o sys tem: area where living things are mutually dependent.
egg: oval bodies laid by birds, fish, and reptiles; reproductive cell.
e lec tric it y: form of energy resulting from the flow of electrons.
e lec trode: material used to make an electric cell.
e lec tro mag net: a piece of iron that becomes a temporary magnet when an electric current passes through wire coiled around it.
e lec tron: particle that moves rapidly around the nucleus of an atom. Every electron has a negative charge.
e lec tro scope: a device for detecting small changes in electricity.
el e ment: a part; that cannot be detected or separated without chemical analysis.
e lim i na tion: the act of getting rid of, removing.
El Niño: major changes in the weather pattern due to abnormally high ocean temperatures.
e lo de a: an aquatic plant often used in aquariums. It floats beneath the surface, but its roots can take hold in the soil under low-water conditions.
em bry o: an unborn or unhatched offspring.
em phy se ma: an abnormal swelling of body tissue, often found in the air sacs in the lungs.
en dan gered species: an organism threatened with extinction.
en er gy: ability to do work or to act; capacity for work.
en vir on ment: surroundings of an organism.
en zyme: a catalyst that helps bring about chemical changes in the body.
e ro sion: process of eating away or of being worn away gradually. In nature, wind and water cause most erosion of rock and soil.
es cape ve loc i ty: the speed of spaceship to overcome earth's gravity.

es tu ar y: wide tidal mouth of a river, an arm of the sea.
Eu sta chian tube: slender canal between the pharynx and the middle ear.
eu troph i ca tion: process(es) of aiding nutrition.
e vap o rate: to change from a liquid into a gas. Molecules of the liquid escape from its surface into the air in the form of vapor.
e vap o ra tion: the process of evaporating.
ev er green: having green leaves throughout the year.
ex cre tion: the act of expelling waste matter.
ex er cise: movement, put into action, train.
ex ert: to use; put into use; use fully.
ex hale: breathe out.
ex pand: to grow large or cause to grow larger.
ex pec to rate: to spit.
ex per i ment: to test; a test that is made to find out something.
ex tinc tion: no longer existing.
ex tin guish: put out a fire.

Fahr en heit: a thermometer on which the boiling point of water is 212° and the freezing point is 32°.
fam ine: scarcity of food, destroy with hunger.
fast food: food that can be prepared and served quickly particularly at a snack bar or restaurant.
fa tigue: tirednes or weariness.
fats: greasy or oily substances of the body. Also oils and parts of meat or other foods that yield oils and grease.
fault: a break in a mass of rock in which one part slides past another part.
fer men ta tion: the chemical change which causes milk to sour, apple juice to turn to vinegar, and starches to turn to sugars.
ferns: any of a group of plants having roots, stems, and leaves, but no flowers, and reproducing by spores instead of seeds.
fer tile: capable of growing, producing fruit or vegetation.
fer til i za tion: the joining of male and female gametes.
fer ti li zer: any material to improve the quality of the soil.
fil a ment: thread-like; part of the stamen bearing the anther.
fil ter: a device for passing liquids or gases through some substance in order to remove certain particles; the material (often paper) through which a liquid or gas passes so that certain things can be removed; to put a material through a filter.
fire: active burning, combustion.
fire box: the place in which fuel is burned in a furnace or boiler.
fire ex tin guish er: device for putting out fires.
fire tri an gle: the three elements needed for fires; heat, material, and oxygen.
fish: vertebrate animals living in water and breathing with gills.
fis sion: a method of reproduction in which one-celled living thing divides, forming two new individuals; the splitting of large atoms such as uranium atoms into smaller atoms, releasing atomic energy.
flesh: the soft part of the body that covers the bones and is covered by skin. Flesh consists mostly of muscles and fat; the soft part of fruits and vegetables.
flood: an overflowing of water on land.
floss ing: act of using dental threads to scrape teeth.
flow er: part of the plant that contains the reproductive organs.
fog: a thick, cloud layer of water suspended in the atmosphere or near the Earth's surface.
food chain: a series of organisms, each of which is eaten by the next organism.
food web: the relationships of many organisms which can be eaten by many other organisms.
force: any cause that produces changes in, starts, or stops motion of, an object.
fore cas ting: predicting, estimating.
form: a shape; to shape or make; a condition or state.
fos sil: preserved remains of a living thing.
fos sil fu els: materials from the past that are used for energy.
frac tion al dis til la tion: removing each material separately by continuing to increase temperature.
frame work: a support or skeleton; the stiff parts that give shape to something.
freez ing point: the temperature at which a liquid freezes or changes to a solid. The freezing point of water at sea level is 32 degrees Fahrenheit or 0 degrees Centigrade.
fre quen cy: the number of times any action occurs.
fric tion: the rubbing of one body against another.
frost: white, frozen dew.
fuel: a substance, or mixture of substances, that can be burned to produce heat or some other form of energy.
ful crum: balance point on a lever.
fun gi: any of a group of plants without flowers, leaves, or green coloring matter.
fu sion: the combining of small atoms, such as hydrogen, forming larger atoms and releasing atomic energy.

gal ax y: a huge group of stars.
gam etes: reproductive cells in plants and animals.
gar ter snake: a common, harmless snake that is brown or green with long yellow stripes.
gas: a material, like air, that is neither a solid nor a liquid, they move about freely, spreading apart until they fill all the available space.
gas, nat u ral: gas that is extracted from the Earth.
gas oline: a fuel from petroleum used in internal combustion engines.
gen er a tor: a device for transforming mechanical energy into electric energy.
ge o graph ic North Pole: one end of the axis about which the Earth rotates. The axis is an imaginary line through the center of the Earth. The geographic North Pole marks the most northerly point on the Earth.
geo graph ic South Pole: one end of the Earth's axis. The geographic South Pole is the most southerly point on the Earth.
ge ol o gist: scientist who studies the Earth.
ge o therm al: relating to the internal heat of the Earth.
ger mi na tion: starting to grow or develop, sprouting.
germs: microscopic animals or plants that cause disease.
gey ser: a spring of hot water that gushes into the air.
gill: in certain water animals, a body structure used for breathing. The gill takes in oxygen from the water habitat and sends out carbon dioxide.
gla cier: a large mass of ice, formed from snow, that moves slowly down a mountainside or sloping valley, or outward from a center as in a continental glacier. The movement of glaciers causes erosion and piling up of soil and rocks.
glands: small organs in the body which produce different substances to be used by or discharged from the body.
gold: heavy, yellow, metallic element that is a precious metal.
gon or rhe a: a serious venereal disease that affects mucous membranes.
gourd: a climbing plant like a squash; hollowed shell of same.
grass es: plants with blade-like leaves, single seed and includes barley, oats, rye, and wheat.
grav i ty: natural force that tends to move objects toward the center of the Earth or other celestial body.
Green house Ef fect: rising of the atmosphere's temperature due to pollutants that reflect Earth's radiant heating back toward Earth.
guin ea pig: a small, fat mammal in the rat family with short ears and short tail.
gul ly: a small valley or a ditch cut by running water.
gup py: a very small, usually brightly colored fish that lives in tropical freshwater.
hab i tat: the place where an animal or plant lives and grows.

half-life: time of a radioactive material to lose half of its original substance.
hal lu ci na tion: apparent perception by senses that are not actually present.
ham ster: small, short-tailed rodent with large cheek pouches.
har mon ics: mixed tones and overtones.
hear ing graph: a graph that shows a person's hearing range or ability.
heart: a small muscle that pumps the blood to all parts of the body and back again.
heat: quality of being hot from molecular action.
Heim lich Ma neu ver: a first aid procedure to help a choking person.
hel i cop ter: type of aircraft that gets its left by horizontal, overhead revolving blades.
he li um: second lightest element, a gas, used in airships and balloons.
hem i sphere: half of a sphere; the Earth is divided into a Northern Hemisphere and a Southern Hemisphere by the equator.
he mo phil i a: a condition in which the blood fails to clot quickly.
hem or rhage: escape of blood from a broken vessel.
herb i cides: chemicals used to destroy unwanted plants.
her bi vore: any animal that feeds on plants.
her pes: a viral infection of the skin or mucous membrane(s).
hi ber nate: to spend the winter in a sleep or in an inactive condition. In true hibernation, body processes are slowed.
highs: high pressure air masses identified with good weather.
ho mog e nized: blended or mixed by force into one part, as homogenized milk.
Ho mo sa pi ens: only living species of the genus Homo is the human being.
hor i zon: the line where the Earth and sky meet.
hu mid i ty: dampness and moisture of the air.
hu mus: soil made from decaying leaves and other vegetable matter.
hur ri cane: a violent storm with winds from 70 to 100 m.p.h. usually with rain and thunder.
hy dro car bons: chemical compounds that contain only hydrogen and carbon. Four groups of hydrocarbons are found in automobile exhausts.
hy dro chlor ic acid: a solution of hydrogen chloride gas in water.
hy dro e lec tric: having to do with the production of electricity by water power.
hy dro gen: a gas, the lightest of all elements.
hy drol o gist: an expert in the study of water.
hy drom e ter: a device to determine the specific gravity of liquids (thickness and weight).
hy drox ide: a metallic compound containing the "OH" ion.
hy poth e sis: an educated guess, a proposition made for reasoning.

ice: solid form of water.
Ice house Ef fect: lowering of the atmosphere's temperature due to pollutants that prevent the sun's radiation from striking the Earth by reflecting back the sun's rays before they strike the Earth.
ig ne ous: of or having to do with fire; produced by fire, great heat, or the action of a volcano.
il lu sion: misapprehension of the state of affairs.
im age: the view seen by the reflection of light rays.
im mu ni za tion: the state of being immune or protected from a disease.
in can des cent: to glow with heat.
in ci sion: a cut or gash.
in ci sor: tooth having a sharp edge for cutting.
in clined plane: sloping, flat surface.
in cu ba tor: an apparatus for hatching eggs artificially.
in er ti a: tendency to remain in the state one is in whether stationary or in motion.
in fec tion: a condition or disease caused by contact with certain harmful organisms.
in flate: distend, puff up.
in fra red: wavelength greater than red end of visible light.
in hale: to breathe in, to draw into the lungs.
in ner ear: the innermost part of the ear. The inner ear is made up of several canals that are filled with fluid. This part of the ear is connected to the brain by a nerve. When the fluid vibrates, it sets up impulses in this nerve which are received in the brain as sound.
in sect any member of a group of small invertebrate animals having a body that has three parts, three pairs of legs, two feelers, and usually two pairs of wings.
in sec ti cides: chemicals used to kill insects.
in stru ment: a tool, mechanical device.
in su la tion: a material or materials that covers another to prevent loss of heat or electricity.
in ten si ty: amount of heat, light, or sound per unit.
in tes tine: the part of the digestive system that extends from the lower end of the stomach. It receives food from the stomach, digests it further, and absorbs it. The intestine consists of two parts: the small intestine, a coiled tube that is about 22 ft. long in the adult; and the large intestine, a thicker tube about 5 ft. long.
in ver sion: act of being inverted or reverse.
in ver te brate: without a backbone; an animal without a backbone. All animals except fishes, amphibians, reptiles, birds, and mammals are invertebrates.
i o dized: having had iodine added.
i ris: the colored area that surrounds the pupil of the eye.
i ron: a metal that rusts easily and is strongly attracted by magnets; a mineral important to the body.
ir ra di a tion: emitting atomic or subatomic rays or particles.

jet stream: strong winds that circle the Earth about 6 miles (10 kilometers) above the Earth.
joint: in an animal, a place where two bones are joined together by ligaments. The movable joints are kept moist by a liquid. Some joints are not movable.

Kel vin: a temperature scale measured in Celsius degrees with absolute zero equal to –273° C.
ki net ic en er gy: the energy of a body that is in motion which includes its mass and its velocity.
king dom: one of the main sub-divisions of all living things.
Kra ka to a: the volcano that produced the greatest noise known.

lac er a tion: a jagged tear or cut.
la goon: enclosed body of water near an ocean or lake.
land fill: waste material used to reclaim land and/or burying rubbish.
lar va: the form in which most insects hatch from the egg, wingless and sometimes wormlike.
lar ynx: a hollow muscular organ forming an air passage to the lungs and holding the vocal cords.
Lat in: language of the ancient Romans. It is still used in science and religion.
lat i tude: distance north or south of the equator, measured in degrees.
la va: molten rock flowing from a volcano; rock formed by the cooling of this molten rock.
lay er: one thickness or fold.
leaf: flat usually green plant part growing from stem.
leg umes: vegetables that have pods, such as peas and beans.

lens: the part of the eye, glasses, or camera, that focuses light to form clear images.
lev er: a bar resting on a pivot used to lift heavy objects.
leu ke mi a: a disease in which there is an extra large number of white blood cells.
lift: upward force on an airplane wing caused by upper curved surface of the wing which thins the air over the wing causing greater pressure below the wing.
lig a ment: a band of strong tissue that connects bones or holds parts of the body in place.
light ning: discharge or flash of electricity in the sky.
lime: calcium oxide, used in neutralizing soil acids.
lime stone: a sedimentary rock formed under water, usually from the remains of sea animals.
lines of force: invisible lines from one pole of a magnet to the other pole that indicate the direction in which the force of the magnet is acting.
liq uid: a material that is not a solid or a gas and that can flow freely like water and take the shape of its container.
li quor: alcoholic beverages.
lit mus pap er: a paper whose dye turns red in acid conditions and blue in alkaline.
lit ter: that which is scattered about needlessly.
liv er wort: a plant that is somewhat amorphous like a moss.
liz ard: large groups of reptiles with thin bodies and four legs, live in hot, dry areas.
loam: vegetable matter with clay and sand.
lo co mo tion: moving from one place to another.
lode stone: a kind of iron ore, called magnetite, that attracts iron and some kinds of steel just as a magnet does.
lows: low pressure air masses identified with poor weather.
lu bri cate: to oil to reduce friction.
lu mi nous: giving off light.
lungs: the breathing organs found in the chest of many animals with backbones.
lymph: colorless fluid containing white blood cells.

ma chine: a mechanical vehicle.
mag gots: wormlike larvae of an insect.
mag ma: liquid, molten rock from the Earth's mantle or crust. It cools to form igneous rock.
mag net: a piece of iron, steel or alloy that attracts or repels iron or other like substances.
mag net ic: having the properties of a magnet.
mag net ic pole: each end of a magnet.
mag ne tize: to give something the properties or qualities of a magnet.
mag ni fy ing glass: a lens which enlarges the viewing area.
mam mal: any number of a group of warm-blooded vertebrates that have fur or hair and that produce milk to feed their young.
mam ma ry: of the human female breast, milk secreting gland.
man u fac tured: having been made by people, and not the result of a natural cause.
mar ble: the metamorphic crystallized form of limestone, white or colored; it is capable of taking a high polish.
mar i jua na: poisonous drug made from hemp leaves and flowers.
mass: volume.
meat: the flesh of an animal, the muscles of an animal.
me di a: the main means of mass communication; the middle layer of the wall of the artery or other vessel.
melt ing point: the temperate at which a solid substance begins to melt or become liquid.
mem brane: a thin, soft layer of tissue in the body of an animal or plant.
met a mor phic: characterized by change of form; having to do with change of form. A metamorphic rock is one that has been changed to a different form by heat, pressure, or both.
met a mor pho sis: change of form, example—tadpoles to frogs.
me te or ite: a large meteor that falls to the earth before it is completely burned up.
mi cro scope: a magnifying instrument that has lens or combination of lenses for making objects appear larger aid of light.
mid dle ear: in humans, the cavity of the ear that is separated from the other ear by the eardrum, and which contains three small bones called the hammer, the stirrup, and the anvil. The cavity of the middle ear is filled with air and is connected to the throat by a tube.
mi gra tion: a move from one place to settle in another.
milk: fluid secreted by female mammals to feed their young.
Milky Way: our galaxy.
mil lion: one thousand thousand; 1,000,000.
min er als: inorganic substances; substances that are neither vegetable nor animal in nature.
mix ture: two or more substances mixed together but not chemically combined. Each of the substances has it own properties and doesn't change when in contact with the other substance or substances present.
moist: slightly wet or damp.
mol e cule: the smallest particle into which a substance can be divided without changing the chemical nature of that substance.
mol lusk: invertebrates that live in water which includes oysters, clams, mussels, snails, squids, and octopi.
mo men tum: force with which a body moves. It is equal to its mass times its velocity.
mo ne ra: one-celled animals without any definite structure; recently named a kingdom.
moss: any of various very small, soft, green or brown plants that grow close together like a carpet on the ground, on rocks, on trees, etc.
moth ball: naphthalene or camphor which repels moths.
moun tain: large mass of earth and rock above ground level.
mul ti sen sor y: pertaining to two or more senses.
mus cle: a bundle of fibers, made up of cells, that contracts or extends to move a part of the body.
musk rats: a North American water rodent, somewhat like a rat but larger.

nar cot ic: a substance that eases pain and may cause sleep.
na sal pas sage: air pathway inside the head extending from the nostrils to the throat.
nat u ral: found in nature, not artificial.
nec tar: a sugary liquid found in the flowers of some plants.
nerv ous sys tem: a network of nerves and nerve centers in a person or animal. In man, the central nervous system is made up of the brain and spinal cord.
neu trons: neutral charge masses that lie within the nucleus of atoms.
New ton: formulator of the Laws of Motion.
ni a cine: nicotine acid, a vitamin, the lack of produces pellagra, (red, dry, skin, and a sore mouth).
niche: area in which an organism usually lives.
nic o tine: the drug contained in tobacco.
ni trates: soluble salts needed by plants and animals for growth; used to fertilize the soil.
ni tro gen: a colorless, odorless gas that constitutes about four-fifths of the Earth's atmosphere.
non mag net ic: lacking the properties of a magnet; not attracted by a magnet.
non re new a ble: any substance that cannot be restored or replaced.
nu cle ar: having to do with the nucleus (center) of the atom.
nu cle us, plural nu cle i: the part of a cell that controls much of what happens in the cell . . . the central part of an atom.

nu tri ent: a food substance that gives nourishment to the body.
nu tri tion: nourishment; food; the act or process of absorbing food or nourishment.

oat: edible seed, small grain, thought to reduce cholesterol.
ob ser va tion: the act of seeing and noting; something seen and noted.
oc clud ed front: where the cold front overtakes the warm front.
oc cu py: to take up; to fill.
o cean: a great body of salt water, there are five main oceans.
o cean og ra pher: scientist who studies the oceans.
Old Faith ful: a natural, large geyser in Yellowstone National Park.
om nivore: animal that eats both plants and other animals.
or bit: the curved path that a planet follows around the sun or one object around another.
or gan: a main part of an animal or plant, made up of several kinds of tissues.
or gan ic: having characteristics of living organisms; natural.
or gan isms: any living beings.
or nith ol o gist: scientist that studies birds.
os mos sis: movement of a liquid through a semi-permeable membrane.
out er ear: in humans, the visible part of the ear and the passageway leading to the middle ear. The eardrum separates the outer ear from the middle ear.
o var y: female reproductive organ where ova are produced.
o vule: part of the ovary of seed plants that contain germ cells.
ox i da tion: the combination of an element with oxygen.
ox ide: compound of oxygen with another element or radical.
ox y gen: a colorless, odorless gas that makes up part (about one fifth) of the air. It supports burning and is necessary to animal life. Oxygen is a chemical element.
ox y gen cy cle: sequence of states that the element passes through.
oys ter: a kind of shellfish or mollusk that has a rough, irregular shell. It is an important food.
o zone: An allotrope of oxygen with three atoms to the molecule; pungent, colorless, unstable gas with powerful oxidizing properties.
o zone lay er: a layer in the stratosphere that absorbs most of the sun's ultraviolet radiation.

pan cre as: gland near the stomach that secretes digestive fluid into the duodenum and insulin into the blood.
pan da: a white and black bearlike animal found in Asia.
par a chute: a rectangular or umbrella-shaped canopy allowing a person or object to descend slowly from a height.
par al lel: at or being the same distance apart like railroad tracks.
par a site: a living thing that must live in or on another living thing in order to get food, shelter, or something else that it needs. A parasite gives nothing in return to the animal or plant it lives on.
par ti cle: a very small bit of material.
pas teur i za tion: a process which is used to destroy harmful bacteria in milk and other liquids. The liquid is kept at a temperature of between 140° and 150° Fahrenheit for a certain period of time, then chilled.
pen du lum: weight suspended by a rod or string to regulate movements.
per en ni als: plants lasting a year or longer.
per i gee: the elliptical point which is closest to the Earth or other orbiting body.
per i scope: an apparatus with tube and mirrors permitting the viewer to see objects on a higher plane; used in submarines.
per ma nent: lasting; intended to last; not for a short time only.
per son al i ty: the quality of being a person, habitual patterns of a person.
per spi ra tion: sweat.
pes ti cides: chemicals used to kill unwanted animals.
pet al: leaf of a corolla.
Pe tri dish: small transparent container (dish and lid) used in scientific research particularly in studying bacterial growth.
phar ynx: tube that connects the mouth with the esophagus.
pher o mones: a chemical substance secreted by one animal to attract another of the same species.
phos phates: salts of phosphorus that stimulate growth, many times excessive such as in ponds and lakes.
phos pho rus: one of the minerals found in and necessary to the health of teeth and bones.
pho to syn the sis: process by which plant cells make sugar from carbon dioxide and water in the presence of chlorophyll and light.
pho to tro pism: attracted toward or away from light.
phy lum: a taxological classification below kingdom.
phy to plank ton: microscopic, aquatic plants that produce most of the world's oxygen supply.
pis til: the seed-bearing part of a flower, contains the ovary, stigma, and often the style.
pitch: tone level.
pith: spongy tissue of corn stalk, or rind fruit.
plague: a contagious, epidemic disease.
plan et: an object or body that travels about the sun in an orbit. The sun's planets are Mercury, Venus, Earth, Mars, Jupiter, Saturn, Uranus, Neptune, and Pluto.
plants: a tree, shrub, or herb; non-mobile organism.
plaque: scum-like substance that covers teeth; main cause of tooth decay.
plas ter of paris: fine, white plaster for making molds.
plas tics: chemicals that can be molded.
poach: catch or trap animals illegally.
poi son: a substance, usually a drug that causes severe sickness or death.
Po la ris: the North Star.
pole: place where the force of a magnet is strongest; either end of the earth's axis.
pol len: grain-like discharge from the male part of the flower containing the gamete that fertilizes the female ovule.
pol lute: contaminate, defile the environment.
pol lu tion: state of being unclean or impure.
pop corn: a variety of Indian Corn with small kernels that pop open when heated.
pore: a very small opening in the skin or in a covering of a plant.
po tas si um: one of the minerals necessary to maintain good health.
po ten tial en er gy: the energy of a body that is obtained by its position in space.
pre cip i ta tion: rain, snow, sleet or hail.
pre da tor: any animal that preys on other animals.
pres er va tion: to keep from injury or destruction.
pres sure: force pushing on a particular area.
prey: a living organism that is eaten by predators.
pri mate: the most highly developed order of animals including humans, apes, lemurs, and monkeys.
pri sm: a triangular, transparent block used to separate light rays.
pro pel ler: a revolving shaft with blades especially to move a ship, boat, or airplane.
pro tein: a nourishing food element, important to all living cells, animal or plant.
pro tis ta: one classification of living things; contains amoebas, euglena, and diatoms has animal and plant characteristics.

pro tons: positive charge masses that lie within the nucleus of atoms.
pro to pla sm: material comprising the living part of a cell.
pro to zo a: a group of one-celled, microscopic animals.
pul ley: a grooved wheel or set of wheels for a rope or chains to lift weights by changing direction and force applied.
pulse: the regular beating of blood against the wall of an artery caused by the pumping of the heart. The pulse is best felt on the wrist near the base of the thumb or at the side of the neck.
pump: a device that moves liquid or gas from one area to another.
pu pa: the cocoon or case stage in the development of an insect; the stage which follows the larva.
pu pil: the opening at the center of the iris of the eye. The pupil regulates the amount of light that enters the eye and expands in dim light and contracts in bright light.
pur pu ra: a disease that colors skin purple from escaping blood from its vessels.
Py rex: hard, heat-resistant type of glass.

qua sar: star-like celestial object that appears very bright and very distant.

rad: a measurement of radiation.
ra di ant en er gy: energy that is given off as rays by a hot object. The sun is a source of radiant energy.
ra di a tion: act or process of giving off light or other kinds of radiant energy; the energy radiated.
ra di a tion de tect or: a device that senses small amounts of radiation.
ra di a tor: a heating device consisting of a set of pipes through which steam or hot water passes; a device for cooling circulating water, i.e., the radiator of an automobile.
rad i o ac tiv i ty: radiation given off by the disintegration of atoms of particular substances.
rain bow: an arc consisting of all colors of the spectrum due to water vapor acting like a prism.
rain for est: tropical woodlands that provide much of the oxygen and mild climates.
re act or: facility where matter is converted into energy.
re claim: to bring back, to keep from being lost or destroyed.
re cycle: to reclaim and reuse needed materials.
re flec tion: the bouncing back of light, heat, or sound from a surface.
ref use: waste material; garbage; rubbish.
rel a tive: having a relationship or connection to one another.
rem: a measure of radiation about one roentgen of an X-ray (*R*adiation *E*quivalent in *M*an.).
re new a ble: capable of being restored to its original state or supply.
re pel: to push away, or to drive back. Magnetic poles that are alike repel each other.
re pro duce: to produce its own kind, as an animal produces young or a plant produces seeds.
rep tile: a cold-blooded vertebrate that creeps or crawls and that is covered with scales or bony plates. Snakes, lizards, turtles, alligators, and crocodiles are reptiles.
re sis tance: opposing, power to resist as force, disease, or electricity.
re sour ces: stock or supply that can be used; available assets.
re spi ra tory: the system of organs used for breathing.
re sus ci ta tion: bring back or come back to consciousness.
ret i na: the membrane lining of the back part of the eyeball; the part of the eye that receives images of vision.
re use: use needed materials over again.
rev o lu tion: a movement of one body around another such as the moon around the Earth or Earth around the sun.
ri bo fla vin: vitamin B-2.
Rich ter Scale: a scale representing the strength of earthquakes (Scale: 0–10).
Ri ker box: container or mount for the collection of insects.
riv er: a large stream of water emptying into a larger body of water.
rock: a piece of mineral material.
roc ket: a self-propelling device operated by means of gas escaping from a nozzle or jet at the rear of a combustion chamber.
ro dent: any of a group of mammals having teeth especially adapted for gnawing wood and similar material. Rats, mice, squirrels, hares, and rabbits are rodents.
roent gen: a unit of X-ray radiaiton.
roll: to move around an object's horizontal axis.
roots: part of plant below surface that provides food, water, and stability to the plant.
ro ta tion: any object that turns around on its own axis.
rud der: a vertical device on a plane or ship for controlling horizontal movements.
rye: a cereal plant, a grass.

sal a man der: an amphibian shaped somewhat like a lizard, closely related to the frogs and toads.
sa li va: a digestive juice produced by glands in the mouth. Saliva keeps the mouth moist and aids in the digestion of food.
sal vage: act of saving reusable materials.
sand dune: a mound or ridge of loose sand heaped up by the wind.
sand stone: a sedimentary rock formed mostly of grains of sand that have been pressed together over a long period of time.
san i ta tion: the elimination of harmful conditions.
sat el lite: any object that revolves around another object.
scald: to burn or injure with a hot liquid or gas.
scale: one of the thin, flat, hard plates forming the outer covering of snakes, lizards, and some fishes; a series of spaces marked by lines and used in measuring distances; an instrument for weighing materials.
scale of dis tance: a scale found on a map or globe for measuring distances between places.
scav en ger: one who, or that which, cleans up dirt and filth.
sci ence prin ci ples: rules or laws of science.
sco li o sis: abnormal lateral curvature of the back.
scor pi on: gray lizard with a curved tail, and poisonous sting.
sea shell: shell of a salt water mollusk, whole or part.
sea son: one of the four periods of the year: spring, summer, autumn, winter.
se cre tions: substances released into the body.
sec tion: a part cut off; part; division; slice.
sed i ment: material that settles to the bottom of a liquid.
sed i men tary: of sediment; having something to do with sediment; formed from sediment as sedimentary rocks.
seed: the part of a flowering plant that will develop into a full plant.
seis mo graph: an instrument that records the force and direction of earthquakes.
son ic boom: the loud, explosive noise from sound waves made by a plane travelling at speeds faster than the speed of sound.
sound ing board: a board with upright nails to test materials for sound.
sen sa tion: the feeling or experience caused by action on the sense organs.
sense or gan: the eye, ear, or other part of the body by which a person or an animal receives information about the surroundings. The messages from such organs are interpreted in the brain as sensations of heat, color, sound, smell, etc.
sen si tive: easily affected or influenced.
se pal: a leafy division of the calyx.
ser ies: objects placed one after the other.

shale: a sedimentary rock formed from hardened clay or mud. Shale splits easily into thin layers.
shoul der: a body joint to which an arm, foreleg, or wing is attached.
silt: fine particles of sand and/or soil.
si phon: a device for transferring liquids from one level to a lower one.
skel e ton: the bony structure of a body. The skeleton is a frame to which muscles and tendons are attached.
skull: the bony framework of the head.
slate: a bluish-gray metamorphic rock, made from shale, that splits easily into thin smooth layers.
smog: air pollution of smoke and fog, also other air pollutants.
smoke: the vaporous and solid materials arising from something burning.
snail: a creepy animal that has curved, protective shell.
snake: legless reptile with an elongated body and tapering tail.
Snel len Chart: eye chart to determine visual acuity.
soil wa ter: water that occurs in the soil. It is absorbed by the roots of plants and provides the minerals they need.
so lar sys tem: the sun and the other heavenly bodies that move around it.
sol id: a kind of material that has shape and size; it is not a liquid or a gas; not hollow; hard; firm; strongly put together.
so lu tion: a combination of substances, especially a liquid formed by dissolving one substance in another; answer to a problem.
space: unlimited room or place extending in all directions; a part or place marked off in some way.
space ship: a rocket-propelled vehicle for travelling in outer space.
space shut tle: a self-contained vehicle that can enter space and return.
space sta tion: a structure designed to orbit above the Earth.
spe cies: a group of animals or plants that have certain permanent characteristics in common.
spec i men: part of a real thing; a representation of a group.
spec trum: series of colored light bands from the division of a prism.
sperm: male gamete; the male reproductive fluid containing the spermatozoa and semen.
spi der: a small animal with eight legs, no wings, and a body with two main divisions. It belongs to the arachnid group.
spi nal col umn: the backbone.
spi nal cord: the thick, whitish bundle of nerves enclosed by the spinal column.
spleen: an abdominal organ that maintains the condition of the blood.
spore: a single cell capable of growing into a new plant or animal. Ferns produce spores.
sprout: to begin to grow; shoot forth; a shoot of a plant.
stag nant: having become dirty and impure from standing still, as of air and water.
sta lac tite: formation of lime, shaped like an icicle hanging from the roof of caves.
sta lag mite: formation of lime, shaped like a cone that is built up from the floor of caves.
sta men: male reproductive organ in flowers, within the petals.
state: the condition of a person or thing; the structure or form of a material; the three states that materials are solid, liquid, and gas.
stat ic e lec tric i ty: electrical discharges that result from moving objects.
stem: stalk of a plant.
ster ile: free from living germs.
steth o scope: an instrument used in examination of a person's chest to convey sounds.
stig ma: the part of the pistil that receives the pollen in fertilization.
stim u lant: anything that increases bodily or mental activity.
stim u lus: whatever makes a living thing act in response to it.
sting: a prick or wound from a plant or animal.
stoma: a small opening such as a pore.
sto ma ta: more than one stoma. The stomata of green leaves regulate the passage of water vapor out of the plant. The carbon dioxide that green leaves use for food making enters through the stomata.
stran ger: a person who is not familiar, a foreigner.
stream: a small river.
strip min ing: surface mining; many times leaving earth scarred.
stron ti um: a pale yellow, metallic element; a by-product of atomic bombs.
struc ture: arrangement of parts; a building or something built.
style: the narrow extension of the ovary in plants.
sub ma rine: a warship that can operate under water and carries torpedoes.
suck ing coil: electrical device that moves a central core.
su crose: a sugar obtained from sugar cane.
suc tion: the creation of a partial vacuum causing a gas or liquid to move from the high pressure area to a lower pressure area.
sug ar: sweet substance from sugar cane or sugar beets, a carbohydrate.
su per clus ter: associated group of galaxies.
sul phur: a pale yellow nonmetallic element.
sul phur di ox ide: an air pollutant that is a nonflammable, nonexplosive, colorless gas: found in acid rain.
sun spot: a dark, cooler area on the surface of the sun.
su per sti tion: a belief or practice based on ignorant fear or mistaken reverence.
sur face ten sion: the cohesion of liquid molecules that act like a "skin" on the surface.
sur viv al: remaining alive.
sur viv al ad ap ta tion: any special means that a species has developed to promote the survival of its kind.
swamp: spongy, low ground filled with water, a marsh or bog.
sweat: moisture given out by glands in the skin of some vertebrates. As sweat evaporates, it lowers the body temperature.
symp toms: signs or indications of a disease or illness.
syn thet ic: not of natural growth or development; made artificially; made of artificial products.
sys tol ic: the contraciton of the heart.

tad pole: an undeveloped frog or toad. At this stage of development, the animal has gills and a tail and must live in water.
tan gent: a straight line that touches an arc, rounded surface.
taste bud: any of certain small groups of cells on the tongue or lining of the mouth that serve as organs of taste.
tel e graph: system of transmitting messages by making and breaking electrical connections.
tel e scope: an instrument for making distant objects appear closer.
tem per a ture: the extent to which anything is hot or cold, given as degrees. The temperature of freezing water is 32° Fahrenheit; the temperature of boiling water is 212° Fahrenheit.
tem po rary: lasting for a short time only.
ten sion: the stress of part of a body or material in equilibrium.
ter ra cing: flattening land from sloped areas to prevent soil erosion.
ter rar i um: an enclosure in which small land plants and/or small animals are kept, contains soil only.
ther mal pol lu tion: pollution of the atmosphere due to abnormal heating.
ther mom e ter: an instrument for measuring temperature.
ther mo stat: device that automatically regulates temperature.
tho ri um: a heavy, gray radioactive element.

thrust: a sudden push or lunge.

thun der: loud, crashing noise due to rapid expansion of heated air usually caused by lightning.

thy roid: pertaining to the large gland which lies near the throat in human beings.

tide: the rise and fall of the ocean; occurs about once every twelve hours.

tis sue: the cells and substance around them which form the bodies of plants and animals.

toad: a small animal somewhat like a frog, which starts life in water but usually leaves it to live on land. The toad returns to the water to deposit its eggs.

top soil: the upper part of the soil; surface soil.

tor na do: violent wind with a funnel-shape cloud that destroys much in its path.

tour ni quet: device for stopping severe bleeding by compressing blood vessel with bandage by twisting with stick.

tox ic: of or relating to poisons.

tox ins: poisons produced by chemical changes in animal and plant tissue.

tra che a: the main tube that carries air to and from the lungs.

trans lu cent: letting light pass through without being transparent.

trans par ent: easily seen through.

tran spi ra tion: passing off vapor from the surface as from leaves of plants or skins of animals.

tree: a tall, woody, perennial plant with many branches.

tri an gle of life: the graphic display of all predator-prey relationships.

tro po sphere: the lowest layer of the Earth's atmosphere between the Earth and the stratosphere about 8 miles (13 kilometers) thick.

tsu na mi: giant waves caused by underground earthquakes.

tu bers: thickened, underground stems of plants, such as in potatoes or dahlias.

tung sten: one of the chemical elements. It is a rare metal used in making steel and for electric-lamp filaments.

tur tle: fresh and salt water reptiles with soft body in a hard shell.

ty phoon: a violent, cyclonic windstorm, usually near the China Sea, a hurricane.

ul tra vi o let light: a type of electromagnetic radiation that is shorter than visible light most blocked out by the ozone layer.

un du lat ing: moving back and forth in waves.

u ni verse: all of the cosmos, totality of space.

up pers: slang term for drugs that are stimulators.

vac ci na tion: the act of injecting killed or weakened organisms into the blood of people to make them immune to a particular disease, such as smallpox or polio.

vac u um: an enclosed empty space from which all of the air has been removed.

vane: pointer showing the direction of the wind; a blade on a windmill or propeller.

vein: one of the three kinds of blood vessels. The veins carry the blood that is returning to the heart from all parts of the body.

ve loc i ty: speed in a particular direction.

ve ne re al dis ease: a disease transmitted by sexual intercourse.

ve nom: poisonous fluid secreted by snakes, scorpions, etc.

ven ti late: to change or purify air in a room by circulating fresh air.

ven tri cle: either of the two lower chambers of the heart that receive blood.

ver te bra: any of the bones of the backbone.

ver te brate: any animal that has a backbone. Fishes, amphibians, reptiles, birds, and mammals are vertebrates.

vet er in ar i an: a doctor who specializes in the treatment of animals.

vi brate: to move rapidly back and forth or up and down.

vi bra tion: quick movement to and fro, up and down, in and out, back and forth as in an earthquake.

vi rus: group of disease producing agents, very small, and dependent upon their host for reproduction and growth.

vis cos i ty: the ease of which a substance flows.

vi su al per sis ten cy: the ability to see an object after it is gone from view.

vi tal: essential or very important to life; having the qualities of living bodies.

vi ta mins: elements found in many foods that are important and necessary to the physical development of man, animals, and plants.

vi var i um: an enclosure in which small plants and/or animals are kept; contains soil(s) and water.

vol ca no: mountain having an opening through which ashes and lava are expelled; an opening in the Earth's surface out of which lava, steam, etc., pour.

volt: electromagnetic force; difference of potential that would carry one ampere of current against one ohm of resistance.

vol ta ic wet cell: a device that produces electricity by chemical change.

vol ume: the amount of space that a material takes up.

warm-blood ed: having warm blood. The body temperature of different warm-blooded animals is from 98° to 112° Fahrenheit. It is relatively constant for each animal.

wasp: winged insect with a slender body and biting mouth parts; has a vicious sting.

wastes: unwanted, formerly used products.

wa ter cy cle: sequence of states that water passes through.

wa ter lev el: the height of the surface of still water.

wa ter shed: area drained by a river or rain.

wa ter ta ble: the level below which the ground is saturated with water.

wa ter va por: water in a gaseous state. The term is used for vapor formed below the boiling point of water. At boiling point and higher it is called steam.

wat tling proc ess: method of conserving land by building fences in gullies to prevent excessive soil erosion.

waves: the up and down movement of water or sound.

wax: dull yellow substance secreted by bees for building cells.

weath er: the state of the atmosphere which includes temperature, pressure, humidity, and winds.

weath er ing: the physical and chemical changes that take place in rocks when they are exposed to conditions at the Earth's surface.

weath er vane: instrument that indicates wind direction.

weight: the amount of force with which gravity pulls down on any object.

wet lands: damp or wet areas of land which include swamps, bogs, lagoons, marshes, etc.

wind: motion of the air.

wind break: a shelter from the wind to prevent soil erosion.

wind pipe: the hollow tube that extends from the throat to the lungs.

wood chuck: a North American marmot; the groundhog.

worm: long, slender, creeping animal with a soft belly living underground.

wreath: a twisted, circular band of flowers or leaves.

X-rays: electro-magnetic radiation; can't be seen; used in medicine and dentistry for examinations.

xy lem: the tissue that carries water through a plant.

yaw: to move back and forth sideways from intended course.

zoo: place where wild animals are kept.

Index